PATROL OPERATIONS

AND

ENFORCEMENT TACTICS

By

Dr. George T. Payton

Emeritus
Evergreen Valley College

Former Patrol Sergeant
San Jose Police Department

and

Michel Amaral

Patrol Sergeant
San Jose Police Department

Published by
CRIMINAL JUSTICE SERVICES

P.O. Box 21115
San Jose, CA 95151
(408) 274-3317

© 1992

by

George T Payton
Criminal Justice Services
All Rights Reserved

§ § §
EIGHTH EDITION
(Formerly Patrol Procedures)
Completely Revised and Updated
§ § §

Standard Book Number 910874-35-2
Library of Congress Card Number 76-53527

Printed in the United States of America

DEDICATION

This book is dedicated to State Commissions on Peace Officer Standards and Training throughout the United States. They have become the motivating force for standardized and quality education and training in the field of criminal justice.

ABOUT THE AUTHORS

Dr. George Payton is a former Patrol Sergeant with the San Jose Police Department. He has a BA and MA from San Jose State University and an Ed.D from the University of Southern California in Los Angeles.

When he left the police department to become Department Chair at a local college, Dr. Payton transferred to the San Jose Police Reserves in order to keep abreast of new developments in the field; he is a Lieutenant in that organization. He also organized the first Regional Criminal Justice Training Academy in Santa Clara County and established the first Campus Police at San Jose City College.

Dr. Payton is a veteran of two wars. He served first in the U.S. Navy and was later commission in the U.S. Military Police. He has written books in the area of California Criminal Law, Criminal Investigation, and Police Supervision. He has also written articles for several law enforcement journals. His biographies are listed in *Leaders in Law Enforcement*, *Who's Who in Law Enforcement*, and *Outstanding Educators*. Dr. Payton has also received the Outstanding Criminal Justice Educator's Award. He recently retired after twenty-seven years with Evergreen Valley College.

Sergeant Mike Amaral is a second generation cop. He is currently a Patrol Sergeant with the San Jose Police Department, and has a BA and MA from San Jose State University. He has been in martial arts for over twenty years.

Sergeant Amaral teaches in the Santa Clara County Regional Criminal Justice Training Center, and is an instructor/consultant for the California Department of Justice. He has taught classes throughout the United States, and has trained over fifteen thousand law enforcement officers. He is recognized throughout the country for his officer survival training courses and has been on nationally syndicated television.

Sergeant Amaral is the author of the book, *Officer Safety*. He also trains police officers in the techniques of instruction as well as in how to pass promotional examinations.

ACKNOWLEDGEMENTS

The authors would like to gratefully acknowledge the assistance of the following persons and groups:

Dr. George Cochern
Emeritus
San Jose State University

Ron Havner
Assistant Dean and Director
Regional Criminal Justice Training Center
Evergreen Valley College

Lou Cobarruviaz
Chief of Police
San Jose Police Department

Stan Edwards
Communications Supervisor
San Jose Police Department

Vera Kalv
Typesetting and Technical Assistance

The Santa Clara County Human Relations Commission
Re-writing Input and Assistance

This book was typeset using XEROX® Ventura Publisher® software.

Preface

This book was written primarily as a text for courses dealing with patrol procedures or patrol operations and techniques.

Patrol officers are the backbone of any police department. They are the first line of defense against crime. They must often possess the patience of Job and the wisdom of Solomon. This book was written to assist them in their endeavor.

This book is not, nor was it intended to be, "The Gospel According to George Payton and Mike Amaral." Because individual people are so different, there is no one answer or method of handling the innumerable problems which humanity creates for itself. Each person and case is unique, and what is good for the goose is not necessarily good for the gander. The procedures set forth in this book are the result of research, personal opinion, and experience.

Patrol officers must take heed of their departments' policies, which usually reflect the needs and feelings of the community in which they serve. Patrol officers must be continually alert for new ideas and techniques that will assist them in their jobs. Officers can be in policework for any number of years and still not know it all. They should plan on receiving knowledge from all levels and all types of people. The authors have seldom taught a class in which they did not learn something from the students.

Although there is no one situation which is exactly the same as another, they do tend to fall into certain patterns, and there seem to be certain procedures and techniques that work better than others. Common sense goes a long way in handling situations with which law enforcement officers are confronted each day. To the new patrol officer, faced for the first time with the realization of how much knowledge and skill is actually required to do modern professional police work, this book is meant to serve as a guide and a reference.

Experience is a wonderful teacher, but in law enforcement, the price paid for experience can be the officer's life. This is too high a price to pay and is not really necessary. The very essence of education is to profit from the mistakes of others. This means that we should start where others have left off and not repeat their mistakes.

Because of more rigorous selection standards, the modern law enforcement officer is far more capable of profiting from instruction than those in the past. Today's officers are the "new breed:" better prepared psychologically for the challenge presented by a more dynamic and demanding society. Citizens today expect more from law enforcement than at any time in the past. It is the intent of all those associated with the field of law enforcement training and education to see that these expectations are met.

G.T.P.
M.A.
24 July 1992

Table of Contents

CHAPTER I
ETHICS AND PROFESSIONAL LAW ENFORCEMENT 3
The Law Enforcement Code of Ethics is broken down passage by passage to analyze its true import. There are illustrations given to show how this code should be put into practice by the patrol officer in the field.

CHAPTER II
THE HISTORY OF POLICE PATROL 33
To provide a background to modern policework, a short history of police patrol is presented.

CHAPTER III
THE PURPOSE AND BASIC DUTIES OF POLICE PATROL 67
The basic duties of preventive and selective enforcement are examined, as well as traffic enforcement, and emergency and routine calls for police service.

CHAPTER IV
THE TYPES OF PATROL 83
The various types of patrol found in today's modern police department are examined. Included are air, automobile, bicycle, boat, dog, foot, horse, motorcycle and television patrol.

CHAPTER V
PREPARATION FOR PATROL 115
Preparation for patrol is an important function. Preparation is covered through the time the officer leaves home, puts on his or her uniform in the locker room, reads the necessary reports in the squad room, and checks out the patrol vehicle. It also includes some background in emergency vehicle procedure.

CHAPTER VI
POLICE COMMUNICATIONS 131
The field of police communications is examined from all angles. Starting out with a brief history of police radio procedures, this chapter thoroughly examines police communications. Also included are standard APCO radio code, the field telephone and the police teletype system. The latest computerized communications systems are examined as well.

CHAPTER VII
'OBSERVATION AND PERCEPTION 163
Since a patrol officer must rely on his or her senses not only to do the job, but to save his or her life as well, this chapter examines each of the five senses as they apply to the officer on patrol duty, and covers some of the "attention getters" that will aid in perception. Faults in human perception are also covered.

Table of Contents

CHAPTER VIII

FIELD NOTE TAKING AND CRIME SCENE RECORDING 183
The purpose of field note-taking is covered along with the equipment needed, the care and use of the notebook, techniques for obtaining notes, and style of note-taking. Techniques of crime scene measurement and sketching are covered along with basic crime scene photography.

CHAPTER IX

IDENTIFICATION & DESCRIPTION OF PERSONS AND PROPERTY . 203
A brief history of criminal identification including Portrait Parle is given, along with general procedures for describing persons and property and an overview of the latest computerized composite sketching systems.

CHAPTER X

FIELD INTERROGATION 225
The legal aspects of field interrogation examined in light of the latest Federal Court decisions. Also discussed are ways of selecting subjects, criminal traits, documents of identification, and some basic techniques of interrogation.

CHAPTER XI

VEHICLE STOPS AND CONTROL OF OCCUPANTS 257
Techniques of police pursuit, the stopping of vehicles (general and high-risk stops), searching and handcuffing of prisoners, and vehicle search are discussed.

CHAPTER XII

PROTECTIVE WEAPONS AND OFFICER SURVIVAL 285
The legal and practical aspects of the use of police weapons, dispatching injured animals, using the police baton, non-lethal weapons, and officer survival are covered.

CHAPTER XIII

TACTICS BY TYPE OF CALL— GENERAL CALLS FOR SERVICE . . 321
The handling of ordinary calls that do not place the officer in a great deal of danger. Examples are intoxication calls, fire calls, civil cases, vandalism, theft, and liquor law violations.

CHAPTER XIV

TACTICS BY TYPE OF CALL—HIGH RISK CONTACTS 381
The handling of calls that place the patrol officer at risk of life or limb. Examples are robbery or burglary in progress, deadly weapons cases, stolen vehicles, and emotional disturbance cases.

CHAPTER XV

COURTROOM TESTIMONY AND DEMEANOR 419
The psychology of court appearance, personal appearance when on the stand, preparation for court, taking the stand, general testimony advice, and use of the chalkboard

Table of Illustrations

CHAPTER I
Fig. I-1; Rodney King Beating, Courtesy: A.P. Worldwide Photo 18
Fig I-2; L.A. Riot After Officers Acquitted, Courtesy: A.P. Worldwide Photo . 19

CHAPTER II
Fig. II-1; Administering Punishment for Petty Theft 34
Fig. II-2, Swedish Watchman, 1400's 35
Fig. II-3; German Watchman, 1500's 36
Fig. II-4; Danish Watchman, 1800's 36
Fig. II-5; Hue and Cry 37
Fig. II-6; Watchman (or Charlie) 38
Fig. II-7; William Anthony, "Last of the Charlies" 38
Fig. II-8; Watch House and Watchmen, 1770's 39
Fig. II-9; Satirical Invitation to Jonathan Wild's Execution in 1725 40
Fig. II-10; Life Saving 40
Fig. II-11; Patrolling Docks 40
Fig. II-12; Picture in Daily Telegraph that led to murderer's arrest. 41
Fig. II-13; Bow Street Runner 41
Fig. II-14; Sketch of Townsend 42
Fig. II-15a; Henry Fielding, Novelist & Magistrate 42
Fig. II-15b; Sir John Fielding, the Blind Bow Street Magistrate 43
Fig. II-16; Highway Robbery 43
Fig. II-17; Bow Street Police Court in 1808 44
Fig. II-18; Sir Robert Peel 45
Fig. II-19, Flyer on New Police 46
Fig. II-20; Reduced Facsimile: Front Page, First Number "Police Gazette" . . . 47
Fig. II-21; Cartoon of Peel attacking Charlies 47
Fig. II-22; Policeman, Old Style 48
Fig. II-23; The "Peeler" 48
Fig. II-24; A Peeler 48
Fig. II-25; Fictitious "Peeler with sword" 49
Fig. II-26; Police at 1837 riots 49
Fig. II-27; Early English Bobby 49
Fig. II-28; Unarmed Bobbies arresting an armed burglar 49
Fig. II-29; Sample of Warrant Card for City of Birmingham 50
Fig. II-30; A "Garde de Paris" 50
Fig. II-31; French Police Patrol Wagons 50
Fig. II-32; French Sergeant de Ville 51
Fig. II-33; French Police Symbol 51
Fig. II-35; French Police Officer 51
Fig. II-34; French Police Officer 51

Table of Illustrations

Fig. II-36; Colonial Watchhouse on corner 52
Fig. II-37; Prank on sleeping watchman 52
Fig. II-38; Police Parade, Broadway 53
Fig. II-39; The "Black Maria" 53
Fig. II-40. Vigilante Symbol 54
Fig. II-41; Cartoon of "Boss" Tweed 56
Fig. II-42; New York City jail known as the Tombs, 1800's 57
Fig. II-43; Postcard of "The Policeman", 1910 57
Fig. II-44; Police and Army responding to the Astor Riots 58
Fig. II-45; Fight between Metropolitan and Municipal police 59
Fig. II-47; Police squad drilling 59
Fig. II-46; Early police equipment 59
Fig. II-48; Photograph showing wide variety of uniforms and badges 60
Fig. II-49; Group Portrait 62
Fig. II-50; San Francisco Police Department on parade 63

CHAPTER III
Fig III-1; Photo of Pin Map 70
Fig III-2; Officer Directing Traffic 71
Fig. III-3; Officer Investigating an Accident 71
Fig. III-4; Officer Offering Courtesy Service 73
Fig. III-5; Courtesy Information Card 73
Fig III-6(b); Using table knife to push spring bolt back 74
Fig III-6(c); Using tool to pull in spring bolt when facing away 74
Fig III-6(a); Table knife under door molding 74
Fig. III-7; Sample Information Booklet 77

CHAPTER IV
Fig. IV-1; A three shift Ten Plan (Dotted line is optional shift) 84
Fig. IV-2; Patrol Automobile 87
Fig. IV-3; Horse drawn paddy wagon, NY 1903 88
Fig. IV-4; Signal answered/Code three, 1886 88
Fig. IV-5; One of the first police vehicles 88
Fig. IV-6; Seatbelts saved this officer 90
Fig. IV-7; Police horse patrol on duty 95
Fig. IV-8; The Bellman of London with dog 96
Fig. IV-9; Police dogs in use 97
Fig. IV-10a; Savoia — Marchetti airplane 99
Fig. IV-10b; Fleet biplane. 99
Fig. IV-10c; Stinson seaplane 99
Fig. IV-10d; Grumman Goose 99

Table of Illustrations

Fig. IV-11; Police helicopter 100
Fig. IV-12; Fixed wing aircraft. 101
Fig. IV-13; Early New York Harbor Patrol 102
Fig. IV-14; New York Harbor Patrol 102
Fig. IV-15; Harbor patrol boat 102
Fig. IV-16; The police tricycle 103
Fig. IV-18; Modern motorcycle officer 104
Fig. IV-17; Motorcycle officers, early 1930's 104
Fig. IV-19; LLLTV Surveillance, remote station on city street 105
Fig. IV-20; Helicopter TV surveillance 106
Fig. IV-21, Monitors for helicopter surveillance 106
Fig. IV-22; Two photos using LLLTV from half a block away 107
Fig. IV-23; Woman patrol officer 108
Fig. IV-24; Woman patrol officer handcuffing a suspect 108
Fig. IV-25; Woman patrol officer questioning subject 109

CHAPTER V
Fig. V-1; Officers in squad room, San Francisco Police Department, 1932 . . 115
Fig. V-2; Officers in squad room, LAPD, 1990 119
Fig. V-4; Vehicle Radio Log 124
Fig. V-5; Smashed police vehicle; driver saved by seat belt 126

CHAPTER VI
Fig. VI-1, Warning bell used in colonial times 131
Fig. VI-2; Photo of rattle and whistles 131
Fig VI-3; FCC Symbol 132
Fig. VI-7; Photo of Cruiser #10 133
Fig. VI-4; Call box and lamp post 133
Fig. VI-5; Telephone and signal box 133
Fig. VI-6; Police telephone signal device 133
Fig. VI-8; Officer using hand set radio (walkie-talkie) 135
Fig. VI-9; Computerized communication center 135
Fig. VI-10; Computer-Aided Dispatch System (CAD) 135
Fig. VI-11; Mobile Display Terminal (MDT) 136
Fig. VI-12; Police radio dispatcher, 1930. SFPD Hist. Soc. 138
Fig. VI-13; Communications officers on the job 140
Fig. VI-14, Car illustration for CYMBALS 146
Fig. VI-15; Police teletype operator, 1920's. SFPD Hist. Soc. 151

CHAPTER VII
Fig. VII-1; Blind spot exercise 166

Table of Illustrations

Fig. VII-2; The Müller-Lyer illusion 167
Fig. VII-3; The Zöllner illusion 167
Fig. VII-4; Optical illusion 167
Fig. VII-5; Optical illusion 167
Fig. VII-6; Optical illusion 168
Fig. VII-7; Optical illusion 168
Fig. VII-8; Optical illusion. 168
Fig. VII-9, Multifaced rear-view mirror 171
Fig. VII-10a; 25mm lens 172
Fig. VII-10b; 50mm lens or 25mm lens with 2X extender 172
Fig. VII-10c; 100mm lens or 50 mm lens with 2X extender 172
Fig. VII-10d; 300mm lens 172
Fig. VII-11; Lock-picking tools 175

CHAPTER VIII
Fig. VIII-1; Offense report form 185
Fig. VIII-2; Juvenile report form 186
Fig. VIII-3, Example report handwritten in notebook 187
Fig. VIII-4; Cross projection sketch 194
Fig. VIII-5; Examples of ways to make measurements 195
Fig. VIII-6; Computerized sketch: COMPUSCENE by Visatex 197

CHAPTER IX
Fig. IX-2; An Unwilling Subject. — Photographing a prisoner 204
Fig. IX-1; Original rogues' gallery 204
Fig. IX-3; Rogues' gallery after use of photography 205
Fig. IX-4; Bertillon's system of identification 206
Fig. IX-5; Ear and head measures (the Bertillon System) 207
Fig. IX-6; Booking card with Bertillon measurements. 208
Fig. IX-7; Computerized composite description system 210
Fig. IX-8; Compusketch Feature Library Illustration 210
Fig. IX-9; "Noted Middle Eatern dictator," Visatech Corp. 211
Fig. IX-10; Standard descriptions of persons 212

CHAPTER X
Fig. X-1; Sample field interrogation card. 233

CHAPTER XI
Fig. XI-1; Approaching the suspect vehicle 263
Fig. XI-2a; Driver suspect opening door quickly 263

Table of Illustrations

Fig. XI-2b; Officer knocked down and into oncoming traffic 263
Fig. XI-3; Officer approaching vehicle from passenger side 264
Fig. XI-4; Concealed firearm visible from passenger side 264
Fig. XI-5; Officer with hand trapped between window and frame 264
Fig. XI-6; Driver reaching for officer's gun 264
Fig. XI-7; Officer writing citation, suspect reaching for gun 265
Fig. XI-8a; First method for stopping vehicles 267
Fig. XI-8b; Second method for stopping vehicles 267
Fig. XI-8c; Third method for stopping vehicles 267
Fig. XI-9; Passenger reaching for gun above sun visor 268
Fig. XI-10; Removing suspect from vehicle in a non-hazardous situation . . . 269
Fig. XI-11f; Search position 272
Fig. XI-11e; Break balance, move in 272
Fig. XI-11b; Grasp hands, break balance, move in 272
Fig. XI-11a; Hands up 272
Fig. XI-11d; Begin hand change 272
Fig. XI-11c; Search position 272
Fig. XI-11k; Search second side 273
Fig. XI-11h; Apply first cuff 273
Fig. XI-11g; Distract, bend finger, establish grip 273
Fig. XI-11j; Search first side 273
Fig. XI-11i; Apply second cuff 273
Fig. XI-12f; Pull hands apart 274
Fig. XI-12e; Search second side 274
Fig. XI-12b; Grasp hands, maintain bowed back, search first side 274
Fig. XI-12a; Hands up 274
Fig. XI-12d; Maintain bowed back 274
Fig. XI-12c; Switch hand position 274
Fig. XI-12h; Secure handcuff link 275
Fig. XI-12g; Apply first cuff 275
Fig. XI-12i; Apply second cuff 275
Fig. XI-13f; First cuff applied 276
Fig. XI-13e; Step over shoulder 276
Fig. XI-13b; hands on ground 276
Fig. XI-13a; Hands up 276
Fig. XI-13d; Gun secured, search back 276
Fig. XI-13c; Pick up hand, gun pointed up 276
Fig. XI-14; Searching multiple suspects if the officer is alone 277
Fig. XI-13h; Lower leg search 277
Fig. XI-13g; Apply second cuff 277
Fig. XI-13j; Stand suspect up 277
Fig. XI-13i; Roll suspect on side, search front of upper legs, groin, and body . 277

Table of Illustrations

Fig. XI-16; Ballpoint pen cartridge made into a handcuff key 278
Fig. XI-15; Search procedure diagrams 278
Fig. XI-17; Handcuff nomenclature 279
Fig. XI-18; Safe-T-Cuffs 279
Fig. XI-19; Safe-T-Cuffs applied 279
Fig. XI-20; Plastic cuffs put to good use in 1992 Los Angeles riots 280

CHAPTER XII
Fig. XII-4; Yawara Stick 293
Fig. XII-1a; Single Handed Position. 294
Fig. XII-1b; Two Handed Position. 294
Fig. XII-1c; Overhand Position. 294
Fig. XII-1d; Chopping Position 294
Fig. XII-1e; Thrusting Position. 295
Fig. XII-1f; Lower Cradle. 295
Fig. XII-1g; Upper Cradle. 295
Fig. XII-1h; Position for Interviewing. 295
Fig. XII-1i-A; Striking hand position, left side view 296
Fig. XII-1i-B; Striking hand position, right side view 296
Fig. XII-1i; Striking Hand Position. 296
Fig. XII-2a, Two Count Baton Technique: distraction 297
Fig. XII-2b; Two Count Baton Technique: drawing back 297
Fig. XII-2c; Two Count Baton Technique: strike to lower leg 297
Fig. XII-3a; Interview Stance—Front 298
Fig. XII-3b; Interview Stance—Side 298
Fig. XII-3c; Horse Stance—Front 298
Fig. XII-3d; Horse Stance—Side 298
Fig. XII-3e; Front Stance 298
Fig. XII-3f; Self Defense Stance 298
Fig. XII-5; Small MACE 300
Fig. XII-6; Spray from pressurized MACE cannister 301
Fig. XII-7; The use of MACE in a dangerous situation 301

CHAPTER XIII
Fig. XIII-1; A punch job 324
Fig. XIII-2; A rip job 325
Fig. XIII-3; A peel job 325
Fig. XIII-4; Another burn job 326
Fig. XIII-4; A burn job 326
Fig. XIII-6; Voiceprints 332
Fig. XIII-7; Medic Alert bracelet 340

Table of Illustrations

Fig. XIII-8; Officer checking Medic Alert bracelet 340

Fig. XIII-9; Officer testing subject for intoxication 345

Fig. XIII-10; Diagram of DUI suspect's ability to walk 346

Fig. XIII-11a; Driving Under the Influence report (front) 347

Fig. XIII-11b; Driving Under the Influence report (back) 348

Fig. XIII-12; Officer administering a manual dexterity test 349

Fig. XIII-13; Photopraph of manual dexterity test 349

Fig. XIII-14; Sample Implied Consent Form 351

Fig. XIII-15; Officer with found missing child 360

Fig. XIII-16; "Missing" child found asleep in closet 360

Fig. XIII-17; Bike frame number 363

Fig. XIII-18; "Bugs" stamped on bike frames 363

Fig. XIII-19; Firetruck 364

Fig. XIII-20; The Fire Triangle 364

Fig. XIII-21; The Fire Quadrangle 365

Fig. XIII-22; Rescue apparatus unit 368

Fig. XIII-23; Aerial ladder unit 368

CHAPTER XIV

Fig. XIV-1; Noise meter 388

Fig. XIV-2; Narcotic user's paraphernalia or "kit" 408

Fig. XIV-3; Marijuana leaf 410

Fig. XIC-4; Marijuana seeds and cigarettes (joints) 410

Fig. XIV-5; Drug identification 412

CHAPTER XV

Fig. XV-1; Proper bearing and attention in court 421

Fig. XV-2; Improper bearing and gun showing. 421

Fig. XV-3; Improper bearing on the stand 421

PATROL OPERATIONS

and

ENFORCEMENT TACTICS

CHAPTER I

ETHICS AND PROFESSIONAL LAW ENFORCEMENT

PROFESSIONAL ETHICS

Today we hear much on the topic of law enforcement becoming the next profession. Most peace officers are in favor of this because such an achievement would lead to an increase in their own personal and social status, not to mention better pay and working conditions. Many steps have been taken in the last thirty years to make this dream a reality. Some of these steps have involved state certification of peace officers for basic, intermediate and advanced levels of proficiency, controlled standards of training and college education, and the setting of minimum recruitment standards.

One of the most important, however, has been the adoption of a professional code of ethics. This code, which originated in California, has been adopted by the International Association of Chiefs of Police, and by most states.

One of the fastest growing vocational programs in colleges today is in the area of criminal justice. This is especially true of the two year community college which seems to be ideally suited for this task because of the proximity of these colleges to local departments, and the lower costs to students.

Still the goal of professional standing is not yet attained. There remain a few difficult problems to overcome. To become professional, law enforcement must have "horizontal mobility", or the ability to move from one department to another when openings exist, and do so without loss of rank and especially retirement benefits. This step presents many problems, the greatest being financial. State or federal subsidies may be a partial answer to this problem. They might finance a single retirement system for all peace officers that would be equal to the system which only the larger cities can now afford.

If all of the basic conditions of a profession were to come about, law enforcement would still not be classed as a true profession without the fulfillment of one necessary condition. This condition must really precede all formal requirements. The condition, simply stated, is that all law enforcement personnel be professional in their actions.

Professional standing must be earned, and in the field of law enforcement, the price can be high. Being a law enforcement officer today is far from being easy, and any recruit who thinks that it is or ever will be, is "riding for a fall". Being a law enforcement officer is not always easy, but being a truly professional officer is considerably more difficult. The job of the enforcement officer is made more difficult by the changing social patterns in American families. There is a trend among parents today to delegate to governmental institutions the responsibilities that, for thousands of years, have been the responsibility of parents themselves or the family structure. They want the church to be responsible for the child's religious foundation, the school, all of the child's general and life education, and they expect the police department to handle the child's discipline problems. They want the county or state to take care of their elderly parents, and the courts to settle arguments that in the past were settled amongst themselves, and so on.

Social institutions cannot replace the family. In any properly functioning society, all segments of that social order must work together for a common good. History books tell us of the many civilizations that have fallen or crumbled because of a basic failure in this area.

A respect for authority and law and order can only be developed in the home. This is a function that law enforcement cannot perform. When the family fails in this area, the job of law enforcement becomes increasingly difficult.

It is interesting to note a study done by criminologists on the west coast just before World War II. Spot maps were made of the major cities on the coast. Each spot indicated a reported crime. In each case the maps became darker with spots as one moved closer to the center of the city. Then in the center of that darkened area would appear a clear zone. This baffled the criminologists until they did a follow-up study and discovered that the area was inhabited by Asians. They were further baffled by the fact that the inhabitants fit catagories that criminologists felt were conducive to crime. They were often first generation foreigners. They were poor. They spoke a language other than English in the home, and their culture and religion were very different from the majority of those living in the city. By all criminological theories, their children should have been highly involved in criminal activities. They were not. Studies were then conducted in an effort to discover the basis for this phenomenon. The answer was that those living in this area had very strong family ties, and a belief that if a member of the family did a dishonest act, that act would bring dishonor upon the whole family. Here we find an example of just how important strong family ties can be.

No law enforcement agency can function properly without public support and assistance. A police department must belong to the people. It must be the "people's police." In today's modern cities, this is most difficult. Too often the police feel that police work is only their business and citizens should stay out of it. On the other hand, resentment and suspicion on the part of those living in high crime areas, especially minorities, further prevent the ideal from becoming reality. In a democracy, the support of the people cannot be forced. It must be won. If the job of law enforcement is to be made more effective, this support must be won, and in a hurry. The best way for officers to win public support is through professional conduct. This is certainly not easy. The desire to act and be professional is a prerequisite, but there are many obstacles between desire and performance.

In some departments there are still supervisors and administrators who are from the "old school", and they often resent the "new breed". It is difficult for them to accept the possibility that their way was wrong. We must understand that it is part of people's nature to resist change as they grow older. After all, we have an investment of ourselves in our past. For that reason change often comes slowly. Many of the "new breed" will become martyrs when their progressive ideas clash with the reactionary thinking of some of those above them in rank. This has always, to some extent, been man's lot, but never in the history of the world has change been so rapidly demanded as it is today.

There has been a constant change over the years in the status of the law enforcement officer. A movement toward professionalization becomes more apparent when we examine the statement of a prominent lawyer of the 1929 era. In the book Cross Examination by A. L. Cornelius, he warns other attorneys about handling police officers as witnesses.

"Policemen as a class are usually not well educated, skilled mechanically or industrious. They are men above the average in physical strength and appearance who have lacked sufficient peresistence to acquire an education or learn a trade. Their contact with the criminal element tends to make them suspicious of human nature. They are daily engaged in the prosecution of others, and of course, in defending their own acts. Their entire attention is focused upon the derelictions of mankind. Therefore it naturally follows that where a person is charged with a crime, the officer is naturally predisposed toward belief in his guilt.

"A policeman's duty also tends to make him officious, dictatorial and arbitrary toward individuals. Policemen as a class are inclined to be vain and somewhat egotistical. They do not, however, lack in courage, as their numerous encounters with the criminal element bear abundant witness."

This viewpoint is rarely valid today and it should be a source of encouragement. It is an indication that progress is being made toward the desired goal of professionalism.

Apart from the problems of an often indifferent public and sometimes reactionary thinking in the occupation, professional minded law enforcement officers must know and face the problems of their own personal weaknesses. They must know and understand their own human nature and how they can prepare themselves for the small pitfalls that await them and which can lead them away from professional standards, not by leaps, but inch by inch. Nearly every department has experienced an older officer whose spirit has been broken; one who started out "full of steam", filled with high ideals and aspirations, but who was totally unprepared to cope with "city hall", public apathy, and the general pitfalls of policework.

The important thing to understand is that although the problems mentioned certainly make professional law enforcement difficult, they also make it more necessary.

Where does one learn to become professional? Some learn it from their parents. Some learn it from schools, colleges, churches and from the writings of great philosophers. Many feel that few of today's youth have digested the lessons that these disciplines offer, or for that matter are even receptive to them. The answer to this will certainly have a great bearing on the future of our country.

Selection is certainly important, and it has been well proven that the expense of a proper and lengthy selection process is a sound investment in the long run. The English Metropolitan Police have been good examples of this concept.

When the Metropolitan Police were first organized, their qualifications were exceptionally high for the small pay that was offered. They continued these high standards of recruitment throughout their history. In 1922, George Orwell, the famous English author, applied for the position of Colonial Policeman under the name Eric Blair. This examination lasted eight days. It not only involved the ability to compose sentences, but included history, mathematics, physics, chemistry, general science, Latin, Greek, drawing, the translation of either French or German, and finally a test in horseback riding.

The total possible points in this series of examinations was 12,400. Orwell scored 8,463 and although he was a gifted writer, his score placed him seventh on the list.

Where does one learn to be a good police officer? Unfortunately, a short recruit Training Academy, as good as it may be, does not properly fill this need. It can only plant seeds in the mind of the recruit. Seeds can become great trees, but they develop best when they are nurtured and given continued care.

To be a good police officer requires constant effort and self evaluation. As a growing tree reaches for the light of the sun, a professional police officer must reach for the idealistic goals that have been set forth as standards for his or her profession.

The most sincere police officer needs professional standards or a set of rules which he or she may look to as a daily guide. One which sets the pattern of professional conduct toward which they can strive. The Law Enforcement Code of Ethics is such a guide.

If one really studies this code, it will soon become evident that adhering to its tenets presents no easy task, for it involves mastering one's own human nature, and this is never an easy goal to attain.

The majority of officers who read the Law Enforcement Code of Ethics will agree with its basic message, and they will accept its basic context as being commensurate with professional standards.

However, if it is to be put into practice, it must first be understood, and we cannot understand the true purpose of the code unless we first understand ourselves.

Although the Code of Ethics was introduced around 1954, it is not a new concept to the field of law enforcement.

In 1829, when Sir Robert Peel, England's Home Secretary, instituted the Metropolitan Police, he gave them a list of instructions that could well be considered a code of ethics. So that we can compare them with our present day Code of Ethics, Peel's Principles are listed as follows:

(1) It should be understood at the outset, the principal object to be obtained is the prevention of crime.

(2) To this, great and every effort of the police is to be directed. The security of persons and property and the preservation of a police establishment will thus be better effected than by the detection and punishment of the offender after he has succeeded in committing crime.

(3) The constable will be civil and obliging to all people of every rank and class.

(4) The constable must be particularly cautious not to interfere idly or unnecessarily in order to make a display of his authority.

(5) When required to act, he will do so with decision and boldness.

(6) On all occasions he may exploit to receive in the fullest, support in the proper exercise of his authority.

(7) He must remember that there is no qualification so indispensable as a perfect command of temper.

(8) He shall never suffer himself to be moved in the slightest degree by any language or threats that may be used.

(9) If he do his duty in a quiet and determined manner, such conduct will probably excite the well-disposed of the bystanders to assist him if he requires them.

(10) Particular care is to be taken that the constables of the police do not form false notions of their duties and powers.

With this as a background, let us examine and analyze our present day Code of Ethics in relation to its practical application in our daily lives. Let us see how we can, by actually putting it into practice, become professional.

Law Enforcement Code of Ethics

As a law enforcement officer, my fundamental duty is to serve the community; to safeguard lives and property; to protect the innocent against deception, the weak against oppression or intimidation and the peaceful against violence or disorder; and to respect the constitutional rights of all to liberty, equality and justice.

I will keep my private life unsullied as an example to all ad will behave in a manner that does not bring discredit to me or to my agency. I will maintain courageous calm in the face of danger, scorn or ridicule; develop self-restraint; and be constantly mindful of the welfare of others. Honest in thought and deed both in my personal and official life, I will be exemplary in obeying the law and the regulations of my department. Whatever I see or hear of a confidential nature or that is confided to me in my official capacity will be kept ever secret unless revelation is necessary in the performance of my duty.

I will never act officiously or permit personal feelings, prejudices, political beliefs, aspirations, animosities or friendships to influence my decisions. With no compromise for crime and with relentless prosecution of criminals, I will enforce the law courteously and appropriately without fear or favor, malice or ill will, never employing unnecessary force or violence and never accepting gratuities.

I recognize the badge of my office as a symbol of public faith, and I accept it as a public trust to be held so long as I am true to the ethics of police service. I will never engage in acts of corruption or bribery, nor will I condone such acts by other police officers. I will cooperate with all legally authorized agencies and their representatives in the pursuit of justice.

I know that I alone am responsible for my own standard of professional performance and will take every reasonable opportunity to enhance and improve my level of knowledge and competence.

I will constantly strive to achieve these objectives and ideals, dedicating myself before God to my chosen profession ... law enforcement.

THE INTERNATIONAL ASSOCIATION OF CHIEFS OF POLICE

The Code of Ethics was the result of extensive research, review and input from many police officer and police administrative organizations. The project was headed by Lieutenant Gene Muehleisen of the San Diego Police Department. Over a period of three years, it was re-written dozens of times. In 1957, after a six month study, the International Association of Chiefs of Police adopted the code. In 1963, the code became part of California law when the State Commission on Peace Officer Standards and Training required that the code be administered as an actual oath to all new officers. Later other states initiated similar laws.

In 1989 an attempt was made to increase the relevance of the code to fit some of the more recent problems. It drew heavily on the Royal Ulster Constabulary's "Professional Policing Ethics."It was adopted by the Executive Committee of the IACP that year. However, it was found to be too long. Many police agencies now require that this oath be part of a swearing in ceremony. The solution was to make minor changes in the basic Code of Ethics, and create a separate document called the "Police Code of Conduct." This was approved by a vote of the membership at the October 1991 Annual IACP Conference.

The new Police Code of Conduct will be covered after the explanation of the basic Code of Ethics.

THE LAW ENFORCEMENT CODE OF ETHICS EXAMINED

"AS A LAW ENFORCEMENT OFFICER, MY FUNDAMENTAL DUTY IS TO SERVE THE COMMUNITY;"

The gist of this passage is contained in two words: "duty" and "serve". Too often we forget that law enforcement is not just a job for which we are hired as one would hire a laborer or tradesperson, it involves a sworn duty. Some progressive departments now require that their officers reaffirm their oath each year in an effort to drive home the message that is contained in this sworn oath, and to again remind the officers of the essential relationship between their job and the free society in which they live.

The word "serve" denotes the denial of one's own pleasures and desires for the good of the person or persons to be served. Service involves dedication and sacrifice, or the giving of one's self. These are words that many find hard to swallow in this present day and age, but the job of professional law enforcement requires a special breed of person. Professional law enforcement has no place for the officer whose philosophy of life is "what's in it for me?" In our present "awakened" society, the crooked or dishonest law enforcement officer is finding it almost impossible to really profit from his or her job in an unprofessional way. This type of officer is rapidly becoming as out-of-place as a horse and buggy on a modern freeway.

Because of this, the officer today, who is not truly dedicated to serving the community, will receive little reward in life. If he or she does not change their job or their philosophy, they will be doomed to hopeless frustration and a total lack of motivation. The very fiber of their soul will suffer from the complete absence of a true purpose in life. This might, to some, sound a little "far out". but the field of law enforcement is truly changing that fast, and to that degree.

As citizens in a country with a free market ecomony, we are able to chose our own doctor, auto mechanic, restaurant or super market. If we don't like them we can chose another. However, this does not apply when we need the services of the police department. When a citizen calls for police assistance, he or she cannot tell the communications officer that they would like Officer Jones to respond. You have to take what you get. Because of this, an officer who treats "customers" badly will not likely lose them. Since the citizen does not have a choice, it is important that the officer be of the highest quality and be well trained.

We are presently living in a world of dynamic change. The field of law enforcement is but one of many that are caught up in this whirlwind of change. Because modern law enforcement is really a combination of many fields, including both the sciences and the humanities, we must be expected to keep pace with the advances in these fields. Both are presently experiencing changes that are so great that there are years of lag between discovery or development and actual practice in the field.

Awareness of change is the key to the future. Today we cannot escape change. It can, however, in some ways escape us, if we are not totally prepared for it. This must never be allowed to happen if we are to truly serve our new and dynamic society.

It is not a matter of yesterday's methods being outdated. If one looks at the overall picture with true perspective and cold realism, one cannot escape the fact that even today's methods are often outdated. This is not too surprising when we look at the field of science where, because development is so rapid, it has become common for a machine or piece of equipment to be outdated on the day that it is first put into use.

"TO SAFEGUARD LIVES AND PROPERTY: TO PROTECT THE INNOCENT AGAINST DECEPTION, THE WEAK AGAINST OPPRESSION OR INTIMIDATION: AND THE PEACEFUL AGAINST VIOLENCE OR DISORDER"

The foregoing, although idealistic,should be a goal in any society that places value on the individual citizen. The Code of Hammurabi, the law of the ancient Babylonians, written over two thousand years before Christ, set forth similar objectives. It was easier to achieve this goal in ancient Babylonia because King Hammurabi was a benevolent dictator who ruled the land with a protective but heavy hand.

We must, however, understand some of the limitations that are present in a truly democratic society. In a society such as ours, this task can often be a difficult one, because protecting the rights of the individual means also protecting the rights of the criminal. This is sometimes a hard pill for law enforcement officers to swallow.

In a totalitarian form of government the people receive a much greater degree of protection. How-ever, they pay for this with the loss of their personal rights and freedoms. The task of efficiently enforcing the laws in a free society is never easy. Because of this, some officers can stray politically to the far right in an effort to either seek a system where their job would be made easier, or to better protect the society that they have sworn to serve. It is easy for an officer to become bitter when he or she has continually witnessed the ends of justice thwarted by red tape, politics and technicalities of the law. The more truly idealistic the officer is, the more frustrated he or she can become, especially if they lack a philosophy or understanding of the officer's true role in American society. Why must the idealistic officer suffer so? When a good carpenter does his best in building a fine house, one that can be seen and admired by all, he can stand back and look at his job with a feeling of accomplishment and satisfaction. The same applies to an artist or anyone in the skilled trades. Why not, then, the police officer? Why must good officers, who work hard for the ends of justice, see the products of their work so often crumble at their feet?

The answer is both simple and complicated. It is simple in that the police officer, unlike the tradesman, works not with objects, but with people. Wonderful and yet fallible people.

It is complicated because the most unpredictable of all things, with which a person can work, is man himself. It is the police officer's relationship with people that necessitates that law enforcement become a profession.

Should a good doctor stop practicing medicine or operating on people because some of his patients die? Should a good lawyer give up practicing law because he or she loses some cases? Should a good teacher give up teaching because some of her students become bad citizens? Obviously not. When the commodity in which we deal is people, we must not, we cannot, expect perfection. The answer to this problem lies in an obvious paradox. That is, we must strive for perfection as though it were actually obtainable, and yet realize that we will never actually achieve it. Failure to understand and practice this philosophy can result in a spirit that is irreparably broken. Examples are abundant in most communities.

There is a lesson to be learned from the legions of officers before us who have suffered so greatly from broken spirits. The lesson, quite simply, is that our satisfaction in law enforcement must come from doing our job to the best of our abilities, and must not be dependent upon the final outcome of our cases.

"TO RESPECT THE CONSTITUTIONAL RIGHT OF ALL MEN TO LIBERTY, EQUALITY AND JUSTICE"

Respecting the rights of others is not one of man's natural qualities. It seems to be part of his nature to suspect and persecute those who are in any way different from himself. We hear much criticism of the United States in this respect, yet there are few, if any, countries in this world where some prejudice and inequality does not exist.

We all want to live in a community where justice prevails, one which adheres to the basic concepts of our constitution. Yet we are often all too ready to make this a conditional justice, one that is just or fair when we want it to be, or when the conditions are what we would regard as favorable.

There is no perfect justice on this earth, nor will there ever be, because man is not all knowing, nor is he himself perfect. Still we must strive for a form of justice that represents our ultimate capability. This involves not only great effort on the part of every person in the community, but individual sacrifice as well.

A greater share of this burden falls upon those whose job it is to enforce and carry out the administration of justice. We can not legislate away personal prejudices. This takes time and careful education. If we cannot rid ourselves of prejudice, then how can we become professional law enforcement officers? This would certainly seem to be one of the prerequisites of being professional. The answer to this lies simply in being aware of our personal prejudices and acknowledging them, but not giving in to them or letting them affect decisions relating to the administration of justice.

One of the greatest faults among police officers generally, is not so much a prejudice against a particular race or religion, as it is a prejudice against the criminal. For example, an officer soon learns from experience that a certain group of persons is often responsible for the majority of the crimes committed. Among the suspects in a case, there is one who has previously committed such an offense. Such a prejudice could lead to the faulty conclusion that he is the guilty person. This soon leads to a general feeling of prejudice against all those who have been convicted of prior offenses, and an almost subconscious refusal to accord them

the same rights that the Constitution provides for all persons. Our present laws provide as fair a deal as is humanly attainable, to all persons subject to that law. Many officers feel that our system of jurisprudence is too lenient, and helps the criminal at the expense of society as a whole. In many cases this is true. One alternative to this would be to have one law for "good" citizens, and another for "criminals". The problem, however, is who decides which person comes under which category. Prior convictions alone cannot be used for qualification. To allow certain persons to have such power over the populace could soon change our form of government into a totalitarian system.

Another alternative would be a "protective" society in which the people would be accorded a high degree of protection, but in return would have few personal rights. This would be the old Roman philosophy of *Salus Populi est Suprema Lex* ("The safety of the people is the supreme law"). Personal rights and public protection are on opposite ends of a fixed scale. If we increase one, we decrease the other. When our society is threatened by a state of emergency, one of the first steps toward protection is restriction. This is usually in the form of a curfew. If no one is allowed on the streets at night, then there is no one to attack the person or property of another and protection is afforded them. However, such conditions are certainly not very conducive to a free democratic society.

We must remember that in the philosophy of American law, it is better that ten guilty persons go free than that one innocent person be convicted. Seeing ten guilty persons go free sticks very hard in the throats of most police officers, yet we must always adhere to the basic tenets of our legal system, even if at times we feel that it might not be warranted in the case at hand. History has shown us that a society is only as great as its laws are just. It is important to remember that the very basis of ethics is that a good result or supposed good end cannot justify the use of a wrong means or action to achieve that end, for no man can guarantee how a thing will end. A system of law that is not ethical will be neither just nor lasting. If we want a lasting society, we must strive toward a just system of law.

We must remember that law enforcement is but one part of the American system of jurisprudence, and that if we do our part in a proper manner, it shouldn't matter what the outcome of the case might be. This, of course, is not easy, because our human nature wants us to carry the case through to the very end, and take a personal interest in it. It is very easy to attempt to be policeman, prosecutor, judge, jury, and corrections officer.

Any game must have rules if there are to be significant results from playing the game. A referee is usually appointed to see that these rules are carried out. In the case of American jurisprudence, the judge and the courts are the referees, and it is their job to see that all parties play by the rules. The continued existence of our society as a democracy depends upon this. In these United States there is such a high respect for the rights of all men to liberty, equality and justice, that a handicap is placed upon law enforcement in favor of the individual person. Those officers who fail to fully understand this concept are the first to become embittered, and later, frustrated. They are then likely to become unprofessional in their chosen work.

"I WILL KEEP MY PRIVATE LIFE UNSULLIED AS AN EXAMPLE TO ALL AND WILL BEHAVE IN A MANNER THAT DOES NOT BRING DISCREDIT TO ME OR TO MY AGENCY."

One of the first things that a law enforcement officer must learn is that he or she has no private life. Every citizen should be entitled to their own private life, yet when a person accepts the calling of law enforcement, as a voluntary measure, they must be willing to offer their privacy as a sacrifice to the good of the community which they serve.

Because Law Enforcement is a position of public trust, the public expects a great deal more from those in that position. These expectations are not always realistic from a practical standpoint, but that doesn't matter to the public. For example if a doctor, plumber, or teacher was convicted of "Driving under the Influence," they would suffer the normal punishment as prescribed by law. They would not lose their jobs. However, if an officer were found guilty of the same offense, not only would there be the normal punishment, but administrative punishment as well. In some cases the officer could suffer the loss of employment.

To illustrate this apparent inequity, there is a recent case of an officer who was having marital difficulties and as a result suffered from low morale. He let his home fall into a state of disrepair. The front lawn was seldom cut. Finally a large group of neighbors went to the Chief of Police and demanded that he make the officer do something about the problem. This would never have happened if the homeowner had been a carpenter or even a teacher. There is an expectation, however unreal, that police officers are or should be different. People feel that they should be examples for the community. Anything short of that is looked upon as a violation of public trust. Many people feel that officers do not look professional when they smoke in public. Some departments will actually list these as undesirable actions in their police manual.

Because of this expectation, officers need to learn which actions seem to offend the public. For example, wearing dark or mirrored sun glasses seems to be one of those things that offend those stopped by officers. They feel that the officer is "hiding behind them." They seem to think that there is something sneaky or unprofessional about it. In our western society it is important to be able to "look a person in the eye." This is not necessarily so in other societies. Another thing that seems to offend people is the officer who goes around with a toothpick sticking out of his mouth. It is a macho type of thing that women seldom do, but one the public looks upon as a sign of arrogance. These things are seldom discussed in police academies. There are so many topics to be covered and so little time. A major amount of time is allotted to topics that are really rare occurences in an average officer's day to day routine. Most police academies are a minimum of 550 hours, but the topic of Ethics averages a one hour class.

The idea of denying oneself for the good of the community is not new. If today's officer thinks that the community demands too much, he or she should read this list of rules posted in 1872 for officers in an upstate New York police department.

(1) Desk officers each day will fill lamps, clean chimneys and trim wicks.

(2) Each officer will bring a bucket of water and a scuttle of coal for each shift.

(3) Make your pens carefully, you may whittle nibs to your individual taste *(the beginning of police officer's individual rights)*.

(4) Officers will be given an evening off each week for courting purposes, or two evenings a week if they go to church regularly.

(5) After thirteen hours on duty, the officers should spend the remaining time reading the Bible or other good books.

(6) Each officer should lay aside from each pay *($18 a month)* a goodly sum of his earnings for his benefit during his declining years so that he will not become a burden on society.

(7) Any officer who smokes Spanish cigars, uses liquor in any form, frequents pool or dance halls, or gets shaved in a barber shop, will give good reason to suspect his worth, intentions, integrity and honesty.

(8) The officer who performs his duties faithfully and without fault for five years will be given an increase of five cents per day in his pay, providing city funds permit.

If law enforcement officers could hide from their neighbors the fact that they are police officers, then their private life could be their own. This, however, is an impossibility. If a police officer has a family, his or her occupation will become known in the neighborhood within a few days at the most. If the officer is single, and avoids contact with others, the secret may be keep a little longer, but if he or she is engaged in active law enforcement within the community, it is inevitable that neighbors will become aware of it. Once this is known, the officer will become the object of constant observation.

Unfortunately, many will be watching the officer, hoping to observe some irregularity that will further justify their negative feeling toward "cops". Others will watch in hopes of catching the officer committing some traffic violation so that they can accuse all policemen of hypocrisy. This will help justify their own misdeeds concerning traffic violations for which they feel they were unjustly given tickets.

There is an unwritten rule in law enforcement that you do not give a traffic ticket to a fellow officer. Because of this, there is a natural tendency for officers to feel that they can violate traffic laws "just a little" without having to pay the consequences. A reporter for the San Diego Evening Tribune decided to conduct a little research on this matter. He found that out of 108,000 traffic citations issued during the six months of his study, not one citation was issued to police officers, their wives, city council members, county supervisors, municipal and superior court judges, and major county and city department heads. The reporter consulted a mathematics professor, and discovered that the chance of 1,100 drivers (the number of officers on the department) not receiving a ticket for a six month period was one in 10,000,000,000,000,000,000,000,000,000,000,000. In an editorial, he concluded that policemen were exceptionally good drivers, since 10 to the 36th power would equal more stars and planets than there are in the sky. As a result of the article, the Mayor of San Diego took immediate measures to correct this inequity.

Many police officers will argue that even doctors give each other "professional courtesies", but the question here is whether or not it is professional conduct. An important issue when covering this particular topic is that officers, being human, will tend to disregard traffic laws when they know that they will not be held responsible for their misdeeds. The driving habits that result, will not only show up in the operation of police vehicles, but will further the reputation of hypocrisy that is so important to avoid.

One of the great ailments of our present society and undoubtedly others before us, is that parents tell their children to do one thing and then they themselves do just the opposite. Then they are surprised at their children's transgressions, and can't understand why they did not heed the good advice given them. The best way to teach something is through example. If this is true, then law enforcement officers could actually make their jobs easier by becoming exemplary citizens. If the example took, there would be less crime, and if the example were a truthful reflection of the officer's personal life, he or she would not only gain the respect of the community, but its cooperation and assistance as well.

There is a little poem by an unknown author that puts it so well that each police officer should have it taped in a place where it could be easily read each night.

> The eye's a better pupil and more willing
>   than the ear;
> Fine counsel is confusing, but example's al-
>   ways clear;
> And the best of all the preachers are the
>   men who live their creeds,
> For to see the good in action is what
>   everybody needs.
> I can soon learn how to do it if you'll let me
>   see it done,
> I can watch your hands in action, but your
>   tongue too fast may run ;
> And the lectures you deliver may be very
>   wise and true,
> But I'd rather get my lesson by observing
>   what you do.
> For I may understand you and the high ad-
>   vice you give,
> But there's no misunderstanding how you
>   act and how you live.

Living a model life as an example for others in your community to follow is not easy. For some it is most difficult. We all have different temptations in varying degrees at varying times. However, it is one of the prerequisites of professional law enforcement, one to which prospective law enforcement officers should give serious thought.

Of great assistance in achieving this goal is an officer's own family. The officer's spouse, or parents if he or she is living at home, should have all of the conditions of the job explained ahead of time, since the spouse plays such an important role in the officer's life. An officer's spouse should clearly understand that an officer is not just holding down a job, but is performing a dedicated service to society, and it is one that requires a spouse's assistance. Society and police administrators in general, are prone to overlook the spouse's part in law enforcement. He or she does play an important role, and great effort must be made to reach them and secure their cooperation. When they understand the true objectives of professional law enforcement, and the sacrifices that are involved, they are very likely to become a partner toward those ends rather than resenting the job because of the many restrictions it places upon the officer and the officer's family. An understanding spouse is a

necessity if a dedicated officer is to achieve his professional goals.

Another area of great danger is the officer's personal morals. An officer spends a great deal of time dealing with moral degenerates and persons of little conscience. If an officer is not constantly on guard, these people can present a negative influence. Female offenders and female friends of offenders are often willing to offer sexual favors to male police officers in hopes of receiving some leniency should they or their friends be arrested. Since most police officers work nights, they come into greater contact with those who might not be of the best moral character. Many have the reputation of being promiscuous, and it is very easy for a law enforcement officer to succumb to these temptations. This can lead to both moral degradation and blackmail, and can have a negative effect in the struggle for professional recognition. It is easy to rationalize and justify transgressions of this nature as just giving vent to natural drives, but these actions do in fact generate moral decay and endanger the officer's family. The citizens of a community are very alert to transgressions of a moral nature among police officers, and they will quickly withdraw their needed support of any law enforcement agency in which the selfish desires of its officers betray their professional calling. Internal Affairs investigators find that this is one of the most common areas where officers endanger their careers.

The section "And will behave in a manner that does not bring discredit to me or to my agency" was added in 1989. This was the result of a great number of officers who felt that they could identify themselves as police officers and at the same time engage in conduct that was demeaning or discrediting to their agency. For example, wearing the department's uniform while engaged in a non-police activity that reflects upon the department in a negative way. When an officer wears the uniform, the average citizen reasonably assumes that the officer is acting in behalf of the department. This also includes lewd and immoral behavior while identifying oneself as a member of their department.

"I WILL MAINTAIN COURAGEOUS CALM IN THE FACE OF DANGER, SCORN OR RIDICULE, AND DEVELOP SELF RESTRAINT;"

Most officers are prepared to face physical danger and the public expects it. This is due to the fact that when most people think of policework, they think of high speed chases with guns blazing and similar situations in which the officer's life is in constant danger. Movies and television with dramatization of the more spectacular aspects of the job are responsible in large degree for this attitude.

Fortunately, danger amounts to but a small fraction of the officer's work routine. Among a listing of the most dangerous occupations in the United States, law enforcement is twentieth on the list. Firefighters rank fifth. Most people see the threat to law enforcement officers in the form of firearms. Some officers in small communities feel that it might be boredom. Actually the automobile can take credit for most officer injuries. The threat for which an officer is not prepared, and one which can have great effect, is public scorn or ridicule. There is no doubt that some have become officers because of a need for power and authority. It comes as quite a shock to them that the badge, uniform and gun mean very little unless there is a person of substance behind those symbols of authority. The first commandment in professional law enforcement should be "A uniform does not a police officer make." Respect must be earned. It cannot be bought with a badge and a uniform.

In a democracy a police officer is a public officer, and as such is a servant to the community. Instead of being above reproach or ridicule, a professional officer must expect to occasionally receive both as part of the job. It is not easy to control one's temper when being subjected to unnecessary and unjustified scorn or ridicule. Punching the perpetrator in the mouth will hurt him physically, but psychologically he will sense victory because he has personally brought the officer off his or her pedestal, and down to his level. One way to handle this is to look upon it as a game. One where, if you lose your temper, you lose the game and your professional standing, and the "scumbag" wins.

Nothing will hurt him more, as he "mouths off", than being ignored. Through practice, even the officer with a wild temper can learn to control it. For the professional law enforcement officer it is a "must." When subjected to scorn and ridicule, it often helps just to consider the source.

A professional police officer must guard against making "retaliatory arrests" or listing multiple and unnecessary charges because the person happened to "mouth off." Most statutes contain small ambiguous sections that can enable an officer to book a person when he is being a "smart ass". Some officers complain that the District Attorney issues criminal complaints on only a few of the many crimes with which an offender was originally charged. Maybe the reason for this action is that the D.A. is keenly aware that the multiplicity of charges were due, not in the interest of justice, but because the officer was angry at the offender. The D.A. knows how juries will view this.

Many of the persons with whom a peace officer deals are either highly emotional or under the influence of alcohol or drugs, and are often not fully responsible for their actions or words. It is not easy to take the brunt of these actions and ignore it, but if the officer will at least try to see the situation in its true perspective, it will help greatly.

Most of the big mistakes we make in our lives are usually when we are in an emotional state or under stress, and we are nearly always sorry later. If we are to play a professional part in anything as important as the administration of criminal justice, then we must constantly guard ourselves against decisions and judgments that are retaliatory in nature and serve only to soothe our damaged ego. Nothing hurts the department's image more than such actions, especially when the public becomes aware of them.

When a citizen approaches an officer who has just taken someone into custody and states "I don't know how you control yourself. If it had've been me, I would have punched that so-and-so in the mouth ten minutes ago", then the officer can take pride in the fact that he or she has earned true public respect because of professional restraint.

"WHATEVER I SEE OR HEAR OF A CONFIDENTIAL NATURE OR THAT IS CONFIDED TO ME IN MY OFFICIAL CAPACITY WILL BE KEPT EVER SECRET UNLESS REVELATON IS NECESSARY IN THE PERFORMANCE OF MY DUTY"

Men will often joke about the tendency of women to gossip, but this is a weakness for all humans. We, by our very nature, love to impress a friend or acquaintance with a confidential piece of gossip or information. It can be a masterpiece of self control, when we are walking down the street with a friend and happen to see some high city official, about whose background we have confidential police information, and we keep walking without mentioning this information to that friend.

If we had a venereal disease that was the result of a chance personal transgression, we would certainly want our doctor to keep this information a professional secret and not broadcast it throughout the community. We would expect the same of our attorney. Yet if law enforcement is to ever achieve professional status, we must acquire the ability to respect confidences that come our way as part of our work. This is another prerequisite for professional standing.

Some officers feel that there is a difference. The information obtained by the doctor and attorney is freely given with the understanding that it will be confidential, whereas the information obtained by the law enforcement officer can be the result of many sources or forms of investigation.

How it was obtained is really not important. The key point is the fact that it was obtained as part of the officer's occupation, and is usually information that the officer would not have otherwise obtained had he or she not been working as a peace officer.

This information should never leave the department or the person retaining it unless it is in the interest of justice. An officer should even be careful not to reveal information to his or her spouse. An officer's wife is often very tempted to reveal information of a confidential nature to neighbor women in an effort to show her neighbors the importance of her husband's job, and to gain status in the eyes of the neighbor women. Husbands of female officers also have trouble keeping

secrets of this nature. It is often looked upon as compensation for what they suffer when they are married to a peace officer. It also makes us feel important when we have access to information that others do not. The authors are aware of a case where the defense attorney obtained a change in venue for a trial because the investigating officer had given confidential information to his wife. Within a week it was common knowledge in the community and the defense attorney claimed it prevented his client from receiving a fair trial.

"I WILL NEVER ACT OFFICIOUSLY"

A fault that is common to new officers is acting officiously. They appear to the public to be overimpressed with their own importance. In a way this is natural because it is associated with pride, and a new officer is usually very proud when he or she first puts on the uniform and badge. They should rightly be proud, for this is a noble undertaking. However, a law enforcement officer must always guard against having this pride misinter-preted by the public as being officious.

The Penal Code is written in black and white, and it allows for no extenuating circumstances. Every human being is, in his own way, different, and every criminal offense is, in its own way, different due to time and place, and because of many human factors. It is therefore up to those who administer the laws of criminal justice to administer them with some feeling for the circumstances and the people involved. If law enforcement officers act like robots, they may someday be replaced by robots.

In most cases of apparent officiousness, it is simply a matter of the officer not knowing how to act. Most police academies greatly neglect the area of teaching officers how to act, or how to play the role that is expected of them. There are so many facts that have to be poured into the recruit's head, that little time is left for this form of role playing.

The majority of people who make contact with a law enforcement officer during a tour of duty are not criminals. Those receiving tickets are normally law abiding, upright citizens in the community, and they are usually embarrassed enough by being caught in a traffic violation without being "talked down to" or treated like criminals.

Judges often report that a common reason for a person appearing in traffic court is not so much to contest the facts of the offense as it is to complain about the demeanor of the officer issuing the citation.

This would support a study conducted by one of the authors in which it was found that certain officers who wrote twice as many citations as other officers had to appear in court only one tenth as often as those other officers. A follow-up sampling of defendants revealed that a major complaint against the officers who appeared most often in court was their attitude. The percentage of convictions for these officers was very low indicating that judges were tired of seeing them in court all the time and were tired of hearing complaints about their demeanor. It is easy for a judge to subconsciously impeach an officer who makes a bad impression.

Sometimes the attitude of an officer is a psychological defense mechanism. It becomes a psychological shield with which to protect his or her own insecurity. Other times the officer is acting out a "parent-child role." When the officer was a child and did something wrong, the parent would make a big issue out of it and rant and rave at the child. Now that the child is a grown officer, it is easy to fall back on that early conditioning. When issuing a ticket, instead of just writing the ticket, the officer feels the need to "chew out" the offender.

Another form of officiousness about which an officer must be on guard, is the "Civil Service" attitude. In private business, the customer is treated with some respect because it can mean a monetary loss or gain. Since city and government employees have civil service protection and are not faced with this alternative, it is easy for them to become very cold and impersonal to those with whom they have dealings. In line with professional thinking, it should be remembered that an officer who has little respect for others seldom has self respect.

"I WILL NEVER PERMIT PERSONAL FEELINGS, PREJUDICE, POLITICAL BELIEFS, ASPIRATIONS, ANIMOSITIES OR FRIENDSHIPS TO INFLUENCE MY DECISIONS"

It is quite difficult to know which desire is strongest in some persons. That of helping our friends or hurting our enemies. Both desires are part of our human nature. Helping our friends can be a very good thing in itself, but when it involves an inequity in the administration of justice, we are defiling the very oath we made to the community in which we serve.

In policework, there is ample opportunity to both hurt enemies and help friends, and it takes a person of strong character to properly perform his or her duties under these circumstances. Without professional convictions, this can be an impossibility.

Sincere, professional police officers are seldom totally aware of the hidden effect that their personal feelings have in influencing daily decisions. Human fallibility prevents us from completely erradicating this fault. However, we may greatly correct it by trying to mentally list all of the personal feelings that might come to play in arriving at a certain decision, and then truthfully ask ourselves what part they play in that final decision.

The words "political beliefs, aspirations," was added in 1989. This was added because some officers were publically expressing political beliefs while in uniform. Again, when an officer is in uniform, the public can reasonably assume that he or she is speaking for the department. We are all free to express ourselves under the United States Constitution, but not while in uniform if it could reasonably be inferred that we are speaking for the department. This also includes acting in a way that would infer departmental approval.

"WITH NO COMPROMISE FOR CRIME AND WITH RELENTLESS PROSECUTION OF CRIMINALS, I WILL ENFORCE THE LAW COURTEOUSLY AND APPROPRIATELY WITHOUT FEAR OR FAVOR, MALICE OR ILL WILL"

The term "with no compromise for crime" means that crime will not be knowingly permitted. It does not mean that the officer must perform all duties to the "letter of the law" without taking into consideration the "spirit of the law."

It is easy for a law enforcement officer to become discouraged. He or she sees arrested persons get off because of some technicality of the law or because of some quirk of fate, and it seems that many of those who are finally convicted, are given light sentences or probation, and are back on the street again in no time at all. It can make their work seem futile. It is therefore easy for the sincere officer to give up and drift with the current because individual efforts seem so unproductive. Why work hard? For what?

If the Code of Ethics will be examined, nothing in that code will be found stating that an officer must obtain convictions and send people to prison for long periods of time. It does state, however, that the officer must do the best of which he or she is capable, and that the actions must, in themselves, be ethical. No person can predict or guarantee the final results of any action. Only God can do this. Man can only be responsible for immediate actions. If an officer does a good job and the criminal is released by the courts, the blame rests upon the courts, the jury or society itself. Not the officer.

There is an old time philosophy in law enforcement that you must treat the criminal in a rough manner. If not, he will think that you are soft or a coward, and will walk all over you. This philo-sophy allows for no in between, no shades of gray. You are either tough or you are soft. If instilling fear in the hearts of criminals was the true purpose of law enforcement the validity of such a philosophy is brought into question when we look at the recorded history of our local departments. Read newspaper clippings covering the criminal aspects of the news during the times when officers were picked for brawn over brains, and when a good officer was measured by how tough he was. One need not read far to find evidence that criminals responded to this treatment by being just as tough themselves.

The modern law enforcement officer has a new motto. "Be firm but fair." The officer does not have to be a "theory bound" sociologist just because he or she treats criminals like human beings One of the authors found that his greatest source of informants was persons he had sent to jail or prison. Because he had treated them fairly, they remembered this when they were released, and often provided very valuable information.

Religious teachings stress the theme that we should hate sin but love man. This means that we may hate crime but not the criminal. For some it is easy to hate the criminal, but in time they are themselves consumed by the flame of this hatred. Some officers feel that their job is to punish, and that in order to punish someone you must vent your anger upon them. Our present system of criminal justice assigns no duties of punishment to the law enforcement officer. The role of punishment belongs to the people in Corrections and Penology.

Getting angry, other than as an interrogative technique, serves no purpose. Anger begets anger. The angry officer only makes the job more difficult.

It is said that the "proof of the pudding is in the tasting". The proof of this theory is in the testing. Try it out. Watch other officers closely when they are making arrests. Why is it that some officers continually have trouble with their prisoners, while others, who make as many arrests, have little or no trouble? Close observation of the techniques of both types of officers will soon reveal the truth.

This does not mean that the modern law enforcement officer has to be a "sissy". On the contrary, he or she must have more courage than their predecessors, if for no other reason than to put up with some of the indignities that officers often encounter without seeking some personal satisfaction through violence or retribution. The modern professional law enforcemant officer lets the criminal call the tune as to his own treatment. The officer can and must be as tough as the situation demands, yet there is no personal vindictiveness in the way in which the criminal is treated. An officer's tone of voice and demeanor usually indicate that he or she will not be walked on, and that they are in charge of the situation.

Some will deny this, but respect can be born out of fairness. Law Enforcement is not a popularity contest. It never has been. Yet liking a person and respecting that person can be two totally different things.

King Charles I was aware of this and indicated it in the Articles of War issued in 1629. "The Provost must have a horse allowed him and some soldiers to attend him and all the rest commanded to obey and assist him, or else the service will suffer; for he is but one man and must correct many and therefore he cannot be beloved."

An officer cannot make friends of all criminals. It would be foolish to try. However, in the majority of cases, an officer can gain respect through "firm but fair" treatment. The officer who can do this has done the job well.

"I WILL NEVER EMPLOY UNNECESSARY FORCE OR VIOLENCE"

At times the use of force in the performance of one's duties is an absolute necessity. There is no escaping it. It can be extremely difficult to judge exactly whether or not the force used in a particular situation was necessary or not.

In 1992 the Associated Press conducted a survey in which it was found that 60% of Americans believed that police officers treated people of all races and ethnic groups equally 22% felt that there was a great amount of police brutality against minorities 70% of those polled believed that the Rodney King verdict did not justify the rioting and anger of those involved.

In 1991, after the video tape of the Rodney King beating was played continually on national television, police chiefs from 10 major U.S. cities met in a committee to investigate the degree of excess force used by police officers. They found that excessive force by officers was national in scope, but that a lot of it tended to be committed by a small group of officers

Society accepts the fact that the police are in the business of using force. Society does not, however, accept the use of excessive force. When they perceive that the police are guilty of excessive force, the credibility of the department and citizen support suffer greatly. In a democracy, citizen support is not only important, it is essential.

When we consider how many arrests are actually made, the number of complaints are relatively low. Less than 2 percent. We live in a democratic society that tends to voice its complaints. Also to be considered is the fact that a large number of complaints are not justified. Yet despite these facts, in 1990, the City of Los Angeles paid out $7 million to settle police brutality and misconduct suits. In 1991 they paid out a record $13 million. By the middle of 1992 it appeared that the year would well exceed 1991. (This is excluding the Rodney King case where attorneys sued for $83 million.) City councilmen have stated that they fear that these suits could bankrupt the city.

Fig. I-1; Rodney King Beating   Courtesy: A.P. Worldwide Photo

Fig I-2; L.A. Riot After Officers Acquitted

Courtesy: A.P. Worldwide

Not only is excessive force morally wrong, it can be extremely expensive. In 1992, after a jury found the officers innocent of criminal charges in the Rodney King case, the rioting in the city of Los Angeles and the arson and looting that took place accounted for losses of almost one billion dollars. That does not include the losses in other major cities where demonstrations took place. That does not include the tremendous cost of overtime for police officers and fire fighters. It does not include the cost of federal officers and the National Guard. It does not include the the unmeasurable grief of the family and friends of the 57 persons killed and 2,383 persons injured. Nor does it include the very high cost of prosecuting the thousands of persons arrested during the riots.

Today, more than at any time in our history, an increasing number of police officers are being successfully sued in court for the excess use of force while performing their duties. These officers will never own a home or acquire any wealth. Monies in excess of their living expenses will go to the plaintiff in the suit.

THE CHRISTOPHER COMMISSION REPORT

In April of 1991, the Mayor of Los Angeles established an independent commision to investigate the use of excessive force under color of law in the L.A.P.D. Although this investigative study involved only one city, its findings and recommendations have importance for cities throughout the U.S.

This commission was headed by former Assistant Attorney General of the United States, Warren Christopher. The commission was assisted by 60 attorneys, modern computers with special software and three accounting firms. They investigated police reports, records and patrol computer transmissions for a four year period. One million documents were reviewed; 700 complaints against officers were reviewed with concentrated efforts toward 87 cases in which the city settled out-of- court with payments of at least $15,000.

As part of this major investigation, 50 expert witnesses appeared before 26 executive sessions (in private); 150 representitives of community organ-izations appeared at 5 public meetings. Then more than 500 current and retired L.A.P.D. officers were interviewed. The findings and recommendations were published in a book entitled the Christopher Commission Report. Members of the commission found that the majority of the 8,450 officers on the department did their arduous job in an exemplary manner. They regretted that this report might reflect upon them in a negative way.

The commission found considerable evidence of excessive force. However, they found that a large number of complaints were lodged against a small number of officers. Of those involved in excessive force, it was found that 5% of the officers were responsible for 20% of the complaints. Despite many written guidelines on proper behavior when dealing with citizens, these officers consistently ignored them. They also found that this problem was aggravated by racism and bias. An important finding by the commission was that those officers who seem to regularly use excessive force have a reputation among their fellow officers for that behavior. Just as important is the fact that this reputation is well known to their supervisors. The investigators also found evidence that the public regularly encountered difficulty when attempting to register complaints against officers. The commission recommended that the complaint office be located away from the police department or sub station. They also felt that the officers receiving complaints should not be in uniform.

The commission felt that the main area of fault was the lack of proper supervision, management and leadership in handling officers charged with excessive force. The department failed to properly deal with officers when complaints against them were sustained. Those with sustained findings were often given positive evaluations by their supervisors. In some cases, their records were ignored when they competed for promotion. Messages sent from patrol cars on the Mobile Digital Terminals (MDT computers) were examined for a 182 day period. Hundreds of messages were found referring to the beating of suspects almost in a form of bragging. Many contained racial slurs. It was found that no attempt was made by the department to audit these messages despite the fact that it would have been easy to do so.

The commission found that many times complaints of excessive force were not investigated by Internal Affairs, but by the officer's supervisors. These investigations were found to be lacking in quality. In those cases where the charges were sustained, the resulting discipline was either light or non-existing.

Of the recommendations issued in this report, the most important was that supervisors and managers must do their jobs properly when it comes to handling excessive force investigations.

An officer has many recourses when confronted with a suspect who is resisting a legal arrest. A great many complaints do not challenge the need for force. It is the type and degree of force used that is the basis for the complaint. Most departments have an Escalation of Force policy which states that an officer should start with a lesser type of force, and if that doesn't work, escalate to a greater force. For example, the first, and by the way, an officer's best weapon, is talking. Most situations can be resolved through talking and patience. Next would be some type of physical restraint, such as an arm or wrist lock. Next would be the use of Mace, and then the baton and finally the firearm. Using a firearm on an unarmed suspect as a first resort would obviously not be following an Escalation of Force policy. In "The Mind and Faith of Justice Holmes", the Justice aptly stated the problem in the following quote:

> The final test . . . is battle in some form. It is one thing to utter a happy phrase from a protected cloister; another to think under fire—to think for action upon which great interests depend.

Those organizations, that are prone to criticize all situations involving the use of force by police officers as "police brutality," seldom do so with complete understanding of all of the factors involved, despite the fact they they might sincerely believe the charges they have made.

Modern law enforcement officers often take offense at unjust charges of police brutality that seem to be continually leveled against the police. It is natural for a person to want to avoid punishment. If you were arrested and charged with a crime, you would want to find some way to escape your unfortunate situation. One of the most successful ways to accomplish this is to accuse the police of brutality during the arrest, and then have your attorney agree to drop the civil suit in return for the District Attorney dropping the criminal charges. This was such a common occurence in the state of California, that a law was passed to the effect that a defendant could not initiate a civil suit against a police department until criminal charges had been resolved. This had a great effect on controlling the blackmail attempts against criminal prosecution.

To really understand this problem, we must accept two facts. First, police brutality, or the unnecessary use of force does in fact exist. A person need not be on the force long to see some examples of this. Many times it is by good police officers who have just "lost their heads" in a particularly stressful situation. The only place we can recruit police officers is the human race. Humans are not perfect. However this should not be used as an excuse to continue unprofessional practices. Second, we in the field of law enforcement have a past that we must live down. The older gen-erations of our society have, in years past, known a different type of law enforcement, one in which unnecessary force was not only accepted but often condoned. Many of our citizens of all ages have come from parts of the United States where, unfortunately, unecessary force and violence may still be an accepted practice. Where there is low pay and the improper selection of police personnel, it is difficult to maintain professional standards. The use of force or violence during interrogations will often produce confessions, but it should be avoided on both ethical and practical grounds. It should be avoided on ethical grounds because the interrogator seldom knows with complete certainty that the suspect is guilty, and the use of force or the "third degree" on an innocent person could and has produced false confessions. The harming of an innocent person is certainly a miscarriage of justice as well as a violation of professional conduct. As a means of punishment for the criminal, it would be out of place for it is not the function of law enforcement to punish criminals. This belongs to the courts and prisons.

From a practical viewpoint, unnecessary force or violence should be avoided during interrogations because if the jury or a judge even suspects that force was used to obtain a confession, it would be thrown out of court, and chances are the case would be lost. It is difficult enough for modern, professional law enforcement officers to convince the courts that their methods of interrogation are "above board", because of the reputation that law enforcement had fifty or more years ago. In a society that is so conscious of its rights as ours is today, the use of force or violence as a common practice would invalidate nearly all of the confessions that reached the courtroom, and would therefore defeat its own purpose.

Confessions are extremely important in the prosecution of criminal cases, so we must insure their validity in our courts, and this can only be done if the public is convinced that the unnecessary use of force and violence in interrogations is a thing of the past and will not be tolerated by the modern, professional law enforcement officer.

The 1991 videotaping of Los Angeles officers beating suspect Rodney King made national headlines. It is a rare citizen who, sitting in their living room watching this on television, did not personally feel each blow that officers administered to the suspect. It will take decades for the general public to forget this incident. It will take longer for good police officers to escape the stigma associated with this act.

It takes training, self control and great presence of mind for an officer to remain completely calm during an emotional crisis. The use of unnecessary force and violence in controlling prisoners and suspects is not uncommon among present day officers, even those who are very ethical in all other respects. Such actions are the result of perfectly natural human traits. When we sense danger, our bodies react by becoming overly alert. We sense the "Fight or Flight" reaction in which our body prepares us to fight or run away. Our hearts beat faster and our emotions rise and impair our intellect or proper thinking. Our salvation in such situations is usually our training or good habits. It is this that can stop us from giving in completely to our emotions.

Because we are emotional, and cannot think as clearly as we normally do, we have a tendency to sink to the animal level in our behavior. It is difficult to fight a resisting prisoner without going all the way. It is very easy to become personally and emotionally involved to the point where there is a feeling of vengeance or retaliation and the officer will give the prisoner one last punch after he has ceased to resist, just to show him who's boss and to work off the affront to the officer's pride.

Fear is another factor. Officers who find themselves in life threatening situations and state that they are not afraid, either don't understand the situation or are lying. Fear can, to a great extent, be partially overcome through proper training in defensive tactics. When officers feel confident in their abilities, they are less likely to "lose their heads". An officer should not try to eliminate fear altogether. Fear has a good purpose. It keeps us alive. As long as it is not completely debilitating, it serves an officer well.

A good police restraint hold will not only secure the prisoner, but will not give bystanders the impression that the officer is "beating up" the suspect .

Fear has an added side effect. Many officers will fight with a prisoner because they are afraid of him and they don't want him to know it. Because of this, they will take absolutely no "guff" or "lip" from him for fear that this will be taken as a sign of weakness, and will reveal their inner feelings. An officer who is not afraid of a prisoner, or who has good presence of mind, will take more lip from the prisoner, and will be more inclined to "talk" him to headquarters rather than fight him there. This "macho" trait is seldom found in female officers.

The key to the problem is control of emotions. Through training and self control, the professional law enforcement officer must learn to keep emotions under control. Officers must take great pains not to lose their tempers or get angry. This takes considerable practice, but it can be done. Once an officer has learned this restraint, that officer gains a degree of self respect in mastering this challenge.

"I WILL NEVER ACCEPT GRATUITIES"

The topic of accepting gratuities causes many long and heated discussions among modern police officers. It is one in which both ethics and rationalization enter the picture.

Those against gratuities of any form state that an officer is cheaply bought when he or she accepts a free cup of coffee. Others feel that the officer has really paid for it dearly in the loss of respect that has been generated from all those who have observed this act.Those in favor of officers accepting small gratuities such as coffee, state that it allows sincere citizens and businessmen in the community an opportunity to offer moral support to the police through some form of overt action. They feel that to refuse their simple gifts would be a slap in the face, and would hurt community relations with these persons. After all, they only want to do their part in the "fight against crime".

Gratuities take two main forms. First is the gratuity given by a person with the sole intent of receiving something in return. The other is the gratuity that is given solely out of a respect for law enforcement and the job that police officers are doing.

It is not always easy to distinguish between the two. There is a variation of the second. The gratuity for favors already performed, or a job well done. The officer who returns stolen property to its owner, a lost child to its parent, or who saves another's life, is likely to be offered some type of gratuity for this service. The history of American law enforcement is filled with the practice of rewards. During earlier times, it was apparently an accepted thing. Today it is a rarity. The general feeling persists that policemen are only doing their duty when they perform some task that helps another.

Those who favor gratuities usually feel that the second form is all right, but not the first. They feel that the key to gratuities is as follows: "Will this in any way affect the proper performance of my duties?" In other words, if the officer were to observe the person giving the gratuity, commit some violation, whether it be an hour or a day later, would he or she, in all conscience, be able to treat that person the same as a total stranger?

When we become personally involved in some action or when we personally profit from it, the process of rationalization plays a great part in our thinking.

The law enforcement officials who developed this code had many years of practical experience in the field and were certainly aware of the complexities of this particular area, but the use of the word "never" in relation to accepting gratuities indicates that they felt that this was a necessary and essential prerequisite to professional law enforcement. To be truly professional we must first be ethical. To be ethical, we must do what is actually desirable, not merely what we would like to be desirable.

Most officers who accept small gratuities such as free coffee and newspapers, would never think of accepting a large bribe. Yet after accepting these gratuities for years, and knowing subconsciously that they have given "breaks" or considerations in the enforcement of the law to the persons involved, a change has taken place. Almost unnoticed by the officer has been a slow weakening in the moral fiber. A person's ethics normally decrease with the years. The frustrations of life and of one's job can have a very discouraging effect on a person's morale. It can mellow the firmness of one's convictions. Especially if, over the years, the officer has failed to nurture them. Under these conditions, it is easy to rationalize that there is really not much difference between the two classifications of gratuities, and that it should be considered a fringe benefit of sorts just as that in private industry. This person has now been conditioned to where he or she will be susceptible to actual bribes, and this can only lead to the loss of one's job and self respect, and damage to the reputation of law enforcement in general.

If law enforcement officers were to immediately refuse further gratuities, there would undoubtedly be many sincere people who would have their feelings hurt. Yet it would be temporary and soon be forgotten. These feelings would change to one of greater respect, and it would go a long way towards building the proper image of the modern law enforcement officer. It is said that respect cannot be bought, that it must be earned. An exception in which it can be both bought and earned is when the law enforcement officer buys his or her own coffee.

"I RECOGNIZE THE BADGE OF MY OFFICE AS A SYMBOL OF PUBLIC FAITH, AND I ACCEPT IT AS A PUBLIC TRUST TO BE HELD SO LONG AS I AM TRUE TO THE ETHICS OF POLICE SERVICE"

The essence of this section is one of the most overlooked and forgotten facets of law enforcement by the those in the field. It is this that distinguishes the difference between law enforcement and the ordinary job. It is this that enables an officer to suffer the difficulties and problems that, at times, can make this field so frustrating and discouraging. If policework is just a job, it is certainly one of the worst.

For an officer to avoid unprofessional conduct, there are three qualities that must be sought as though they were precious jewels. They are integrity (moral excellence and conduct), virtue (soundness of moral principle and character) and honesty. An officer may not be rich, have super intelligence, good looks, talent or other sought after qualities, but any sincere officer can achieve these qualities so valued by mankind. The first step is recognizing their true value, and then making an effort to develop them. A person possesses very few things in life that cannot be taken away. Money, good looks, health, a job. All of these things are temporary and can pass away. However, if an officer develops the qualities of integrity, virtue and honesty, and works hard to maintain them, no one can ever take them away. They can be lost, but only by the officer. These qualities are closely related to, and actually enchance, self respect and dignity— attributes so lacking in today's society.

Police administrators would do well to place more emphasis upon the swearing-in process. It should be made very formal and similar to the initiation of fraternal organizations. The Chief of Police or Sheriff should see that the recruit is not issued a badge or allowed to put on a uniform until he or she is thoroughly familiar with the code of ethics and especially the above section. Officers should be made to understand that they are one of a select few, and that this job is a public trust that must be earned. The new officer should also understand that any personal reward will not be obtained from the public itself, for the public is a difficult master. They expect too much of the police. Their expectations go far beyond anything the police officer, as a human being, under existing conditions, can deliver. If there is to be a personal reward, it can only come from the job itself or from knowing the true significance of the job and the essential role that it plays in society. Perhaps the greatest reward is the self respect and satisfaction that comes from the knowledge that the job was done in a truly professional manner.

"I WILL NEVER ENGAGE IN ACTS OF CORRUPTION OR BRIBERY, NOR WILL I CONDONE SUCH ACTS BY OTHER POLICE OFFICERS."

This part was added in 1989. In the past it was covered under "never accepting gratuities" Bribery and corruption are criminal acts, and all officers are aware that they are forbidden. The important part of this section is "nor will I condone such acts by other police officers." One of the most difficult obstacles in the path of police professionalism is the "Code of Silence." Because each officer's life may depend on the actions of another, there is a very close camaraderie amongst police officers. This causes many officers to look the other way when they observe a fellow officer doing acts that are either criminal or non-professional. This is really a substantial problem and the answers are not easy.

It must be understood that when one officer violates the ethics of the profession, it does not just affect that one person. It affects all of the other officers on the department and neighboring departments. It affects that officer's family and the families of all the other officers on the department. No officer can really be an individual when it comes to improper behavior.

This concept is emphasized in the 1989 "White Paper" issued by the Philadelphia Police Department. It states that: "It is not enough that our personal integrity remain untarnished. Since our own reputations are tied so closely to the conduct of our brother and sister officers, we must ensure that those who work with us remain free from corruption..... Each time an officer engages in an unethical or corrupt act, every officer in the department, in addition to our families, suffers injury... It weakens our image before the general public, destroys their confidence in us and makes our mission more difficult."

Today the opportunities for corruption are very limited when compared to past eras. Chapter Two will cover the social conditions necessary for wholesale police corruption to occur. They do not exist in our present society. Officers today are more often disciplined for such things as drug and alcohol abuse, disclosure of confidential information, lying or making false reports to protect other officers, unwanted sexual harassment, planting evidence, lying to obtain search warrants, the harassment of minorities, lying in court, failure to protect the rights of citizens, and tricking suspects into signing waivers of their rights. There are just two areas of modern law enforcement where officers seem to get caught up in serious corruption. They are narcotics and vice investigation. The temptations present in work of this type can be so great as to challenge the imagination. It is not uncommon for narcotic officers to make a raid in which they seize millions of dollars in small bills. The amount of money is so great that it would take a week for a group of officers to count it. The best of humans can be tested in situations like this. It is not uncommon today for officers to seize thousands of pounds of narcotics in one raid. This is in addition to millions of dollars.

In December of 1990 a jury convicted a sergeant and six deputies from the Los Angeles County Sheriff's Department of 25 felonies. They were members of a special narcotics investigation team. The IRS estimates that they skimmed about 1.4 million dollars from money seized in raids. What went wrong? Apparently rationalization played an important part. Those arrested in a raid will deny ownership of both the money and narcotics. Who does it belong to then? Do we repeat to ourselves the old saying "finders keepers. " Do we tell ourselves that it will go to those greedy politicians in City Hall? The human mind is very adept at the use of rationalization in justifying our misdeeds.

Let us examine the officers involved. Were they the result of inferior selection? The Los Angeles County Sheriff's Department selects only 4 % of all applicants. That is pretty selective. Were they new officers? Their average age was 45 and they had from 14 to 23 years experience. Was their performance poor? One deputy had 15 commendations, two had 18, another had 21; another had won the department's Medal of Valor twice. They were good cops, but they lacked moral strength when presented with the temptation of a lifetime.

Were they prepared for the temptations they encountered? Absolutely not. Sometimes the longer an officer is in policework, the more injustice he or she observes. They do things that are improper, in order to achieve a supposed good end. Life becomes a system of plea bargaining. Without a constant effort to maintain ethical standards, an officer's moral fibre can become weak. The fine edges of what every child knows as being right or wrong become blurred. The officer sees only shades of gray, yet there are things in life that are either black or white. For example, it is wrong to steal. It is not wrong to steal under certain circumstances but OK to steal under others. Lying on reports or in court is always wrong. Law enforcement is filled with situations that are either right or wrong. There are no shades of gray. There is no need to list them here. We learned them in grade school and at our mothers' knees. We know right from wrong.

In most cases, the first violation is a small one. However, once the wall has been breached there is no limit. Each time it is easier to do, and each time it is easier to extend the limits of the violation. Remember, honesty is like pregnancy, there are no degrees. Edwin Delattre, author of <u>Character and Cops: Ethics in Policing</u>, emphasized the importance of character in police officers when he stated:

> "The mission of policing can safely be entrusted only to those who grasp what is morally important and who resect integrity. Without this kind of personal character in police, no set of codes or rules or laws can safeguard that mission from the ravages of police misconduct."

At no time in the history of law enforcement has the need for ethical officers been so great. In 1992 a former Detroit Chief of Police was found guilty of embezzling $2.6 million from his department. He had over 40 years with that department.

When the author was in charge of a police academy, an investigator from Internal Affairs made an hour presentation on his job. This was only about a month into the academy, and few if any of the cadets had any active police experience. Yet they all hissed when the I.A. investigator entered the classroom. They looked upon him as the ememy. When questioned, everyone in the class

wanted to be a professional. They all wanted unworthy officers removed from the department. They were all against police corruption. Yet they had already, even after only one month in the academy, formed a prejudice against the one person whose job it is to keep the department clean and professional. Would they cooperate with this investigator when a fellow officer has violated his or her public trust?

"I WILL COOPERATE WITH ALL LEGALLY AUTHORIZED AGENCIES AND THEIR REPRESENTATIVES IN THE PURSUIT OF JUSTICE."

This section was also added in 1989. It was obviously influenced by police adminstrators who are frustrated with the power of police unions. This section is sure to bring about heated debate among police officers and their protective or benevolent associations. Some would argue that it does not belong in the code. Another purpose is to provide ammunition for breaking the police "Code of Silence" which for so long has protected unprofessional peace officers.

"I KNOW THAT I ALONE AM RESPONSIBLE FOR MY OWN STANDARD OF PROFESSIONAL PERFORMANCE AND WILL TAKE EVERY REASONABLE OPPORTUNITY TO ENHANCE AND IMPROVE MY LEVEL OF KNOWLEDGE AND COMPETENCE. I WILL CONSTANTLY STRIVE TO ACHIEVE THESE OBJECTIVES AND IDEALS, DEDICATING MYSELF BEFORE GOD TO MY CHOSEN PROFESSION . . . LAW ENFORCEMENT"

When we try to overcome the basic elements of our human nature and exert mastery over self, we find that it is a constant battle, and if the goal is to be attained, we must be ever alert and continually strive for self improvement. We could use the analogy of keeping ourselves in good physical condition. How easy it is to slip out of condition, and once we have slipped, how difficult it is to get back into shape. The key is not to relax, but to make conditioning a continuing effort.

Proficiency in law enforcement involves many factors. It involves mental, moral and physical conditioning. They are all important aspects. The officer who becomes physically unfit is certainly not able to protect society. The officer who is in good physical condition has more confidence in his or her ability, and this is sensed by those with whom the officer deals. As a result it will be found that it is not necessary to exert authority as much as it might otherwise be. Unfortunately, most police departments require a stiff physical agility examination before the officer is selected. Once the selection is made and the officer is actually working in the field, this area is either forgotten or greatly neglected. It is left up to the individual officer to keep in shape.

In regard to morals, most people feel that there is no conditioning involved, that you are either moral or you are not. They fail to realize that we all change from day to day, even though it is ever so slight. If we look around us, it is easy to find examples of persons who were at one time very moral, and because of one reason or another have slipped into one or more habit patterns that would be classed as immoral. There are also many examples of those who have worked very hard to overcome bad habits or vices and have finally achieved their goal.

Because of the nature of law enforcement, an officer is in contact with persons who are often lacking in good morals. At first the new officer is shocked, but later accepts what he or she sees as commonplace. An officer must continually guard against accepting the moral standards of criminals in the field. Should this immoral standard involve a vice that the officer finds personally pleasurable, then it becomes that much easier. The divorce rate among police officers is very high, and one of the reasons for these divorces is the failure of the officer to practice moral conditioning. This applies to both sexes.

Of all the challenges faced by the modern law enforcement officer, one of the greatest involves keeping mentally abreast of the latest developments and concepts in the field. Today an officer needs to be as handy with a computer as with a firearm. It is not uncommon for departments to require from one to four years of college as an entrance requirement for new police officers. We are living in an era of change that is greater than at any time in the history of the world. Keeping abreast of these developments not only involves certain mental capabilities, it involves much time, effort, and personal expense outside of normal working hours.

Since most law enforcement jobs are now under civil service, it is easy for an officer to relax after a few years of service and rest on prior laurels. If this happens, the officer will soon be left behind, and it will be most difficult to catch up.

Just how does a modern law enforcement officer keep abreast? This can be done in many ways. First should be the joining of professional law enforcement oreganizations. Such organizations are found on the local, state and national levels. Those not yet in the field, but who are enrolled in a college training program, may join a law enforcement association such as Lambda Alpha Epsilon, which has both collegiate and professional chapters. This allows the student to transfer to a professional chapter upon graduation. The advantages of such organizations are many. They not only provide the opportunity for a personal exchange of ideas and techniques, they also establish progressive standards that are not only idealistic, but realistic as well, because they are the product of people who are doing the job.

Officers should not only belong to general law enforcement organizations, but specialized organizations if they are working in one of these specialized areas of law enforcement. There are many such organizations. They serve areas of particular skills and knowledge such as narcotics and homicide investigation or the field of identification. The exchange of ideas and techniques is especially important to persons in this category. Examples of such organizations would be the International Association for Identification and the International Juvenile Officers Association. Belonging is not enough. The professional officer should thoroughly read all of the journals sponsored by the organization, and should make every effort to attend the quarterly meetings and especially the annual conferences where experts discuss the latest developments in that field.

Another way in which the professional officer may keep abreast is to devote so many hours each week to reading the many books and professional law enforcement journals or magazines that are now available. Much good reading material is now available for law enforcement personnel. Because there is so much to read, an officer might profit from the book review sections of the major police journals. This will enable him or her to better use alloted "improvement reading" time.

Good intentions are not enough. It is easy to put our feet on the table and say "tomorrow we are going to get organized". The best way to find time for personal improvement is to schedule it. Make out a written schedule and post it in a place where everyone in the family can read it and can assist the officer in adhering to the schedule. It is best to set aside several short reading times rather than just one long session per week or month. This makes the task more pleasant, and it increases the degree of perception. It is difficult at first to start a new habit, but once it is formed, it can become a routine matter.

The actual amount of time spent on "improvement reading" is dependent upon the individual. If the officer is attending college classes before or after a working shift, he or she will be very short on extra time. The reading speed of each person is different, and this is an important factor. In a few years, police departments will have to give special classes in speed reading as is done in private industry or business. The reason for this is the greatly increased volume of forms, bulletins and announcements that an officer must read before going out on the beat. This, plus the amount of reading that will be necessary in order to keep abreast of the recent developments in the field, will make speed reading as essential to the law enforcement officer as knowing how to properly shoot a weapon.

Since most of this reading will be on the officer's own time, it is essential to develop the initiative that is so common to other professions. Law enforcement is, at present, undergoing changes that are revolutionary, yet its future development will be so dynamic that our present advancements will appear stagnant. It is imperative that the field of law enforcement recruit only those with professional capabilities and then develop them to maximum proficiency.

The Law Enforcement Code of Ethics has been broken down and discussed in some detail. It has been done in an effort to awaken in the reader a greater awareness of the importance of the code. It is a means of achieving professional standing. However, knowing and understanding the Code of Ethics is not enough. It must actually be practiced. It must be lived.

To profess a doctrine or way of life, and not adhere to it is hypocrisy. Law enforcement can never achieve the respect that it needs through hypocrisy. This respect must be won by living the Code of Ethics. Law enforcement officers must make it a way of life, difficult though it may be at times. There is no other way.

POLICE OFFICERS AND THE BILL OF RIGHTS

Being a police officer in a democracy is seldom an easy job. In order for the average citizen to have rights, we must also grant the criminal the same rights. The police officer is told to do a job, but it must be done under a very strict set of rules, and many times these rules make the job considerably more difficult. That is the price that one must pay in order to be a police officer in a democracy.

In our society, the first consideration in law enforcement is written or established law. Laws are proposed by elected representatives and are then voted on by a legislature of similarily elected representatives. If the laws are bad, or are not suitable, they can be changed, should the voting public feel strongly about the issue. There is no doubt that changes come slowly, but a study of legal history will reveal that laws quickly enacted or changed, seldom serve the best interests of the people or the community.

Since the printed law is rigid, the democratic police officer must not only consider the "Letter of the Law" but the "Spirit of the Law" as well. The "Spirit of the Law" is also referred to as the "Legislative Intent" or the reason the law was written in the first place.

Since this is also a constitutional democracy, another factor must be taken into consideration. That factor is the constitutionality of the laws that are passed. These laws may be the result of democratic action, but if they violate the constitution, they are unacceptable. We may not always be happy with the outcome, but if we want to continue living in a Constitutional Democracy, we must abide by the Constitution.

Police Code of Conduct

All law enforcement officers must be fully aware of the ethical responsibilities of their position and must strive constantly to live up to the highest possible standards of professional policing.

The International Association of Chiefs of Police believes it important that police officers have clear advice and counsel available to assist them in performing their duties consistent with these standards, and has adopted the following ethical mandates as guidelines to meet these ends.

Primary Responsibilities of a Police Officer

A police officer acts as an official representative of government who is required and trusted to work within the law. The officer's powers and duties are conferred by statute. The fundamental duties of a police officer include serving the community, safeguarding lives and property, protecting the innocent, keeping the peace and ensuring the rights of all to liberty, equality and justice.

Performance of the Duties of a Police Officer

A police officer shall perform all duties impartially, without favor or affection or ill will and without regard to status, sex, race, religion, political belief or aspiration. All citizens will be treated equally with courtesy, consideration and dignity.

Officers will never allow personal feelings, animosities or friendships to influence official conduct. Laws will be enforced appropriately and courteously and, in carrying out their responsibilities, officers will strive to obtain maximum cooperation from the public. They will conduct themselves in appearance and deportment in such a manner as to inspire confidence and respect for the position of public trust they hold.

Discretion

A police officer till use responsibly the discretion vested in his position and exercise it within the law. the principle of reasonableness will guide the officer's determinations, and the officer will consider all surrounding circumstances in determining whether any legal action shall be taken.

Consistent and wise use of discretion, based on professional policing competence, will do much to preserve good relationships and retain the confidence of the public. There can be difficulty in choosing between conflicting courses of action. It is important to remember that a timely word of advice rather than arrest - which may be correct in appropriate circumstances - can be a more effective means of achieving a desired end.

Use of Force

A police officer will never employ unnecessary force or violence and will use only such force in the discharge of duty as is reasonable in all circumstances.

The use of force should be used only with the greatest restraint and only after discussion, negotiation and persuasion have been found to be inappropriate or ineffective. While the use of force is occasionally unavoidable, every police officer will refrain from unnecessary infliction of pain or suffering and will never engage in cruel, degrading or inhuman treatment of any person.

Confidentiality

Whatever a police officer sees, hears or learns of that is of a confidential nature will be kept secret unless the performance of duty or legal provision requires otherwise.

Members of the public have a right to security and privacy, and information obtained about them must not be improperly divulged.

Integrity

A police officer will not engage in acts of corruption or bribery, nor will an officer condone such acts by other police officers.

The public demands that the integrity of police officers be above reproach. Police officers must, therefore, avoid any conduct that might compromise integrity and thus undercut the public confidence in a law enforcement agency. officers will refuse to accept any gifts, presents, subscriptions, favors, gratuities or promises that could be interpreted as seeking to cause the officer to refrain from performing official responsibilities honestly and within the law. Police officers must no receive private or special advantage from their official status. Respect from the public cannot be bought; it can only be earned and cultivated.

Cooperation with Other Police Officers and Agencies

Police officers will cooperate with all legally authorized agencies and their representatives in the pursuit of justice.

An officer or agency may be one among many organizations that may provide law enforcement services to a jurisdiction. It is imperative that a police officer assist colleagues fully and completely with respect and consideration at all times.

Personal-Professional Capabilities

Police officers will be responsible for their own standard of professional performance and will take every reasonable opportunity to enhance and improve their level of knowledge and competence.

Through study and experience, a police officer can acquire the high level of knowledge and competence that is essential for the efficient and effective performance of duty. The acquisition of knowledge is a never-ending process of personal and professional development that should be pursued constantly.

Private Life

Police officers will behave in a manner that does not bring discredit to their agencies or themselves.

A police officer's character and conduct while off duty must always be exemplary, thus maintaining a position of respect in the community in which he or she lives and serves. The officer's personal behavior must be beyond reproach.

THE INTERNATIONAL ASSOCIATION OF CHIEFS OF POLICE

The purpose of the Constitution is to offer protection to the citizens of this country by establishing a set of legal guidelines. If these guidelines are bad or unworkable, they can be changed by the democratic process. We have many amendments to the Constitution.

Unfortunately these guidelines are subject to interpretation, and because they were written over 200 years ago, it can, at times, be difficult to decide what the writers of the Bill of Rights would have thought had they been alive today. This is undoubtedly why we have so many split decisions by the Supreme Court.

To help insure that decisions of the Supreme Court are objective, we were the first country to establish an independent Judiciary. Our Supreme Court is a separate branch of government whose duty it is to interpret the Constitution without being influenced by the Executive branch of government.

There have been a considerable number of volumes written on the interpretation of just a few words in one of the Amendments of our "Bill of Rights." For example, what does the word "unreasonable" mean as it pertains to the Fourth Amendment protection against unreasonable search and seizure? As the makeup of the Supreme Court changes, so do some of the interpretations.

It has often been said that a police officer in the field must make split second decisions, at night and under adverse conditions, upon which a life may depend, and it will take the Supreme Court of the United States six months to decide whether the decision was constitutionally right, and then they will split on a four to five vote.

In the last decade, law enforcement officers have been very much affected by Supreme Court decisions regarding their procedures, yet, many officers are still unfamiliar with the Constitution under which they must work. Because of this, the first ten Amendments and the fourteenth are listed here for ready reference. It will, however, take considerable time on an officer's part to keep abreast of how the local, state and U.S. Supreme Courts interpret these rights as they apply to everyday situations.

AMENDMENTS TO THE U.S. CONSTITUTION

"BILL OF RIGHTS"

1. Congress shall make no law respecting an establishment of religion, or prohibiting the free exercise thereof; or abridging the freedom of speech or of the press; or the right of the people peaceably to assemble, and to petition the government for a redress of grievances.

2. A well-regulated militia being necessary to the security of a free state, the right of the people to keep and bear arms shall not be infringed.

3. No soldier shall, in time of peace, be quartered in any house without the consent of the owner, nor in time of war but in a manner prescribed by law.

4. The right of the people to be secure in their persons, houses, papers and effects, against unreasonable searches and seizures, shall not be violated, and no warrants shall be issued but upon probable cause, supported by oath or affirmation, and particularly describing the place to be searched, and the person or things to be seized.

5. No person shall be held to answer for a capital or other infamous crime unless on a presentment or indictment of a grand jury, except in cases arising in the land or naval forces, or in the militia, when in actual service, in time of war or public danger; nor shall any person be subject for the same offense to be twice put in jeopardy of life or limb, nor shall he be compelled in any criminal case to be a witness against himself, nor be deprived of life, liberty, or property, without due process of law; nor shall private property be taken for public use without just compensation.

6. In all criminal prosecutions, the accused shall enjoy the right to a speedy and public trial, by an impartial jury of the state and district wherein the crime shall have been committed, which district shall have previously ascertained by law, and to be informed of the nature and cause of the accusation; to be confronted with the witnesses against him; to have compulsory process for obtaining witnesses in his favor, and to have the assistance of counsel for his defense.

7. In suits at common law, where the value in controversy shall exceed twenty dollars, the right of trial by jury shall be preserved, and no fact tried by a jury shall be otherwise re-examined in any court of the United States than according to the rules of the common law.

8. Excessive bail shall not be required, nor excessive fines imposed, nor cruel and unusual punishments inflicted.

9 The enumeration in the Constitution of certain rights shall not be construed to deny or disparage others retained by the people.

10. The powers not delegated to the United States by the Constitution, nor prohibited by it to the states, are reserved to the states respectively, or to the people.

FOURTEENTH AMENDMENT

Section 1.

All persons born or naturalized in the United States, and subject to the jurisdiction thereof, are citizens of the United States and of the State wherein they reside. No State shall make or enforce any law which shall abridge the privileges or immunities of citizens of the United States; nor shall any State deprive any person of life, liberty or property, without due process of law; nor deny to any person within its jurisdiction the equal protection of the law.

REFERENCES AND RECOMMENDED READING

The Police Chief, Journal of the IACP, Vol. LIX 1992,Charles Higginbotham, Editor.

Delattre, Edwin J.,Character and Cops: Ethics in Policing, AEIPPR Washington D.C. 1989.

Kleinig, John, "Teaching and Learning Police Ethics," Journal of Criminal Justice, 1990

Cohen, Howard, "Teaching Police Ethics," Teaching Philosophy, 1983 vol. 6

Lawrence, Sherman, "Learning Police Ethics," Criminal Justice Ethics, Winter/Spring 1982

____ "The Mind and Faith of Justice Holmes"

STUDY QUESTIONS for Patrol Operations

CHAPTER 1

1. The Code of Ethics that has been accepted nationwide was first developed in what state?

    _____

2. Officers from the "Old School" tend to resent the newer educated officer.   T or F

3. In his book <u>Cross Examination</u>, A.L. Cornelius states that police officers, as a rule, are very sharp(1929).   T or F

4. When the metropolitan police were first instituted in London in 1829, there were no regulations in written form because the officers could not read and write.   T or F

5. According to the Code of Ethics, an officer's job is to serve the public.   T or F

6. The idea of protecting the innocent and weak was not really expressed in writing until the metropolitan police in 1829.   T or F

7. Police officers find that protecting the constitutional rights of criminals is a very hard task.   T or F

8. The Roman philosophy of law, "*Salus Populi Est Suprema Lex*" means? _____

    _____

9. In New York State in the late 1800's the rules for police officers were much less strict than they are in the present day.   T or F

10. A reporter in San Diego did some research and found that officers tended to give traffic citations to important people more than they did citizens in general.   T or F

11. Television and movies prepare new officers for the danger in policework, but not for the scorn and ridicule.   T or F

12. Keeping bits of confidential information to yourself is really very easy if you are a police officer.   T or F

13. When public employees have a "civil service" attitude toward the public, they are, in effect, being "officious."   T or F

14. In policework it is difficult for officers to help their friends and hurt their enemies.   T or F

15. The term "With No Compromise For Crime" means that an officer must carry out the letter of the law very strictly.   T or F

16. The key to professional enforcement is to be "fair but firm."   T or F

17. Justice Holmes once stated "It is one thing to utter a happy phrase from a protected cloister; another to think under fire, to think for action upon which great interests depend." What did he mean?_____

_____

18. King Charles I, even before Gilbert & Sullivan, stated that a policeman's lot is not a happy one.   T or F

19. A good professional police officer never loses his temper.   T or F

20. Vice officers who are guilty of graft, were usually poor patrol officers in the past.   T or F

21. Most officers found guilty of graft have few years with the department.   T or F

22 How many general headings of gratuities are there? _____

23. The book recommends that chiefs of police make the swearing-in ceremonies very formal   T or F
    and invite relatives.

24. Because of the First Amendment rule of separating church and state, the Code of Ethics   T or F
    cannot mention the word "God."

25. The term "Spirit of the Law" is also referred to as the:

    a. _ Spiritus Lex
    b. _ Legislative Intent
    c. _ the Elements of the Law
    d. _ Corpus Delicti

26. Match the below rights under the Constitution with the amendment under which they are found.

    ___ (1) freedom of religion   A. First Amendment
    ___ (2) right to a speedy trial   B. Fourth Amendment
    ___ (3) freedom of speech   C. Fifth Amendment
    ___ (4) right to an attorney   D. Sixth Amendment
    ___ (5) right to bail that is not excessive   E. Eighth Amendment
    ___ (6) protection against cruel punishment
    ___ (7) protection against self incrimination
    ___ (8) protection against illegal search and seizure
    ___ (9) right to cross examine witnesses against you
    ___ (10)right to due process of law

CHAPTER II

THE HISTORY OF POLICE PATROL

The history of police patrol is as old as organized society. Man has always needed protection, first from animals, and then from his own kind. His first attempts to protect himself and his family involved barricading the entrance to his cave.

Then as mankind multiplied, they grouped together in small communities and protection developed into a community affair. As the communities enlarged, so did the need for developing a specialized group or agency to handle protection.

Since warfare has been a part of man's social history, and since each community has had to have soldiers or warriors to carry out the tasks of war, the duties of police protection usually fell upon their shoulders. This form of protection usually involved night patrols of soldiers about the town or city, and groups of soldiers stationed at various posts around the perimeter, and at major points within the same town or city. Most communities of any size were encircled with walls, and the gates were kept locked at night. As a further means of protection, curfew laws were enacted and strictly enforced.

The key to the development of police patrol is closely associated with the congestion of popula-

tion. Where the population is sparse or spread out the justification of a police patrol becomes less warranted. As towns become cities and the cities grow in population, both the justification and need for a police patrol becomes greater. It is therefore understandable that police patrol as we know it today is a relatively new innovation in the history of man.

The word "Police" originated from the Greek word "Politeia", meaning government of a city. It applied to civil officers and not necessarily policemen. The Romans changed the word slightly to "Politia". The French changed the word to "Police" and applied it to those persons who actually enforced the law. The English and Americans borrowed the word intact from the French and used it to describe a law enforcement officer. Since the police in Western civilizations started wearing uniforms, they have used the French military terms for rank such as sergeant, lieutenant and captain.

Many police terms are much harder to trace, for example, the word "cop," which is so commonly used to describe a police officer. In England they use the word "copper". Today we hear many different origins of the word such as "Chief Of Police", "Constable On Patrol", or some sources trace the word to the copper badge that early policemen wore in New York. This would not account for the English terminology though.

It is more likely that it originated from the early English word "cop" meaning to catch or to seize.

Although the words themselves could be traced back further, it is interesting to note that it was the French who gave them to us in their law enforcement context. Not only did we get the word "constable" from the French, but the word "patrol" as well. Patrol is from the French "Patrouiller" meaning to go through puddles. Even today with our highly mechanized patrol units, the definition is one that is very apt.

THE ANCIENT POLICE

If we search recorded history, we can find many documents and archeological finds that would support the existence of a form of organized police. For example, there is the ancient Babylonian clay tablet, dated around about 2,000 B.C., which contained a report from a Babylonian officer to his superiors, notifying them that he had proceeded to the man's house as ordered, arrested him, taken his fingerprints and then taken control of his property. Likewise, the discovery in the Indus Valley, also about 2,000 B.C., revealed not only that this city had sewers and a bathroom in each house, but that there were special "watch-houses" which were used by officials whose duty it was to patrol the streets and maintain order.

In both the Old Testament (Song of Solomon, Isaiah and Jeremiah) and the New Testament (Matthew and John) we find references to "watchmen" whose duty it was to protect the city and arrest offenders.

There are many indications in the hieroglyphics of the ancient Egyptians that they had police officers. They even had a special flag with a distinctive emblem; it was a gazelle with a large ostrich feather attached to its neck. (see illustration II-1). Because of the great treasures hidden in the many tombs, there was a constant need for some

Fig. II-1; Administering Punishment for Petty Theft

type of protective police patrol. Because of this the Egyptians became the first people to use police dogs on patrol. They also invented the lock.

The police were called "Medjay", and although they were civilians, they were headed by an Egyptian military officer. They were black Nubians from the tribe and village of Medjay. Traditionally they hired out to the Egyptians as mercenaries whenever they were at war. After the war was over, the Medjay were hired as policemen to guard the war booty (if they won). After a while the name Medjay came to mean the same as "police."

Emperor Augustus formed the "Vigiles" of Rome just before the time of Christ. It consisted of a group of over two thousand men, armed with staves and short-swords, whose duty it was to keep the peace and fight fires.

In the early historical references to law enforcement duties, we seldom know whether the personnel assigned to these tasks were actually policemen, or members of the military. For example, the special police flag used by the early Egyptians contained an ostrich feather. This same symbol was often used by the military. However, the Egyptian goddess of truth and justice is usually pictured with the same type of ostrich feather in her headband.

POLICE IN THE MIDDLE AGES

THE WATCHMEN

In the early part of the middle ages, law enforcement was mostly handled by the military. Near the end of the middle ages, a system was developed in towns and cities throughout Europe and England, based on the use of watchmen.

There were three pieces of equipment that were commonly carried by watchmen of this era. First was the pointed or bladed staff. Although it was basically a weapon of defense, it was also a symbol of authority. It would have been more practical for them to carry a short sword. Early in the middle ages, the Christian church became more organized and formal. As a symbol of the church's mission, bishops and those of higher rank carried a shepherd's crook to indicate that they were

shepherds of Christ's flock. Later on this staff, called a crosier, became more of a symbol of authority. Only those of higher rank were allowed to carry them. About the same time, persons of civil authority began carrying a special staff as a symbol of their high position. The mayor of each town had one. It was called a "scepter" when used to show regal or imperial power. It was always carried on important occasions of state. The idea was not completely new as ancient history does reveal examples of those in authority having such an ornamental staff to represent their authority.

Since watchmen were representatives of local government, they needed some symbol to show their authority and the staff served that purpose as well as providing some form of defensive weapon.

The second piece of equipment carried by all watchmen was a lantern. This was the flashlight of early times. The third common piece of equipment was some type of warning device. In Europe, the horn or bell was the most commonly used device (in England a "rattle" was used.) Since watchmen were out at night, in what was usually quite cold

Fig. II-2, Swedish Watchman, 1400's

Fig. II-3; German Watchman, 1500's

Ten O'clock

Master, maid and boy, would you the hour
    know?
It is the time that you to rest should go
Trust in the Lord with faith, and careful be
Of fire and light, for ten o'clock has struck.

Three O'clock

Black night departs, and day begins to dawn
Keep them far off, O God, who wish us harm.
The clock has stricken three
Father, Thine aid we seek, and of Thy grace
Give us abundantly.

(Translated by Mr. R.S. Ellis, clergyman at the
English church in Copenhagen.)

weather, they wore very heavy coats and hats that would offer them some protection from the elements.

In Europe this position was looked upon as being more important than it was in England. As a result, the European watchmen had more ornamentation on their uniforms. Bright metal buttons were considered a basic. (See illustrations II-2, II-3, and II-4) In Scandinavian towns it was common for the watchman to wear a shiny emblemed breastplate. It was further evidence of his authority.

A major problem for watchmen was staying awake during their night watch. It was rare for them to work during the daytime. One way for them to stay awake was to call out the time each hour during the night, and give some type of information such as the weather. For example, "Two o'clock and all's well. The weather is cloudy but no rain."

In Scandinavian countries the watchmen would often sing a different, short song each hour. Some, such as this Danish watchman's song, had strong religious significance.

Fig. II-4; Danish Watchman, 1800's

ENGLAND

In the early Middle Ages (a period from the 5th Century A.D. to about 1350) a system of mutual protection was developed called the "Frankpledge". Under this system a community was divided into tythings or groups of 10 families, each member of which was responsible for the conduct of the other members of his group and for the assurance that a member charged with a breach of the law would be produced at court. Thus we see that the individual was not only responsible for his own behavior and protection, but his neighbor's as well. He was indeed his brother's keeper!

This system has in some ways prevailed until modern times in the British military. If one man makes a mistake, the whole group to which he belongs is punished.

In England this system of mutual protection reached an early development as each petty kingdom was divided into shires or counties. Each shire was the responsibility of a "Reeve", who in turn was responsible to the King for law and order in his respective district. This responsibility often endowed this officer with wide powers. The shire Reeve was later called the Sheriff.

Each Shire was broken down into Hundreds (100 households) headed by a Hundredman, later known as a High Constable.

Each Hundred was further broken down into Tythings (10 families) headed by a Tythingman or Chief Tythingman who was elected by the group. He served as a combination constable and judge. In the Twelfth Century he was replaced by the Constable.

Although this system focused the responsibility of law and order on each individual, the fact that the whole Tything was held responsible for the criminal acts of each member of the group reduced the number of crimes that were actually reported.

Another form of police protection used at the end of this era was for each able-bodied man to serve so much time patrolling the town at night as a "Watchman." Since this job was not too well liked, and since the law allowed a person to hire a replacement, it was handled mostly by persons who were selected not for ability, but because they would work cheaper than anyone else. Although they were officially under the control of the Constable, he seldom came out at night to check on them, so they often slept on the job. Later, as was done with European watchmen, it was required that they call out the time and weather on the hour in an effort to stop them from sleeping.

THE HUE AND CRY

The Hue and Cry was an ancient Saxon practice that the invaders brought over to England with them. When a person committed a crime, or a felon escaped, and it was detected, an alarm was sounded by the oldest known warning device in history, the horn. When the others heard the alarm, they raised a cry, sounded their horns, and by law had to lay aside their work and join in the pursuit. If any able-bodied man failed to take up the pursuit, he was considered to have taken the part of the escaping person and would be liable to arrest. (See illustration II-5)

Fig. II-5; Hue and Cry

The law stated that those chasing the fugitive must continue in pursuit until he was caught or until they reached the sea.

KEEPERS OF THE PEACE

At the end of the Twelfth Century (1195) King Richard issued a proclamation entitled "Keepers of the Peace". This document required the appointment of knights to keep the King's Peace. They often did this by standing guard at bridges and gates and checking on people entering and leaving the town.

Some believe that the present "shield" type badge used by some police departments had its origin with the shields carried by these knights.

STATUTE OF WINCHESTER (WATCH AND WARD ACT)

Near the end of the Thirteenth Century (1285) the Statute of Winchester was enacted to beef up law and order. It introduced the system of Watch and Ward, where a watch was stationed between sunset and sunrise at each gate of a walled town. It also revived the practice of Hue and Cry. Some watches grouped together for protection and patrolled the town in "Marching Watches". These watchmen were selected from a roster, and as before, substitutes could be hired, with the same unfortunate results.

It also contained a curfew law. When the bell tolled at St. Martin's Le Grand Church, all those found on the streets were taken into custody by the Keepers of the Peace (Watchmen or Constables). No taverns were allowed to be open after curfew. The law also forbade fencing schools on the grounds that they promoted violence and injury.

Fig. II-7; William Anthony, "Last of the Charlies"

THE CHARLIES

Near the middle of the Seventeenth Century (1663), King Charles II passed an act which provided for the employment in London of one thousand Night Watchmen or Bellmen to be on duty from sunset to sunrise (See illustrations II-6 & II-7).

They were called Charlies because of King Charles. They carried long staves with dimly lit lanterns, and they called out the hour and the weather conditions. They were also referred to by the local citizens as the "Shiver and Shake" watch because they were often old and decrepit and would run off if they saw any trouble, or heard a cry for help. Some were not too honest, and were often looking for an extra shilling. They would sometimes work for criminals as lookouts, or would even "case" jobs for them. Because they were basically ineffective, many merchants hired their own watchman who were known as the "Merchant Police."

Despite the watchmen, crime was rampant. A letter written in 1690 by Richard Lapthorne stated:

Fig. II-6; Watchman (or Charlie)

Fig. II-8; Watch House and Watchmen, 1770's

"Never was there such beare faced outrages committed in and about London. Not a day or night passes but robberies, if not murders, are committed in our very streets."

In 1777 the 14th act of George III enlarged upon the Watch and Ward Act. It went into some detail concerning the staffing and equipping of the watches. It stated that: "A watchman shall carry a rattle, stave and lantern. He will proclaim the time loudly and audibly. He will see that all doors are safe and well secure. He will prevent to the utmost of his power, all murders, burglaries, robberies, and affraies. He is to apprehend all loose, idle and disorderly persons and deliver them to the constable or Headborough of the Night at the watch houses."

Although the Act had excellent intentions, in reality, it failed in its execution. One of the problems was low pay. The other was poor selection.

When Sir John Fielding was questioned in 1772 about the failure of the watchmen, he stated: "Their duty was too hard and their pay too small."

THE THIEF TAKERS

The disposal of stolen goods was so common that fences gave very little money for stolen items. This brought rise to the lucrative occupation of stolen goods broker. These brokers would study the newspapers for advertisements regarding stolen property. In return for a "fee", they would negotiate between the victim and the thief for the return of the property. Sometimes the reward for the thief was greater than that for the return of the property. In this case the broker would now become a "Thief Taker."

Because watchmen were so ineffective, both victims and the Crown would offer rewards for wanted criminals. This system started with the Act of 1693, in which rewards were given for the arrest of noted criminals, especially highwaymen. If your apprehension led to the conviction of a highwayman, you were given 40 pounds, the highwayman's horse, arms and his money.

This brought about the occupation of "Thief Taker." Today we call them "Bounty Hunters."

They were very successful because they filled the need for a proper law enforcement agency.

One of the most famous Stolen Goods Brokers and Thief Takers was Jonathan Wild (1683-1725). He had a gift for organization, and developed the brokering of stolen goods into a science. His business was so large that he had several warehouses, and his own ship for taking stolen goods to Europe. As a form of insurance he also became a Thief Taker and was able to provide authorities with considerable information that led to the arrest of numerous criminals. In fact, he was humorously given the unofficial title "Thief Taker General of Great Britain & Ireland." (see illustration II-9)

Fig. II-9; Satirical Invitation to Jonathan Wild's Execution in 1725

THE THAMES RIVER POLICE

England was becoming a major importer of goods from its vast empire. The Thames River was loaded with ships bearing riches from the colonies. Without proper police protection, wholesale theft became a major problem.

Fig. II-10; Life Saving

As a result, the large shipping companies formed a private police agency called the Thames River Police. Their uniform was similar to that of the navy. They wore round straw hats. Since it was a private enterprise, they were well equipped, and were armed. They were also effective. Thefts dropped significantly after they were put into operation. They did such a good job that when the Metropolitan Police were formed, the Thames River Police did not merge with them.

Fig. II-11; Patrolling Docks

BOW STREET RUNNERS

Near the middle of the Eighteenth Century (1748), Henry Fielding became Chief Magistrate at Bow Street Court in London. This court is still in existence in London today. Fielding often sat on the bench for 16 hours a day. He would return after dinner and work from 7pm until midnight. He set up night courts for working people. At first he received no pay, only fees. Although it was a widespread practice, no biographer has been able to find any evidence that Henry Fielding ever took a bribe.

From the moment of his appointment, Henry Fielding set a goal for himself to fight crime, corruption and hypocrisy. He was against the system of Thief Takers because he felt that they even encouraged crime in order to catch people. His first step was to invite the public to come to his office, or send a messenger with information about stolen and robbed property and the descriptions of the perpetrators. He placed this information in the newspapers with the result that a large number of criminals were apprehended. This system was widely supported by the public who had no faith in the watchmen.

He then took six constables of high integrity and placed them under the leadership of himself and a High Constable. By the end of the century, the number had increased to seventy, and they were known as the "Bow Street Runners." (See illustration II-13). They presented a new philosophy in the field of law enforcement. The watchman hoped to prevent crime just by walking his assigned beat.

Fig. II-12; Picture in Daily Telegraph that led to murderer's arrest.

"The Runners", on the other hand, actually went after the criminal. They developed informants, and placed notices in local taverns and places of business, describing crimes that had occurred and descriptions of those responsible for the crimes. This led to numerous arrests.

The following is an example of one of the notices posted by magistrate John Fielding:

> **WHEREAS** many Thieves and Robbers daily escape justice for want of immediate pursuit, it is therefore recommended to all persons who shall henceforth be robbed on the highways or in the streets, or whose shops or houses shall be broken open, that

they give immediate notice thereof, together with as accurate a description of the offenders as possible, to JOHN FIELDING, Esq; at his house in Bowstreet, Covent Garden: By which means, joined to an advertisement, containing an account of the things lost (which is also taken in there) Thieves and Robbers will seldom escape; as most of the principal pawnbrokers take in this paper, and by the intelligence they get from it, assist daily in discovering and apprehending rogues.

Fig. II-13; Bow Street Runner

And if they would send a special messenger on these occasions, Mr. Fielding would not only pay that messenger for his trouble, but would immediately dispatch a set of brave fellows in pursuit, who had been long engaged for such purposes, and were always ready to set out to any part of this town or kingdom, on a quarter of an hour's notice.

Henry Fielding did not have the funds to pay his officers. As a result they had to survive by being Thief Takers on the side. At first they were called "Fielding's People," but were later called the Bow Street Runners

Henry Fielding was the first person to set up a criminal records bureau in England. He started a register of criminals and the crimes they committed. He believed in the old Saxon system of every citizen being responsible for the control of crime.

The British constable never adopted the chest badge or shield as a symbol of authority, as was done in the United States. The Bow Street Runner's symbol of authority was a gilt crown on the top of his baton.

Because attacks had been made on members of the Royal Family, the Bow Street Runners were eventually called upon to become Royal body guards like our Secret Service. At least two Runners were assigned full time to this duty.

Fig. II-14; Sketch of Townsend

To catch criminals and develop informants, the Runners had to associate with the criminal element, and this often brought public outcry. They were offered bribes quite often. A famous Runner named Townsend (See illustration II-14) reported that he was constantly offered bribes, and at one time was offered 1,000 pounds just to keep back one witness. Although some Runners were convicted of crimes, and one of them left a very large estate which certainly didn't come from his salary, the reputation of the Bow Street Runners was generally quite favorable. They were considered to be bold, courageous, faithful and resourceful. However, when the New Police were formed, very few of them applied for the job. They were used to operating under their own methods, and didn't want to conform to the strict rules laid down by Sir Robert Peel.

Fig. II-15a; Henry Fielding, Novelist & Magistrate

JOHN FIELDING AND THE BOW STREET HORSE PATROL (ROBIN RED-BREASTS)

John Fielding, the brother of Henry Fielding, had been blinded at the age of nineteen. He worked with his brother at the Bow Street Court, and learned law from him. Eventually he too was appointed a magistrate. While at the Bow Street Court he received the nickname the "Blind Beak". Some think that this was due to his large nose, but "beak" is an old Anglo Saxon word for a person in authority. When he took over the Bow Street Runners, the were called the "Beak Runners" for a while.

Fielding was the first to invite newspaper reporters to his court. He also started an exchange of information between county justices, who before this time paid no attention to the goings on in nearby courts. He was generally not easy with criminals, and sent many to the gallows. He was however, very lenient with first offenders, and with women and children

Like his brother, he believed that publicizing information about crimes and criminals would help in apprehension. He had his men place notices at turnpikes, pawn brokers stores, taverns and stables. When a crime was reported, he often went in person to interview the victim. Because he was blind, he developed a high degree of concentration, and was an excellent interrogator. Nothing slipped by him in court. He was knighted in 1760.

THE HORSE PATROL

At the turn of the century, a number of adventurous criminals became highwaymen. They frequented the main roads leading into London, and were responsible for a considerable number of robberies. Armed with pistols, they would approach carriages with the demand "Stand and deliver," meaning that victims should stop their carriages and hand over their valuables.

This became such a problem, that a special unit of the Bow Street Runners was formed by John Fielding. It was called the Bow Street Horse Patrol. They wore a blue coat with brass buttons and a scarlet waistcoat (vest) as sort of a uniform or means of identification. Because of this they were often called "Robin Redbreasts". They were armed with both sword and pistols as well as truncheons

Fig. II-15b; Sir John Fielding, the Blind Bow Street Magistrate

An Exact Representation of MACLAINE the Highwayman Robbing LORD EGLINGTON on Hounslow Heath on the 26th of June 1750.

Fig. II-16; Highway Robbery

(clubs). Their routine duty was to patrol the main roads leading into London from 5 to 10 miles out. They normally worked from 5pm until midnight. They were to try and intercept highwaymen and to be on the lookout for persons fitting the description of those committing the robberies. If the victim of a robbery reported the crime soon enough, the Robin Redbreasts would ride out in pursuit, often with success.

When they approached a carriage or horseman, they cried out "Bow Street Patrol" This let citizens know that first, they were not highwaymen, and second that they were protecting them. This had a very positive effect on public relations, and it greatly reduced the crime of highway robbery.

By the end of the 1700's budget problems caused the Horse Patrol to fall upon hard times. In 1805 it was re-instated by the new Chief Magistrate. New officers were recruited exclusively from old cavalry soldiers.

The Bow Street Runners were small in number, and the main form of police protection at the time was the constable and watchman. They were not especially effective, and during the big riot at Parliament in 1780, only 6 out of 80 constables could be found. (Merchants continued to hire their own police) With the fast rising crime rate, something much more effective was needed.

THE METROPOLITAN POLICE

From 1770 to 1828, various committees in Parliament looked into the possibility of forming a new system of policing. Little was done. London, though very rich, relied upon the parish watch and privately hired police.

The prime effort behind a new police system was Sir Robert Peel, England's Home Secretary. Peel had been Secretary for Ireland from 1812 to 1818, and while in that position, had formed a regular Irish Constabulary. This gave him some experience in forming a police force. They were called Peelers as were the later Metropolitan Police officers. Still there was much resistance to the idea. Even though the system of watchmen was not very efficient, people had come to accept it and believe that without the watchmen, crime would be even greater.

Fig. II-17; Bow Street Police Court in 1808

Fig. II-18; Sir Robert Peel

In 1822 Robert Peel wrote "I want to teach people that liberty does not consist of having your house robbed by organized gangs of thieves. His intention was to form a preventive police system to replace capital punishment as a deterrent to crime. When he became Home Secretary in 1822, there were over 200 offenses punishable by death. Still the crime rate continued to rise.

By this time it had become apparent that none of the previous methods of maintaining law and order were adequate to cope with the rising tide of crime in the cities of that day. Robbers and burglars were responsible for a loss of 10 million pounds a year (After the forming of the Metropolitan Police, the loss dropped to 100,000 pounds.) From the period of 1821 to 1828, there was a 15% increase in the population of London. In the same period, there was a 41% increase in crime. The time was ripe for a change in the system of policing.

The Industrial Revolution and the great movement of the masses to the cities, plus crop failures, had created new conditions of poverty and suffering among the masses that were unprecedented in English history. The conservative government at that time responded to the problem by increasing the penalties. Capital punishment reached an historical peak of over forty persons a day being executed. This included men, women and children, and with no apparent effect on the crime rate.

The theft of a loaf of bread or twelve pence was punishable by death. The placing of graffiti on Westminster Bridge was also punishable by death. Not since the Draconian Code of ancient Greece has Western history recorded a set of laws so severe. Draco had justified his severities on the basis that minor crimes deserved death, and he could find no higher punishment for the more severe crimes. The existing systems of police protection such as the Watch and Ward, the Parish Police, the Bow Street Runners, vigilante groups, the privately financed Merchant Police and Marine Police were haphazard and generally inefficient.

Seeking at least a partial solution to the problem Robert Peel introduced into Parliament "An Act for Improving the Police In and Near the Metropolis". It is more commonly referred to as the 1829 Metropolitan Police Act.

The result was that in September of that year, England had its first real, uniformed, municipal police department. The constables wore a blue, swallow tailed coat, blue trousers in the winter and white in the summer, and a black top hat. The coat had a single row of bright white buttons down the front, and a military type belt with a large brass buckle. They carried a wooden rattle which was used to call for help, and a truncheon (club) for self defense. (see illustrations)

The first police headquarters was at 4 Whitehall Place, in small quarters behind Scotland Yard. It was called Scotland Yard because that is where the Kings of Scotland stayed when they came to London. The Metropolitan Police, or "New Police" as they were more commonly referred to by the majority of Londoners, were not well received at first.

People from all levels of society were against them. This included the London Times. A large number of Irishmen were recruited, and they were mostly Catholic. At this time there was considerable prejudice against both the Irish and Catholics. This added fuel to the fire of resentment. The English were not used to strict policing as were the French, and because of past English history, the people were very sensitive to any form of governmental oppression. Peel was accused of being a dictator, and plotting to overthrow the government and put General Wellington in power. His "New Police" were often referred to as "Peel's Bloody Gang," "Blue Devils" and "Dirty Papists."

One handbill that encouraged a mob to attack Parliament and the police stated: "LIBERTY OR DEATH. Come armed. We assure you, from ocular evidence, that 6000 cutlasses have been removed from the Tower for the use of Peel's bloody gang." When a mob of 400 people attacked the police, many were stabbed and one died from wounds. Despite this, the police responded with a baton charge and the rioters ran off into the night. In the first few years, in the Whitechapel division, 20% of all constables were injured annually. At any time, 9% of the force was on sick leave due to savage assaults.

The New Police were looked upon as a "disguised military force" who were opposed to the free institutions of the country which gave parish authority sole control in keeping and securing the peace. It was felt that if people were to have a new police system at all, it should be under local control, and not controlled by the government. In looking back, it may have been a good thing. By making the police responsible to the Home Office in the federal government, the chance of corruption was greatly reduced. Had the United States adopted a national police, it would most certainly have avoided the terrible scandal of corruption and dirty politics that is such a stain on its early reputation.

The New Police.

PARISHIONERS.---Ask yourselves the following *Questions*:

Why is an Englishman, if he complains of an outrage or an insult, referred for redress to a Commissioner of Police?

Why is a Commissioner of Police delegated to administer Justice?

Why are the proceedings of this new POLICE COURT *unpublished* and *unknown*? and by what Law of the Land is it recognized?

Why is the British Magistrate stripped of his power? and why is Justice transferred from the Justice Bench?

Why is the Sword of Justice placed in the hands of a MILITARY Man?

Consider these constitutional questions: consider the additional burthen **saddled** on you---consider all these points, then UNITE in removing such **a** powerful force from the hands of Government, and let us institute a Police System in the hands of the PEOPLE under *parochial* appointments---

UNITY IS STRENGTH;

THEREFORE,

   I.---Let each Parish convene a Meeting.

   II.---Let a Committee be chosen, instructed to communicate with other Parishes.

   III.---Let Delegates be elected from each Committe to form a

CENTRAL COMMITTEE,

To join your Brother Londoners in one heart, one hand, for the

Abolition of the New Police

These Bills may be had at the Printer's, at 4d. per Dozen; 2s. per Hundred; or, 17s. 6d per Thousand, and the enemies of oppression requested to aid its circulation.   ELLIOT, Printer, 14 Holywell St. Strand.

Fig. II-19, Flyer on New Police

POLICE GAZETTE;
OR, HUE AND CRY.
Published by Authority.

FRIDAY, JANUARY 18, 1828.   [PRICE SEVENPENCE.

taining the Substance of all Informations received in Cases of Felonies, and Misdemeanors of an aggravated nature; and against Receivers of Stolen Goods, reputed Thieves and Offenders escaped from Custody, with the time, the place, and every particular circumstance marking the Offence. The Names of Persons charged, who are known but not in Custody, and of those who are not known, their Appearance, Dress, and every other mark of identity that can be described. The Names of Accomplices and Accessaries, with every other particular which may lead to their Apprehension. The Names of all Persons brought before the Magistrates, charged with any of the Offences mentioned, and whether committed for Trial, Re-examination; or how otherwise disposed of. Also a Description of Property that has been Stolen, and particularly of Stolen Horses with as much particularity as can be given, with every circumstance that may be useful for the purpose of Tracing and Recovering it.

DESERTERS.

FROM THE ROYAL MARINES.

CHATHAM DIVISION.

JAMES OATLEY, aged 25, private, 5 feet 8, dark complexion, hazel eyes, black hair, uniform coat, waistcoat, and p. blue trowsers: born at Kelvedon Hatch, near Chipping ongar, in Essex, labourer. Deserted 7th January, from ad quarters.—Third time of desertion.

WOOLWICH DIVISION.

ARCHIBALD BLAIR, aged 38, private, 5 feet 8, dark complexion, hazel eyes, brown hair, red round jacket, blue trowsers, forage cap: born at Kilbride, Lanark, Ireland, raver. Deserted 11th January, from Head quarters.—third time of desertion.

MURDER.

WHITEHALL, JANUARY 10, 1828.

WHEREAS it hath been humbly represented to the KING, that on the night of Monday, 31st December last, Elizabeth Jells was most inhumanly murdered by some person or persons at present unknown, in the house No. 11, Montague-place, Russell-square, which was left under her care.

His Majesty, for the better apprehending and bringing to justice the person or persons guilty of the said atrocious Murder, is hereby pleased to promise His most gracious Pardon to any one of the Offenders (except the Person who actually committed the said Murder) who shall discover his or their Accomplice or Accomplices therein, so that he, she, or they may be apprehended and convicted thereof.

LANSDOWNE.

And as a further encouragement, a Reward of ONE HUNDRED POUNDS is hereby offered by the Parish Officers of St. Giles in the Fields, and St. George, Bloomsbury, to any person making such discovery as aforesaid except as before excepted, to be paid on conviction of the offender or offenders. Information to be given to Mr. Stafford, Chief Clerk at the Public Office, Bow-street.

Information is requested to be given to Mr. Stafford, Chief Clerk at the above Office; and a Reward of Ten Pounds will be paid on the apprehension of the Offender.

WHITEHALL, JANUARY 19, 1828.

adjoining; and whereas it hath been also represented to the King, that on Saturday night the 22d, or early on Sunday morning the 23d day of December last, a fire broke out on the premises of Mr. William Bayliss, of Welford, in the county of Gloucester, which consumed five wheat ricks, a bean rick, a hay rick, a straw rick, part of a barn, a granary, and a cow-shed; and whereas it hath been further represented unto the King, that, on the 1st of January instant, a fire broke out in the rick-yard of Mr. John Baldwin, of the parish of Alveston, near Stratford-upon-Avon, in the county of Warwick, and destroyed property therein; and that there is every reason to believe, that the several fires before mentioned were the act of some evil-disposed person or persons unknown;

His Majesty, for the better apprehending and bringing to justice the persons concerned in the felonies above mentioned, is hereby pleased to promise His most gracious pardon to any one of them (except the person or persons who actually set fire to the said respective premises) who shall discover their accomplice or accomplices therein, so that he, she, or they may be apprehended and convicted thereof.

LANSDOWNE.

And, as a further encouragement, the following rewards are hereby offered, viz. ONE HUNDRED POUNDS, by the County Fire-office, to any person (except as aforesaid) who shall discover the said offender or offenders who set fire to the premises of Mrs. Blick, so that he, she, or they may

Fig. II-20; Reduced Facsimile of Part of Fron Page of the First Number of the "Police Gazette"

Sir Robert Peel felt that the Fieldings were right in their belief that advertising the descriptions of crimes and criminals would result in arrests and convictions. As a result, a special police newspaper was printed for that purpose. It was called the Hue and Cry. (See illustration II-20) The first issue appeared in January of 1828.

It was common for people to throw rotten apples and bricks at them when they patrolled the streets. It took a lot of guts just to go out on patrol in those days. Drinking by officers was both heavy and understandable. Of the first 2800 men recruited, 1790 were dismissed for being drunk on duty.

Most English citizens were aware of the Continental police systems where the police had tremendous powers and were often government spies. They were concerned about so much power being placed under one person in the federal government.

Because of fears that the New Police might be too militaristic, an effort was made to avoid military type uniforms. They chose a blue swallow tail coat and trousers, and a top hat made of leather. It was similar to the police uniform for the small City of London Day Police. Many people were familiar with this uniform because they saw it when they attended the many public hangings outside Newgate Prison which was in that inner section of London

Fig. II-21; Cartoon of Peel attacking Charlies

proper. To avoid people's suspicion that the New Police were government spies, they wore their uniforms at all times, even when off duty. A blue and white armlet was worn when the officer was on duty, so that citizens would know that he was available.

Recruits had to be under 35 years of age, at least 5 foot 8 inches tall, and be in good physical condition. They also had to be able to read and write. Considering that qualification, the pay was not good. In 1828 a literate person could make more money elsewhere.

A constable was paid three shillings a day. Each week two shillings were deducted his pay for uniform costs. Even by contemporary standards, the

Fig. II-23; The "Peeler"

Fig. II-22; Policeman, Old Style

pay was barely above the subsistence level. To help out, the government provided quarters for married constables, and single officers were allowed to stay in military style barracks and were provided with a dining hall where the meals were highly subsidized by the government.

Although an effort was made to avoid a military association, the constables were regularly drilled, marched and paraded through the streets. Discipline was enforced by fines or reduction to a lower pay scale. To avoid possible corruption, as happened with the watchmen, discipline was strongly maintained. If a constable was off sick, he was fined one shilling. There was no pension system.

The "Peelers" took a terrible beating at first. Because of rumors, the general populace thought they were armed, even though they carried nothing but their truncheons. They were advised to use those only in dire emergency. When Londoners learned that they were, in fact, not armed, their attitude began to change. Another factor that weighed heavily in changing the attitude of the public was the unprecedented high standards demanded of the police by their superiors. These standards were quite similar to our present day Code of Ethics. This is undoubtedly one reason why we often hear that our modern American police system has been adapted from the Metropolitan Police.

Fig. II-24; A Peeler

Fig. II-25; Fictitious "Peeler with sword"

Fig. II-27; Early English Bobby

The London Times, which had earlier attacked the formation of the New Police, now came to its defense. In a later editorial, after the constables did excellent work in controlling a riot, they stated:

A military force supposes military weapons of some kind. The police have neither swords nor pistols to defend themselves; and recent circumstances suffice to prove that for the preservation of their own lives, to say nothing of the public, the bits of stick with which they are at present provided are anything but adequate. We ourselves have seen nothing of the police but exemplary courtesy, forbearance, propriety, great willingness to act and, when occasion calls for it, to refrain from acting.

Within four years after the formation of the Metropolitan Police, the most common complaint against the constables concerned their habit of talking to servant girls while on duty, a trait that seems to have persisted to this day when officers flirt with waitresses or clerks.

Fig. II-26; Police at 1837 riots

Fig. II-28; Unarmed Bobbies arresting an armed burglar

THE WARRANT CARD

Unlike American Police, British officers did not use a chest badge to show their authority. Officially their authority rested in what was called a Warrant Card. When an officer was officially sworn in for the position of constable, he also signed an oath card. This became his identification and his basis for making legal arrests. Later, when the stove top hat was replaced by the helmet, an ornate badge was placed on the front of the helmet. The warrant card, however, was still used as the symbol of authority.

I _John Lloyd_ do swear that I will well and truly serve our sovereign Lady the Queen, in the office of Constable, for preserving the peace and preventing robberies and other felonies and apprehending offenders against the peace, not only within the Borough of Birmingham, but also withing the County in which such Borough is situated and also within every county being within seven miles of any part of such borough and also within all liberties in any such county, in pursuance of an Act of Parliament passed in the 5th and 6th years of the Reign of His late Majesty King William the Fourth, entitled,"An Act to provide for the regulation of Municipal Corporations in England and Wales," during so long as I shall continue to hold the office of Constable under the said Act, and that while I continue to hold the said office, I will faithfully discharge the duties thereof to the best of my skill and knowledge, without favour or affection, malice or ill will.

SO HELP ME GOD

Fig. II-29; Sample of Warrant Card for City of Birmingham

FRANCE

The French Police institution is quite old. In the days of the Roman Empire, France was the Roman province of Gaul, and the French expanded on Augustus Caesar's idea of police by giving them very wide powers.

These powers included such duties as price control, welfare, public morals, and even sitting in judgment of these offenders. They handled duties that today we would consider "civil" matters. The power of the police came directly from the king and not from the community as with the English and later the Americans. This resulted in strong central control.

Fig. II-30; A "Garde de Paris"

In the sixth century, Paris had two patrols. The Citizen Night Guard, (similar to English Watchmen) and the Royal Guard, which was probably there more for the protection of the King.

It was at this time that Saint-Louis gave the Guard the motto that is even today on the French police emblem. "Vigilat ut Quiescant" (He watches that they may sleep). (See illustration II-35). The essence of this motto still holds true today, and could be considered an international motto for police patrol.

Because of their wide powers and such strong central control, the French police unfortunately have a history of not only being overly strict, but also as being political agents of the ruling powers. Until the French Revolution, the police were quite oppressive. We have obtained the word "dossier" from the French because of the sinister practice by the French police, over the centuries, of compiling such thick dossiers on just about everyone. Police spying became a way of life. Most officers were recruited from the army.

Fig. II-31; French Police Patrol Wagons

Fig. II-33; French Police Symbol

Fig. II-32; French Sergeant de Ville

Fig. II-34; French Police Officer

Fig. II-35; French Police Officer

On the positive side, the French police were responsible for conceiving street signs, house numbers, street lighting, emergency rescue services and a system of police ambulances. They are also the first to have patrol wagons. (see illustration II-31, previous page) They set up state pawn shops to relieve the gouging of poor people.

They also founded children's hospitals and schools for the poor and even assumed the duty of finding work for the unemployed.

At the end of the eighteenth century (1791) the position of "Officers de Paix" was formed (the origin of our present term "Peace Officer).

At first only officers and the military wore uniforms, the major form of identification was a "Warrant Card." The English used the same method. It gave the policeman the authority to make arrests, and was used as a combination "Loyalty Oath" and police identification card.

Though most people consider the Metropolitan Police as being the first uniformed municipal police organization, it is a fact that Louis-Marie Debelleyme, who was appointed Prefect of Police in 1828, formed the first such organization in March of 1829, six months before Peel's Metropolitan Police. It consisted of one hundred uniformed policemen called "Sergents de Ville" (Servants of the City). They wore tall cocked hats, and blue uniforms. They carried canes in the daytime and sabres at night. (See illustration) At night they were doubled in number.

THE UNITED STATES

COLONIAL TIMES

Since the United States started as an English colony, it was natural for its leaders to borrow from the country of its origin.

There seemed to be two main trends in this country as far as law enforcement was concerned. In the north, life was more urban oriented, and the Watch or Constable system seemed to be best suited. In the south the development was more rural because of agriculture, and the Sheriff system of enforcement became the trend.

Fig. II-36; Colonial Watchhouse on corner

Since many colonists came to this country as convicts, sent here in "Banishment" (a form of English punishment at that time), there was a reluctance among many concerning the formalizing of any type of police protection.

In the towns and ports, however, the need for some type of protection, especially at night, became apparent. The development, like the growth of the towns themselves, was slow. At the end of the eighteenth century there were really very few cities in the United States with large populations.

Although Boston formed the first "Night Watch" in 1636, there is a record of a constable being chosen for the town of Plymouth in 1634. A little over twenty years later the Dutch colonists formed the "Ratlewacht" (rattle watch) in New York.

It was not until the turn of the century that Philadelphia set up a system of obligated duty in which citizens had to serve as watchmen.

Fig. II-37; Prank on sleeping watchman

Like their counterparts in England, our early watchmen were not much to boast about. They were mostly volunteers, but some were forced to do watchman duty as a form of punishment for certain transgressions. Those who were paid for the job were not paid much, and therefore didn't feel that they had to do much. As in England, the watchmen were often subjected to pranks and jokes by groups of young men who were "out on the town." Since it was common for watchmen to sleep on duty, it was considered quite a prank to push over a watchhouse with the watchmen asleep inside. (see illustration II-37, previous page) American watchmen were called "Leatherheads" because they wore varnished leather hats. By the early part of the eighteenth century, the "night watch" was well established in towns and cities.

THE INTERMEDIATE PERIOD

It was not until 1833 that the city of Philadelphia instituted the first daytime, paid, police service. This occurred because a large amount of money was willed to the city to provide more effectively for the safety of persons and property in that city. Two interesting provisions of the will were

that watchmen were to patrol in pairs at night, and that promotions were to be made from within the ranks and not by outside political appointments.

The idea of paid, full time police departments became more popular, and within the next three decades most major cities in the East and Midwest followed suit. About this time there were a series of major mob riots that swept the country, and this had a very definite effect on both the establishment of full time police departments, and the increase of personnel in those departments already existing.

Fig. II-39; The "Black Maria"

New York organized the first modern American police force in 1844 based on the English Metropolitan Police system. It was soon followed by San Francisco, Chicago, Cincinnati, New Orleans, Philadelphia and Boston.

In the frontier areas of the United States, law enforcement was developed on a local level without many established rules. Enforcement was aided by the use of the old legal process "Posse Comitatus" (the power of the state to summon assistance in enforcing the law), and the "posse" became a part of "law in the West."

Unlike Canada, which used the federal "Mounties" to maintain law and order in frontier areas, the United States federal government restricted their involvement to the use of troops when things got completely out-of-hand.

To assist in law enforcement, frontier areas relied upon such methods as the "Wanted Poster" and "Bounty Hunters." The bounty hunter tracked down wanted criminals, especially those wanted

Fig. II-38; Police Parade, Broadway

"dead or alive" and they were often shot from ambush without danger to the bounty hunter.

The sheriff and local marshals were poorly paid, and relied on the reward system to augment their regular pay. Despite the fictional stories of our school days and those represented in popular movies, some of the noted law officers were far from professional in carrying out their duties.

The West developed so fast and the population was so transient, that the problems of law enforcement in the new frontier seemed at times almost insurmountable. Despite the colorful stories of some of our early Western lawmen, serious research into the history of the West reveals that some of them were as bad as the criminals they sought.

In those areas that failed to establish organized police protection, or where the police became politically ineffective, citizens often took things into their own hands by the formation of "Vigilance Committees." The most famous example of this was the San Francisco "Committee of Vigilance" that formed during the years 1848 and 1849 due to the great influx of fly-by-night gold seekers.

The Vigilance Committee adopted the symbol of a watchful eye (see illustration II-40) and used the motto made famous by Lord Mansfield in 1770, "Fit justitia ruat coelum" (Let justice be done though the heavens fall). Unfortunately, as happens with any organization that is not responsible to the people, they often sought their own personal and political ends through this committee, and justice was not always served.

Frontier Law enforcement was handled by a sheriff on the local level and by marshals on the Territorial level. Since there was no federal police organization, private detective agencies, such as Pinkerton, filled the gap between local and federal law enforcement. Unfortunately this was a service provided only for those who could afford it.

Fig. II-40. Vigilante Symbol

CORRUPTION IN RAPIDLY GROWING AMERICAN CITIES

The latter part of the nineteenth century and into the early part of the twentieth century was a difficult time for organized law enforcement in the United States. Politics reigned supreme and police appointments were political. Without civil service protection, an officer's job was at the whim of the mayor, the city council, or local ward bosses.

Social scientists argue the pros and cons of local police control as opposed to central or national control. But few can dispute the terrible effect that local control has had on police corruption. It is unfortunate, but the Intermediate Period of American Police history was a time when the standards of professional police work had sunk to its lowest level. It is not a pleasant topic to cover, but if we can learn from history, then it is important that it be covered.

Having hindsight, we can examine the factors that brought about this unfortunate condition. There were three basic factors involved. The first was the fact that the police were locally controlled. The second was the "Jacksonian philosophy," and the third was "Bossism".

LOCAL CONTROL

Most early Americans originated from Europe, and experiences there often shaped their feelings about government in their new country. Most came from countries where the government had a system of strong central control. Unfortunately, some of those governments often oppressed the people. Because of this many came to this country seeking an opportunity to live under a more democratic form of government where local communities held more political power. As we will see, when this system is also applied to policing, problems can occur.

THE JACKSONIAN PHILOSOPHY

Andrew Jackson was the 7th President of the United States. He was a great military hero and quite popular with the people. He was looked upon as a symbol of the democratic feelings at that time. Those in power and those having political influence, looked upon him unfavorably. They considered him an uncouth and dangerous "upstart." Jackson had many enemies, and they opposed his every action. This further encouraged his desire to get even. To overcome this handicap, he made a great many promises to those who helped him in his campaign. (Not unusual in politics.)

He was elected in 1828 and became President in 1829. Once in office he carried to extremes the Roman philosophy, "to the victor go the spoils." He used this philosophy to hand out numerous government posts, jobs, and lucrative contracts. Quite simply, he fired all those working for the government and gave their jobs to his friends and supporters. These jobs were considered to be rewards that the victor handed out to those who helped him get elected. Often this is called the "Spoils System." Friends helped friends. Personal relationships were of the utmost importance. Who you knew and recommended was the key. This obviously had to have a terrible effect on the efficiency of government when employees had no real job security. As a result, in 1883, Congress passed the Pendleton Act which established civil service. However, this applied only to federal employees. To this day, it is considered the President's right to hand out well paid administrative jobs to his supporters.

Under the "spoils system", on the local level, jobs on the police department became part of the pie to be divided after the election. This resulted in "soft" police jobs for those who supported the winning candidate for office. Those who did have political protection would often work all day at another job and sleep all night on their police job.

BOSSISM

Bossism was a system of political control used to pervert the democratic process of government. It gained control of cities through misuse of the voting process. In large cities, bossism centered around one powerful figure who was called the "Boss." Under him was a complex network of lesser figures called the "Machine."

The original purpose of the Machine was to promote the political aims of the group as well as further their social interests. As it became more powerful, the main objective became financial corruption. When applied to Bossism, the old saying that "Power corrupts and absolute power corrupts absolutely" could not be more true. Bossism depends upon the manipulation of voters to elect candidates supported by the Machine, who in turn do the bidding of the Machine. Like a benevolent dictatorship, Bossism did much good for those in the community. Once in power, the Machine could provide jobs and offer political protection to its supporters.

In large cities such as New York, all of the newly arrived immigrants settled in certain parts of the city. There was an Italian section, an Irish section, a Russian Jewish section and so on. Each section was called a Ward. Those living in a Ward would elect a representative to help govern the city. In theory this sounds good. An example of the democratic process. But in practice the votes of these immigrants were bought by the politicians. The Machine would win their favor by helping them find jobs, assisting them when they went to court, and when they were unemployed, providing food and necessities. If this didn't work, the votes were either purchased with money or obtained by threats, which were carried out by the police.

Most major cities had their political bosses. For example: Abraham Ruef of San Francisco, Thomas Pendergast of Kansas City, James Curley of Boston, Frank Hague of New Jersey, William Thompson of Chicago, William Vare of Philadelphia, and William Tweed of New York, to name some of the more notable. Their power reached every part of government. The police, the courts, the District Attorney, all of those working for local government owed their jobs to the Machine. Their complete loyalty was not only expected, but demanded. The police department became the enforcing agency for the Machine. Like the "soldiers" in organized crime, the police arrested, beat up, and jailed those who resisted the Machine, and the courts convicted them, despite their innocence.

TAMMANY HALL

One of the most notorious political machines in American history was that of Tammany Hall in New York City. Tammany was a popular name for the Democratic political machine in Manhattan, New York. It started as a patriotic society after the American Revolution. It took its name from the Delaware Indian Chief Tamanend. It was sometimes called the Tammany Society or the Columbian Order of New York City.

At first its activities were more social. But because it supported Andrew Jackson for President in 1828, it received so many political favors that it became an important power and the dominant political force in the City of New York. Originally it promoted political reforms on behalf of the common man, and was therefore very popular with the average person. It gained considerable strength through helping newly arrived immigrants find jobs. They nearly always voted for Tammany candidates despite the obvious corruption, election fraud and other abuses.

With the increase in power, Tammany Hall engaged in corruption on a scale never before seen in American history. It reached the pinnacle of power and abuse in the 1870's under the leadership of William Tweed, better known as "Boss Tweed." Like an octopus, it had tentacles in all branches of local government, including the courts. To challenge the organization was very dangerous because a policeman's very job was dependent on Tammany Hall. They made short work of those who caused trouble for the Machine.

If an honest police officer wanted to make changes or complain about the system, there was not only no one to listen, but many who would gladly take action against any officer who was trying to "rock the boat."

At times, when major scandals would be revealed by the newspapers, Tammany politicians would be voted out of office, but in the next election they would be back in the driver's seat. By 1933, the citizens of New York City had finally had enough. Tammany hall suffered a major defeat. Even though an occasional Tammany candidate was elected, the organization was no longer a power.

BOSS TWEED

Fig. II-41; Cartoon of "Boss" Tweed

In 1848, William Tweed became a volunteer fireman and acquired a number of influential contacts within the Ward. He seemed well suited to politics, and was soon elected as an Alderman. He later served a term in Congress. By 1857 he controlled Tammany and the City of New York. He and his associates in the political machine called the "Tweed Ring" looted the City of New York of 30 million dollars through fraud, forgery, bribery and kickbacks. Like most "Bosses", he was very generous to the poor and had the support of the people. The New York Times and the political cartoonist Thomas Nast took on Boss Tweed in the newspapers with little success. (See Nast's political cartoon on defying the law)

Then a county bookkeeper, who was brave enough to provide documentary evidence against Boss Tweed, was able to expose the wholesale graft in Tammany Hall and arouse great public indignation. Boss Tweed was tried twice and finally sentenced to 12 years in prison. He appealed and was able to have the sentence reduced to one year. Later, he was arrested on another charge but escaped from custody and fled the country. He was extradited and imprisoned, where he died in 1878

Even though the City of New York finally enacted a Civil Service system, those running Civil Service were appointed by the Machine, and didn't follow the proper rules. Major A. Griffins, a famous English author on international police systems at the turn of the century, did a study of New York police departments. He found that under Tammany, no one could become a police officer unless he paid for it, or had political connections. The Civil Service rules stated that all appointments were to be made by open competition, but if a candidate did not pay the right person $300, he would never pass the examination. He found that it cost $1,600 to make Sergeant, and $15,000 to make Captain.

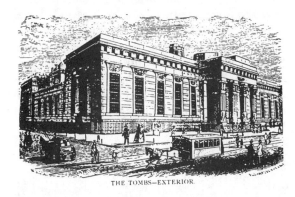

Fig. II-42; New York City jail known as the Tombs, 1800's

When the Machine had a prominent minister falsely arrested for attacking the political system, the state legislature formed the Lexow Commission to investigate the situation. Despite serious threats to their persons and families, 687 Witnesses testified under oath. Witnesses were "abused, clubbed and falsely imprisoned" based on false police testimony. There were 10,576 pages of court testimony. The city politicians were able to stall the commission report for nine months. When the report was finally published, it documented a scandalous political system gone wild. Police departments were called "slaughter houses, and police corruption was declared appalling.

A reporter from the New York Herald was falsely arrested and badly beaten at the station because he wrote an article attacking the system. He was later asked why he did not sue the police department. His reply was " It's no use going to law with the Devil when the court is in hell."

THE POLICEMAN

You're the bummest old policeman—
Running when there's trouble near,
Always grabbing kids and poodles,
Courting housemaids all the year.

Fig. II-43; Postcard of "The Policeman", 1910

Although we have examined some of the negative aspects of police departments during those difficult times, it should be mentioned that research will show that on a day-to-day basis, police officers did a good job of investigating crimes and catching criminals.

There was reluctance on the part of some policemen to wear uniforms and especially visible badges. Those who did wear uniforms, were likely to wear only part of one.

It was common to see several varieties of uniforms in one department if you saw any at all. Chief George Walling of the New York Police Department in the late 1800's stated in his book Recollections of a New York Chief of Police, that during the Astor Place Riots in 1849, the police officers did not wear uniforms. They did have a badge which they attached to their jackets.(See illustration II-44, next page)

POLITICS AND THE BATTLE BETWEEN THE TWO NEW YORK CITY POLICE DEPARTMENTS

Probably one of the saddest events in American police history was the battle between the two New York City police departments. In 1857, Fernando Wood became the mayor of New York City. He turned the police department into his own political tool. It became so bad that the New York state legislature declared in 1857 that the city was too corrupt to govern itself. Control of the police department was transferred from the city to the state. The State of New York established a new Metropolitan Police Department comprised of New York County and two other counties. The members of the old police department were then told that they now belonged to the new department. The Governor established a police commission of five people. This ruling was challenged all the way to the State Supreme Court, which upheld the decision. Despite this, fifteen captains and over seven hundred policemen proclaimed their loyalty to Mayor Wood who refused to accept the decision.

He had "his" policemen start throwing newly appointed city officials out oeir offices. As a result, a warrant of arrest was issued for Mayor Wood. Fifty of the new Metropolitan Police officers were dispatched to carry out the warrant. At Mayor Wood's headquarters, there were about 800 uniformed officers from the old Municipal Police Department. As the Metropolitan officers approached, the Municipals attacked them, and a fierce and bloody battle ensued (see illustration II-45). Many were badly hurt and a few were almost killed. The Police Commission contacted General Sanford of the Seventh New York Regiment (who were at that time in the city.) When the Seventh Regiment approached city hall, Mayor Wood saw that it was futile to resist the arrest warrant any further, so he submitted. In a settlement between the conflicting parties, the Municipal Police were allowed to remain in their jobs for a period of one month. As a result, New York City had two functioning police departments for that period. Morale was very low, and little policework was accomplished during that time. Citizens lost what remaining respect they had for the police, and crime rose to an all time high despite the city having two police departments

Fig. II-44; Police and Army responding to the Astor Riots

Fig. II-45; Fight between Metropolitan and Municipal police

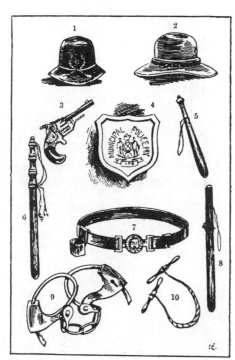

EQUIPMENTS OF THE NEW YORK POLICE.

1. Winter Helmet. 2. Summer Hat. 3. Revolver.
4. Shield. 5. Day Stick. 6. Rosewood Bâton for
Parade. 7. Belt and Frog. 8. Night Stick. 9.
Handcuffs (new style). 10. Nippers.

Fig. II-46; Early police equipment

Many solutions were offered to solve the problem of politics and policework, including the election of policemen. Although this had its merits, under a system of this type, the officer would do nothing to offend anyone for fear of losing the next election. Anyone today, who is familiar with sheriff departments, knows the conflicts that often arise between a sheriff's desire to be re-elected and his duty to enforce the laws of the county he serves.

Some major cities throughout the United States experimented with metropolitan police systems or state police boards, but not all met with success. One of the greatest steps in solving the problem of

Fig. II-47; Police squad drilling

corrupt local control was the passing of Civil Service protection for city employees. As was previously stated, the rules were not always followed, but in most cases they were. The Pendleton Act of 1883, which established Civil Service for federal employees, became the model and slowly, state and local governments followed suit. Many city governments were reluctant to establish Civil Service for policemen because it meant losing political control over them, and some held out as long as possible. It is sometimes argued that Civil Service protects the "goof-off", but it has had more of an effect in breaking the political stranglehold on police departments than any other factor.

As the immigrant tides came to this country, its members sought and obtained jobs on local police departments. Studies of early police records show that when large numbers of immigrants settled in a particular urban area, their representation on the local police department increased.

The photograph below shows the variety of uniform styles found in many departments at the turn of the century. It was taken in San Francisco after the 1906 earthquake. There are two different colors of uniforms, three different styles of uniforms, two different types of sergeant's stripes and three different styles of badges.

THE MODERN PERIOD

The Modern period began in the 1920's with the use of automobile patrol and voice radio communications. It was here that general police tactics took on a greater change than at any other period. As things improved for policework in the United States, fate suddenly dealt a new hand in the form of Prohibition. Prohibition was not only unpopular with the average citizen, but was rarely enforced by the police. The "fast buck" to be made by "bootlegging" brought about an era of gangsterism. Mob leaders divided up sections of cities like feudal lords divided up kingdoms in the middle ages. Again the police were in the middle. Prohibition made breaking the law a popular thing, and contributed to breaking down respect for police and the law. Working in a frustrating situation like this caused some normally good policeman to succumb to the "payoff." It takes a lot of courage to fight a whole system by yourself. Political machines, seeking large donations of money to their causes, developed an "unholy alliance" with rich gangsters. Once more it was truly a difficult time for those in police work who wan-ted to be professional. Apart from enforcement connected with prohibition, the police on a day-to-day basis did good policework. Through the use of federal agents and the end of Prohibition, the era of gangsterism passed, and law enforcement gained a breathing spell.

Fig. II-48; Photograph showing wide variety of uniforms and badges

WORLD WAR II AND ITS EFFECT ON THE POLICE

World War II had many effects on American law enforcement. From a negative aspect, it was hard to get personnel, and many departments had to "scrape the bottom of the barrel" to maintain their strength. Civil service later protected their jobs.

On the good side, great numbers of young men became members of the military police which stimulated their interest in making a career of policework. Large amounts of money were spent on new methods of police training and the development of both equipment and tactics. After the war, these were applied to non-military policework.

The Second World War brought about great shifts in population. Small towns became cities in short periods of time. There was a great movement of population to the West and to cities. This large influx of new people made the political control so common to the older cities impossible. Things grew too fast to establish the network of political intrigue. Because communities grew so fast, young officers found themselves being promoted to high positions in unprecedented numbers. With youth goes innovation, and in the soil of a nonpolitical environment, it grows to great heights.

Another product of the Second World War was the GI Bill. Before this time, college was thought of as being only for the rich. This picture was now changed and policemen were starting to get a college education. The "New Breed" was being born.

By the end of the Korean War college programs specializing in Police Science began to sprout like weeds. Today they are one of the fastest growing college programs in the nation. The Law Enforcement Education Program (LEEP) initiated by Congress in the 1960's to help pay for the education of prospective law enforcement officers was one of the many contributing factors. Incentive pay based on the numbers of college units taken was another factor.

Despite the great strides toward professionalization in the field of law enforcement, there are still police agencies in some parts of the country where poor selection and inadequate training hamper professional standards. However, recent research shows that great changes are taking place for the better.

To achieve better standards, most states have established State Commissions on Peace Officer Standards and Training in an effort to regulate proper training. This is usually accomplished through a state subsidy to police departments in return for adhering to proper standards.

Today's police are finding that science, both social and physical, is becoming an important ally. Policework is still basically dealing with people, but in the investigation and solving of crimes, science has proven to be especially helpful. Today's officer must understand computers and technical equipment. In a few years he or she will be lost without this knowledge. No longer is muscle the key factor; now it is brainpower.

Today there are approximately 40,000 Law Enforcement agencies in the United States, and well over 500,000 peace officers. Law enforcement has become a big operation. Unlike times past, law enforcement officers today are paid a decent wage and proper benefits. Despite the increased cost, few citizens really understand that police protection can be one of the best bargains available to the taxpayer.

It is difficult to set a fixed scale on the cost of police protection. There are two important factors to be considered. First, is the size and makeup of the community served. The cost is higher in very small communities and in very large cities. Sea ports also place a greater demand on police departments because there always seems to be more crime in sea ports. Towns or cities near large military posts or bases usually have more need for police officers. In large cities, the number of visitors that are temporarily attracted to the city can be important. While there, they commit crimes or are victimized by criminals. They also increase traffic problems that require more police personnel.

The second factor is the ratio of officers per thousand population. This varies throughout the country, but averages about two officers per thousand population in major sea ports, to less than one officer per thousand population in small towns.

THE PRESENT MODERN PERIOD

The present modern period began in the 1980's. The key to the early modern period was the development of the police radio and its use with the patrol car. This present period was brought about by the phenomenal advances in the sciences. The development of DNA sciences has revolutionized the field of criminal identification. Not since the development of fingerprint identification in the late 1800's has a development so affected this field.

This is also true of advancements in the field of computers. Today, most large cities have computers in their patrol cars. The prediction of crime location is done through probability software. There are programs that draw accident scenes and crime scenes and programs that allow a person of little artistic ability to develop good sketches of criminal suspects. In the booking procedure, officers can photograph and record all of the important information about an arrested person by computer. It can then be stored on disks that take up a small fraction of the room needed for the old records. Police Communications officers use computers to assist in assigning the right car for each assignment. They can also determin the location of a particular police car and show that location on a computer screen map. Although computers were not new to the 1980's, the advances in both hardware and software have changed the field of law enforcement and will continue to do so in the future.

Fig. II-49; Group Portrait

Fig. II-50; San Francisco Police Department on parade

Criminal Justice Services would like to acknowledge the following sources for non-original prints used in Chapter Two:

Griffiths, Major A. *Mysteries of Police and Crime*. London: Cassell & Co. Ltd., 1895.
    Figures 8, 10-12, 14, 15, 17-22, 24-28, 30, 31, 34, and 41

Jones, Willoughby. *Lights and Shadows of New York Life*. Cincinnatti, Ohio: Union Publishers, 1872.
    Figures 42, 46, and 47

Lee, M. *History of Police in England*. London: 1901.
    Figure 7

San Francisco Police Historical Society
    Figures 48, 49, and 50

Walling, George. *Recollections of a New York Chief of Police*. New York: Caxton Books, 1888
    Figures 38, 39, 44, and 45

Waters, M. *Recollections of a Policeman*. London: Hassett Publ., 1884
    Figures 9 and 16

STUDY QUESTIONS for Patrol Operations

CHAPTER 2

1. The word "police" originally came from what country? _____

2. The Romans then changed the word to "politia," the _____ changed it to "police" and the English adopted it from them.

3. Name one of the supposed origins of the word "cop." _____

4. The word "patrol" came from the French word "patrouiller" which means _____
   _____

5. There is evidence on clay tablets that the ancient Babylonians had policemen.   T or F

6. The Old Testament has references to "watchmen", who protected the cities of the   T or F
   ancient Hebrews.

7. The first organized, uniformed, municipal police force was formed in ancient _____.
   They were called _____ which is the district in Nubia from which they came.

8. In ancient Rome, the Emperor Augustus, formed a police force that also watched for fires
   They were called the _____.

9. In England, in the middle ages, each citizen was considered to be a policeman. Each person
   belonged to a group of ten, which was then placed in groups of one hundred. This was called the
   _____.

10. In the middle ages, in England, each county was called a shire. The law enforcement officer in
    charge of each shire was called a reeve. He was very powerful. Later this person was called a
    _____.

11. In England, in the middle ages, there was a requirement that all persons, when they heard the
    alarm sound, were required to stop everything and chase the criminal or they would be arrested.
    This alarm was called the " _____ and _____."

12. In 1195, King Richard instituted a group of law enforcers called "Keepers of the Peace."
    They were recruited from _____.

13. It is thought that one of our police symbols from today has its origin in the "Keepers of the
    Peace." It is the _____.

14. The "Statute of Winchester" in 1285, was called the " _____ and
    _____ Act."

15. In 1663, King Charles II, passed an act that established a force of one thousand night watchmen.
    They were called _____ after him.

16. This group was also old and fearful of criminals.Because of this they had the nickname, the
    "_____ and _____ watch".

17. The "Bow Street Runners" got their name from the judge who hired them.   T or F

18. The "Bow Street Runners" were also called the "_____ takers."

19. They later started a horse patrol to combat the large number of highwaymen on the approaches
    to London. They were nicknamed the "_____."

20. In 1780, there was a riot at Parliament. Only 6 constables could be found out of 80   T or F
    that were supposedly available.

21. There will only be two dates you have to remember. One of them is the date that the
    Metropolitan Police were formed in London.

22. The first London Metropolitan Police wore "stove top" hats.   T or F

23. The only weapon the Metropolitan Police carried was a "_____."

24. The name that seemed to stick to the Metropolitan Police was the one given to them after
    the person who started the police. Today they are still called "_____."

25. The ancient French had a police system adopted from the Roman vigiles.   T or F

26. In the sixth century the French police were given a motto that is still used today.
    It is "Vigilat Ut Quiescant".This motto means: "_____."

27. The word "Dossier" came from the French police.   T or F

28. The French police were responsible for the implementation of street numbers.   T or F

29. The French police were responsible for the institution of house numbers.   T or F

30. The early French police did not wear uniforms (except for officers). Their means
    of identification was a "_____ card".

31. Actually the French had a uniformed, municipal police force on duty in Paris six   T or F
    months before the London Metropolitan Police.

32. The above officers were called the "Sergeants De Ville." This means
    "_____ of the City."

33. In the United States, in 1636, the first night watch was established in the town of
    _____.

34. About 1654, the city of New York established a system of watchmen. They were called "Ratlewacht",
    which means "_____."

35. Because of their hats, American watchmen were called "_____."

36. The establishment of the first day and night police force occurred in 1833 in the city of
_____.

37. The first modern police force, patterned after the London Metropolitan Police, was established in 1844 in the city of _____.

38. In the western United States, the citizens, tired of lawlessness, took the law into their own hands and formed "_____ committees."

39. The early police in the United States suffered because of the Jacksonian philosophy   T or F
of the "spoils system."

40. Civil service was finally brought to federal employees in 1883 with the "_____
Act."

41. The modern era of policework began with the combination of the _____
and the newly invented police _____.

42. One of the advantages of World War II was the high quality of officers that were hired   T or F
during this era.

43. The movement west of great numbers of people had a very negative effect on   T or F
police departments because of increased crime.

44. Name one of the advantages of World War II for policework._____
_____

45. The term "Leep" stands for "law enforcement _____."

46. Post stands for "peace officer _____ and _____."

47. There are approximately _____ police agencies in the U.S.

CHAPTER III

THE PURPOSE AND BASIC DUTIES OF POLICE PATROL

THE PURPOSE OF POLICE PATROL

PATROL IS THE BACKBONE OF THE POLICE DEPARTMENT

The statement is often made that the Patrol Division is the "backbone of the police department." This statement is true for the following reasons:

First of all, it is the only division that cannot be eliminated. All other divisions of the police department may, if necessary, be eliminated.

The great majority of police departments and many sheriff's departments in this country are so small that they do not have, nor could they justify, separate divisions for Traffic, Investigation, Juvenile and other specialized areas. Their size and case-load require that all duties be handled by the patrol officer. In many small departments, the Chief of Police must also carry out a share of the patrol duties as well as administer the department.

Even in those departments that have specialized divisions, they seldom operate twenty-four hours a day as does the Patrol Division. Their Detective and Juvenile units often operate from 08:00 until 01:00. After that time all of their cases are handled by the patrol Officer.

THE BASIC DUTIES OF POLICE PATROL

The duties and objectives of police patrol are many, but the basic duties could probably be summed up in two words: protection and service.

To properly understand the purposes of patrol, it might be worthwhile to discuss each fundamental objective of the patrol division.

PREVENTIVE ENFORCEMENT

Preventive enforcement falls under the heading of protection, and involves the prevention of crime through the noticeable presence of police vehicles and personnel.

It has proven its value and continues to do so in the area of accident prevention. It is a statistical fact that where the police have purposely made their presence known by parking their patrol vehicles at or near hazardous intersections, or by heavily patrolling critical areas, a reduction in offenses occurs. Many state Highway Patrols have found this technique quite effective by parking "dummy" vehicles, that are painted to simulate regular Highway Patrol vehicles, in critical spots along the highway. This causes most people to slow down when they see the black and white vehicle on the side of the road.

Preventive enforcement, as a criminological philosophy, was first presented by Sir Robert Peel just prior to 1829 when he suggested the formation of the Metropolitan Police to Parliament. It was Peel's contention that when London criminals saw a group of able bodied uniformed policemen patrolling the streets, that they would throw up their hands in fear and run off to the nearest form of honest employment. Sir Peel and his associates had little real understanding of the true and basic causes of crime and they believed that all criminals were criminals solely by choice. They failed to comprehend the sociological implications of the Industrial Revolution. Although the resulting effect of the Metropolitan Police fell quite a bit below the high expectations of Peel and the members of Parliament, it still showed positive results and proved the value of preventive enforcement.

Prevention of crime is the soundest of all criminological theories. It is much easier to patch a crack in the dike than it is to repair the dike after it has broken. The old saying about "an ounce of prevention" being "worth a pound of cure" could not find a better example than in the prevention of crime. The cost of prevention when compared with the cost of crime is insignificant even when human suffering, injury and the loss of life are not weighed. Strictly from a monetary standpoint, society stands to lose greatly once a crime has been committed. There is the loss of taxes when the victim is injured and the perpetrator jailed. There is the increased cost of enforcement when crime increases. There is the cost of jails and their upkeep, the high cost of trials and prisons and the cost to the community of supporting families when the breadwinner is incarcerated. These, plus the financial loss to the victim, are but a part of the true cost to society when a crime has actually been committed.

When patrol officers and their vehicles are readily observed, this can and does reduce criminal activity. On the average, a police car, with red lights, that has stopped a motorist in fairly heavy traffic, is passed by over 100 cars per minute. Each one of these drivers becomes aware of the law enforcement presence in that area, and will drive more carefully for about half an hour. This can and does reduce accidents.

Professional criminals, especially burglars, will often admit that they avoid an area or community when their "casing" has indicated heavy and thorough police patrols. In some cases this does not stop the crime itself, it just changes the location of the crime. Yet because many crimes are committed on so-called impulse, the deterrence of preventive enforcement has great effect.

THE OFF DUTY POLICE CAR PLAN
(24 Hour Patrol Power)

A concept of preventive enforcement was put into operation by the Indianapolis Police Department. Officers were told to take their police cars home and to use them for their everyday personal use. Indianapolis quadrupled the number of police cars so that each patrol officer could have his or her own police car. It was a bold experiment and the cost was quite high. With such an expenditure, heads would surely roll if the experiment failed.

The only requirement made on patrol officers was that they keep an accurate log and have the radio on whenever in the car, on or off duty. If the officer was to hear a serious call over the air, and it was in the immediate vicinity, a response was expected. If the officer had family members in the car when a serious call was broadcast, they would be let out while the officer responded to the call, and then picked up after the call was resolved.

There have been some interesting results. First of all, the officers took better care of police cars, resulting in a definite drop in cost-per-mile expenses. Traffic accidents, injuries and deaths dropped, but overall crime slightly increased. This could be due to many factors such as an increase in population, or the fact that more crimes were now reported. Some people will report a crime to an officer in a police car, but not take the trouble to go to police headquarters to make that report.

A very significant statistic was the 35% increase in the number of arrests made over the preceding year. When off duty and in their police cars, officers made over 100 felony apprehensions. These arrests could, in the long run, have quite an effect on the reduction of criminal activity.

THE KANSAS CITY PREVENTIVE PATROL EXPERIMENT

A one year study of preventive patrol in the city of Kansas City, Missouri was completed by the Police Foundation. The report has become a point of heated argument among police chiefs, police officers, and research specialists.

Basically the study involved dividing fifteen of the police beats into three groups. One group was called "Reactive" and preventive patrol was eliminated in that area. In a second group of beats labeled "Proactive," the preventive patrol was increased by two to three times. The third group of beats was a "Control" group in which preventive patrol was maintained at its regular level.

The apparent outcome of the study was that preventive patrol made no difference to crime (excluding traffic offenses) and citizen feelings about police service. The researchers of this study have, however, advised caution in applying its results to all police departments.

The Los Angeles Police Department and Dr. Lyle Knowles, research specialist at Pepperdine University, have taken special exception to this study. They have challenged the accuracy, reliability, validity and general research techniques used.

There were many important factors that could have affected the outcome of the study, such as specialized units that could work in any beat, and beats that were only five blocks wide, and that were often crossed by units not assigned to that beat. This would in effect, increase the patrol car visibility on that beat. There were also main thoroughfares going through these beats to reach headquarters. Citizens who were not aware of the boundaries for this study, crossed the boundaries to go to work or to the store or for recreation purposes, and would then observe regular or increased police patrol, unaware that there was no preventive patrol on the beat in which they resided.

Officers from "Proactive" beats were not prevented from responding to calls in the "Reactive" beats. This could give the impression of increased patrol in the "Reactive" beats.

In an article in the magazine, Police Chief, the study was criticised and the researchers were allowed to respond. After carefully reading the responses to the criticism, the authors feel that the original researchers did not adequately respond to the criticism presented, and that the study should be taken very cautiously.

In the same issue of the Police Chief, there was an article by Charles Brown, a member of the Kansas City Police Department, and a member of the department staff assigned to this project. It revealed the great number of interpersonal problems that developed between police officers and researchers, and explained the initial resistance from the police officers who were to take part in the study. He indicated that the problem was never fully resolved. These are factors that could greatly affect a study of this nature.

If all the problems regarding research techniques were resolved, and, for the sake of argument, they showed that preventive patrol really made no difference, it would not change this system of patrol. This prediction is based on the fact that the average citizen wants to see visible patrol enforcement. One of the greatest concerns of citizens today is the prevalent and rising crime rate. If they are told that visible patrol has been reduced, and they see that crime is still a problem, you can be sure that they will be pounding the doors at city hall, demanding protection that they can actually see. After all, they are paying taxes for police services.

It is interesting to note that in the same year as the Kansas City study, the Cherry Hill, New Jersey department of Public Safety experimented with a program of "high visibility patrol" which resulted in a 31% reduction in residential burglaries as well as other crime.

In 1980 the Justice Department conducted a similar experiment and found that visible, marked patrol cars had a definite deterrent effect on crime.

SELECTIVE ENFORCEMENT

Even though our present patrol division is extremely mobile, it cannot completely cover all of the area or beats assigned to its patrol units. The only logical solution to the problem is selective enforcement. In other words, go to either where the trouble is, or where the trouble is likely to occur.

Fig III-1; Photo of Pin Map

In order to properly apply selective enforcement, we must rely on an administrative function of patrol, that of statistical research. An officer working just eight hours a day, and relying solely on memory cannot properly formulate an overall picture of criminal trends. Statistical charts and maps, on the other hand, can be a great help because they show trends that occur 24 hours a day, seven days a week, not just when the officer is on duty.

Selective enforcement has proven to be a very effective technique in patrol operations. If a certain area is subject to a high crime rate, the patrol officer will spend a greater amount of time in that area. If a nearby beat has a low incidence of crime, the officers from that beat might be assigned to cruise through the "high rate" area two or three times a night. This will usually result in a drop in the crime rate.

Today, with the widespread use of computers, police departments are in a much better position to apply the techniques of selective enforcement through the use of modern computer software. Computers can not only pinpoint locations and times, but can be used to predict potential hazards and trends. This information will allow patrol commanders to use their personnel and equipment to maximum efficiency.

Selective enforcement when combined with preventive enforcement and used in accident prevention has proven itself quite useful. When statistical research shows a particular area or intersection to have a high accident rate, the patrol commander assigns one or more marked patrol cars to give that area special attention. The results have proven this technique has value in the mission of the patrol division and the police department as a whole.

TRAFFIC ENFORCEMENT

Larger police departments have special traffic divisions, but the majority of the departments in the United States are small, and have only the patrol division to handle traffic enforcement. Even in large departments with traffic divisions, they cannot handle all accidents and traffic enforcement during rush or peak hours. Because of this, traffic remains basically a patrol function. The investigation of an accident involves considerable knowledge and skill, and since the patrol officer cannot escape the responsibility of accident investigation, it falls upon the department and the officer to see that he or she acquires this knowledge and skill.

Some officers complain that accident investigation amounts to "working for the insurance companies," and that the police should not waste time with borderline civil cases when they could be devoting the time to the detection and apprehension of criminals. It is true that insurance companies are served through accident investigations by the police. Yet the public and the interests of justice are better served through police skills. After all, service is one of the basic purposes of police patrol.

Traffic enforcement is strongly dependent upon personal contact between the patrol officers and the violators. There is much argument about the effectiveness of giving verbal warnings vs. the issuing of citations. There are good points to both sides of the argument, but department policy usually has the last word. The important thing is that the violator is stopped and the violation brought to his attention. As was mentioned previously, there is great preventive enforcement value in stopping traffic violators on a main thoroughfare. Here the situation can be observed by many passing vehicles. This makes traffic enforcement a valuable part of the patrol officer's duties.

Fig III-2; Officer Directing Traffic

Some police administrators are concerned with the effect of traffic enforcement on "police image." They feel that traffic enforcement should be separated from "policework", because this is a main cause of alienation between the public and the police. It is true that many law abiding citizens become quite upset at being stopped by a police officer. They will often later berate the police in front of their friends in order to compensate for having

been caught and cited. No one enjoys receiving a traffic citation. It is undoubtedly true that certain citizens would cooperate better with the police if it were not for the fact that they still have a bad taste in their mouth from the last citation they received. It has been pointed out that in some foreign countries where the police image was originally high, that their image has recently dropped. Studies have shown this attitude to be commensurate with the increase in vehicle traffic and the need for police to enforce traffic laws. These suggestions and theories might sound good, but the practical hurdles that would have to be overcome in separating traffic enforcement from general policework, make the idea impractical.

An alternate solution to the problem, although far from being the only answer, is to increase the officer's ability to issue citations without further offending the violator. This can be done through proper training. A very effective method is through the use of "role playing." In this form of training, the officer acts out the role of an officer issuing a citation in front of the class. From the critique of the class, and from observing the manner and procedures of others when they are role playing, officers can gain new insight into their own interpersonal behavior. This can enable them to bring about changes in their attitudes and approach.

EMERGENCY CALLS FOR SERVICE

One of the duties and purposes of patrol is the handling of emergency calls for service. The police vehicle has been equipped as an emergency vehicle, and special laws have been passed exempting the police officer from the normal rules of the road when responding to emergencies. (Emergency Vehicle laws and operation will be covered in Chapter IV.)

Of all public agencies, the patrol officer is usually the first at the scene of an emergency. This applies to fires, accidents, drownings, and attempted suicides just to name a few. These emergencies can be very trying for patrol officers. They are usually the first at the scene because they are already in the area and are mobile. A great responsibility rests on the shoulders of the first person of public authority who arrives at the scene of an emergency. The average citizen is not prepared for these situations, and is prone to panic. They can

Fig. III-3; Officer Investigating an Accident

often compound the problem until someone of authority takes command. When officers arrive at the scene, their uniform and badge establish them as the logical leaders. People will look to them for advice and instructions. In a split second an officer must decide on a proper course of action that can save or cost a life. This same decision may take a panel of judges several months of meditation and research before they can arrive at a conclusion as to whether the officer's decision was right. Even then, their respective conclusions may be different.

Since the handling of emergency calls for service is one of the basic duties of patrol officers, they should be trained in first aid, mouth-to-mouth resuscitation, and water life-saving procedures. They must be able to keep their heads during these emergencies. If they appear to know what they are doing, the general public will usually accept their decisions and be less prone to panic. The patrol officer must often be a good actor.

When handling an emergency child birth, the officer should tell the woman that he or she has handled many such situations before, and that everything appears to be coming along fine. Even though, in reality, it is the officer's first involvement in child birth, it makes the woman feel much better to believe that she is in experienced hands.

ROUTINE CALLS FOR SERVICE

Routine calls account for the majority of services provided by the patrol division. Because of this, officers have to guard against becoming callous and indifferent to these calls. To the complainant, this case is a very important matter and deserves the attention of no less than the Chief of Police. Again officers must be good actors and show the complainant that they are interested in the situation, although they may have heard the same story a thousand times and are bored to tears. It is natural for the patrol officer to become bored with petty complaints. The fact that the officer chose policework in the first place is usually indicative of a desire for excitement and stimulating experiences.

The patrol officer must learn to politely bring conversations to an end. Otherwise some complainants will talk for hours. At times, the real reason the citizen has called the police is a need for someone to talk to. The officer can sense this and must develop a skill at both steering and concluding a conversation. In communities with a high population and a small number of officers, economy of time is quite important. Naturally the more serious offenses should receive preference. The officer can tell a complainant that it has been pleasant talking to him, but that there is another call waiting, and that he or she will give the complainant's problem their personal attention on a follow-up basis.

Officers should fully record all calls to which they respond. Even on what might appear to them as a very minor situation, not worthy of recording. There are many cases on record of minor arguments that later turned into homicides. It can be of great help to the District Attorney to have some recorded information of the prior calls. This is also a form of protection. There have been cases where the officer did not record a particular call and later the person who requested the police made an unjustified complaint about the officer's demeanor. Because the call was not recorded, it could appear that the officer was trying to hide something.

COURTESY SERVICES

Most contact that citizens have with the police department is usually in the form of receiving a traffic citation. This often leaves them with a negative feeling toward the department. This feeling can in some ways be compensated through a conscious effort by the patrol officer to offer as many courtesy services as possible.

Although most departments today are very public relations conscious, they are often caught in a severe time bind. In larger cities, the calls for criminal service are so great at times, that they have to suspend public service type calls. When a system of priorities must be maintained, criminal calls have to be given preference over the courtesy service type of call. This is unfortunate because citizens who request courtesy services fully expect the department to provide them. When they are refused this service, or when it takes hours for the patrol car to arrive, they can only remember that the last time they drove past the local Drive Inn, they saw three patrol cars parked there and the officers drinking coffee and "shooting the bull." Police administrators should utilize police reserves or cadets during rush hours to handle public service type calls.

Fig. III-4; Officer Offering Courtesy Service

Many citizens believe that when they have a problem for which they need an immediate answer, the police department will be able to resolve it. This is true even when it is not criminal in nature. In many cases, the citizen is aware that the police department maintains phone communications on a twenty-four hour basis. They feel they can at least talk to someone regarding their problem. But deeper is the feeling that the police department is a service agency, and that information to the public is one of their basic duties.

GENERAL INFORMATION

Both visitors and local residents will look for a police officer when they desire information regarding directions, social events or special gatherings. It is usually the foot and traffic control officers who receive most of these requests. An officer should be prepared for this type of courtesy service by having

---

It has been the pleasure of the
Evergreen Police Department
to serve you.
If you are a Visitor to Evergreen
Please drive safely
and
make your stay a pleasant one.
Thank You.
Bill Harrison
Chief of Police

OFFICER #

Fig. III-5; Courtesy Information Card

---

in his or her possession a map of the city and a list of events put out by the local chamber of commerce. Another item that will assist both the citizen requesting information and the officer giving it, is the Courtesy Information Card. On one side of the card is printed a public relations greeting with a special space for the officer's badge number. The other side is blank. This side is used for writing down the information requested, or for drawing a map of directions. It must be understood that most people have average to poor mem-ories, and when hurriedly given directions, they usually forget by the time they arrive at the first street. When directions are written down on the back of the Courtesy Information Card, they can refer to them at their leisure.

The value does not end there. An officer can also profit from the use of this card. The person receiving the card usually keeps it. It will later remind him of the courtesy extended by the officer. It will also give him the badge number of that officer. When one of the authors did research on his department, it was found that about one in fifteen persons who received these cards wrote to the department expressing their thanks. Since the officer's badge number is included, the letter of thanks goes into his or her personnel folder. When an officer is called into the Chief's office regarding a situation demanding disciplinary action, and the Chief reviews the officer's personnel folder and finds several letters of appreciation from various citizens, he is quite likely to give the matter more favorable consideration.

LOCKOUTS

When citizens lock themselves out of their home and all keys are inside of the house, they usually call the police department. Unfortunately many citizens believe that all police officers carry passkeys to all doors in the city. They expect the officer to drive up and simply open their doors with a twist of the passkey. Others are aware of the limitations, and call the department because they don't know what else to do. An officer who receives a call to assist a citizen locked out of his home, is faced with three general possibilities:

(1) Call a locksmith (some communities demand this since the locksmith has paid the city for

a license to practice, and any other action, would be an infringement of free enterprise).

(2) Make a "Break" entry by smashing a window or forcing a door or lock. In this case the officer should be careful that no one is injured by flying glass. This should not be attempted without the owner's written permission.

(3) Pick or slip the lock. The picking of locks is a skill that requires much practice and patience. In many cases the officer can slip the lock using a common table knife that can easily be carried in his or her duty briefcase. This can only be done on cheaper door locks that do not have a "deadbolt" device. Usually the door leading from the garage into the home can be slipped in this manner. If there is a piece of molding in the way, the knife can be forced under the molding in most cases.

FigIII-6(a); Table knife under door molding

If the garage door is locked, and it is of the single piece, double car garage type, and it is not locked on both sides (it rarely is), entry may be made by pulling out on the corner of the door that is not locked. The torque of the wide door will allow it to pull out far enough for a small person to crawl through. Once entry is made, the person entering can open the side door of the garage, and the inner door can be attacked.

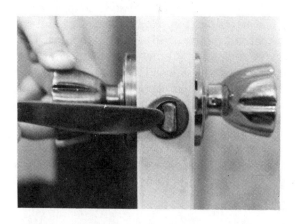

FigIII-6(b); Using table knife to push spring bolt back

It is most important that an officer obtain proper identification from a person requesting assistance in gaining entry to a house or building. There have been cases where the person did not have the authority to enter the building, and did so in order to remove some property. This can be quite embarrassing to the officer and to the department.

Another consideration is the fact that the householder wants badly to enter his home. As a result he may consent to any means of gaining entry. Once he is inside the home, it is no longer a matter of urgency, and he may look at the broken window, made for purposes of entry, as a rash decision. He will then accuse the officer of bad judgment. Some departments require the citizen to sign a release card before the officer is allowed to force an entry.

FigIII-6(c); Using tool to pull in spring bolt when facing away

POLICE ESCORTS

Police escorts involve a common misunderstanding between the average citizen and the police. In movies the police are always giving motorists police escorts, so it is natural that they have come to expect such a courtesy service. In cases of this nature the officer will have to make a judgment call as to whether or not the request is really an emergency. Police escorts with red light and siren can be dangerous to both the officer and citizens in the car being escorted. It can also involve civil liability if the car being escorted is involved in a crash.

A citizen will often stop a police officer and request an escort when there is someone in the car who is ill or is having labor pains. This can often be a legitimate request. It should be remembered that this person is usually nervous and under strong emotional pressure. It can be expected that he will neither think in a rational manner nor follow instructions as he might normally do. That person's driving skills are also affected. The officer must first decide whether the situation might better be handled by calling an ambulance, escorting the victim, or transporting the victim in the police car. The latter is frowned upon by many departments because of the possible lia-bility involved, yet it can be safer if the driver is an officer who is experienced in emergency driving.

By using sympathetic introspection, an officer may understand the pressures and thoughts of the citizen requesting the escort. The officer must make a greater effort to facilitate communication through semantics and patience. Any instructions between the officer and the citizen should be short and to the point. This will reduce the possibility of the instructions being confused or forgotten.

Escorts are not normally permitted beyond the nearest hospital, the reasoning being that, in an emergency, the nearest hospital is the best place for the victim. Sometimes problems arise in cases where the victim is of a particular faith that operates its own hospital. If this hospital is some distance past the nearest hospital, the officer has a decision to make. Many doctors cooperate with certain hospitals, and want their patients sent there. It places a big responsibility on the officer. He or she must decide on need versus want, or whether the seriousness of the emergency would prohibit extending the escort beyond the nearest hospital.

An officer must remember that an escort is different than driving a police vehicle on an emergency call. The officer must anticipate the possible danger to both the police vehicle and that of the person being escorted. Many times the person being escorted is not conditioned for fast driving and is fearful of its dangers. He can easily get left behind if the escorting officer has a heavy foot. The opposite can be true if the officer drives in a cautious manner and the person being escorted drives wildly due to his emotional condition.

Although it is done, the laws in most states do not allow the use of red light and siren for the escorting of dignitaries or "VIP's".

INVALIDS

A common courtesy service involves assisting elderly invalids. Some fall out of bed and cannot be lifted by the persons caring for them because they too are elderly and are not physically capable of performing this task. This same type of case occurs occasionally when an invalid becomes ill while bathing, and cannot get out of the tub. The spouse or person living with him also lacks the strength to lift him out. In handling calls of this nature, the officer should always fill out a report and see that a copy goes to whatever agency would normally handle a follow up. The agency would contact relatives who could make a decision about the need for some type of in-home care.

Unfortunately some officers resent this type of call. They feel that they are crime fighters and not nursemaids. This attitude, and the remarks that often accompany it, can do much to hurt the victim, who is usually embarrassed and humiliated by being in this sort of situation. This is especially true if at one time the victim was quite physically agile, and independent. In this country of wealth it is often hard to find an opportunity to dispense true charity; this type of case can often provide that opportunity. To those officers who are not overflowing with the milk of human kindness, it might be well to remember that someday they too might be in the same situation and have to rely upon the physical help of some uniformed stranger who may either openly show resentment, or give that person the respect and courtesy that is due all members of the human race. There is no greater way to show the community the professional standing of police officers.

DEATH MESSAGES

One of the most difficult duties for an officer who has any compassion for those who suffer is that of delivering a death message. Sometimes a person dies as a result of a criminal offense or a traffic accident and the next of kin does not have a phone. In some cases the next of kin are not immediately known. The police in the city where the victim lived often assume the duty of finding the next of kin and then notifying them of the death.

In cases of this type, it is important that the officer not "hit and run." It is an unpleasant duty. Therefore it is natural to want to present the message and get out. But the officer here has an extended responsibility toward the next of kin. This is especially true if they are alone. The relative will often need some type of comfort or care, and sometimes a female relative will faint. If this happens, the officer should try to find some household ammonia. It will often bring the victim back to a conscious state. It is usually located under the kitchen sink, or in the bathroom.

It would be wise to contact neighbors and ask them for assistance. Even if the neighbors have not been on speaking terms, they will usually respond to a situation of this type in a generous way. There have been cases of neighborhood enemies becoming the best of friends as the result of a family tragedy that caused one of them to forget their animosities and assist the other in their hour of need.

As much as the officer dislikes this duty, "beating around the bush" is not the proper way to perform it. The best approach is to see that the next-of-kin is properly seated, and then come straight to the point. For example; "Mrs Jones, I'm afraid I have some bad news. Your husband has been killed in an automobile accident." It is a good idea for the officer to write down instructions as to who to contact in order to recover the body. Also include other information that will assist the next-of-kin. It must be realized that in their state of mind, they might not remember instructions, or in some cases perceive what is being said.

As a parting gesture, the officer might call the family minister, priest or rabbi so that they too might assist in the matter. Relatives might also be contacted to provide assistance.

HOUSE CHECKS AND VACATION CHECKS

A common courtesy service extended by most police departments is that of checking vacant houses when the occupants are temporarily away because of vacation or illness. Although this is classed as a courtesy service, it is also an important part of Preventive Enforcement.

In the summer, a patrol officer might have so many vacation house checks to make, that it would be physically impossible to check them all during one shift. In cases such as this, the patrol officer should get together with the other officers who have the same beat but on different shifts, and then split up the vacation houses and alternate checking on them. In this way they may all be checked at least once a day. If there are still too many, the officer can divide his list and alternate it by checking the houses on one list one night and then the houses on the other list the following night. Many departments utilize police reserve officers and cadets for this task.

When checking out vacation homes, look for newspapers or other handouts laying about. Place them where potential burglars would not see them and know that the residents are away. It is good policy to make a personal contact when it is observed that the people have returned. They should be asked if everything is in proper order. It gives them a feeling of receiving good service and leads to better public relations.

NEIGHBORHOOD TROUBLESHOOTER
CONTENTS

Emergency Telephone Numbers 1
Introduction 2
Government 2
Streets 2
Sidewalk Repair 2
Water 3
Sewers 3
Storm Drain/Curb Inlet Stoppage 3
Gas Leaks 3
Street Signs 4
Traffic Signals 4
Street Lights 4
Street Cleaning 4
Abandoned Automobiles 5
Injured or Stray Animals 5
Licensing 5
Lost Pets 5
Dead Animal Removal 6
Barking Dogs 6
Weeds and Litter 6
Street Trees 6
Garbage and Trash Collection 6
Stolen Bicycles 7
Housing Authority 7
Building Permits 7
Relocation Policies 7
Multiple Dwellings 7
Vacant and Hazardous Buildings 7

Table of Contents

Introduction — Government — Streets — Sidewalk Repairs ... 1

Introduction — Government — Streets — Sidewalk Repairs ... 2

Water — Sewers — Storm Sewer Stoppage — Curb Inlet
Curb Inlet Stoppage — Gas Leaks ... 3

Street Signs — Traffic Signals — Street Lights
Street Cleaning — Abandoned Automobiles ... 4

Injured or Stray Animals — Licensing — Lost Pets
Dead Animal Removal — Barking Dogs ... 5

Weeds and Litter — Street Trees — Garbage and
Trash Collection — Stolen Bicycles ... 6

Housing Authority—Building Permits—Relocation Policies
Multiple Dwellings — Vacant/Hazardous Buildings ... 7

Streets

The City is responsible for maintaining all streets and will send a crew to repair dangerous areas. Call the Public Works Department at 292-3141, Extension 881. If your street is so rough that it requires complete resurfacing or reconstruction, call the street resurfacing and reconstruction section, Department of Public Works, 292-3141, Extension 701. The City has a regularly established program for maintaining worn-out streets, and will send an inspector to determine whether your street should be on the list. If your street has never been paved, the City will still maintain it, but at a limited level. If you and your neighbors should wish to have permanent pavement and curbs and sidewalks installed in an unimproved street, the City will help you form an assessment district. The property owners along the street must bear most of the cost of such construction. Write the Director of Public Works, City Hall, 801 North 1st Street, San Jose, California 95110.

Sidewalk Repair

The property owner is responsible for keeping the sidewalks in front of his property in good repair. If you are a tenant or a neighbor, first call a broken sidewalk to the attention of the landlord. If the repairs are not made, call the sidewalk inspection division of the Public Works Department, 292-3141, Extension 701. If an on-site inspection indicates the necessity for repairs, the City will issue a notice calling for the repair of hazardous conditions.

Introduction — Government — Streets — Sidewalk Repairs ... 2

Water — Sewers — Storm Sewer Stoppage — Curb Inlet
Curb Inlet Stoppage — Gas Leaks ... 3

Street Signs — Traffic Signals — Street Lights
Street Cleaning — Abandoned Automobiles ... 4

Injured or Stray Animals — Licensing — Lost Pets
Dead Animal Removal — Barking Dogs ... 5

Weeds and Litter — Street Trees — Garbage and
Trash Collection — Stolen Bicycles ... 6

Housing Authority—Building Permits—Relocation Policies
Multiple Dwellings — Vacant/Hazardous Buildings ... 7

Sewers

The property owner is responsible for the maintenance and repair of plumbing and sewer lines inside his building and out to the main sewer in the street. If a property owner is having problems with his plumbing and suspects the reason is a blockage of the sewer main on the street, he may call the Department of Public Works, 292-3141, Extension 881, and the Department will send a crew to determine whether or not the main is clear. If it is determined that the main sewer line et the street is clear, the property owner will be so advised and may either clear the lateral himself or hire a plumber to do the job. If your sewer backs up and the landlord is unwilling to fix it, call the housing sanitarian at the City Housing and Community Development Department. Call 292-3141, Extension 504.

Storm Sewer Stoppage....Curb Inlet Stoppage

During a rainstorm water may rise over the curb and go onto private property. Such a problem should be reported to the Public Works Operations Department, 292-3141, Extension 881. A crew will be dispatched to clean the storm sewer. These stoppages generally occur during the first storm of the season when leaves and other debris clog the inlets. A property owner may help by keeping his gutter clean of debris and by refraining from sweeping leaves into curb inlets.

Gas Leaks

If you smell gas . . . either indoors or out in the street . . . call the Customer Service Department of the Pacific Gas and Electric Company, any time of the day or night, at 298-2811. If the leak is so severe as to pose a danger of imminent fire or explosion, call the Fire Department, 294-4664.

Water — Sewers — Storm Sewer Stoppage — Curb Inlet
Curb Inlet Stoppage — Gas Leaks ... 3

Street Signs — Traffic Signals — Street Lights
Street Cleaning — Abandoned Automobiles ... 4

Injured or Stray Animals — Licensing — Lost Pets
Dead Animal Removal — Barking Dogs ... 5

Weeds and Litter — Street Trees — Garbage and
Trash Collection — Stolen Bicycles ... 6

Housing Authority—Building Permits—Relocation Policies
Multiple Dwellings — Vacant/Hazardous Buildings ... 7

Fig. III-7; Sample Information Booklet

Chapter Three

ASSISTING OTHER CITY AGENCIES

Since patrol officers are constantly moving about their beats, they see many things that are not criminal but should be brought to someone's attention. This is particularly true of defects in equipment and services that are handled by other city departments. Even though it is not criminal in nature, it is the patrol officer's job to report these situations to communications, (if it is of an emergency nature) or on a department form so it may be directed to the proper agency handling these matters. Some of the more common example are:

(1) Street lights out.

(2) Fire hazards.

(3) Leaking water mains.

(4) Defects in the street and sidewalks.

(5) Conducting business without a license.

(6) Health hazards.

(7) Illegal display of advertising/election posters.

(8) Traffic signals out or defective.

(9) Dead animals in the street.

(10) Barricade lights out at construction site.

(11) Stopped up or flooding drains and sewers.

(12) Building or adding without a permit.

On the preceding page is a sample of a booklet issued to officers showing the responsibilities and phone numbers of other municipal and county departments.

In some cases, the officer must use good judgment in estimating the seriousness of the situation. Otherwise a public works employee can be called out of bed in the middle of the night for a matter that could just as easily be handled in the morning.

PRESERVATION OF EVIDENCE

If an officer is in a department where a specialized investigative division handles major crimes, he or she can still perform an essential function by protecting the crime scene. Failure to properly perform this function can often result in the whole case being lost. Since the patrol officer is usually the first officer to arrive at the scene, there is a greater responsibility for preserving all evidence and protecting it from contamination and damage. It is not necessary to know a lot about investigation or evidence preservation to perform this task. Common sense goes a long way. The first step should involve determining the reasonable limits of the crime scene. Then some effort should be made to protect it from:

(1) **Patrol officers**. Patrol officers wouldn't be in police work if they did not enjoy being "where the action is." As a result, When they hear of a crime over the police radio, they often leave their beats and rush to the crime scene to "get in on the action." As a result, officers often unwittingly destroy evidence. Usually by stepping on it.

(2) **Relatives and householders**. They feel that since it is their house, or that of a relative, that they have a constitutional right to free access. If the relative has been killed, they also feel that they have the right to "steal the place blind" before the other relatives arrive. In doing this, they often unwittingly take items that can be important evidence.

(3) **Neighbors and onlookers**. Curiosity is a strong driving force, and as neighbors, they feel that they have a God given right to find out what is going on. They also take things.

(4) **The perpetrator**. He may want to destroy or remove incriminating evidence. Sometimes he may pose as a witness and give false information in an effort to throw off investigating officers.

In protecting the scene, the officer can either call for more assistance, or set up physical barricades such as rope, or furniture. The individual situation will determine whether one or both methods should be used.

PREPARATION OF REPORTS

An essential function of the patrol officer is the recording of all basic information concerning the call for service or the case handled. This information must be transferred to a standardized report form. It is important that the happenings be documented and supported by complete and carefully prepared reports. Since the patrol officer is the primary contact in the field, this report can be of the utmost importance when it comes to both evaluating and prosecuting the case.

The key to a complete report is answering the following questions:

(1) WHO　　　　　(4) WHERE
(2) WHAT　　　　 (5) WHY
(3) WHEN　　　　 (6) HOW

If the officer is taking a preliminary report on a case that will involve some follow-up the next day, it would be very helpful to the follow-up investigator if the officer would list the place where the person works and the phone number at his place of occupation. This information is very easy to obtain while the officer is taking the initial report, but can be difficult to obtain the following day.

STUDY QUESTIONS for Patrol Operations

CHAPTER 3

1. The patrol division is the "_____" of the police department.

2. The duties and objectives of police patrol are summed up in two words. They are
    "_____ and _____."

3. The California Highway Patrol at one time used preventive enforcement by placing
    _____ along the state's highways.

4. Patrol cars parked next to the curb with their red lights on do not have a "preventive   **T or F**
    enforcement" value toward oncoming traffic.

5. The Indianapolis police department experimented with an innovative "preventive
    enforcement" of placing more police cars on the streets. They let officers take their
    police cars home with them and allowed them to use the cars for personal business.
    Arrests increased by what percent?

    (a) __ fifty   (b) __ thirty-five   (c) __ twenty-two   (d) __ four

6. The experiment on "preventive patrol" in Kansas City was widely accepted by police   **T or F**
    departments and their administrators throughout the United States.

7. In the above experiment, the researchers broke the city into special districts that were
    classed into three types of enforcement. They were:

    (1) _____ (only answered calls)

    (2) _____ (increased patrol in area)

    (3) _____ (patrolled in regular way)

8. The Cherry Hill, New Jersey, Department of Public Safety experimented with increased   **T or F**
    "preventive enforcement" with very good results in the reduction of burglaries.

9. "Selective Enforcement" is most often used in the area of _____.

10. It is often complained that accident investigation amounts to working for the
    _____ companies.

11. The main source of alienation between the police and the public seems to be the enforcement
    of _____ laws.

12. This problem can be somewhat eased by having the officers practice _____
    _____ in the giving of citations.

13. Most officers would prefer "the routine call" rather than the "dangerous emergency" call.   T or F

14. Often citizens will call for an officer just to have someone to talk to and use some little   T or F
incident as the excuse.

15. In crowded, busy cities police departments are forced to cut down on the handling of
"courtesy services." Some citizens have trouble with this excuse when they drive by
certain locations and see _____.

16. The best use of the "courtesy information card" is to write what on the back?

_____

17. Few people who receive "courtesy information cards" write the police department and   T or F
thank the officer.

18. The first priority in handling a citizen who has locked himself out of his house is to
call _____.

19. Why?_____

20. Where is the best place to "slip" a lock in an older tract home? _____

21. Most states' vehicle codes allow police "code three" escorts of "VIP's" (e.g. governor   T or F
or president.)

22. In giving "death messages" it is best to give the relative the information and leave quickly.   T or F

23. If a person faints when given a "death message", there is a household item that can be used
to "bring them to." It is: _____.

24. Another problem of increased calls for criminal services is the inability to conduct "vacation
checks" which is good public relations. Name one of the ways mentioned to help carry out
this need.

25. Name one of the situations in which an officer is required to make a special report to other city
agencies.

26. Name another one?

27. Name one of the persons who tend to destroy evidence, whether they intend to or not.

28. In report writing it is important to always include the five W's and the _____sign.

29. Fill in the below:

(1) W_____   (2) W_____   (3) W_____

(4) W_____   (5) W_____   (6) H_____

CHAPTER IV

THE TYPES OF PATROL

In the modern police department there are many types of patrol. This chapter will discuss the various types, the advantages and disadvantages of each and the various techniques that may be utilized. Most patrols are assigned to a particular area called a BEAT, and are called BEAT PATROLS. The size of the beat is determined by:

(1) Type of area to be patrolled. (e.g. Business, farming, residential, recreation.)

(2) Type of criminal activity in the area.

(3) The frequency of crime in that area.

If a beat has a large number of night clubs, there will be an increased need for patrol officers. The same applies to beats containing public housing developments, a large number of convenience stores, or liquor stores in the inner city. These are just a few examples of establishments that attract criminal activity and need police patrol services.

To properly cover the beat when needed, patrols are assigned in SHIFTS. Shifts are usually determined by the number of personnel available and the frequency of calls for police service.

Most communities have three main 8 hour shifts to offer twenty-four hour service. In larger communities special shifts are assigned to help with peak loads. These shifts should be constantly re-evaluated according to need. In many communities the crime peak is Between 7 p.m. and 3 a.m., so a special shift is assigned during this time. Traffic problems in the early morning and late afternoon will sometimes necessitate a split shift, but this usually results in a morale problem because officers do not like a split shift.

THE TEN PLAN

A popular breakdown in shift assignments is the "Ten Plan." This system of shift assignments started in Huntington Beach, California, and has spread to many departments throughout the country. It has been recognized for some time that the eight hour shift has not completely met the need for police service. The overlap system of assigning special shifts at peak hours helped with this problem, but didn't completely meet the needs of some communities. Although there are variations in this plan, basically it involves three ten hour shifts that overlap during the peak hours of need.

The essence of the plan is that fewer men are put on each shift, so that it does not require an added number of personnel to account for the overlap and for the extra days off that the officers receive. Even though the shifts are "thinner" because they contain fewer men, they still put a maximum number of men into the field during the peak hours of need.

Below is an example of an overlapping shift plan using this system. Each department must adjust its plan to suit its own varying crime peaks or rush traffic hours. The dotted line represents an extra shift that might be needed in larger cities where there is a heavy crime peak during the late evening and early morning hours.

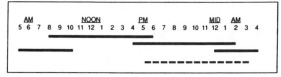

A THREE SHIFT TEN PLAN
(Dotted line is optional shift)

Fig. IV-1; A three shift Ten Plan (Dotted line is optional)

The major advantage for patrol officers is that they work only four days a week and have three days off. In some departments this overlap of time enables the officer to conduct the briefing period on city time rather than showing up half an hour early on his or her own time.

Advantages

(1) More men in the field during peak hours.

(2) Three days off.

(3) Quicker response to calls.

(4) More days off helps family relations.

(5) Better for attending college or other extracurricular endeavors.

(6) Increased morale.

(7) In-Service or "roll call training" can be conducted during overlap times on "low peak" days, saving the agency the cost of time-and-a-half paid training sessions.

Disadvantages

(1) Overtime makes shifts too long, and increased injuries can occur.

(2) Overtime can interfere with school attendance.

(3) More officers are needed on shift III.

(4) Lack of sleep on court days can affect officer efficiency at a later time.

(5) Problems with radio dispatchers. They are usually on an eight hour shift which does not mesh with officer's shifts.

(6) After three days off, officers seem to lose touch with what has been happening on their beat. It takes a long time to read all reports.

Many administrators have found this plan does not serve the better interests of the department. However, the plan has been so well accepted by patrol officers that it has become a union issue when departments attempt to go back to the old eight hour shifts. Some agencies have even carried this plan further. They have gone to a twelve hour shift three days one week and four days the following week. It is nice to have all those days off, but in large cities where a shift can result in a lot of pressure on the patrol officer, the question of officer safety can arise.

FOOT PATROL

Foot patrol is the most expensive patrol type. Because of this, most departments have either eliminated or reduced foot patrols to a minimum. However, it does have some advantages that warrant its continued use even if on a limited basis.

Usually a foot patrol is assigned to an area of dense population such as the downtown area. Also where there is heavy traffic congestion and the assistance of an officer is needed to help eliminate traffic jams. The main intersection of a city is often an excellent location. It is also where out-of-town visitors find themselves in need of information that an officer on foot could readily provide. In some cities, the foot patrol officer spends part of the shift walking the beat or providing traffic control, and when things are quiet (i.e. early morning hours) he or she is assigned to ride as a second officer in the beat patrol car.

FOOT PATROL MAKING A COMEBACK

There have been several recent examples where cities have re-instituted foot patrols because they feel that they are worth the expense.

In cities such as San Jose, California, merchants have hired regular police officers on their off duty hours to provide foot patrol in the downtown area in hopes of encouraging customers to return there for their shopping.

In Des Moines, Iowa, at the request of leaders in high crime, low rent areas, city officials have appropriated about $240,000 to establish foot patrols in those areas.

Officers working this detail report that they have received encouragement and support from about 90 percent of the residents. Although they have made numerous arrests, their low key approach and attempt to "negotiate" arrests has gained further community support in an area thought to be highly anti-police.

PUBLIC ATTITUDE TOWARD FOOT PATROL

A one-year study by the Police Foundation of police departments in the state of New Jersey revealed that when officers walk a foot beat it reduces citizen's fear of crime. HOWEVER, IT DOES NOT ACTUALLY REDUCE CRIME.

Although businessmen, as a group, did not believe that foot patrol reduced crime, citizens in general perceived a reduction of street disorders, attacks on the elderly, and auto theft. They also felt that their personal safety had increased. A study of criminal statistics however, showed this perception to be false. It is interesting to note that the study also showed that "generally foot patrol officers are more satisfied with policework. They have a more benign view of citizens, a lower absentee record and a more community-based view of the police function."

SOME ADVANTAGES OF FOOT PATROL

(1) Foot patrol officers can provide immediate traffic control when it is needed. Being in a close proximity to problem areas, they will know when assistance is needed. Also there is no parking problem. Too many officers park wherever they feel like it, but this usually causes more traffic problems than it solves. However, sometimes there is no choice in crowded downtown areas apart from parking on the sidewalk.

(2) More person-to-person contact can be made with the public. This provides greater chances to promote good public relations. However, if the wrong type of officer is given this assignment it can backfire and harm public relations. Too often an officer is taken out of a patrol car because of some type of misdeed and assigned to a foot beat as a form of punishment. It is then natural for the officer to have an attitude problem and take it out on the public. The foot patrol officer makes more personal contacts and is seen more by the public than any other type of patrol, and therefore becomes an important link between the department and the public. Extreme care should be used in selecting an officer for this duty.

(3) The officer can actually get to know the physical layout of the beat much better. There are many things that an officer misses by patrolling the beat in a police car.

(4) Getting to know people on the beat, and developing criminal informants is much easier. A rendezvous with informants can be made without being noticed. It is easy to slip into a doorway or an alley. When there is a police car parked nearby, informants are understandably reluctant to be seen in the area.

(5) A foot officer can sneak up on a situation, where a patrol car is easily noticed when it approaches. Officers who have been promoted to a non-uniform assignment, and are driving an unmarked car, often remark about the criminal activity they observe since they are out of a marked patrol car.

(6) By use of walkie-talkies, officers can maintain communication with the department and mobile units. The lack of communication was once a major disadvantage of foot pat-rol. Now officers can be directed to trouble situations along with patrol cars and can also make immediate reports to communications.

FOOT PATROL PROCEDURES AND TECHNI-QUES

(1) Don't establish set patterns of patrol. We are creatures of habit, so it's very easy to patrol certain areas according to an unconscious schedule. We usually start with the first part of the beat we approach after leaving head-quarters. Coffee stops and lunch at particular establishments also tend to create patterns in the way we walk the beat. If criminals can clock our movements, we are bound to have trouble on the beat because they know how long we will be away from certain places. A conscious effort should be made to break up patterns by doubling back occasionally.

(2) When checking doors for forced entry, use a flashlight on the area around the lock to see if there are fresh or noticeable jimmy marks. Don't get into the habit of grabbing the handle, and twisting and leaning on the door. This technique will enable the officer to cover ground faster, but occasionally the door will be unlocked and the officer will fall in the entrance way. This can be embarrassing.

(3) When an open door is found, NEVER ENTER ALONE. Call for assistance, even though it may simply be a matter of the owner forgetting to lock the door. Any advantage gained through immediate entry cannot compensate for the loss of an officer's life. Having another officer present will also avert the possibility of a store owner claiming that some items are missing and that they were probably taken by the beat officer. When there is more than one officer present, it reduces the possibility of such a situation actually happening, and it gives added testimony that it did not happen. (Techniques of handling an "open door" case will be cov-ered later in Chapter XIV.)

(4) At least once a night use the fire escapes to check the roofs of businesses located on the beat for possible "cut-through" burglaries or "roof jobs" as they are sometimes called. Many burglaries are perpetrated in this manner in order to prevent detection by the patrol officer who normally checks the doors and windows for jimmy marks. While on the roof, officers should take advantage of the position to look over the beat. At night an officer can see many things take place on the street when concealed in a high position.

(5) Since burglars need some device to assist them in gaining entry to second stories and above, the patrol officer should be alert for boxes piled behind or ropes hanging down the sides of buildings, or ladders that might have been used to gain access to a roof.

(6) At night the foot patrol officer should occasionally step into an alley or store entrance and get out of the light as much as possible. Because sound travels better at night, an officer who is quiet and listens carefully can hear locks or windows being broken or people's conversations. It is interesting that in Boston in 1636, an order was put out regarding the patrol procedure of the Watchmen. It stated "Watchmen are required to walk their rounds slowly and silently, and now and then stand still and listen."

(7) Foot patrol officers spend most of the shift on their feet, so proper care of the feet cannot be overemphasized. When walking, an officer should maintain good posture. Not only does this impress the public, but it helps the officer's back, legs, and feet. It is also important when walking not to put all of the body weight on the heel as it shocks the bone structure and can cause back trou-ble. A good pair of walking shoes is essential and a wise investment if an officer is assigned to a permanent walking beat. Thick socks will also help. It is also important for officers to get off their feet at regular intervals. If at all possible, they should go to a back room where and elevate their feet for a short period of time. NEVER DO THIS IN PUBLIC. Nothing looks worse to the average citizen. Washing the feet daily and using foot powder liberally will also pay dividends.

(8) During the winter, the foot patrol officer must walk during all types of weather. Therefore every possible precaution should be taken to protect the officer's health. Good, heavy, long winter underwear and heavy wool socks not only protect health, but make the tour of duty more comfortable. Officers should also have some place where a raincoat can be stored so it doesn't have to be carried all the time. It should be in a place where it can be quickly retrieved. Most cafes will be glad to assist the officer. If it is cold, the officer should wear lined leather gloves. Hands should be kept out of uniform pockets. It does not look professional, and is bad for public relations.

(9) A patrol officer should never smoke or chew gum while in uniform on the street. It looks unmilitary and creates a poor public image. In restaurants or restrooms it is not so bad.

(10) The foot patrol officer should make a conscious effort to make friends on the beat. This is not only for good public relations, but is a good way to develop informants. It is also nice to have friends in case the officer is jumped by members of a gang. Because most walking beats are in or near lower class areas, some officers feel that it is beneath them to make friends with bums, winos and persons from "halfway houses". Other officers feel that these people are terrible bores and that they should only talk to persons who can carry on a stimulating conversation. Attitudes like this are quickly sensed and the people living in this area will react in a way that will soon reduce an officer's efficiency and development.

(11) Use all five senses while walking the beat. Observation is a skill that requires continued effort to develop. Too often officers, when walking, will only look straight ahead. As a result, they will miss much of what goes on and efficiency will drop. They should develop the habit of looking up and down while walking, and occasionally look over and under things. Sight is the patrol officer's greatest sense, but it is seldom used to full capacity. Walking beats usually have tall buildings and much of what takes place on them is seldom in a straight line of sight.

(12) When things are slow, the officer should plan strategies. Once the mind has solved a problem, it becomes easier the next time that or a similar problem is presented. The more a problem is presented to the brain to solve, the quicker the answers will come. If an officer imagines various types of situations that may occur on the beat, and then asks him or herself what steps should be taken in responding to the situation, This is, in effect, practicing problem solving. When the real situation arises, it is not really new to the brain. Memory circuits have been formed, resulting in a more sound and speedy reaction. This is because the solution was resolved, not under the pressure of the emergency, but when the officer was relaxed and had ample time to evaluate the various possibilities.

AUTOMOBILE PATROL

Fig. IV-2; Patrol Automobile

The use of automobiles for patrol began about the time automobiles first became popular in the United States. There are cases of the use of automobiles by police departments as early as 1904, but not for patrol. The Indianapolis Police Department started to replace horse drawn "paddy wagons" with automobiles in 1904. Before this time, horse drawn wagons were used to respond to emergency calls. Later, when police call booths were installed, they would respond to the walking officer's called in signal.

In 1917, the Detroit Police Department began using automobiles with two men per car, but not to go out on patrol. They were stationed in "Police Booths" along the streets. The "Police Booths" contained a desk, a telephone, a pot-bellied stove and a coal bin. They left the booth only upon a telephone request for assistance.

Fig. IV-3; Horse drawn paddy wagon, NY 1903

It was not until the advent of the workable mobile radio receiver that police vehicles became patrol vehicles as we know them today. The automobile is the most economical type of patrol, and offers the greatest tactical ability when used in numbers. In the last four decades it has replaced all but the most essential of the walking patrols.

SOME ADVANTAGES OF AUTOMOBILE PATROL

(1) Where speed and mobility are needed, such as in a large area that must be covered by few officers, the speed of the automobile allows service to the whole area in an efficient manner. Where hills and grades are part of the beat, it allows a mobility with which neither horse nor foot patrolman could compete.

A multi million dollar report was issued by the President's Crime Commission. This report has had more effect on modern police work than any other government effort. As a result of the extensive research preceding this report, one of its many recommendations emphasized the importance of speed in responding to calls for assistance. It brought out a definite relationship between speed of response and the possibility of arrest. In citing

Fig. IV-4; Signal answered/Code three, 1886

Los Angeles statistics, it showed that response time in cases where an arrest was made averaged 4.1 minutes, whereas the response time in cases resulting in no arrest averaged 6.3 minutes. A difference of 2.2 minutes does not seem like much, but if arrest of the perpetrator is important, these statistics certainly reinforce the value of every minute.

Fig. IV-5; One of the first police vehicles

In the same Crime Commission report, it was suggested that the country have one set phone number, like the British, for police emergency calls. It was felt that this would reduce response time. As our suburbs continued to grow, the number of calls to the wrong police department became a serious problem. On the edge of cities, residents considered themselves a part of the city, but really lived in the county. As a result they would call the police department rather than the sheriff's office. This resulted in a further time delay. Today, the 9ll system, after innumerable technical problems, is well established throughout the United States. It has turned out to be an exceptional tool of policework. When a dispatcher receives a call, this system allows him to obtain the complainant's phone number, and from this the address. This has greatly increased the patrol officer's efficiency, and improved the service that citizens expect from their police departments.

(2) The marked police car is one of the best means of Preventive Enforcement. With its distinctive colors, red lights and door insignia, it is very effective in deterring criminal activity by making people conscious of the presence of police enforcement, and by creating an awareness of punitive action.

(3) It offers the officer protection from the weather and to some extent from traffic. If hit by a car, the officer would suffer less injury in a police car than when walking on the street. It also offers an officer better protection when being shot at.

(4) It permits the officer to carry extra equipment such as rain gear, clothing, a shotgun and extra ammunition, first aid equipment, flares and camera equipment. It also has room for a briefcase that is so greatly needed for the many forms, ticket books, cards and manuals that might be needed in the field.

(5) The patrol car allows the police officer to have a partner when needed, and to transport one or several prisoners. It can also be used to transport evidence and in some cases bi-cycles. Many departments have small metal holders attached to the rear or front bumper of the police car so bicycles may be easily attached for transportation to headquarters.

(6) In the case of station wagons, which are used quite often when an officer has a police dog, they can be used as emergency ambulances when a disaster occurs. They can also carry larger pieces of evidence.

(7) Patrol vehicles can be used as barricades in roadblocks, and they also offer a higher degree of safety during high speed pursuit. Especially when compared with motorcycles

GENERAL TECHNIQUES AND PROCEDURES FOR AUTOMOBILE PATROL.

Many of the techniques and procedures mentioned for foot patrol are also applicable to automobile patrol.

(1) Check the police car thoroughly before leaving the garage. It could mean your very life if the car proved faulty during an emergency.

(2) As in foot patrol, the beat should not be traveled the same way each night. If a criminal is able to time your movements, some place on your beat may be "knocked off."

(3) Don't spend too much time in drive-ins or coffee spots., go for coffee when there is another police car already there, or meet another car at one of these places for a conference. The public sees it as a waste of manpower and vehicles, and feels that the officers are "goofing off". Conferences between patrol cars should take place on a main thoroughfare where they can be seen by passing motorists. This has a Preventive Enforcement effect because the motorist feels that the police are looking for violators, and the cars are ready for immediate pursuit.

(4) Do not drive too fast on general patrol. It wastes gasoline and very little is seen by the driver. The recommended speed for patrolling is between 15 and 20 miles per hour, but it should be adjusted to suit the situation. Don't patrol too slowly in heavy traffic. Most motorists are hesitant to pass a police car and as a result traffic may back up.

(5) During normal patrol, observe the rules of the road. A police officer is exempt from traffic laws only in an emergency. Officers are civilly liable when an accident is caused that is not the result of emergency driving, and which could have been prevented by the use of caution on the part of the officer.

(6) The license numbers of all strange or suspicious cars should be jotted down; it takes only a few seconds. Many times an officer is on a call and cannot stop to question a suspicious driver, but can jot down the license number and later check it out or follow up on the matter. This should be done with all strange or unknown cars that are parked near places that are likely to be victims of robberies and burglaries. If it later turns out that a crime was committed, the license number would provide a good follow-up clue.

(7) Make it a habit to never leave the keys in the police car, even just for a minute. There are many cases on record of police cars be-ing stolen. Every one of them had the keys in the ignition. In an emergency, it is easy to jump out of the car to chase a suspect and leave the keys in the car. The important word here is habit. When it becomes a habit to grab the

Fig. IV-6; Seatbelts saved this officer

keys whenever you leave the police car, you don't even have to think about it anymore. Having your police car stolen is quite embarrassing. Other officers will never let you forget it.

(8) When working nights, it is a good idea to have a small pack of commercial nerve stimulant pills such as "No-Doz". They should not be used regularly. When some situation arises where you were not able to get the proper amount of sleep, they may be taken to keep you sufficiently awake. This not only allows you to perform the job better, but to possibly save your life or prevent serious injury should you fall asleep at the wheel. This is a common occurrence among new police officers who are not used to sleeping in the daytime, or who are taking college classes during the day. Spending a lot of time in donut shops drinking coffee will also help you stay awake, but can easily damage public relations.

(9) Since we are creatures of habit, a police officer must make it a habit to use a seat belt at all times. It should be an automatic reaction when getting into a police car. The use of seatbelts can make a driver less tired at the end of a shift. This is due to not having to fight gravity on each turn. During a full shift, this can amount to a lot of turns. The above

photo shows a police car that was responding to an "officer needs help" call. The driver lost control on an off ramp and drove through the air into a creek bed. Needless to say he was of little help to the officer needing assistance. However, the officer was not hurt, despite "totaling out" the car, because he was wearing his seat belt.

(10) The beat officer should learn the whereabouts of all safes, safe lights, nightlights and outside locks in commercial buildings on the beat. They should be checked at least once each night. If a nightlight is found to be out, the owner should be called, even if it is two o'clock in the morning. The owner will be upset as would any person called at two o'clock in the morning, but it will pro-bably make him replace the light bulb reg-ularly. When it is first noticed that the night- light is out, communications should be no-tified, and then a close inspection of the outside of the building conducted to see if a forced entry has been made. The checking of locks and nightlights as a regular procedure is a good means of both apprehending bur-glars, and of preventing the occurrence of burglaries. When a burglar "cases" a place before committing the job, he also times the police cars on beat patrol, and sees if the officer checks doors for jimmy marks and goes around the backs of buildings.

(11) A 3x5" card file should be carried in the patrol car and, among other things, it should list all cars belonging to night workers on the beat. The cars should be listed by license number, and should have the name of the owner, and where and what hours he works. When the car is noticed parked after the normal time, further investigation is warranted. It is possible that the worker might be ill, or even tied up in a back room while some criminal is working on the safe. (Always refer to a janitor as a custodian. The term "custodian" sounds better and will assist in establishing rapport.) This card file should also list known criminals who live or work on the beat, and pertinent information concerning them, such as the cars they drive, their friends, and the types of crimes that they usually commit.

(12) If the officer's beat contains factories and warehouses, it is important to know what they produce or contain. In the event that a car is stopped for a traffic citation or due to suspicious circumstances and it is noticed that the back seat contains certain items, the officer will know that these items could have been taken from a burglary on this beat, and would also have a good idea of where to check for a possible forced entry.

(13) The officer on automobile patrol must, like the foot patrol officer, always be on the alert for possible informants. Members of the detective division usually have access to funds for the purpose of paying informants. The patrol officer does not and therefore must develop informants whose sole motive is friendship, or possibly the feeling that it doesn't hurt to befriend the beat officer. If the approach is right, these people will give information to the officer on a voluntary basis. The officer must not push for information as is often done with a paid informant, but must first establish rapport and then develop a feeling of confidence towards the officer on the part of the informant

A new officer must watch out for the "con" informant who states that he has important information and "suckers" the officer into buying him a meal or a few drinks in the hopes of obtaining that information. Some of these people approach each new officer on

the beat with a hush-hush story about some "big narcotic deal." They can keep the officer on the string for weeks or longer through the belief that this information will make headlines and that the officer will undoubtedly be transferred to the detective division when the case is cracked. In the meantime the so-called informant suckers the officer for a couple dollars on each contact. Later when the officer becomes impatient, the informant states that someone has told the conspirators that he was revealing information and as a result they left town.

The following people are good persons to develop as contacts and possible informants.

(1) **Service station attendants** Especially all-night stations.

(2) **Custodians and maintenance persons**

(3) **Window washers** Especially those who work early in the morning.

(4) **Newspaper vendors and paper boys**

(5) **Deaf persons** There are often a few who hang out in downtown areas of major cities. The criminal element will sometimes make fun of them, but they fail to realize that deaf persons can read lips and actually see conversations from a distance. As a result, crim-inals will often say things amongst them- selves, such as plans for a crime that they would never say if someone were close by.

A means of establishing rapport with a deaf person is to learn sign language. This is not difficult, but takes practice. Many dictionaries contain the fingerspelling alphabet. Most deaf persons carry a pencil and paper, but in an emergency, such as a fire, they might run out without these items. Apart from the fact that a deaf person can be a good informant, an officer should provide this person with the respect and consideration afforded all citizens in the course of professional police work.

(6) **Delivery men** (Milk men, garbage men, etc.)

THE "TABS" PROGRAM

The term TABS stands for Truancy Abatement System. It is based on the theory that juveniles who are supposed to be in school, but who instead are roaming the streets, are probably responsible for a lot of criminal activity. When a patrol officer observes a person roaming the streets during a legal school day who seems to be of school age, the officer checks the person's age and school status. If he or she is supposed to be in school, the officer takes the juvenile into custody and to a special TABS facility. The juvenile is then processed through the necessary paperwork. If this is a repeat offense, the juvenile is booked into Juvenile Hall. If not, the juvenile is released to his or her parents.

This program is usually started with some type of grant because it involves renting and staffing an office. In some departments volunteers are used. If there is a college nearby with a Criminal Justice program, students are given units in a field work class when they volunteer to work in TABS part-time. Departments can also assign injured officers to TABS on a temporary basis while they are recuperating. When a TABS program has been instituted by a department, and property enforced, there has been a noticeable drop in day-time residential burglaries, vandalism and thefts. This program is so effective, that departments are including it in their regular budgets when their grants expire.

COMPUTER DIRECTED PATROL

THE GAME THEORY APPLIED TO POLICE PATROL

Professional gamblers and insurance companies have long known that probability is a science. The more information is received, the greater is the chance of predictability. This sci-ence is being applied to police patrol. Roulette wheels and computers are combined to put the patrol officer where crime is most likely to occur.

On the beat, the patrol officer is careful not to develop a set pattern of patrol. A good pattern of patrol is usually haphazard. The officer patrols according to whim or intuition.

By carefully charting the past activity of a beat, and then feeding the information into a computer, each part of the beat may be evaluated as to the probability of criminal acts occurring. This information is then used to determine how much of a roulette wheel is assigned to certain parts of the beat. If there are areas of high activity on, there is a larger wedge on the roulette wheel that covers that particular area. This increases the chance that the wheel will stop on that area. When the officer goes out on patrol, a list is carried showing which areas to cover and how many times. The pattern is changed according to the day and time. Those cities and towns trying this technique of patrol report that it does work.

A NEW APPROACH

The New Orleans Police Department has developed a new twist to computer directed patrol. When the computer indicates that a particular area of the city will be subjected to increased burglaries, the department publicizes this information in newspapers and on TV. They then have the computer determine the alternate areas bur-glars will likely go once they become aware of the prediction. This other area is saturated with extra plain-clothes officers. The result has been a 13% drop in burglaries and a 12% increase in burglary arrests. Another result of the media announce-ments is that citizens who live in the predicted crime area become more alert to strangers. As a result there is an increase in the amount of citizen reports when unusual circumstances are observed. This has resulted in a greater number of arrests by the "beefed up" patrol force.

ONE PERSON VS. TWO PERSON AUTOMOBILE PATROL

Since there is much controversy concerning one and two officer patrol cars, the pros and cons will be covered briefly.

ADVANTAGES OF TWO OFFICER PATROL CARS

(1) A two officer patrol car provides a greater safety factor by doubling firepower and physical protection. The presence of two officers prevents trouble in many cases.

(2) The mistake that one officer makes may be caught by the other. We all have our bad days, and we are all different. A weakness of one officer can be a strength of the other.

(3) One officer does not have to drive a full shift, and is therefore more rested and can do a better job. The variety of tasks makes the job more interesting.

(4) Two pairs of eyes are better than one. It is difficult enough to drive in today's traffic, let alone devote much attention to what is going on around us while we are driving.

(5) One officer can operate the radio while the other drives.

(6) On quiet nights the driver can have someone to talk to, helping the driver stay awake.

(7) Morale can be improved through companionship if the officers are compatible.

THE SAN DIEGO STUDY

The System Development Corporation of Santa Monica, under the direction of the Police Foundation, completed a one year study of one-officer patrol cars in the city of San Diego. There were 22 two-officer patrol units and 22 single-officer units in this study. The study concluded that one-officer patrol cars had fewer problems with resisting arrest, fewer citizen complaints, were more likely to make an arrest, write up a formal crime report, and were more cost efficient.

The study received immediate criticism from peace officer associations which favor the use of two-officer cars. Most of the criticism came from sheriff's departments. The feeling was that their patrol units were different from city units because they had more territory to cover and could not count on another unit to assist them in time.

ONE OFFICER PATROL CARS

The modern use of the one-officer patrol car involves the team concept. Just as fighter pilots use team tactics, so must one-officer patrol cars, in order to achieve maximum effect. Each beat is as-

signed two patrol cars. They work separately or when the occasion arises, work as a team. This requires special training on the part of the officers just as it would for members of a football team. Although this concept was first introduced in Wichita, Kansas in 1928, it has not been used too widely until recent years. Some people think of this concept as just taking one officer out of a patrol car for economy purposes. That is not the case. The second officer is given another patrol car to cover the same beat that was originally covered by a single two-officer car. The coverage of the same area is now doubled. Cities that have experimented with this concept have reported good results.

ADVANTAGES OF ONE-OFFICER PATROL CARS

(1) The Preventive Enforcement is doubled by having twice as many visible police cars.

(2) When the officer is alone, full attention is devoted to driving and the beat rather than to conversation with the other officer. It often happens that the two officers become so involved in their conversation that they become oblivious to everything else.

(3) In a two officer car, the officers begin to rely on each other. Unfortunately, an officer may expect support which isn't there. An officer working alone develops self reliance.

(4) In the two-officer car, an officer is more likely to take greater chances than when alone. This can be caused by a false sense of security. It can also be caused by a fear of appearing cowardly in the partner's eyes. More officers have been killed when riding in two-officer cars than when riding alone.

(5) Personality clashes are reduced. Riding in a small patrol car with another person for an entire shift will soon reveal the most intimate faults of both partners. In a short time these faults can get on the other person's nerves. It is very unusual for a two-officer team to last much over a year or two. It is not uncommon for members of a two-officer team to spend more hours with each other than with their spouses.

THE TEAM CONCEPT OF PATROL

Today we often hear older citizens complain that we don't have the good old beat officer who walked his beat and knew everyone by name. Like ice boxes and Victrolas, the old fashioned foot patrol officer is a thing of the past. The officer who controlled juvenile delinquency by leaving his footprint on the britches of errant youngsters would today find himself involved in endless civil suits. However the need for personal contact with the people who live on an officer's beat is even greater. One answer to this problem is a new concept first developed in Detroit and then deve-loped further in New York. It has been called the "Team Concept", the "Beat Commander" system, or the "Neighborhood Police Team" system.

The early history of law enforcement, as covered in Chapter II, reflected conditions that were far from professional. One of the efforts to discourage graft, corruption and "shakedowns" was to move an officer frequently to prevent his becoming too friendly with the criminal elements on his beat and succumbing to temptation.

Today we have a different type of officer, and departments that are more professional. Internal Affairs units are more active and sophisticated than in the past. Today, if police administrators want to prevent corruption, they are able to control it. Therefore the need of rotating officers for this purpose is no longer essential.

The problem with rotating officers today, in their mobile units, is that they seldom get to know the people on their beats. More important is the fact that the people on the beat don't get to know the officer. The "Team" concept corrects this fault by assigning a team of officers to one particular part of the city. It encourages them to get out of their cars as much as possible, to introduce themselves to people on their beats and let them know that they are available when they are needed. This seems to change the image of the police department. What was previously "THE police officer" now becomes "OUR police officer." Distributing business cards with the officer's name and the department's phone number results in an increase in calls for police service. This could give the impression of an increasing crime rate, but it helps policework and the community in general.

It is interesting to note that the officers themselves seem to get more satisfaction out of this type of system. To illustrate one effect, departments using this system have noticed that sick leave has been reduced by up to one third.

UNMARKED CAR PATROL

When a patrol officer is first promoted to the Detective or Juvenile Divisions and drives an unmarked car, an unusual phenomenon occurs. He or she observes a greatly increased amount of criminal activity, much more than they ever saw while driving the "black and white" or marked police car. The preventive enforcement aspects of the marked patrol car are of proven value. However, if there is a disadvantage to this type of pat-rol, it is the fact that criminals who are cautious and alert can spot a marked car blocks away. To correct this, many departments have instituted a patrol shift where uniformed officers ride in unmarked police cars during peak crime hours. To further their objective of not being noticed, they do not wear hats while in the car. Their objective is not to prevent crime, but to catch criminals. Since this type of patrol has been used, it has been very effective in achieving this objective.

THE "METRO" OR PLAIN-CLOTHES FOOT PATROL

A type of patrol in larger cities is the "Metro" squad. The purpose of this group is to patrol the downtown and "skid row" areas in plain clothes, and to contact hotel clerks and bartenders as of-ten as possible. The purpose of this patrol is twofold. First is the gathering of information and "police intelligence." The second is to let business men in these areas know that the police are present and aware of their problems. They make it a point to introduce themselves to businessmen and workers in the downtown area and listen to their complaints and suggestions as well as gather information. In past years, however, many of these squads have strayed from their original purpose, gathering instead "intelligence" on subversive groups and planned violent acts or demon-strations. This has brought criticism from civil liberties groups that these units are a form of Gestapo. They use the same tactics as undercover narcotic agents, but generate a lot more criticism.

HORSE PATROL

Horse patrol, next to foot patrol, is one of the oldest types of patrol. Although we associate horse patrol with times past, there is still a need for this type of service. In communities where there are large open areas and a lack of roads, and where the terrain is steep and rough, the use of police horses can be quite beneficial.

To increase the safety of both horse and rider, the Philadelphia Police Department has outfitted its horses with white luminous leg stockings and a rump sheet to make them more visible to motorists at night. They have also equipped the officers riding the horses with battery operated lights that are mounted on their backs.

Fig. IV-7; Police horse patrol on duty

The disadvantage of the horse patrol is the cost of stables and upkeep, and their limited use in a city. They are not much good at chasing criminals driving an automobile down city streets. They tire easily and require close physical attention. Some cities have partly overcome this problem by renting their horses just for special occasions. Although this has resulted in a monetary savings, its disadvantage is that the horses might not be available exactly when they are needed. With the use of small compact transistorized radios, the horse patrol can maintain the same communications as the patrol car.

The following are some of the more common uses of horse patrol:

(1) **Park Patrol** In most parks of any size, there are trails that are too narrow, steep, and winding, for automobile patrol, or even jeep patrol. In terrain of this sort, there is a great need for horse patrol. In parks within large cities there is a tendency for deviates to congregate. Some are attracted to the children who play there. Here the need for some type of patrol to go off the beaten path becomes more important. The horse also provides its rider with a higher and better plane of vision than the driver of a patrol car.

(2) **Beach Patrol** In communities with large beaches, it has been found that the sand and water can make vehicle patrols difficult. Horse patrol, however, is quite suitable. There is also the added problem of unruly crowds, and of "beach bums" who gather at the beaches in the summer and cause disturbances and other forms of trouble. The horse patrol seems to be very effective in controlling crowds of this sort. Walkie-talkie radios increase their effectiveness. Because the beaches are so crowded in the summer, it is important that only well-trained horses be used in order to avoid civil suits resulting from injuries to innocent persons.

(3) **Posse and Search duty** Any community that is close to or part of a mountainous area has the problem of chasing down escaped or wanted persons who have fled to these areas. They also have the problem of children, hunters, and fishermen becoming lost in these areas. The mounted posse is undoubtedly the best means of locating these persons when used in conjunction with the helicopter. Since the need for such a posse is not too frequent, it is wise for the department to start a police reserve posse made up of ranchers and persons living in the mountainous area who already have their horses, and who would readily volunteer to assist the department when requested.

(4) **Parade and Crowd Control** Horses have been used for parade and crowd control for centuries. People seem to have a healthy respect for horses and their hoofs. They might challenge a man because they know that he is a rational and responsible being possessing an intellect that will in some way often control

his actions. Horses, on the other hand, are not expected to possess these qualities, and there is an uncertainty regarding their behavior that will make people hesitant to challenge them. Their height and size has a strong psychological advantage in dealing with unruly mobs.

DOG PATROL

Records show us that dogs have been used as a means of personal protection throughout recorded history.

THE BELMAN OF LONDON.

Bringing to light the moſt notorious villanies that are now practiſed in the KINGDOME.

Profitable for Gentlemen, Lawyers, Merchants, Citizens, Farmers, Maſters of Houſholds, and all ſortes of ſeruants, to marke, and delightfull for all men to Reade.

Lege, Perlege, Relege.

Printed at London for NATHANIEL BVTTER. 1 6 0 8.

The Bellman of London, 1608

Fig. IV-8; The Bellman of London with dog

As was mentioned in Chapter II, the ancient Egyptians used dogs to help patrol treasure-laden tombs. In our early history they were used to protect the U.S Mint. There is a record in Philadelphia showing that in 1793, three dollars were paid for a savage dog named Nero to Protect "Ye Olde Mint" (nameplate on the United States Mint in Philadelphia). He accompanied the guard as he made his hourly rounds. Nero's food came from the same budget as the horses that were used to provide power for the Mint's machinery

During World War II, the military on all sides widely used dogs as a means of security and protection. In the United States military, the K-9 Corps was a major operation. It was natural to expect this training and knowledge to be converted to civilian use after the war. After the war, the biggest development and use of dogs for police work occurred in Europe. Their wide use in policework in the United States was slow in starting. There are isolated examples of the successful use of police dogs in var-ious parts of the country, but it wasn't until after the Korean War that their use became widely popular.

Today they have become commonplace. Many police administrators were at first cautious, and waited for other departments to be the first to experiment with them. When their success in the field was quite apparent they too adopted their use. Some administrators, unfortunately, jumped into using police dogs without proper preparation or training. As a result many programs were dropped when they didn't work out as expected. The key to the successful use of police dogs in patrol is based, first of all, on an understanding and willing master. Second, on the proper selection and training of the dogs, and finally, on preparing the general public for their use. Some administrators feel that the last idea is the most important.

To become a dog's master or handler, the officer must first have an understanding of animals. He or she must be willing to make personal sacrifices in keeping the dog. Acceptance by the officer's family is also important. There have already been cases of police dogs coming between officer and spouse. When an officers' spouses realizes that the dog can save their lives, it can sometimes change their attitudes from indifference to acceptance.

The selection and training of dogs is very important, but can present many problems. When a program is first announced, many well meaning citizens, some of them politically influential, will offer their dogs to the department for this purpose. Not all breeds of dogs are suited for police-work. Even among those most suited for police- work there are many that don't work out. The type of dog that is the best suited for all-around police work is the German Shepherd. Refusing a person's dog or rejecting it during training, can cause hurt feelings. Therefore great care must be exercised in accepting a dog for training. Training police dogs is a special field. Well-meaning cit-izens will offer to train dogs for the police department. Because training can be expensive, the city council will sometimes accept a citizen's offer to train police dogs at a reasonable price. This can be false economy and result in the failure of the program. Training is not enough. It must be proper training.

Fig. IV-9; Police dogs in use

Dog patrol may be fine as far as the department is concerned, but if the public thinks that dogs are a danger to the community as well as criminals, they will not last. A well-planned pub-lic relations campaign must be conducted to show that the police dog is gentle except when commanded by his master, and that his use will be restricted to more serious offenses. A poorly informed public can imagine all sorts of misuses such as attacking traffic offenders and shoplifters. It must be informed through proper press cover-age and public exhibitions. Due to their misuse in civil rights demonstrations in the South, the NAACP has tried to have the use of police dogs outlawed. Because of this, it is important that strong control be exercised over the indiscrimi-nate use of these dogs, or it is quite possible that they might be eliminated altogether.

Although the use of police dogs is unlimited, they seem best suited to locating prowlers, burglars hiding in large buildings or stores, and the control of unruly crowds and riots. Dog patrol cars should be evenly spaced throughout the city. POLICE DOGS SHOULD NEVER BE USED TO REPLACE POLICE OFFICERS. They are a supplementary force that can aid officers in better performing their duty. They should never be used as an economy measure to reduce personnel. If this were ever attempted, police unions would very quickly eliminate them.

It is interesting to note that the report of the President's Commission on Law Enforcement and Administration of Justice, stated that police dogs are very effective in patrolling industrial areas against burglaries, but a question arises as to their effectiveness when used on routine patrol in minority-group areas. The Commission felt that they tend to antagonize the community, and can result in more harm than good. This presents police administrators with a dilemma. They have a tool that will help protect the police officer from hostile attack, and yet this same tool promotes the hostility that causes attacks by minorities on police officers.

There is a great need for public relations work in this area, for there exists a gross fear and misunderstanding among minorities about the true purpose of the police dog. Communication is extremely important in all interpersonal relationships, but between minorities and the police it is essential. It must be shown that police dogs are not an offensive weapon in the "war against minorities", but a defensive weapon, one to be used in protecting both officer and citizen alike.

Unfortunately, there has been a tendency among some "dog" officers to promote a fear among hoodlums that the dog will be "sicced" on anyone the officer doesn't like. This is supposedly done in the interest of insuring their own personal safety. Also for the purpose of "teaching them respect". The only "respect" taught by this method is fear and hate. Fear is the main force for control in a dictatorship, but in a democracy, even though the fear of punishment can never be eliminated we must strive for more professional means to achieve our ends.

NARCOTIC DETECTION BY USE OF DOGS

Although not necessarily a normal patrol function, dogs have been successfully used in the detection of narcotics. This special use is based on their keen sense of smell. When properly trained, they are able to detect opiates, cocaine, marijuana, and other dangerous drugs. In one case, detection occurred when 5 pounds of heroin was heavily sealed and placed in the gas tank of an automobile. In Savannah, Georgia, a police dog named "Sergeant Blitz" was so successful in drug sniffing, that the underworld put out a $10,000 "contract" on the dog.

Although dogs have been used for this purpose on a local level, usually by narcotic investigators, the major use of these specially trained dogs has been with the United States Customs Inspectors. They have been so successful at customs inspection stations that U.S. Customs now has over 100 of these very useful dogs in their canine unit.

BOMB DETECTION DOGS

Police dogs can also be used for the detection of explosives. German Shepherds are best suited for this job because they have an especially keen sense of smell. They are also reliable, predictable, adaptable to weather conditions, good at responding to commands, and have the needed ability to discriminate between friend and foe. One of the best training centers for this special skill is Lackland Air Force Base in San Antonio. Dogs trained at this base can identify by smell, TNT, gelatin dynamite, plastic explosives, smokeless powder, and nitro-glycerin. The dogs and their handlers are trained together. It is most important that these dogs receive continued training in order for this special skill to be retained. The Allegheny County Police in Pennsylvania have been using police dogs for explosive detection since 1973. Their dogs are also trained for other patrol functions so they can be used in the field on a regular patrol basis.

When a special work collar is placed on the dog and he is released, it is a signal for him to begin the search. When he smells an explosive, he immediately "sits" at that location, and waits for his handler. Once the bomb is located, the bomb squad is called and a further search is conducted in case there are more explosives at that location.

These specially trained dogs can contribute greatly to the patrol function in view of the large number of bomb calls received by police departments today.

ULTRASONIC DOG CHASERS

Patrol officers should be aware of an electronic device developed by Electronics for Industry Inc. of Miami. It produces an ultrasonic sound that cannot be heard by humans, but is so severe to dogs that they run off very quickly. The company has sold thousands of units in the United States and Canada, mostly to mailmen and meter readers. The device does not affect farm animals, but a prolonged use can be harmful to children. This device can be used by patrol officers who have a continuing problem with a neighborhood dog. However, criminals can also use it against police dogs. It is about the size of a cassette tape recorder.

PRIVATELY OWNED SECURITY DOGS

Because of the great increase in burglaries, businessmen and citizens are requesting guard dogs almost as fast as they can be trained. Unfortunately, not all dogs are suited for this type of training, and the average person doesn't know the difference. If the dog looks big or mean, he is accepted as being a good guard dog.

This is mentioned because of the potential danger to officers on patrol. There is an increasing number of patrol officers being bitten by private guard dogs when they respond to burglary or prowler calls. Since dogs are not affected by mace, the riot baton held out horizontally in front of the body can be a good defense. If the dog jumps at the officer, the baton can be directed to the dog's mouth or jaws.

AIR PATROL

Air patrol is not a new concept in policework. As early as 1929 the New York Police Department started their Air Service Division at Glen Curtis Airport (now La Guardia Field) with a Savoia-Marchetti biplane.

Fig. IV-10a; Savoia — Marchetti was an odd three-seater. Third seat was the unusable "angel seat."

Fig. IV-10b; Fleet biplane, a land type, replaced a Savoia — Marchetti that washed out.

Fig. IV-10c; Stinson seaplane rejuvenated bureau after World War II.

Fig. IV-10d; Faster and more powerful, Grumman Goose was last fixed-wing aircraft.

Until recently, air patrol was a service that only very large cities or State agencies could afford. Today it is rapidly becoming an important type of patrol service. Those departments that cannot afford it are now looking into the possibility of going together with other nearby agencies in an effort to make such a venture financially feasible. If the area to be serviced is large enough, air patrol can actually be as economical as the automobile. The more use it receives, the lower is the cost per mile. Light aircraft and helicopters are today proving themselves very useful. They are effective in the area of traffic control because they can cover miles of highway in a short period of time without being bothered by traffic jams or signals. As our traffic congestion has increased, so has the use of air traffic patrol.

HELICOPTERS

Fig. IV-11; Police helicopter

Today the most advocated type of air patrol involves the use of helicopters. Since this type of operation does involve quite an expense, any department thinking of such a service should carefully weigh all of the factors, since not all departments are suited to this type of service. The main considerations are geography, terrain, the number and type of people in the area, and the rate and type of crime in that area. The most important consideration under geography would certainly be the number of square miles to be covered.

FLIRS (Forward Looking Infra Red System)

Modern science has made the helicopter even more valuable. Borrowing from the military, scientists have developed a sensing device called FLIRS (Forward Looking Infra Red System). When mounted in a helicopter, it can use infra red sensors to locate human beings on the ground. This can be invaluable when searching for lost persons in wooded areas. The device is so sensitive that it can even locate persons inside buildings. This would be of great value to officers who are responding to a silent alarm in a very large building, and have to spend considerable time searching for a suspect. It would also increase officer safety by allowing the officer to know the exact location of a suspect. It can also tell from the air whether or not a parked vehicle has been driven recently by the heat still present in the vehicle. In some cases it can even locate buried bodies.

Any discussion about the use of helicopter patrol would not be complete without properly looking into the advantages and disadvantages of such an operation.

ADVANTAGES OF HELICOPTER PATROL

(1) Improved response time to emergency calls.

(2) Increased apprehension of offenders.

(3) Increased prevention of crime.

(4) Improved efficiency of regular patrol units through receiving airborne information.

(5) Ability to easily conduct roof searches for forced entries and suspected felons. This could be difficult for officers in cars.

(6) Easier location of lost and escaped persons.

(7) More efficient rescue operations and emergency ambulance service.

(8) Better floodlighting of large areas at night.

(9) By using airborne loudspeakers, information can be broadcast to large areas.

(10) Rapid emergency transportation of injured personnel.

(11) Added security for patrol officers through "backup" offered by air borne patrol.

(12) Possible use in fire fighting.

(13) It can be used to assist other public agencies and save the city money.

DISADVANTAGES OF HELICOPTER PATROL

(1) Bad weather will ground the helicopter.

(2) Smog and light or intermittent clouds might affect vision.

(3) This type of service requires special skills and training.

(4) There is a danger from high wires, trees and similar objects.

(5) Can be difficulty in landing in urban areas.

(6) Pilots are subject to fatigue and must work shorter periods of time than regular shifts.

(7) Refueling problems.

(8) Special facilities required for housing/repair.

(9) There are many tactical problems to overcome such as location of police units on ground, and the exact locations of addresses from the air. Many departments paint large numbers on top of patrol cars so that helicopters can properly identify them.

(10) Adverse public reaction due to the fear of "Spying from the sky" or just simple objection to the noise involved.

(11) Criminals can hear the helicopter coming and surprise is lost.

(12) It is the most expensive type of patrol.

PROJECT SKY KNIGHT

One of the most notable experiments in the use of helicopters for patrol service was conducted, in the early years, by the Los Angeles County Sheriff's Department. Under a federal grant, the City of Lakewood in California was selected for this experiment.

Using a two-man team, one pilot and an observer, a Hughes helicopter patrolled the city at an altitude of between 500 to 700 feet. Unfortunately the noise caused residents to complain, and the altitude had to be raised to 1500 feet. Engineers resolved the problem by designing a new rotor and an engine muffler, and the helicopter resumed patrolling at the lower altitudes and at faster speeds with no noise complaints resulting.

Within six months there was no doubt as to the effectiveness of the helicopter as an aid to police patrol and the overall protection of the city. The statistical evidence of both crime prevention and arrests were quite significant. This experiment has paved the way for a much wider use of police helicopter patrol.

FIXED WING AIRCRAFT

Recent developments in a new prototype of light fixed wing aircraft have shown great promise for use in air patrol.

Fig. IV-12; Fixed wing aircraft.

One example is the modified Cessna 172 developed by World Associates Inc. in southern California. Referred to as the "Sky Sentinel", this light plane has many advantages over the helicopter. The first, and most important to any administrator, is economy. It not only initially costs considerably less than a helicopter, it also costs much less to operate. Some of the other advantages are: *

(1) Can travel at airspeeds as slow as 35 mph.

(2) Can remain airborne for seven—eight hours.

(3) Can go at least 40 miles per hour faster than a helicopter in case of a "hot pursuit."

(4) Has a new type of muffler that causes the engine to be practically unheard when flying at a height of 1000 feet. This also allows much clearer audibility in the loudspeaker when transmitting messages to the ground.

Like the helicopter, it carries a 3.5 million candlepower searchlight. It is ideally suited for the patrol of highways and freeways. Its major disadvantage is that it cannot hover, or fly in tight circles like the helicopter or it would lose altitude.

REMOTE CONTROLLED AIR PATROL

When police aircraft crash, and they do crash, death or serious injury usually result. Because of this, there has been much talk about some form of unmanned, remote-controlled air surveillance.

One answer is the Remote Piloted Miniblimp developed for, and tested by, the Bell Gardens Police Department in California. The Miniblimp is 45 feet in length and 11 feet in diameter. It can fly up to 55 miles per hour, and usually cruises at about 500 feet, where the wind velocity is not very great. Although its gas tank holds only 4 gallons, it can stay in the air for 24 hours at a time. The Miniblimp is guided by a police dispatcher who sits at a television console that duplicates the blimp's control panel, and can observe whatever the blimp's zoom camera is aimed at. The camera can take pictures of persons and license plates, and, through the blimp's loudspeaker and receiver, the dispatcher can carry on a conversation with people at the scene. Since it is not highly pressurized, it does not explode if hit by bullets, but very slowly sinks to the ground depending upon how many bullets hit it.

Eglen Hovercraft of Terre Haute, Indiana, has developed a Mini RPV (Remotely Piloted Vehicle) which has a speed of 80 to 100 MPH. This rear mounted "pusher-prop" type aircraft can be equipped with a TV camera and video tape recorder for fly-over type surveillance.

BOAT PATROL

Fig. IV-13; Early New York Harbor Patrol

Since man has usually founded and built cities next to rivers or some body of water, it is conceivable that the use of boats in the enforcement of the law has been a type of patrol since the dawn of history. The recorded history of our earliest civilizations indicate the use of tariffs. Where there are tariffs there is smuggling, and the control of smuggling in any community near water necessitates the use of a water patrol. The ancient Egyptians had this problem, according to their records.

POLICE AND RIVER PIRATES.

Fig. IV-14; New York Harbor Patrol

In the United States our standard of living has risen to the point where the boat has become the status symbol that was once assigned to the second car. It is not only a status symbol, but it is becoming one of the major forms of recreation in a country whose leisure time is steadily increasing with the advent of a shorter work week and the automation of many household tasks. As people flock to the water with boats of all sizes and shapes, traffic control has now become a problem. In communities on the west coast, the great increase in population has necessitated the building of large dams and reservoirs for the* storage of water. Many of these facilities have been opened to the public as recreation areas. Now police departments, who had never thought of the necessity of a boat or water patrol in their landlocked community, now find that they must form such a patrol. When a boat patrol becomes necessary, it is wise to also form a Scuba diving team. Where there is water, there will also be drownings and evidence disposed of by throwing it into the water. In most cases the department provides the equipment for the team, and then pays them overtime while they are on diving assignments.

Fig. IV-15; \harbor patrol boat

In large seaports, the duties of the boat patrol, usually referred to as the Harbor Patrol, are manyfold. Where there are large piers and warehouses, there is also the danger of theft and burglary. Many times it is easier to patrol these piers from the water than to have patrol cars drive out on the pier, although a combination of the two is often better. Most large boats in the harbor patrol are equipped with fire fighting equipment so they can also be used for controlling or putting out fires that might be discovered while on patrol.

Those officers assigned to this duty should be as familiar with the seagoing "Rules of the road" and the Harbor and Navigation Code as a traffic officer would be familiar with the Vehicle Code.

BICYCLE PATROL

THE POLICE TRICYCLE.

Fig. IV-16; The police tricycle

Bicycle patrol has long been a part of the patrol services of most countries throughout the world. In the United States, the rapid development of the automobile and the wider streets has limited and almost eliminated the use of the bicycle as a patrol vehicle. However, many communities have retained the use of the bicycle for the following reasons. First of all it is economical. Secondly it is quiet and can be used to patrol an area without alerting criminals. With the use of a small compact hand radio, the bicycle can have the same communications capabilities as the patrol car.

The public relations aspect of bicycle patrol should not be overlooked. Although not as good as foot patrol, bicycle patrol allows the officer to make numerous contacts on the street. It seems to be a natural "conversation piece." People will often stop the officer and ask questions about the bicycle and its effectiveness in law enforcement. Those who would not normally stop an officer who is walking the beat, seem to have no hesitation at stopping an officer riding a bicycle and starting a conversation.

A large number of departments in the United States have successfully used bicycle patrols to control burglaries and muggings that were getting out of hand. When officers have worked in teams and used some type of team strategy or tactic, along with the utilization of mobile communications, the use of bicycles has been very effective.

The Military Police at Fort Dix, New Jersey, experimented with bicycle patrols, after seeing the success the Military Police had with it in Germany. They found that its use in the housing area of the fort resulted in reduction of crime and an increase in public relations. The patrolman riding the bike seemed to have a better opportunity to stop and chat with people in the neighborhood than he would when patrolling in a car.

MOTOR SCOOTERS AND MOPEDS

When this type of patrol was first suggested, there was much resistance to the use of motor scooters and mopeds by police officers. It just didn't seem to fit their "macho" image. There are, however, certain types of terrain and facilities that are ideally suited for this type of vehicle. Once officers discovered how much better their jobs could be performed when using these vehicles, the resistance seemed to decline. Major cities across the nation use them for patrolling airports, major shopping centers and areas or locations that are inaccessible to normal vehicles. For example, the moped weighs about 100 pounds, and can be taken up and down stairs, escalators, and even lifted over small walls and hedges. Although the speed of a moped is only about 30 MPH, it can catch any running suspect over a distance. When the officer gets to a running suspect, he is usually out of breath and can be more easily restrained.

TRAFFIC PATROL

The first problem with vehicular control occurred in France in 1769. A man by the name of George Cugnot invented the first self powered vehicle. It was steam driven and quite slow. He developed it on a contract with the French army, but it didn't go as fast as a horse, so the military was upset after spending so much money. He tried to make it go faster, and ran off the road, hitting a stone wall belonging to the army (First vehicle accident). He was tried for reckless driving and destruction of government property, and banished from France. The first ticket for speeding in the United States occurred in New York in 1911. A cab driver, Jacob German, was arrested for driving 12 miles an hour in New York City.

Fig. IV-18; Modern motorcycle officer

The two-wheel motorcycle is useful in traffic enforcement, parades and escort duty. It has the disadvantages of being able to be used only in fair weather, of causing a greater number of accidents which are usually more serious, and in the long run, costing the department almost as much as a patrol vehicle, despite the initial low cost. A report from the Health Insurance Institute reveals that in recent years, motorcycle accidents have increased. The report showed that nearly 90 % of all motorcycle crashes have resulted in injury or death. Compare this to only 10 % of automobile crashes resulting in injury or death.

MOTORCYCLE PATROL

The use of the motorcycle as a means of police transportation is almost as old as that of the automobile. It was in 1909 that motorcycles were first used in law enforcement. The wide use of the side-car motorcycle in World War I set the stage for its use in policework following that war. Although the use of motorcycles has lost ground in recent years, their need in congested traffic will insure their continued use as a form of police patrol.

Fig. IV-17; Motorcycle officers, early 1930's

THREE WHEEL MOTORCYCLES AND SCOOTERS

The old three wheel motorcycle, commonly used in the enforcement of parking, is being used less and less in police work today. It has the disadvantage of high cost and upkeep when compared to scooters, and does not provide the rider with protection against weather. Most parking control today is handled by the covered, three wheel scooter. It is easier on gas, and easier to operate. It also costs less initially, and maintenance costs are lower. Although it is used mostly on parking enforcement, its mobility and dependability has resulted in increased use at airports and parks.

TELEVISION PATROL

Television patrol, though probably suggested in the Dick Tracy comic strip, was first used in police work on a practical basis in West Germany. Its use was basically for purposes of traffic control. It involved a television panel with a capacity for thirty television receivers, situated in front of a control board manned by a single operator.

In the field, at key points, television cameras were mounted in weatherproof housings. They were equipped with Zoom lenses and were controlled remotely by the operator at the control board who could adjust each camera to a panoramic view of 270 degrees. As situations developed in the field he could direct officers to the exact location. With the use of the zoom lens, it is possible to pick up the license numbers of fleeing automobiles. The possibilities are unlimited.

It is obvious that this type of operation is only adaptable to cities or areas containing great concentrations of people or traffic, but the idea is not only sound but economical. In the United States this system has been used with considerable success in the control of prisoners in jail.

Many cities in the United States have experimented with the system of placing TV cameras at strategic locations in an effort to either curb crime or assist in apprehending criminals. One of the first was Orleans, New York. They started with four stationary cameras mounted 20 feet high on utility poles along each side of a five block stretch of their main street.

The major problems encountered were lighting and the fact that only the front doors of stores were covered. Since most crime occurs at night, this was the major problem. The Orleans PD did find it useful in knowing when a traffic jam was developing, so they could dispatch someone to resolve it.

LOW LIGHT LEVEL TV SURVEILLANCE

One development that has helped this area of surveillance is a TV camera that can operate in just about any lighting condition, from full sunlight to starlight. It is the apparent answer to the problem of downtown TV surveillance. This type of camera was first developed for the military, and was later released for civilian use. The first city to experiment with this low light system was Mount Vernon, New York.

Fig. IV-19; LLLTV Surveillance, remote station on city

The LLLTV camera is a passive device and does not radiate or emit a beam that would give away its location. The camera operates on a light amplification principle. Very little light can be greatly amplified. It can be used with any combination of lenses, and it can be easily adapted to video tape for a permanent recording. The control box at the police station can turn the set on or off, and can focus the picture, control the zoom lens, move it up and down to the right or left, and can even turn the windshield wipers on and off. It can be easily installed in a weather proof housing that will withstand all types of weather. This unit can be used not only for downtown surveillance, but for automobiles and helicopter patrol as well.

The field of electronics continues to offer great promise as an important aid to law enforcement. Because of the vast amount of research money being spent in that area, startling technical advances are developed every year. Electronic manufacturers now have a television camera three inches in diameter and seven inches long. This size not only makes the camera suitable for still surveillance purposes, but also makes it adaptable for mobile work such as in police vehicles and helicopters.

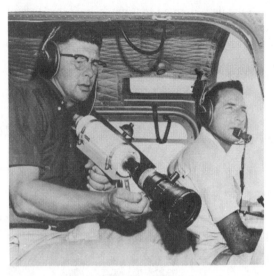

Fig. IV-20; Helicopter TV surveillance

The "Telecopter," so widely used by news services, proved its great value as a patrol and surveillance device during the Watts and Rodney King riots in Los Angeles. Because the telephoto lenses worked so well, one could make positive identification of the perpetrators who were looting and setting fires. Clothing identification gained by such means greatly assisted in the apprehension of law breakers. It also proved to be of great tactical value by enabling the patrol supervisors to properly direct officers to a particular scene on the television screen and thus intercept and arrest the perpetrators.

With the use of video tape recorders, these same cameras are being used as very effective training devices. The officer is able to perform some action, and then immediately review that action and offer constructive self criticism. The same equipment is now being used as an economical means of recording the actions and sounds of suspected drunken drivers.

Fig. IV-21, Monitors for helicopter surveillance

During the Mideast operation, Desert Storm, our military showed how successful "robot" tanks can be. Although they are certainly expensive, the reduced loss of human life can make it worth while. These tanks contain television cameras that enable military leaders to view battle scenes without endangering themselves

Such devices have been adapted to law enforcement use on a minor scale. Unfortunately, only larger departments can afford them because of the high expense. They have proved very valuable in cases involving the surveillance of barricaded fugitives, riots, civil disturbances, and breaking into narcotic "safe houses." The possibilities of using television in future patrol work will only be limited by our own imagination.

Fig. IV-22; Two photos using LLLTV from half a block away

A HISTORY OF WOMEN AND PATROL DUTIES

In England during World War I, because all able-bodied men were in the military, women were temporarily hired for patrol duty. After the war, they were removed from that assignment. Here in the United States it was not until 1968 that the Indianapolis, Indiana Police Department assigned the first female police officer to patrol duty.

It was not until the 1960's that an honest effort was made to bring women into police officer ranks. Prior to that they were assigned to working in records and identification offices. They were usually given the title of Police Matron, and paid considerably less money than a patrol officer. The major stumbling blocks to recruiting female candidates were first the agility test, and second the attitude of police administrators. Because females do not have the same upper body strength as males, they had difficulty passing the pull up and push up parts of the police physical agility test.

Fig. IV-23; Woman patrol officer

Why did police agencies suddenly open their patrol ranks to women in the 1960's? The major reason was that the federal government mandated that cities either hire women for patrol duty or face the loss of federal funding. Large cities were so heavily dependent upon federal funding that they had practically no choice.

Still the majority of women were failing the physical agility test. The federal government demanded that police departments prove that pull ups and push ups really tested a quality essential to everyday duties in police work. As a result, these two parts of the physical agility test were removed. An attempt was also made to remove the part of the agility test involving the six foot wall, as this was also a means of eliminating female candidates. This met with little success because it was felt that chasing suspects over fences was a valid part of police work. With these changes in the physical agility test, great numbers of women were, for the first time, passing patrol officer tests. Since that time, the majority of women have shown that they are able to adequately perform in the patrol function.

Fig. IV-24; Woman patrol officer handcuffing a suspect

A study of the performance of women in patrol has been conducted by the Urban Institute for the Police Foundation. This four month study of the Washington D.C. Police Department revealed that most male partners working with women tend to display "honest protectiveness", and that the women made fewer arrests, took more orders from their male partners and as a rule let the male drive the police car.

Dr. Lewis J. Sherman, Professor of Psychology at the University of Missouri, also conducted a study of women in patrol work. He found that women patrol officers use less force in making arrests than do male officers. The women officers seem to have approaches, techniques and strategies that can better defuse violent or emotionally tense situations. They also seemed to show more patience with people who were involved in conflict situations, and did not see a quick arrest as the immediate solution. In checking the responses to family fights, Dr. Sherman found that there were fewer repeater calls regarding family fights when the call was handled by a woman officer. He also found that the presence of policewomen often seemed to cool things down, where the presence of male officers would often aggravate the situation.

THE LEGAL BASIS FOR HIRING FEMALE PATROL OFFICERS

In the 1960's, most police administrators were hesitant to hire women as patrol officers. Since they had not worked in this position before, there was a fear that they might fail in the task and that public opinion might oppose such a move. The 60's were a time of change, but those promoting change were few in number and not very popular with the general public. What was it then, that brought about the wholesale recruitment of women into the ranks of police patrol? The moving force was first, legal, and second, federal. The legal force for this movement started with Title VII of the Civil Rights Act of 1964, later amended in 1972 by the Equal Employment Opportunity Act. This extended the act to public employees and allowed the Attorney General of the United States to bring suit for violations. It also established an Equal Employment Opportunity Commission to see that the regulations were carried out. They also established guides pertaining to such areas as entrance examinations, pay and promotion and fringe benefits.

Another legal basis is the "Equal Protection Clause" of the Fourteenth Amendment of the United States Constitution. It is seldom used however, because such an action would take too long to go through the courts. In fact there are few cases dealing with the recruitment and assignment of women in police work that have reached the high courts. This is because cities have attempted to avoid lengthy and expensive trials by giving in to the demands of the EEOC.

The importance of the Federal Government in bringing about change was due to the fact that they handed out millions of dollars to police agencies. In 1973 the Crime Control Act prohibited recipients of LEAA funds from discriminating against women in employment. Since most police agencies re-ceived a considerable amount of funds from LEAA, the loss of such funds would be a serious threat to the continued fiscal operation of departments.

The decisions of the EEOC could be contested in the courts, but this would be expensive and time consuming. As a result, cities agreed to the hiring of large numbers of women to avoid lengthy litigation and the loss of federal funds. These laws were basically not directed toward the hiring of women, but to correct imbalances in the hiring of racial minorities. Women were considered to be minorities because of past hiring practices, and were included in the laws. To correct the problem many departments established hiring quotas for women and minorities. However this resulted in "Reverse Discrimination" suits. In these suits it was claimed that the rights of white males were being denied under the 14th Amendment of the United States Constitution. (Equal protection under the law) These suits were being filed by both police officers and fire fighters, but the first one to reach the United States Supreme Court involved a student who was passed over for medical school in favor of a minority who had received a lower score on the entrance examination. (University of California v. Allan Bakke). In this case, the Supreme Court found in favor of Bakke. The main issue here, however, was that Bakke received a higher score on the entrance exam, and because of this, was a victim of "Reverse Discrimination." From a legal standpoint, this is not a simple matter. Each case can be different, and it will take years for the courts to lay out rules that police administrators will be able to apply in the majority of cases.

Women working in private industry complain about a "glass ceiling" that prevents them from attaining top positions. This is not true in the field of police work. Today women are filling all ranks, and some have been appointed to the position of Chief of Police in large cities.

Fig. IV-25; Woman patrol officer questioning subject

STUDY QUESTIONS for Patrol Operations

CHAPTER 4

1. The area in which an officer patrols is called a _____.

2. When an officer is assigned to a particular watch that covers a certain time of the day, it is called a _____.

3. In the "Ten Plan", an officer works less hours per week.   T or F

4. Name one advantage of the "Ten Plan" for officers. _____.

6. The most expensive type of patrol is _____.

7. Foot patrol seems to be making a comeback.   T or F

8. The Police Foundation study in New Jersey revealed that, with the reinstatement of foot patrol, there was a decrease in crime.   T or F

9. Name an advantage of foot patrol. _____.

10. The best way to walk a foot patrol is to follow exactly the same pattern so that the sergeant can find you easily.   T or F

11. When an open door is found, it is permissible for the officer to enter alone only if the front door is the only exit.   T or F

12. A foot patrolman should, when possible, check the roofs of businesses. Why? _____.

13. Unlike times past, today it is permissible for an officer to smoke in uniform, when on duty, and in public.   T or F

14. When things are slow, an officer should conduct a mental exercise of planning _____.

15. When automobiles were first used by police departments, they did not go out on patrol, but remained in a garage waiting for calls.   T or F

16. Modern police tactics were born when the police automobile was first equipped with a workable _____.

17. The advantage of the automobile patrol is speed and _____.

18. Police cars do little in the way of preventive enforcement.   T or F

19. While in a marked police car, officers are immune from the Vehicle Code "Rules of the Road."   T or F

20. If officers don't drink coffee, the book recommends the occasional use of _____ when working the night shift.

21. Seat belts are not only a safety device, but also cause the officer to feel less tired after a shift.   T or F

22. An officer should always refer to a janitor as a _____.

23. New officers should be leery of "set up" informants who offer to give the new officer important information in return for meals and money.   T or F

24. Name one of the persons mentioned in the book as a possible informant that a beat officer should develop. _____

25. In New Orleans, the police have a computer figure out where there is likely to be an increase in crime, and then broadcast it over the local media.   T or F

26. Name one advantage of a two-man patrol car. _____.

27. A San Diego police study showed that officers in one-man cars were more efficient.   T or F

28. The proper use of one-man patrol cars requires special training.   T or F

29. More police officers have been killed when riding in two-man cars than in one-man cars.   T or F

30. Originally, officers were required to change beats regularly. Why? _____
_____.

31. A problem with the downtown "metro" squads was:

     a. _ they didn't arrest anyone.
     b. _ they violated the rights of demonstrators.
     c. _ they hassled businessmen.
     d. _ they spent all their time in downtown movies.

32. Horse patrol is an expensive type of patrol.   T or F

33. Dog patrol was used by the ancient Egyptians.   T or F

34. Dog patrol was used by the U.S. Mint in Philadelphia in 1793.   T or F

35. Most of the development in the use of police dogs occurred in our military in World War II and the Korean War.   T or F

36. Police dogs were used by watchmen and bellmen in England in the 1600's.   T or F

37. The dog that seems to be best suited to policework is the _____.

38. Police dogs have come under attack by minorities because of their misuse in certain states.   T or F

39. The president's Commission of Law Enforcement and the Administration of Justice   T or F
recommended that the use of police dogs in minority neighborhoods be restricted.

40. Police dogs can be successfully used to detect narcotics.   T or F

41. In Savannah, Georgia, a police dog was so good in detecting narcotics that _____
_____. (what happened?)

42. The best dog for sniffing explosives is the _____.

43. The major training facility for explosive sniffing dogs is _____ AFB.

44. Privately owned security dogs present a real danger for police officers responding to   T or F
burglar alarm calls and prowler calls.

45. The first use of airplanes in policework occurred in the state of _____ in 1929.

46. Name a disadvantage of helicopter patrol. _____

47. Name an advantage of helicopter patrol. _____

48. The first experimental use of helicopters in police patrol occurred in 1966 in the city of
_____.

49. Name one advantage of the newly developed "sky sentinel" fixed wing aircraft. _____
_____

50. The new experimental "remote piloted miniblimp" can stay in the air for _____ hours
at a time.

51. The problem with the above miniblimp is that if it is hit with a bullet fired from the   T or F
ground, it will explode.

52. The only departments that have boat patrols are those situated next to the ocean or   T or F
natural harbors.

53. The use of bicycles in patrol work seems to be best for what type of criminal offense?
_____

54. The Los Angeles police department uses mopeds at their International Airport with good   T or F
success.

55. Motorcycles were first used in policework in the early 1900's.   T or F

56. Name one disadvantage of motorcycles in police work. _____

57. Nearly _____ percent of all motorcycle accidents result in death or injury as opposed to ten percent for automobiles.

58. Because of the cost and the weather, three-wheeled motorcycles have been replaced, in most departments, by covered motor scooters.   T or F

59. The practical use of television for patrol observation was first developed in what country?
    _____

60. When TV was first used for patrol observation, there was a major problem that was later solved by science. It was:

    a. _ Television cameras were too heavy, and large to properly mount.
    b. _ At night the light was too low to pick up a decent picture.
    c. _ When it rained, the TV's shorted out.
    d. _ The cameras could only pick up things that were no more than 50 feet away.

61. The first policewoman was assigned to patrol duties in 1968 on the _____ police department.

62. The study completed by the urban institute for the police foundation showed that policewomen:

    a. _ made fewer arrests than their male counterpart.
    b. _ took more orders from their male partner.
    c. _ tended to let the male officer do most of the driving.
    d. _ all of the above

63. The study done by Dr. Lewis Sherman from the University of Missouri showed that women officers showed more patience than male officers.   T or F

64. The above study showed that women officers, when responding to family fights, tended to have fewer repeat calls.   T or F

65. The legal basis for female patrol officers is:

    a. _ LEAA   b. _ LEEP
    c. _ Title VII of the Civil Rights Act 1964   d. _ POST

66. Another legal basis for female patrol officers is the "equal protection" clause of the _____ Amendment.

67. These laws not only apply to women, but to minorities as well.   T or F

68. The important U.S. Supreme Court case, University of California v. Allan Bakke, deals with:

    a. _ women police officers.   b. _ entrance tests for policemen.
    c. _ reverse discrimination   d. _ police physical agility tests.

CHAPTER V

PREPARATION FOR PATROL

An officer who does not properly prepare for patrol duty is not only doing the community a disservice, but is actually increasing the possibility of danger while on duty. By failing to obtain information about a wanted and dangerous person, the officer may later stop that person and be shot in the back, solely because of a lack of being forewarned of this particular danger.

Fig. V-1; Officers in squad room, San Francisco Police Department, 1932

It is as important for a police officer to prepare for duty as it is for a surgeon to prepare for an operation. In reality, they both can begin their tasks without any preparation. But if quality and results are important as they are in both cases, then any information or awareness gained through preparation is time well spent.

It has been long observed by supervisors in the field, that there is a definite relationship between the ability to perform, and the amount of time spent in preparation. Just when does this preparedness start? Preparation for patrol duty should start before the officer leaves home.

WHAT TO CHECK BEFORE LEAVING HOME

Many times an officer lives some distance from the police department, so it is important to stop for a minute, just before leaving for work, and make sure that he or she has everything that will be needed. Some of the following are things that are most commonly forgotten:

(1) **Check shoes and socks for color** Quite often an officer, being in a hurry or almost late, will rush out of the house wearing brown shoes and socks when the uniform requires black shoes and socks. Shoes should always be shined. This takes time and should not be a last minute task.

(2) **Off duty gun** A check should be made for the off duty gun if the department requires that it be worn to and from work. It is easy to forget.

(3) **Writing implements** An officer should always have at least two writing implements in case one should run out of ink. If it looks like rain, a pencil should be carried to write citations, as this eliminates the problem of running ink.

(4) **Wristwatch** If an officer has been working in the garden or has just taken a shower, a watch is easy to forget. If it is a spring-type watch, it should be wound just before leaving the house. The officer should make this habit automatic.

(5) **Fingernails** Check fingernails and have a fingernail file. Police officers are looked upon by the general public as "White Collar" workers. They are expected to have a clean and neat appearance before the public. A fingernail file will help an officer's appearance. Sometimes an officer will be involved in a dirty job just before going to work, such as working in the garden or on a car. Time must be allowed to properly clean up. Dirty grease may be removed from under the fingernails by use of a fingernail file and one of the special cleaning compounds containing a special detergent. Merely washing the hands in this compound is not enough. The compound must be worked under the nail with the fingernail file.

(6) **Shave** Male officers who work at different hours around the clock might shave in the morning and then forget to shave again before they start the afternoon shift. It is not too noticeable at first, but by the end of the shift, it becomes quite noticeable. Officers should make it a habit to look in the mirror and rub their faces for the feel of whiskers just before leaving for work.

(7) **Lunch** When an officer is married and his or her spouse is nice enough to make a lunch, it can be dangerous to forget it. He or she will not only have to buy lunch, but will be in trouble when getting home. No one likes to perform a task for nothing. With all of the things to remember before leaving for duty, it is easy to forget something.

(8) **Forms** At times an officer will take home a form or file so that it can be properly filled out and returned. Because of a busy shift, or overtime, the officer feels that more time is needed to do the job properly. Sometimes a court notice is taken home so that it may be recorded on a wall calendar. Care must be exercised to see that it is signed and returned to the District Attorney if required by policy. It is best to place all forms and similar materials in one set location near the front door, and to form the habit of checking that location each time when leaving for work.

(9) **Fresh Uniforms** Fresh uniforms from the cleaners should be taken to the officer's locker as soon as possible. Sometimes an emergency occurs, such as a flood or searching a dirty building, in which the officer's uniform becomes too wet or dirty to wear in public. This requires changing into a clean uniform, and there should always be one handy.

CHECKOUT BEFORE LEAVING THE LOCKER ROOM

When the officer is dressed, certain items should be checked before leaving the locker room. An officer would be wise to make a typewritten list and tape it to the inside of the locker so that it may be quickly checked off mentally just before leaving for the squad room.

When we are in a hurry, pressure tends to make us forget things. If we make it an automatic habit to read the list each day, it will insure our preparedness.

(1) **Check the locker calendar** Every officer should have a large calendar on the inside of the locker door. It should be the type with large blocks for each date, so important items can be written in the squares. The following are examples of what should be indicated on the calendar.

(a) **Uniform cleaning** An officer's uniform should be cleaned every so many days. It should not be left to the officer to decide when the uniform needs cleaning, for when it looks dirty, it is too late. Since time goes by fast, the calendar will help the officer remember.

(b) **Haircuts** Although styles of hair do change, many departments allow their officers some leeway by allowing longer styles of hair. It should be noted that the Supreme Court ruled that a police department can set hair standards as a condition of employment. The key is not so much the length as it is how neat it looks. The author is very aware of how important it is for young people to maintain contemporary hair styles. He has observed good students, with long hair, change their college majors after giving full consideration to the fact that they would have to cut their long hair to become an officer. Long hair can have some tactical disadvantages. An officer who becomes involved in a fight can find himself or herself being swung around by the hair. In one fight, in which the author was involved, a heavily built construction worker grabbed another officer by the hair and swung him "every which way but loose." The next day the officer cut his hair.

It should be remembered that a peace officer is a public servant. He or she has sworn an oath to serve the community. This community does have some expectations about the appearance of peace officers. Whatever the length and style of an officer's hair, it does require certain care and trimming, and this should be done on a regular basis. One way for an officer to insure this, is to use a calendar to indicate the last time it was trimmed.

(c) **Locker cleaning** An officer's locker should be cleaned out once a month. If this is done, it becomes a fairly easy job. The officer may also find important papers that have become lost in the pile of other papers. Time slips by fast, and it is nothing for a year to go by without accomplishing this task. Then it becomes a monumental duty, and important papers are found that can no longer help the officer or are outdated. It is a "stitch in time saves nine" affair. If an officer spends a little time at regular intervals straightening out his or her locker, it will be found that much time is saved looking for things.

(d) **Court dates** As soon as the officer receives a court notice or subpoena, the date should be indicated on the locker calendar. Then every time the locker is opened, it is there to be seen as a reminder.

(e) **Other important dates** One way to maintain good personal relations with those you love or respect, is to remember them on special dates such as birthdays, wedding anniversaries and other important dates. The locker calendar can remind you to get a card for this person during lunch break or on the way home.

Before you throw away the old calendar, be sure to transfer these important dates to the new one. This calendar could also help you to remember doctor and dentist appointments. A good businessman lives by his date calendar. A good police officer should rely on it.

THE POLICE OFFICER'S LOCKER

The policeman's locker is a personal office and storeroom. If everything is in the locker that should be there, it must be neat. If one were to list all the items that an officer might need in the field or during an emergency, it would take a small moving van to hold them, but the following list contains some basic items.

(1) **An extra uniform** Having a uniform ripped or torn is an occupational hazard for the police officer. Therefore an extra one in the locker can be smart. Since it is for emergencies, it need not be one of the best, but one that is still serviceable.

(2) **Black shoes and socks** Since an officer is human and can sometimes come to work wearing brown shoes and yellow socks, there should be an extra pair of black shoes and socks.(or matching whatever uniform the department has). There are times when an officer is away on business and does not have time to return home to change shoes.

(3) **Batteries, flashlight bulbs and an extra flashlight lens** Some departments provide flashlight batteries, but not the bulbs and lens. yet because of the dangerous nature of the work, an officer's flashlight receives many broken lenses and bulbs. Sometimes at night these items are hard to obtain, so there should be spares in the locker.

(4) **Extra ammunition** With the increasing possibility of a police officer becoming involved in a shooting, it is important to keep extra ammunition in the locker. It would be embarrassing for an officer to have to go home for more ammunition after being involved in a gun battle.

(5) **Extra handkerchiefs** In the field, an officer has many uses for a handkerchief. Therefore extras should be stored in the locker.

(6) **Shoe laces** Few officers stop to think of the consequences if one of their shoe laces were to break in a couple of places, especially when chasing someone. The best insurance against this is to change them regularly. Traffic signals seldom burn out because they are replaced on a regular schedule before their expected life runs out. An officer should do the same with shoe laces. They are so inexpensive and yet so important. Some officers carry a spare set with them in their duty briefcase.

(7) **Shaving gear and toothbrush** When emergencies and special duties arise, such as stakeouts, a male officer might be called to work overtime. Should this occur it would be well for the officer to have a simple and economical safety razor in his locker. The same applies to a toothbrush and toothpaste. Female officers should be prepared for similar emergencies.

(8) **Thermos bottle** A thermos bottle can be a godsend when an officer is given an unexpected stakeout assignment. On the way to the stakeout he or she can stop off and have the thermos filled with coffee. Stakeouts are usually at night and can last a long time.

(9) **A wide-mouthed jug or jar** A wide mouthed jug or jar can be well appreciated if the officer is assigned to an unexpected stakeout where there are no toilet facilities, especially if a thermos of coffee is brought along. A mayonnaise jar of the quart size should do the trick. Stakeouts are often assigned to a patrol officer on a moment's no-tice, and can last beyond the normal shift.

(10) **Suit of underwear** There are times when an officer will fall into water, or jump in, to save someone's life. In areas prone to floods, an officer might have to wade through water. In these cases, especially if it is in the win-ter, an extra set of underwear back at headquarters will be most welcome.

(11) **Extra notebook paper and pen refills** These items do not cost much, yet many officers who have been in policework for a while have had the unfortunate experience of unexpectedly running out. They take up little space, so if they are never needed, there is little loss. They should also be carried in the duty brief case.

(12) **Plastic raincoat** At times the weather can change quite suddenly, A plastic raincoat has several advantages. First, it can be folded into a very small package. Secondly, it is so thin that an officer can actually grab a holstered weapon, draw it and fire it from the inside of the raincoat. Another advantage is that because it is clear, the uniform and badge show underneath the raincoat. Some departments require that officers wear the heavy yellow rain gear because it can be more easily seen by motorists.

(13) **Handcuff key and whistle** If these items are carried on the belt snap, they are probably the most often lost items of police equipment. Because they are quite essential when they are needed, spares should be kept in the officer's locker and duty briefcase.

WHEN THE OFFICER IS IN UNIFORM AND READY TO GO TO THE SQUAD ROOM

When the officer is in uniform and is ready to go to the squad room, stand in front of a mirror and check for the following items before leaving.

(1) Is the badge on the uniform?

(2) Is the gun in the holster?

(3) Do the shoes match the uniform?

(4) If a tie is required, is it on? (with a black uniform and tie, it is often hard to notice.)

(5) Does the officer have a flashlight and baton?

(6) Does the officer have a hat, if required?

The novice might laugh and say that this is silly, but these are the main areas of forgetfulness among patrol officers. It is quite embarrassing to enter a squadroom full of fellow officers and have them laughingly ask you which cab company you work for because one of these items is missing.

(7) Writing implements (always carry two in case one runs out).

(8) Citation book and street map.

Before you leave the locker room, stop and look at yourself in the full length mirror by the door and ask yourself "ARE YOU PROUD OF YOUR APPEARANCE." If not, why not. If you can find some fault in your appearance, you can be sure that the public will. In fact the public will find fault in your appearance and uniform before you will, so be very critical.

Deputy Dale E. Curry, of the Santa Barbara County Sheriff's Office, has conducted an extensive study of the killing of peace officers. His study included interviews with men in prison who had shot officers. One point of inquiry was the decision of the criminal as to whether or not he should shoot. His inquiry revealed that an officer's appearance has a lot to do with this decision. He was told that if an officer appeared to be sharp in his appearance, the chances were that he was also a "sharp" shooter. If he appeared to be sloppy in dress and appearance, he was probably also a sloppy shooter, and the odds were therefore in favor of the criminal. Remember, it is a rare criminal who is not also a gambler. He is always considering the odds when making an important decision such as whether or not to shoot. Personal appearance then has more value than just personal pride and self respect.

Fig. V-2; Officers in squad room, LAPD, 1990

OBTAINING THE NECESSARY INFORMATION FOR PATROL DUTY

You should arrive at the squad room, dressed for duty, at least twenty minutes before the watch begins. If it is a large watch section, some officers go to the squad room early before getting dressed, and read the reports at least ten minutes before the briefing begins. In order to obtain the information necessary to properly prepare for duty, the officer should take the following steps.

(1) **Mail slots or box** An officer should first look in the personal mail slot or folder before entering the squad room. There could be important messages or court notices. If there are court notices, they should be taken to the records unit so a copy can be made of all the reports involved in the case. By the time the officer is ready to go out on duty they may have been copied and be ready for pick up.

(2) **Daily Offense Bulletin** The daily offense bulletin lists the basic and minimum information for each crime committed within the last twenty-four hours. In large departments, when it is an important case on or near the officer's beat, he or she can take the case number and later look up the complete report. In smaller departments, it is expected that all reports be read by all officers.

(3) **Beat File (or Offense Report File)** In smaller departments the Offense Report File contains copies of all the offense reports. In larger departments, there are too many offense reports for each officer to read them all. They are therefore divided up by beat, and put in a beat file. If an officer has time after reading the reports for the assigned beat, those for adjoining beats can be read. If it is the first day back to work, the officer should arrive earlier in order to read the reports covering the days off.

(4) **Bulletin Board** The bulletin board should be checked once a day, preferably at the beginning of the watch. The bulletin board usually contains the following sections:

(a) **Training** Roll call bulletins. Latest developments. Special classes.

(b) **Range Schedule** Who goes to the range, at what time, and on what date.

(c) **Hit and Run Information** Descriptions of hit and run accidents and possible vehicles.

(d) **Watch Notices and Schedules** Who is assigned to what watch.

(e) **Cases Cleared** Supplementary reports listing arrests and crimes cleared by arrest.

(f) **Announcements** Any new announcements for the patrol division as a whole.

(g) **Wanted Persons** Descriptions and mug shots of wanted persons.

(h) **Orders** This section lists all of the Special, General, and Division orders.

(i) **Well Done** Letters of recommendation and commendation for patrol officers.

(5) **Annexations** With population increases, most communities are undergoing rapid changes in their borders. Once an area is annexed into a particular jurisdiction, that jurisdiction is immediately responsible for offering the area police protection. It is therefore important that the patrol officer continually check the Annexation file to see if new territory has been added to the beat.

(6) **Missing Persons** Descriptions of missing persons should be jotted down in the officer's notebook, especially those involving persons who live, or hang out on the beat.

(7) **Daily Arrest Sheet** The daily arrest sheet contains the names of all persons arrested during the last 24 hours, and the offenses for which they were arrested. Sometimes it lists pertinent information about them. This can provide the patrol officer with valuable information because it tells which criminals are in town, and can give hints as to who might have been committing crimes on the beat.

DAILY BULLETIN

VOLUME 52	BULLETIN 171	PAGE TWO	8-3-95
CASE #	BEAT #	WATCH COMMANDER – G. SMITH	OFFICER ASSIGNED

N-84031
PETTY THEFT
18
(8-3-95 - 21:30 Hrs)
John F. KARRAS, 541 S 14th St., reports instamatic camera taken from parked car behind BERNIE'S PIZZA, 458 Jackson St.
LOPEZ

N-84033
FORCIBLE RAPE
9
(8-3-95 - 19:00 Hrs)
Alice B. FIZZER, 1650 Melody Ln. Victim of forcible rape by son-in-law, Arvin DUDLEY.
SMITH

N-84034
PEEPING TOM
11
(8-3-95 - 20:35 Hrs)
Sally RAND, 958 N. Runway, reports that when she got out of shower, a tall male was looking at her through bathroom window. Desc. WMA, 30's, 6', 175, BRN, Brn. "V" has seen "S" in neighborhood before.
PAYTON

N-84035
BURGL.
20
(8-3-95 - 21:36 Hrs)
WILSON LUMBER CO. 940 Sunol, reports burglary. The company was closed for remodeling. $300 and adding machine (# 3087932) taken. Entry—front door.
PERRY

N-84029
INJURED PERS.
5
(8-3-95 - 15:30 Hrs)
Tommy WOOSTER, 10 yrs., 4460 Mt. Wilson Dr. fell from swing at Happy Hollow City Park. Taken to County Hospital for X-rays.
HARRIS

N-84032
BATTERY
1
(8-3-95 - 21:30 Hrs)
Harold HORTON, 349 Willow Ave. victim of battery at Last Hole Bar, 385 Lexon St. Perpetrator, John L. SULLIVAN, left bar after fight. Has long record for battery.
SANCHEZ

N-84036
ADW
13
(8-3-95 - 22:00 Hrs)
Manuel GONZALES, 2154 Tremont St. During birthday party, his cousin, Jose GONZALES stabbed him after short argument. Taken to County Hospital. Jose GONZALES booked at County Jail.
JUAREZ

NOTE**
12
Bill SELLERS, 4960 Clover, is going on vacation for 5 days. House broken into last two times he has left for over two days. Suspects local kids.
WILSON

N-84028
IND. EXPOS.
20
(8-3-95 - 15:00 Hrs)
Helen BIGLUBS, 849 N 22nd, reports while she was in branch library at 22nd St., a WMA 40, 6', 175, BLK, Brn. Blue trousers, yellow shirt exposed himself in NW corner of 2nd floor stacks.
PERRY

N-84030
MISSING JUV.
18
(8-3-95 - 19:20 Hrs)
Linda Marie JULIAN, WF 16 yrs, 4830 Golf Dr. left house after fight with mother, Mrs. Gloria WILFORTH. 5'4", 110, Blu slacks, W sweater, Brn shoes.
LOPEZ

(8) **Computer Printouts** Computer printouts should be scanned for wanted persons and warnings to the local area that certain criminals might be in their area, or headed that way. Lists of stolen property from nearby areas can also be important. Should there be a notice of a wanted person who lives or possibly visits on the officer's beat, a mug shot of the person should be obtained from Records and Identification. Any teletypes that are specially directed to the officer are usually put in his or her mail slot.

(9) **Pin Maps.** Most modern police departments keep up to date pin maps on major offenses, or those that are becoming a nuisance. Since an officer works only part of the twenty-four hour day, and not seven days a week, The whole, overall picture can be difficult to perceive based just on personal experience. The pin map and spot map are good devices for showing patterns in criminal activity. An officer can profit greatly by keeping abreast of criminal patterns that are beat oriented and anticipating the criminal's next move.

(10) **Instructions from the watch sergeant** At about ten minutes before the watch starts, or twenty minutes before, if roll call training is to be given, the watch sergeant reads the latest orders and instructions, and relates any recent criminal information just obtained from police communications by phone, including the most recent hot cars and cancellations. Roll is then taken.

(11) **Obtaining needed forms** The modern police officer uses a multitude of forms for various reports and accident investigations. It is therefore important to make sure that the officer's beat brief case has an ample supply for the coming watch. There are also certain books that should be carried, such as the Penal Code, Vehicle Code and some type of a peace officer handbook.

(12) **Shotgun** If an officer is required to carry a shotgun, it should be picked up on the way to the car. In departments that keep their shotguns stored in the police building, it should be remembered that they SHOULD NEVER BE LOADED IN THE BUILDING.

They should be loaded next to the patrol car, but never in the car. Both hands should be used for loading the shotgun, and the barrel should always be pointing up. More shotguns are accidentally fired than any other police weapon. The shotgun ammunition should be carefully checked. Loading and unloading shells for each watch tends to wear the paper out, and this can cause a jam. The plastic casings are better.

INSPECTION

It would be nice if police officers would, of their own accord, keep their uniforms clean and their equipment in proper shape. Many of them do. But police officers are human beings, and some tend to rationalize their way out of any extra work at times. because of this, they need someone to apply a little pressure as far as their uniform and appearance is concerned. Nothing will do this like an inspection. Some human beings, when judging themselves, tend to be a little bit lenient, and it is easy for some officers to convince themselves that their uniforms could probably go two more days before needing to be cleaned. This can also apply to hair grooming. It is so easy to say that it can probably get by until payday. When faced with a daily inspection, the officer tends to be more realistic in self evaluation, especially when faced with the possibility of being chastised in front of fellow officers.

LEAVING THE SQUAD ROOM

Should the police vehicles be located outside the building or in another building, the officers of the new watch should try and maintain a military bearing while they are en route to their police vehicles. It looks quite bad for a group of men in uniform to be "clomping" along like a herd of apes. Some departments require that the watch actually march to their vehicles in a military formation. The larger the watch, the greater is the need for this military bearing and uniformity in movement.

CHECKING OUT THE VEHICLE BEFORE LEAVING THE GARAGE

The law requires that ALL drivers make sure that their vehicle is in proper condition before they drive it. Many times an officer will neglect this duty because it is a city vehicle and a city mechanic is supposed to keep it in proper running condition. It should be remembered that few vehicles undergo rougher treatment than a police car. A car could be in top condition at eight am and need major repairs at midnight. Apart from the fact that it is a legal requirement, an officer should properly check the vehicle for the following reasons:

(1) This is an emergency vehicle and is likely to be operated under emergency conditions. Faulty equipment or conditions may result in an officer's death. Most people think of the criminal as presenting the greatest danger to the police officer, but automobiles take a greater toll than do criminals.

(2) At times an officer can slightly damage the vehicle while on patrol. Sometimes it is just a scratch on the paint. It is possible that the officer is not aware of the damage. At the end of the shift the vehicle is returned to the police garage without a mention of vehicle damage. If the next officer to get the vehicle does not properly check it out, he or she can be easily blamed, and possibly charged for the damage. This should be such a habit that it is automatic, without any thought involved.

When the officer has checked the vehicle and found it to be in proper order, the following things should be done:

(1) Adjust the seat and rear view mirror.

(2) Adjust the seat belt and fasten it.

(3) Record the speedometer mileage on the vehicle radio log.

(4) Record the date, the beat assigned, and the car number.

(5) Notify communications that the vehicle is in service and ready for calls.

VEHICLE CARE

Before an officer takes a police vehicle out in the field, he or she should have some training in vehicle care. Many officers feel that since it is not their vehicle and since they are not paying for the gas, that they need have no concern for these matters. Nothing could be further from the truth. As a taxpayer, the officer is in fact paying for the gasoline used. More important is the fact that a police chief receives only so much money for the department's yearly budget. If a considerable sum of it must be spent on unnecessary gasoline and vehicle repair bills, it greatly reduces the chance of an increase in wages or benefits for the police officer. The following are some of the ways in which an officer can cut down on gasoline and vehicle repairs.

(1) Drive as if the vehicle is the officer's own.

(2) See that the tires are properly inflated. This can increase gas mileage by about one mile per gallon and decrease the possibility of a blowout. Since the average mileage for a police vehicle is around 11 mpg, an increase of one mpg would amount to a 10% saving. A 10% saving in gasoline for a department of any size can be quite a lot.

(3) Avoid quick starts and stops unless it is an emergency.

(4) Do not idle the engine too long. This is the greatest consumer of gasoline. If a vehicle is parked for over two minutes in a non-emergency situation, the engine should be turned off and the radio switched to battery. (In many cars this is automatic.) Often, two officers will meet for a conference and will both leave their engines idle for a half hour or more. It is also common for an officer who is "sandbagging" a stop sign for traffic violators to park with the engine idling. If things are slow, the engine will not only burn a lot of gas, but will often heat up to the point where it will stall when the officer takes off after the violator. Field sergeants can usually check on the amount of time that a police vehicle has been idling by the heat gauge and by the amount of water dripping from the bottom of the radiator when the car starts off.

VEHICLE RADIO LOG					
MILAGE					
OUT	12541				
IN	12460	DATE	CAR#	BEAT	SHIFT
TOTAL	81	2-11-95	51	B-14	SWING
TIME IN	TIME OUT	OFF-ENSE	LOCATION & INFORMATION		
16:15	16:30	10·70	314 S 2ND· MISS S. RAND - GOA		
17:05	17:50	11·82	1ST & VIRGINIA - FORM 16 ON FILE		
18:00	18:50	10·51	3RD & ST JAMES· ARR. JOE WALL WM-45		
19:30	20:00	Code 7	MANNY'S 6TH & WILSON		
20:30	20:45	10·70	1120 N JACKSON· MRS L. HARRIS GOA		
21:10	21:20	10·51	3RD & ST JOHN - UNABLE TO LOCATE		
21:45	22:30	415·F	270 JOLSON - ARR BILL JARVIS - NM- 40		
23:00	23:40	415	JOE'S BAR - S 1ST - ARR · JOHN BARR WM-50		
23:45	23:55	CITE	BILL LAKE - RUNNING STOP SIGN - 5TH & JAY		
	24:00	OD			

REMARKS & OTHER INFORMATION:

17:55 STOLEN JKR-459 - 85 CHEV SW W/GRN HEAVY DENT RR DOOR

20:55 MISSING WFJ-15 JANE WILBER 5'6" - 110 - BRN - BLU - RED SWEATER, PINK SKIRT WHITE SHOES. FREQUENTS WINCHELL'S ON MERIDIAN

Fig. V-4; Vehicle Radio Log

EMERGENCY VEHICLE PROCEDURES

The operation of an emergency vehicle is so important that police academies now heavily stress the techniques involved in high speed driving. All officers should have a good basic knowledge of the procedures and laws pertaining to emergency driving. Emergency driving presents a great danger to the police officer, and can also present a danger to the general public. This issue has become so important from a political standpoint, that some cities are planning to eliminate "hot pursuits" in heavily populated areas. An officer under great pressure must often make split second decisions based upon a legal term which may have taken the courts a considerable time to interpret. Since the majority of police car accidents occur during an officer's first year, departments are pursuing more intensive training programs in the area of emergency driving for new officers.

The average new officer, when first hired, often has the mistaken belief that the criminal is the greatest danger in policework. Later, it is learned (and often the hard way) that this dubious honor belongs to the vehicle and modern traffic rather than the criminal.

The National Safety Council recently reported that more Americans have died in accidents on our streets and highways than on all of the battlefields on which we have fought since the war of 1812. Since the beginning of the century, there have been 1.9 million deaths from traffic accidents compared to 648,952 combat deaths in the last nine major wars.

The nine major wars and their battle fatalities were:

War of 1812	2,260
Revolutionary War	4,435
Mexican War	1,733
Civil War	214,938
Spanish-American War	385
World War 1	53,513
World War 2	292,131
Korean War	33,629
Vietnam War	45,928
Total	648,952

WHAT IS AN EMERGENCY VEHICLE?

The Vehicle Code of each state will define an emergency vehicle. Officers can make a safe assumption that the police car they drive will come under this classification. An emergency vehicle is usually exempt from regular traffic laws (called Rules of the Road) when it is displaying acceptable red (or in some cases blue) lights AND the driver sounds a siren.

If the communications officer declares the call to be an emergency and recommends that the officer respond to the call code 3, the officer to whom the call is directed is fully protected from a legal standpoint. This is true even if it turns out that the call really did not justify that classification, and a collision resulted. To use the words of one state appellate court, "The officer has the right to believe the information he receives to be true and to act accordingly." (36 CA 2d 244) Most states allow a police car to violate traffic laws when in pursuit of a suspected violator. However, the burden of proof is on the officer to show that there was more than just mere suspicion. There should be some set condition or overt act that would cause a normal reasonable, prudent person to believe the suspect had violated some law.

FIRE ALARMS

Police cars do not normally respond to fire alarms under code three conditions. Their own sirens might drown out the siren of an approaching fire engine and a serious collision could occur at a blind intersection. Code two is sufficient for police vehicles since it is not a split second emergency.

CIVIL LIABILITY

Most states provide legal protection against civil liability when damage or injury results from an emergency response that is in the line of duty. The most common conditions for this exemption are:

(1) Red light (or blue light) and siren are used.

(2) The officer is pursuing an actual or suspected violator.

(3) It is a response to (but not from) a fire.

CRIMINAL LIABILITY

The above conditions do not excuse an officer from criminal liability if it can be shown that the officer was criminally negligent. What this means is that even though the officer is protected, the protection ceases when he or she fails to employ good sense or is obviously negligent and careless in the operation of the vehicle. Negligent operation by the driver of a police vehicle can result in a judgment against the city, and the city can, in turn, recover the monies from the officer through civil suit.

THE DUTY OF A MOTORIST TO YIELD THE RIGHT OF WAY.

A motorist must yield the right of way to a police vehicle ONLY WHEN HE OR SHE HAS KNOWLEDGE OF ITS APPROACH. They are under no obligation to anticipate its approach. This would be too difficult to enforce and would not be just. REMEMBER, A DEAF PERSON CAN OBTAIN A DRIVER'S LICENSE. (They are usually better drivers, since they make up for their lack of hearing by being overly alert.)

THE TIME DIFFERENCE BETWEEN CODE 2 AND CODE 3

In a study conducted by the author, it was found that a vehicle going code three through the city from one end to the other (not using freeways), arrived at the other side less than one minute ahead of another vehicle going code two. An officer must

be aware of the true purpose of the red light and siren. That purpose is to minimize traffic delay. It is not a magic plow that creates a path in the traffic ahead as some new officers believe.

DANGEROUS FACTORS INVOLVED IN CODE THREE DRIVING

One of the reasons that new officers become involved in so many traffic accidents in their vehicles is because they don't fully understand the limitations involved in such driving. The following are some factors that must be taken into consideration:

(1) **Siren Audibility.** Even with the window down, the average motorist can only hear an under-the-hood siren for about 1000 feet IF THE VEHICLE IS STRAIGHT AHEAD. If it is to the side, the distance is cut by half. The electronic external siren is over twice as loud as the under-the-hood siren. In order to increase audibility, the officer should always vary the cycle of the siren rather than keep it at a high pitch. Most siren controls have a switch for varied responses. The electronic sirens are very good in this respect, especially the "warbler" or similar type sirens.

A study conducted by the Acoustical Society of America discovered that when the average driver is sitting in his car with the windows open, and a siren is heard, three out of four times, there is confusion about the direction of the siren.

Fig. V-5; Smashed police vehicle due to unsafe code three driving; driver saved by seat belt

(2) Sound Barriers. Modern cities present a multitude of barriers that reduce the audibility of police sirens. Some of them are:

(a) Buildings.

(b) Background noises such as traffic, industry or even heavy rain.

(c) Personal hearing limitations.

(d) Automobile insulation. (Windows rolled up reduce audibility by about one third.)

(e) Radio in the automobile. (Especially if the music is loud.)

(f) Children playing or fighting in back seat.

(g) Arguing spouse.

(h) Motor noise and body noise.

(i) Sound-proofed automobiles. Ford advertises a car which can shut out railroad noise with rolled up windows. Fire departments are increasingly concerned about this condition as fewer drivers hear even their air horns.

DIFFICULTY IN STOPPING

Many departments are now conducting special courses in defensive driving. Telephone companies have been successfully giving these courses to their personnel for years. One area of instruction involves a marking device that fires a yellow powder charge into the street when the brakes of the vehicle are applied, and again when it has stopped. It gives the driver some idea of how long it takes to stop while driving at various speeds. To some, this distance comes as quite a shock. In city driving, there are many blind intersections. This greatly increases the chance of an intersection collision. One must consider the time it takes in applying brakes, and then coming to a complete stop. A police car traveling at 60 miles per hour is going about 88 feet per second. One traveling at 45 miles per hour is going about 66 feet per second. When one takes into consideration the width of the average street, it soon becomes obvious that even driving under the most cautious code three conditions, an officer would not be able to stop before the vehicle had completely gone through the intersection.

PASSING OTHER VEHICLES WHEN GOING CODE THREE

(1) Always pass on the left. The vehicle might hear your siren at the last minute and suddenly pull to the right into your path.

(2) Be careful that you do not follow other emergency vehicles too closely. A vehicle that has yielded for the first emergency vehicle might suddenly pull back into the lane when the other vehicle has passed, and can sideswipe your vehicle.

(3) Use the siren sparingly when passing. The motorist can panic and cause a traffic hazard. Use the emergency lights and, if the driver doesn't see them, use the horn, especially in the daytime. If it is night, use the spotlight, but don't flash it on the rear view mirror. It may blind the driver and cause an accident, and the officer could be liable.

CAUTION IS AN ESSENTIAL PART OF EMERGENCY DRIVING

Appellate courts have decided that an officer can be sued when it is shown that the accident could have reasonably been prevented. This is true even though the officer had the right-of-way. For example, an officer sees a vehicle ahead, but because he or she has the legal right-of-way, no effort is made to drive around or avoid that vehicle, and an accident occurs, the officer could be liable. An officer is required to use extreme caution when driving an emergency vehicle under emergency conditions. Automobile manufacturers are building faster and more powerful automobiles and more of them, but the human body is still the same.

IT IS IMPORTANT TO REMEMBER AT ALL TIMES WHEN DRIVING, EMERGENCY OR NOT, THAT THE FOLLOWING EPITAPH WILL BE OF LITTLE CONSOLATION TO AN OFFICER'S FAMILY.

OFFICER SMITH

HE HAD THE RIGHT OF WAY

STUDY QUESTIONS for Patrol Operations

CHAPTER 5

1. When should "preparation for patrol duty" start? _____

2. An officer should always carry two _____.

3. The general public looks upon police officers as _____ collar workers.

4. The United States Supreme Court ruled that a police department can set hair standards   T or F
   as a condition of employment.

5. The community has certain set standards of appearance that they expect of their officers.   T or F

6. Which of the following items should be stored in an officer's locker?

   a._ batteries for his flashlight   b._extra handkerchiefs
   c._ shoe laces   d._all of these

7. Why should an officer keep a wide-mouth mayonnaise jar in his locker?
   _____

8. Name an item on an officer's belt snap that is often lost? _____

9. It is common for an officer to leave the locker room with something missing.
   Name one item. _____

10. Dale Curry did a study of criminals who shot officers. What did he discover about the way
    an officer's appearance affected criminals? _____
    _____

11. What is the map called that has pins or spots showing the locations of individual crimes?
    _____

12. In case an emergency should arise outside, it is wise to load the shotgun before leaving   T or F
    the building.

13. There is a very good practical reason for checking the outside of your police car before leaving
    the garage. It is _____.

14. Keeping the tires of a police car properly inflated can increase the mileage by _____
    mile(s) per gallon.

15. The greatest consumer of gasoline in a patrol car is _____.

16. The criminal is not an officer's greatest hazard, it is the _____.

17. More people have been killed in the United States in traffic accidents than in all our wars since the War of 1812.   T or F

18. An emergency vehicle is usually exempt from regular traffic laws when the emergency light is displayed and _____.

19. Communications mistakenly gives a call that is classed as "Code 3", and an accident occurs.   T or F
Later it is determined that the call should have been "Code 2". The officer is responsible.

20. Why do police cars seldom respond to fire alarms Code 3? _____

21. Fire engines can respond "Code 3" when leaving a fire or even when changing stations.   T or F

22. As far as civil liability is concerned, an officer is exempt when (1) responding Code 3 (2) responding to a fire, or (3) _____.

23. These conditions do not excuse an officer from criminal liability if it can be shown that the officer was _____ in his or her actions.

24. When does a motorist have the legal duty to yield the right of way? _____

25. A deaf person can obtain a driver's license.   T or F

26. The Acoustical Society of America discovered that the average driver is confused about the direction of a siren _____ out of _____ times.

27. Name three things that will interfere with a driver's ability to hear a police siren.
(1) _____ (2) _____ (3) _____

28. An automobile traveling at 60 MPH is going about _____ feet per second.

29. An automobile traveling at 45 MPH is going about _____ feet per second.

30. When going "Code 3" an officer can pass on the right safely.   T or F

31. Heavy use of the siren can panic some motorists.   T or F

32. Because the siren might cause a motorist to panic, it is best to stop a normal traffic violator by shining your spotlight on the back of the rear window and the rear view mirror. However, it should not be left on the rear view mirror too long because _____
_____.

33. Why is having the "right-of-way" not the most important thing in the long run? _____
_____

CHAPTER VI

POLICE COMMUNICATIONS

HISTORY

Communications has always been a part of law enforcement. Since man's existence on this earth, there has been a need for a system by which one person could warn another of existing or pending danger. There was also a need for some way to send messages to members of a nearby group.

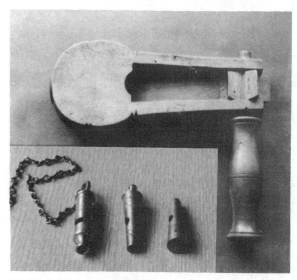
Fig. VI-2; Photo of rattle and whistles

Fig. VI-1, Warning bell used in colonial times

In primitive times, the pounding of hollow logs or the beating of animal skin drums was used to convey a message. Later, man discovered that when he cut the tip from the horn of an animal and blew through it, the sound carried for quite a distance. We find its use mentioned throughout the Bible, and it was certainly the main warning instrument used in the "Hue and Cry" even into the twelfth century. In the Orient, the brass gong and finally the bell, became the warning instrument.

In western civilization, until very recently, the church bell, high in the steeple, not only called the people to church services, but warned the town or village of imminent dangers. The American Indian used smoke signals, bird calls and drums in his effort to communicate and send out warnings. In the history of Anglo-American police patrol, we find the horn replaced by the hand-bell and rattle, and then the metal whistle. (see Fig. VI-2, prev. pg)

Police communications are the backbone of police tactics. Without proper communications, the modern police department would be lost. When police vehicles were first used, there was no radio communication as we know it today. The system of notifying patrol vehicles of emergencies and calls for service was handled by the installation of red lights at the major intersections of the town or city. When headquarters wanted to contact a police car, they would pull a switch. It would send power to the red lights at the intersections. The next time the patrol car passed the intersection and saw the red light on, he would drive to headquarters for the assignment. When telephones became more common, the officer would call headquarters when he observed the light signal.

Fig VI-3; FCC Symbol

When radios were first installed in police vehicles, they were usually just receivers and did not have transmitters for answering the calls. The radio operator would broadcast the call and hope that it was received.

The police have always been keenly aware of the importance of communication, and because of this, they, along with the military, have been leaders in the development and adoption of new methods of communication. In the early days of electronic communication the departments themselves had to develop their own communications equipment because there was little or no commercial equipment available to suit police needs. Today the situation is different. Because of military and space development programs, the police are able to readily adapt existing commercial equipment to their needs. This has the great advantage of eliminating the many years of costly and time consuming experiments and failures that the early police departments had to suffer in their development of police communications. A brief history of the development of police communications is as follows:

1877 The Albany New York Police Department installed five telephones in the mayor's office connected to precinct stations. This was only two years after Alexander Graham Bell developed the telephone. This indicates how quickly the police saw the value of the telephone and how promptly it was utilized as a tool of law enforcement.

1880 The Chicago Police Department installed the first "Police Call Box" on a city street. Only officers and "reputable citizens" were given keys to the booth. Before this time a signal box was used that would signal the emergency without voice communications. Detroit made such installations in 1884 and Indianapolis in 1895.

A code wheel was installed in the box so that when the beat man called in for his time check, it would register at headquarters with the proper signal for that call box. This insured that the beat officer was in fact at the location from which he claimed to be calling

1883 The Detroit, Michigan Police Department installed one police telephone. This was significant when one considers the fact that there were only seven telephones in the whole city at that time. In 1889 the department established a new division to handle communications. It was called the Police Signal Bureau.

1916 The New York Harbor Police installed spark transmitters so they could communicate with their police boats while they were patrolling the harbor. This also enabled them to communicate with other boats and ships in the harbor.

1923 The Pennsylvania State Police installed point-to-point radio telegraph between their headquarters and various posts throughout the state.

1928 On April 7, 1928, the world's first workable police radio system went on the air. The Detroit Police Department went on the air as station WBFS. The transmitter was installed on Belle Isle in the Detroit River, and the receiver was installed in cruiser No. 5. This was the climax of seven years of work and development under the direction of Police Commissioner William P. Rutledge.

The major problems in making a radio receiver work reliably in a police car were receiver instability and lack of sensitivity. Added to this were problems involving red tape with the Federal Radio Commission (predecessor to the Federal Communications Commission).

Fig. VI-4; Call box and lamp post

By **1927** the prohibition era had seen the development of big-time crime and the gangsters were making wide use of automobiles as "getaway

Fig. VI-6; Police telephone signal device

cars." The police were under great pressure to control the situation, but always arrived at the scene too late. Commissioner Rutledge then persuaded Robert L. Batts, a young radio technician and student at Purdue University, to come to Detroit and work on a radio receiver that would operate in a police car. It was through this effort that the first workable police radio setup was developed. Tests of the new radio receiver were more than successful, and Detroit Police Cruiser No. 10 was equipped with the second new receiver.

The result in terms of criminal apprehension was exciting. Police cruisers were catching holdup men, car thieves, and burglars often seconds after the crime was reported. Police communications

Fig. VI-5; Telephone and signal box

Fig. VI-7; Photo of Cruiser #10

Used by permission. From the files of the Chicago Police Department.

Chapter Six

had now brought about a new phase of police work. Early gangster movies, glorified the "hot pursuit" chase as they depicted the interception of gangster-loaded sedans leaving the crime scene, to the accompaniment of screeching tires, and the staccato sound of sub-machine guns, as the vehicles raced through city streets at high speeds.

The new Detroit Police Radio system was so successful that it drew worldwide publicity. Visitors came from police departments throughout the U.S. and the world to observe this new tactical police weapon. Unfortunately other departments desiring to install police radio systems had to develop their own equipment because there were no commercial police radio receivers available.

1929 In September, 1929, the Cleveland Police Department went on the air with a few cars. In December of the same year, Indianapolis became the third police department in the world to set up a workable police radio system.

1930 The Michigan State Police became the first state police organization to go on the air in October of 1930. It proved very effective in apprehending bank robbers and other gangsters. Twenty-three police stations were now on the air, including San Francisco, Berkeley and Pasadena.

1931 The first police motorcycle was equipped with a radio by the Indianapolis Police Department in September, 1931.

1933 In March, 1933, the Bayonne New Jersey Police Department went on the air with the first two-way, mobile police radio system.

1934 By 1934 so many police departments had police radio systems that they were being used as inter-city communications for general police and personal messages. The Federal Communications Commission had to intervene and establish strict control of police radio communications, restricting non-emergency messages to wire communications.

1935 Because police departments did not understand the government restrictions, they at first refused to obey them and police radio officers from all over the country banded together to form the APCO (Association of Police Communications Officers.) Later they changed to the Associated

Public-Safety Communications Officers). There was a great need for such an organization. It enabled police radio officers to exchange ideas and information and thus develop better equipment, techniques and performance.

1939 Daniel E. Noble, of Connecticut State College, developed the first FM mobile two-way radio system for the Connecticut State Police. This brought about a change in the whole mobile radio picture. (FM means Frequency Modulation.)

1940 Motorola President, Paul Galvin, saw the value of FM over AM for mobile police communications, and hired Dan Noble to develop two-way FM for Motorola Police Radio Sales. One of Noble's first developments was the remarkable Differential Squelch Circuit which demonstrated a greatly increased range in fringe areas. This was to signal the changeover in police communications to FM, even though the FCC would only accept applications for FM on an experimental basis.

1945 The FCC allocated frequencies for FM and it became the established system for police radio communications. Most departments now have three-way radios so the patrol car may not only carry on a two-way conversation with the base radio, but may also carry on the same type of conversation with other vehicles in the field. Developments by the military, in the area of communications, promise that law enforcement communication will have an interesting future.

OFFICER HAND SETS

A generation ago, one of the major complaints regarding foot patrol was the fact that the officer lacked communications. Many times patrol cars would rush to the scene of some disturbance and upon arrival would find that the foot patrol officer was just two doors away, completely unaware that there was a need for police assistance.

Today, with small handi-pack radios, the patrol officer can easily maintain contact with police communicatons and other officers. A common problem with the handi-pack portable radio is the officer's failure to turn it on. This is especially true when the officer is in a patrol car and leaves the car to handle a call or some other situation. Turning on the handi-pack radio must be an automatic habit when leaving the car. Just as common an occurrence is the officer who turns down the radio while talking to a citizen and forgets to turn it back up. This portable radio can be an important safety aid for the patrol officer. But only if it is used.

Fig. VI-8; Officer using hand set radio (walkie-talkie)

THE CONVENTIONAL COMMUNI-CATIONS & COMMAND CENTER USING THE MANUAL DISPATCH SYSTEM

Many small police communication centers operate in a two-stage manual process. Since 90 % of all police departments in the U.S. have 10 or less officers, this applies to the majoritiy. When a call is made to the police department, the officer at the complaint desk first determines the need for police action, and then records the details on a card. The card is routed to a dispatch console where the operator has control of one or more radio channels. In very small agencies, this is usually accomplished by handing the card from one person to another. In larger departments using a manual system, it is customary to use a conveyor belt system between the two positions.

The operator at the dispatch console then establishes radio contact with the patrol unit and relays the details of the complaint. The dispatcher also has the duty of maintaining a record of the status of the police vehicles under his or her control. If information is needed from the records division or from some computer source, the operator must phone for this information.

THE MODERN COMPUTERIZED COMMUNICATION CENTER

Fig. VI-9; Computerized communication center

Large departments which are growing usually have a problem with their communications centers. They simply cannot handle the increased load. At one point, the City of New York purchased 400 vehicles without radios due to the overloaded frequencies. The problem continues. Some are suggesting the use of communications satelites just for police agencies.

In the 1990's most cities have found themselves in a tight bind, financially. This has prompted city governments to take a closer look at increased efficiency and cost accounting. An answer to the problem of communications can, in many cases, be a switch to a Computer-Aided Dispatch (CAD) system. Although the initial cost of equipment is rather high (if not leased), it not only increases overall efficiency, but can actually save money. The

Fig. VI-10; Computer-Aided Dispatch System (CAD)

major saving is in time, and time is money. When all of the hidden backup expenses are taken into consideration, the average cost of a police officer in a large city is fairly high.. In the multi-million dollar budgets of today's urban police departments, salaries account for the major portion. With a shortage of qualified police officers throughout the United States today, any device that can cut down on person-hours is sorely needed.

The Task Force Report to the President's Commission on Law Enforcement and Administration of Justice stated; "staffing is a perennial problem for the police and, as the size and complexity of an operation grows, merely adding more people is not the answer." The same report stated that "A computer assisted Command and Control system offers many new possibilities for deployment and control of a police force."

The United States has tremendous technical capability in computers. It is now being applied to the field of criminal justice by the major systems companies. Most companies are conducting their development on an "evolutionary" basis. This means that development occurs in individual, specialized units. These can be added to future systems one at a time until a whole system is complete. Each unit is compatible with the existing system.

A TYPICAL COMPUTER AIDED DISPATCH (CAD) SYSTEM

In a Computer Aided Dispatch (CAD) system, each telecommunicator console or position has at least one computer terminal. The complaint taker enters the appropriate information into a preformatted screen and the computer then reads the location and transfers the information to the appropriate radio dispatcher for action. CAD can include resource files, address verification files, special note files, etc. Additionally, the CAD system produces management reports that are analyzed continually. This ongoing analysis usually results in beat boundaries being moved to compensate for changes in crime statistics. This type of police communications center has resulted in the development of centralized answering points for requests for emergency assistance. The Public Safety Answering Point (PSAP) ususaly functions as complaint-taker in the communication center.

Recent law changes have mandated that 911 be designated as the emergency number nationwide. 911 is already in place in most areas across the nation. With enhanced 911 (E911), the caller's telephone number and location are displayed on a screen at the complaint taker's position. This decreases the time required to determine the caller's location. This can be important if the caller is unable or refuses to provide this information. E911 also ensures that the caller is automatically connected to the proper law enforcement agency.

Advantages of the automated system

(1) It reduces the response time of the complaint phase by 80%.

(2) 911 is a universal number for emergencies so the caller does not need to look up the number or go through the operator.

(3) It greatly reduces (but does not eliminate) human error.

(4) It allows a more efficient dispatching of police units, saving time, and wear and tear on motorized equipment and wasted gasoline.

(5) Provides adequate information for proper and efficient realignment of beats.

(6) Adequate records maintenance.

Fig. VI-11; Mobile Display Terminal (MDT)

MOBILE TELEPRINTERS & MOBILE DISPLAY TERMINALS (MDT's)

Many agencies are now moving their communications efforts in the direction of the mobile teleprinter and/or Mobile Display Terminal (MDT). The feasibility of such a system is the cost of installation versus overall future savings. To this can be added increased efficiency on the part of the patrol officer and better officer security.

When considering potential savings, the major factor is time. Time is money. With the trend toward increased salaries and benefits for police officers, the time involved in each function during an officer's shift becomes important.

The President's Commission on Law Enforcement indicated that time is the worst enemy of law enforcement. The longer the elapsed time after the commission of a crime, the more it costs. This is not only in apprehending the criminal, but to secure a conviction in court.

It is estimated that six minutes out of every hour of a patrol officer's effective law enforcement time is lost to writing down messages. This also includes obtaining messages that were sent when the officer was out of the car. There is also the wasted time resulting from misunderstood radio messages. This amounts to 10% of an officer's time. If a mobile teleprinter or MDT can save just 10% of the patrol officer's time, it will result in a saving for the department. This is because the hourly cost of a teleprinter or MDT is much less than that of a police officer.

With the increase in both population and crime, our police communication centers are becoming overworked. They were not designed to handle the traffic they now experience. The mobile teleprinter or MDT is one answer. The Associated Public-Safety Communications Officers (APCO) predicts that soon, teleprinters and MDT's will be as common as regular police radios.

The mobile teleprinter, which has the appearance of being an oversized adding machine, is attached to the regular in-use mobile radio receiver. Printed messages are sent to the patrol car at 280 words per minute. The MDT is a TV type screen on which the officer receives messages or calls. A keyboard is attached which allowd the officer to send messages to the dispatcher, or to other MDT-equipped units. It also allows an officer to make data-base inquiries such as to NCIC. Some of the advantages and disadvantages of the teleprinter and MDT are as follows:

Advantages

(1) Hard copy data that can be Xeroxed or attached to reports.

(2) Messages are received ten times faster than if they were sent verbally.

(3) Virtually eliminates problems with semantics, phonetics and interference.

(4) Names and long identification numbers are accurate. Reduces error.

(5) Messages are received even while moving at high speeds.

(6) Added security from outside monitoring and from prisoners in the patrol car overhearing transmitted information.

(7) No overlapping transmission from far-out units.

(8) Messages can be sent to individual patrol units, selected groups or to all mobile units in the field.

(9) Messages are received even when the officer is out of the car. (During busy periods, officers are out of their cars about 50% of the time.) The message waiting for the officer could be of a life-saving nature.

(10) It operates automatically, the officer need do nothing.

(11) It can provide instant and confidential legal advice to the officer in the field from legal information in the computer.

Disadvantages

(1) It increases the amount of valuable equipment in a patrol car that can be damaged during riot situations or stolen when officers leave the car to answer calls.

(2) During high speed chases the driver of a one-officer car will not be able to read messages.

TECHNIQUES IN RADIO COMMUNICATION

Fig. VI-12; Police radio dispatcher, 1930. SFPD Hist. Soc.

Communication over a police radio can present many problems. The following information is intended to help the patrol officer in this endeavor. A department can have some of the finest communication equipment in the country, but its use becomes greatly impaired if the officers in the field are not familiar with its proper use or the basic rules of radio procedure. The increase in population has resulted in an increase in crime and an increase in the need for diminishing air time. Even smaller departments have been forced to use two or more frequencies because of increased air traffic. With air time so valuable, it has become increasingly important that it not be wasted. One of the best ways to ensure the proper use of air time, is to follow the ABC's of radio transmission.

The ABC's Of Radio Transmission

(A) **Accuracy** Accuracy is necessary to get the desired information to the receiving party without having the message later re-checked over the air for possible errors. There is also the danger to officers in the field, should improper information lead them to believe that there are "no wants" on a suspect, when in fact that suspect is wanted and classed as dangerous. This lack of accuracy can be the fault of either the officer who first file checked the suspect, or the records and radio personnel at communications. The major cause of inaccuracy is haste and impatience. The old saying that "haste makes waste" certainly applies to police communications.

(B) **Brevity** Brevity is increasingly important due to the expanding volume of radio traffic. This makes it essential that there be no unnecessary or repetitious words in the transmission. Half of the words in the English language are not needed in order to understand the message. There is certainly no need to add to the communication problem. The important point is understanding and clarity. Sometimes we can make a simple message confusing just by saying too much.

Officers should avoid starting "word battles" over the air because of personal animosity. If an officer has some legitimate gripe, it should be handled through proper channels rather than make smart remarks over the air. It is difficult not to reply in kind when someone makes an offending remark over the air. There is the knowledge that possibly all the officers in the field heard the remark, and this further injures an officer's pride. It takes a real professional officer to just remain silent when bearing the brunt of some derogatory remark over the air. Sometimes the tone of the transmitter's voice can be sarcastic or cynical. It is easy to take this as a personal attack. Don't waste air time with anything that does not contribute to better communications. The use of the police code can help maintain brevity.

(C) **Courtesy** Courtesy is necessary for rapid and efficient service. Courtesy begets courtesy. Anger begets anger. The courtesy in police communications is more of a form of respect than it is flowery words. In fact, brevity demands that courtesy not be expressed in words. The officer who says "Thank you very much" over the air is practicing good human relations, but is taking up very valuable air time. Courtesy can be shown in the tone of voice. Anger and disrespect can also be shown in the tone of voice, and it should be guarded against since it promotes a similar reply. There is a practice in many departments of jiggling the transmitter button when someone "goofs up" on the air, or says something that is humorous to the other officers. This is bad procedure, and can jam up the frequency just when a fellow officer is trying to call for help. There have been many instances, where, on crowded frequencies, officers in trouble could not get through to transmit their call for help.

Clarity, The Second "C"

Police administrators have long felt the need for the second "C" Clarity is often mentioned in report writing and notetaking, but it is also an essential in police communications. There is an old proverb that states "Clear knowledge is more valuable than profound knowledge." Clarity can be enhanced in two main areas:

(1) **Semantics:** What is semantics? Webster says "Significant meaning, the science of meanings as contrasted with phonetics, the science of sound." Proper semantics would be the transference of thoughts or ideas between people through communication without a loss or perversion of the original mean ing or intent.

(a) **Improving Semantics** There are two ways to improve semantics. Learn which errors are common. If an officer tries to communicate with someone and finds that he or she is misunderstood or has trouble getting the idea across, that officer can give the problem some thought with the intent of finding a better way of expressing it next time. Talking to others can help. Find out how they would express this thought, or just listen to others when they try to communicate in the same or similar situations. Experience helps considerably since in law enforcement, as in all fields, there is eventually a repetition of most situations and problems.

(b) **Think before talking** An officer should spend a few seconds thinking before transmitting. It will be found that the result will be

fewer problems with most communications. Officers should always put their brains in gear before releasing the clutch on their mouths. Too many officers grab the mike, press the transmit button and then think of what they want to say. This is easy to do when the situation involves an urgent matter. The important thing to remember is that the message be received and UNDERSTOOD. If not, the time made precious by the emergency will be wasted.

(2) **Phonetics:** Phonetics is the science of sounds. The understanding of a communication through the proper sounding of words. There are three main areas that hinder phonetics and good police communication:

(a) **Radio interference and distortion** This can often be corrected to some extent by proper adjusting of the squelch control. Changing position and having the message relayed by other units can also help.

(b) **Poor pronunciation** An officer should not transmit when chewing gum or eating. If it is an emergency, the gum or food should be spit out for the sake of clarity. When transmitting a message, officers should face the mike at all times. The mike should be held about two inches from the mouth. When speeding with the siren going, noise may be cut out by placing the mike on the side of the throat and then transmitting the message.

(c) **Similar sounding words and letters**. There are many words in the English language that have a similar sound. There are also many letters in the alphabet that sound the same: e.g.

B C D E G P T V Z   M N
A J K   Q U
I Y

Phonetics may be improved by:

(1) Not speaking too quickly, or in a slovenly manner. Talk with the mouth open. Mouth the words. It seems that telephone operators sometimes go to extremes in this area, but it is well justified.

(2) Use the phonetic alphabet when the word is likely to cause trouble. Unusual surnames should be spelled phonetically.

(3) Use similes. This can be done by saying that something is like something else. The name WOOD could be pronounced "WOOD as in FIREWOOD." Associations can also be used, e.g. "GREEN like GRASS".

(4) Indicate "common spelling." There are some words that are spelled differently from the most common spelling. e.g. SMITH can be SMITHE. BROWN can be BROWNE, WHITE can be WHYTE. For example, when broadcasting the word SMITH, state "SMITH, common spelling" rather than spelling it out.

(5) Use phonetic spelling for letters that sound the same. NOT FOR ALL LETTERS. For example, PAYTON is a name that can be spelled different ways. You would broadcast "PAYTON", P as in Paul, A-Y T as in Tom, O-N. This is because the "P" and the "T" are letters that are often misinterpreted.

COMPLAINTS OF COMMUNICATIONS OFFICERS

Fig. VI-13; Communications officers on the job

The author conducted a study in which police radio communications officers were asked to state some of their more common "gripes" about the way in which patrol officers use the police radio. The letter sent to each radio operator contained one sheet of paper on which they were requested to list the main problems that they, as police communications operators, had observed as being the most common. Not only was the return on this survey extremely high, but most of those responding added one or two extra sheets of paper to their list of complaints. Along with the returned questionnaire were many letters of appreciation expressing thanks for the opportunity, at long last, to vent their frustrations. Frustrations brought on by the continued misuse of the police radio by patrol officers.

Although the communications officers questioned were from different agencies, the complaints were basically the same. This would seem to indicate that problems concerning radio communications are common to most departments. Assuming this to be true, a list of the complaints most often mentioned have been compiled as follows:

(1) Record requests on more than three subjects at one time should be run on a secondary radio channel unless it is a real emergency. If possible, this information should be handled by telephone. This places an excessive work load on the radio operator even in normal hours of traffic. It ties up valuable air time.

Requests involving time consuming tasks should be handled by phone unless it is an emergency. Many of these requests could be handled later by the officer upon returning to headquarters; especially abandoned vehicles.

(2) Avoid personality conflicts over the air. If an officer has a gripe against a communications officer, the operator's supervisor should be contacted. Do not "chew out" the operator over the air. The information transmitted by communications officers has been given to them by someone else. If it is wrong or incomplete, don't become antagonistic toward them. It is outside of their control in most cases.

(3) Officers often fail to realize that communications officers do not have a crystal ball. They cannot fully understand what is going on in the field unless they have been fully informed. It is easy for the patrol officer to assume that the communications officer understands the situation exactly as he or she does.

(4) Let communications know your location each time you leave the car. Be sure to turn on the pack-set or handi-pack radio. Much air time can be wasted calling officers who have left their cars and have forgotten to turn on their portable radios. Dispatchers have a sincere concern for the safety of officers.

(5) Don't keep asking communications if they have further information on a crime. If they get information, they will broadcast it as soon as possible. They are not trying to hide information from patrol officers. They're on the same team.

(6) Some officers jump into the car, grab the mike and report themselves back in service without listening to see if anyone else is transmitting, often blocking emergency traffic. In larger cities or communities, two cars on the fringe of a frequency range may broadcast simultaneously without hearing each other.

(7) Make sure that communications is fully informed when information is requested from a third party over the phone. Too often the officer will ask radio to call someone to obtain information. For example, whether they gave permission for a certain person to use their car. The party called may have questions that the radio operator cannot answer. The result is another use of valuable air time to obtain these answers from the officer. These three way conversations are very time consuming. Often the officer in the field could have a partner stay with the subject, and use a phone to make the call. It would resuslt in a faster and better job.

Along the same line, officers will often ask the communications officer to obtain information from someone over the phone. Once the information is obtained, they usually hang up and transmits it to the officer who then asks for further information. The radio operator has to call the person back. This can make him appear inefficient or stupid. Request all information at once, or ask the operator to hold the party on the phone.

(8) Officers sometimes talk so fast that the radio operator is forced to ask for a repeat. This takes more time in the long run than if one spoke slowly to begin with. It is a rare commications officer who takes shorthand.

(9) Learn to use radio code. Avoid long sentences. Know what to say before pressing the transmission button.

(10) Too many officers receive radio messages without writing them down. They later call radio for a repeat on an address or name or some other detail.

(11) Officers should develop an understanding of what takes place when they request information and should not keep impatiently checking to find out why they haven't received it. Most information must be obtained from other sources over which communications officers have little control. Since the primary task of a communications officer is the operation of the radio, this takes precedence.

(12) When Officers are out on a call longer than usual, they should phone radio control to let them know they are OK. Otherwise another car might have to be sent to check on the original unit when it is not really necessary.

(13) Officers on a hot pursuit will often fail to report their location as they change direction or pass major landmarks. Without this information a communications officer cannot direct proper assistance or tactical interception.

(14) Officers who are involved in traffic accidents should state the accident's seriousness and what personal injuries, if any, resulted. The lack of information may cause other officers, upon hearing of the accident, to rush to their assistance, placing themselves at risk, when no assistance is needed.

(15) There are officers who articulate quite well in normal speech, but for some reason seem to mumble when they talk into the mike. It is as though they feel that no one will notice their mistakes if they mumble quietly. This can be overcome by concentrated effort and practice.

The great danger is that radio operators may get tired of asking certain officers for repeats all the time and start guessing at what was said. If the officer leaves the car and does not report back for some time, the radio operator might send help to the wrong location. If the officer were shot, he or she could bleed to death due to the delay.

(16) Redundancy, or the unnecessary use of words. For example the officer who states "Please be advised that this unit will be 10-7 for a few moments" instead of "B-3, 10-7." It must be remembered that the police radio is not a telephone. The patrol officer should avoid superfluous transmissions. The best alternative is to meet the other officer at some location and discuss the matter in person.

(17) The patrol officer should learn the names and locations of streets on the beat. At least use the beat map rather than call radio for the exact location of each street in a given assignment. One of the best ways to learn the streets is to look them up. If the call is an emergency, and the street is new, it is a different matter. The communications officer will not mind looking up a street or a cross street in an emergency.

OTHER AIDS TO BETTER COMMUNICATION

(1) Don't assume anything. In the field of law enforcement, matters are often of a serious nature. Make sure that it is plainly stated, and that all the important facts are included.

(2) Don't make extra long transmissions. Someone may have an emergency message and not be able to cut in. It is best to take breathing spells between sentences in case an emergency should arise. This will allow others to cut in between sentences. It also makes it easier on the person who is copying the message.

(3) Don't hang your hat on the mike. Someimes an officer will place a hat on a secured mike because it seems to hold it nicely. It is convenient. Sometimes the weight of the hat will depress the mike button, and two things can result. First, activating the transmitter can interfere with other messages being transmitted. Second (and it has happened), everything the officer says to his partner will be broadcast. There have been some very embarrassing conversations because of this,. where the officers have called down everyone, from the supervising sergeant to the chief of police, and it was broadcast to headquarters and all police units in the field.

(4) Don't shout into the "mike." If the voice transmissions are weak, turn up the volume.

(5) Pronounce words slowly and distinctly. The normal speaking rate is between 40 and 60 words per minute.

(6) Proper use of the microphone. Keep the microphone about 2 to 3 inches away from the mouth and speak across the its face in order to maintain a proper modulation level.

(7) Keep your voice as emotionless as possible. This is because a monotone voice is more easily understood.

(8) Be impersonal. A police radio station is not licensed for person-to-person communication. Personal names should not be used. Refer to the person being called by the radio call number or car number.

(9) Use the Standard Phonetic Alphabet. Since numbers are often confused when spoken over the radio, use the Standard Phonetic Alphabet for Numerals developed by the Bell Telephone Company. Always use "zero" instead of "oh" for the number "0".

1 – Wun	2 – Too
3 – Thuh-ree	4 – Fo-wer
5 – Fie-yiv	6 – Siks
7 – Sev-ven	8 – Ate
9 – Nie-yen	0 – Zero
	(Never "oh")

OPERATING THE POLICE RADIO

They are many different companies that make radios for police agencies but since many police departments use Motorola equipment in their vehicles, this will be the type of equipment discussed. Despite their differences, most police radios are basically the same.

(1) SINGLE CHANNEL AND TWO CHANNEL RADIOS

(a) On-Off Switch. This switch can be located at almost any position on the control panel. It is usually a toggle switch that moves either up and down or sideways. When the switch is turned on, a green light, next to it, will light up. This light should always be checked. It is common for patrol officers, with many things on their mind, to forget to turn the radio on. Hours later, they wonder why they havn't received any calls.

(b) Volume Control Knob. This knob is used to control the volume of the loudspeaker. It increases the volume when turned clockwise. Some older models combine this knob with the on/off switch so the radio is turned off by turning the knob counter-clockwise until it clicks and the small green light goes out. Patrol officers should constantly check this knob to be sure that it is properly adjusted. Sometimes officers will turn it down while listening to a citizen or giving him information. Then they forget to turn it back up. There is also the possibility of rubbing against the knob and turning the volume down. Sometimes a communications officer will try to reach a police unit in the field and cannot do so. Later, communication is mysteriously reestablished. The officer, to save face, will blame it on a faulty radio, but it is usually a case of the volume knob being turned down.

(c) Squelch Control Knob. The squelch control knob can eliminate the objectionable background noise of the receiver. To properly utilize this device, the knob should be turned counter-clockwise until static is heard. Then it should be turned back just enough to eliminate the static. It is then at the right position to promote full reception on the radio's receiver. This control should be checked regularly throughout the shift. Especially if the officer is having trouble receiving a message from another police unit or from radio control.

(d) Frequency switch. The frequency switch is almost a standard item on police radios. Increasing population has forced many departments to use two or more frequencies, and increasing air traffic has caused special units such as detective and juvenile to operate on another frequency. The frequency switch is usually located in the upper left-hand corner of the control head or on a special frequency control switch just below the control head. It is marked with F-1, F-2, etc.

(e) Receiver pilot lamp. The receiver pilot lamp is green in color, and is usually on the right side of the control head. When on, it indicates that the equipment is in the standby position, ready to receive or transmit.

(f) Transmitter pilot lamp. The transmitter pilot lamp is red in color, and is to the left of the receiver pilot lamp. When it is lit, it indicates that the transmitter button on the mike has been depressed and that the transmitter is working. Officers should learn to check this light occasionally. If the transmitter button ever accidentally stick or jam, it would be noticed and the situation corrected.

(2) MULTIPLE CHANNEL RADIOS

Many cities are now finding that the one and two channel radios are not filling their needs.They have switched to the multi-channel radio. It is basically the same as the single channel radio except that it has a series of push buttons or a rotary knob. This allows the officer to select a radio channel. An added advantage of the multiple channel radio is that when an officer is in trouble and needs to call for help, the assigned channel can be in use. With the multiple channel, the officer can quickly switch to another channel and give that radio operator the message. The operator can then take the emergency action necessary, or notify the officer's assigned operator of the Code 3 traffic.

(3) THE ELECTRONIC CONSOLE

Many patrol cars are now being equipped with the electronic console. This type of device enables the patrol officer to perform many tasks from one central control box. The functions of this device are as follows:

(a) Emergency lights control. This control is found on the left hand side of the console. It contains a lever with four positions, Off, Light f#1 (rear flasher), Light f#2 (ALL emergency lights), and electronic siren. It also contains four colored instrument lights that indicate which position the lever is on.

(b) Locking releases. In the upper right corner of the console are located one or two buttons that release the locks on the shotgun holder and/or the rear doors of the vehicle.

(c) Siren control. This control is found in the left hand knob, and gives the officer the different types of siren or puts it on manual control so that the siren only sounds when the horn is pressed or a floorboard button is depressed.

(d) Public address system. This control is found in the right hand knob, and will turn the unit into an outside public address system. It can also broadcast the regular police radio transmissions on an outside speaker so that the officer can leave the car and still hear the radio.

POLICE UNIT IDENTIFICATION

In order for a police communications network to properly function, there needs to be a system of unit identification so that inter-unit communications can identify the sender and receiver. Three systems will be mentioned here.

(1) **The police unit identification system.** When a department is small and has its own communications system apart from the county, it can simply assign each car a number. This number is usually the vehicle number that is painted on the door or fender. Any officer using this car will answer calls using the car number. The unit would be addressed as "Car 26" or "Unit 26." When the department grows to the point where it has many specialized units such as detective, juvenile, vice, traffic, motorcycle, and others, it may assign letter designations to be placed before the call number. For example, "B" for beat car, "I" for investigative unit, and "J" for juvenile. Each specialized division would have its own series of numbers, each division having a car with the number 1, 2, 3, or 4. Communications would refer to the units as "J-1."

(2) **The individual and department identification system.** When a department reaches the size of a major city, or when communication is handled by a county-wide control center, there is a need to further break down the identification call number. One of the best systems is the Number-Letter-Number system. As the name indicates, it is composed of one number, one letter and one number.

(a) Key number: The key number refers to the individual department or organization. For example:

Sheriff's Department would be 1
Los Gatos Police would be 2
Campbell Police would be 3

(b) Function Letter: The function letter refers to the function or assignment. For example:

Ranking officers above sergeant = A
Patrol beats = B
Detective Division = C

(c) Personal Number: This is an individual number assigned to officers as long as they are a member of a particular division. Often it is the same as the officer's badge number. This system is very helpful when a county is composed of many small departments and specialized agencies that use the same communications center. A unit that called radio control using the identification 1-A-2 would immediately be recognized as the number two man in the administration of the Sheriff's Department, who would probably be the Under-sheriff.

(3) **The All Number Computer Identification System.** Some of the larger departments have been feeding their "calls for police service" into a computer for analysis. Others are planning to do this in the future. There is also a movement toward using computerized car dispatching systems. In order for the identification number to be best assimilated by the computer, it should be composed of only numbers rather than numbers and letters.

There are numerous ways of using this system, but basically they are the same as the two systems mentioned previously. Part of the number indicates the purpose or specialized type of service rendered by the unit. Part of the number can indicate the district and/or the detailed location of the beat. Usually four numbers are sufficient for full identification, and can be used for both computer analysis and computerized dispatching.

PRIORITY CODES

Because of the mixed nature of police calls, there must be a system whereby the officer receiving the call may expedite the vehicle according to the degree of emergency. Since the officer seldom receives all of the information over the air concerning the call, it is the responsibility of the complaint officer, who originally received the call over the phone, to assign that call a code, if one is necessary.

No Code. When no code has been assigned, or in departments where a "Code 0" is used, this call has the lowest priority and usually involves picking up some papers or information that isn't too important. In this case there is no one anxiously awaiting the arrival of the officer. It can be answered almost any time during the shift, and all later calls with a numbered priority should be given preference over it.

Code 1. This is a routine call, and is to be answered with strict observance of all traffic laws. The red lights and siren may not be used on a code 1 call. If officers in the field are aware of circumstances unknown to radio control, they may use code 2 or 3, but the legal responsibility for the decision is strictly their own.

Code 2. Code two means URGENT, and is to be answered immediately in a manner that will enable the unit to get to the scene as quickly (and safely) as possible. All traffic laws are to be observed, and the siren is not to be used. Some officers will use red lights during a code two call in order to expedite movement through traffic if it is fairly heavy. It must be emphasized that the red light by itself offers no basis for emergency exemption while responding to the call. It must be used in conjunction with the siren.

Code 3. Code three means EMERGENCY, and like code two, is to be answered immediately by driving to the scene as quickly and safely as possible. In this case, however, the red lights and the siren are to be used to obtain the right-of-way. It must be remembered that code three is not a magic wand that clears all traffic ahead. The important thing is to get there. If code three is assigned by radio control, and it later turns out that the code assignment wasn't justified, the officer is not held responsible. In accident cases, the courts have held that the officer is not liable if radio control assigned the code and later it was shown that the call itself did not justify the emergency code.

Officers who wish to clear the air, may announce "Code three traffic." All other communications should cease until the emergency message is transmitted. Radio control will often repeat the warning, in the event that units on the far edge of town might not hear the original call. They could easily interfere with control's radio reception of the emergency message.

RADIO PROCEDURES

(1) All things being equal, communications officers have supreme authority and priority on police communications. However, there are two exceptions. First, any mobile unit that announces code three traffic, receives top priority. Second, a field supervisor who is involved in a tactical situation can take command of immediate communications because, by being there in the field he or she is in a better position to assume command.

(2) When radio control desires to call a unit, or when any unit desires to contact another unit, they will first use the identification of the unit being called. They will then identify themselves. For example: "B-2 from B-6" or just "B-2, B-6." There should be a pause to enable the officer being called to be alerted to the fact that this particular traffic is directed to that unit. Patrol officers who have worked in the field for some time condition themselves to be immediately alerted when their call number is sounded. When officers hear their call numbers (and/or letters) and want the calling unit to know that they are ready, the officer being called will reply by giving the unit's call number. For example, "B-2." Some officers will respond with "B-2, go ahead." This might be fine in a small community, but where air time is limited, the "go-ahead" is unnecessary and should be left out.

(3) Whenever a mobile unit is out of service, or the driver leaves the car to approach a stopped vehicle, he or she should notify radio control of the location of the stop and the license number of the vehicle. Not only is this a safety measure in case the officer should get into trouble, but it saves the unnecessary use of valuable air time by repeatedly calling the unit without receiving an answer.

(4) According to Federal law (Ch. 8, section 605, Communications Act of 1934), any message is the property of the one who originates it. Cancellation can be made only by that party or department. Legally however, this authority may be delegated. The essence of this matter is that it is the responsibility of a person originating a message or alert, to issue a cancellation or a change in the original message when appropriate.

(5) When a vehicle has just been stolen, and there is a great likelihood that it is still in the area, or when it is believed that it might be headed toward a certain area, it can be very important to broadcast the pertinent information as soon as possible. The Associated Public Safety Communications Officers recommends that the acronym CYMBALS be used.

CYMBALS

Color
Year
Make
Body style
Additional
License
State

Fig. VI-14, Car illustration for CYMBALS

Added to this information should be (1) Other descriptive information (e.g. stickers, radio antenna), and (2) The authority or jurisdiction where car was stolen. It is important, for liability reasons, to state whether or not the legal owner has signed a waiver.

(6) Missing persons, runways, wanted persons and escapees present a problem to police communications. They are quite frequent, and in order to give a proper description, a minimum of information should be broadcast. Examples would be the name, subject classification and age. The descriptions of other persons should be basically the same as that listed in Chapter VIII. It should adhere to the following form:

(a) — Authority.
(b) — Reason wanted.
(c) — Name.
(d) — Sex.
(e) — Race-class.
(f) — Height.
(g) — Weight.

(h) — Hair color.
(i) — Eye color.
(j) — Complexion.
(k) — Build.
(l) — Clothing description, from head down.
(m) — Where and when last seen.
(n) — Description of vehicle, if one was used.
(o) — Whether armed, if known.
(p) — Possible location or destination.

Subject Classification

In report writing, the common way to classify a subject is to use symbols that represent the race, sex and age. e.g. WMA — 32 is a White Male Adult — 32 years old. In radio description, however, the term Adult or Juvenile should be left out as being an unnecessary waste of air time. The age 32 indicates that the person is an adult, so the word adult would be superfluous. The proper classification would be White Male-32. Race classifications are as follows:

White — Those whose skin is light or of the so-called white race. The letter designation would be "W."

Black — Those whose skin is dark enough to approach the Negroid race. The letter used would be "B." The term "Afro-American" is not used because the "A" would be confused with "Asian."

Asian — Those whose background is obviously Asian. The letter used would be "A."

Hispanic — Those of obvious Mexican or Latin American descent. The letter used would be "H."

Indian — Those of American Indian descent. The letter used would be "I."

Filipino — Those of Filipino descent. The letter used would be "F."

Other races and their letter symbol are to be listed as follows:

A — Other Asian.
C — Chinese.
D — Cambodian.
G — Guamanian.
J — Japanese.
K — Korean.
L — Laotian.
O — Other.
P — Pacific Islander.
S — Samoan
U — Hawaiian.
V — Vietnamese.
X — Unknown race.
Z — Asian or East Indian.

(7) When an officer in the field desires registration information on a vehicle, radio control should be contacted. They in turn can radio state records. Registration information may be obtained from the Department of Motor Vehicles when the officer can provide either:

(a) Vehicle license number.
(b) Make and motor number of the vehicle.
(c) Name and address of the suspected registered owner.

In order for the officer to obtain this information over the air, it must be of an official nature. Follow-up information and driver's license information should be obtained through the use of the teletype rather than the police radio. The telephone should also be utilized to save air time.

(8) Abbreviations should be used whenever possible and the employment of a standardized set of abbreviations is important if clarity and brevity is to be achieved. Crimes should be referred to by the penal code section number for the same reason. Some of the more common abbreviations are:

GENERAL

ABV — Above
ACK — Acknowledgement
ADD — Address
ADM — Administrative
ADW — Assault with a Deadly Weapon
AKA — Also Known As
APB — All Points Bulletin

APPROX – Approximate
APT – Apartment
ARR – Arrest
ATT or A/ – Attempt
ATTN or ATN – Attention
BET or BETN or BETW – Between
BKG – Booking
BLDG or BLD – Building
BLKS – Blocks
BUR – Bureau
BURG – Burglary
CCW – Carrying a Concealed Weapon
CITE – Citation
CITZ – Citizen
CMDR – Commander
CONT'D – Continued
COP – Chief of Police
CURR – Currency
DA – District Attorney
DESC – Description
DISP – Dispatcher
DIST – District
DIV – Division
DL – Driver's License
DOA – Dead on arrival.
DOB – Date of Birth
DOT – Direction of Travel
DUI – Driving Under the Influence
EMER – Emergency
ETA – Estimated Time of Arrival.
EVID – Evidence
EXP – Expired
FEL – Felony
FI – Field Interrogation
GOA – Gone on Arrival.
HBD – Had Been Drinking.
HOSP – Hospital
HQ – Headquarters
IA – Internal Affairs
ID – Identify
IMP – Impound
INJ – Injury
INV – Investigator
L/F – Left Front
L/R – Left Rear
L/S – Long Sleeve
LIC – License
MAX – Maximum
MED – Medium
MISD – Misdemeanor
MO – Method of Operation
OFCR or OFR – Officer
PASS – Passneger

PKD – Parked
PLT – Plate
POE – Point of Entry
POI – Point of Impact
POSS – Possible
PROB – Probation
PROP – Property
PVT – Private
QOA – Quiet on Arrival.
QOD – Quiet on Departure.
R/F – Right Front
R/R – Right Rear
RE – Regarding
RECD – Received
REG – Registration
RES – Residence
RP – Reporting Party
RPT – Report
SIG – Signal
SUBJ – Subject
TRAF – Traffic
UNK – Unknown
UNMKD – Unmarked
UTC – Unable to Contact
VIC – Victim
VIN – Vehicle Identification Number
WARR – Warrant
WIT or W-1 – Witness
X-ING – Crossing
X-WALK – Crosswalk
YR – Year

COLORS

BLK – Black
BLN – Blond (hair)
BLU – Blue
BRN – Brown
DK – Dark
GRN – Green
GRY – Gray
HZL – Hazel
LT – Light
RUD – Ruddy
YEL – Yellow

THE LAKEWOOD, COLORADO TEN CODE EXPERIMENT

The Public Safety Department at Lakewood, Colorado conducted an experiment to test the effectiveness of the Ten Code. After comparing the Ten Code with a "clear speech" system, they found that messages were transmitted faster and with fewer errors. A random sampling of radio tapes revealed that of 200 calls, there were 113 errors when using the Ten Code. As a result the patrol officers were given a refresher course in the Ten Code. Another random sampling of the radio tapes showed a drop in errors, but there were still 85 errors in 200 calls. As a result, a new system using plain English was developed and put into practice. After the new system was used for a while, a random sampling of tapes revealed only 14 errors.

The next consideration was time. A test was conducted where dispatchers and officers were shown flash cards with typical messages in both Ten Code and plain English. These messages were read into a microphone while the time was measured by a sensitive timing device. The results of the test showed that using plain English saved 2 hours and 53 minutes in each 24 hour day. It would be worthwhile for some departments to further test the validity of this innovative experiment.

APCO TEN CODE

For those agencies that do use a radio code, the Associated Public-Safety Communications Officers recommend the Ten Code. Their latest revised Ten-Code is listed as follows:

10-1 – Signal Weak
10-2 – Signal Good
10-3 – Stop Transmitting
10-4 – Affirmative (OK)
10-5 – Relay (To)
10-6 – Busy
10-7 – Out of Service
10-8 – In Service
10-9 – Say Again (repeat)
10-10 – Negative
10-11 – _____ On Duty
10-12 – Stand By (Stop)
10-13 – Existing Conditions
10-14 – Message/Information
10-15 – Message Delivered

10-16 – Reply to Message
10-17 – En Route
10-18 – Urgent (Quickly)
10-19 – (In) Contact
10-20 – Location
10-21 – Call (_____) By Phone
10-22 – Disregard
10-23 – Arrived At Scene
10-24 – Assignment Completed
10-25 – Report to (Meet)
10-26 – Estimated Arrival Time
10-27 – License/Permit Information
10-28 – Ownership Information
10-29 – Records Clerk
10-30 – Danger/Caution
10-31 – Pick Up
10-32 – _____ Units Needed (Specify)
10-33 – Help Me Quick (Emergency)
10-34 – Time
10-35 – 10-39 – Reserved

Radio users are urged to incorporate the use of the APCO TEN SIGNALS in their radio operating procedure. They are short, easily understood and convey maximum meaningful information in minimum time. The proper use of these signals contributes significantly to the conservation of airtime by restricting free choice of words. It forces the officer to use prescribed forms when transmitting information which constitutes the major portion of daily radio traffic. These signals serve a dual purpose as they can be used to make a statement, or ask a question, simply by voice inflection.

In concert with the APCO ten code, the patrol officer should avoid phrases and words that may be difficult for the listener to understand. Preferred words and phrases include:

Poor	Preferred
Yes	Affirmative
No	Negative
Want	Desire
Can't	Unable
Buy	Purchase
Get	Obtain
Send	Forward
Wait	Stand by
Do you want . . .	Advise if . . .
Find out	Ascertain
Call and see	Check

PHONETIC ALPHABET FOR LAW ENFORCEMENT

A – ADAM	N – NORA
B – BOY	O – OCEAN
C – CHARLES	P – PAUL
D – DAVID	Q – QUEEN
E – EDWARD	R – ROBERT
F – FRANK	S – SAM
G – GEORGE	T – TOM
H – HENRY	U – UNION
I – IDA	V – VICTOR
J – JOHN	W – WILLIAM
K – KING	X – X-RAY
L – LINCOLN	Y – YOUNG
M – MARY	Z – ZEBRA

FIELD TELEPHONES (CALL BOX)

The field telephone is expensive to maintain. Because of this, there has been a tendency in many cities to discontinue them. They are usually found in the downtown area where foot patrol beats are located. Some communities have kept or added these boxes because the federal government will now pay half their cost through Civil Defense funds. These funds are available for all police communications equipment because the government feels that during a national emergency the equipment will be of great value. Some advantages are:

(1) They can be used by the general public as emergency telephones.

(2) They can be used to call in fires. Some cities make them combination fire alarm and police call boxes since they both go into the same communications center.

(3) They can be used for confidential messages that should not be transmitted over the air. Many people have police radios, including criminals. An officer should not assume that a message transmitted over a police radio frequency will be secure.

(4) They allow foot patrol officers to check with headquarters to obtain the latest information, or to call for a police vehicle when an arrest is made, saving the portable hand-pak and reducing radio traffic.

THE USE OF PUBLIC TELEPHONES

In recent years there has been an increased use of public telephones as a means of transmitting lengthy or confidential calls. The officer on the beat simply stops at a public telephone, preferably at a gas station. This is so the police vehicle can be parked next to the phone. The officer then radios the phone number to communications where an operator can phone the number. The officer answers the phone and gives the message to the police operator who in turn transfers it to its proper destination. The communications officer can also connect the phone to a regular outside phone line. Some departments require that officers phone in their offense reports from the field. They would make good use of public telephones in this manner.

TELEVISION

Educational television has been with us for some time, but the use of television as a means of police communication is relatively new. Basically it involves broadcasts throughout a county, just before the major shifts start. A large TV set is placed in each squad room and specialized police division. The broadcasts contain information on wanted persons and identification lineups. They also include an unlimited number of training sessions and training films. Some states already have a statewide hookup. Some use satelites for this purpose.

TELETYPES AND COMPUTER MESSAGES

With the American public becoming ever more mobile, there is the increasing need for inter-community police communications. The backbone of this form of communications has been the police teletype. Today computer modems and fax machines are taking over. There have been many innovations in the teletype since it was first started, many of them because of the increasing loads that teletype systems are now required to handle. Most modern teletypes are now able to automatically take a message and hold it until there is a line clear on which to transmit. In the past, the operator had to keep trying until she found the line clear.

Fig. VI-15; Police teletype operator, 1920's. SFPD Hist. Soc.

Many police officers fail to use inter-agency messages to their full advantage. The police teletype or fax system is not just an administrative function as is sometimes thought. It is a police tool that will greatly aid the officer in the field. However, the officer must first realize its true value, and then take advantage of it.

When new officers first read a police teletype or fax message, the form looks like Greek. Because it is a little strange, officers tend to shy away from it. Knowing how to read police teletype messages is important to proper performance in the job. Patrol officers should make a conscious effort to learn the format and terminology of teletype messages so they may become one of the tools of the trade.

Since the format of a police teletype message is similar throughout the nation, the examples used for illustration will be from the state of California.

THE FORMAT OF POLICE TELETYPE MESSAGES

Generally speaking, there are five parts to the police teletype:

(1) The heading.

(2) The area designation or station being sent to.

(3) The type of message.

(4) The body of the report.

(5) The identification of sender.

(1) **THE HEADING.** The heading consists of (a) The message number: assigned by order of teletype during each 24 hour period, and listed before station designation; e.g. 4-SJS. (b) The sending station: each department or agency has a three letter identification; e.g. SJS-San Jose Sheriff. (c) Date and time: time is listed by the military 24 hr. system; e.g. 5-28-95 0118 hrs. PDT. (d) Class of message: the class of message would be:

CRIM – Criminal
CII – State Bureau of Identification
APB – All Points Bulletin
BUS – Business
SVC – Service
CORR – Correction

The heading should read: 3 CII 5-28-95 0118 hrs. PDT CRIM. This means that it is the third message sent out by the State Bureau of Identification on May 28, 1995, at 1:18 A.M. Pacific Daylight Savings time, and is of a criminal nature.

(2) **AREA DESIGNATION OR STATION TO WHICH SENT.** The area designation is not always used, but it is the general area to which the teletype is of concern. Sometimes it is listed first. The station to which the message is being sent is listed by three letters: e.g. CII, Bureau of Criminal Identification; MVS, Motor Vehicle Section; DDL, Division of Drivers Licenses.

(3) **TYPE OF MESSAGE.** The type of message is broken down into the (a) primary subject, and (b) secondary subject.

(a) **Primary Subject.** The primary subject would be the type of offense, or area of concern, such as:

ASSAULT, MISSING PERSON
BURGLARY INFO., WANTED
BUNCO, CHECKS, etc.

(b) **The Secondary Subject.** The secondary subject would be a further breakdown of the primary subject. e.g.

BURGLARY: BUSINESS
IN CUSTODY: SAFE
WANTED: SUPL (SUPPLEMENTARY)
RESIDENCE

(4) **BODY OF THE REPORT.** The body of the report gives the message or the information to be transmitted to the receiving agencies. The body of the report should be brief and include proper standardized abbreviations (See prior list) For example a requested record of a suspect might read: 12- 10-95 FED CORR INST SEAGOVILLE TEX 5153 ST VIOL NATL MTR VEH THFT ACT. This means that on December 10, 1995 he was sentenced to the Federal Correctional Institution at Seagoville, Texas for violation of the National Motor Vehicle Act.

The body of the report should include:
(a) Names of persons involved.
(b) Descriptions of subjects.
(c) Identification numbers of subjects.
(d) Listing of subjects as "Suspect No. 1, Suspect No. 2, or S-1 and S-2."
(e) Property involved.
(f) Vehicles used.
(g) Modus operandi.
(h) Department case number, so other agencies may refer to it without using a lengthy description.

If the message is of special importance to any one department or area, the symbol "— ATTN" and the name of the department should be placed at the bottom of the message. e.g. — ATTN SANTA CLARA PD.

(5) **THE IDENTIFICATION OF THE SENDER** should include:

(a) Name of the sender or authority—-e.g. J. SMITH
(b) The title of the sender —-e.g. COP (Chief of Police) SGT. Sergeant
(c) Location of the sender —-e.g. SAN JOSE
(d) Call letters of originating stations—e.g. SJP (San Jose Police)
(e) Phone number (including area code)
(f) Initials of attendant AND sender if different--e.g. KTW (/RB)

The Identification section should look like the following: J. SMITH COP SAN JOSE SJP KTW

EXAMPLES OF MESSAGES SENT

The most common teletype sent by the patrol officer is one requesting information on vehicle registration. It is usually very short and to the point. To save time and space, the operator sending the teletype might include several requests on the same message, and then later disseminate the information to the various officers requesting it. In a larger department with many patrol officers, this is more difficult. Individual requests are usually sent.

Example:
11 SJP 12-29-95 0959 hrs. PST
MVS
REG ON CBT 329
408-227-4156
L. COBARRUVIAZ COP SAN JOSE/SMITH/ MR

This message was the eleventh message sent by the San Jose Police Department on December 29, 1995. It was sent at 9:59 a.m., PST, and was sent to the Motor Vehicle Section requesting registration information on the vehicle with the license number CBT 329. The authority for sending the teletype was L.Cobarruviaz, Chief of Police at San Jose. The officer requesting the information was officer Smith, and the initials of the clerk actually sending the teletype were MR.

EXAMPLES OF MESSAGES RECEIVED

The patrol officer should carefully scan the latest teletypes in the squad room just before goeing on duty. There are so many that all of them cannot all be read. but by scanning the headings and the "Special Attention" notations, officers can pick out the one that may be pertinent to their beat or immediate area. Whenever a sending station feels that the teletype has a message of special importance to one or more particular areas, they will use the notation "—ATTN" and the name of the department or agency. This is usually placed at the bottom of the message. e.g.

5 UKP 5-28-95 1400 hrs. CRIM
AREA B
MISSING OR RUNAWAY JUVENILE
MISSING FROM UKIAH, DIANE WATERS WF 16

5-3 115 RED, BRN OLVE COMPL LAST WEARING BLK SLACKS WHT BLOUSE SUBJECT MENT ILL MISSING SINCE 5-26-95 POSS IN COMPANY OF UNK SUBJ WM DRIVING YELLOW 60 FORD CONV

—ATTN SAN JOSE PD—HAS AUNT AT 1156 WELCH AVE.
—ATTN CAMPBELL PD—FOUND AT 114 RAILROAD ON LAST RUNAWAY.
—ATTN STOCKTON PD—HAS SISTER, BETTY SMITH AT 5567 SHASTA.

REFER RICKART, JUV DIV
707-555-1212
P L JACKSON COP UKIAH PD BOG

An officer on the Campbell Police Department, when scanning the report, would notice the —ATTN CAMPBELL PD, and would immediately check the address to see if it was on his beat. If it was, he would then either contact the people at that address for assistance, or stake out the area.

OTHER EXAMPLES:

3 SDP 6-14-95 1330 hrs. PDT CRIM
PD LOS GATOS
PETTY THEFT

THIS DEPT HOLDS MISD WARRANT NO 3671 CHARGING 488 PC/PETTY THEFT/ SIGNED BY JUDGE WALLACE L SNARK DATED 6-13-95 BAIL $525.00 ON HARRY CLEFT AKA HAROLD CARLSON WM 57 5-8, 150, BLK BRN. UR NBR C15487. LAST KNOWN ADDR 415 MAIN ST UR CITY.

REFER JACKSON
619-555-1212
R M MILLER COP SAN DIEGO PM BLC

It notifies the Los Gatos Police Department that San Diego has a warrant for Harry Cleft, also known as Harold Carlson, White male, 57 years, 5 feet 8 inches tall, 150 lbs. with black hair and brown eyes. He has been previously booked in Los Gatos under the number C15487.

Obtain copies of teletype messages from your department and practice reading them.

MAJOR SOURCES OF TELETYPE INFORMATION (all mostly computerized now)

(1) **State Records Bureau** Wanted persons, criminal record checks, bad checks, stolen property, gun records.

(2) **State Highway Patrol (Police)** Stolen and wanted vehicle checks. Give license and/or vehicle identification number. Files will contain many out of state "wants" not listed in APB's.

(3) **State Motor Vehicle Department** Registration of vehicles available through three methods. (a) License number. (b) Vehicle identification number. (c) Alphabetically by the name of registered owner. If there is some doubt as to accuracy, include all three if available.

(4) **State Drivers License Department** Can be searched by Driver's License number or name.

Do not list more than one different license request on one teletype, as it can cause delays and mix-ups.

COMPUTERIZED SWITCHING SYSTEMS

All states have one or more computerized switching systems. For example, the National Law Enforcement Telecommunications System (N-LETS) is located in Phoenix, Arizona. If an officer requests an out-of-state vehicle check, the dispatcher enters the information and sends it off by computer. Since it is an out-of-state request, it goes to NLETS which then forwards it to the state in question for the want check. A request concerning vehicles should include license and engine or serial numbers if possible. If the vehicle is stored, its running condition and place of storage should be included. When requesting registration information, and only the motor, serial or identification number is available, always include the make and model of the vehicle. If the license plate has a symbol between numbers or letters such as the bucking horse on the Wyoming license plate, it is omitted when the license number is entered in.

These services are available to any law enforcement agency desiring out-of-state information, and can be obtained by teletype request to the relay station for the state in which the department is located. This usually includes information requested from any area outside the normal radiotelephone or teletype communications limits.

COMPUTERIZED SOURCES OF INFORMATION FOR THE PATROL OFFICER

Few areas offer more promise to general law enforcement than that of computers. Although they are primarily being used in the area of police records, their ultimate use will be much wider. Present computer systems are being developed on three levels, hut their planning is such that they will eventually all be joined together.

(1) **NATIONAL** On the national level, **NCIC (The National Crime Information Center)** is the major computer system. It is administered by the FBI in Washington, and is linked to existing computer systems throughout the United States by leased lines or microwave. In order for this system to be of maximum effectiveness, the International Association of Chiefs of Police has worked with the FBI to develop a common computer language and a uniform crime reporting system for federal, state, and local police agencies. This system contains information on wanted persons, stolen articles, gun files, and stolen and felony associated vehicles. There are about 16 million records relating to wanted persons and stolen property. Each day NCIC handles about 1,000,000 transactions involving wanted persons, stolen property, and criminal history records. "Hits" or positive responses on stolen property and wanted persons average over 40,000 per day making it worthwhile.

(2) **STATEWIDE** There are two types of state computer systems. They are (a) Specialized and (b) General. Examples of each type are as follows:

(a) Specialized

AMIS (Automated Management Information System) The information obtained from this computer system pertains only to the specialized areas of Vehicle Registration and Driver's Licence Information.

AUTO STATIS (Automated Statewide Auto Theft Inquiry Service) This system specializes in information about stolen, impounded, and repossessed vehicles. It also includes plates and identifiable parts. It operates in conjunction with NCIC. It uses an IBM 7740 computer system and services over 400 police agencies in several western states.

(b) General

CJIC (Criminal Justice Information Control) pronounced See-jiss. This system covers a wide area of criminal justice information and includes sub-systems dealing with wanted persons, stolen articles and gun files. On a local level, this system ties together information about the overall progress of a criminal case that has in the past always frustrated officers seeking follow-up information. It follows an arrested person all the way through the various agencies involved in the administration of criminal justice.

In the past, there have been problems in finding out the final dispositions of cases handled by an officer. Now this information can be retrieved instantaneously. The major areas covered are Field, Investigative, Booking, In-Custody, Court, District Attorney, Probation and Public Defender operations.

(3) **LOCAL** It is usually not financially feasible for a local agency or even a county to set up a computerized information system. To resolve this problem, many major metropolitan areas have grouped together to form such a system. The PIN system in the San Francisco Bay area is a good example.

PIN (Police Information Network) PIN serves 93 agencies in the Greater Bay Area. It is sophisticated enough to locate names when the contributor has misspelled the name. It deals with outstanding criminal and traffic warrants. Parole violators are now being added to this system. If there are special conditions of probation for particular persons, they are listed. It also carries a list of persons who have resisted arrest in the past or have shown violent tendencies when dealing with peace officers. It has already been effective in substantially reducing the half million outstanding warrants for arrest that amount to more than $5,000,000 in bail money.

OTHER POLICE USES OF COMPUTERS

New York State has been running tests on a field tactical use of a computer and scanner. It involves an automatic license plate scanner that is set up alongside a well-traveled road and hooked up to a computer. The scanner transmits license numbers to the computer which then searches its files against a "wanted" list. It immediately flashes its findings back to the patrol officer stationed near the scanner, all in "Real Time." Dick McDonnell, an ex-policeman now working for IBM, describes "Real Time" as "information returned fast enough to help you alter the outcome of an event."

In Chicago, all police files except fingerprints are stored in IBM computers. Many large agencies and state identification bureaus have installed the new computerized fingerprint and latent print systems.

Police jurisdictions all over the country are now taking advantage of computers to assist them in doing a better job of police work. It is hoped that in the future all of these systems will be tied into a major information computer system like the one presently administered by the FBI.

COMMUNICATION OF TRANSIENTS

Throughout history, people whose way of life involved being "on-the-move" or in transit have had a form of written communication. It changes from time to time and from place to place, but if officers will take the time to learn the meaning of these signs, they can do their job a little better. These signs are usually left at the entrance of towns or cities and on the gates or fences of residences. They are left there as a means of either warning others of dangers, or letting them know the type of person living in a particular house or in a community as a whole.

Dr. Hans Gross, the famous German (Bavarian) criminologist, was one of the first to note this in writing when he observed that roaming gypsies left signs and symbols at the entrances of towns which would tell other gypsies which houses were "soft touches" or would warn them of very strict police enforcement.

In the United States the hobo developed his own set of symbols and would leave them around the railroad yards. This is where he would arrive and leave, since his major means of transportation involved "hopping a freight train."

Today we find the transient person following a similar pattern, though his main form of transportation is "hitch-hiking." Because of this the marks and symbols are left in places such as the concrete embankments of freeway overpasses, freeway off-ramps and telephone poles near entrances to towns and cities. Their purpose, like the gypsy and hobo marks, is to tell other transients something about the particular city, house, town or farm.

Transient Symbols

Out of Date		**Modern**	
	You will be shot.		Stay clear. It's a long jail term if caught.
	People at this house are not friendly. Watch the dog.		Religious people and considerate on the whole.
	There have been too many transients stopping here. The place is ruined.		Kind hearted woman here.
	Stop here if you have anything to sell. Watch them, they're pretty sharp.		Act good. Be religious at this house.
			This is a safe camp.
	Not a good place to stop. The people are poor		If you are sick, they will care for you.
	Good place to stop. Kind people. Will give food and maybe money.		This place is under surveillance.
	Keep going. Police are tough here.		You will be beaten.
	Be careful. If the police stop you, it's jail.		Tell a pitiful story.
	They throw you in jail here so they can make you work.		Fink.

STUDY QUESTIONS for Patrol Operations

CHAPTER 6

1. What was used as a means of communication in ancient times? _____

2. In the Middle Ages, the church _____ became a means of communication.

3. Police _____ is the backbone of police tactics.

4. At first, before the police radio, patrol cars were notified by _____.

5. In 1880 the _____ police department installed the first call box.

6. In 1916 the New York Harbor police installed the first _____ transmitter.

7. In the year _____ the Detroit police department went on the air with the first workable police car radio.

8. Police departments wishing to install police radios like Detroit had to make their own because no one manufactured them at that time.   T or F

9. It was 1933 before the first _____ - _____ mobile police radio system was established.

10. At first police departments abused the privilege of using the police radios, and the Federal Communications Commission had to intervene.   T or F

11. In order for police departments to have some unity in communications, communications officers formed a national organization called _____ (initials).

12. In 1939 the first _____ mobile two-way transmitters and receivers were developed.

13. What does "FM" stand for? _____ _____

14. What does a "squelch circuit" do? _____

15. As cities grow they need proper radio _____ to handle all the calls.

16. In the "ABC's of radio transmission", the "A" stands for _____.

17. In the "ABC's of radio transmission", the "B" stands for _____.

18. In the above, the first "C" stands for _____.

19. The second "C" stands for _____.

20. Semantics is the science of _____.

21. Officers, when transmitting over the radio, should always put their brains into gear before releasing the clutch on their _____.

22. The important thing to remember is that the message be (1) received and (2) _____.

23. Phonetics is the science of _____.

24. When transmitting, the officer should hold the mike about _____ inches from the mouth.

25. If you are going Code 3 on a "hot pursuit", and the radio operator is having trouble understanding you, what alternative do you have with the mike? _____

26. To improve phonetics an officer should use similes. Give an example. _____

27. When transmitting the name "Jones", rather than spell it, you should, instead say "Jones" _____ _____.

28. The book states that officers who are on a hot chase often fail to notify the radio operator of what? _____

29. When officers are involved in an accident, they should give the location and _____ _____.

30. What does the word "redundancy" mean? _____

31. When transmitting, your words should be between _____ and _____ words per minute.

32. To increase proper communication, the officer should use a lot of emotion in his voice for emphasis.   T or F

33. The number "0" should be pronounced _____.

34. If you are having trouble hearing a distant car transmitting, adjust the _____.

35. Name an advantage of the multiple channel radio to the patrol officer during an emergency. _____

36. The problem with the electronic console is that it does not have a public address system.   T or F

37. In the "Letter-Number-Letter" system of radio identification, the call identification 1-A-1 would be which person? _____

38. Code 1 means _____.

39. In responding to a "Code 2" call, the officer must obey all traffic laws.   **T or F**

40. All things being equal _____ _____
    has the supreme authority and priority over police communications.

41. Name an exception to the above. _____

42. When one unit is calling another, they should first identify themselves. Example "Unit   **T or F**
    One to Unit Two"?

43. According to federal law any message is the property of _____.

44. The authority to cancel or change radio messages can be delegated.   **T or F**

45. Missing persons, runaways, wanted persons and escapees present a time problem to police
    communications in that they are quite _____.

46. A missing person's report describes the person as an "OMJ". What does this mean?

    _____

47. What does "WMA" mean? _____

48. What is the meaning of the following abbreviations?

    ETA _____   QOA _____
    HBD _____   ETA _____
    QOD _____   GOA _____

49. The Lakewood, Colorado Department of Public Safety found that the Ten Code resulted in   **T or F**
    fewer errors than a "Clear Speech" system.

50. Know the radio code for your community.

51. What is the phonetic alphabet for C & D? _____ & _____
    (learn by reading a paragraph on a page and using the phonetic alphabet for each letter).

52. In the multi-million dollar budget of a large police department _____
    counts for by far the largest portion.

53. The President's Commission Task Force stated "the answer to police problems in cities is   **T or F**
    adding more people."

54. The advantage of the automated command and control dispatch system is that it reduces the response time of the complaint phase by:

    a._ 20%   b.__ 40%

    c._ 50%   d.__ 60%

55. The above system reduces human error (but does not eliminate it).   T or F

56. Name one of the other uses for a "field telephone" (call box). _____

57. How can an officer use a public pay phone without putting in money? _____
    _____

58. You are reading a teletype with the heading: 3 CII 2-28-95 0118.HRS, PDT CRIM

    The "3" means _____.
    The "CII" means _____.
    The "0118.HRS" means _____.

59. Give the AM and PM times for the following 24-hour times.

    23:40 _____   07:20 _____   12:00 _____
    17:30 _____   09:45 _____   13:15 _____
    20:20 _____   19:35 _____   14:40 _____

60. When requesting information about driver's licenses, you should contact the DMV (Dept. of Motor Vehicles) with a subheading of:

    a._ DLS   b.__ DDL
    c._ DLB   d.__ DLU

61. Under the "Type of Message", there is both a "primary" and a "secondary" subject. With a "primary" subject of burglary, what would be a "secondary" heading? _____

62. AKA means _____.

63. In a teletype the abbreviation "S-1" and "S-2" would refer to _____ & _____.

64. What would "V-1" mean? _____

65. A teletype message ends with "J. Smith, Cop Evergreen EPD GTP/SS." What is the meaning of "GTP/SS"? _____

66. What does "PST" in a message mean? _____ _____ _____

67. How about "EDT"? _____ _____ _____

68. What does the message "WF 16 5-3 115, BRN" mean? _____

69. In police terminology, A "J" is a _____; an "X" is a _____.

70. Name one of three ways in which the State Department of Motor Vehicles registers vehicles.

    (1) _____ (2) _____ (3) _____

71. When sending license info and the license has a symbol separating its numbers (such as the bucking horse for Wyoming), the license number would be given as:

    a.__3333   b.__3-333
    c.__3 symbol 333   d.__3 horse 333

72. The NCIC is run by what federal agency? _____

73. NCIC means:

    a.__Nationwide Communications Information Center
    b.__National Center For Information On Crimes
    c.__Nationwide Criminal Identification Center
    d.__National Crime Information Center

74. Autostatis means:

    a.__Automobile Statewide Teletype System
    b.__Automatic Statewide Auto Theft Inquiry Service
    c.__Automobile Statewide Automatic Teletype Service
    d.__Automatic Statewide Auto Theft Search

75. The local computer system that follows a defendant through the criminal justice system is:

    a.__CJIC   b.__FCOC
    c.__PIN   d.__AMIS

76. PIN stands for _____ _____ _____.

77. A term used in police computers is "real time", it means:

    a.__that the information is received before the office closes
    b.__that the information is returned fast enough to help alter the outcome of an event
    c.__that the information pertains to the technology of the present time
    d.__all of the above

78. Where did hobos leave their symbols to tell others about a particular location?

_____

79. Where do present day transients leave their symbols about a particular town? _____

_____

80. Who was the German criminologist and judge who first wrote about these symbols?

_____

CHAPTER VII

OBSERVATION AND PERCEPTION

The success of good patrol procedures rests heavily upon observation, yet few of us really observe things around us. Observation is a skill that every police officer should develop. Any field sergeant can verify that some patrol officers thoroughly cover their beats, yet do not observe what takes place on those beats. The important thing is that all police officers, new and old, can improve their powers of observation. Speed reading has shown that with practice, the average person can perceive, with a high degree of comprehension, entire sentences and more at a glance. Before this training most persons take in one word at a time.

To increase powers of perception, the military has used the Tachistoscope since World War II. It is a short-exposure projecting device. It flashes pictures of ships, tanks and aircraft on a screen, starting at one per second and increasing the speed until servicemen are able to perceive and properly identify the objects at one hundredth of a second. Police departments are now experimenting with this same device to train officers to observe license numbers at speeds of a fraction of a second. This device holds much promise for law enforcement.

The idea of improving perception is not new. There are many recorded instances of individuals developing this power. Houdini and his son perfected a high degree of perception by stopping at store windows, giving a quick glance, and then looking away and describing the articles inside. At first they were lucky to identify more than two objects, but with continued practice, they were able to take one quick glance at a window containing a dozen articles, and to fully describe each article. They found this to be very helpful on the stage when they performed their feats of magic. This same technique can be applied by foot patrol officers as they walk a beat in the downtown area. It is best to start with window displays containing a few large articles. As skill develops, this technique can be used on windows containing many small objects.

Observation can become one of the most useful skills of the patrol officer. It is one of the abilities that is first noticed by the new patrol officer who is riding with a more experience officer as part of the "breaking in" period. When the experienced officer points out certain quick observations, the newer officer cannot help but marvel at what appears to be an unbelievable degree of perception. The new officer often fails to realize that, through application and practice, he or she too may, within as little as six months, develop a degree of skill in observation comparable to that of the experienced officer.

DEFINITION

Webster's unabridged dictionary defines Observation as:

The inspection of, taking note of
To watch and pay attention to
The act or practice of taking notice
The act of seeing or fixing the mind on
To notice closely
To scrutinize with the view of discovering or determining
To perceive. (The dictionary describes perceive as: To have or receive knowledge through the five senses.)

What is the actual process of human observation? First we perceive some external stimulus through one or more of the five senses. Second, the nervous system transmits this perception from that particular sense to the brain where it is registered.

There is more to perception than the actual physical qualities of our individual senses. For example, if we hear a noise to our right side, it is heard by the right ear first and then by the left ear. However, we do not hear the noise as two separate sounds as we should, since the sound does not arrive at both ears at the same time. Our nervous system regulates the two receptions into one and then transfers it to the brain. Should our nervous system become faulty, our perception could also suffer.

Too often we see the process of perception as being photographic. We think that the external stimulus registers on the brain exactly as it is in real life. This is far from true. There is much in the external world that never registers on the senses, and what does register can be far from an exact duplication of that external stimulus. It is possible for something to be added to the perception when it reaches the brain and is processed and recorded. It is also part of human perception for blank spots to be filled in. This enables us to see a movie as a moving perception when in reality it is a series of still pictures. Because of past experiences, we can also add to a stimulus that we briefly perceive, or do not fully perceive. Our brains record it as being the same as other stimuli we have received in the past. Especially if that stimuli was similar in may respects.

Why is it, that when our senses are presented with a multitude of external stimuli, we only select certain of these stimuli? The basic factor is probably attention. Why do we pay attention to one thing and not another? The following are some basic reasons why our attention is given to one particular form of stimulus.

(1) **EXTERNAL REASONS FOR SELECTIVE PERCEPTION**

(a) **Intensity and size**. Whatever the stimulus may be, if it is loud enough or big enough, it will get our attention. This is because it is not normal, and its intensity and size quickly stimulates our senses.

(b) **Contrast**. Contrast causes a very strong stimulus to register with our senses. If we see a bum who is dirty and unshaven in a high class residential district, we are automatically alerted. An officer who notices a young juvenile in old clothes and badly needing a haircut driving a shiny new expensive car is immediately stimulated to the obvious contrast between the driver and the automobile. A well dressed woman of obvious class, in a skid row bar, would immediately stimulate an officer's senses because of the obvious contrast.

(c) **Repetition**. As things repeat themselves, our attention is quickly focused on them. This can be quick repetition such as a gun that is fired ten times, or slow repetition as in the case of a person who is seen loitering on a corner for five straight nights. The first night he might not attract our attention, but each night that he repeats the act, the more intensely will the memory patterns in the brain react to the situation. This will cause us to be more alert to this particular stimulus.

(d) **Movement**. Movement can stimulate our perception because it is easier to notice movement from all parts of the eye, even from the periphery. Stationary objects are not so easily noticed. There is also the contrast of the moving object with the stationary background.

(e) Proximity. The closer something is, the more we notice it. It can be caused by the fear of possible danger or by a positive feeling such as love. This is part of humans' basic animal nature.

(f) Similarity. Because similarities are generally unusual or significant, they stimulate our attention. This can be based on many motives, such as curiosity or fear. If we saw one man wearing a black suit, it might mean nothing. But if ten men were together in black suits, the similarity would cause a mental alert. If an officer noticed a man wearing two pair of trousers, memory would serve as a reminder of all the bums from past arrests who had also worn two pair of trousers. The officer would now become alerted to the possibility of this person also being a bum.

(2) **INTERNAL REASONS FOR SELECTIVE PERCEPTION**

(a) Personal Drives. When an officer sees an exceptionally good-looking person, that person receives immediate attention because of the basic sex drive. If the officer is hungry and passes a hamburger stand, this will stimulate attention.

(b) Personal Interests. An officer who has an interest in cars will be immediately stimulated by a new custom-made car with a special paint job. The officer who is adding a room to a house will pay particular attention to construction jobs on the beat. An officer who raises flowers will be stimulated by gardens that he or she passes, but might not even notice the other stimuli.

(c) Conditioning. Police officers are especially subject to stimuli for which they have been trained. When an officer hears a car "peel out," or hears someone "rap his pipes," there is an immediate mental alert. The tinkling of glass is another. One thing that amazes the average citizen is how officers know immediately when their car is being called on the radio. It is simply a matter of conditioning. New officers who are not conditioned to the stimulus of their call number may have to be called several times.

THE SENSES

Since we achieve observation through the senses, it might be well to discuss the five senses and how they affect our perception.

(1) **SIGHT (VISUAL SENSE).** An officer on patrol must use all five senses and sometimes a sixth. Yet of all the senses, sight is an officer's greatest asset. Few people, including police officers, use their sense of sight to even a fraction of its full capacity.

(a) The rods and cones. There are two parts of the eye that are used for seeing. They are the rods and the cones. The rods are used for night vision and the cones for day vision, the cones are located near the center and the rods around the edge of the eye. The rods cannot distinguish hues of color. Color is perceived only when the illumination is increased to a high enough level to bring the cones into action. Because of this, visual observation at night will usually lack color definition. Thus the old saying "When all candles be out, all cats be gray."

(b) Color blindness. True color blindness is rare. Dichromatism (two colors) which is the most common, allows the subject to see only in two hues, yellow and blue. They confuse red, green and yellow. Color blindness is not an all-or-nothing situation, but occurs in varying degrees of weakness. About one in twenty-five people suffer from some degree of color blindness. Due to the way this condition (Dalton's Dichromatism or Daltonism) is genetically linked, about 99% of "red-green" color blind people are men.

This can be a very dangerous situation when observing traffic signals. This applies whether the person is actually driving, or is a witness to an intersection collision. This should cause the police officer to be suspicious of color identifications during investigations. Even normal eyes will see colors differently from the corner of the eye than they will from a front view. In 1881, Lord Rayleigh, in England, invented a standardized way of testing how colors are perceived by different persons.

In the early 1990's Dr. John Mollon of Cambridge University, and Dr. Samir Deeb of the University of Washington conducted molecular studies of the human eye. They discovered that the cause of different perceptions of red was due to one single amino acid in the red-sensitive pigments of the eye.

(c) Visual acuity. Visual acuity enables us to determine size and shape, but the best acuity is obtained from using the center or fovea rather than the side of the retina. The fovea is that part of the retina directly behind the lens of the eye. Staring or looking directly ahead increases visual acuity because the object becomes focused directly on the fovea. But staring straight ahead causes a decrease in visual acuity just slightly to the right or left of the object at which we stare. For example, if an officer stares straight ahead at the road while driving, he or she will probably not be able to read the signs on either side. Just 5 degrees off the fovea will reduce acuity by one half. At 45 degrees from the fovea, visual acuity will only be one twentieth as good.

During general patrol, officers should neither fix their eyes straight ahead nor should they stare as they might lose part of their peripheral vision. Peripheral vision is most important to patrol officers, for there are times when they literally need eyes in the backs of their heads, and any side vision that might be attained should be utilized to the fullest. Should something alert an officer, he or she can then focus a fixed attention on the object, but when identification has been made, the stare should be relaxed to obtain better visual acuity.

(d) The blind spot. In the retina of the eye there is a place that has no rods or cones. This is where the blood vessels enter the eyeball and the nerves leave. Since there are no rods or cones, we cannot see from this spot. This is called the blind spot. It occurs about 1/4 of the distance from the fovea toward the nose. Each person can locate the blind spot by looking at the drawings below and following the instructions.

We do not normally notice this blind spot because our right eye sees the object when it is in the blind spot of the left eye, and vice versa. This suggests the need for an officer to constantly use both eyes for observation. Both eyes are also needed for any judgment of depth.

Fig. VII-1; Blind spot exercise

Close the left eye by placing the left hand over it. Now look at the star with the right eye. With the right hand, move the book away from you until the hand disappears, or largely disappears, from view. This is the position at which the image of the hand falls on the blind spot of the right eye.

(e) Recognition of persons. There are limitations in our ability to recognize one another under certain conditions. An officer must be aware of them when judging the statements of witnesses regarding their observations.

(i) At night, even during a full moon, a person must be within 30 feet to be recognized by features alone.

(ii) During daylight hours, a little known person may have to be within 90 feet in order to be recognized.

(iii) During daylight hours, a well-known person may be recognized at about 130 feet.

(iv) During daylight hours, a relative, friend, or person whom we know very well (including mannerisms) can be recognized at 300 feet.

(f) Night Vision. At night or when there is less light, the rods of the eye are used for seeing. Since they are around the edge of the retina, it would be wise not to look directly at the object since it would then be focused on the center of the retina where the cones are located. This would result in the object fading out. Therefore, if you were to look slightly above, below or to the side, the object would appear sharper.

When an officer is going from one room to another, and one room is dark and the other lighted, a good technique would be to close one eye upon entering the lighted room. This will prevent the loss of night vision in that eye. This technique involves a certain gamble because safety might be lost by entering the lighted room with one eye.

(g) Color. Since color changes from dawn to dusk, and under different kinds of lighting, such as mercury and sodium, it is wise to show witnesses a color chart under the same conditions in order to obtain a better color description.

(h) Optical illusions. Illusions are false or distorted perceptions. Optical illusions are caused by the relationship of objects to one another, or by background or the pattern or angle of lines.

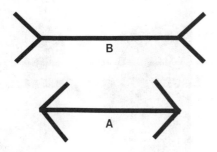

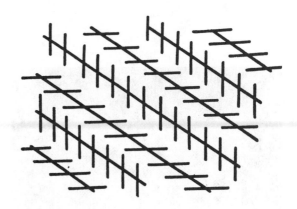

Fig. VII-3; The Zöllner illusion

In Figure VII-3, the Zöllner Illusion, the long lines are all parallel, but the small cross lines give the illusion that they are not. (see below and next page for more optical illusions)

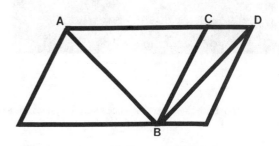

Fig. VII-4; AB and BD are the same length

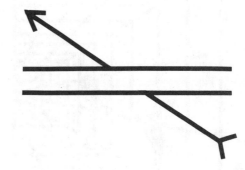

Fig. VII-5; The arrow is really straight

Background can be very important in judging tone and quality. In Figure VII-6 on the next page, the shields enclosed in squares are exactly the same shade. It is the background that makes one appear darker.

Fig. VII-2; The Müller-Lyer illusion

In Figure VII-2, the Müller-Lyer illusion gives the impression that the two lines are of unequal length when in fact they are the same. It is the direction of the spur lines that causes this illusion.

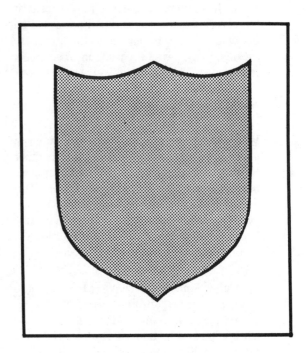

Fig. VII-6; Both shields are the same shade. Why does one look darker?

Fig. VII-7; All figures are the same height.   Fig. VII-8; What do you see? Look again.

(2) **HEARING (AURAL SENSE).** Next to sight, hearing is the most reliable sense. Hearing can be invaluable to both defensive and offensive action. It can warn the officer of impending danger, or give away the whereabouts of someone trying to evade police detection. It can also make a suspect aware of an approaching officer.

(a) **Direction and distance.** Where it takes two eyes to properly perceive distance, and only one eye to determine direction, the ears are just the opposite. It takes two ears to properly perceive direction and only one to determine distance.

To experiment with this, close both eyes and cover one ear. Then try to judge the direction of a certain sound. When a guess has been ventured as to the direction, open both eyes and uncover the other ear to see how close you were.

At night when we are deprived of our full visual perception, we can be easily fooled by the direction of sound if there is too much wax in one ear, or if one ear is affected by a head cold. Direction may be better determined by turning the head so that both ears are involved.

(b) **Hearing in the blind.** When we suffer the loss of one sense, we usually make up for it by developing our other senses to a fuller capacity. This is usually the case with blind persons. In the blind, the sense of hearing is very acute, and is responsible for what we often consider to be a sixth sense. Blind persons can often turn away before walking into a wall. This is because they can hear sounds reflected off of the surface of the wall.

The courts have accepted the testimony of blind persons as to what they have heard as proof of identification. Voice identification is a good example. Most blind persons can identify a person by his or her footsteps.

Things affecting what we hear

Although hearing is considered to be a fairly reliable sense, there are many common factors that will affect what we hear. They are:

1. Volume
2. Direction
3. Acoustics
4. Quality of the sound
5. Condition of listener's ears
6. Outside interference (noise, etc.)

Even if we properly perceive a sound as it actually is, human error can change it by the time it is recorded in the mind. If it should be repeated, it is subject to even greater error. One of the most dangerous forms of testimony is when a person is asked to repeat a conversation that was overheard. In law this is called Hearsay Testimony, and the courts will not accept it except under very special circumstances. Even the ancient Egyptians would not allow its use in court.

If you have ever played the party game of "tell a secret", you have some idea of how the spoken word can be unintentionally changed. In this game, a sentence is written down on a piece of paper and given to one person at the party. He reads it and then whispers the sentence to someone else who in turn whispers it to another person. The last person in the crowd to receive the spoken message then writes it down and the two sentences are compared. If as many as ten persons are involved in this experiment, the sentence will usually have completely lost its original meaning and context.

(3) **SMELL (OLFACTORY SENSE).** The sense of smell is dependent on the olfactory nerves which are located high up in the nasal passages leading from the nostrils to the throat. In normal breathing, little air passes by these receptors, but a sudden sniff will stir up the air in these passages and if the air contains any chemical substances, the olfactory receptors will detect them.

Although the sense of smell is unreliable, it can be extremely sensitive, actually beyond measurement. The olfactory receptors have been noted to detect an odor of a substance that was 400 millionths (1/400,000,000) of an ounce when mixed with a liter of air. Yet animals have an even higher degree of smell. The sense of smell is highly individual. It fatigues faster than any other sense.

Both smell and taste rapidly lose their sensitivity because the nerves fatigue more rapidly than do the other senses. When we first put on a shaving lotion or cologne, the smell is strong, but a short while later it seems to disappear. Actually it hasn't disappeared, it is just that the olfactory sense for this particular smell has fatigued. When we meet someone an hour later, they might remark about the fragrance because it is new to them. This is actually a good thing, for many times we are subjected to unpleasant smells that would make us quite sick if it were not for the fact that our olfactory senses easily fatigue. For all practical purposes, the smell disappears.

Officers must rely on their sense of smell combined with their memory to assist them in the job. Once an officer knows the smell of marijuana, or of chloral hydrate (knock-out drops) it will be helpful in the job. Detecting the odor of natural gas or gasoline can help an officer save lives by locating the source and eliminating it, or just by stopping someone from lighting a match.

(4) **TASTE (GUSTATORY SENSE).** Taste is determined by small taste buds that are located below the surface of the tongue. In order for them to detect taste, the substance must be in solution (dissolved) and penetrate the tongue to reach these taste buds.

There are basically four qualities of taste:

1. Salty Detected on tip and sides of tongue
2. Sweet Detected on tip of tongue
3. Sour Detected on the sides of the tongue
4. Bitter Detected on the back of the tongue.

Taste is highly individual. We all have a preference for a large variety of foods and liquors if they are available. Taste is more sensitive to acids and bitter substances than it is to sweet and salty substances. This might be for the purpose of self protection, since most poisons are acid or bitter.

Smell and taste are mentioned together because they are closely related. Taste is heavily dependent upon smell. Often we think we taste something, when in fact it is mostly a matter of smelling it. To test this, block the nasal passages of a subject with cotton and blindfold him. Then have him taste a drop of vinegar. The subject will know that it is sour, but will not be able to identify it. Under the same circumstances, a piece of potato will not be distinguishable from a piece of apple. It sounds strange, but try it. Colds often ruin the taste of food. They block up the nasal passages and make the food taste different due to the lack of its distinctive odor. There are certain substances that will deaden the sense of smell. Gasoline, kerosene and ether are examples.

(5) **TOUCH (TACTILE SENSE).** The sense of touch is actually four senses which are often referred to as the skin senses. These are:

(a) **Touch or pressure:** Caused by bending of the skin surface or hair.

(b) **Pain:** Caused by injury or damage to the skin.

(c) **Heat** and

(d) **Cold:** The sensation of heat and cold is due to the variation of the temperature of the object touching the skin, and the temperature of the skin. Even a one or two degree variation from the temperature of the skin can be noticed.

The most sensitive parts of the body are the lips, tip of tongue and fingertips.

POLICE OBSERVATION

Many police officers who make a large number of good arrests will often tell you that they know of no one thing that led them to the arrest or caused suspicion. They will reply that they just sensed something was wrong and looked further into the matter. This is a sort of sixth sense that develops after being in police work a while. There are many believers in this theory. To deny the existence of a so-called sixth sense would be foolish in view of all the evidence on extrasensory perception and in view of how little we really know about the human mind at this present date. Yet much of a police officer's so-called sixth sense is really the use of the five senses without realizing it.

Officers may not be able to tell you exactly what it was that alerted them, because it was apparently so insignificant, or possibly a combination of small sensory perceptions. They often can't put their finger on it, so they call it a sixth sense for lack of being able to identify it. If an officer were to closely examine the situation right after it happened, he or she might find some clues to sensory perception that could actually be identified. These clues could then be used to help fellow officers establish probable cause in future field stops.

OBSERVATION FROM A PATROL CAR

Observation from a patrol car involves a paradox. The vehicle code requires that a person give full attention to driving and the road ahead. Yet the basic purpose of the patrol requires a police officer to give attention to what is happening on all sides of the police car. In order to satisfy both requirements, the average officer settles for giving half of his or her attention to the road and driving, and half to beat observation. It is a wonder that more police vehicles are not involved in accidents. There are two reasons why accidents of this type are not more prevalent. They are the development of good peripheral vision, and the ability to make "split second" observations and react to them. Both require attention and practice.

There is a recent innovation that offers much promise in the area of visual perception for the patrol officer. It is the multifaced rear view mirror. First used by European police departments, and re-engineered for American automobiles, this device allows the patrol officer to have almost 180 degree vision to the rear while on patrol duty. It not only reduces accidents by allowing the officers to see spots that are normally blind, but it prevents anyone from sneaking up on the parked patrol car without the officer being aware.

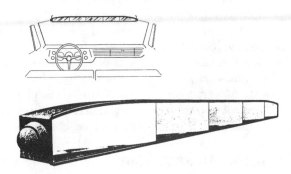

Fig. VII-9, Multifaced rear-view mirror. Illustration courtesy of Winkelman Racing

THE USE OF BINOCULARS

As mentioned previously, a disadvantage of a marked patrol car is that those persons planning a criminal action can spot the patrol car some distance away and temporarily cease their activities or hide any incriminating evidence. One way to overcome this is for each patrol car to have a set of binoculars in the glove compartment. Since sight is the patrol officers greatest asset, this asset is thus streng-thened. Detectives widely use binoculars for their "stakeout" work, but departments seldom provide them for the patrol officer. This is undoubtedly due to the large expenditure that would be involved. Many patrol officers seeing the value of increased vision have purchased their own binoculars.

The courts have made it clear that observations made through the use of binoculars are not illegal since it is an extension of normal vision. As long as the officer has the legal right to be at the location where the binoculars are being used. It does not fall under the same category as wire tapping or invasion of privacy. Although legal, local citizens might feel that this use is in fact an invasion of privacy, and in a democracy the feelings and attitudes of the people can certainly affect police policy. In view of this, the patrol officer should exercise caution in the use of binoculars. Scanning bedroom windows while on patrol would certainly bring this privilege to a halt.

LIGHT INTENSIFYING BINOCULARS

Another useful tool for the patrol officer is the Night Viewing Device. It is a passive device which amplifies light like a loud speaker system amplifies sound. No supplemental light is needed other than starlight, moonlight and sky glow. It enables an officer to detect man-sized objects more than one-third of a mile away under moonlight conditions. It can see in total darkness with infra-red illumination. It is adaptable to TV cameras, 16 mm motion picture cameras, and 35 mm photographic cameras. Most models utilize an Automatic Brightness Control which automatically adjusts the gain to the illumination level of the scene being observed.

USING THE SPOTLIGHT

The use of the spotlight is basically a mechanical skill, but just as important is the ability to know when to use it and under what conditions. The purpose of the spotlight is to obtain concentrated illumination, but using the spotlight can do two things:

1. Locate objects and persons in the darkness.

    a. Persons hiding or getting away.
    b. Locks, safes and signs of forced entry.

2. Give your position away, or make your presence known.

The spotlight should be used sparingly. With practice, an officer can aim the spotlight at something, press the button, and be right on the mark. An officer can develop a high level of skill in the use of the spotlight, and can develop the manual dexterity needed to follow a moving object without jerking the light.

In using the spotlight, officers should be very careful not to shine it in the eyes of the drivers of oncoming cars. The officer would be liable for any accidents that result from a driver being temporarily blinded in this manner.

NIGHT VIEWING DEVICE WITH DIFFERENT LENSES

Fig. VII-10a; 25mm lens

Fig. VII-10b; 50mm lens or 25mm lens with 2X extender

Fig. VII-10c; 100mm lens or 50 mm lens with 2X extender

Fig. VII-10d; 300mm lens

PORTABLE LIGHTS

Most patrol cars carry a plug-in type of extension cord floodlight in the trunk. It is usually plugged into an AC receptacle that has been installed in the dashboard.

Some patrol cars have a special high intensity wide angle flood light on each side of the car roof. Sometimes it is on either end of the emergency light bar. When turned on, it lights up the entire surrounding area on either side of the car.

A recent development is the portable high intensity hand lamp. Through the use of a new gated optical system, this pistol grip lamp is capable of a controlled light output of up to 200,000 candlepower. It is a compact, weatherproof, durable, and valuable tool for the night patrol officer.

ATTENTION GETTERS

None of these attention getters are the basis for either an arrest or a search. They are just reasons for further investigation. The approach to these persons should be friendly and courteous. This type of approach will usually obtain the best results.

An officer cannot legally stop everyone on the street at night to determine whether they might be doing something wrong. In a busy city this is also a physical impossibility. Yet there are many people who are out at night under circumstances that bear watching or checking. From a legal standpoint, there must be some definite suspicious action or behavior (probable cause), along with reasonable belief that a crime has been committed, before the officer can search a suspect. This must be articulable. That means that the officer must be able to verbally explain the reason in court. Yet an officer is justified in stopping and talking to a person whose actions have aroused the officer's keen perceptive nature. The action must be one that causes reasonable concern for either the suspect or the officer. It can also be a concern for the safety of property and persons in the neighborhood. These are sometimes called suspicion arousers. The number of suspicion arousers is unlimited, but the following list will give the new officer some idea of what to look for.

The approach to these persons should not be one of suspicion, but explained to them as one of concern for their safety

(1) **Cars parked with occupants.** It may be a stakeout, casing a place for future criminal acts, or for purposes of illegal sex, such as adultery, rape, oral copulation and sodomy. If there are juveniles in the car, it could involve a case of Contributing to the Delinquency of a Minor. It may also be a getaway car. Be particularly alert if there is one person in the front seat and one in the back, as this arrangement usually means a robbery getaway or sometimes a sexual offense. If there are juveniles in the car, determine their age and relationship to others in the car. Explain that you are concerned because people have been attacked in parked cars recently.

When preliminary observation indicates only one person in the car, but on driving closer, another head pops up, this should arouse suspicion of an act of oral copulation. To confirm this suspicion, the officer should immediately use a flashlight to determine whether there are any undone zippers. In states with "consenting adult" laws, this would not be a violation. Officers who ignore occupied parked cars on their beat will soon have an increase in rape cases.

(2) **Juvenile gangs loitering.** Juvenile gangs or groups loitering around a corner or one special location usually means that they have nothing to do. If they haven't committed some criminal offense, it usually means that they haven't thought of one yet. However, if a group of active, red-blooded youth stand around long enough, someone is bound to think of something daring to do, and chances are that it will be criminal in nature. A close eye should be kept on such groups, and if it can be tactfully done, they should be moved on. If an officer untactfully rousts them on their way, it is quite likely that they will cause many acts of vandalism en route to their next location when they are sure that the police car is not around. If the community has curfew laws, the officer might announce that the next time he or she goes by, identification will be checked. This usually thins out the crowd.

(3) **Persons moving from car to car.** A person who is moving from door to door, or from car to car, could be handing out advertising brochures, but chances are he is looking for an open door, valuables inside a vehicle, or keys in an ignition. Even if he is handing out advertising brochures, it might be a violation of a local ordinance.

(4) **Clerks with frozen looks.** Whenever an officer observes a clerk in a store with a frozen look on his face, a possible holdup should be suspected. If it is the officer's regular beat, the clerk should be contacted and arrangements made to use a set of simple signals such as scratching the nose or pulling the ear, to indicate a holdup. The officer should also advise the clerk to remove large cardboard advertising signs that will block the officer's view of the clerk and cash register when driving by.

(5) **Persons whose faces show fear or are blank.** When a person has done something wrong, they often feel that everyone knows about it, and the expression on their faces can show guilt. When they see a police officer, the guilt reaction can cause an expression of fear. They will often stare straight ahead. Most people will look at a police car as it drives by. An ex-convict will seldom do this, but will maintain a poker face expression as though the police car were not actually there. This is something that is often learned in prison, and should arouse an officer's suspicion as much as the guilty stare.

(6) **Cars being driven without lights.** An automobile driving without lights can mean many things. It can mean that the driver is trying to get away without being seen, or having his license number taken. It can also mean that the driver is drunk, or even sick, or it can simply mean that the driver was careless and forgot to turn the lights on. In any case, the car should be stopped and the driver checked out. Technically it is a violation of traffic law, even though a minor one.

(7) **Cars being driven in a damaged condition.** Cars with old damage should be checked out against the "wanted hit and run" file. Those with fresh damage or leaking radiators should be stopped as possible hit and run vehicles fleeing the scene. Cars with signs of bullet damage should always be stopped for investigation. Sometimes it is caused by the driver attempting petty theft from some farm or ranch, and having the farmer shoot at the car with a shotgun. These incidents are often not reported to the police. Repairing bullet holes in a vehicle without first clearing them with the police is a criminal offense. So is driving a damaged or unsafe vehicle on a street or highway.

(8) **Persons running at night.** Persons running at night may have committed a crime, but it could also be that they are running from someone who is trying to assault them. Of course they may also be running to catch a bus, but the way to find out is to stop and ask them. They may also be running to obtain medical help or call the fire department. In these cases the officer can be of great help. It should be noted that it is a common Modus Operandi of some residential burglars to wear a jogging suit and case the neighborhood while jogging. If it turns out to be a local resident, the officer should introduce himself or herself and explain that he or she wants to serve the neighborhood by getting to know the local residents. This can turn a touchy situation into a good public relations move.

(9) **Barking dogs.** Barking dogs in a residential neighborhood can be quite a headache to the patrol officer. They often get call after call to a particular location. Some dogs just love to bark all of the time. But sometimes it is an indication that someone strange is in the neighborhood. An officer should never overlook the fact that a burglar or prowler could be causing the dog to bark. A careful examination of yards and lawns in the area might reveal fresh footprints.

(10)**lFlagrant traffic violators.** Flagrant traffic violators require the patrol officer's immediate attention. The safety of the public demands it. There are many reasons for this type of driving. The driver may be leaving a crime scene in a hurry; he may be drunk; the car may be stolen, and the driver is not used to the car; the driver may be underage and unlicensed; the driver may be taking someone to the hospital; or it may just be a case of reckless driving.

(11)**Cars that won't pass a police car.** Many law abiding citizens will not pass a police car because they are afraid they might get a ticket. There are also many criminal violators who are afraid to pass a police car because they fear possible recognition. These drivers will usually turn off at the next intersection. The patrol officer should be alert to these actions, and try to get a look at the driver. This can sometimes determine whether the driver is a law abiding citizen or some known or suspected criminal. The act of not passing a police car by itself is certainly not grounds for stopping a car, but it can be a basis for getting a closer look at the car and the driver. If the driver has done something wrong, he might be nervous and commit some minor traffic violation which would allow the officer to stop the vehicle and identify the driver.

(12)**Drivers who don't fit the cars they are driving.** A person who is not used to a particular car may have some trouble in driving it. His appearance may also not match the type of car he is driving. This also applies to drivers who appear to be too young to have a license. Today this presents more of a problem due to the large number of middle and upper class young persons who dress in raggedy clothes. It is now more common to see an expensive car driven by a person who looks like a transient just up from the freeway. They seem to want to turn their backs on all the material things in life except automobiles.

(13)**Person dressed as a burglar.** A burglar does not wear a sign saying "burglar," nor does he intend to wear clothes that will give him away. However, in order to best commit the burglary, he will wear clothes that are adaptable to the performance of his task. Silence can be very important to the burglar, so he usually wears tennis shoes. This type of shoe also gives him better footing for climbing on roofs or for running from the scene. Since he doesn't· want to leave fingerprints at the scene, he will either wear or have in his possession a pair of gloves, even in warm summer weather. In order not to be readily seen, he will usually wear dark clothes. When a patdown is justified under the "Terry v. Ohio" decision, it may reveal the possession of burglar tools or devices for picking or slipping locks. Since they are made of metal, they would feel like weapons. Possession of such tools is usually a felony in most states.

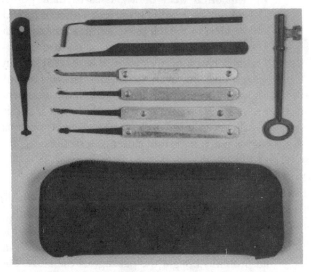

Fig. VII-11; Lock-picking tools

(14)**Persons carrying things at night.** It doesn't take but a few seconds to stop a person who is carrying things at night to determine what he is carrying and where he is taking it. During this process, the questions are not nearly as important as the expression of the suspect or his answers to the questions. It could explain the fact that there have been a large number of thefts in the area.

(15) **Persons with bulges under their clothing.** A person who has nothing to hide will readily explain why he is hiding something under his clothing. Unless it is raining, most people will not do this. Sometimes the object is small and requires close observation on the part of the officer to notice it.

(16) **Cars parked with the motor running.** This is a vehicle code violation because it can cause property damage, injury and even death should the gears accidentally engage. An officer should also be alert to the possibility of its being used as a getaway car or an attempt at suicide by carbon monoxide poisoning.

(17) **Persons wearing dark glasses at night.** Some people with special eye problems may have to wear dark glasses at night. However, this is rare. Those who have used narcotics recently will often wear dark glasses so their pupils cannot be readily observed. Officers should be alert to the tell-tale contraction or dilation of the pupils that accompany the use of certain types of narcotics. There are certain groups, however, that wear dark glasses at night because it is "cool" and all the members of their group wear them. Although it is not illegal to wear dark glasses at night, persons who do so warrant closer observation.

RATIONALIZATION

Some officers rationalize every situation that occurs in the field. They can find an excuse for every suspicion arouser mentioned. They think "Oh he probably bought the package at the store. He probably lives in the neighborhood even if I haven't seen him before. He's stopping everyone on the street, but he's probably just asking for the time. Or maybe he's asking people for directions." Officers who rationalize every suspicious action will make few arrests and crime will increase on their beats.

FAULTS IN OBSERVATION

If perception was strictly physical, there would be little distortion in our observations, providing our senses were working properly. But perception is not strictly physical, and it is so strongly affected by emotion, environment and conditioning, that it is often difficult to know exactly what to believe.

There is an old saying, "believe nothing you hear and only half of what you see." The longer an officer is in police work, the more truth will be found in this saying.

A person seldom realizes at the time an observation is made that he or she might later be required to appear in court as a witness to that incident. Yet studies show that even intelligent people, who are pre-warned about an impending incident, will testify with considerable discrepancy as to what they saw.

THE MÜNSTERBERG EXPERIMENTS

Hugo Münsterberg, professor of psychology at Harvard University in the early 1900's was quite concerned about the conflicts in testimony at a trial that he attended. Being an experimental psychologist, he decided to conduct experiments in human perception and testimony at Harvard University. He used several hundred law students from his psychology classes to conduct experiments in visual perception, time judgment, sound perception and distraction.

Visual Perception

For 5 seconds, he showed the students a white piece of cardboard with 50 black squares, that were unevenly spaced. This was to represent a crowd of people in a room. The students were asked to write down the number of squares. The answers were between 25 and 200 black squares. The answers of over 100 were more frequent than those below 50. This further confirms other experiments that indicate that people tend to overestimate or to exaggerate numbers of things or people.

Time Judgment

He clicked two objects together and then ten seconds later he clicked them together again. The students were asked to write down the time that lapsed between the two clicks. The students reported the time as being between one half second and 60 seconds.

Sound Determination

He struck a tuning fork below the desk out of sight of the class. He then asked them to write down what device made the sound. They reported it was a bell, an organ pipe, a muffled gong, a brazen instrument, a horn, a cello string, a violin, the growl of a lion, a steam whistle, a fog horn, a fly wheel, and a human song. Only two students described it as a tuning fork. He also asked them to describe the tone and got responses like soft, mellow, humming, deep, dull, solemn, low, resonant, clear, penetrating, full, rumbling, rough, sharp, and whistling.

Distraction

He held up a revolving disk in his right hand, high above his head, and watched it very eagerly. He then took a pencil from his pocket and wrote something on the desk with his left hand. He took his watch out and laid it on the table. He then took his cigarette case out and removed a cigarette and then snapped the case shut with a click. 18 out of the 100 students saw nothing done with the left hand. This knowledge of the power of distraction has been used for centuries by ma-gicians. The same techniques are used by criminals such as pickpockets.

The author conducted similar experiments in his Criminal Investigation classes of about fifty students, using the same format as Münsterberg, and obtained basically the same variation in answers.

MECHANICS OF FAULTY PERCEPTION

Human testimony involves five stages:

1. We **PERCEIVE** stimuli through the five senses.

2. We **EVALUATE** what we perceive from our own experiences and reasoning.

3. We **RECORD** it in our minds according to our evaluation.

4. We **RECALL** it according to our degree of memory.

5. We **RELATE** it to others.

Between all five steps lies an abyss of human error, and it is most important that all police officers be aware of this so they can better judge statements and testimony.

Between perceiving something and fixing it in our minds, we alter it to meet the following conditions:

1. We sense things based on our wants and needs.

2. We sense things based on what we already believe or want to believe.

3. We sense things based on what we already expect to sense.

In other words we inject a part of ourselves and our environment into what we perceive. Our perception is conditioned to our desires, beliefs and expectations.

1. **We sense things based on our wants and needs.** Those who have served in the military overseas understand how important mail is. This is especially true when it arrives after a long period of time without receiving mail. The following story shows how what we hear can be affected by what we want to hear.

During the Korean War, the author was on a small ship that had just tied up alongside the Battleship Missouri to transfer a load of 16 inch shells which it had just brought from Japan. The Missouri had been shelling an enemy airfield inland from Inchon harbor, and had just about run out of shells. Because the Missouri had been at sea and on the move for a long time, it had been over two months since its personnel had received any mail.

An officer from the battleship yelled across to the captain of the small ship asking if they were carrying any mail for the Missouri. The captain replied that he had seventy-five sacks of mail, and that none of it was for the Missouri. The officer from the Missouri turned to another officer and stated, "They said that there were seventy-five sacks of mail, and they're not sure but they think there might be some for us." The other officer called to someone else stating, "They have at least seventy-five sacks of mail for us on that ship." He in turn yelled to another sailor. "They have almost a hundred sacks of mail for us and probably more." In twenty minutes a large working party boarded the small ship to pick up the several hundred sacks of mail that they insisted belonged to the Missouri.

2. **We sense things based on what we want to believe.** Toulouse-Lautrec, a famous French painter, was standing by one of his paintings depicting a woman getting out of bed, and a man half undressed sitting on the edge of the bed. A woman looked at the painting and told her companion how disgusting and immoral the painting was. Lautrec turned to the woman and said, "Madam, this painting is of a man and wife who are getting up in the morning, and their happiness is not due to sensual lust, but to the fact that it is their twenty-fifth wedding anniversary, and that their son is taking them out to dinner that evening. Madam, please take your filthy mind and go look at someone else's painting."

3. **We sense things based on what we already believe.** There are many experiments that can demonstrate this fact. One of them is the experiment where a person is shown a picture of a streetcar scene. On the streetcar is a Caucasian who is bent over. Next to him is an African-American with a loaf of bread in his hand. Next to him is a Caucasian woman. Next to her is a Caucasian with a knife in his hand. The person who is shown this picture is asked to privately tell the next person what he saw. That person in turn tells the next one and so on. If there is the belief among the members of the class that African-Americans carry knives, before the description of the picture goes very far, the knife will appear in the hand of the African-American, and the bread will be in the hand of the Caucasian.

4. **We sense things based on what we expect to sense.** Preconditioning strongly affects sensory perception. For instance, you are shown a bowl of worms at a fraternity initiation. You are blindfolded. A forkful of clean spaghetti is put in your mouth. You will firmly believe that you have a mouth full of worms.

Again, you are at a fraternity initiation. You see a branding iron sitting in some hot coals. You are blindfolded, and a piece of ice is put on your arm. You would swear that you have just been branded with a hot iron.

OTHER FACTORS THAT AFFECT OBSERVATION

To make an observation known, it must be expressed. Unless it is being related as it happens, it must be expressed through recalling the observation from the memory center. Our memory picture will often suffer change through the following:

1. If it is given much thought.

2. Each time it is expressed orally.

3. Each time it is written.

4. If much time elapses between the observation and the telling.

5. If many others disagree with what we believe we observed.

It is common for us to look back to our childhood and remember something that brought us much enjoyment, such as the old swimming hole. As the years pass, our memory changes the swimming hole into a crystal clear lake. When we return to our old home town, we are shocked at how it has changed in size and purity. It is really still the same small mudhole that it was in our childhood, it is just that time has changed it in our minds.

COURTROOM TESTIMONY

As all humans are different, so human testimony can be different. Studies of experimental psychology show us that it is natural for a large group of people seeing a situation, to report it in many different ways.

Yet when ten people report something as being exactly the same, verbatim, we are inclined to accept it as being the gospel truth. In fact it defies human nature and common error for ten people to see a single situation in exactly the same way.

Why does this happen? Basically it can be due to witnesses discussing what they saw and to the insecurity of some people's convictions when challenged by the testimony of others. When we hear someone else give their story, we can unconsciously change our perception to match that of the other witnesses. It seems to follow the rule that "there is safety in numbers."

An interesting class experiment is often conducted with the student who is continually late. The instructor enters into a conspiracy with the class in which he presents a problem on the board which is obviously wrong such as 4 and 4 equals 9. When the whole class agrees with the instructor that 4 and 4 equals 9, the latecomer, who is not in on the joke, will seldom raise his hand and object because he feels that if the whole class agrees with the answer, then he must have done something wrong in his figuring even though he knows that 4 and 4 do not equal 9.

This illustrates the need for a patrol officer to separate witnesses at the scene until their individual statements can be obtained.

STUDY QUESTIONS for Patrol Operations

CHAPTER 7

1. Powers of observation are inborn and cannot be improved.   T or F

2. The tachistoscope does what?

    a._ measures the distance between the eyes
    b._ improves the speed of perception
    c._ measures the distance between the iris and the fovea
    d._ all of the above

3. Who was it who developed a very high degree of visual perception by looking in store windows and identifying the objects inside, during shorter and shorter times?

    a._ H. Gross   b. __H. Houdini
    c._ G. Payton   d. __A. Volmer

4. Perception applies to all five senses.   T or F

5. In the process of perception, the brain records exactly what the stimuli is in a photographic   T or F
    manner.

6. Which of the following cause selective perception?

    a._ intensity and size   b. __movement
    c._ repetition   d. __all of these

7. Which of the following cause selective perception?

    a._ proximity   b. __contrast
    c._ similarity   d. __all of these

8. Of all the senses, _____ is the patrol officer's greatest asset.

9. The rods are for _____ vision and the cones are for _____ vision.

10. Visual observation at night will usually lack color identification.   T or F

11. The most common type of color blindness involving two colors is called:

    a._ dichromatism   b. __bilocation
    c._ dicotomism   d. __bichromism

12. About one person in _____ suffers from some degree of color blindness.

13. Visual acuity enables us to determine:

     a.__ distance   b.__height
     c.__size and shape   d.__shades of white and black

14. Staring straight ahead increases visual acuity, but reduces overall vision (peripheral).   T or F

15. All persons have a blind spot in each eye.   T or F

16. Both eyes are needed for any judgment of depth.   T or F

17. At night, even during the full moon, a person must be within 30 feet to be recognized by features alone.   T or F

18. At night it is not wise to look directly at an object because at night we are using the rods, and they are on the side of the retina. Instead we should look slightly to one side.   T or F

19. Next to sight _____ is the most reliable sense.

20. It takes two ears to perceive direction (the opposite of the eyes).   T or F

21. Direction may be better determined by turning the head slightly.   T or F

22. Hearing is referred to as the _____ sense.

23. The ancient Egyptians did not allow hearsay testimony in court.   T or F

24. The sense of smell is dependent upon what nerves?

     a.__nostralia   b.__olfactory
     c.__nasal   d.__proboscia

25. The sense of smell is very individual and usually unreliable.   T or F

26. The sense of smell fatigues faster than any other sense.   T or F

27. Where are the taste buds located? _____

28. There are _____ qualities of taste.

29. Taste is more sensitive to _____ and _____ substances.

30. Taste is heavily dependent upon smell.   T or F

31. _____ tends to deaden the sense of smell.

32. Touch is basically _____ senses.

33. The most sensitive parts of the body are the _____, tip of the
    _____, and the _____.

34. Much of the so-called sixth sense of experienced policemen is really the use of the five   T or F
    senses without realizing it.

35. The courts have declared the use of binoculars by police officers to be unconstitutional.   T or F

36. The only light needed for the new "light intensifying binoculars" is sky glow, stars or
    _____.

37. The spotlight should be used sparingly because it can _____.

38. There are now new portable spotlights with candlepower as high as _____.

39. An officer who aggressively moves a group of juveniles away from a particular location
    is likely to cause them to commit what offense? _____

40. Name one of the ways in which burglars dress._____

41. The Harvard University professor who did experiments in human perception was:

    a. _Wilson   b. _Volmer
    c._Munsterberg   d. _Hoover

42. How many stages are there in human testimony?

    a. _three   b. _four
    c._five   d. _six

43. Between which steps in the above procedure is there the greatest danger of error?

    a. _perception and evaluation   b. _evaluation and recording
    c._recording and recalling   d. _recalling and testifying

44. We sense what we? (three answers) Name two.

    (1) _____ & (2) _____

45. Name two conditions that change how we normally perceive things.
    _____ & _____

46. When we remember things from our childhood, we tend to think of them as being better   T or F
    than they actually were.

CHAPTER VIII

FIELD NOTE TAKING AND CRIME SCENE RECORDING

PURPOSE OF FIELD NOTE TAKING

If all police officers were gifted with photographic memories, there would still be the need for note taking. It is extremely important to an officer's investigative duties while working in the field. It is an essential tool of the trade in law enforcement. Since we are creatures of habit, it is important that new police officers begin by forming proper habits in the use of field note taking so that it will eventually become second nature to them. Some of the major reasons for field note taking are as follows:

(1) **To make a permanent record of events**. Very few police officers have photographic memories. Yet sometimes an officer will be called to testify years after an incident has occurred. He or she must rely on these notes because memory alone will not suffice. In Chapter VII on Observation and Perception, the factors that effect memory were discussed. The author was once subpoenaed to testify regarding a fatal accident that had occurred six years before. The jury is made up of human beings, and they know the limitations of memory. When they see an officer refer to notes that were taken at the scene, they give this testimony more weight. This is especially true if the officer impresses them as being a capable and reliable person. They know that the notes have not changed with time and personal feeling. Most Codes of Civil Procedure state something similar to the following: "A witness is allowed to refresh his memory respecting a fact, by anything written by himself, or under his direction, at the time when the fact occurred, or immediately thereafter, or at any other time when the fact was fresh in his memory and he knew that the same was correctly stated in the writing. But in such case, the writing must be produced, and may be seen by the adverse party, who may, if he chooses, cross-examine the witness upon it, and may read it to the jury. So, also, a witness may testify from such a writing, though he retain no recollection of the particular facts, but such evidence must be received with caution."

(2) **To Aid Memory for Report Writing and Investigation.** An officer will often not be able to write the actual offense report until after other immediate calls have been handled. Not only will time have its effect on forgetting certain facts, but it will tend to distort them. There will also be the other more recent cases to confuse the first. Often if we can just bring one little hint of a situation back to our minds, the entire picture seems to follow. Notes can serve as memory hooks on which to bring back whole pictures, scenes or incidents. This can be especially true if the incident is to be recalled the same night before writing a complete offense report.

As an aid to investigation, notes can tell an officer whether all the duties required at a crime scene were performed. By looking back at the notes, the officer can see if there were some areas that were overlooked in the investigation. The notes also contain opinions that might not be listed in the completed offense report. They may also record little simple acts of behavior or statements by the defendant that could be very damaging in court. Especially if they tend to show intent. The mere writing down of happenings tends to further impress them on our memory. This point is stressed by psychologists who have conducted studies on note taking in college.

(3) **As An Aid to Interrogation.** Many times a patrol officer will arrest someone in the field and will bring the suspect to headquarters to be interrogated by an expert interrogator. It is most important for the interrogator to have some background information on the suspect. Because the case is fresh, an offense report has not yet been written. The officer should not rely on memory alone to brief the interrogator. In an interrogation it is quite important to have every piece of information about the case and the suspect. Many expert interrogators have reported that during an interrogation they have felt something wrong. They sensed a missing key. On talking to the officer again, and searching for details, they discovered some small piece of information that enabled them to return and successfully interrogate the suspect. Good notes taken at the scene can often mean the difference between a successful or failed interrogation.

(4) **To counteract changes in a person's story.** A police officer soon learns that the saying "It is a woman's prerogative to change her mind," applies to all persons. Many people will make statements to an officer and then later change their statements or even completely deny what they said. During the hustle-bustle of an emotion-filled investigation, it is possible for an officer to get certain statements confused, and then possibly doubt the authenticity of the statements because of basic human uncertainty. One of the best ways to correct this is through the taking of notes at the scene. <u>If an officer suspects that the person will later change his statement, the statement should be put in writing in the field notebook, and the person should sign it.</u> Many months can pass between the original investigation and the final court appearance. Witnesses can unconsciously change their own concept of what they said and believe their new viewpoint to be correct. Notes taken at the scene can correct this error.

(5) **To lay out an overall picture.** An officer at the scene is often under great pressure. This is a result of trying to protect the scene, obtain statements from witnesses, and talk to the complainant while they are all often seeking the officer's attention. Naturally it is difficult to think under these conditions. If an officer takes as many notes as possible, he or she can go to some quiet spot and from these notes form an overall picture. If it appears that the situation is still unclear, re-interviewing the witnesses may help. Many things may become clearer to an officer during the course of a difficult investigation when notes are re-read. They may suddenly reveal something that was originally overlooked.

EQUIPMENT NEEDED

The equipment needed for field notetaking is not extensive. It should consist of the following:

(1) **A notebook.** The notebook should be about 3 x 6 inches. One of the most common is the six ring looseleaf memo book #K-25 put out by the McMillan Co. This size enables the book to be carried in the officer's pocket. It should be available at all times.

The looseleaf type of notebook is best. Certain pages may be removed for use in court without taking the whole book. The paper should be thin lined, as this allows more to be put on the page. This also promotes neatness.

(2) **Writing implements.** The patrol officer should always carry two writing implements. It could be embarrassing to run out of ink in the middle of a notetaking session and have to ask someone else for a pen. It would be more embarrassing if no one else had one. It would be extremely embarrassing if the officer was writing a traffic citation and had to ask the violator for a pen. Always carry a spare. An officer should also carry a lead pencil so that the writing will not run when writing or taking measurements in the rain.

(3) **Tape measure.** In order for a patrol officer to make good reports, it is often required that certain measurements, such as the width of a jimmy mark, or the size of a broken window, or the length of a knife blade be recorded. Some officers carry the large 10 foot steel tapes with them at all times, but this can soon wear a hole in the pocket.

There are several companies that put out a very thin steel tape measure, that will extend to ten feet, but is only about 1/4″ in width. Since the width of the tape is seldom important, this type is recommended. To further save the pocket, it is recommended that a small cloth bag be sewn in which to carry the tape measure.

(4) **Graph paper.** Few policemen seem to be artists. Yet with a sheet of graph paper, a very neat and accurate drawing can be made by even an amateur. It requires only a little practice. Graph paper not only enables an officer to draw a good overhead view of the object, but it is also good for three dimensional views.

(5) **Tracing paper.** Many times an officer wishes to describe an object that was stolen, and the victim has a catalog showing a picture of the object taken. By using a sheet of tracing paper, the officer can obtain a reasonable facsimile to attach to the report.

(6) **Printed forms.** Using pre-printed forms ensures that information required for the particular type of report is obtained. At a crime scene there can be many emotional pressures that may cause an officer to forget an item that might be required on the final offense report. By using a pre-printed form, the officer simply fills in the spaces. The report will have the essential information.

OFFENSE FORM

TYPE OF CRIME	DATE COMMITTED
THEFT	3-18-95

NAME OF VICTIM (FIRM NAME IF BUSINESS)	TIME COMMITTED
JOHN HARRISON	1300 HRS

RESIDENCE ADDRESS	PHONE
1234 JACKSON	427-1810

BUSINESS ADDRESS	PHONE
567 S FIRST ST.	528-1132

PERSON ATTACKED	PROPERTY ATTACKED
N/A	1 STORY RES. YARD

HOW ATTACKED
TAKING PANTIES FROM CLOTHES LINE

MEANS OF ATTACK
HANDS

OBJECT OF ATTACK
POSSIBLE SEXUAL GRATIFICATION

TRADEMARK OR PECULIARITY
"S" TOOK ONLY COLORED PANTIES

WHAT DID SUSPECT SAY?
N/A

TRANSPORTATION USED
ON FOOT

WHERE COMMITTED
1234 JACKSON

REPORTED BY (W)	ADDRESS	PHONE
MARY SMITH	1236 JACKSON	427-1927

DATE/TIME REPORTED	REPORTED TO
3-18-95 - 1310 HRS	POLICE DESK

NAME OF SUSPECT	SEX	DESCENT
UNKNOWN	M	W

HEIGHT	WEIGHT	AGE	HAIR COLOR	EYE COLOR
5'8"	160	13-16	BRN	UNK

MARKS, SCARS
NONE NOTICED BY WITNESS

OCCUPATION	DISGUISE OR DRESS
POSS. STUDENT	BL JEANS- W. TSHIRT

FORM 200-29

PERSONS ARRESTED
NONE

Fig. VIII-1; Offense report form

(7) **Compass or map.** Sometimes when it is important that an officer obtain the true compass headings when describing the relation of things. The proper way to determine this would be through the use of a small magnetic compass. Another way would be to use a street map. Most street maps have indicators marking north. By orienting the street in relation with the street map, it is a simple matter to determine compass direction.

(8) **Chalk.** In the investigation and taking of information at a crime scene or accident, there are times when evidence must be moved, for example: a victim in a stabbing where death is not instantaneous must be taken to the hospital in a hurry, or an automobile (in an accident) which is blocking traffic and causing a traffic jam must be moved. In these cases, the officer may quickly outline the position of the victim with chalk for later reference, or chalk the position of the wheels of the vehicle, and then allow removal. This will still allow measurements to be taken later, at the officer's convenience.

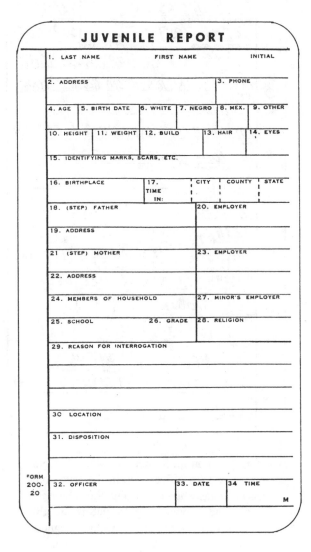

Fig. VIII-2; Juvenile report form

THE CARE AND USE OF THE NOTEBOOK

There are certain procedures that should be followed in the care and use of the notebook. They are as follows:

(1) **Make sure that your name is in the book.** Since the covers of most police type notebooks have a grained surfaced, it is difficult to put a name on them. Because of this, notebooks are continually found lying around the squad room or at crime scenes, and it presents a problem in identifying the owner. Sometimes they can be traced through case numbers. A spot check at one department revealed that almost 50% of the officers did not have names in their notebooks.

(2) **Keep it filled with paper.** If notebooks aren't checked regularly, it is easy to run out of paper. Officers should carry extra paper in their cases. When an officer runs out of paper, 3 x 5 cards or the backs of printed forms are often used. This is the start of a bad procedure.

(3) **Don't start a "vest pocket file."** One of the best indications of a lazy and disoriented officer is the use of the so-called "vest pocket file." This involves using standard 3 x 5 notecards as a notebook. Because of their small size, they hold a minimum of information. The officer using these cards as a notebook will usually take the basic information such as the name, address, and phone number of the victim or complainant and the type of offense and sometimes the date, in order to fill out the initial contact form at police headquarters. The disadvantages of this system, apart from promoting a minimum of information, is that the cards are easily lost and they are not kept together in any way that ensures continuity.

(4) **File old notes properly.** When the notebook becomes full, the pages should be stored in the officer's locker in proper order so they may be located when needed. An officer should never throw notes away. Some officers feel that, when the statute of limitations has run out, the notes are of little value. However, the officer may be subpoenaed to testify

in a civil trial where the statute of limitations is different. It is also easy for an officer to throw the old notes into a locker without placing them in proper order. The amount of time it takes to file them properly is a fraction of the time it takes to locate improperly filed notes. It is a universal rule that when old notes are needed, it is an emergency and they are needed immediately.

(5) **Don't crowd paper.** Paper is cheap. Do not sacrifice clarity for economy of space. The only time this should be done, is when there are only a few pages left, and this shouldn't happen. It is good for officers to develop the habit of checking their notebook before each shift to ensure an adequate supply of paper.

(6) **Don't use an individual style of shorthand.** Remember that something can happen to you and if the notes are not legible, justice may suffer. Always consider this possibility when taking notes. Abbreviations may be used if they are common in policework and easily understood by other officers..

(7) **Use a rubber band as a marker.** Officers should place a thick rubber band around the cover of their notebooks and the last page used. It will be very easy to open the book to the next clean page. This will save the officer a lot of unnecessary thumbing of pages in trying to locate a place to start writing.

(8) **Be generous with time notations.** When an officer is taking notes at the scene, it is easy to obtain time estimates. The next day or in the days to follow, this becomes increasingly more difficult. In court, the defense attorney will often spend time harping on the exact or estimated times of certain happenings.

(9) **Use capital letters to denote persons in the report.** Rather than referring to each person in the report by name each time, a capital letter should be used to denote this person. For example, "C" for Complainant, "V" for Victim and "S" for suspect. If there are several victims or suspects, they should be numbered "S-1," "S-2" and so on. They may be indicated by putting the circled letter in front of the name. This is often a matter of department policy. Some agencies want the names to be spelled out in full each time they are used.

(10) **Use uniform habits in the location of certain pieces of information.** If each piece of information is written in the same spot each time a report is taken, it will be easy to check on the possibility of missing something. Each officer can set up an individual system, just as long as it is consistently followed. As illustrated at left, the example has the case number in the upper right hand corner, the type of offense right under it, and under that the location of the offense. In the upper left hand corner is the date, and under it is the time of arrival at the scene. The circled times are the times that the complainant and the victim were questioned.

Fig. VIII-3, Example report handwritten in notebook

Make sure the day of the week is listed along with the date. For follow-up purposes, this information can be of great value. This is especially true if the report is examined a year or more later. For example, instead of "3-21-96," it should be "(Sat) 3-21-96."

(11) **Make sure that the notes are legible**. understandable, concise, accurate, and complete. They should be legible so that the officer, a partner or the jury can understand them. If an officer scribbles in an effort to speed up the writing, it may be wasted effort. If scribbling is necessary in an emergency, the notes should be re-copied in a legible manner immediately after the emergency situation is over. The second set of notes will still be acceptable in court. The law will allow two officers to make just one set of notes for both of them to use, so this makes it even more important that they be legible.

Field notes will be considered understandable if they convey the intended message and do not mislead. The officer should always be mindful, when writing, that others may have to read and understand the notes. They should be concise (contain no unnecessary material and not be repetitious in content.) Striving for the facts will help in this matter. They should always be accurate because if an officer's memory fails him, the notes are what will be sworn to when testifying under oath. They can be considered complete if they answer the basic questions of: who, what, when, where, why and how.

WHEN TO TAKE NOTES

Generally speaking, officers should not start taking notes right away. First hear what the complainant has to say. Many people restrict their information when they see it all being written down. There is also the possibility that after the officer has written several pages, it will be realized that the complainant is mentally ill and is expressing a delusion, and that the note taking was a waste of time and effort. Let the person talk for a little while until the gist of the problem is obtained. The officer then has had a chance to size up the complainant. When the whole story is heard once, it can make a difference to the legibility of the notes because the

officer now has a general picture of the problem. Notes are taken whenever there is information to be obtained, but generally they are taken when:

(1) **Receiving a routine complaint.**

(2) **Investigating a crime scene for evidence.** Unless the officer is the criminal investigator, note taking should be restricted to identifying and writing down the location of evidence, not collecting it. The key is "Record, but don't touch."

(3) **When meeting possible informants.** An officer should always write down the names of people, and their possible use as informants.

(4) **The patrol officer notices something suspicious.** Notes should include all known people and the license numbers of cars that may be associated with the incident. This should be done before the cars leave the scene. If some of them are leaving when the officer arrives, these numbers should be recorded first.

HOW TO OBTAIN INFORMATION

Apart from a complainant, who is normally willing to give information, the patrol officer must also interview reluctant witnesses. These are usually persons who do not wish to get involved because they are afraid of being subpoenaed into court and missing work; they may also be afraid of retaliation by criminals should they testify against them. Many officers will walk up to a crowd of witnesses and say, "All right, who saw anything." When no one answers, they write down "no witnesses" in their reports. There are techniques to assist patrol officers in obtaining information.

(1) Upon arrival, the officer should write down the license numbers of all vehicles leaving the scene. The cars could be driven by the perpetrator or witnesses. With license numbers, it is easy to later locate drivers for interviews.

(2) The officer should stand back and view the whole crowd, looking for people who are explaining things to others. A good approach would be "They tell me that you saw this happen, would you mind telling me what you

saw?" Under these circumstances, a witness is more likely to give information. Sometimes officers can use a little psychology by playing the "dummy." They can scratch their heads and say "Boy, this is really a tough one to figure out, we're really stymied." This is an open invitation for someone to be "important" and tell the "experts" how it all happened.

(3) When the crowd is large, and there are many witnesses, the investigating officer should not spend too much time with one person. It is best to obtain a quick general statement of what happened from one, and then go around obtaining the names, addresses and phone numbers of the rest. Otherwise, by the time the officer is finished with one long-winded witness, the others may have left. When the officer has talked to one witness, he can be questioned as to whether or not he saw anyone else at the scene when the incident happened. He will often point out another witness.

(4) The officer should always be alert for planted witnesses, especially in traffic cases. There are cases on record where a passenger of one car jumped out and mixed with the crowd. Then, when the officers arrived, volunteered information as a witness that would help the driver of the car in which he was riding. Others at the scene, when questioned, can identify him as a passenger in one of the cars.

(5) An officer should realize that the average citizen is not an expert witness. Some officers are poor witnesses themselves, so they should not expect too much from the average citizen. The citizen can, however, be helped to a great extent by receiving a series of guidelines from the patrol officer. The officer must be very careful not to suggest answers to the victim or witness. The best method of determining height and weight is through comparison. The officer can point out someone else, and say, "Was he as tall as him?", or "Was he thinner than him?" Each officer should know the exact height of his or her hairline, nose, eyes and other parts of the body. They can be used for comparisons. For example, the officer could ask the witness "Was he as tall as me? No. How about my chin?" This will make it easier for the witness

to estimate height, weight and even age. If the witness states that he can't describe the suspect, and is probably sincere in his belief, the officer should not let it drop there. Very good descriptions can be obtained from witnesses when the officer tries to draw out particulars. The officer might start with the various aspects of Portrait Parle, and when each possibility is presented, it might help stimulate his memory and enable him to remember forgotten details. For example, "Was his hair curly? What color was it? Did he have a receding hairline? Was it long?"

When questioning young children it is extremely important not to lead them. Young children are highly susceptible to suggestion. The officer could ask them "Do you know anyone else who looks like the man that did this? Maybe a relative or neighbor will have similar features. If you ask a child "Was he tall?", the child will often agree. They want to please adults and will often look for some sign that the interviewer is pleased with the answer. It is best to use the narrative type of interview, and let the young witness talk with a little guidance, but avoid suggestions.

(6) In sex cases, especially obscene phone calls, the M.O. is most important. This means that the victim must relate the exact words of the phone call. It is often the M.O. alone that will identify the suspect, since they usually stick to one method of operation. Sometimes a woman, the usual victim of such calls, is embarrassed to repeat the exact language used in the phone call. Depending upon her age, she may even be reluctant to go into the general theme of the calls, and just refer to them as "nasty." There are two techniques that can be used here. First, the woman can tell her husband or boyfriend and he can repeat it to the officer. Second, the woman can write down on paper the exact wording of the message. Female officers can often handle this type of case without causing the victim undue embarrassment. Today this is becoming less of a problem due to the openness among young people about sex. Still an officer should be sensitive to the possibility that a victim might be embarrassed.

WHAT NOTES TO TAKE

The officer need not be a literary genius to write a good report. If an officer obtains the 5 W's and the Indian sign, (WHO, WHAT, WHEN, WHERE, WHY AND HOW), the report will be complete though not a literary masterpiece. The following is a list of variations that can be derived.

WHO

Who was the victim?
Who was the complainant?
Who discovered the crime?
Who saw or heard anything of importance?
Who had a motive for committing the crime?
Who committed the crime?
Who helped him?
Who was talked to?
Who had means of committing the crime?
Who worked on the case?
Who had access to the crime scene?
Who searched for, identified and gathered the evidence?
To whom was the evidence turned over?
With whom did the victim associate?
With whom did the suspect associate?
With whom was the victim last seen?
With whom do the witnesses associate?
With whom did the suspect commit the crime?

WHAT

What was the crime that was committed?
What are the elements of the crime?
What actions did the suspect take before and after the crime?
What actually happened?
What do the witnesses know about it?
What evidence was obtained?
What was done with the evidence?
What tools were used?
What action did the officers take?
What further action should be taken?
What knowledge, skill or strength was needed to commit the crime?
What agencies were/should be notified?
What witnesses were not contacted?
What time was the crime committed?
What time was it reported?
What time officers and investigators arrived?

What time were the witnesses contacted?
What type of transportation was used by the suspect(s)?
What was the motive for the crime?
What weapons were used?
What crime may be associated with this one?

WHERE

Where was the crime committed?
Where was the crime discovered?
Where was the entry made?
Where was the exit made?
Where were tools used in the crime gotten?
Where was the victim found?
Where were the witnesses during the crime?
Where was the suspect last seen?
Where was he seen at the time of the crime?
Where did he live; where does he now live?
Where did and does he now "hang out?"
Where was he when he cased the job?
Where is the suspect now?
Where would the suspect likely go?
Where was the evidence marked?
Where was the evidence found?
Where was the evidence stored?

WHEN

When was the crime committed?
When was it discovered?
When were the authorities notified?
When did they arrive at the scene?
When was the victim last seen?
When did the officers arrive?
When was any arrest made?
When will a complaint be signed?
When did witnesses hear anything unusual?
When did the suspect "case" the job?

HOW

How was the crime committed?
How did the suspect get to the scene?
How did the suspect leave the scene?
How did the suspect obtain the information necessary to commit the crime?
How was the crime discovered?
How were the tools for the job obtained?
How were the tools or weapons used?
How was the crime reported?
How was the arrest made?

How much damage was done?
How much property or money was taken?
How much did the victim claim was taken?
How much information is being withheld?

WHY

Why was the crime committed?
Why were certain tools used?
Why was the crime reported?
Why was the crime reported late?
Why are witnesses reluctant to give information?
Why is the suspect lying?
Why did the suspect pick the particular time to commit the crime
Why did the suspect pick the particular place for the crime?
Why did the suspect pick the particular day for the crime?

PROCEDURES IN NOTE TAKING

(1) Always use the exact terminology of the person giving the statement. If it is an actual statement, use quotation marks. Do not correct it grammatically, or interpret it. The defense attorney will make a great fuss in court if it is discovered that the officer did not record the exact words given by the witness or defendant. He will insinuate that if the officer "changed" the wording, what else was "changed" in the report. It could look bad for the officer. If the statement contains profanity, the exact wording should be in the report. If later, in court the officer is asked to quote from the report, it is a smart tactic to turn first to the jury and state, "If the ladies and gentlemen of the jury will excuse the profanity, the defendant stated "stick it up your ass cop." This impresses the jury with the officer's professional demeanor and moral concern.

(2) When taking statements from several witnesses, separate the witnesses so that they cannot hear each other's statements. If they can hear the others, it will affect their own statements. Sometimes people are reluctant to talk freely in front of other people.

(3) Strive for facts rather than opinions, and never label an opinion as a fact. Sometimes it is important to a case to obtain personal opinions, but they should be very carefully labeled as opinions.

(4) Since these notes are usually the basis of an offense report, it is important to obtain everything that would be needed for a complete offense report. One way to do this is through the use of pre-printed forms.

(5) Since an investigator might have to follow up on the case the next day, it is most important that phone numbers be obtained on all witnesses. Not only should the home phone number be obtained, but also the work phone. The next day a follow-up investigator who wants to talk to the witness, might spend half an hour driving to the witness's home just to find out that he is not there. Another half an hour is spent driving back to headquarters. An hour of valuable time would be wasted where one phone call would have saved the trip.

(6) Don't be skimpy in the details. It might look complete right now, but how will it look a year from now? Will the officer be able to recall the whole case at a future time just from the notes?

(7) If possible, print notes in block letters. More departments are now requiring officers to write their reports in block letters. This is because some officers have very bad handwriting. If someone else had to read the notes there could be a problem. Sometimes a partner has to read notes in court written by the other partner. If machine copies are made of the notes, block lettering records better.

THE STYLES OF NOTE TAKING

There are three basic styles of notetaking. They are:

(1) **The narrative style.** This is in the language of the witness taken down as he tells it. It has the advantage of giving him free rein and not restricting him to the point where he leaves out important information. It has the disadvantage of being too long and a burden in notetaking.

(2) **The question and answer style.** This style is usually restricted to obtaining specific information from witnesses, such as in the investigation of traffic accidents. It has a limited use. It is commonly used in confessions and statements of admission. Its advantage is brevity and the fact that it only contains the meat of the matter. The disadvantage is that something important can be easily left out.

(3) **The chronological style.** The chronological style is often used in taking notes from a suspect or person whose time must be accounted for. It is also used in taking notes on occurrences covering a long period of time.

Examples:

(A) 0920 Hrs. Victim received first phone call.
0950 Hrs. Victim received second phone call.
1015 Hrs. Victim heard a knock at the door.

(B) 10-12-96 — 1200 Hrs(Noon) Suspect approached victim's car at 2nd and Santa Clara and asked for a match.

10-13-96 — 1230 Hrs. Suspect was waiting in parking lot when victim came out to her car. He again asked her for a match.

10-15-96 — 1240 Hrs. Suspect was waiting at victim's car. When she approached, he exposed himself to her.

TWENTY-FOUR-HOUR TIME

Since police officers work around the clock, it is customary for officers to use Twenty-four-hour time in their reports. This can be a little confusing to those who have not been in the military or have not worked with this system before.

Basically time starts counting after midnight. 1:00am would be 0100 Hrs. (Pronounced Zero one hundred hours. Sometimes Oh one hundred hours) 3:00am would be 0300 Hrs. 12:00 Noon would be 1200 Hrs (Pronounced Twelve hundred hours). After 12:00 Noon, each hour is added onto the twelve. For example, 2:00pm would be 1400 Hrs (Fourteen hundred hours), 7:00pm would be 1900 Hrs (Nineteen hundred hours). To change it back, you simply subtract twelve from anything over twelve. For example 2015 Hrs. would be 8:15 pm. 2015 minus 1200 equals 8:15.

SKETCHING THE CRIME SCENE

THE PURPOSE OF SKETCHING

Many officers in the field feel that photographs are all that are necessary in order to properly record the crime scene. Photographs, as will be explained later, are a very good means of recording the crime scene, but they do have faults that are corrected by the use of sketches. The advantages of sketches are as follows:

(1) The sketch does not distort the scene as will a photograph. Different lenses and camera angles can distort photographs. It is important that evidence be free from distortions. For example a telephoto lens will make objects in the distance appear to be closer together. It can make skid marks appear to be shorter than they really are. A sketch will not distort distances or angles.

(2) The sketch can be as simple or as complicated as the need requires. Where the photograph records everything that is present, the sketch can record only that which is essential.

The sketch can have transparent overlays that will allow the addition of items at will. By the use of colored or heavier inks, certain points or objects in the sketch can be brought to the viewer's immediate attention. Colored inks can also show relationships when it is important.

(3) The sketch can show direction. The direction of north can be accurately shown on a sketch because it is usually an overhead view.

(4) The sketch will show more than the view from one direction. The photograph will show a view from only one direction. The sketch will show all directions at once. It can even show the ceiling in certain types of cross projection sketches. The sketch will permit the jury to obtain an overall picture.

(5) The sketch can be used in conjunction with photographs. The sketch and the photograph should go together, just as the skeleton and the flesh of the body are part of a whole.

HOW THE SKETCH MAY BE USED

The crime scene sketch has many uses, the following are some of the more common:

(1) It enables the investigators to obtain a set, permanent picture of the scene which can aid them in putting pieces together and seeing relationships long after the crime scene has changed or been destroyed. Sometimes it is difficult to see relationships at the scene because of the various pressures during the investigation. But later a complete sketch will enable the investigators to reenact the crime and check out statements and alibis against certain obvious facts.

(2) It can greatly aid witnesses in explaining where they were standing when they observed certain happenings. They can show exactly where a certain object was located when they entered the room. Police officers can better explain the duties they performed at the scene, when testifying in court, when they have a sketch to use as a guide.

(3) It can better help the judge and the jury in more clearly understanding the relationships at the crime scene. It can also help in understanding testimony regarding the crime.

(4) It can help the prosecution by impressing the jury. Juries gain respect for the police when they see the extent to which they go to in order to prove facts. In other words, a good crime scene sketch impresses the jury, and impressing the jury is a most important step toward prosecuting the defendant.

THE MATERIALS

The materials needed for the sketch are broken down into two categories. First those needed at the scene, and then those needed for the final sketch. The patrol officer will be concerned with the first group, but not necessarily the second. Some small departments will of necessity, allow the patrol officer to make the final sketch if talent permits. It is often best to turn the rough sketch, made at the scene, over to the city engineering department. They have both the materials and the qualified personnel to properly draw a final sketch.

THE ROUGH SKETCH

The rough sketch will require the following materials:

(1) A hard back clipboard.

(2) Graph paper.

(3) A soft pencil (number 2B).

(4) A small hand pencil sharpener (or a pocket knife).

(5) A steel tape measure.

(6) A directional compass.

THE TYPE OF SKETCH BEST USED FOR CRIME SCENES

The type of sketch used depends upon the location of the crime. In outdoor areas, the Outdoor Plan type of sketch is best. Inside a house there are two major types of sketches. If there are several rooms, the Floor Plan type of sketch is best. If there is one room, the Cross Projection type of sketch is best. This is also referred to as the Exploded Sketch by the FBI. The Cross Projection sketch shows the walls as an extension of the floor. In some cases the ceiling is drawn as an extension of one of the walls.

The Cross Projection sketch can also be made into a three dimensional display by scoring the underside and cutting out the cardboard so that the walls fold up. This makes the sketch into sort of doll house, and gives the jurors a more complete picture of the scene. Usually one wall is left down so the jurors can look into the room.

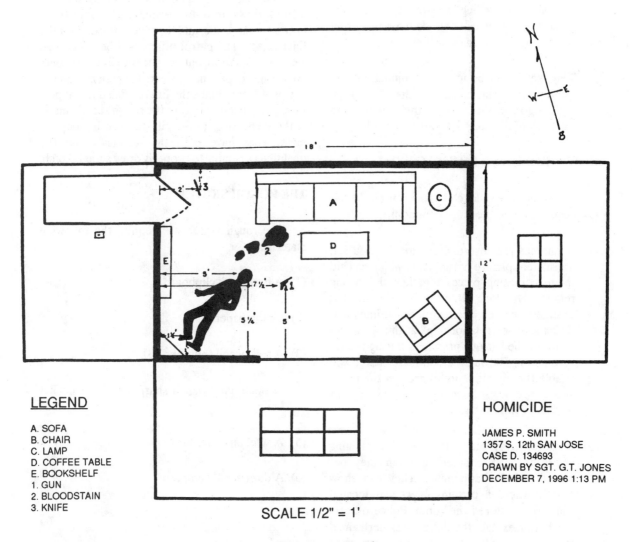

LEGEND

A. SOFA
B. CHAIR
C. LAMP
D. COFFEE TABLE
E. BOOKSHELF
1. GUN
2. BLOODSTAIN
3. KNIFE

SCALE 1/2" = 1'

HOMICIDE

JAMES P. SMITH
1357 S. 12th SAN JOSE
CASE D. 134693
DRAWN BY SGT. G.T. JONES
DECEMBER 7, 1996 1:13 PM

Cross projection sketch

Fig. VIII-4; Cross projection sketch

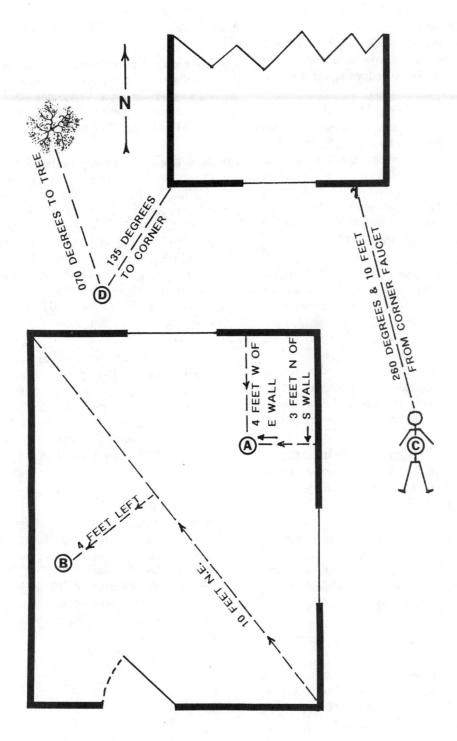

EXAMPLES OF WAYS TO MAKE MEASUREMENTS

Fig. VIII-5; Examples of ways to make measurements

RULES OF MEASUREMENT

In crime scene sketching, there is a cardinal rule. Decide WHAT is to be sketched before taking measurements and drawing objects. When the officer has decided what is to be sketched, the rules below should be followed in drawing the sketch.

(1) All measurements should be made from permanent objects. If measurements are made from temporary objects such as furniture, it is possible that the objects might be moved. Should someone wish to re-measure the scene, the measurements would be different. Outdoors, the officer should use fire plugs, lamp standards, and trees. Inside a room, the walls or corners should be used.

(2) Verify all measurements. No human being including the best police officer is infallible. We all make mistakes, and it is embarrassing to have these mistakes brought out in court. It can also lose the case. When two officers can verify that they both made the measurements on different occasions and arrived at the same conclusion, the jury will more readily accept those measurements. Just as important is the fact that they will be more exact.

(3) If the measurement is to be made outdoors, and there are not many permanent objects from which to measure, then it is best to bring in a professional surveyor.

(4) In measuring bodies, two measurements should be made, one at the head, and another at one foot. This will better show the exact angle of the body. In the rough sketch, all bodies should be shown as stick figures.

(5) Always show north on the rough sketch.

(6) Identify all objects in the rough sketch with a letter or number, and then in the notebook, describe that object in detail. Don't clutter up the sketch with these details.

(7) If photographs are taken, show the position of the camera on the sketch. A number at that location will show which numbered photo it was.

METHODS OF MEASURING

There are four basic types of measurements made at the crime scene. They are as follows:

(1) **Rectangular Coordinate.** The rectangular coordinate is two measurements at right angles from the object being measured to the nearest permanent objects, usually walls. See "A" in Figure VIII-5 on page.

(2) **Plane line or Thrust line.** In the Plane line or Thrust line measurement, an imaginary or real line is drawn between two permanent objects such as the corners of a room or between the corner of a house and a tree. To obtain the measurement, the officer starts at one of the permanent objects and follows the line for a set number of feet, and then goes at right angles to the right or left to the object in question. See "B" in Figure VIII-5 on the previous page.

(3) **Polar Coordinate.** In the Polar coordinate, one permanent object is chosen, and with the use of a compass, the direction of the object to be measured is determined. The officer then measures the number of feet to that object when following the bearing of the compass. See "C" in Figure VIII-5 on the previous page.

(4) **Triangulation.** In triangulation, the officer uses a compass to obtain bearings of two noticeable permanent objects. Later it is easy to locate these objects on an engineer's map, and by using the reverse bearing, lines are drawn in the direction of the object to be measured, and when they intersect, it marks the location. See "D" in Figure VIII-5 on the previous page.

SCALES USED IN MEASUREMENTS

The following scales are those most often used in crime scene sketching, but they are not mandatory. If the situation demands another scale, or the officer can justify it, another scale may be used.

Small rooms ½" = 1 ft.
Large rooms ¼" = 1 ft.
Small building ⅛" = 1 ft.
Large buildings/outdoor scenes ½" = 10 ft

FORMAT OF THE CRIME SCENE SKETCH

There are six parts to the crime scene sketch.

(1) **The drawing of the scene.** This is the immediate scene, room, or building, and includes the essential environment.

(2) **The legend.** The legend has two purposes.

(a) Identifies numbered articles on the drawing.
(b) It can describe the articles and give the location of measurements if these measurements clutter up the drawing.

(3) **The title.** The title identifies the drawing with the scene and the investigators. It includes:

(a) Case number.
(b) Type of offense.
(c) Identification of victim or of the scene.
(d) Detailed location of the scene.
    (Northeast bedroom of second floor.)
(e) Date and hour that sketch was made.
(f) Name of the sketcher and witnesses if any.

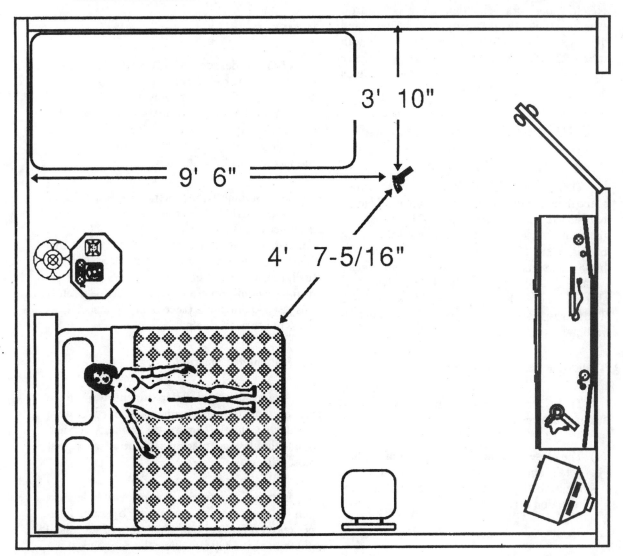

Fig. VIII-6; Computerized sketch: COMPUSCENE by Visatex

(4) **The compass heading.** North should always be at the top of the sketch.

(5) **The scale.**

(6) **Other pertinent data.** This would include the slope of the ground, or the floor, or the composition of the soil such as muddy or gravel.

Figures VIII-4, VIII-5, and VIII-6 show examples of finished crime scene sketches.

COMPUTERIZED SKETCHING

Officers no longer need artistic or graphic skills in order to compose and construct crime scene sketches. Computer software is now available that will allow officers to make a presentable sketch in considerable less time than it took to draw such a sketch in the past. Errors can be easily and quickly corrected. Changes can also be made with speed. The sketch on the previous page (Figure VIII-6) is an example of a computerized sketch developed by Visatex corporation.

PHOTOGRAPHING THE CRIME SCENE

There is no quicker way to record the crime scene than to photograph it. Nothing can add more realism to a court presentation than to supplement the delivery with adequate photographs. Because of this, every officer should be familiar with the basic elements in the use of standard police photographic equipment. Whenever a crime scene sketch is made, photographs should also be taken. The two go together. Photography is a valuable investigative tool.

TYPES OF PHOTOGRAPHS

There are two basic types of photographs taken at a crime scene:

(1) **The close up.** The close up is taken to show detail and possible words or numbers of identification either on the object or identification card.

(2) **The over-all shot.** The over-all shot is taken to show relationships of certain evidence to the crime scene as a whole. Otherwise it might be difficult to show that the particular piece of evidence came from the crime scene. It is important to place numbered or lettered cards next to pieces of evidence. Sometimes evidence is so small that it cannot be seen or recognized in an overall photo. The identifying number or letter on the cards should be printed large enough to be seen. The officer's notes will describe the evidence and indicate the number or letter associated with that evidence. In the final sketch, this information will be listed under the "Legend."

A patrol officer should always use a flash in the field even though it is daylight. This will reduce the number of shadows and result in a better picture.

CAMERAS

For many decades the 4 X 5 Graphic camera was the "workhorse" of police photography. It was adopted by police departments for many reasons. First of all the "Press" or news media used this camera as their "Press camera." Secondly there was the feeling that the larger the negative, the better was its evidence value in court.

The Graphic type camera involved a lot of skill, and it was bulky. In order for the officer to use it properly, there were a great number of things to remember. If an officer mastered the use of this camera, the photographs were excellent. Few actually did, however. The average failure rate for officers using this camera was about fifty percent. It was just too difficult a piece of equipment for officers to use occasionally.

The Instamatic Camera

As a result nearly all departments went to the use of the instamatic camera. The costs were reasonable, and the camera was compact. It could fit into the glove compartment or the briefcase that most officers use.

Instamatic cameras are considerably less expensive, and are very simple to operate. Inexperienced officers obtain a high rate of successful photographs. They also allow the economical use of color film. As a result, departments rapidly switched to the instamatic type camera. The disadvantages of this type of camera are the lack of distance when taking flash pictures at night, and the small size of the negative if enlargements are needed for court.

Common Problems In The Use Of The Instamatic Type Camera

Even though the use of the instamatic type camera has reduced the number of problems, there are still some errors that are repeated often enough to merit mention. They are as follows:

(1) Carelessness in handling of the camera and failure to protect it from dust, dirt and excess heat. (These cameras are plastic and should not be left in direct sunlight for a long time)

(2) Failure to check the batteries for freshness.

(3) Failure to use a flash. (even in daylight)

(4) Failure to advance film all the way until shutter is reset.

(5) Taking pictures of evidence from so far away that necessary detail is lost.

(6) Taking pictures of evidence so close as to lose overall identification value.

The Polaroid Camera

Because of the expense, patrol divisions seem reluctant to use the Polaroid camera. Detective divisions use them extensively. Although the cost per photo is higher than the instamatic type camera, it can be lower when considering the fact that fewer photographs have to be taken. With the instamatic, the officer will take numerous shots in the hopes that one or some of them will come out good. This is because no one knows how the prints will look until the film is developed. With the Polaroid camera, you know how the print looks in a matter of seconds. If it is good, no more shots are taken. The result is a saving in money. There is also the problem of storage. With the instamatic camera, thousands of negatives and prints have to be stored, and this is an added expense. Some

departments have experimented with Polaroid cameras in the patrol car but due to abuse by some officers, have discontinued this practice. They were using large amounts of the film for personal use. This would certainly be a disadvantage. The greatest advantage is in knowing that you have proper photographs of a crime scene that can change in hours or days. Once a body has been removed from the scene, that scene can never be photographed in its original condition.

PROFESSIONAL PHOTOGRAPHERS

In some smaller departments there is not enough need of photographs for officers to develop the skills necessary in important cases. In a homicide that has generated considerable publicity, the costs of prosecution can be extremely high. All of that money could go down the drain if the case was lost due to poor quality photographs. Because of this, smaller departments should not hesitate, because of the expense, to hire a professional photographer.

ADMISSIBILITY OF PHOTOGRAPHS

The admissibility of photographs in a trial is usually dependent upon several basic rules:

(1) Is the photograph relevant to the case? Film should not be wasted on photographs that are not relevant to the case. Before taking the picture, the officer must first think "What will this picture prove?"

(2) Will it cause undue prejudice or sympathy? Judges will often refuse photographs as evidence if they serve no purpose but to inflame the jury.

(3) Is it properly identified? If the photo is to be presented in court, proper identification would include not only the identification of the photo as being taken at the scene, but with what piece of equipment. All the details of the processing should also be included.

TESTIMONY ON PHOTOGRAPHS TAKEN

In times past, having a photograph admitted as evidence was quite a problem. The defense attorney would spend hours cross examining the officer as to every minute detail. He would want to know everything about the camera, lens, filter, film and the type of processing.

Today the courts are more liberal in their acceptance of photographs. The key question now asked of the officer on the stand is whether or not the photograph is a "fair representation of the scene" or what the officer saw at the time the photo was taken.

Because of this, the officer need only admit to knowing the basic operation of the camera. Any technical details, if requested, can be obtained from the lab technician or a specialist.

The late Harris Tuttle, Eastman Kodak's law enforcement photography expert, was probably the most knowledgeable person in the country on this subject. Yet many times he warned officers against qualifying themselves as "experts" on photography when on the stand.

This field is so extensive, that even experts can get caught up on cross examination. The officer is better off just stating that the camera was aimed in the proper direction and the shutter pressed. It should then be stated that the photograph is a fair representation of the scene as it was when the officer took the picture.

Once the photograph is taken at the scene, the officer should give careful attention to the proper identification of the film. Next. care should be taken to insure the "Chain of Control." It must be protected from damage, mix-up or contamination between the crime scene and the evidence locker or photo lab. It must then be later protected during its transportation to court.

The officer should make the following notes at the crime scene just in case the court requests more information on the mechanics of the photograph taken.

NOTEBOOK INFORMATION

Whenever a photograph is taken, the officer should record the following information. It should accompany the photo if it is submitted as evidence:

(1) Date and time taken.

(2) Location of scene.

(3) Exact location of camera.

(4) Compass bearing indicating the direction the camera is facing.

(5) Complete description of the camera.

(6) Description of camera lens.

(7) Exposure data.

(8) Type of film.

(9) Name of officer taking photograph.

(10) Case number of crime or accident.

STUDY QUESTIONS for Patrol Operations

CHAPTER 8

1. Most police officers have photographic memories.   T or F

2. The rule that "a witness is allowed to refresh his memory from his written notes" is found in the:

   a._ penal code   b. _vehicle code
   c._ code of civil procedure   d. __probate code

3. The standard police notebook is about 3 x 6 inches in size.   T or F

4. An officer's notebook should always be the looseleaf type.   T or F

5. An officer should always carry two _____ and a _____
   in case he has to write citations in damp weather.

6. According to the book, a sharp officer should always carry a "vest pocket file" of 3 x 5 cards.   T or F

7. Why should an officer keep notes beyond the criminal Statutes of Limitations? _____
   _____

8. How does an officer open a notebook to the last page used? _____
   _____

9. The letter "C" in an officer's notes stands for _____.

10. An officer should start taking notes just as soon as the witness starts talking.   T or F

11. Name one of the techniques that an officer can use to get witnesses to give statements.
    _____

12. Without leading the witness an officer can ask questions that will help in obtaining a
    description of the suspect. List one of the questions that can be asked of the witness.
    _____

13. If a woman victim of obscene language is embarrassed to repeat exactly what she heard, the
    officer can ask her to _____.

14. It is best not to write down exactly what the witness stated, but to write down a general   T or F
    statement of an overall nature.

15. When taking statements, an officer should always separate _____.

16. When writing a report that investigators will follow up on the next day, be sure to include
    _____

17. The type of report that lists happenings by the exact time is called a _____ report.

18. The type of report that states what the witness says just as he tells it to you is the:

    a. _ narrative style   b. __question and answer style
    c. _ chronological style   d. __neither of these

19. Name one advantage of a sketch over a photograph. _____

20. The FBI refers to the "cross projection sketch" as the _____ sketch.

21. In crime scene sketching, there is a cardinal rule. Decide _____ is to be sketched first before taking measurements and putting anything down on paper.

22. All measurements should be made from permanent objects.   **T or F**

23. In measuring dead bodies, use _____ measurements.

24. On sketches, north should always be _____.

25. When an object is located in a room by making two measurements at right angles from the object to the walls, it is called a _____.

26. An officer should not waste money by using camera flashes in the daylight.   **T or F**

27. If the "D.A." submitted a photograph that showed gory blood and wounds just to upset the jury against the defendant, when it was not relevant to any issue, the defense attorney could object on the grounds that it would cause undue _____ or sympathy.

28. Today the key phrase for the admission of photographs as evidence is whether or not the photograph is a _____ _____ of the scene.

29. Harris Tuttle, from Eastman Kodak, felt that an officer who is knowledgeable about photography should testify as an expert, and in that way impress the jury.   **T or F**

30. One of the main considerations for officers who take photographs for evidence is that they protect the film by proper "chain of _____."

CHAPTER IX

IDENTIFICATION & DESCRIPTION OF PERSONS AND PROPERTY

The description of persons was not a problem until people formed communities and populations greatly increased. As a result, it was common for one member of the community to be unknown to other members. This same problem arose in wars involving a large number of soldiers. How could a soldier know who was his enemy? This problem was solved by the wearing of distinctive uniforms.

As trade developed among people, and cities were formed near bodies of water, the number of strangers and foreigners in these cities increased. To this was added the migration of those persons who left or were forced to leave their own communities because of crimes they had committed. There were also those who were attracted to the city to "seek their fortune." Since this increased the possibility of one person not knowing the other, there was the tendency not to feel bound by tradition or rules of smaller communities. Nor was there the fear that every move was being watched by someone who knew you. Naturally this resulted in an increase in crime, and also an increase in the possibility of getting away with criminal actions. It was this anonymity that brought about the need for a good system of crim-inal identification.

HISTORY OF CRIMINAL IDENTIFICATION

Early criminal identification took two forms. One was to identify the individual criminal, and the other to identify all criminals in general. The first amounted to a complete physical description of the person, and the second involved branding or scarring the cheek or forehead of the criminal with a symbol indicating the type of offense committed.

The ancient Egyptians had a well-developed system of identification by personal description which was used in identifying criminals. However, criminals in ancient Egypt were few in number.

The inhumane system of branding criminals remained in our western Christian world until the nineteenth century. It was later replaced by a system of personal description. About the same time the Rogues' Gallery was developed. Recently arrested criminals were paraded in a gallery or courtyard for the public to view. It was hoped that some citizen might recognize one or more of them as being responsible for some criminal action in which the citizen had been the victim or a witness. This later developed into a display of criminal photographs or "mug shots."

Fig. IX-1; Original rogues' gallery

In 1840, photography was introduced as a means of criminal identification, but due to a lack of control and standardization, it was not a very valid means of identification. There was no set position for the criminal to assume, and many times the subject would make faces or fight the process and would have to be held down by five jailers while the picture was being taken.

It was not until about 35 years later that Alphonse Bertillon, a French identification clerk, standardized criminal identification photography. He did this by setting up strict rules of position for the subject's head so that it would always be photographed at the same angle and from the same direction. Because of his work in this area, and in crime scene photography, he has often been referred to as the "Father of Police Photography."

Criminals did not always like the idea of being photographed. Two main reasons were a fear of being later identified from the photograph, and a superstition against being photographed. This type of superstition seemed to prevail in both Europe and the United States.

A study of the early history of photo identification reveals that France, England and the United States had problems with prisoners who were reluctant to have their photographs taken, and would sometimes fight "tooth and nail" to prevent this. The illustration below shows six officers holding one prisoner so a mug shot can be taken.

Fig. IX-2; An Unwilling Subject. — Photographing a prisoner for the rogues' gallery at police headquarters.

Chapter Nine

Fig. IX-3; Rogues' gallery after use of photography

CRIMINAL ANTHROPOMETRY

Criminal anthropometry, or Bertillonage as it is sometimes referred to, has an important place in the history of personal identification. It was through this development that man, for the first time in history, was able to positively identify each single person as being individual.

In the year 1875, Alphonse Bertillon, son of a noted anthropologist, and an apparent social misfit, was badly in need of a job. Had he, in that day, consulted a job counselor, it is highly improbable that they would have recommended him for a career in law enforcement. However, since his father did wield some political influence he was able to obtain a job as a police clerk of the twentieth grade. He worked in the office of the Prefect of the Paris Police (Chief of Police).

Because of his stubborn nature, Alphonse did not do well in school, and as a result, he bordered on becoming what today we would call a juvenile delinquent. When he was old enough to work, he had developed a personality problem that resulted in his moving from one job to another. He finally ended up in London as a French teacher. While there he formed an admiration for the Metropolitan Police which might have helped him in accepting his job with the Paris Police. When he lost his job in London, he almost starved. He wrote his father for help and then returned home like the prodigal son, more mature and determined to hold down a steady job, much to his father's satisfaction. Bertillon Senior still had misgivings about his son, and this was probably the reason he obtained this particular job for him. As a file clerk in an out-of-the-way place, he hoped that Alphonse could not get into any trouble.

The job consisted of filing the photographs and descriptions of arrested persons. At first Alphonse, a quiet person, did his job in the manner expected of him, until he realized how useless his task was, and it caused him great distress. In order to retain his sanity, he decided to devise a system of positive identification. He worked on it night after night without much success. He then remembered helping his father as a boy, and how his father would measure all of the bones in the laboratory and derive information from them, and he remembered his father stating that they were all different. He was soon convinced that the key to personal identification was in the measurement of the bones of the body.

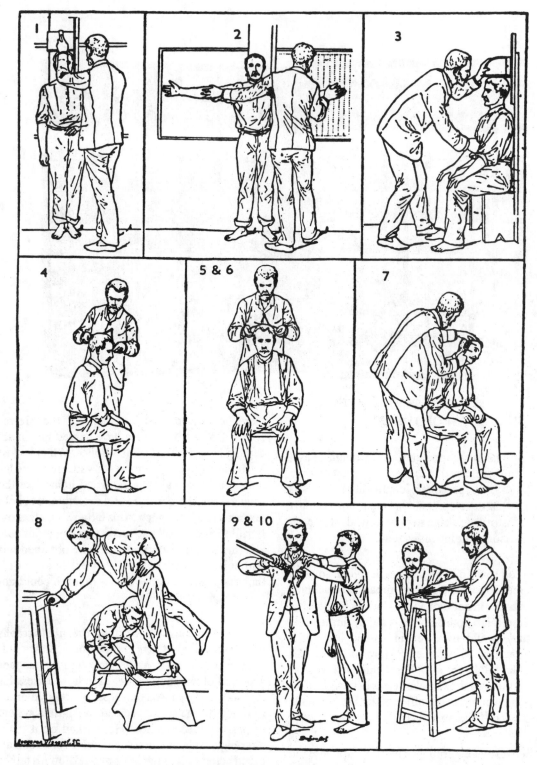

1. Height
2. Reach
3. Trunk
4. Length of head
5. Width of head
6. Width at temple
7. Right ear
8. Left foot
9. Left middle finger
10. Little finger
11. Left forearm

Fig. IX-4; Bertillon's system of identification

When he had worked out the rough details, he proudly strutted into the Prefect's office and told him of the new discovery. The Prefect was a political appointee, and had no scientific knowledge or appreciation of it. His sole interest was in keeping things running as smoothly as possible at the prefecture. This precluded adopting the crazy ideas of any clerk in the twentieth grade. He was firmly convinced of that

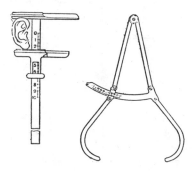

Fig. IX-5; Ear and head measures (the Bertillon System)

Alphonse had "slipped his trolley." His reply to Alphonse's idea was, "Bertillon, your report reads like a practical joke. Do you think that you, a clerk of the twentieth grade, and with no police experience, could improve on a system so long in development, and one which works so well." Bertillon untactfully told him the present system was useless and was promptly thrown out of his office. He was warned not to trouble the Prefect again with such foolishness.

Because Bertillon was stubborn, he did not drop the matter, and the Prefecture wrote his father stating that Alphonse was not only a troublemaker, but possibly of unsound mind. Bertillon senior, fearful that the Prefect was right, called Alphonse home for a "father-to-son" talk. Alphonse apologized for the trouble that he had caused, explaining that if he had sought his father's advice in the first place, his system would have been more easily understood. He then showed the research papers to his father who glanced at them with interest. Alphonse left the room so his father could read them. An hour later his father came out of the den. The look of anger on his face had been replaced with one of pride. The old scientist, unemotional by French standards, approached Alphonse with tears in his eyes and hugged him. Being a scientist, he realized that his son, for whom he had little hope, had developed one of the greatest discoveries in the history of criminology.

For the first time in the recorded history of man, a person could be permanently identified through eleven body measurements. This was certainly a milestone in criminology and social justice.

Bertillon decided not to press his idea until a new Prefecture of Police had been appointed. In the meantime he went over his development with hopes of improving it. Alphonse tried to measure his system statistically to determine the possibility of two persons having exactly the same set of measurements. Because statistics was a new science, Bertillon was not that familiar with it, his figures underestimated the validity of the system.

This was really a fortunate error on his part, because to supplement his system of bodily measurements, he devised another system of breaking down the features of the head which could be added to his anthropometric measurements. This was his "Portrait Parle" or speaking picture.

This was really his greatest personal achievement, because the science of anthropometry was not his invention. He merely applied it to the identification of criminals. Portrait Parle, on the other hand, was solely a product of his own genius. It was used long after his system of criminal anthropometry was replaced by fingerprints.

In the few years that followed, his system of identification became common in most of the police departments throughout the world. However, during the next twenty years, the awareness and use of fingerprints as a better means of identification continued to develop until in 1903 there occurred a case in Leavenworth Prison where a Will West and William West were found to not only have the same name, but appeared to be physical twins with almost the same Bertillon measurements. Their fingerprints, however, were quite different, and this seemed to sound the death knell for Bertillon's system of identification, for it was but a short time after this that the changeover to fingerprints began. Another disadvantage of the Bertillon system was that the human skeleton does not stop growing until the person is about twenty years old, and is therefore limited to those criminals over twenty.

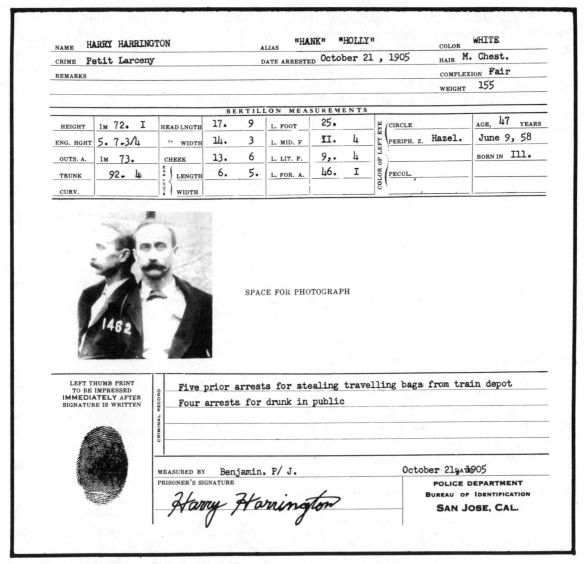

NAME	HARRY HARRINGTON		ALIAS	"HANK" "HOLLY"		COLOR	WHITE
CRIME	Petit Larceny		DATE ARRESTED	October 21 , 1905		HAIR	M. Chest.
REMARKS						COMPLEXION	Fair
						WEIGHT	155

B E R T I L L O N   M E A S U R E M E N T S

HEIGHT	1M 72. I	HEAD LNGTH	17. 9	L. FOOT	25.	CIRCLE		AGE, 47 YEARS
ENG. HGHT	5. 7.3/4	" WIDTH	14. 3	L. MID. F	II. 4	PERIPH. Z. Hazel.		June 9, 58
OUTS. A.	1M 73.	CHEEK	13. 6	L. LIT. F.	9,. 4			BORN IN Ill.
TRUNK	92. 4	LENGTH	6. 5.	L. FOR. A.	46. I	PECUL.		
CURV.		WIDTH						

SPACE FOR PHOTOGRAPH

1482

LEFT THUMB PRINT
TO BE IMPRESSED
IMMEDIATELY AFTER
SIGNATURE IS WRITTEN

CRIMINAL RECORD

Five prior arrests for stealing travelling bags from train depot

Four arrests for drunk in public

MEASURED BY   Benjamin. P/ J.   October 21, 1905

PRISONER'S SIGNATURE

Harry Harrington

POLICE DEPARTMENT
BUREAU OF IDENTIFICATION
SAN JOSE, CAL.

Fig. IX-6; Booking card with Bertillon measurements.

The unfortunate part about the switching over from the Bertillon system to the use of fingerprints as a means of personal identification, is that there was a tendency to also drop his Portrait Parle. This is unfortunate in that his Portrait Parle is a practical system that can easily be used by the man in the field who would find difficulty in stopping each person in a crowd and examining their fingerprints.

THE PORTRAIT PARLE

In his observation of prisoners and people in general, Bertillon noticed that there are more variations to the parts of the face and head than would be normally assumed. He took the main parts of the head such as the face, forehead, nose, ear, mouth, lips, chin, eyes, neck, hairlines, and the general shape of the head itself, and by closely examining them from both side and front views found that there was a great variation in the parts of each section of the human head when one individual was compared with another. By giving definitions to each peculiarity such as the shape, angle, slope, color or relationship to something else, he developed his Portrait Parle or "speaking picture."

The use of Portrait Parle is dependent upon an officer's ability to develop an awareness of the many differences that can be found in the face and head of each individual. He can then use it to assist in making visual identification of wanted persons. When the author began a class in facial identification, he would have each student in the class write down the description of another student. On the average, the paper would contain one paragraph. After as little as two hours training in Portrait Parle, the same students would fill up two full pages with a physical description on one of their fellow students. Bertillon developed his breakdown of features to an almost infinitesimal degree. He classified the human eye as having 54 different color variations. He was able to break the human ear down into so many different classifications, that he claimed he could make identification of a person from the ear alone. Recent scientific investigations have indicated that the human ear remains the same throughout life except if changed by injury or atomic radiation.

To show the value of the ear in personal identification, in 1928, a woman claimed that she was the Grand Duchess Anastasia Nikolaievna, the youngest daughter of the Czar, and claimant to the Russian throne. She had quite a bit of support from other Russian refugees. The Portrait Parle system of identification was used in comparing her photograph with one taken of the real Duchess, ten years earlier. By this method it was shown that she was a fraud. When the photographs were enlarged, the side view of the ears were noticeably different when using Bertillon's system of ear identification.

The general breakdown of Portrait Parle is as follows:

(1) **The Forehead.** A. The slope of the forehead. B. The height of the forehead. C. The width of the forehead. D. The peculiarities of the forehead, (wrinkles, etc).

(2) **The Nose.** A. The root or bridge of the nose. It depresses from a side view. B. The line or curvature of the nose from the side view. C. The base of the nose. The slant of the underpart. D. The length of the nose, from root to base. E. The projection of the nose. How far out from the face. F. Width of the nose from the front view. G. Peculiarities of the nose. Marks, breaks, twists, etc.

(3) **The Ear.** A. Separation of ear from head from the front view. B. Size of the ear compared to the head, from the side view. c. Shape of the ear from the side view, (round, square, triangular). D. Position of ear in relation to the eye, from a side view. Up or down.

E. Vertical set of ears, from side view. Front or back of center-line. F. Lobes of the ear. Their shape and how they connect to head. G. Slope of the ear. What angle is it on its axis. H. Peculiarities of the ear. (Soars, curls, deformities.)

(4) **The Mouth.** A. Length of lips. From nose base to lip and from chin to lip. B. Thickness of the lips. C. Peculiarities of the lips. D. Width of the mouth.

(5) **Teeth.** A. Size. B. Peculiarities: 1. discoloration, 2. spaces or missing teeth, 3. crooked teeth, 4. noticeable decay, 5. protruding teeth.

(6) **The Chin.** A. Slope of the chin from side view. B. Size of the chin. C. Shape of the chin. D. Peculiarities of the chin, (dimples, scars, etc.).

(7) **The Face.** A. The shape of face. B. Peculiarities of the face, (expression, boniness, high checks). C. The eyebrows and mustache, beard (color, slant, thickness).

(8) **The Head.** A. The shape of the head, (round, egg shaped, pointed, square). B. The size of the head in relation to the body.

(9) **The Neck.** A. Length. B. Width. C. Adam's apple (protruding, flat).

(10) **The Shoulders.** A. The slope from the neck down. B. The width.

COMPOSITE DRAWINGS OF SUSPECTS

The first composite device in criminal identification was the Identi-Kit. The Identi-Kit was developed by Hugh C. McDonald, Division Chief at the Los Angeles County Sheriff's Office. It is based on a system of transparent overlays, each transparency or "foil" containing a part of the human face such as the lips, nose, eyes, etc. In the kit, each part of the face is represented by a large number of different foils. the large number of foils shows how many variations can be found among human facial features.

To begin constructing the composite picture, the operator carefully questions the witness or victim as to the description of the hair, and then selects a foil containing the proper hair style. Next a foil is selected containing the proper chin and ears. The outline of the head is now formed. Then foils containing the nose, lips, eyes, eyebrows and wrinkles are laid on top, forming a distinctive picture of a human face according to the description of the victim or witness. Through careful and skillful questioning, the Identi-Kit operator selects the proper foils or replaces selected ones until the witness feels that the picture is representative of the perpetrator.

Although an exact likeness is not the prime objective of the kit, many composites are exceptionally like the person they represent. The Identi-Kit is not meant to be a photograph, but a composite showing feature similarities.

COMPUTERIZED COMPOSITE DESCRIPTIONS OF WANTED AND MISSING PERSONS

Fig. IX-7; Computerized composite description system

Unlike the Ideni-Kit, the police artist tries to make the likeness in a sketch as close to the person as possible. As a result, this task requires certain artistic skills which not too many officers have. Again, computers come to the rescue. With minimal training, an officer can use computer software to compose a good likeness of a suspect or missing

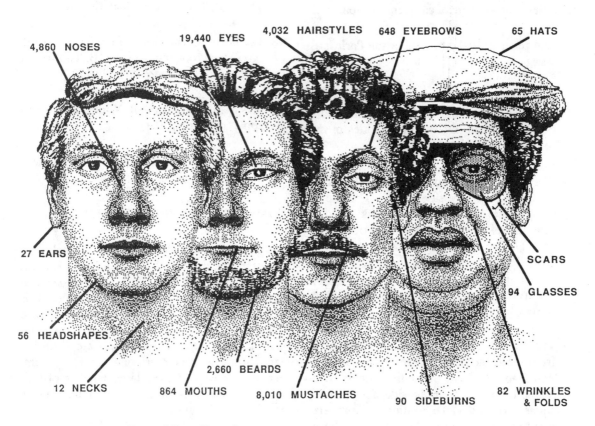

Fig. IX-8; Compusketch Feature Library Illustration

person. The advantage of a computer sketch over the Identi-Kit is the almost infinite number of variationsthat can be composed. It also takes less time.

The process begins with an on-screen, interactive interview. Both multiple-choice and carefully designed free-form questions are used. Upon completion of the interview, the sketch is automatically assembled from a comprehensive library of images. There are over 40,000 features. Then, the sketch is further modified to satisfy the witness' further description.

Another advantage over the Identi-Kit is that a feature, say the nose, can be changed in part only. Instead of having to apply a new nose, the nose can just be given say a more narrow tip, etc.

Figure IX-8 on the previous page shows the number of different features available with Compusketch software. Figure IX-9 is a Compusketch composite of a noted Middle-Eastern dictator.

Fig. IX-9; "Noted Middle Eatern dictator," Visatech Corp.

GENERAL DESCRIPTIONS OF PERSONS

The description of persons should follow a standard form. Figure IX-10 on the following page shows the form of description that is most popular. The purpose of this particular form is to make automatic the officer's procedure in obtaining information regarding the description of persons. When an officer takes a report that involves the description of a suspect and uses this system, it can be quickly determined if a piece of information has been left out. The officer simply runs down the memorized list and checks it off in the notebook. It is very important that this be a habit. Many times at a crime scene an officer is under pressure from the victim and witnesses. The excitement can easily lead an officer to forget something. When emotion blocks our thinking, we have to rely on good habits.

General Form

1. Name (Nickname).
2. Sex.
3. Race.
4. Age.
5. Height.
6. Weight.
7. Hair.
8. Eyes.
9. Complexion.
10. Physical marks (scars, limp, mustache, tattoos).
11. Clothing from head to foot.
    a. Cap or hat.
    b. Shirt and tie.
    c. Jacket or coat.
    d. Dress or trousers.
    e. Shoes.
12. Jewelry and glasses.

To help in remembering the order, a memory aid may be of assistance. Since the form is broken down into two sections, two aids can be used:

(1) **N-S-R-A** (Names, sex, race and age). **Numb-Skulls-Rarely-Agree.**

(2) **H-W-H-E-C-P-C-J** (Height, weight, hair, eyes, complexion, physical marks, clothing and jewelry). **Have-We-Had-Escaping-Criminals-Pull-Cunning-Jobs?**

STANDARD DESCRIPTIONS OF PERSONS

1. **NAME**

2. **SEX**

3. **RACE**

4. **AGE**

5. **HEIGHT**

6. **WEIGHT**

7. **HAIR**

8. **EYES**

9. **COMPLEXION**

10. **PHYSICAL MARKS, SCARS, ETC.**

11. **CLOTHING**

   A. **Hat/Cap**

   B. **Shirt & Tie**

   C. **Jacket/Coat**

   D. **Dress/Trousers**

   E. **Shoes**

   F. **Jewelry**

     (1) **Ring**
     (2) **Watch**

Fig. IX-10; Standard descriptions of persons

Breakdown Of Description

(1) **Name:** Can be the full name if known, or the first name or nickname if overheard.

(2) **Sex:** Although this seems simple, there are cases where a person has dressed as a member of the opposite sex to avoid detection. In these cases there is usually something about the suspect that makes the victim uncertain.

(3) **Race:** Race should include apparent race and also nationality if it is noticeable through accent or dress. Sometimes the suspect's terminology will reveal nationality.

(4) **Age:** Age presents one of the greatest problems in identification. It is an area where mistakes are easily made. If the perpetrator is of another race, it makes it more difficult. Probably the best method of determining age is to find another person who looks about the same age as the perpetrator and ask his age. Otherwise it is best to stick to general age groups such as middle aged or elderly.

(5) **Height:** Most people, including police officers, are poor judges of height. The best way to determine height is to establish approximate height by moving the hand up and down until the victim says to stop. Another way is to have the victim point out another person of approximately the same height.

(6) **Weight:** Weight is similar to height in regard to difficulty of judgment. Probably the best method is by comparing the perpetrator to another person of similar build. Weight guessing can be accurate as is evidenced by carnival weight guessers. However, the average citizen has not developed this skill. An officer should be satisfied with a general description such as thin, medium or fat.

(7) **Hair:** The description of hair should be detailed. The average police officer will often accept a description of "Blond" as sufficient. The description of the hair should contain the following :

(a) **Color,** including streaks.
(b) **Thickness** and baldness. It should include exact location of baldness.
(c) **Texture,** such as kinky, curly or straight.
(d) **Style and part.** Crew cut, or part on left side, or no parting.

(8) **Eyes:** The description of the eyes should contain more than just the color. If the eyes protrude or bulge like the actor Marty Feldman, it should be included in the description along with size of the eyes. Also include any bags under the eyes, watery eyes, or bloodshot eyes as accompanies a cold, cross eyes, missing eye, slant of eyes or squinting eyes.

(9) **Complexion:** Complexion should include the color of the skin, such as fair, dark, ruddy, chalky, pale. Descriptions of persons of color should include the degree of darkness such as dark or light complected. It should also include presence of birthmarks, freckles, pockmarks, blackheads and pimples, and should list their location number and degree.

(10) **Marks:** Physical marks should include, scars, limps, deformities, tattoos, mustache, beard, teeth, etc. and should include a detailed description as to exaction location and degree.

(11) **Clothing:** The description of clothing should include the color, style, shape, condition, open or closed, and material.

(12) **Jewelry and glasses:** The jewelry should include color, material, stones, where worn and design, and glasses should include the description of the frame, such as style, color, and material, and the lenses should be described as to thickness and, if it is noticed, whether or not they are bifocal. Sometimes glasses have designs on the frame.

PROBLEMS IN IDENTIFICATION WHEN USING SPANISH SURNAMES

Because of the large influx of Spanish surnamed persons to the United States in the last fifty years, there can often be problems in identification when using the American system of last name identification.

Many persons of Spanish decent who were born in the United States and have lived here for a while, have dropped the Spanish system of last names. In these cases there is little problem. However, there are many who do follow the old system, or who switch back and forth. It would therefore be wise for officers working in communities where there are a large number of Hispanics, to learn the difference in the two systems.

In the Spanish system, two last names are used. The first last name is that of the father's family, and the second last name is that of the mother's family. For example:

(1) Father's name before and after marriage

Jose Manuel Torres Rivera

(First names) (Father's family name)
(Mother's family name)

(2) Mother's name before marriage

Maria Lucia Martinez Gonzales

(First names) (Father's family name)
(Mother's family name)

(2A) Mother's name AFTER marriage

Maria Lucia Martinez de Torres

(First names) (Father's family name) de
(Husband's family name)

If Jose and Maria get married and have a son, his name will be:

(3) Son's name

Pedro Miguel Torres Martinez

(First names) (Father's family name)
(Mother's family name)

Sons never change their names. However, they may occasionally (or permanently) refer to themselves only by their father's last name. E.g. PEDRO TORRES. When requesting identification information on a Spanish surname, the person should be asked his mother's family name and whether or not he has used that as part of his name before. If so, it should be considered as an AKA (Also Known As) and the name checked both ways.

In the case of a female, her name changes upon marriage. For example, Pedro's mother's name changed when she married his father. She dropped her mother's maiden name Gonzalez (the second part of her last name), and replaced it with the last name of her husband's father's family (Torres).

Example: **Maria Lucia Martinez de Torres**

The "de" is not considered a part of the name for purposes of identification. It simply means that she is the wife of a man whose father's family name is Torres. If, however, the "D" is capitalized, it is then part of the last name and would be filed under the letter "D."

Example: **Juanita Rodriguez De Jesus**

This woman would be a single female whose mother's family name is De Jesus. If her name was JUANITA RODRIGUEZ de De JESUS, you would know that she was married to a man whose first part of his last name was De Jesus.

Sometimes the two last names are hyphenated, such as TORRES-RIVERA, or they can have a "y" between them such as MARTINEZ y GONZALEZ (The "y" means "and").

FINGERPRINTS ARE THE BEST MEANS OF IDENTIFICATION.

Sometimes it is easy to jump to conclusions when establishing identity. As mentioned earlier in the chapter, two men with the same name, and whose photographs looked the same, were identified as being the same person. Their fingerprints, however, were not the same. Whenever a suspect claims that he is not the person wanted, as they very often do, it would be wise to make a check of his fingerprints. This leaves no doubt.

A man was arrested in California as a parole violator. He had the same first, middle and last name as well as the exact same birthdate as another person wanted for parole violation. At his arraignment, he insisted that he was not on parole. The judge ordered the suspect's fingerprints to be examined and then it was discovered that they had arrested the wrong man. Under these circumstances, it would be an easy assumption to make. There are not too many persons with the same full name and birthdate. An officer does not have to be a fingerprint expert to compare a suspect's prints with those on a "Rap Sheet." It takes little time to learn the three basic types of fingerprint patterns and the peculiarities or "minutiae" that distinguish one from another.

LINEUP IDENTIFICATION

Lineup identification has long been an important part of criminal identification. Criminologists have been aware of the dangers of improper lineups for a long time and some of these dangers have been covered in the Chapter on "Observation and Perception."

In the past, policemen were too often prone to preparing lineups that were not always fair to the suspect and they seemed to ignore the possibility that the witness could be "set up." It was not uncommon to prepare a lineup where only one person fit the description given by the victim or witness. Finding four other unknown persons to put in a lineup could be difficult for a smaller department. It would be even harder to find four persons who fit the description of the suspect. As a result, the procedure in many cases, was to get four or five winos from the drunk tank. It was also common to place one or two policemen in the lineup. Often the policemen wore sportcoats over their uniforms in a half-hearted attempt to disguise the fact that they were policemen. All of these tactics tended to "set up" the witness. He would often pick out the person the police had brought in as their number one suspect. After all he was the only one that fit the description. To make matters worse, the witness was often asked "Which one of them did it?" This has the effect of telling the witness that the guilty person is in the lineup so he or she must pick them out.

The proper procedure, and one that will better stand up in court is, "Do you recognize anyone in the room?", and if they answer yes, ask them when they last saw the person and under what conditions. Anything that approaches "leading the witness" or is suggestive in nature, will be promptly thrown out of court.

THE WADE DECISION

Three important Supreme Court cases regarding lineups were Wade, Gilbert and Stovall. They are now referred to as the Wade Decision. These cases reached the Supreme Court on the grounds that they involved a violation of the Sixth Amendment. Basically the decision stated that a defendant has a right to have his attorney present at any lineup or any confrontation for identification purposes.

As in the Miranda Decision, the suspect may voluntarily and intelligently waive his right to have an attorney present. Like Miranda, he must be notified of his basic rights as follows:

(1) What time and place the lineup will be held.

(2) That the results of the lineup can and will be used against him in court.

(3) That he has a right to have his counsel present during the lineup.

(4) That if he cannot afford an attorney, one will be provided.

The defendant should then be asked if he understands these rights, and if so, does he wish to waive his right to have an attorney present.

When Does Wade Not Apply?

Both Wade and Gilbert state that the right to counsel before the trial applies only to "critical stages of the criminal proceedings", and does not apply to showing the witness a photograph of the suspect if done in a fair manner. This also includes the taking of blood, fingerprints, handwriting examples, clothing, and having him speak for identification purposes.

Modification Of Wade By Kirby ("Critical Stages Of The Criminal Proceedings")

Five years later, the United States Supreme Court modified the rules under the Wade Decision. In Kirby v. Illinois (406 U.S. 682) the court stated that the identification of a suspect on a one-on-one basis, at a police station, after the arrest, but before criminal proceedings had been initiated, did not constitute a "critical stage in criminal prosecution", as used in the Wade Decision.

Two years later, the New York Supreme Court ruled that the police do not have to use a "blank" lineup (Where none of the persons in the lineup is the suspect) even though that would minimize suggestibility. (People v. Guerea 358 N.Y.S. 2d 925)

If a suspect's attorney is present at the lineup and ensures that his rights are protected, that attorney does not have the right to also be present when the witnesses are separately interviewed after the lineup. If there are irregularities in the interviews, these can be readily brought out under cross examination at the trial. (U.S. v. Banks, 485 F 2d 545) (1973).

AT THE SCENE IDENTIFICATION OF SUSPECTS

In a California Supreme Court decision (People v. Floyd, 1 Cal 3rd 694), the suspect was picked up two and one half hours after the crime had been committed. He was then shown to the victim for purposes of identification without benefit of counsel. On appeal, the high court upheld the conviction. There are several higher court decisions involving a one hour lapse of time before identification was made, so this time period seems to certainly be on safe ground.

Two years later the Federal Court of Appeals, 10th Circuit, in Spencer v. Turner, (468 F. 2d 599) ruled that the police did not violate a suspect's rights under Wade when they stopped him thirty-five minutes after an armed robbery because he fit the description of the robber. In this case, the suspect refused to accompany the police to the scene, so they brought the victim to the scene of the arrest, where he made positive identification.

PHOTOGRAPH IDENTIFICATION

Showing the victim or witness a series of photographs is permissible providing there is a similarity between the photographs. To play it safe, a total of six photographs should be shown to the victim or witness. Sometimes, to show the reliability of the witness, the officer will show a group of photographs that do not include the suspect. This shows that the witness is not overly suggestible if he does not pick out one of the photographs. The fact that this routine was used can be presented in court to substantiate the witness's reliability.

Years ago, the United States Supreme Court ruled that photographic displays do not require an extraordinary system of safeguards as would a physical lineup. It felt that if there were unfair influences used in the identification, that they could readily be reconstructed at the trial and exposed. (U.S. v. Ash 93 S.Ct. 2568)

The U.S. Court of Appeals, 3rd Circuit, ruled that the Sixth Amendment covers the "right of an accused to be confronted with the witness against him," and that there was no "confrontation" when a pretrial photographic identification of the accused takes place after his arrest. (U.S. ex rel. Reed v. Anderson, 461 F2d 739)

If a lineup is conducted with the suspect's attorney present, it is not a violation of his rights if later a photograph of that lineup is shown to witnesses who were not able to attend the original lineup. (U.S. v. Collins, 461 F2d 696)

TALKING ROGUES' GALLERY

An innovation in the use of "Mug Shots" as a means of identification has been developed by the Nassau County Police Department in New York.

Using the 3M Sound Slide System, all suspects and arrestees are photographed in color and in full view. They are then asked to read a standard question form that asks six pieces of information. Their name, address, place of birth, age, date of birth and height. This information is then recorded on a plastic recording disc that is imbedded on a card which holds a 35mm slide. When the slide is projected on a screen for a witness or victim to view, the suspect's voice is also played over a loudspeaker. If the suspect did not say anything during the crime, the sound part of the slide is not used. In Nassau County they have made over 60,000 of these sound slides, and have had them filed by computer so that if a witness or victim can give a good description of the suspect, the computer will show only slides of persons fitting that description. This saves considerable time. Slides can also be shown by type of crime if the computer is so programmed.

DESCRIPTION OF PROPERTY

The minimum description of any article listed in a crime report should cover:

1. Quantity of the article.
2. Kind of the article.
3. Physical description.
    a. Model.
    b. Style.
    c. Design.
    d. Shape.
    e. Size.
4. Material (gold, silver, wool, etc.).
5. Color.
6. Condition, including age.
7. Value.
8. Trade name.
9. Identifying numbers, initials, marks.

If this description was adhered to, perhaps 50% more property would be returned to the owner. Every six months, the police department auctions off huge supplies of stolen and lost items that cannot be returned to the rightful owners due to a lack of description in reports. If properly described, the articles could be matched with the owner who may be in another part of the state. All such reports go to the State Bureau of Criminal Records. Most states now have a major computer bank that holds these records. If the description is complete, the computer will be able to match the property with the owner. The following is an example of a report on a stolen sweater:

One sweater, buttonless, long sleeve, bulky knit, size 10, wool, blue, new, value $12, made by Capri, has red rose knitted on the left side.

Should there be a number of articles that must be described in the report, the officer should give each one a number. Should it ever be located in another part of the state, it may be referred to by report or case number, and then the item number. This would save the finding agency the trouble of listing the whole description when referring to it.

Description By Article

A. **Firearms**
    1. Manufacturer's name and model.
    2. Type, such as single or double action revolver, semi-automatic, etc.
    3. Caliber, or gauge.
    4. Barrel length.
    5. Serial number.
    6. Finish, (nickel plated, blued).
    7. Stock, (material: pearl, ivory, wood; and color)
    8. Engravings.

B. **Watches**
    1. Manufacturer's name.
    2. Movement (e.g. Swiss).
    3. Type of watch.
        a. men's or women's.
        b. wrist, pocket, lapel.
    4. Case numbers.
    5. Marks or initials. Monograms.
    6. Metal or material.
    7. Number of jewels.
    8. Number of stones and description.

C. **Rings**
    1. Whether man's, woman's or child's.
    2. Kind of metal or other material.
    3. Mounting and setting.
    4. Plain or engraved.
    5. Jeweler's or manufacturer's code marks.
    6. Engraved initials or inscriptions.
    7. Size.
    8. Weight of stones and value.

D. **Silverware**
1. Kind.
2. Trade name.
3. Number of articles.
4. Design.
5. Code marks.
6. Solid or plated.
7. Engraving or initials.
8. Condition.
9. Value.

E. **Cameras**
1. Name of manufacturer.
2. Type and model.
3. Size of film used.
4. Still or movie.
5. Serial numbers.
6. Color.
7. Covering materials.
8. Attachments (e.g. light meter as part of camera).
9. The lens description (the most valuable part of the camera).
   a. Serial number.
   b. Make.
   c. Size.
   d. Type.

F. **Clothing**
1. Kind, (suit, dress, hat, under garments, overcoat).
2. Man's, woman's, or child's.
3. Manufacturer's name.
4. Trade name.
5. Size.
6. Style.
7. Material.
8. Color.
9. Age and condition.
10. Where purchased.
11. Laundry or cleaners where clothing is taken (to obtain their ultraviolet mark).
12. Any repairs or alterations.

G. **Vessels** Note* This has become an increasingly important item as far as theft is concerned. The Boating Industry Assn. estimates that there are 10.1 million pleasure boats in the U.S.)

The following identification information can often be obtained from a copy of the owner's vessel registration certificate. If he does not have a copy (often it is on the stolen vessel) the State central records bureau will have a copy, usually in the Division of Motor Vehicles.

(1) **CF number.** This is usually a four digit number followed by two letters.

(2) **Name of builder.** In many cases this is found on a name plate at the rear of the vessel.

(3) **Builder's hull number.** This is found on the name plate.

(4) **Type.** Categories are: sailboat, rowboat, cruiser, runabout, barge, kayak canoe and other.

(5) **Length.**

(6) **Beam** (width).

(7) **Color(s).**

(8) **Hull material.** Categories are: wood, aluminum, steel, fiberglass or plastic and other.

(9) **Propulsion.** Categories are: inboard, outboard, inboard/outboard combination, sail only, jet, hand propelled, auxiliary and sail and other.

(10) **Motor number.**

(11) **Other distinguishing features** that would be an aid to identity.

(12) **Name and address of registered owner.**

PROPERTY LISTS

Every citizen and especially every officer should keep a list of all valuables owned, and the serial numbers of those articles along with a description of each article. Very few people actually do this, and when some of their articles are stolen, they frantically try to obtain the serial number from some other source, which is extremely difficult if not impossible. A copy should be made so one may be placed in the home, and the other at work or in a safe deposit box. This procedure doesn't take long.

Since a police officer usually has more than one gun, he or she should have all gun serial numbers and handcuff serial numbers written down and kept in a fireproof box.

PHOTOGRAPHS/PICTURES OF PROPERTY

Because the average citizen victimized by theft or burglary seldom knows the exact model number or style of most of the items taken, the officer might suggest to him that he try to obtain a photograph or magazine picture of the same model. Most of the items that we buy today are advertised in one way or another, usually with an accompanying picture or photograph. If the victim can find an advertisement in a magazine, newspaper, or catalogue, he could bring it to the police department, and it can be stapled to the offense report.

Many times a burglar is arrested, and in a search of his home or garage, hundreds of items are discovered that have been stolen from numerous places. In talking to the burglar, he states that he has committed so many jobs, that he honestly can't remember where each item was taken. Without a full description from the victim on the offense report, it is difficult to connect the items with their rightful owners. However, if a picture of the article was attached to the offense report, the task of matching the recovered articles with those reported stolen would be a much easier task. The Chinese proverb that "one picture is worth a thousand words," could well apply here.

Ultra Microfiche In-car Identification System

UMF systems in Los Angeles has developed a portable microfiche viewer that can be used in a patrol car. It is an "Ultra" microfiche system that can imprint up to 8,000 high quality images on a 4-by-6-inch transparent film card called a fiche. This could make the patrol car a mobile records department. This same information could be transmitted to the patrol car equipped with a computer terminal. This, however is expensive and requires considerable maintenance. The microfiche viewer runs about $100 which is quite low. If the

transparent film cards were produced on a metropolitan basis, the cost of this "software" would also be low. Maintenance on this equipment is, at the most, minimal.

To illustrate how much information can be capsulized, the Manhattan telephone directory has already been reproduced on a 4-by-6-inch fiche. Having the city directory, telephone directory, fingerprint cards of local criminals, mug shots, rap sheets (just to name a few items of information) would be invaluable to the patrol officer working in the field. Once a fiche has been made, it can be reproduced quite easily and economically. This would give unlimited fingertip information to patrol officers and reduce the amount of air traffic.

HYPNOSIS AND IDENTIFICATION

Hypnosis is a tool that is now being used by law enforcement agencies to assist witnesses in recalling details of crimes, and better identifying suspects.

The Winter Park, Florida Police Department began training the whole department in hypnosis. It was to be used not only in assisting witnesses to recall details, but to also assist police officers in refreshing their memories before testifying in court. It has also been used to increase officers' power of concentration.

Emotional shock often causes a memory block on the conscious level. Hypnosis has been very successful in penetrating this block. It has been used to investigate cases of murder, robbery, rape, assault, arson and kidnapping.

Dr. Martin Reiser, clinical psychologist for the LAPD conducted a year of research with this tool before initiating a special unit for the department. The new unit consisted of two captains and eleven lieutenants, all with a good background in criminal investigation. They started with a 48 hour course and then underwent a period of internship under the supervision of consultants. In its initial stages, the use of hypnotism resulted in a 60 to 65 percent increase in success over traditional investigative techniques. It has turned out so well that Dr. Reiser has recommended that the unit be doubled in size.

A basic text in this area is "Hypnosis in Criminal Investigation" by Harry Arons. After this book was written, the technique of using hypnosis increased among police agencies throughout the United States, including the FBI.

An organization has been formed by which techniques and ideas on the investigative use of hypnosis can be exchanged. It is the Society for Investigative and Forensic Hypnosis (c/o Capt. Mike Nielsen, Devonshire Div. LAPD, 10250 Etiwanda Ave, Northridge CA 91324)

There are certain rules that must be followed in the professional use of this tool. First, it is done only on a volunteer basis, and it is used to gain leads, not confessions (It cannot be used in court). It is a memory aid to be used when witnesses possess information that they are not able to consciously recall.

Not everyone can be hypnotized. Even those who are willing to cooperate. It is estimated that about 3 out of 5 persons are capable of being hypnotized.

This estimate naturally varies dependent upon the ability of the hypnotist. There are some who claim that with the use of Biofeedback equipment, they can hypnotize anyone. Children are often the best subjects. There has been some success in enabling persons to recall incidents that occurred when they were so intoxicated they normally would have very little recall.

If this use of hypnotism is scientifically developed and professionally controlled, it could be of great service to the field of criminal justice.

STUDY QUESTIONS for Patrol Operations

CHAPTER 9

1. Early identification of criminals took two forms. (1) to identify the individual criminal, and (2) to identify _____ _____ in general.

2. The first was handled by a description of the person, the second by _____.

3. In early times, criminals were paraded in a courtyard to see if someone could identify them by recognition or identify them as having committed certain crimes. This was called the " _____ _____ ".

4. In 1840 photography was used as a means of identification with excellent results.   **T or F**

5. In 1875, criminal identification photographs were standardized by:

   a. _ Bertillon   b. __ Henry
   c. _ Gross   d. __ Volmer

6. The above person later became known as the father of criminal photography.   **T or F**

7. Criminals did not always like to be photographed and often resisted it.   **T or F**

8. The system of positively identifying a person through 11 measurements is call Bertillonage after its inventor. It is also called:

   a. _ anthrometrics   b. __ criminal signetics
   c. _ criminal anthropometry   d. __ criminal angetromity

9. In 1875, Alphonse _____ developed the first system of positive identification.

10. Up to this time fingerprints had not been accepted as a positive means of ID.   **T or F**

11. To supplement his system of bodily measurements, Bertillon added a system of detailed identification of the head. He called this his _____ _____.(in French)

12. Name a disadvantage of the Bertillon system of criminal anthropometry. _____ _____

13. Bertillon claimed that he could make identification of a person by examining just his _____ alone.

14. Hugh McDonald, Division Chief at the Los Angeles Sheriff's Office, developed a system of identification that involves overlays. It is called:

   a. _ identi-code   b. __ map-a-face
   c. _ identi-kit   d. __ identi-foil

15. The memory aid "numb-skulls rarely agree" stands for:

    N _____ S _____ R _____ A _____

16. The memory key "Have we had escaping criminals pull cunning jobs?" stands for:

    H _____ W _____ H _____ E _____
    C _____ M _____ C _____ J _____

17. In the Spanish system of names, two last names are used.   T or F

18. The first last name is that of the _____ family.

19. The second last name is that of the _____ family.

20. When running a want check on a Latin suspect, it is a good idea to ask him his mother's   T or F
    family name.

21. What is the difference between the name "Maria Lucia Martinez de Torres" and "Maria Lucia
    Martinez De Torres"? _____

22. In a "lineup" for purposes of identifying a suspect, if all of the other persons in the "lineup"
    are much taller or of another race than the suspect, it is called a _____
    and is illegal.

23. The proper procedure in talking to witnesses who are observing a "lineup" is to ask them   T or F
    "Which one of them did it?"

24. The "Wade" decision pertains to "lineups." It states that:

    a. _There must be at least six people in the lineup.
    b. _Suspects have the right to an attorney during a lineup.
    c. _Photographs cannot be used to replace the lineup.
    d. _A suspect cannot be placed in a lineup against his will.

25. The "Wade" decision only applies to the _____ stages of the investigation.

26. In the "Kirby" decision, the U.S. Supreme Court modified the "Wade" decision by moving   T or F
    the critical stage past the arrest.

27. Under "Kirby" the defense attorney has the right to be present when the witnesses are   T or F
    interviewed after the lineup.

28. Based on several high-court decisions, it appears that it would be safe to place a suspect in   T or F
    a one-on-one "field lineup" up to one hour after the crime had been committed.

29. To be on the safe side, it is best to show witnesses _____ photographs
    when using a photographic lineup.

30. The United States Supreme Court stated that photo displays do not require as stringent   T or F
safeguards as do physical lineups.

31. A photograph of a physical lineup can later be shown to witnesses who could not be present   T or F
at the original lineup.

32. The 3M Sound Slide System of identification, not only shows a colored slide of the suspect,   T or F
but also plays a recording of his voice at the same time the slide is shown.

33. How many pleasure boats are there in the United States?

     a.__5 million   b.__7 million
     c.__9 million   d.__10.1 million

34. In the new "ultra-microfiche" identification system that can be carried in police cars, each
4 x 6 transparent film can carry 8,000 images. The name for this small piece of film is

     _____.

35. The Los Angeles Police Department, a leader in the field of investigative hypnosis, requires   T or F
that hypnosis not be used for confessions, but for gaining leads.

36. It is estimated that _____ out of _____ Persons can be hypnotized.

37. _____ seem to be the best subjects for hypnosis.

CHAPTER X

FIELD INTERROGATION

One of the important tasks of the police officer in American society is the protection of citizens. One of the ways in which this is accomplished is through conducting field interrogations. Another very important duty for officers is to safeguard the Constitutional rights of citizens in the community in which the officer serves. At times these duties can seem to be in conflict. Protecting rights and catching criminals are at the opposite end of a fixed balancing rod. When one increases, the other decreases, and vice versa. Many court decisions have restricted the way in which police officers carry out their duties. The question is "Can we still make good arrests from field interrogations and maintain the democratic philosophy of respecting personal rights?" The answer is undoubtedly yes, but it hinges upon being able to make field interrogations without gross infringement upon the basic rights of the persons involved. This involves skill, personal control, courtesy and mental alertness. These are qualities that mark the professional law enforcement officer.

If patrol officers continue to press the established legal or proper limits of their actions to the breaking point, they will unfortunately bring the walls of adverse court decisions down upon them. Nearly every court decision that adversely affects

police officers is the result of the improper actions of some officer somewhere in the United States. Through his or her own actions, the patrol officer may exert a profound effect upon the future decisions of the court. This in turn affects the restrictions under which they must work.

There is no doubt that the use of field interrogation has been abused by police officers. At night, when things are slow, it has been a common practice to use a numerical formula as a means of stopping vehicles or pedestrians for field interrogation. Every fifth vehicle or every third person on the street is stopped without real cause other than the feeling that the person "might be up to something." Often a stop is made in the hope that by talking to the person, something might be found wrong. Some feel that this is especially true if the interrogation is long enough and thorough enough. This does not mean that an officer should not stop cars and people on the street unless they have actually been observed committing a crime. There is a happy medium. Some of the "suspicion arousers" that will assist an officer in justly stopping suspects will be covered later in the chapter. There is no doubt that those officers who practice mass or saturation "field stops" will make more arrests than those officers who don't. However, this indiscriminate stopping of passersby causes much ill feeling among the citizenry and could have an adverse effect upon police-community relations. It should also be mentioned that although this type of officer might make a large number of arrests, the number of convictions in court are few. This officer is also more likely to be sued.

The population of American communities, and especially the large cities, are undergoing changes. Every year the percentage of minority citizens is increasing. Unlike the white middle-class citizen, they do not seem ready to accept the number of criminals arrested from improper tactics as justification for continuing this practice. They are the ones most often stopped during field interrogations. They are the ones who seem to be more often subjected to improper treatment.

Because of this, officers making field stops must always bear in mind that they will be required to firmly justify their suspicions in court. No longer will "He just didn't look right" be justification for a field interrogation. Officers should therefore train themselves to base their suspicions upon a firm and explainable foundation. No relying on a so-called sixth sense. This can be done with the proper training and effort.

One must realize however, that almost all of the Appellate Court decisions, which some consider adverse to the field of law enforcement, are often the result of a split decision. This means that four of the nine justices of the Supreme Court of the United States felt that the decision was wrong. Yet these decisions have become the "law of the land." We must adhere to them for they are now the rules of this game that we play. Since interpretation of the Constitution is based on opinion, some feel that the pendulum is swinging the other way. Especially since conservatives are now the majority on the U.S. Supreme court. Despite the political makeup of the court, there has been no evidence whatsoever, based on its prior decisions, that it will make major changes in the interpretation of the Constitution. The Burger court publicly stated that even though it would not have overturned the Miranda conviction, it has seen that it has done more good than bad and would therefore not reverse it.

To face the situation honestly, we must admit that most of these adverse decisions were brought about because of the indiscretions of police officers in many jurisdictions. Since police officers are human, it is easy for them to justify their wrong actions by pointing to the good that these actions will achieve in the end. Our court justices have become painfully aware of this "police philosophy", and it is certainly reflected in their decisions.

There is presently a strong trend in the United States toward eliminating injustices. This is especially true in the area of civil rights, not only for minorities, but for all citizens. In the field of law enforcement, this trend gained momentum with court decisions which placed strict controls on the way in which evidence was obtained. This is especially true regarding evidence obtained during field interrogations or "shakedowns." It is the feeling of some that this would never have happened if law enforcement officers had practiced more discretion in the performance of their duties, especially in the area of field interrogation.

When these decisions were first handed down, police officers protested that they would never be able to make another narcotics arrest, and that field interrogation was now a waste of time. Today we are able to look back and find that we were wrong. Some decisions did hurt law enforcement in certain areas. However, we now see that the number of arrests have not been that greatly affected. In fact some of those decisions have made policemen do a better job in a more just and professional manner.

DISCRETION ON THE PART OF THE OFFICER

Field interrogation is an important part of the patrol officer's job. yet success in this endeavor requires both knowledge and skill. The knowledge required involves the changing laws and court decisions as well as the proper techniques to be used for each individual situation. The skill involved is that of talking to people and sensing their true reactions to probing questions or remarks. It involves being able to "match wits," and to use discretion in selecting subjects. It also involves the ability to ask questions in such a manner as not to offend those stopped.

In field interrogation, much is left to the individual officer's discretion. Interrogations can be very productive in the arrests that can result. It is therefore natural for new officers to try and copy the more experienced officer. Making arrests is what law enforcement is all about and new officers want their share in this fertile endeavor. It must be remembered, however, that discretion is an important part of this skill. Officers who fail to exercise it, may eventually lose the right to practice it. It is therefore important that the patrol officer have a good understanding of the latest court decisions. These are the "ground rules" by which he or she must play. Failure to either understand or apply them can result in the whole case being lost in court.

MAJOR COURT DECISIONS THAT AFFECT FIELD INTERROGATION

The Miranda Decision (Miranda v. Arizona, 384 U.S. 436.)

Since any appeal to the United States Supreme Court must be based on a violation of the constitution, Miranda was appealed on the basis that it violated the Fifth Amendment (self incrimination) and the Sixth Amendment (Due Process - Right to Counsel)

When Miranda was first handed down, the guidelines were not too clear. There was a tendency for judges to throw out any statement or confession that was not preceded by the Miranda warning, regardless of the circumstances surrounding the situation.

Since the original Miranda decision, there has been a general body of law that has developed regarding the application of that decision. The general premise of the decision is now accepted as being a means of protecting a person from "formal interrogation." This has certainly changed things since the decision was first handed down. At first, departments, as a form of insurance, required their officers to "Mirandize" all suspects under all conditions as a blanket policy. The decision stated that once a suspect has been "taken into custody or otherwise deprived of his freedom of action in any significant way," he must be notified of his rights. He must then voluntarily waive these rights in order for any statement to be admissible in court."

The major point of interpretation today is the question of whether or not the accused was "in custody." The officer's suspicions or intentions have nothing to do with the definition of custody. It is the defendant's state of mind that is important.

What the jury must consider is: Would an ordinary person under those circumstances have felt that he was in custody of the police? If so, the warnings have to be given. Therefore the officer's exact words to the suspect are very important. Through knowledge, the officer may "avoid" Miranda which is perfectly legal. It is when Miranda is "evaded" that the law has been violated. One of the ways to avoid Miranda is in the way the officer conducts the conversation. Does it make the suspect feel that it is a formal interrogation, or that he is in custody.

The Waiver Of Rights

Since Miranda requires the person to first understand his rights and then intelligently waive them, several problems can arise. For example, can young juveniles, intoxicated persons or people who don't speak English intelligently waive their rights?

With the first two, the officer must do the best he or she can to explain the rights and then leave the final decision to the court. With the non-English speaking person, the officer can enlist the aid of someone who can speak the language. Some officers carry a Miranda warning card printed in the language most common in that area. It can still present difficult problems in court.

Miranda And The Field Stop

Does Miranda apply to field interrogation or stop and frisk cases? Under ordinary circumstances, in a field interrogation, there is no custody within the meaning of the Fifth Amendment. Although there certainly is custody within the meaning of the Fourth Amendment. Miranda clearly states that "General on-the-scene questioning as to facts surrounding a crime or other general questioning of citizens in the fact-finding process is not affected." A field stop does come under the Fourth Amendment. However, even if it is for a very brief and temporary detention, the officer must be able to substantiate the stop with reasonable cause. The probable cause for an arrest requires a greater weight of evidence.

The courts have so far resolved the issue of field stops by saying that if there are no special coercive circumstances attached to the stop, no Miranda warnings are required. Some examples of situations that could bring Miranda into the picture are as follows:

(1) A large number of officers interrogating one suspect.

(2) The officer talking to the suspect with his gun drawn.

(3) Taking the suspect some distance from the scene in order to talk to him.

(4) Talking to the suspect while he is handcuffed.

(5) The officer makes statements which are indicative of custody or arrest. The conversation should be kept as friendly and casual as the circumstances permit. The officer might say "its kind of unusual to find someone here at this time. Would you mind telling us what you are doing here?"

The Rights Warning Under Miranda

When a suspect does come within the jurisdiction of the Miranda decision, he must be notified of his rights before any statement will be admitted in court. Those rights are as follows:

(1) His right to remain silent.

(2) Notification that if he does say anything, it can and will be used against him in court.

(3) His right to counsel prior to or during any statements.

(4) Notification that if he cannot afford one, a lawyer will be appointed to represent him.

It is important to note that warning the suspect of his rights is not enough. He must have clearly understood what was said. The burden of proof in this regard is upon the questioning officer. The suspect must then intelligently waive his rights.

Although the present court has stated that they will not reverse Miranda, they do seem to be chipping away at it. The following are cases that have changed Miranda in some ways.

HARRIS v. NEW YORK. (401 U.S. 222) The U.S. Supreme Court allowed a statement, given before Miranda warnings, to be used to impeach the defendant's credibility. This was accepted even though it was not allowed in evidence for conviction.

U.S. v. CASTELLANA (500 F2d 325) Federal agents raided a suspect's store and immediately asked him if he had any guns within reach. He told them where guns were hidden. Later he contested his conviction on the grounds that his statement was used in violation of his Fifth Amendment rights. The high court upheld the conviction based on the fact the question was not an interrogation, but a question concerning safety.

MICHIGAN v. MOSLEY (90 S.Ct. 321) The U.S. Supreme Court upheld a conviction based on a voluntary statement that was made more than two hours after the suspect had been Mirandized and declined to give a statement. His later statement occurred during a new interrogation regarding another unrelated crime, after he had again been Mirandized.

U.S. v. RINKA (512 F 2d 425) The high court accepted a confession made after a lineup, despite the fact that after his arrest the day before, the suspect refused to answer any questions. In this case he was again Mirandized after the lineup. The court based its decision on the "voluntariness" of the confession.

OWENS v. U.S. (340 A 2d 821) The high court upheld a conviction where an officer arrested a suspect in a tire store after a silent alarm sounded. Without giving the suspect Miranda warnings, he asked him why he was there. The suspect admitted that he was there to steal tires. The court upheld the conviction based on their feeling that the suspect was still in the process of being apprehended, and was not in the words of Miranda being "held for interrogation".

WARRANTLESS VEHICLE SEARCHES

CARROLL v. U.S. (267 U.S. 132 (1925)) This decision set the basis for officers being able to stop and search a car when there was reasonable cause to believe that it contained contraband, intruments of the crime or fruits of the crime that were subject to seizure. The search was justified on the theory that the car was immediately movable, and that unless the police took action right there on the highway, the car could be moved and the contraband would escape seizure. By the time that a warrant was obtained, the vehicle could also be in another jurisdiction.

CHAMBERS v. MARONEY (399 U.S. 42 (1970)) Officers stopped an auto occupied by four men fitting the description of those responsible for a robbery which had occurred less than one hour before. A warrantless search revealed weapons, stolen property and other incriminating evidence. The court upheld the search on the grounds that the officers had sufficient descriptive information. The court also felt that carrying out the immediate search would be no more of a constitutional intrusion than holding the car until a search warrant was obtained.

Under Chambers, if the police have information upon which a search warrant could eventually be obtained, they have a right to search that car without a warrant, even at a time and place away from the scene of the arrest, or even without an arrest.

Under Chambers, the Chimel theory of "search incident to arrest" does not apply because it is an automobile. Even in Carroll the courts distinguished the difference between an automobile and a home or office.

Before Chambers, the police resorted to subterfuge in order to justify a delayed search of an automobile after the time and place of arrest. Today, if you have probable cause, you simply arrest the driver, take the car to the station and search it.

Chambers is the first case in which the Supreme Court has explicitly recognized the practicality of its rules involving police procedure. It stated that if the police are to be made to resort to the warrant procedure, that it should be under circumstances that would make the procedure practical and workable. Chambers also expands the type of evidence that can be seized beyond the previous "contraband" classification. The range of items that can now be seized in a search of a car is very broad.

U.S. v. ROBINSON (414 U.S. 218) (1973) "By a 6-3 decision, the Supreme Court greatly eased the restrictions ·on searching a person arrested for a minor traffic offense. In this decision the court stated that "It is the fact of the lawful arrest which establishes the authority to search, and we hold that in the case of a lawful custodial arrest, a full search of the person is not only an exception to the warrant requirements of the Fourth Amendment, but is also a 'reasonable search' under that amendment." In this case, Robinson, of Washington D.C., was stopped on an outstanding traffic warrant. Upon arrest, a search of his person reveled a packet of heroin.

GUSTAFSON v. FLORIDA (414 U.S. 260) (1973) Just after Robinson, the Supreme Court again affirmed the legality of a search after a traffic arrest. The major difference between Robinson and Gustafson is that in Robinson's case, it was a department policy to make a custodial arrest, whereas in Gustafson's, the department did not require a custodial arrest, but left it up to the officer.

The Supreme Court stated that "It is sufficient that the officer had probable cause to arrest the petitioners and that he lawfully effectuated the arrest and placed the petitioner in custody. The court further stated that "he was entitled to make a full search of the petitioner's person incident to that lawful arrest."

NEW YORK v. BELTON (1981) The Belton decision applies only when an arrest has been made. It was based on the officer safety aspects of Chimel v. California (395 U.S. 762.) It went a bit further by allowing officers to search closed containers within the passenger area of a vehicle. To quote the court: "We hold that when a policeman has made a lawful custodial arrest, he may, as a contemporaneous incident of that arrest, search the passenger compartment. The police may also examine the contents of any containers found within the passenger compartment."

U.S. v. ROSS (456 U.S. 798) (1982) The Ross Decision made it easier for patrol officers who had difficulty deciding courses of action under prior court rulings. Now, if an officer has reasonable cause to believe that there is contraband or evidence in a vehicle, the vehicle and its closed containers may be searched. This decision further diminished the "expectation of privacy" rule associated with homes.

The scope of the search is based on what the officer has reasonable cause to believe is in the vehicle. If it is believed that the vehicle contains stolen TV consoles, a search in the glove compartment would not be justified. If the suspected evidence is found in the driver or passenger compartment, a search of the trunk would probably not be legal because the suspected evidence has now been located. A search of the trunk would be a "fishing expedition."

If the suspected evidence is a small packet of heroin, then the whole vehicle could be searched until it is found. If the driver is a suspected narcotic dealer, it would be reasonable to assume that there would be more narcotics in the vehicle. A search of the trunk would probably be justified. Trunks require "independent probable cause," so there must be special probable cause to search that area. There must be a "Nexus" or legal connection between the probable cause and the trunk. For example, three bags of money were taken in a holdup. A search of the passenger compartment reveals two bags. Since there is still one bag missing, a search of the trunk would be reasonable.

In Ross, an informant told officers that Ross was selling narcotics out of the trunk of his car. The officers stopped him and searched the trunk and then opened two closed containers found inside the trunk. Inside were narcotics and money. The appellate court overturned the conviction. The U.S. Supreme Court overruled the appellate court and said the search was legal. Here, the high court, for the first time, stated that if an officer had enough probable cause to obtain a search warrant from a magistrate, that a warrantless search was justified. Of course this applies only to vehicles.

MOTOR HOMES AND CAMPERS

In 1987, the U.S. Supreme court in **California v. Carney,** stated that a motor home or camper was a vehicle as long as it was on a roadway or parked in a location that was readily accessible to the roadway. Examples would be a driveway or a parking lot. Suppose it is parked at a campground and hooked up to utilities, or parked in a back yard? It is then classed as a dwelling and does not come under the vehicle exception to the Fourth Amendment rules on search and seizure.

IMPOUND-INVENTORY SEARCHES OF VEHICLES

When a vehicle has been towed under police control, and after it has been impounded, the U.S. Supreme court in **Colorado v. Bertine** (1987), stated that an inventory search may be made of the vehicle. Any contraband, fruits of the crime or instruments of the crime, or other evidence found in the vehicle may be legally seized. Examples would be after an arrest; when a vehicle has been abandoned after a chase; or when a vehicle has been disabled in a traffic accident; and even when a vehicle has been towed as the result of a parking violation.

SEARCHING FOR EVIDENCE WITHOUT A WARRANT

MAPP v. OHIO (367 U.S. 643 (1961)) This ruling is based on the "exclusionary rule" under the 4th Amendment. This decision brought all of the states under the federal ruling that illegally searched and seized evidence is inadmissible in court. Although illegal searches and seizures are, in some places, common practice during field interrogations and car stops, little has been said or done about it. The trend today, however, is toward increasing personal and civil rights. There are many organizations that are looking for cases they can take to court to establish a precedent. As a result, patrol officers who make a practice of such illegal searches will unfortunately find themselves involved in litigation under the 1968 Civil Rights Act. Patrol officers must, of their own accord, become overly sensitive to the two words "reasonable cause." It is the key as to whether or not a case will hold up in court.

CHIMEL v. CALIFORNIA (395 U.S. 762 (1969)) The Chimel decision is one of the most restrictive dealing with warrantless searches during an arrest. At one time, when an arrest was made in a person's home, that whole home could be searched. In this particular case the officers arrested the defendant on a burglary warrant at his home. They searched the whole house and the garage, turning up evidence of other crimes.

The Supreme Court overturned the conviction and stated as grounds that a warrantless search incident to arrest is strictly limited to the person and the immediate vicinity of the arrestee (within his immediate control). The court defined this as meaning the area from within which he might gain possession of a weapon or destructible evidence. Originally called the "reach rule," it has now been expanded to where it is called the "lunge-and-reach rule," which means that it now includes areas where the suspect might jump or lunge in order to grab a weapon or destroy evidence.

Exceptions To Chimel

There are certain conditions under which the search and seizure restrictions of Chimel do not apply. Four of them are:

(1) Automobiles. The courts have long set forth this distinction.

(2) Hot Pursuit. When a suspect has committed a crime and is being pursued and runs into a house, he may be followed inside. Any evidence observed inside may be legally seized.

(3) Evidence found in plain view.

(4) Emergency situations. Mainly this would cover the entry into a house or building for the purpose of saving a life. For example, a man is found outside a residence in an unconscious state. You enter to look for medicines or poisons. Any criminal evidence observed inside is seizable.

This also includes searching an unconscious person for identification or medicines and finding some criminal evidence.

STOPPING AND FRISKING AT THE SCENE OR IN THE FIELD

The term "Stop and Frisk" is widely used in policework. From a legal standpoint it is quite misleading. This is because it involves two separate and distinct powers that are not necessarily dependent upon each other. There are occasions when officers would be completely within their rights to detain a person for a brief interrogation. They may, however, have no power to frisk the suspect. Such an action would be unconstitutional. The Supreme Court has defined the term "Frisk" as the "patting down of the outside of the clothing." Under present law, any frisk not asso-ciated with arrest or a search warrant can only be done for purposes of self defense based on reason-able cause.

TERRY v. OHIO (392 U.S. 1 (1968)) The Terry decision has become the guiding law regarding the frisking of a suspect. In the Terry case, an experienced officer noted two men acting very suspicious in front of a jewelry store. From his observations, plus his many years of experience, he became convinced that they were casing the jewelry store for an armed robbery. He stopped and questioned the suspects and then patted them from the outside. The frisk detected a metal object. It not only felt like a gun but actually was a gun. The case was appealed on the grounds of illegal search, but the Supreme Court upheld the conviction.

The court set down certain guidelines in the Terry decision. First, there must be a reasonable belief that the suspect is armed with a deadly weapon. There must also be the belief that if the suspect is not frisked and disarmed, harm will come to the officer or to another person. This can be based upon either a combination of observation and experience, or upon legitimate prior information. A reliable informant or an all-points-bulletin would be an example. Once these conditions are met, the officer can pat the suspect's outer clothing for deadly wea-pons. If any are located, an inside search may be conducted to recover the weapon. If during the frisk, the officer feels a soft lump that later turns out to be a bag of marijuana, this would not be a legal search under Terry. It would be inadmissible in court because the object did not feel like a weapon. However, if it was wrapped in heavy foil, it might feel like a weapon and would be admissible.

INSLAW STUDY ON PATROL ARRESTS

A study by the Institute of Law and Social Research (INSLAW) for the Justice Department, showed that 15 percent of officers accounted for 50 percent of all arrests THAT LED TO CONVICTIONS. The last part is very important because there are many officers who make large numbers of arrests. However, they seldom obtain convictions in court either because of the way the arrest was made or the way evidence was seized. The study stressed the importance of gathering evidence properly and of obtaining witnesses. These are two areas of weakness in general patrol work. It was found that the conviction rate for robbery jumped from 25% to 40% of those arrested when the officer gathered some type of tangible evidence. The conviction rates also increased in proportion to the officer's ability to obtain cooperative witnesses.

THE PURPOSE OF FIELD INTERROGATION

There are four main functions of the field interrogation:

(1) **The developing of information and informants.** An officer cannot possibly see everything that goes on all over the beat. An officer can, however, use others to obtain information. In this sense, field interrogation involves more than just talking to people who are suspicious, or who are suspects. It involves talking to people and obtaining information from them. Especially those persons on the beat who might have had access to various types of information. Obtaining this information is a skill and can be done without damaging public relations, but only if the officer has developed a knowledge of human nature and the ability to relate to people of different backgrounds. The importance of informants in policework is seldom stressed. This is because officers are afraid to let it be known that about 50 to 60 percent of all major crime is solved through the use of police informants. This includes paid informants and citizens in the community who want to help because it is the right thing to do. This seems to have been the case for centuries.

(2) **Identification.** Good patrol officers know the people on their beat. They learn how to develop friendships on the beat in a manner that doesn't arouse suspicion. A field interrogation is simply the obtaining of information. It does not have to be aggressive in its manner or approach.

Once an officer obtains the name of a person through normal conversation, it should be run through the Records Division to see if that person might have a criminal record. An effort should be made to obtain as much background information as possible from those on the beat. To avoid suspicion when trying to obtain information on a certain person, an approach like this might be used. "Say Bill, Fred Jones seems like a nice person. I'd like to get to know him better. What do you know about him?" If Bill tells you something negative about Fred, you could reply "You're kidding me. He seems like such a nice person." It's unfortunate, but people love to demonstrate how wrong we are. When negative information is given on a suspect, the response could be "I find that hard to believe." This puts the informant in a position of defending his statement. He will often provide more information just to prove he's right.

All of this information should be put on 3 x 5 cards and filed by name and beat in a plastic file box that can be carried in the patrol car. The name of the informant should also be included with the background information obtained on that person. Later the names of the suspect's friends and associates can be added. It is also good to list all of the automobiles owned by or associated with the suspect. Good arrests have been made when an officer hears the description of a person and vehicle involved in a crime, and is able to identify him from information in the file box. Even more important is when the arrest is accomplished by knowing those persons with whom the suspect associates, and knowing where they live. When a person commits a crime, he often goes first to someone else's house to "hide out."

| Last Name First—PRINT | | Date | | |
| | | Mo | Day | Year |

| Address | | Phone |

| Social Security No. | Military I.D. No. | Veh. Oper. Lic. No. |

Place of Employment

| Location of Occurrence | Time | U. C. Student |
| | | Yes ☐ No ☐ |

Parent or
Local Ref.

| Age | Date and Place of Birth | Height | Weight | Build | Complexion |

| Race | Hair Color | Eye Color | Marks or Scars | | |

Clothing

| Make of Car | Year | Type | Color | License No. | State |

POLICE DEPARTMENT, UNIVERSITY OF CALIFORNIA · BERKELEY · FIELD INTERROGATION REPORT

FRONT

List names of all persons with suspect at time of interrogation:

_____

_____

_____

_____

Reason for Interrogation:

_____

_____

Disposition:

_____

Officers' Names:

Series 3666

BACKSIDE

Fig. X-1; Sample filed interrogation card.

Many times officers can obtain the names of persons on the beat without actually talking to them by asking persons they already know. These can be gas station attendants, newspaper vendors, or waitresses in local cafes. The officer can point out the person whose name is desired and state "What's the name of that guy over there? He looks like someone I used to know." The person asked will not only name him, but will probably give some background information. This will be to assist the officer in making a connection with the past association. It is also good to ask, "Does he still live over on the East side on Jackson Street? The informant will probably reply "Oh no, he lives on 15th street on the Northeast corner of Harrison."

The patrol officer should make a list of who associates with known criminals on the beat. Every time a known criminal is observed with an unknown person, an effort should be make to identify that person. Once the name is obtained, it should be added to the officer's 3 X 5 card on that criminal. If the officer stops a car at night under suspicious circumstances, and makes out field interrogation cards on the occupants, the associates names should be listed on the back of each person's FI card. These cards can be referred to later if one of the suspects is arrested and his unknown associates escape the police. The beat officer will now have an idea who the associates might be.

(3) **Development of suspects.** When a crime has been committed and there are no suspects and few leads, the officer who is assigned to follow up on the case should rely heavily on the field interrogation cards. Those that have been turned in on the night of the crime should be given close examination. The cards should also be checked for several days prior in the event that the suspect "cased" the job during that time. Traffic citations are also useful, since many times a perpetrator will be in such a hurry to leave the scene of the crime, he will commit traffic violations and attract the attention of an officer who will either cite him or take his name.

Whenever an officer cites a person for a traffic violation, and that person arouses the officer's suspicion, in addition to the citation, a field interrogation card should be filled out. A duplicate should be kept for the officer's file box and the original turned into the department.

(4) **Crime prevention.** This comes under the heading of Preventive Enforcement. When criminals "case a job," they look to see if the patrol officers in that particular area are thorough in covering their beat. Do they check locks on doors and gates and make sure safe lights are working? Do they check on strangers and suspicious persons? If so, they will be hesitant about committing crimes in that area. A criminal does not actually have to be stopped for this to have effect. When friends and acquaintances tell him about being stopped, they usually exaggerate the number of times and the length of the stops. This is often done to show the injustice of the action, and how the police pick on them. This, along with actually seeing a number of cars stopped for field interrogation, will usually cause criminals to steer clear of the area. After all, there are many other beats where the patrol officers are lax in their duties. So why should they take a chance on this beat?

Again this does not mean that the patrol officer is to engage in wholesale "shakedowns" or "fishing trips" of vehicles and pedestrians. The quality of field interrogations is of much more value than the quantity.

SELECTING THE SUBJECT

There are hundreds of people walking or driving back and forth on an officer's beat. It is physically impossible to stop all of them for interrogation. The phone in the Chief's office would be ringing off the hook if officers were even to attempt stopping great numbers of people. Yet many new officers will try this. They will stop many cars out of ignorance. They hear what seems to be innumerable police cars going out of service all night on car stops. They also hear some of them telling communications that they are on the way to jail with a prisoner. They ask themselves why they are not making the same arrests? Maybe they need to stop more cars? When they develop good patrol skills, they will know that selection is important. Car stops MUST be justified by reasonable cause.

In large cities with increasing populations and large numbers of calls for police service, many patrol officers are finding less time for field interrogation. Most of it is done during the quiet hours of early morning.

Time is becoming very valuable to the patrol officer, especially in the urban areas. Therefore it is important that it be used wisely. Vehicles or pedestrians should not be stopped just "for kicks." Field stops should not be make just because things are quiet, but because an officer's trained eyes detect something measurably suspicious.

Chiefs of Police often report that when citizens complain to them that they were stopped for a traffic citation, the officer made them feel like a criminal. A respectable citizen is usually most offended when he is stopped for a field interrogation and is treated poorly. In Los Angeles, a study revealed this complaint to be the most frequent and strongest cause of poor public relations.

In a democracy, how the public feels is very important. The voice of the people can bring about changes in both governmental and police departmental policy. If the people are upset, those changes may not always be conducive to efficient policework.

What then are the clues by which an officer will know who to stop and when to stop him? Such a list would be endless, but some of the more common are:

(1) **A subject who is out of place.** By knowing the beat and the people on that beat, an officer can be more cognizant of a person who does not fit the situation. For example, an exceptionally well dressed man who is noticed hanging around "Skid row." He may be a homosexual who is soliciting partners, or he may be a heterosexual seeking a prostitute, or a gambler looking for a dice game. He may just be "slumming," wanting to see how the other half lives. In any event, he will soon be picked out as a "mark" by the local inhabitants who are always looking for a fast buck. Before long this person can be the victim of some sort of crime. In an effort to prevent this crime, or to stop the subject from becoming involved in a criminal action, the beat officer should make an effort to have the subject leave the area. This may be done in many ways. The conversation could be started with, "Good evening, sir. Are you looking for some particular place? Maybe I can help you." This will set the stage by establishing the fact that it is obvious to the officer that the subject does not belong in this setting. The officer's next move will depend upon the subject's answer to his offer of help. If he states that he is just passing through, the matter can be dropped, because he will now leave the area even if he hadn't originally intended to. He will naturally not reveal his true purpose for being in the area, as it is more than likely illegal.

Should he simply state that he is "just looking around," the officer should be direct and explain the dangers that are involved. When a person of obvious means hangs around an area where the majority of the people have little or no means, and fewer scruples as to how they obtain their means it will mean trouble. If he does not respond to this technique, and merely replies that he can take care of himself, there is little that the officer can do but keep a close eye on the subject. It will probably not be long before he becomes involved in some sort of trouble.

At the other end of the scale we find a person who is obviously a bum in a high class or residential area. His true purpose may be to beg for money or handouts, or to case the area for petty theft or burglary. When there was a vagrancy law in effect, it was simply a matter of telling the subject that if he didn't leave the area, he would be "booked for vag." With this law declared unconstitutional, the officer must use other means. Often just stopping the subject and talking to him will solve the problem. He may explain that he is lost and would the officer kindly tell him the direction to "Skid row" or the local "jungle." As a safety measure, the officer should transport him from the area. In any event, a field interrogation card should be filled out. It may later be found that a residence has been entered, or an attempt at entry made.

Should the subject be "con wise" and tell the officer that he is just out walking and has done nothing wrong, the officer may use a little subterfuge. He or she may indicate that there has been a "peeping Tom" in that area, and that the local residents are really upset. Some of them have even threatened to shoot him on sight. The officer could explain that he is sure that the subject is not a "peeping Tom," but that a stranger who hangs around this area under the circumstances is really sticking his neck out. There are any number of similar subterfuges that can be used.

(2) **A subject who is carrying something suspicious.** This is especially true if the object is hidden under his clothing. An officer cannot stop every person carrying some object, but can be alert to this situation when it is combined with other circumstances. The obvious bum carrying an expensive item should certainly be stopped and questioned. The person who makes a special effort to conceal the object when he sees an officer or police car should definitely be stopped. This would certainly be an example of probable cause.

Passenger cars that appear heavily weighted down in the trunk are worth stopping. If nothing else, there may be a vehicle defect or traffic hazard involved. There have been cases of officers stopping vehicles with heavily loaded trunks only to find a stolen safe.

It takes only a minute to stop a person and inquire about the nature of the object being carried. If the citizen becomes irate at being stopped, the officer can politely explain that he or she had just received a report from another citizen that someone had been going through parked cars in the neighborhood, and that it was the officer's duty to check the area thoroughly. The officer can explain that if the person stopped were the victim, he would surely appreciate the officer's effort. The officer's tone of voice often sets the mood of the interrogation, and how the subject will accept it.

(3) **A subject who acts strangely.** A subject who acts strangely or has rumpled clothes could either be the victim of a crime or could be suffering from some mental problem. He may also be sick or injured. In any case, the subject should receive police attention. This type of person could not only injure others but could also injure himself. There are many cases of persons who have been victims of strong arm robberies and have been left in such a daze that they have walked in front of passing vehicles. It is important to remember that acting strangely is not in itself a crime, nor is it grounds for incarceration. Under the emergency commitment section for the emotionally disturbed, the person may not be taken into custody unless they present a danger to themselves or to others. Every beat has persons who act very strangely but are not a danger to themselves or others. The beat officer should be aware of these persons and know their names. They should be kept under loose surveillance to detect changes in behavior patterns. Under the continued teasing and ha-rassment of their peers, it is possible for some of them to react violently.

(4) **A suspicious looking person who stays in the same place for quite a while.** Many times a patrol officer will notice a person standing at a certain place as he drives by, and the next time he passes by, the person is still there. The same is true of a person in a parked automobile. The beat officer should park at a distance and observe the subject. A person who is waiting for another, and has been waiting for some time will usually keep looking at their watch, although this act could be

performed by the subject to throw off suspicion. A short surveillance will often suggest reasons for the person to be there. It will also provide a foundation for the field interview if the officer decides to talk to the subject.

The patrol officer should be alert to the following possibilities when a person is loitering in one location for a long time.

(a) A lookout for some crime being committed.
(b) A person who may be ill, physically or mentally. A catatonic state in psychosis can result in complete immobility.
(c) A "peeping Tom."
(d) A sexual deviate soliciting passersby for participation in sexual fantasies.
(e) If the subject is loitering near a playground or school, he may be a molester. Most states have laws against loitering about schools and playgrounds.
(f) The subject may be "casing" a place for a future crime.
(g) The subject may be trying to pick up women that pass by.
(h) The subject may be passing out political or religious leaflets to passersby. Not a crime in itself.

At times the patrol officer will notice a vehicle driving around the block or in one small area. In a downtown area, the driver may be looking for a parking place, but a short surveillance will usually verify or eliminate this possibility. Many times his purpose is one of the prior nine listed.

(5) **Subjects who stop people on the street.** Sometimes through a citizen's complaint, or from a short observation, the patrol officer finds that the subject is stopping people on the street. There can be many reasons for this action. Some of them are as follows:

(a) **Panhandling.** Usually the panhandler is poorly dressed and often under the influence of alcohol. The United States Supreme Court in 1991, declared begging or "panhandling" laws unconstitutional. They felt that such laws violated a person's First Amendment right to free speech.

Most citizens are quite irritated by street beggars, but won't complain directly to the police because they don't want to appear uncharitable. Still they feel the police should do something about them. The majority of panhandlers are after wine money and will soon end up passed-out on the street, and will then be arrested for being drunk in public. Most cities have soup kitchens or similar institutions such as the Salvation Army where transients can obtain a meal. The City of Berkeley, California had such a problem with begging, that it developed a coupon system. Under this system, citizens could purchase coupons that could be redeemed for food. When approached by a "panhandler", they would give him a coupon. Naturally this was not too popular with winos who wanted cash.

Many officers will give a panhandler the "bum's rush" by telling him to get out of town before he is booked for some unstated violation. There have been cases of officers going under bridges where transients sleep and throwing all their belongings into the creek. There have also been Civil Rights suits for acts of this nature. An officer must be careful. In most cases an officer will do this with the belief that the hobos will move on to another town. They feel that they are helping public relations by clearing the streets of a person who would annoy citizens and give them the impression that the police department is not on the job. Despite their appearance and the lives that they live, they are still human beings and deserving of proper treatment. About the only legal recourse left is a violation of the trespassing laws.

This has been a problem for society since before the Middle Ages. It was in those times that the laws on vagrancy were first enacted. History shows us that even with harsh laws, the problem was never properly resolved. It was more of a social problem than a police problem, as it is today.

(b) Pimping. When the vice squad in a community is active, its raids will usually eliminate permanent houses of prostitution. Those who continue their operation must constantly move about from room to room or from motel to motel. They often must rely upon pimps to steer customers to their new abode. Most pimps hang out in bars and are selective in choosing their customers. They usually watch for big spenders, or those with large denominations of money. There are those pimps however, who are after quantity rather than quality. It is these people who ply the streets for customers, especially if there are a large number of servicemen in town.

These operants are fly-by-night, and are not in the least bit hesitant about robbing the customers. It is common for an accomplice to sneak into the room and go through the customer's trouser pockets while he is in bed. The feeling prevails that the victim will not complain to the police because he is afraid to admit that he was involved in something illegal. Prostitutes involved in this type of operation are more often infected with a venereal disease, and often with AIDS. This presents another reason why the patrol officer should be alert to possible pimping.

(c) Selling stolen goods. It is common for "winos" to steal items from the Five and Dime store or a local hardware store. They will then peddle them on the street to passersby in order to get wine money. When an officer books a wine bum, he often finds his pockets full of small items that have been stolen from local stores for this purpose. Places that are frequented by juveniles are often good for selling stolen items.

The patrol officer should be alert to juveniles that go from car to car in drive-in movies. This type of surveillance should be done with binoculars from a distance because they are very cautious when they see a patrol car. The favorite items to be sold at these places are automobile parts, electronic parts, car stereos, tires and alcoholic beverages. Although the conversation may not be heard, it may be noticed that after the subject approaches each car, the driver or the occupants will shake their heads indicating that they are not in the market for whatever he has to sell. The officer should write down the license numbers of those who have been approached. If the suspects are in a vehicle, their license number should be recorded.

Later, when one of the vehicles that had been approached leaves the drive-in, the patrol officer may follow it for a while. If a minor traffic violation is observed, the vehicle may be stopped and the occupants interrogated regarding the suspected selling. Often information can be gained that would provide probable cause to later search the suspect's vehicle. From the license number of the suspect's car, his address might be obtained. A stakeout on this residence might reveal that the suspect has many cars follow him home, and that they drive around to the back of the house and leave shortly after. This, plus information gained from one of the "customers" who were stopped, would be grounds for a search warrant for the suspect's residence.

A thorn in the patrol officer's side is the person who obtains a peddler's permit from the city, and then sneaks around the beat, stopping people on the street and insinuating that the item he has for sale is "hot" and that he will let it go for little money providing that no questions are asked. The item is usually a very cheap second or irregular. The most common items are watches, furs and clothing. The watches are usually quite ornate on the outside and cost the seller a few dollars each. By passing it off as a hundred dollar watch, he can usually get at least $10 for it, although he will go as low as $5.

Some of these con men drive a panel truck and pass themselves off as delivery men who have accidentally been given one too many items in the last delivery. They tell the "mark" that they hate to take it back to the money-grabbing outfit that gave it to them. As a result they will sell it for next to nothing. Apart from stopping people on the street, they will often hit service stations and bars. This type of operation is borderline illegal, but a prosecution is hard to obtain. Just as difficult to prosecute is the case where the subject insinuates, but does not actually state, that the item is stolen. Both of the schemes mentioned rely upon the larceny in the blood of the victim.

In these cases, there is little that the patrol officer can do, for the only crime committed is in the mind of the victim. The seller has obtained a peddler's permit. Should this situation get out of hand, the city can print a special notice on the peddler's permit that it can be revoked by any police officer on the complaint of a citizen.

Since prosecution is so difficult, the best procedure is to chase the suspect out of town, or watch him closely for some other violation. If things are quiet, the patrol officer could follow the subject everywhere he goes. Since this would crimp his sales, he will leave the community for greener pastures.

(6) **Older men in the company of young females.** Older men in the company of young females can mean trouble. It may be a father and daughter. It doesn't take a long surveillance to determine if that is so. Their expressions and gestures will soon tell. Many times the young girl is a prostitute who has run away from home. Many officers feel that until a statutory rape has actually been committed, there is little that they can do.

(7) **Transvestites.** Officers who work beats in the downtown areas of big cities or in skid rows should know the transvestites on their beats. They often have a high incidence of venereal disease and AIDS. They are also the cause of fights. When one is picked up by a "John" who does not know that "she" is a man, there is often a good fight when the "John" discovers that he has been wasting his time on what he thought was a woman. Not all transvestites are homosexual. Some just suffer from a sexual aberration where they have a strong desire to wear women's clothes. Most of those who walk the streets and make pickups are homosexual.

Actually the laws on contributing to the delinquency of a minor are quite broad. There are also usually violations of the alcohol beverage control and narcotic laws involved in these situations. A record check of the parties involved will often reveal prior offenses, and will help the officer in deciding how the case should be handled.

THE INITIAL CONTACT IN FIELD INTERROGATION

When the patrol officer has selected a proper subject for Field interrogation, based on probable cause, the next problem is where to stop him. The fact that the subject was selected by the officer indicates that the officer noticed something wrong. If the subject has just committed a crime, he might believe that the officer has information linking him with the crime. It is possible he will flee in an effort to escape arrest. The patrol officer should therefore take care in selecting the proper location at which to stop the suspect. The basic concern is in finding a place that has the least number of escape routes, and the least number of people who could be injured or used as hostages.

The fact that the subject aroused the officer's suspicion should cause the officer to proceed with caution when approaching the subject. Caution does not mean approaching with gun drawn or baton in hand in all cases. It does mean being mentally alert to every possibility and the positioning of oneself for tactical superiority. Since most people are right handed, it is usually best to approach the subject from his right side. This reduces the chance of the suspect bringing his right fist across his body with a right handed "haymaker" as he could if the officer were to his left.

Once the location for stopping has been selected, and caution observed, the next problem is the proper conversational approach. It is most difficult for a police officer to stop a person and not have that person be on guard. Yet it is possible to obtain a greater amount of truthful information if the subject does not feel that he is under suspicion. A person who has done something wrong is usually reluctant to talk to the police, but if he feels that he is not under suspicion, he will often talk to them in an effort not to attract suspicion.

An officer should not spend too much time talking to any one person in the field. There are many other duties to perform. The initial approach should involve fishing for nibbles. If there are no nibbles, the officer should cut it short and look for another fishing spot. If the officer does receive nibbles, then it is worth talking to the subject longer. The field interview could now change to the field interrogation. When it comes to nibbles, there are two things to look for: deception and lying. When the subject makes an effort to deceive the officer or to tell lies, there is usually a reason. The officer's job now is to find out why. The officer, like a fisherman, will use skill to hook the "fish" and reel him in.

Roger Bennett, a researcher at Ohio State University, conducted a three year study on facial expressions as lie detectors based on the prior research of two psychologists, Dr. Paul Ekman and Dr. Wallace Friesen. The results of this study indicate that the key to unmasking a liar is spotting lightning-fast changes in expression. This is caused when the subconscious mind reacts to the conscious lie.

The following are some signs for which officers should be alert.

(1) Eyes blinking very rapidly.

(2) The quick movement of eyeballs to one side and then back again.

(3) The moving of the jaw quickly from side to side.

(4) A smile that suddenly switches to a frown then quickly snaps back to a smile.

When the person lying notices that you are studying his face, he is very likely to use some type of "smokescreen" to distract your attention. For example, he might start licking his lips to cover up his mouth and jaw movement. He may also pull at his collar, his clothing or ear as a distraction.

Customs officials must often pick one or two persons out of a large crowd, when they believe they are trying to sneak something past customs. One of their techniques is to closely study the blinking of people's eyes. The average person under average conditions will blink his eyes about 12 times per minute. If someone is under emotional strain such as when they are trying to deceive a customs official or the police, the number of blinks will greatly increase. Because the eye is the most sensitive part of the body, it is difficult to control such a nervous reflex. Although the increase of smog in major customs cities has caused an increase in the number of blinks per minute, the officials still report good success with this method. It is important to remember that increased blinking is a sign of nervousness, but not necessarily a sign of guilt. There can be many reasons for this nervousness other than guilt. Just being stopped by a police officer will cause nervousness in many people. If rapid blinking does occur, it just means that the officer should talk to them a little longer. If officers will give extra attention to this technique, they will find themselves becoming proficient and will eventually be able to make judgments without counting the blinks.

When a subject first lies or attempts to deceive, the officer should not bring this to his attention. It is best to let the conversation continue until he has told more lies. If the officer were to jump on the subject after the first lie, he might be able to come up with some excuse or possible explanation. He might even state that the officer heard him wrong. The officer's suspicion would have now been exposed. There is no way that the officer could now return to or assume the prior relationship with the subject on a mere conversational basis. On the other hand, if the subject were allowed to tell several lies or errors before he was called on it, it would be more difficult to explain.

Most of us can come up with one excuse out of thin air, but not several all at once. It is easy to change the conversation from one of simple inquiry to one of an aggressive interrogative nature, but the reverse is almost impossible. For this reason, the officer should make sure that as much information as possible has been obtained from the subject through a simple inquiry approach before switching to a more aggressive one.

A friendly approach is very important in establishing a simple inquiry relationship. The friendly approach causes the subject to lower his guard or defenses a little. Maybe not completely, but enough to obtain information that would not otherwise be obtained.

The key to the preliminary conversation is subterfuge. Subterfuge is limited only by the officer's mental capacity and acting ability. When things are slow, an officer should develop various techniques of subterfuge as a means of mental exercise.

The key to acting, if not an oversimplification, is to live the part as though it were actually true. Acting is an important skill for patrol officers to develop. Because of this, officers should use every opportunity to practice and improve this skill.

The minute an officer uses the "Hey you, come here" approach, a mental wall is set up and the stage is set for a "me versus you" engagement. In this approach, the subject will tell the officer as little as possible. Some examples of subterfuge that could be used in the initial conversation are as follows:

(1) A person has been loitering in one place for a long time.

"Pardon me, were you the person who called for the police? You didn't?" (The officer goes "hmmm" and looks intently at the subject) "We received a call to meet a citizen here. Have you seen anyone else here? How long have you been here?" (If the subject states that he has been there just a few minutes, and the officer has observed him there for 15 or 20 minutes, it is an indication of deception on the part of the subject.)

(2) A person has been walking back and forth in a small area for over an hour.

"Pardon me, I'm new on this beat. Can you tell me where Jackson's Machine Shop is? It's supposed to be in this neighborhood. I didn't get the address. You don't know? Then you must be new in the neighborhood. Where did you originally come from?" etc.

(3) A person has been sitting at a bus stop for three quarters of an hour, and all the buses have passed without him getting on one. He also talks to every woman that passes.

"Pardon me, did you see a short man with a red jacket go by here a couple of minutes ago? How long have you been here? Are you sure? He was headed right this way. Maybe you know him, most of the people in the area do. They call him 'Shorty Joe'. You don't? Then you must be new in this area. How long have you been here? Where did you originally come from?" (The name "Shorty Joe" and the description should be fictitious. If the subject states that he did see him or states that he does know him, it would be an indication of deception.) If he is up to no good, he will probably engage in some deception.

The advantage of subterfuge is that it enables the officer to engage in a conversation with the subject without it appearing to be a deliberate effort to question the subject in a suspicious way. It is the best way not to arouse the subject's defenses. Even a very short conversation with the subject or suspect will enable the experienced and alert officer to detect or sense that something is wrong and that the matter warrants further inquiry.

In the case of parked automobiles, the approach should be one of offering assistance on the assumption that the subject is having mechanical difficulties or some other problem. This puts the driver in the position of explaining why he or she is parked there. The patrol officer should never use the "what in hell are you doing here" approach. There is an old saying, "You catch more flies with honey than with vinegar.

In a short conversation with the subject, an officer can very often detect some clue that will indicate criminal traits. Maybe the subject will display a pattern of behavior common to criminals. It is a game of cat and mouse.

CRIMINAL TRAITS

We are creatures of habit and victims of our environment. A person who has spent a long time in jail or prison has certain characteristics such as word usage, tattoos or dress that will give clues to his spending time in prison. Sociologists and some criminologists are very sensitive about the term "criminal trait." They feel that there is no such thing as a criminal trait, because the biggest criminals in our society are not now, nor ever have been, in jail. They claim that some of them are looked upon with great social favor. There is no doubt that some big businessmen in this country are guilty of greater crimes than many of those in our prisons. Prisons hold but a small percentage of what could be technically classed as criminals. However, when we in law enforcement speak of criminal traits, we are referring to those traits practiced by the type of criminal who has spent much time in jail.

Recidivism is quite high in the United States as a whole. About 80% of all persons sent to prison will later return there. One of the reasons for this high rate of recidivism is that few people today are sent to prison for their first offense. Most of them are either given probation or given a county jail sentence when they are caught and finally sentenced. Because of this, a person who is sent to prison has already formed a pretty solid criminal habit. He has had many chances to get his act together in the past. He has also had a lot of association with other criminals. Few criminals are caught on their first offense. It is most difficult for him to break this habit pattern even if he actually wants to. Through long association with other criminals, he has formed habits that are peculiar to that particular segment of society.

Whenever anyone has been subjected to a homogeneous society or a special closed group, they will emulate the speech and habits of that group. If there are special physical conditions that exist in that society, the member's actions will reflect that condition. For example two persons of Japanese ancestry are walking side by side on a San Francisco street. One of them was born in the United States, and the other recently arrived from Japan. the recent arrival might raise his feet slightly as he walked, even though the sidewalk was smooth and he was wearing shoes. This would be due to the many years that he had worn clog type sandals and had walked on uneven surfaces. This may be also observed, to some extent, in many new immigrants who come from a third world country where there are few sidewalks. Most of us have some peculiarity that could distinguish us from others, and tell something about our present and past environment. For example, an American is visiting Europe and is observed eating in a restaurant. A European will immediately know that he is an American. This is because Americans hold their knives and forks differently than Europeans.

Sherlock Holmes stories have thrilled readers for many years because of Sherlock's astute powers of observation, and the feats of deduction that resulted from these observations. These deductions are certainly not "elementary" to the average reader, but in law enforcement we should strive to develop an awareness of the differences in people and what these differences can tell us about those people. A person who has herded cattle on the range for most of his life will probably have legs that are bowed and a face that is weather-beaten. He will use a terminology that is peculiar to cowboys. A serviceman in uniform, with a very short haircut, has probably just finished basic training. This is because it is common for basic trainees to have their heads shaved during their basic training.

If the patrol officer were to be assigned to assist in crowd control at a protest demonstration, he or she could quickly pick out the average citizen who has joined the group just because he feels the cause is just and wants to voice his opinion. This is the right of every American. The distinction becomes obvious when observing dress and listening to the language used. The professional "revolutionary" type protestor will dress in the same manner as others who have long belonged to those organizations. It is almost like a uniform They will also use the standard phrases and terminology so common to those groups.

There are certain characteristics that are common to bums. An officer soon learns these characteristics after booking enough of them. The bum who is transient will usually be wearing two pairs of trousers and two shirts to keep him warm at night. In his pocket he will usually have an unassembled safety razor in a cloth tobacco bag such as the type containing Bull Durham.

It is common for some women to insist that they have never been arrested before in hopes that the officer will feel sorry for them and give them a break. Often their terminology will give them away. They might ask what "charge" they are to be "booked" on, and ask what the "bail" will be. These are terms that are uncommon to a woman who has never been arrested before.

In China, it is common practice for two persons to walk down the street in tandem and carry on a conversation with both of them looking straight ahead. In this country, the same trait is indicative of a long time in prison. Because prisoners are always passing secret messages back and forth, they do not want the guards to see the person to whom they are talking. As a result, they develop the habit of not looking at the person to whom they are talking. A person who has been in prison a long time becomes quite adept at talking through the side of his mouth. He also develops a way to hide inner emotion through the display of a poker face.

It can be quite noticeable when a police officer passes this person on the street. Other people passing will at least give the officer a glance. The ex-con will walk by as though the police officer were not even there. His effort to conceal his concern will actually give him away.

If a young person, just released from a Youth Authority facility, is stopped by an officer, he will often stand in a half attention position, and will not look the officer in the face. Most of his replies will be "yes sir" and "no sir." His tone of voice will reflect that of a captive audience. His head will usually be half down, looking at the ground. This will change after he has been out for awhile.

TATTOOS

It is common for inmates to tattoo themselves while in prison. The tattoos from each prison are different. They can also indicate the gang to which they belong. Prison tattoos are different from other tattoos. They are seldom in color, and they are not professional in appearance. They are made with a needle or a pin and ink that is sometimes made from newspaper print. The ink is placed on the surface and the needle is punched rapidly into the skin. A professional tattoo is done with a machine which makes even lines. The lines in prison tattooing are wider and rougher than professional tattooing. An officer who works in a city with a large number of ex-cons should make an extra effort to learn the meaning of prison tattoos. It is not as though it were some sort of secret. Those with prison tattoos are proud of them and will gladly explain them to anyone.

Narcotic addicts will often use tattoos to hide needle marks on their arms. The twisting scar on an addict's arm is caused by the vein collapsing from the powerful narcotic. In narcotic terminology, it is called a "snake" or "track." Some addicts with a sense of humor will have a snake tattooed over their needle scars.

SPECIAL PARAPHERNALIA

Under present search and seizure laws, evidence obtained in a forced search will not be admissible in court. Neither will the law allow evidence that is illegally seized to be used as the basis for an arrest. Sometimes the subject can be talked into allowing a search. This is called a "Consent Search." It is legal, but the burden of proof to show that the waiver of rights was truly voluntary rests with the officer. He may be asked "are you hiding anything from us?" If he says no, the officer may then state "if you are not hiding anything from us, would you consent to a search?" he may be asked to show what he has in his pockets to prove it. If he does this voluntarily, without any threats, any evidence that is found is legal. Like any tradesman, criminals need certain tools or equipment in order to perform their task. Officers should be alert for the following articles:

(1) **Hot wires or jump wires.** There are two types of jump wires. The simple type is a wire with two small alligator clamps at each end. The more complicated type is used on automobiles that have a separate starter button. This jump wire has several alligator clamp wires that lead to a push button device so the starter may be activated by pushing the button when the clips are attached to the back of the ignition. There are an unlimited number of devices for starting vehicles such as chewing gum wrapped in tinfoil wrappers, fifty cent pieces, screwdrivers, and a recent device has been a hypodermic needle filled with water. It is injected into the keyhole making the points at the rear of the ignition switch contact to start the engine. When it dries out, a new injection is inserted.

Another common tool for car thieves is the dent puller. It is screwed into the keyway and the whole ignition switch is then pulled out of the dash or steering column.

(2) **Glue sniffing apparatus.** A dangerous fad that has been practiced by many juveniles and some adults is glue sniffing. It is used as an economical means of becoming intoxicated. Airplane glue is poured into a rag or handkerchief and then quickly rubbed between the hands to create heat which in turn creates fumes. The hands are cupped and then brought up to the face where the fumes are inhaled.

Unfortunately, if this practice is continued, brain damage will result. Juveniles can be arrested under the protective sections of the Welfare and Institutions code. Some officers are concerned about which booking section should be used to book an adult who has been sniffing glue. If he is actually intoxicated from the fumes, he can be booked for drunkenness.

(3) **Narcotics.** Apart from the regular narcotics mentioned in Chapter XIV, the patrol officer should be watchful for prescription type drugs. They are usually in multicolored gelatin capsules. Needles and a large bulb used to inject "crystal" or "meth" may also be found on a suspect or in his car. At night a flashlight should be used to shine oblique light across the floorboards. Marijuana seeds can often be seen. They are probable cause to search further in the car. Any group of pills rolled up in tinfoil would be suspicious. LSD breaks down in sunlight and is often wrapped in tinfoil to prevent this.

(4) **Lock picking devices.** Lock picks that are professionally made are illegal. They can only be possessed by locksmiths and police officers. If a suspect is caught inside a building with these devices, they can be used to show intent in a charge of burglary. There are many special car opening tools that are commercially produced. They are used by police officers and tow truck drivers. Anyone else carrying these items should be suspected of auto theft, although many private citizens do carry them in their cars. A wire coat hanger can be bent and used in the same manner as the commercial tools. If the tools are not commercially made, the state must be able to prove that they were carried with the intent to be used as burglar tools.

(5) **Obscene pictures and materials.** The possession of obscene pictures and materials, even those depicting abnormal sex acts, are not illegal except when they depict young children engaged in such acts. However, they are indicative that the possessor might be a sexual deviate, one who is a pedophile or even a sexual sadist. These people can be dangerous. The descriptions of persons found carrying such paraphernalia should be checked against recent sexual offenses.

An officer should be especially alert for pictures showing sadistic tendencies. Examples would be photographs of naked women who have their eyes blackened, chains drawn on their arms and legs, or which have pin and knife holes punched into the picture. This should indicate to the officer that the subject could be dangerous to society. Any legal basis should be used to book this person. A search warrant should then be obtained for his room where further evidence may be found. In some cases officers have found articles belonging to women who have been murdered in a sadistic manner. The suspect could be booked under the Welfare and Institutions Code as being mentally ill and a danger to others. The photographs would be the basis for probable cause.

(6) **Criminally associated calling/business cards.** Calling cards or business cards of attorneys, bail bondsmen, parole or probation officers, betting slips, and pawn tickets are items that are commonly carried by the criminal element. They are certainly not a basis for arrest, but they tell you something about the person stopped. If a person has the business card for a parole or probation officer, those persons can be an unlimited source of information about the suspect.

(7) **Gambling devices.** Betting stubs, dice and decks of cards are often carried by the criminal element. Gambling seems to be one of the most common traits among criminals. They almost seem to be gamblers by nature. It is part of their philosophy of life, to make a quick buck. They seem to have a feeling that everything in life rests on luck rather than ability. They hope that one day they are going to hit the jackpot. They believe that their ship will come in someday and all their troubles will end.

DOCUMENTS OF IDENTIFICATION

Since one of the objectives of field interrogation is to detect deception on the part of the subject, the patrol officer should spend more time in the examination of documents of identification. Allen Bristow's book on Field Interrogation con-

tains an excellent chapter on this topic. This book is highly recommended for patrol officers.

It takes so little time to properly check out an item of identification. Yet the average patrol officer will often give it a cursory glance and then use it to fill out a field interrogation card; or it will be used to write a citation. If the card has a fingerprint, it will state under the fingerprinting exactly which finger or thumb it represents. An officer need not be a fingerprint expert to compare the fingerprint on the card with the subject's finger or thumb. It does take a little practice to hold a finger at the right angle to the light so the ridge pattern becomes apparent. At night the flashlight will do a good job when held at an oblique angle to the finger.

If the identification contains a photograph, it sometimes presents problems, Many times the identification photographs do not look like the subject. In the case of a driver's license, which can be good for five years, the photograph might have been taken five years ago when the subject had a full head of hair and his face was covered with acne. Now he is balding and his complexion is good. Rather than overall appearance, the officer should look for details such as the size and angle of the ears, the shape of the eyebrow, the width of the nose, and the shape of the chin and mouth. The most deceptive part of the head is the hair. It can and does change the person's appearance.

In checking any document of identification in the field, the officer should never handle the wallet. The subject should be asked to take the identification out of the wallet. By handling the wallet, the officer can easily be accused of removing money or something of value. If the suspect is arrested and booked, it is permissible for the officer to handle the wallet at booking, but it is always wise to do so in the presence of a witness.

FALSE INFORMATION

The FBI estimates that half of the wanted criminals in the United States have in their possession, carefully chosen false credentials. If there are no outstanding warrants on the name used, those using the false identification are safe from our computer systems. Today, with modern technology (especially the new color copy machines), false documents can be made easily and quickly.

There is no sure way to detect all pieces of false identification in the field. When officers conduct a thorough search of a suspect, they will often find identification for different persons. It is common for a person carrying false identification, to be arrested under the name on his false identification, and then bail out before a check of fingerprints reveals his true identify. Modern technology will help correct this problem. Today there are computers that can record a person's fingerprint at a county jail and then search the state and federal fingerprint systems in a matter of minutes.

A patrol officer should never reach the point where he or she automatically accepts proper looking identification as being valid. Especially when there are other circumstances to the situation that should arouse suspicion.

There is an underground publication called "The Paper Trip" which gives all the "know how" needed to obtain false identification. All the members of the Symbionese Liberation Army, who kidnapped Patricia Hearst, had documents of false identification. These were used to rent apartments and getaway cars.

The most common method is called the "Tombstone Theory." The person who wants false identification obtains a name from a tombstone (or obituary) of a person who, had he or she lived, would be about the age of the person wanting the identification. Since birth certificates and death certificates are not cross referenced, there is no way for a clerk to know that someone is requesting a birth certificate of a deceased person. Once the birth certificate is obtained, it becomes the basis for obtaining all of the other identification needed. Because of this, the birth certificate is called a "breeder" document.

The Immigration Service estimates that a large number of the over 8 million illegal aliens in the United States have some type of false identification. Border cities do a brisk business in false identification. Some of those involved even offer money back guarantees because they feel that their ID's are so good.

THE DRIVER'S LICENSE (OPERATORS LICENSES)

This is one of the most common types of identification. There are various classes of licenses according to the type of vehicle and the purpose for driving. There are also various restrictions that may be typed or printed on the front or back of the license. For example, restrictions on driving without glasses are usually on the front of the license. Restrictions that limit the holder to driving only to and from work, or only during the daylight hours are usually stamped on the back of the license.

When examining a license for alterations, the officer should look for differences in the size of the type. The type on a driver's license is smaller than normal. The major type of alteration is usually the birthdate so the holder can purchase alcoholic beverages. There is quite a demand around most large college and university campuses for forged identification. When this is done with a photographic process it makes detection quite difficult. Officers who suspect that a college student does have an altered driver's license should take down the student's name and description. A call to the college records office the next day will usually reveal the true date of birth. The back of the license should also be checked for an official seal.

Many states are changing to a new tamper proof license. The 3M Company has developed a "top secret" process in which they can seal a driver's license into a permanent plastic container. This plastic coating has a normally invisible state seal imbedded in the plastic. However, it can be seen when exposed to a special light carried by the patrol officer. The detection light is very inexpensive, and sometimes the oblique beam from the officer's flashlight will reveal the seal. The machine that embeds the license costs over $200,000. It is doubtful that college students will be buying this machine for their "bootleg" identification businesses.

When stopping a suspicious vehicle, it would be a good policy to ask both the driver and the passenger for their driver's licenses. In many cases a driver who has had his license suspended will quickly borrow his friend's license if stopped by the police. If the passenger states that he does not have a license, the officer should check the description on the license presented by the driver to see if the description also fits the passenger. If the prima facie description fits, the passenger and the driver should be asked to step out of the car so their height may be checked against the driver's license.

If the subject has a temporary driver's license, he and the license should be more thoroughly checked. The temporary license is almost worthless as a means of identification because it is so easily obtained, and has no photograph. Many persons who have had their license suspended will keep applying for temporary licenses in order to continue driving. To obtain the regular driver's license, the subject must reside in one place for at least a couple of months until it is sent through the mail. The temporary license can be obtained at once, and the subject can move immediately.

In some states, a minor's driver's license photograph is taken with a side view. This helps prevent date alterations, because an officer knows that all side view photographs are of minors.

THE SOCIAL SECURITY CARD

This is often the only means of identification that the transient or person of limited means will normally carry on their person. In booking bums, the officer will usually find no ID, but somewhere on his person there will usually be a dirty folded Social Security card. He doesn't want to work, but he knows that if he ever does have to work, he will need the card.

It is a very unreliable form of identification because it can be obtained just by applying for it, and it contains no photograph. Criminals have been known to apply for and receive dozens of them under different names. Check passers will use different cards to back up other phony identification that they carry.

It is quite common for the cards to be stolen and borrowed. The first element or three digits of the card number indicate where the card was issued. The numbers start in the New England states and go down to Florida. They then zigzag across the United States and end up on the West coast in the 500's. The 600 and 700 series are for railroad employees who have a special retirement act. A subject who has a very low number, say 020, but states that he has never been to the East coast may not be the rightful owner of that Social Security card. If it is his card, he may be denying that he came from the East coast because he is wanted there. On the other hand, he might have just borrowed the card from a friend in order to obtain employment until he can obtain a duplicate of the one that he lost. It is a trait of this type of person not to be concerned about the future and the building up of retirement points under social security. Because of this, they often look at the card only as something that they must have in order to work rather than as a means of retirement.

IMMIGRATION IDENTIFICATION

Because of the agricultural nature of the Southern part of the United States, there is a need in these areas for farm laborers during the growing season. In the past this need has been largely filled through the use of Mexican Nationals who have been issued special work permits and have been granted temporary immigration privileges. Today these workers have been restricted through small quotas. This, along with difficult economic times in Mexico and Central America, has resulted in large waves of illegal workers sneaking across the border in hopes of finding employment.

The border between Mexico and the United States is a long one, and because it is largely unguarded and unpatrolled, it is impossible to stop the flow of illegal entrants. The United States Immigration authorities have special officers whose job it is to seek out illegal entrants and return them to Mexico. Still, local law enforcement agencies are expected to assist in this endeavor. If a person of Mexican descent, who cannot speak English, is arrested and does not have proper identification, Immigration authorities should be contacted. The next day their experienced personnel can properly check out his status.

All alien laborers should have in their possession either or both the Alien Laborer's Permit and the Alien Identification Card. The Laborer's Permit is 3"x 5" and contains the bearer's photograph and other basic information. Included is information about the work contract. The Identification card is 2 x 3 1/2" and it has a photograph on the back and general identification information on the front.

If an officer stops a Mexican National and wishes to see his identification, he can just use the word "Papeles" (pah-peh-lays) Which means "papers." The subject will understand and will produce the identification papers if he has them.

TECHNIQUES OF INTERROGATION

The key to interrogation is an understanding of human nature and the ability to use sympathetic introspection. Sympathetic introspection is placing yourself in the position of the subject or suspect. Officers who attempt to understand the feelings of a person they are about to question, will soon understand why a suspect does not respond to the approaches used by so many officers.

COMMUNICATION

Without proper communication, interrogation would be ineffective. If an officer who spoke no Spanish were to interrogate a Spanish-speaking person who spoke no English, he or she could talk for days and achieve nothing. A large number of field interrogations deal with subjects from an entirely different background than the officer. As a result, there can be a great lack of understanding and that can interfere with successful communication. Even when we deal with those of similar education and background there can be problems in semantics. The English language contains many words that have a number of meanings. For example:

RUNNER

(1) One who runs in a race.
(2) One who runs errands.
(3) A smuggler.
(4) An operator or director.
(5) The bottom of a sled.
(6) A groove on which something slides.
(7) A long strip of roofing material.
(8) A ravel in a stocking.
(9) A shoot forming new plants.

There are just some of the meanings of one word. If the patrol officer does not make every effort to be clearly understood, efforts at interrogation will be wasted, or the information obtained might be false.

META-COMMUNICATION

Meta-communication is the message that is transmitted apart from the actual words that are spoken. Actually we can receive meta-communication without any words being spoken.

In law enforcement we sometimes have a tendency to be overly word conscious. We want to get the exact wording down in our report because in court this is what will be demanded of us. Sometimes we are so anxious to get the exact wording that we miss the hidden or underlying message.

An officer who is observant and sensitive to meta-communication, will know that the subject is admitting guilt when he says nothing, but slightly hangs his head, has an "oh well" expression on his face and shrugs his shoulders and sighs when asked a guilt assuming question.

This should be the key for the officer to let the subject know that he or she understands, and maybe give him a little pep talk to the effect that it takes a man to admit it when he has done something wrong, and that even though it is difficult, the subject appears to have that quality and is man enough or has courage enough to admit it.

At times a suspect stopped near the scene of a crime will have his alibi memorized. When questioned, he will often recite his alibi from memory like a little school boy reciting a poem. An officer whose senses are tuned to word content alone, might not catch the undertone of the message.

TONE OF VOICE

Through empathy, a good actor can, by tone of voice, control the emotions of his audience. He can make the audience happy, sad or angry by transmitting this feeling called empathy. A police officer can do the same during an interrogation. A smooth, low and relaxed tone of voice creates less of a danger reaction in the subject, and he is less likely to be on the defensive. When the officer wants the subject to become emotional, this can be accomplished through the officer's tone of voice becoming emotional. Emotion blocks our intellect and makes clear thinking more difficult. It can be advantageous at times to make the subject emotional.

SALESMANSHIP

Once the interrogating officer senses or realizes that the subject is guilty or might be involved, the task becomes one of salesmanship. The subject must be sold into making a statement or confession. It is no different than the salesman who is selling a set of encyclopedias. The householder does not want to buy a set of encyclopedias, and the subject does not want to confess. The salesman must convince the householder that the thing he wants more than anything else in the world right now is a set of encyclopedias. The interrogator has the same task. It is to convince the subject that right at this minute the thing that he wants more than anything else is to get this thing off his chest and give the officer a statement or confession. The next morning both the householder and the subject will be sorry that they were talked into it. The salesman has a contract and the officer a recorded statement. It happens every day of the year. People are sold things that they don't want. It was accomplished through salesmanship. Some smooth talker convinced them that it was what they really wanted.

Salesmanship is a skill. It is a skill that all patrol officers should develop. All phases of their work require it to some degree.

MAKE IT EASY FOR THE SUBJECT TO ADMIT GUILT

One of the cardinal rules in interrogation is to make it easy for the subject to admit what he has done. Yet every day of the year patrol officers and detectives violate this rule. A patrol officer will pick up a suspect who was pointed out as a child molester. The officer will then take the approach of an irate mother scolding her child. "Shame, shame. How could you do anything so low? Why, what you have done is just terrible. You should be horsewhipped." The suspect is often quite ashamed of what he has done. He may have been fighting this urge for years. He might like to admit it and get it off of his chest. However, the officer's scolding and tone of voice make it that much more difficult for him to admit it. If the officer could only use introspection, the true effect of this type of approach would become clear. The officer should control his voice, and if he suspects that the subject might be the type of person who would be remorseful for his actions, the following approaches may be used:

(1) **Minimize the crime.** It is common logic that if the crime is minimized, it will be easier for the subject to admit it. This works quite well with juveniles who have committed acts of malicious mischief and have done considerable damage. To a young kid $50 can seem like all the money in the world. If an officer makes a statement like "Do you realize that you have done over $500 worth of damage?" the kid will be so scared that his mouth will shut like a clam. How much easier it would be for the youth to admit what he had done if the officer stated that he didn't know exactly how much the damage was, but he was sure that it wasn't much. Once the kid admits the act, then the details of the exact damage can be worked out.

The sex offender who, because of his religious background, feels that he is some kind of a fiend, will be more prone to admitting his acts if he is told that it is quite common and that some very prominent people have done the same thing. By showing or pretending to show a little understanding, the officer can create the confidence that is often necessary for a sex offender to reveal his offenses.

(2) **Sympathize with the suspect.** The suspect will naturally admit his offense more readily if the interrogator sympathizes with him rather than condemns him. The officer can suggest to the suspect that the victim probably deserved what he or she got. Another sympathizing statement might be "You know, under the same circumstances, who knows what I might have done." Once the statement has been obtained and the confession recorded, the true gravity of the offense can be brought home to the suspect.

(3) **Avoid sensitive words.** The officer should avoid words that would interfere with the suspect's confession by making him sensitive to the gravity of the offense. Words like rape, murder, kill and torture are harsh. Less offensive words should be substituted. For example: Why did you do IT? or Why did you do THIS THING? When did THIS occur? When did IT happen?

(4) **Avoid discussing punishment.** The good encyclopedia salesman never discusses the cost of the set. When asked, he avoids it and talks about everything else because it might cool the sale. The interrogator must never discuss punishment. If asked about the punishment, the reply should be "I'm glad you asked that, because it shows me that you are a person who is concerned with honesty, blah blah blah." Talk on and on but do not answer the question. If you were to say "Well the Penal Code says fifteen years in state prison," Your subject would go into a state of shock and the conversation would probably end. The truth of the matter is that no one knows what the punishment will be in the early stages of investigation. There are too many factors that the judge will take into consideration before passing sentence. This is what you should tell the subject. Be very careful about making promises. Do not make statements like " You will probably get off with probation." Any hint of making promises can invalidate a confession. During interrogation, an officer must be a politician. A good politician, when asked a very sensitive question, will talk about everything under the sun but will avoid answering that particular question.

BLUFFING

When Miranda first came out, the Supreme Court chastised the police for using "tricks" to obtain confessions. The present Supreme Court seems to be more interested in whether or not the confession is free and voluntary, and whether or not an innocent person could be coerced into making a false confession by the techniques used.

Bluffing is a dangerous game when used in interrogation. It is used by officers who lack the skills for good interrogation. It is a gamble. If the subject calls the bluff, all is lost. For example, when an officers states "We have a witness who saw you coming out the side door," and the suspect really came out the back door, he knows the interrogator is bluffing, and the game is over.

(1) **The indirect bluff.** There is a type of bluff called the indirect bluff that will allow the officer to back off and not lose face if the bluff is called. The officer presents the bluff to the suspect for confirmation rather than as a threat. The indirect bluff is best used in breaking down alibis. If the suspect states that he was in Portland during the time the crime was committed, and that he stayed in the Elite Hotel on River St., the officer can reply, "Didn't I read in the paper that one of those hotels caught on fire on River St.? Was that near the hotel that burned? It must have been quite a fire." If the suspect firmly replies that there was no hotel fire there, the officer can back off by saying "I could have sworn that the paper said Portland. I'll have to look at the paper again." This technique puts the suspect in a bad spot. The bluff was not presented in a threatening manner, but as a point of information. If he was not actually there, what reply should he make? If the suspect replies "Yeah, that was some fire. I never saw nothing like it." The officer knows the suspect is lying. This will then change the course of the interrogation.

(2) **The physiological bluff.** This bluff is effective with juveniles and persons who are nervous. It can be pointed out to them that their guilt is obvious because experience has taught the interrogating officer that when a person is guilty, the carotid artery on the side of the neck will swell and pulsate. The Adam's apple will also move up and down. Because of the power of suggestion, the suspect's Adam's apple will respond when this is mentioned. These are not signs of guilt, but signs of nervousness. They are not readily visible, but the suspect is very much aware of them when they are brought to his attention by the officer. As a result, he feels that his guilt is obvious to the whole world.

(3) **The separation bluff.** If there is more than one suspect, they should be immediately separated and interrogated individually. Criminals do not trust each other. Once the suspects have been separated, the officer can make statements like "I was just talking to your buddy, Fred, boy is he dumping it on you. He's blaming everything on you." An innocent person would not be concerned and would reply "I don't know what you're talking about. I've done nothing wrong." However, a subject who was involved would try saving his own neck by blaming the others.

Little tricks could be planned that would make it appear that one person has talked. In a large group, the leader of the gang is usually obvious by his demeanor. If you talk to anyone in the group, they seem to look sideways toward the leader before they answer. Pick one of the suspects who is the most cooperative. Take him into another room, and explain that there is some confusion as to who is who. It should be mentioned that the officers have everyone's name, but that they are not sure which one is Bill Smith (the obvious leader). The subject is then asked if he would point out Bill Smith. When he does, the officer thanks him out loud for his cooperation. The group now thinks that he has talked and they will be fighting to be the next one to "cooperate" in an effort to save their own necks now that the ice has been broken. If an officer is talking to one of the suspects in the police car he should be asked to step out for a minute. When he does the officer should shake his hand so that the others can see. Then in a loud voice, the officer should say "Thank you for your cooperation, if there is anything I can do for you let me know." The others will now believe that he has talked to the police, and will be more willing to talk themselves.

A more simple bluff would be to leave one suspect with another officer and then go over to the other suspect and state "I've heard his side of it, how about hearing your side now. I'm not sure that I believe everything he said about you." Criminals know each other for what they really are, and even though they talk about a "code of honor," they really don't trust each other. This feeling of distrust may be used to advantage. An officer should be careful when using this type of bluff. One suspect might ask what the other one did say. If the officer is not careful in the reply, something might be said that would let the suspect know the officer was not telling the truth. The bluff would then be over. It is best not to tell one suspect what the other suspect said.

DON'T GIVE MORE INFORMATION THAN YOU RECEIVE

Unfortunately many officers give the suspect more information than they receive. When a suspect is stopped, he will naturally say, "What's this all about?" Rather than give him a complete rundown on what has occurred, the officer should reply, "I just want to ask you a few questions. If you haven't been involved in anything, there's nothing to worry about. I'll explain everything after we've talked for a little bit." If the suspect supposedly knows nothing about the crime, he might accidentally slip in his conversation and mention something that he could learn only by being at the scene or by participating in the crime.

Another good reason for not giving information to the suspect, is that he might have just committed another unrelated crime and feels that he is being stopped about that offense. The patrol officer might be looking for someone who has just pulled a "purse snatch." A block away a youth is spotted who fits the description. When the officer stops him, he might believe that the reason is that someone had seen him break into the store down the street. Under the officer's questioning, he might admit to the break-in, unaware that the officer stopped him because he looked like the suspect who had committed the "purse snatch."

USE PRESUMPTIVE QUESTIONS WHEN INTERROGATING A SUSPECT

In questioning suspects, the officer should always use presumptive questions. Never ask the suspect if he committed the crime. Ask him WHY he committed the crime? He could be asked what he did with the money? He may also be asked what he did with the tools, such as the jimmy bar or even the gun or knife. Sometimes a good approach would be to use flattery. For example; "Boy you certainly have a lot of guts to pull something like that. I'd be afraid of being shot." This approach seems to catch them off guard. They expect a direct approach like "You stole the money didn't you?"

When questions containing presumptive guilt are presented to the suspect, he might think that the officer has information linking him with the crime. It is best to ask this type of question in a normal voice that does not alert his defenses. Quite often the suspect will answer the question and then stop and realize that he just admitted his guilt. You can tell by the look of surprise on his face.

STUDY QUESTIONS for Patrol Operations

CHAPTER 10

1. The use of field interrogation has been abused by police officers.   T or F

2. In dealing with field interrogation, it must be remembered, however, that _____ is an important part of this skill.

3. When "Miranda" was first handed down, the guidelines were not too clear.   T or F

4. An officer can "avoid" Miranda, but not "evade" Miranda.   T or F

5. There is a problem dealing with Miranda that has not yet been fully resolved when it comes to "intelligently waiving his rights." This applies to two classes of persons. _____ & _____

6. "On-the-scene questioning" does not apply to Miranda, all things being equal.   T or F

7. Give an exception to question #6. _____

8. List the rights under Miranda.

   (1)_____
   (2)_____
   (3)_____
   (4)_____

9. When a suspect's rights have been read, what do you then ask him? _____
   _____

10. When an officer asks a suspect where his gun is hidden, the statement violates "Miranda."   T or F

11. Unlike the "Warren Court", the present "Burger Court" seems to be more interested in knowing if the confession was truly _____.

12. In the "Carroll" decision, the U.S. Supreme Court stated that an automobile was different than a house when it came to search and seizure because the automobile was _____.

13. The "Chambers" decision is considered a "practical" decision in that the court stated that   T or F
    if the officers have information that would be the basis of a search warrant on an automobile, they can go ahead and search it.

14. Under the Robinson & Gustafson decisions, if an officer has "probable cause" to arrest a   T or F
    motorist, he can search his car.

15. The famous "Mapp v. Ohio" decision established the _____ rule which states that illegally seized evidence will be excluded in court.

16. Officers who make a practice of illegal searches will soon find themselves involved in a civil suit under the 1968 _____ _____ Act.

17. A patrol officer must, of his own accord, become overly sensitive to the two words "_____ & _____".

18. According to the "Chimel v. California" decision, if an officer arrests a suspect without a warrant, his search is limited to the _____ and immediate vicinity of the arrestee.

19. The "Chimel" decision is also called the "_____ & _____" rule.

20. Name two exceptions to the "Chimel" rule.
    (a)_____
    (b)_____

21. The terms "stop and frisk" involve legally the same thing.   T or F

22. Any "frisk" not associated with arrest or a search warrant can only be done for the purpose of _____ based on reasonable cause.

23. The famous "Terry v. Ohio" decision dealt with:

    a. _ patting down suspects.   b. __police brutality.
    c. _ improper use of an officers club.   d. __putting handcuffs on too tight.

24. The "INSLAW" study found that only 15% of officers accounted for _____ of all arrests that led to convictions.

25. A field interrogation is the obtaining of information, and it does not have to be aggressive.   T or F

26. Detectives and follow-up officers make very good use of the "FI" cards in developing suspects. Another good source is _____.

27. The "_____" of field interrogation is much more important than the "_____."

28. A study by the Los Angeles Police Department found that the #1 cause of complaints and   T or F poor public relations was the field interrogation.

29. An obvious bum, who is not intoxicated, is found walking in a high class neighborhood Can you arrest him. (YES)_____ (NO)_____

30. What technique or subterfuge can be used if he refuses to leave on your suggestion?
    _____

31. Give two examples of persons who seem to be staying in the same place for a very long time, and can be committing crimes.
    (a)_____
    (b)_____

32. If you get complaints of a "wino" panhandling, it is normally easy to get the victim involved   T or F
in the case by testifying against him.

33. It is common for a person to try and sell items on the street or in bars with the insinuation that
the items are stolen. In reality, this person is playing games and carries a _____ permit.

34. Older men in the company of young females (apart from parents) are usually guilty of violating
the law on _____ to the _____ of a _____.

35. When approaching a suspicious person in the field, it is best to approach on his _____ side.

36. What is the reason for doing what you do in question #35? _____
_____

37. Name two signs of nervousness that could be indications of lying.
(a)_____
(b)_____

38. The normal eye blinks about _____ times per minute. Customs officers have found that
persons trying to sneak items through customs, have an increased number of blinks per minute.

39. During field interrogation, when a suspect lies to you, you should bring it to his attention and   T or F
demand the truth.

40. The key to acting is to _____ the _____.

41. It is important for an officer to show suspects in the field that he is tough, so the best   T or F
approach is for the officer to yell, "Hey you, come here."

42. Give one of the examples listed in the book as a means of talking to a suspicious person without
giving him the idea that you suspect him of something criminal. _____
_____

43. Recidivism in the United States is about _____%.

44. There is no such thing as a "criminal trait" as far as the patrol officer is concerned.   T or F

45. Name one of the things about a bum that will let you know that he is "on the road."
_____

46. Name one of the things about a prison tattoo that is different from one done by a commercial artist.
_____

47. What is the narcotic (heroin) scar on an addict's arm called? _____

48. If you stop a suspect in the field and find that he has some pills that are wrapped in tinfoil, they
are probably _____.

49. Give an example of a "criminally associated calling card. _____

50. In identification photographs, the most deceptive part of the head is the _____.

51. In checking a suspect's identification, an officer should not handle the suspect's wallet. Why? _____

52. The FBI estimates that half of the criminals at large in the United States have carefully   T or F
chosen false credentials.

53. The book, <u>The Paper Trip</u>, states that one of the most common methods of obtaining new identification is to obtain a _____ that belongs to a person who is about the same age but has died.

54. The above procedure is called the " _____ Theory."

55. Because it is the basis for obtaining all other documents, the birth certificate is called a
" _____ " document.

56. One of the most common types of identification is the _____.

57. Restrictions on a driver's license are located _____.

58. The typing on a driver's license is normally larger than normal.   T or F

59. Today, a modern driver's license is easy to counterfeit.   T or F

60. The temporary driver's license is worthless as a means of identification.   T or F

61. What part of the social security number contains information as to the state in which the card was obtained? _____

62. The 600 and 700 series on the "S.S." card are for _____ employees."

63. What is the Spanish word for "papers"? _____

64. When a foreign national is in this country, he has a special card that allows him to stay. This card has a nickname based on its color. It is " _____ _____ ".

65. When we say certain words, but by our expression and tone of voice, we transmit another message, it is called:

a. _psycho-communication.   b. _para-communication.
c._meta-communication.   d. _quasi-communication.

66. When a person transmits emotion to another person by the way he acts, it is called:

a. _empathy.   b. _caliphony.
c._transference.   d. _para-communication.

67. Interrogation is really a form of salesmanship.   T or F

68. One of the cardinal rules in interrogation is:

    a.__have more than one officer present.   b.__talk tough
    c.__make it easy for the suspect to talk about it.   d.__threaten the suspect.

69. With the sex offender, the minimize-sympathize technique is very good.   **T or F**

70. A rule in interrogation is not to use sensitive words. Give an example. _____
_____

71. In the interest of honesty and professionalism, when the suspect asks during interrogation-   **T or F**
what the punishment will be, an officer should tell him.

72. Bluffing is a dangerous game in interrogation.   **T or F**

73. The indirect bluff is used best in breaking down alibis.   **T or F**

74. Give an example of a psychological bluff. _____

75. The success of the "separation bluff" is based on:

    a.__anger.   b.__distrust.
    c.__envy.   d.__fear.

76. Give an example of a "presumptive question." _____
_____

77. When an officer stops a suspect, he or she should, in all fairness, give him a detailed   **T or F**
explanation of why he was stopped.

CHAPTER XI

VEHICLE STOPS AND CONTROL OF OCCUPANTS

VEHICLE PURSUITS

The ancient philosophy of law, "Salus Populi est Suprema Lex," or "The safety of the people is the supreme law," seems to be giving way to a philosophy of "The safety of the individual is greater than the safety of the people." American law has always given more importance to the individual than other societies. However, it seems that we have lost sight of the fact that there must be a balance between rights and responsibilities. Many people have, in the name of individual rights, put their own personal selfishness above the safety of the community. There is the story of the Desk Sergeant who received a telephone complaint from an irate citizen about the noise from a jet bomber that flew over the city. The Desk Sergeant asked the complainant if it was a Russian bomber. The complainant replied no, that it was one of ours. To this the Desk Sergeant simply replied, "Be thankful." In a democracy, people's complaints are both important and powerful. There are examples of air bases that have been moved because of public pressure, even though these air bases were to protect the citizens who were complaining.

In a similar vein, police departments are receiving an increasing number of complaints whenever newspapers play up a big pursuit through the city. Letters are written to the editor of the local newspaper. The Chief of Police is visited by both individuals and committees. The gist of their complaint is simple. Police cars should not endanger the lives of innocent citizens by chasing criminals at high speeds through populated communities. Some feel that it is better to let the suspect escape rather than endanger innocent persons. There are certainly many examples of people who are killed by a fleeing suspect. Some are crossing the street, and some may be driving through an intersection when hit by the escaping suspect.

In the early 1990's a study by the AAA Foundation for Traffic Safety found that there were 50,000 high speed pursuits each year. Twenty-four percent of these pursuits results in traffic injuries. Between 1 and 3 % of the pursuits ended in death. The foundation also discovered that twenty-five % of those killed were innocent motorists or pedestrians.

Police departments are servants of the public. Because of this, wise police administrators lend an attentive ear to public demands when they feel that their own positions may be in danger. Since our towns and cities are growing so fast, the problem will become more acute as areas become more populated. It boils down to the safety of the general public versus the safety of the individual. Many cities in the U.S. have department policies against high speed pursuits through highly populated areas. It is difficult for police officers to accept these policies because they feel that it is making a game out of apprehending criminals. It is giving them another edge in escaping responsibility for their criminal acts.

The solution to this problem is not simple. It can be helped, however, through proper training and new attitudes on the part of patrol officers.

EMOTIONAL INVOLVEMENT OF PATROL OFFICERS DURING A PURSUIT

It is quite easy for officers pursuing a suspect to become emotionally involved in the pursuit. When they do this, they will take chances and often endanger their own safety and subject their vehicle to serious damage. There is also the safety of citizens to consider.

It is wise to remember that when we become emotional, our intellect is either impaired or blocked. We are at the mercy of our emotions and our habits. In situations like a police pursuit, officers need every bit of intelligent thought they can muster. A pursuit can often amount to a battle of wits. Officers must, therefore, learn to control their emotions and remain cool during emergencies. This takes considerable practice and is harder for some than it is for others. But it is something that can be developed in every officer. Habits can be of great help to an officer if they are good habits. All officers should carefully develop good habits in driving and general police procedures. If officers will do this, and later find themselves in an emergency situation, they will automatically perform their tasks in a proper manner. This will be the result of proper habit training.

In a police pursuit the officer usually has the advantage. Because of this, there is no need to take unnecessary chances.

Advantages in a Police Pursuit:

(a) Police communications to be used for general coordination and tactical operations such as interceptions and roadblocks.

(b) Numerical superiority. Officers can call on other units from their own department and those from other agencies and neighboring communities.

(c) The officer has a better knowledge of individual streets and the general area.

(d) The officer has more experience and skill at high speed driving.

Police officers "lose their heads" during a hot pursuit more than most types of police action. Studies have shown that a great number of suspects are assaulted by police officers when the pursuit comes to a climax. It is natural for an officer to build up internal tension during the pursuit. This tension is difficult to turn off when the pursuit ends. The driver of the pursued vehicle experiences the same feelings. Many times he will come out of the car fighting because his body is also stimulated by adrenaline as a result of the pursuit. Pride also enters into the picture. If an officer has pursued a suspect for some time, and the pursuit finally ends, the officer exits the patrol vehicle in a "pumped up" state. Any move on the part of the suspect that could be interpreted as being aggressive, will surely receive an aggressive response from the officer. It is hard for anyone to turn their emotions on and off like a faucet. The responsibility that a police officer holds demands that he or she give it their total concentration. The police supervisor can also play an important role in controlling officers in the field.

PURSUIT CONSIDERATIONS

It is wise to consider the emotions of the person being pursued and analyze their thought processes.

(1) The persons being pursued are under pressure to escape and make decisions. Decisions made under pressure are often not the best ones.

(2) Unless the persons are under the influence of alcohol or drugs or a combination of both, they are usually very emotional and scared and will take more chances. Often the fact that they are fleeing is a sign of panic. Many officers will play this to their advantage by staying on their tail rather than trying to overtake them through dangerous maneuvers. The result is that the officer ensures greater safety, and the suspects often crash their vehicle or loose control because they took too many chances. Keeping a safe distance also prevents the officer from rear ending the pursued car, allows more room for the officer to maneuver if a split second decision is required and can give the officer a better view of overall traffic so he or she can prevent collisions with other cars.

(3) If the pursued driver is under the influence of drugs or alcohol, his senses and reactions will be slower, and sometimes non-responsive.

(4) Because of movies and television, the suspect may have the added fear that officers will shoot at him. It is uncommon that officers today will shoot at a vehicle being pursued. It would have to be a very serious crime or a case where the suspects are shooting at the officers. The suspect doesn't know this and it will add to the pressure he is experiencing.

(5) The siren and red lights tend to make the suspect think that the patrol vehicle is closer and is going much faster than it really is. As a result the pursued driver, in order to escape, will take unnecessary chances in his driving.

TACTICAL CONSIDERATIONS

Police officers should review the following tactics on a regular basis. They will probably not remember all of them during the first pursuit, but through continual review, these actions will eventually become part of the normal habit response.

(1) Notify headquarters immediately when the pursuit begins. Notify radio control of the nature of the offense committed. If the pursuing officer knows of no crime other than traffic violations, communications should be notified that the car is wanted for traffic viola-

tions only at this time. The reason for this is that other units might join the pursuit believing that the suspect is wanted for a serious offense. It may be a case of juveniles who are just scared and want to avoid getting a ticket.

(2) Weigh the seriousness of the violation against the possibility of wrecking the patrol vehicle and causing self injury. Some violations are just not serious enough that an officer should gamble so much to apprehend the fleeing vehicle. This is extremely difficult for officers because it is their job to catch criminals. If the officer can get the license number, or possibly recognize the vehicle and occupants, they can be apprehended later when circumstances are more favorable, with the added charge of evading a police officer.

(3) Do not begin the pursuit until the safety belt is on and secure. It takes only seconds. Those few seconds are not that important.

(4) Don't pursue a vehicle when carrying passengers or prisoners unless it's a dire emergency. The courts could award them a considerable sum if they were injured. An officer may follow the suspect for a short distance if it is possible to see the license number, report it to communications, then stop the pursuit.

(5) Don't make quick starts or floor the accelerator pedal when starting a pursuit. It can stall the engine, and also cause an accident due to pulling into traffic too fast. Those first few seconds are not as important as safety.

(6) When not accelerating, keep your foot on top of the brake pedal without depressing it. The split second that will be saved in applying the brakes will mean that the patrol vehicle will stop many feet sooner. When approaching an intersection this could save your life.

(7) Take into consideration the condition of the road, the degree of traffic and the weather conditions. All of these conditions should have a conservative effect on your driving. The driver of the fleeing vehicle will pay little attention to them and as a result he may have an accident. This will shorten the pursuit and lessen the danger to the officers involved.

(8) When entering a blind intersection, plan on another car entering from the side street. Remember how easy it is for a person in a noisy car, with the windows rolled up, not to hear your siren.

(9) Keep communications informed of each change in direction so that the other patrol units may be directed to a proper interception. When updating radio, make sure it is done on straightaways and not during turning movements.

(10) Don't use the siren unless you are the immediate pursuing patrol unit. It is unfortunately common for one emergency vehicle to collide with another at a blind intersection because they both had their sirens on and could not hear each other.

(11) Don't accelerate on oil slicks, ice, or slippery parts of the road. It causes slip outs and loss of control.

(12) If you have a partner, let him or her operate the radio. If it is at night, the partner should sweep the approaching intersections with the spotlight. This can warn vehicles approaching from side streets that you are approaching the intersection. Do not shine your spotlight into oncoming vehicles. This can blind the driver and cause him to drive into the patrol unit or another vehicle .

(13) When approaching another vehicle from behind, slow down gradually before actually arriving just behind him. Whenever brakes are applied at the last minute, it presents a greater danger of accidents. It also results in a greater loss of speed. It is harder to regain this speed if you have to pass. It would be better if the police vehicle was slowed slightly when the vehicle ahead was first noticed, and then the speed gauged accordingly.

(14) Give all cars ahead plenty of forewarning when you are about to pass them. This can be done with the horn or spotlight if the siren is not being used. When driving at fast speeds, it is difficult to take evasive action when one of the vehicles ahead suddenly decides to make a turn.

(15) Avoid passing vehicles at intersections. These locations present the greatest danger to officers. This requires planning, but the safety factor is worth it. Don't pass on the right. If it is a necessity, it should be done very slowly and only when the car ahead has had some warning and seems to be aware of what is taking place. This is a very dangerous man-euver.

(16) Don't brake during turning movements. Pump or fan the brake pedal intermittently. Don't jam the brakes. This causes skidding and overheating to the point where the brakes may fail completely.

(17) When going into a turn at high speeds, accelerate slightly. This gives the rear wheels a little traction and will help the vehicle stay on the road. Race drivers use this technique on the track.

(18) If there is a strong wind blowing, plan on the patrol vehicle swerving sharply when passing large trucks or when going into an underpass. These act as wind blocks, and have the same effect as if a person were pushing against you with his arm, and then suddenly pulled his arm away.

(19) In a long pursuit, the accelerator should not be given full throttle for long periods of time. The pedal should be released for a second to give the pistons, rings, and cylinder an oil bath. This little precaution may ensure that the patrol vehicle does not have an engine failure and thus end the pursuit.

(20) If the officer sees that a collision with an oncoming vehicle is imminent, it would be better, if possible, to run off the road. It is better to hit something on the side of the road at 65 miles per hour than another car at a combined speed of 130 miles an hour. It would result in a less forceful impact. Sometimes, when the patrol vehicle runs off the road, there are small fences and bushes that could slow it down. In such a case the officer should face down and to the right, toward the seat, to avoid being cut by flying glass.

(21) Officers often forget to use turn signals during a pursuit. It is easy to do when one's whole attention is centered on the pursuit. The other drivers on the road are not mind-readers. Using turning signals will further ensure an officer's safety. After all, the job can present enough danger without officers themselves adding to it.

(22) Officers should not join in a pursuit unless ordered to. Setting up a roadblock position at a major intersection is a good move. One of the most common problems in a pursuit is too many patrol vehicles from too many agencies. When there are over four police cars in the pursuit, they get in each other's way. They also cause many accidents and create communication problems. It is not uncommon to have 20 to 30 cars involved in a pursuit on a quiet night. It is very appealing to a patrol officer to go "where the action is." Few of the officers responding are really needed and they are also leaving their beats unprotected.

RAMMING THE SUSPECT VEHICLE

This is an area of much controversy. There can be a time when all of the factors involved would warrant the police officer endangering his or her safety and the patrol vehicle by ramming the car being pursued. It must be remembered however that this would be a rare situation. It is a difficult decision to make. An officer could never guarantee that a supervisor or administrator would later agree with the decision. It could be quite difficult to justify to a "Monday morning Review Board" that the suspect was such a great danger to officers and citizens alike that his vehicle had to be stopped at all costs. If the matter was truly analyzed, the costs could also include the life of both the officer and the suspect, the "totaling out" of both cars, plus an undetermined amount of property damage. At the time, during the heat of the pursuit, an officer's emotions and ego play a great part in that decision. Sometimes the bottom line is "That S.O.B. is not going to get away from me."

The speed of the fleeing vehicle should certainly be an important factor. If the vehicle has "spun out" and is temporarily immobile, but capable of again taking off, the ramming might be justified if the front end was rammed causing damage to the radiator. This could limit the pursuit because the engine would overheat without water. It would certainly be more acceptable than ramming it at 100 miles per hour. In the above situation, it would be more acceptable for the patrol vehicles to drive to a position where the suspect vehicle is blocked from further escape.

STOPPING THE VEHICLE

When it is expected that the vehicle might respond to your command to pull over, the first consideration is picking the best location. When a location is picked, communications should be notified of this proposed location. It will also enable other vehicles to intercept if the occasion demanded it. Prime considerations in picking a location are:

(a) As few escape routes as possible (such as side streets.)

(b) As little traffic hazard as possible. The street should be wide enough to make the stop without danger from passing cars.

(c) As little populated as possible. There have been cases where officers have stopped a suspect in a heavily populated ghetto or barrio area and large groups of bystanders have surrounded the patrol vehicle. Because they believed that the stop was racially motivated, they attacked the officers. The Watts Riot in Los Angeles started with just such a stop.

In cases where the suspects might start shooting, officers could be injured because they are hesitant to return fire with large crowds standing around. If there is a choice, it is best that it be where there are fewer people.

TYPES OF STOPS

There are three general classifications of stops made by the patrol officer. They are:

(1) Traffic stops
(2) Investigative stops
(3) High Risk stops

TRAFFIC STOPS

The majority of vehicle stops made by the average officer are for minor violations, mainly traffic violations. Unfortunately these types of stops cause officers to let their guard down. Several times a year, the price for this carelessness is paid when an officer is found lying dead in the street.

It is quite impractical to treat each person or vehicle stopped as you would a known or dangerous criminal. It is bad enough stopping the average citizen for a traffic citation. One of the major complaints against officers issuing citations is that they make the violator, normally a law-abiding citizen, feel like a criminal. If the officer were to approach each traffic violator with gun drawn and then order the driver and passengers out with their hands up, the phones of the Chief of Police, the Sheriff, and the Mayor would never stop ringing. Granted, there would be fewer officers shot by criminals when stopped for minor violations, but the citizens, who in our democracy have the final say, would see that the practice was soon brought to a halt. This does not mean that the officer must be left to the mercy of all criminals. There are basic procedures which, if followed, would greatly reduce the hazard involved in making so-called traffic stops. Before discussing these, it might be well to first look into the definitions of traffic stops and the other types of stops. Traffic stops involve police contacts with persons who have committed traffic violations.

INVESTIGATIVE STOPS

Investigative stops involve those situations when a police officer stops a vehicle based on probable cause. An example of probable cause would be when the officer believes that the individual(s) in the vehicle might possibly be connected with some type of criminal activity. The car could fit the description of a vehicle that had been involved in some crime. The driver or suspects could fit the description of someone wanted for questioning or criminal activity.

HIGH RISK STOPS

High risk stops are vehicle contacts which are conducted involving known criminals. In this case the officer knows they are criminally involved or believes, based upon good probable cause, that they are armed and dangerous.

TECHNIQUES FOR STOPPING VEHICLES

ALL TYPES OF STOPS

Pre-planning

(1) Always call in the license number on all vehicles stopped. Be sure to include a description of the vehicle. This could help if the plates were stolen or later changed. This does not stop the driver from shooting the officer, but it might mean that assistance will arrive at the scene sooner and get the officer to the hospital in time to save his life. Even in the worst scenario, if the officer were to die, the license number might lead to the eventual arrest of the perpetrator and possibly save the lives of future victims. Be sure that a sign is received from radio before proceeding.

(2) Keep an eye on the driver of the stopped vehicle. Even though it appears to be a traffic stop, the officer may observe him hiding something, or changing places with his passenger. He may also observe something being thrown out of the window. The driver does not always know exactly why he was stopped. He might have just committed a crime and believe that he has been identified.

(3) If it is at night, turn one spotlight on the subject's rear view mirror only when the vehicle has stopped. Then shine the light along the side of the car to observe whether or not objects are being thrown out. If it is an isolated area, and the officer is alone, it is a good idea to open and slam both doors to make the driver of the stopped vehicle believe that there are two officers.

(4) If the stop takes place at night on a highway or freeway, park as close to the right as possible and turn off the rear flashing yellow lights. A study done by the California Highway Patrol proved that a yellow/amber light served as an attention getter. There was a tendency for intoxicated drivers to become fixated by the light and attracted to it. The result was a rear-end collision. They learned that the normal parking lights served as a warning without the collision potential.

Approaching The Vehicle

(1) Check the trunk during the approach. Is it ajar? If so why? Is it weighted down? What is it that is so heavy?

(2) Check the back seat and the floorboard during the approach.

(3) If it is at night, the flashlight should not be held in the gun hand. It should be held in the striker position rather than the carrying position. In this way it can be used as a flashlight for checking identification, and in an emergency, it can be quickly used as a striker, but only under the same restrictions as the baton.

(4) Stop just before the doorpost and check the ignition. If the key is missing, it could be that the car has been hot-wired.

Fig. XI-1; Approaching the suspect vehicle

(5) Do not go further than the doorpost. Why?

(a) If the subject were to open the door quickly, it would knock the officer down, or possibly into oncoming traffic.

Fig. XI-2a; Driver suspect opening door quickly

Fig. XI-2b; Officer knocked down and into oncoming traffic

(b) If the subject has to turn in order to talk to the officer, it puts him at a psychological disadvantage. A criminal usually weighs all of the facts before taking overt action against an officer, and will take this action only when he feels that the odds are in his favor, or when it is a last resort.

(6) The male officer should always stand with his side facing the subject. Should the subject decide to kick or deliver a blow to the groin, the hip would take the blow instead.

(7) If the officer senses something is wrong, it might be best to approach the vehicle from the right side. In this way the officer would have a clear view of the driver, and would also be able to see a hidden weapon.

Fig. XI-3; Officer approaching vehicle from passenger side

Fig. XI-4; Concealed firearm visible from passenger side

Contact With The Driver

(1) Ask him to turn the engine off if it is still running. This will prevent the driver suddenly taking off and promote better communication.

(2) Don't reach in for the ignition keys. An officer would be at a great disadvantage when reaching through the window and down to the key. The officer's arm could be broken, or an armlock could be placed on it. If the driver is trying to get the car started, it might be warranted to grab for the keys, but caution should be taken. If the car has electric windows, the officer could get his or her arm

trapped between the window and window frame. It would be better to grab the fingers on the driver's left hand and peel them off the steering wheel and then into an arm lock. This would prevent him from driving off unless he chose to leave his arm behind. It is also possible for the driver to grab the officer's gun from that position.

Fig. XI-5; Officer with hand trapped between window and frame

Fig. XI-6; Driver reaching for officer's gun

(3) Explain the purpose for the stop and ask the subject to step out of the car. Then ask the subject to step over to the edge of the road or to the sidewalk. This prevents:

(a) The subject driving off.
(b) The officer being hit by passing cars.
(c) The driver pushing the officer into traffic.

(4) Instruct passengers to remain in the car if it appears that they might be getting out. If the officer is alone and the passengers appear to be the type to cause trouble, they can quickly encircle the officer in an innocent manner. If there were several of them, it would be too late for the officer to grab a weapon once they were on all sides. If they were to get within several feet, the officer would have little chance to draw a gun. Keeping them in the car is a good preventive measure. However, if the situation were such that the officer suspected some type of felony, it would then be wise to draw his or her gun order everyone to stay in the car. They should be told to place their hands on their heads.

(5) If it is at night, and the officer is alone, and something arouses suspicion, a good tactic would be to call back to the patrol vehicle as though a partner were still in it. The imaginary partner could be given some type of instructions such as calling headquarters, or to get the shotgun and stand behind the police car. This bluff might be the deciding factor for suspects who had originally intended to attack the officer. The author stopped an armed robber at night on one occasion and was later told by that suspect that he would have shot him except for the fact that he could not see the exact position of his partner. He was never told that the partner was nonexistent.

(6) A firm habit should be developed to never stand in a position where the subject is on the same side as the officer's gun. At first this requires a conscious effort, but after a while it becomes second nature. When writing a citation, the officer could put the gun toward the vehicle so it cannot be easily grabbed.

Fig. XI-7; Officer writing citation, suspect reaching for gun

INVESTIGATIVE/HIGH RISK VEHICLE STOPS

This is a topic of great controversy. There seems to be no one approach that suits all police officers. The purpose here is to present some of the more common methods used. They can be adopted or modified as officers see fit.

Observing The Suspects

Spotting criminal suspects requires that patrol officers be constantly alert, not just when a crime has been committed and a radio alert broadast. It is common for the criminal to change automobiles for the "getaway." Because of this, an officer should be alert for persons who fit the description of the perpetrators, not just the automobile. The officer should plan on there being slight variations in the description of the vehicle because:

(1) The suspects may change things on the car or change to another car.

(2) Human error may occur in:

(a) The victim's or the witness's description.
(b) The officers recording of the description .
(c) The radio dispatcher's transcription of the description.

Notify Communications When The Suspect Vehicle Is Observed

When a patrol officer spots a suspected vehicle, radio control should be immediately notified of the following information:

(1) The fact that the vehicle has been observed.

(2) The location of the vehicle at the time of reporting.

(3) The direction in which the vehicle is going.

(4) The relationship of the police unit to the suspect vehicle.

(5) The speed of the suspect vehicle if known.

Chapter Eleven

It is important that the suspect vehicle not be immediately stopped. It is possible that the driver has not seen the patrol vehicle, and this would give the patrol officer time to plan a proper strategy before the suspect can take evasive action.

METHODS OF STOPPING

There are several methods of stopping suspected vehicles. Three of the main methods will be covered here. In stopping a vehicle where a crime is suspected, all pretense is dropped. The approach is made with the intent of providing the officers with maximum protection.

First Method For Stopping Vehicles

When the traffic is heavy, or the officer is alone in the car, it is sometimes best not to park the vehicle out in the traffic lane, or too close to the suspect vehicle. In a case of this type, the police vehicle should be parked directly behind the suspect vehicle, with the left rear slightly jutting out toward traffic. This will offer a little protection for the officer from passing traffic. In the case of the one officer car, it prevents the suspect from seeing how many officers are actually in the vehicle. At night this method has the advantage of allowing both spotlights to be played along the side of the suspect vehicle. The headlights should be on high beam to increase visibility into the suspect vehicle. (See Fig. XI-8a, next page)

Second Method For Stopping Vehicles

The purpose of this method of stopping the suspect vehicle is to provide the officers with some type of physical barrier. In this case, the patrol vehicle is turned at an angle behind the suspect vehicle, so that the front left end of the patrol vehicle is jutting out in the traffic lane. In this way, the driver can use the hood of the car for a barrier and protection, and the passenger officer can use the rear right fender for the same purpose. This adds greatly to the psychological pressure on the suspects not to resist arrest or initiate a gun battle. (See Fig. XI-8b, next page)

Third Method Of Stopping Vehicles

This method will be covered in more detail in order to follow through with the complete procedure to be used in stopping vehicles with felony suspects.

Step 1. Turn on the red lights and sound the siren or horn. Use the spotlight if it is night.

Step 2. If a two officer car, the passenger officer should project his weapon out of and between the opened passenger door and window frame toward the suspect's vehicle. If a shotgun or rifle is carried in the car, it should be used. These weapons have a stronger psychological effect then a handgun. The rifle has a higher velocity and more penetration, and the shotgun has a wider target coverage.

If the suspect(s) open fire, officers may return fire immediately. It is best to first look over the area for possible innocent bystanders. Sometimes the immediate return of fire makes the suspects realize that the game is "for keeps" and they had better change their minds about resisting. When the suspects can see a rifle, shotgun or revolver pointing directly at them, and it is in the hands of someone they believe to be an expert, it has a strong psychological effect. They feel that the police "have the drop on them."

Step 3. Stop the police unit one car width to the left of, and slightly behind the suspect vehicle. This will allow a better view of the driver. It will also provide some protection for the officers if they order the suspects to come out from the left side of their vehicle. It is important that the rear flashing light be on. It is preferable that all emergency lights be on so that passing motorists and pedestrians may be warned of the potential danger. It also has a psychological effect on the suspect(s). (See Fig. XI-8c, next page)

In making stops of any type, always remember that automobiles approaching from the rear can kill the officers just as quickly as the criminals in the suspect vehicle.

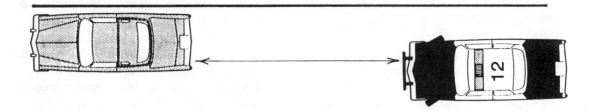

Fig. XI-8a; First method for stopping vehicles

★ = OFFICER

● = SUSPECT

Fig. XI-8b; Second method for stopping vehicles

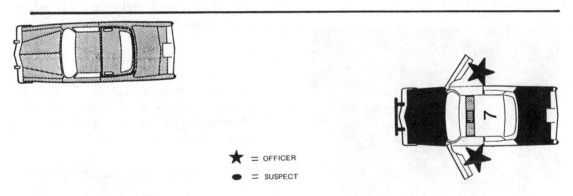

★ = OFFICER

● = SUSPECT

Fig. XI-8c; Third method for stopping vehicles

Step 4. Give the following orders to the suspects in a LOUD, CLEAR and STEADY voice:

"POLICE OFFICERS, DON'T LEAVE THE VEHICLE. DON'T MOVE UNLESS WE ORDER YOU TO. KEEP LOOKING STRAIGHT AHEAD."

The orders should be loud to be heard, clear to be understood and steady to show that the officers mean business. Tone of voice is always important in police work and will often determine how suspects will react. The term "we" should always be used in talking to the suspects, even if it is a one officer car.

At this point a decision must be made. If the windows are not rolled down and they are dirty, or if the light is reflected off the windows making vision poor, it might be advantageous to have the suspects roll the windows down. This should be done immediately before the shock of being stopped wears off and they have time to think. It should be done before the officers leave the police car. A disadvantage in rolling the windows down, is that the suspects might throw evidence out of the windows on the far side. Officers should be alert to this possibility.

Step 5. Continue giving the suspects the following instructions:

(a) "DRIVER, LAY BOTH HANDS ON TOP OF THE STEERING WHEEL, PALMS UP."

(b) "YOU IN THE RIGHT FRONT PASSENGER SEAT, PUT YOUR HANDS ON THE WINDSHIELD, PALMS AGAINST THE GLASS."

(c) "YOU IN THE REAR SEAT, LAY YOUR HANDS ON THE BACK OF THE FRONT SEAT, PALMS UP."

(d) "ALL OF YOU, KEEP LOOKING STRAIGHT AHEAD. DON'T MOVE UNTIL TOLD TO DO SO."

The suspects should not be told "Put your hands up." while they are in the vehicle. This puts their hands out of sight and within reach of the sun visor, and possible weapons.

Leaving The Police Vehicle

Fig. XI-9; Passenger reaching for gun above sun visor

(1) Turn the radio volume down so that it may still be heard. It should not be on too loud, or the suspects might be confused between the radio and the officer's commands. Take your portable, hand-held radio with you.

(2) Remove the ignition key from the patrol vehicle. More than one suspect has escaped the scene in a police vehicle because the officer has left the keys in the ignition. An officer would have a difficult time living this down.

(3) Communications dispatcher should be notified when the officers exit the police vehicle.

(4) The doors of the police vehicle should be used as shields until it is felt that it is safe to advance. The doors offer limited protection against bullets, but they can deflect bullets that come at an angle. They do offer a certain psychological advantage because suspects believe that the officers are protected. It might prevent them from shooting at officers.

(5) If using a flashlight, it should be held out from the body in the hand other than the gun hand. If the light becomes a target, it should be as far away from the body as possible.

(6) Handguns should be drawn, but not cocked. In an emergency, the officer can fire the gun double action in a hurry. If it is cocked, it may go off accidentally. This could injure someone unintentionally. It could also instigate gunfire on the part of the suspects who feel that they must return the fire in order to protect themselves.

(7) The suspect vehicle should never be approached by going between it and the police vehicle. The suspects could place their vehicle in reverse and back up, crushing the officer. There is also the disadvantage of being outlined by the headlights of the police vehicle.

IMMOBILIZING THE SUSPECT VEHICLE

To make sure that the pursuit does not start all over again, the suspect vehicle must be immobilized. This is best done by removing the keys to the vehicle. This can be dangerous because any removal of the suspect's hands from view can mean that the suspect is reaching for a weapon. There are two methods used in removing the keys from the suspect vehicle.

Method 1. When the Driver's Window is Rolled Down

Step 1. Order the driver to slowly move his left arm out the window.

Step 2. Order the driver to slowly move his right hand from the steering wheel and out the window to open the door from the outside with his right hand. This puts him at a physical disadvantage.

Step 3. Order the driver to put his right hand back on top of the steering wheel.

Step 4. Order the driver to slowly reach for the keys with his left hand, and slowly reach out and drop them on the ground.

Method 2. When the Driver's Window is Rolled Up

In this situation, the driver would have to remove his hands from sight to roll the window down anyway, so this movement might as well be utilized to open the door. He should be ordered to raise his left elbow up in the air, then keeping his elbow high, open the door with his right hand. In this position the driver would find it more difficult than if his arm were completely out of sight while opening the door. Once the door is open, Steps 3 and 4 would be the same.

Method 3. To Save Time

While the officers are fully protected by using the patrol vehicle as a barricade, simply order the driver to open the door and drop the ignition keys out into the road.

REMOVING SUSPECTS FROM THE VEHICLE

Approaching The Suspect Vehicle

In taking control of the suspect's vehicle, the following steps should be observed:

(1) Don't give the suspects so much attention that you are oblivious to oncoming traffic. Traffic can kill just as well as the criminal, and often does.

(2) Watch that you don't get into a position where you are in your partner's line of fire.

(3) Watch for the trunk lid being slightly ajar. Someone might be hiding in the trunk.

Removing the suspects when the officer believes the stop is non-hazardous.

If there is only one person in the vehicle and the officer believes that the stop is non-hazardous, a good approach is the one illustrated in Figure XI-10 below. It places both persons out of the way of traffic and gives the officer a chance to observe the driver as he comes between the two vehicles. it also allows the officer to take cover behind the police vehicle if the situation should suddenly become dangerous.

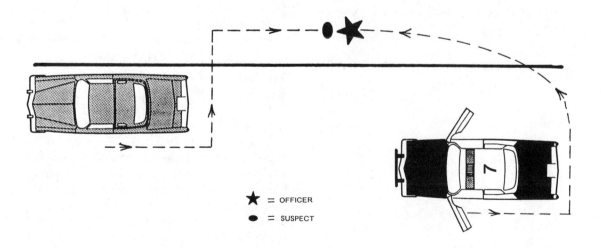

★ = OFFICER
● = SUSPECT

Fig. XI-10; Removing a suspect from a vehicle in a non-hazardous situation

Removing the suspects when the officer believes the stop is hazardous.

In removing possibly dangerous suspects from the vehicle, observe the following procedures.

(a) THE DRIVER The driver should always be removed first. He is usually the leader. Have him grab the top of the steering wheel with both hands, and then back out of the open door with his hands still on the steering wheel. When his feet are on the ground, have him place his hands high in the air and slowly back up to you. He must then be placed in a position where he may be watched and later searched.

(b) THE FRONT PASSENGER Have the front seat passenger slide over to the driver's side of the car and put his hands on top of the steering wheel. Then have him repeat the same procedure as the driver.

(c) THE REAR SEAT PASSENGER(S) Have the rear seat passengers put both hands out of the door windows and open the doors from the outside with their hands remaining on the outside. When their feet are on the ground, have them raise their hands high and back up toward you. If the windows are rolled up, have the passenger on the rear left side raise his left elbow and open the door with his right hand, then place both hands back on top of the front seat. He can then back out in the normal way. The passenger in the right rear seat should then slide over to the left and repeat the process.

SEARCHING AND HANDCUFFING OCCUPANTS

Searching

There are three main types of searching positions:

(1) The Standing Search.
(2) The Kneeling Search.
(3) The Prone Search.

THE STANDING SEARCH AND HANDCUFFING PROCEDURE

The standing search is a safe technique to use in most misdemeanor arrests. It offers adequate control for an officer to search and handcuff most suspects. This search is generally not used for felonies or when the officer has determined that there is a need to draw a firearm. In such a case, it is recommended that the officer use either a kneeling or prone search and handcuffing procedure. The latter searches offer more control than the standing search. (See Figs. XI-11a-k, pp 272-273)

THE KNEELING SEARCH AND HANDCUFFING PROCEDURE

The kneeling search offers an officer more protection and greater advantage by placing the suspect in a more awkward, off-balance position. This is a suggested technique that should be used when faced with multiple suspects and high-risk situations. If possible, this search should be conducted with the aid of a cover officer. The kneeling search is generally used when it is undesirable to place the suspect in a prone position. Examples would be when there is deep snow, tall grass, or mud. It also applies in cases where the suspect and officer are confined to a very small space. The initial commands or instructions should be given from a position of cover or concealment if available. If none is available, keep a distance of about 10-15 feet during the initial stages. At this point, the gun may be drawn. (See Figs. XI-12a-i, pp 274-275)

THE PRONE SEARCH AND HANDCUFFING PROCEDURE

The prone search and handcuffing procedure offers the officer the most control and gives greater advantage during the application of handcuffs than any other technique. It is best used when the officer knows, or has good reason to believe, that the suspect is dangerous. If at all possible, a cover officer should be present during this procedure. As with the kneeling search, officers should take advantage of cover or distance during the initial stages of commands and until the suspect is actually in the prone position. In this technique, the suspect should remain facing the officer so that his hands may be observed at all times. At this point, the officer's gun should be drawn. (See Figs. XI-13a-j, pp 276-277)

CONSIDERATIONS IN SEARCHING

(a) **IF THE OFFICER IS ALONE** If officers are alone, they should only conduct searches of felony suspects as a last resort. It is best to wait until some assistance arrives. If assistance is not available, the officer should order one suspect to remain by the car for search, and have the others lay in the road in a "spread eagle" position, facing the other direction. It is important that they are facing away from the officer. If they cannot see the officer, it is difficult to plan counter measures. The suspect should be told in a firm manner to remain in that position and not to turn around. (See Fig. XI-14, pg 277)

(b) **IF THERE ARE TWO OR MORE OFFICERS** If there are two or more officers, one officer should secure his or her weapon and conduct the search while the other officer stands off at some distance and keeps the suspects covered.

The officer holding the gun (cover officer) should be careful that the searching officer is not in a line of crossfire should any of the suspects try some countermeasure.

In searching the suspect, the patting type search should be avoided. It will detect large weapons, but it is possible to miss a flat object such as a blade or hacksaw with this type of search. The grasping type of search is better.

(c) **MALE OFFICERS SEARCHING WOMEN AT THE SCENE** When male officers have a female suspect, the law allows a proper search, but the search depends upon the situation. It is best to obtain witnesses to the search to counter later accusations of molestation. The main concern is locating concealed weapons. It is common for criminals in the company of their girlfriends to pass weapons to them. Weapons such as a gun or knife can be detected by a grasping type search. Anything concealed in the body cavities can be found later by a female officer at the jail. If a woman is properly handcuffed with her hands behind her back, it would be difficult to gain access to these items. There-

fore, in the field, the search should be restricted to her purse, hair and torso. If she is wearing spiked heels, remove them. They can be dangerous weapons.

A favorite hiding place for guns is in a woman's underwear. At one time it was common for criminals' girlfriends to hide small knives in their large hairdos. If a woman has a large hairdo, a grasping pat of the hair will detect anything that can be dangerous.

CLOTHING SEARCH

Many criminals plan for their eventual capture or arrest. They will hide both escape tools and narcotics in their clothing. They will also occasionally hide money in the clothing to be used for bribing and the buying of favors. Some of the favorite parts of the clothing used for hiding articles are:

1. Hat band
2. Tie
3. Lapels (underside)
4. Inside belt
5. Pant cuffs
6. Socks
7. Instep of shoe
8. Heel of shoe (false cavity)
9. Rings
10. Narcotics in handkerchief hem

BODY SEARCH

When the suspect is taken to headquarters or to jail, the search should be more intensive and should include the body itself. Some of the more common hiding places are:

1. the hair
2. the ear
3. the mouth
4. the nose
5. the armpit
6. under skin bandages
7. under the soles of the feet
8. under the testicles or foreskin of the penis if not circumcised.
9. in the anus
10. between the toes

STANDING SEARCH

Fig. XI-11a; Hands up

Fig. XI-11b; Grasp hands, break balance, move in

Fig. XI-11c; Search position

Fig. XI-11d; Begin hand change, slide thumb under, replace fingers, maintain pressure

Fig. XI-11e; Break balance, move in

Fig. XI-11f; Search position

STANDING SEARCH, CONT'D

Fig. XI-11g; Distract, bend finger, establish grip

Fig. XI-11h; Apply first cuff

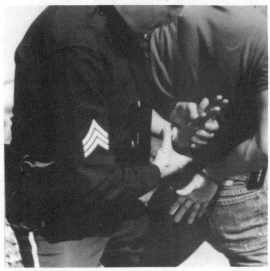

Fig. XI-11i; Apply second cuff

Fig. XI-11j; Search first side

Fig. XI-11k; Search second side

KNEELING SEARCH

Fig. XI-12a; Hands up

Fig. XI-12b; Grasp hands, maintain bowed back, search first side

Fig. XI-12c; Switch hand position

Fig. XI-12d; Maintain bowed back

Fig. XI-12e; Search second side

Fig. XI-12f; Pull hands apart

KNEELING SEARCH, CONT'D

Fig. XI-12g; Apply first cuff

Fig. XI-12h; Secure handcuff link

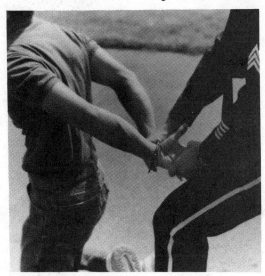

Fig. XI-12i; Apply second cuff

PRONE SEARCH

Fig. XI-13a; Hands up

Fig. XI-13b; hands on ground

Fig. XI-13c; Pick up hand, gun pointed up

Fig. XI-13d; Gun secured, search back

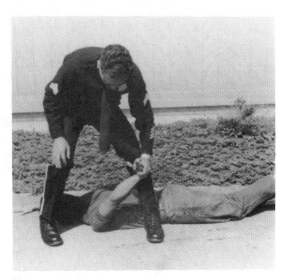

Fig. XI-13e; Step over shoulder

Fig. XI-13f; First cuff applied

PRONE SEARCH, CONT'D

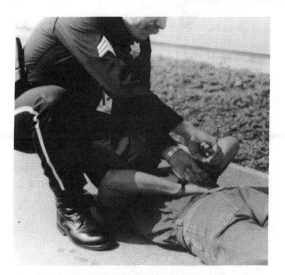

Fig. XI-13g; Apply second cuff

Fig. XI-13h; Lower leg search

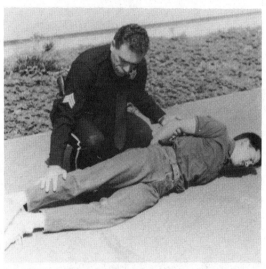

Fig. XI-13i; Roll suspect on side, search front of upper legs, groin, and body

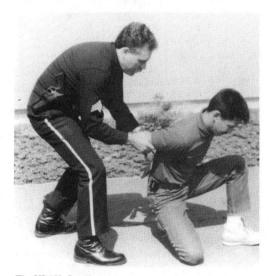

Fig. XI-13j; Stand suspect up

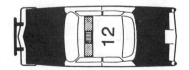

★ = OFFICER

● = SUSPECT

Fig. XI-14; Searching multiple suspects if the officer is alone

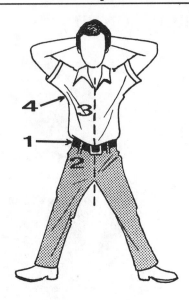

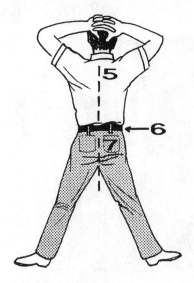

SEARCH FRONT HALF OF SUSPECT FIRST

1.   FRONT WAISTBAND
2.   FRONT POCKET
3.   UP THE CHEST
4.   ARMPIT & DOWN SIDE TO WAIST

SEARCH BACK HALF OF SUSPECT LAST

5.   NECK/SHOULDER AREA AND DOWN BACK
6.   LOWER BACK & REAR WAISTBAND
7.   REAR POCKET
8.   Repeat 1 — 7 on suspect's other side

Fig. XI-15; Search procedure diagrams

HANDCUFFING

POINTERS ON HANDCUFFS

(1) Always handcuff the suspect's hands behind his back unless transporting a long distance, in which case use a transportation chain.

(2) Handcuff the hands back to back. This prevents manipulation of the handcuffs.

(3) Double lock both cuffs. This (a) prevents shimming. Otherwise any thin metal object such as a hairpin can be used to shim the ratchet and release the cuff. (b) It prevents unnecessary injury to the wrist if the cuffs tighten up on the suspect. If this happens, it can cut the prisoner's wrist. This could instigate a police brutality charge.

(4) When going some distance, put the suspect's belt through the cuffs. Then move the belt buckle on the opposite side of the body from the cuffs. This prevents the suspect from swinging his arms against the officer. The arms, even though cuffed, can cause a heavy blow.

(5) Search prisoners for handcuff keys and ball point pens. Check the mouth. Ball point pens can be used as both (a) weapons (they can be used to stab) and (b) handcuff keys.

Fig. XI-16; Ballpoint pen cartridge made into a handcuff key

(6) When a prisoner is handcuffed and in the car, use seat belts to secure him to the seat. This is for both safety and security.

(7) Handcuffs are not escape proof. They are meant to be a temporary restraint. Don't put too much faith in them.

(8) Always carry an extra handcuff key. They are easily lost.

HANDCUFF NOMENCLATURE

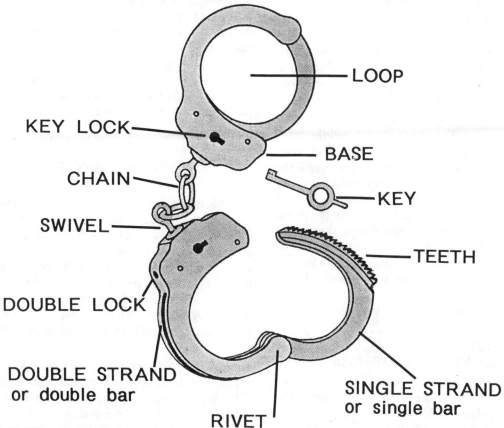

Fig. XI-17; Handcuff nomenclature

PLASTIC STRAP HANDCUFFS

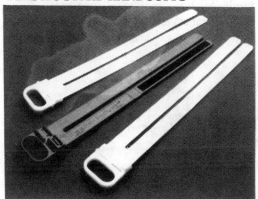

Fig. XI-18; Safe-T-Cuffs

Few officers carry an extra pair of handcuffs, yet many times an officer arrests more than one person. Multiple arrests are becoming more common than in past decades. One answer to the problem of multiple arrests is the plastic handcuff. This type of restraining device has many advantages. First, it is relatively inexpensive. Second, these devices will fit the wrist or ankle of any person. Some people's wrists or ankles are so large that normal handcuffs will not fit. Finally, they are easily

stored. Some officers store several of them in their carrying case. Some place one or two inside their gun belt. One can be stored inside the officer's cap.

The only problem with plastic strap handcuffs is that some type of cutting pliers are needed to remove them. Because of their wide use today, most booking officers have a pair of snippers for this purpose.

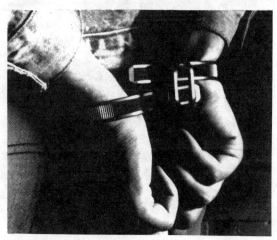

Fig. XI-19; Safe-T-Cuffs applied

MORE THAN ONE PRISONER. ONE OFFICER. ONE PAIR OF CUFFS.

(1) Put them both in the back seat with the left hand of the left seated prisoner cuffed to the right hand of the other prisoner. Secure both prisoners with seat belts.

(2) Put one in the right front seat, and the other in the right rear seat, then handcuff both their left hands together, but through the open windows of the doors and around the doorpost on the right side of the police car. This position is one of the safest to the police officer. Some do not recommend this technique because they feel that in case of an accident or fire, the prisoners would not be able to escape from the car. It is a good policy to never handcuff a person to a permanent part of the car for this same reason.

WHEN THERE ARE TWO OFFICERS, TWO PRISONERS AND TWO SETS OF CUFFS.

Both prisoners are handcuffed behind their backs and placed in the back seat. They are secured with seat belts. The other officer sits in the back seat behind the driver. It is suggested that an officer buy an extra set of handcuffs. They could be carried in the officer's briefcase. Occasionally the situation will arise where the officer will really need the extra pair. Also, it is not too uncommon for a handcuffed prisoner to run off. If it is a misdemeanor, the officer cannot shoot. If the prisoner is a better runner than the officer, the officer would lose both the prisoner and the handcuffs. In a case such as this, the officer would have to continue on duty for the rest of the night without a pair of handcuffs. This further points out the advantage of carrying plastic strip handcuffs.

VEHICLE SEARCHES

Whenever suspects are arrested in a vehicle, a search of that vehicle should be a matter of habit. Since the vehicle will be impounded, a preliminary search is all that is necessary in the field. There are a limited number of places in which a person could hide things after being stopped by officers. Most of the objects hidden in automobiles are put in places where they can easily be accessible to the person hiding them. Some of the more common places are:

1. Glove compartment.   2. Back of sun visor.
3. Under/in arm rests.   4 .Behind dash board.
5. Under floormat.   6. Behind seat lining.
7. Under back seat.   8. Ash trays.
9.. Under hood.   10. Under frame.

11. Under fenders ("hide-away" magnets).
12.Under front seat, in stuffing, around springs.
13. Behind back seat, through back seat to trunk

Fig. XI-20; Plastic cuffs put to good use in 1992 Los Angeles riots   Courtesy: A.P. Worldwide Photo

STUDY QUESTIONS for Patrol Operations

CHAPTER 11

1. "Salus Populi Est Suprema Lex" is a Latin saying that means:

   a.___The safety of the people is the supreme law.   b.___The popular law is the best law.
   c.___The law that is supreme is popular.   d.___All law is supreme if it is popular.

2. Many citizens today feel that officers should not become involved in hot pursuits.   T or F

3. Name one reason why an officer has the advantage in a hot pursuit. _____

4. When officers state that they are involved in a hot pursuit, they should also state the reason   T or F
   for which they are pursuing the car.

5. For safety reasons it is best to pass at intersections in hot pursuits.   T or F

6. When going into a turn at high speeds, it is best to accelerate slightly.   T or F

7. In a long pursuit it is best to give the accelerator full throttle for as long as possible as this   T or F
   gives more oil to the pistons and rings.

8. Even though an officer is going Code 3, turn signals should be used.   T or F

9. There is much controversy about ramming a suspect vehicle.   T or F

10. If you are going to ram a suspect vehicle, it is best to do this when the vehicle has
    _____; the best place to ram it is _____.

11. The word "routine" means "any regular procedure adhered to by habit".   T or F

12. When you have stopped a vehicle for a traffic violation, the first thing you do before leaving
    the car is _____ & _____.

13. How can you make the suspect believe that you are a two-man car if it is at night?
    _____

14. Your flashing lights should be left on even if you are parked safely off the roadway.   T or F

15. The CHP uses what alternative? _____

16. Before approaching the driver of the stopped vehicle, you should first check the _____.

17. If it is at night, the flashlight should be held in which way? _____

18. When talking to a driver, it is best to stand even with him so that you can look at the   T or F
    floorboard.

19. What can happen if you do the above? _____

20. If you are talking to the driver on the curb or sidewalk, it is best to stand with your
    _____ facing him.

21. When an officer is approaching a car and he senses something wrong, he might approach
    the car in what way? _____

22. To make sure the driver doesn't drive off, you should reach in and take the keys out of   T or F
    the ignition while the driver is still sitting behind the wheel.

23. If you stop a suspected vehicle at night and use the first method it has the advantage of
    using both. _____

24. The advantage of stopping method #2 is that it provides the officers better _____.

25. The visible use of the shotgun in felony stops has a stronger _____ power.

26. In making a felony stop, the suspects should be told to get out of the vehicle as soon as   T or F
    possible.

27. When giving instructions to suspects during a felony stop, the term _____
    should be used, especially if it is at night.

28. The first command to suspects in a car is to tell them to "put your hands up."   T or F

29. What is the problem with turning up your police radio too loud when leaving your car
    in a felony stop? _____

30. How should your flashlight be held when approaching a suspect vehicle at night?

    _____

31. When approaching a felony suspect, the hand gun should be drawn and cocked.   T or F

32. The _____ of the police vehicle should be used as shields.

33. If it is at night and you are leaving the driver's side of the patrol car and you wish to   T or F
    approach the suspect's passenger side, you should go between your headlights and the
    rear of his car.

34. When working with a partner, and you are approaching suspects who have been ordered
    out of the car, you have to watch your position so that you are not in your partner's
    _____.

35. When approaching a suspect car, you should always automatically look for the _____
    being slightly ajar.

36. When stopping a felony suspect car, you should have the _____ exit first
    if there are four people in the car.

37. When felony suspects exit a car, they should be told to exit with their _____ facing you.

38. When searching a suspect, you should give your partner your _____.

39. During a wall search, a suspect tells you that his feet are as far back as he can put them, you should do what? _____

40. If you wish to immobilize a serious felony suspect (and embarrass him as well) you could (especially if you are alone) _____.

41. When conducting a standing search, always have the suspect lift his _____ so you can check for contraband or handcuff keys.

42. If an officer is alone and has several felony suspects stopped, it may be best to have them exit the car and lay in the street or sidewalk with their arms and legs spread out. This position is called the _____ _____.

43. The patting type of search can miss _____.

44. To avoid criticism when searching women, you should search in what manner? _____
    _____.

45. Always peel a suspect's bandages to see what is under them.   T or F

46. In the "kneeling search" the officer should put his _____ on top of the suspect's top leg.

47. A major fault in the kneeling search is that the suspect can hide a knife _____ and it can go undetected.

48. Where is the control point in the spread-leg-standing-with-hands-clasped-behind-head search?
    _____

49. If possible, the suspect's hands should be handcuffed _____ of hand to _____ of hand, although this can be difficult when the suspect is resisting.

50. To stop the suspect from using a "shim" on his handcuffs, you should _____ the handcuffs.

51. To prevent injury to the suspect's wrists from handcuffs, you should _____.

52. Name a common item on that can be used as a handcuff key. _____

53. Handcuffs are just meant to be temporary restraints.   T or F

54. The best way to apply handcuffs is to hit the suspect's wrists hard with the lower swinging   T or F
    arm of the handcuffs so they swing around by themselves.

Chapter Eleven

55. Few officers carry an extra pair of handcuffs.   T or F

56. How can this problem be solved in an inexpensive way? _____

57. Where can they be carried? _____

58. Four prisoners can be handcuffed with _____ pair of handcuffs.

59. If there is no cage or plastic shield between the front and back seats of the police car, never seat a prisoner _____.

60. You should never move a suspect vehicle to headquarters until a complete and thorough   T or F
    search has been made of the vehicle and all of its contents.

CHAPTER XII

PROTECTIVE WEAPONS AND OFFICER SURVIVAL

Thirty years ago it was common for a police department to issue each officer a badge, gun, and baton, and then tell that officer to "go out and enforce the law." Only major cities had a Basic Police Training Academy. New officers were teamed with an older officer who usually taught the "rookie" the ropes. Today each state has a State Commission on Peace Officer's Standards and Training, whose objective it is to improve both the standards and training of police officers. There is also an increasing feeling in the general public that they not only deserve top quality law enforcement, but that they should actually receive it.

The courts have made it quite clear that towns, cities and counties have a definite responsibility to properly train their law enforcement personnel. This is especially true for training in the skillful use of protective weapons. A lack of training that results in injury to the public at large makes the department employing that officer liable for civil damages for any injuries.

A landmark decision in this area was Linda Peer v. City of Newark, New Jersey. More than any other decision, this one was responsible for police departments ensuring that officers were properly trained before they were let loose on the public. In this case an officer, who had received no firearms training, accidentally shot a young girl. The courts held the city negligent in its training obligation.

FIREARMS

One of the greatest misconceptions among new police officers relates to the use of their side arms. Because of TV, the movies, and comic strips, many young officers get into serious trouble because they lack an understanding of both the practical as well as the legal aspects of using their firearm.

WHAT IS THE PURPOSE OF THE POLICE FIREARM?

The purpose of the firearm is to kill. That is what it is made for. If an officer wishes to maim or disable a person there are other weapons such as the baton that could be used for this purpose.

What about just wounding the suspects by shooting them in the leg or arm? It happens all the time. The papers are full of examples. More criminals are wounded by police officers than are actually killed by them. The answer lies in chance or fate. It is a very rare and skilled officer who, under combat conditions, can say with 100% accuracy that he or she can shoot a person and not kill him, or can hit him in the leg or arm only. This is stuff for movies and TV and not real life. If this is true, officers should only fire their weapons when it is their intent to kill the person. They must be willing to accept responsibility if that person dies as a result of the weapon being fired.

The next problem that confronts officers is WHEN they should use their firearms. This problem will be addressed in two ways. First it will be discussed from the legal, and then from the practical standpoint.

LEGAL ASPECTS OF USING FIREARMS

Since we cannot guarantee that a bullet will not kill the person at whom it is fired, we must seek refuge in the law that allows peace officers to kill another person. Generally the law states that homicide by a peace officer is justifiable under the following conditions (however, these laws do vary from state to state):

(1) When necessarily committed in overcoming actual resistance to the execution of some legal process, or in the discharge of any other legal duty.

(2) When necessarily committed in retaking felons who have been rescued or have escaped, or when necessarily committed in arresting persons charged with a felony who are fleeing from justice or resisting such arrest.

It is important for an officer to realize that this law does not give carte blanche privileges in such cases. The firing of an officer's weapon should be a last resort when all other means have failed, or when it is obvious that this is the only course open. If it would appear to a prudent and reasonable person that such extreme force was not necessary, then the law would not protect the officer. (People v. Newsome 51 C.A. 42)

Recently, a federal appeals court ruled that an officer cannot shoot a person based solely on the fact that he has committed a felony. The 8th U.S. Circuit Court of Appeals in St. Louis overturned a Missouri law that allowed officers to use deadly force to arrest any person suspected of a felony. Although not a U.S. Supreme Court ruling, it reflects the direction that higher courts may be taking. It should also be pointed out that this section applies only to felonies, not misdemeanors. The law feels it is better that a misdemeanant escape than be killed. This would be a punishment far in excess of the crime and would violate the Eighth Amendment.

Laws usually give further justifications for committing homicide. These apply not only to police officers, but to all citizens. Examples of such laws are as follows:

(1) When resisting any attempt to murder any person, or to commit a felony, or to do some great bodily injury upon any person.

(2) When committed in defense of habitation, property, or person, against one who manifestly intends or endeavors, by violence or surprise, to commit a felony, or against one who manifestly intends or endeavors, in a violent, riotous or tumultuous manner, to enter the habitation of another for the purpose of offering violence to any person therein.

(3) When committed in the lawful defense of such person, or of a wife or husband, parent, child, master, mistress, or servant of such person, when there is reasonable ground to apprehend a design to commit a felony or to do some great bodily injury, and imminent danger of such design being accomplished; but such person, or the person in whose behalf the defense was made, if he was the assailant or engaged in mutual combat, must really and in good faith have endeavored to decline any further struggle before the homicide was continued.

(4) When necessarily committed in attempting, by lawful ways and means, to apprehend any person for any felony committed, or in lawfully suppressing any riots, or in lawfully keeping and preserving the peace.

Again, it must be remembered that these laws are to be relied upon only when the killing was a last resort. It is also expected that a police officer would exercise greater care than the average citizen in these matters. His or her training and judgment should better prepare them to handle the situation with a cool head. The legal defenses are quite explicit in justifying homicides. They are justified only when the intentions of the perpetrator are manifestly exhibited or when the controlling actions are reasonable.

PRACTICAL ASPECTS OF FIREARM USE

The practical aspects regarding the use of a firearm can be condensed into two rules:

(1) Use it to save your own life.
(2) Use it to save the life of another.

These rules are certainly more restrictive than those allowed in the Penal Code. One should consider that illegal defenses in the Penal Code are a last resort. They are an attempt to set down in writing, rules that would lay the boundaries on the unlimited combination of human circumstances that are possible in such situations. It would be wise to consider the taking of a human life from a more conservative viewpoint.

A professional police officer should be a person of conscience. A person of conscience does not lightly weigh the taking of a human life. An officer's action might be approved by a court or re-view board as falling within the limits of justifiable homicide, but in the mind of the officer there might be present for a lifetime a question as to whether this action was truly a last resort. There have been good police officers who have quit the department after killing someone, although their actions were justified from both a legal and practical standpoint.

WHY ARE PRACTICAL ASPECTS PRACTICAL?

The answer is that we are all human beings. As such, we are fallible and can perceive a chance appearance or circumstance in various ways. It is quite possible to take an innocent life while performing what we consider to be a legal duty. Is the case actually a felony, or does it just appear to be one? The following are examples of actual cases:

(1) An armed robber held up a grocery store. There were several people inside the store. As the robber left by the front door, one of the people ran out the back door and over to a gas station to call the police. In the station getting gas was an off-duty officer. Upon hearing what had happened, he ran to the front of the store. In the meantime, the owner of the store had picked up a revolver and took off after the perpetrator. When the officer arrived at the front of the store, he saw the owner running with the firearm in his hand. He yelled for him to stop. The owner turned and saw the officer, in plain clothes, with a firearm in his hand. and thinking that he was the partner of the other gunman, he fired at the off-duty officer. The officer, in turn, returned the fire, and a firearm battle ensued while the real perpetrator got away. Luckily no one was killed. If someone had been killed, it would have been declared excusable or justifiable homicide. The person doing the killing, however, would have had it on his conscience for life.

(2) Two persons held up a downtown bank and the alarm was tripped. As a businessman was about to enter the bank with a bag of money, he saw one of the perpetrators fire a shot, and he turned and ran down the street. Just then a police car arrived at the scene and saw the businessman running down the street with a money bag in his hand. The officer yelled at him to halt, but the running had apparently jarred the businessman's hearing aid loose, and he didn't hear the order. The officer fired at the businessman and killed him.

(3) At a bank holdup, the perpetrators, while going through drawers, accidentally set off the silent alarm. When the first officers arrived, a firearm battle ensued. A man living next door to the bank, saw what was going on and grabbed his revolver so he could assist the police. As he ran across the parking lot of the bank with his firearm in his hand, another police car drove up. The officers jumped out, and one of them started shooting at the citizen with the firearm in his hand. Fortunately the officer was a bad shot and the citizen was not hit.

(4) A man and his wife were walking down the street. Some kids threw several firecrackers on the sidewalk, and the woman fainted because of the shock. Her husband ran toward their house so he could get her a glass of water and some medication she had been taking. A police car was just around the corner when the firecrackers went off. To them it sounded like shots. As they turned the corner, they saw the woman lying on the sidewalk and the man running. One officer jumped out and yelled for the man to halt and since he was now quite a distance away, fired a shot which fortunately missed him.

Apart from the cases of mistaken or supposed identity, an officer should also consider the possibility of hitting innocent bystanders if a firearm battle takes place. There are, unfortunately, cases of innocent bystanders being shot when am officer fired at a criminal and missed. This seems to happen more often when officers are firing from their cars during a pursuit. Extreme caution should be used when firing a weapon in a congested area. Here the practical rule of shooting only to save a life should be applied.

SHOOTING AT JUVENILES

Shooting at juveniles presents many problems for the police officer. An officer should never underestimate the capabilities of a juvenile or the potential danger that the juvenile might present. There are many times when an officer is completely justified, from the legal standpoint, in shooting at juveniles and yet, from the practical standpoint, it is ill advised.

It used to be common for police officers, when they were chasing a stolen car containing obvious juveniles, to start shooting at them. This was especially so if they finally stopped the car and started running. Officers would justify the shooting by the magic word "felony." They would say "If it is a felony you can shoot at them." It should be remembered that the majority of juvenile car theft cases are reduced to a misdemeanor, "joy riding." Many departments now prohibit officers from firing at stolen cars unless they are fired upon from the stolen car first (the safety of the public is an important factor here.) Some of the practical considerations regarding shooting at juveniles are:

(1) **MONDAY MORNING QUARTERBACKS.** After an officer has shot a juvenile, even if it was justified, there are many people, including fellow officers, who will question the wisdom of the shooting. They will state that, "It seems quite obvious now that he didn't really have to shoot him." It is easy for the "armchair strategist," who was not at the scene during the heat of battle, to evaluate the actions in terms of what is now known.

Since we all look at things from different perspectives, all officers should expect a certain amount of criticism when a shooting occurs. It is unfortunate, but there are those who have a dislike for cops, and they will criticize officers even if their actions are clearly justified. There are also those who are very sincere in their negative beliefs about officers. Some may have a legitimate basis for their beliefs. Policework is a public service, and as such, officers are certainly subject to criticism from citizens. Unfortunately it is part of the job. Because of the politics involved, critics can often damage an officer's career. This is especially true if the critic has some position or office in local government.

(2) **PUBLIC PRESSURE GROUPS.** The general public is often in sympathy with young people and concerned with the protection of our youth. Because of this, minority pressure groups, some of whom believe that officers shoot minorities without legal basis, seldom pass up the opportunity to make "political hay" when an officer has shot a minority juvenile.

(3) **HEADLINE HAPPY MEDIA.** In large communities, there is usually one paper that builds up circulation by attacking the local police. This technique does sell papers. Anyone who has ever had a negative contact with the police is anxious for proof that the police are not just in their actions. This confirms their belief that the officer citing them was wrong.

A good example occurred some time ago. A series of liquor stores had been held up regularly by the same perpetrator. As a result the Chief of Police put stakeouts in almost every liquor store in town. A few nights later, the perpetrator, a 17 year old who was large for his age, held up another liquor store. The officer, who was staked out in the back, jumped out armed with a sub-machine gun, and told the robber to drop his gun. Instead, the suspect turned and fired at the officer. As the suspect ran from the store, the officer opened up with the sub-machine gun, and hit everything but the perpetrator. The officer then ran outside, drew his .38 caliber revolver, fired at the suspect a half block away and killed him. The next day the headlines were "COP KILLS KID." On the front page was a picture of the officer holding the sub-machine gun, and next to that was a picture of the perpetrator, taken when he was 14 years old. As a result, the officer and the department were subject to public criticism and abuse for some time after that.

PANIC FIRING

The Second World War, Korean War, Viet Nam war, the Gulf War (and most likely every other war that has ever been fought) were punctuated with examples of panic firing. Panic firing is where one person opens fire and everyone else follows suit. The first shot can be, and in many cases has been, an accident. It seems that when the first shot is fired, everyone panics. They are under great pressure and are fearful for their lives. They feel that there must be some good reason for the first shot being fired. In wars and in police work there have been numerous examples of members of the same team firing at each other. The strength of the panic reaction is greater at night when darkness breeds insecurity and often hides the reality of the situation. Another danger in panic firing is that officers quickly empty their firearms. They are then left with an unloaded weapon when a new and real danger could suddenly present itself.

WARNING SHOTS

Most departments have orders forbidding the firing of warning shots. Still, officers violate these orders. It is probably the result of frustration on the part of officers at having someone running away from them. They are reluctant to shoot the fleeing suspect, but feel that they should do something. Despite written orders to the contrary, some of-ficers will use a warning shot because they feel that the orders are not sound and that some situations demand their use. What is wrong with warning shots?

(1) **WHAT GOES UP MUST COME DOWN.** The question is, where will it come down. The chances of a warning shot coming down and hitting a person in the head are rather remote, yet it has actually happened.

(2) **ANGLE SHOTS CAN CAUSE DAMAGE.** Many officers fire their warning shots over the suspect's head. This is more dangerous because it can easily ricochet and cause property damage as well as injury and death.

(3) **IT SELDOM STOPS THE SUSPECT.** Officers usually fire warning shots when the suspect is too far away to chase. When the suspect is that far away, he will seldom stop when the shot is fired. If anything, he will run faster because the shot has stimulated the production of adrenalin in his body, and has given him more energy.

(4) **A REPORT MUST BE FILED.** Usually a copy of this report goes into the officer's personal folder. Even if the officer feels the warning shot was justified, the report will probably be considered derogatory in nature by the officer's superiors.

AN EXCEPTION TO WARNING SHOTS RULE

Some departments have come under intense public criticism when an officer has shot a suspect who was coming at him without first firing a warning shot. Because of this, some departments have recently changed their policy on warning shots. They now allow the officer one warning shot before firing a fatal shot at an oncoming suspect. This can be done only in cases where the officer would normally be justified in shooting to kill. Cities could quickly change this policy when an innocent bystander is hit by one of these warning shots.

USE OF FIREARMS IN "DISPATCHING" INJURED ANIMALS

Most officers seldom fire their sidearms in an actual combat situation. Many, however, will use their firearms to put injured animals out of their misery when it is obvious that nothing can be done for them. In dealing with animals under any conditions, remember that some people love animals more than they love other people. They will be very critical of any decision that involves shooting them.

The following steps are recommended when it appears that an officer will have to shoot an animal that is injured.

(1) **OBTAIN THE OWNER'S PERMISSION IF POSSIBLE.** If the owner is not around, or is unknown, obtain the names of witnesses who can verify that the animal was in a condition that warranted its being put out of its misery. If the owner of the animal later sues the officer on the grounds that the killing of the animal was unjust, the officer can call on the witnesses to back up the action.

(2) **USE SPECIAL AMMUNITION.** An officer should carry one or two extra "wad cutter" type bullets to be used in dispatching injured animals. It is very embarrassing for an officer to shoot an animal and then have it jump up and go yelping down the street. A magnum load should not be used because it has a greater chance of going through the animal and ricocheting to cause injury or damage.

(3) **CLEAR ALL CHILDREN FROM THE SCENE.** Young children do not understand the situation. It is possible that they might subconsciously hate all police officers for the rest of their lives because they remember a police officer in uniform shooting the pet that they loved so much. They might have forgotten that the animal was injured. They might not have been present when it was actually hit by the car. The thing that sticks in their minds is the police officer shooting it.

(4) **MOVE THE ANIMAL OFF THE PAVEMENT.** To reduce the chance of the bullet ricocheting, it is best to remove it to a dirt or lawn area.

(5) **MUZZLE THE ANIMAL.** For safety's sake, it is best to muzzle the animal even though it may appear to be almost dead or even unconscious. The animal should not be moved without first muzzling it. This can be done with a belt, handkerchief, or piece of rope.

(6) **LIFT THE ANIMAL BY THE SCRUFF OF THE NECK.** This is the safest position for the officer, and it is the least painful to the animal. It will also reduce the chance of criticism from bystanders.

(7) **DON'T SHOOT THE ANIMAL IN THE HEAD.** If it is possible that the animal is rabid, the lab must have the head intact in order to perform tests. If there is no suspicion of rabies, then it may be shot in the head, down into the body. This increases the likelihood of killing the animal and helps prevent the bullet coming out the other side. If the animal is suspected of rabies, it should be shot in the neck, down into the body.

(8) **BREAKING THE NECK IS ANOTHER WAY.** An officer may be reluctant to shoot the animal because the area is congested with people, and there is no unpaved area. In this case, hold the animal up by the hind legs in one hand until the neck arches back, then take the baton in the other hand and give a snapping blow to the back of the neck. This reduces the danger of shooting and is less messy. It does, however, require some skill.

(9) **WHEN THE ANIMAL IS DEAD.** Many times an officer will shoot an injured animal, notify headquarters to call Animal Control, give the location, and then leave. Under such conditions, a dead animal has lain in the gutter for days. The reaction of neighborhood residents is often quite strong. They feel that the officer's job was only half done. People expect more from the modern police officer than ever before. After the animal is dead, if the officer is notified that an Animal Control officer is not available, one of the neighbors should be solicited to allow the animal to be put in a garbage can (if it fits) until Animal Control can remove it. If the animal is too large, one of the neighbors might be asked to provide a large garbage bag.

LIABILITY WHEN USING FIREARMS

An officer who shoots an innocent bystander during a gun battle, may not be found criminally guilty. The District Attorney, when examining all of the evidence, might feel that there was not present the intent or negligence necessary to a crime. It could be classified as a case of excusable homicide resulting from accident or misfortune. If later, in a civil action, the jury were to find that the officer did not exercise reasonable care and caution, the officer could be successfully sued in civil court for damages. It is important to remember that the review board or jury that decides on the action is taking a "Monday morning" view of the shooting. They were not there during the heat of battle. Their thinking can be quite different. When the law refers to actions as being those of a "reasonable and prudent person," it usually means the viewpoint of a group of persons who are sitting at a table without pressure or fear. This can be a considerably different state of mind from that of an officer who is operating under combat pressure. When an officer feels as though the only way to stop a suspect is to shoot at him, it might be best to swallow one's pride and let the suspect escape rather than risk a civil suit. If the situation is borderline, the officer should always err on the side of caution. A career can be at stake.

FAILURE OF OFFICERS TO USE FIREARMS

Today police administrators are as much concerned with officers who fail to use their firearms when they should as they are with those who use their firearms recklessly. Police administrators are becoming more aware of situations where police officers have suffered from "buck fever." Under combat conditions, they cannot fire their weapons. In some cases the officer has been wounded or killed as a result. The killing of another human being is a serious matter and should not be taken lightly. However, an officer's life and safety is much more important than that of a criminal. Steps must be taken to discover these tendencies and either correct them or direct the officer into another field of employment. Since average officers rarely fire their weapons in a real combat situation, it is conceivable that an officer could spend years in the department without being aware of this problem. Another thing to consider is that this problem could endanger a fellow officer.

One solution to the problem is training. Using wax bullets and a reverse projection movie screen, or some of the modern electronic training devices, it is possible to train officers to react to real danger situations by having them draw their firearms and fire them when various situations are presented on the screen. With enough practice, this becomes a "conditioned response." Officers will automatically react when faced with dangerous situations. The officer's central nervous system and memory system will respond in a proper way to the previous conditioning.

INTRODUCTION TO THE BATON

The baton is an intermediate weapon whose use falls between weaponless control and the use of the firearm (deadly force).

The baton is a weapon. Whether an arrest technique or a baton is used, control is the goal. The baton is to be used in a defensive manner.

The baton offers safe and effective control over an assaultive or resisting subject who cannot be controlled by conventional arrest control techniques. When used properly, the baton is an additional resource available to the law enforcement officer. An officer's option to use the baton is based upon departmental policy and state statutes.

To become proficient in the use of the baton, a minimum of forty hours of training is required. An ongoing program of continued training and routine practice is required for officers to become confident in the use of the police baton. Individual practice will develop self-confidence and control along with the ability to apply basic baton techniques.

When the baton is used, the suspect is likely to suffer physical injury. However, if the baton is used properly, injuries sustained by the suspect will be minor. If the baton is used properly, the officer will avoid public criticism and reduce liability complaints. When deciding whether to use the baton, the officer must consider appropriate response and escalation of force. The decision must be based on the circumstances surrounding the incident.

CONSIDERATIONS IN THE USE OF THE BATON

The baton may be used when:

(1) The officer is attacked and needs to defend himself and cannot overcome resistance or assault by means of weaponless control.

(2) The suspect demonstrates training or experience in hand to hand combat and the officer believes that he cannot overcome his resistance or assault by means of weaponless control.

(3) The officer is threatened by multiple unarmed suspects and an overt act is made to carry out the threats. The officer believes he must use the baton to defend himself.

(4) The officer is a team member in a crowd control situation and movement is used to separate or disperse persons or to deny them access to an area.

TARGET AREAS TO AVOID:

(1) Head, neck and throat
(2) Spinal column
(3) Groin
(4) Kidney area

TARGET AREAS TO STRIKE:

(1) Arms, backs of hands, wrists, elbows
(2) Lower legs, below the knees, shins, ankles
(3) Chest and rib cage
(4) Midsection
(5) Collarbone

THE USE OF THE POLICE BATON

Like the revolver, the police baton can present problems to the new officer. This is because of prior conditioning from movies, TV, and the comic strips. The "Dirty Harry" approach has no place in modern policework.

HOW SHOULD THE BATON BE USED?

There is much confusion about the use of the police baton. If a word association test were given to the average citizen, and the words "police baton" were spoken, the word that would likely come to their minds would be "head." It seems natural for the baton to be used in this manner, yet if there were a cardinal rule for its use, it would be "Do not hit a person in the head with the baton." So natural is this reaction that veteran officers, who know better, have hit their opponents on the head in the excitement of a fight. Why then, if this tendency is so natural, should an officer avoid this tactic?

(1) **IT CAN KILL THEM.** If you want to kill the person, use the firearm. That's what the firearm is for. It is possible that the suspect might have a metal plate in his head, or have some deformity of the brain. A good whack on the head with the baton might well kill him.

(2) **YOU SELDOM KNOCK THEM OUT.** In most cases, the baton is used to subdue the opponent. With the police baton, this seldom occurs. Sometimes the baton will even break and still not knock the person unconscious.

(3) **IF THE BATON BREAKS, IT IS PSYCHOLOGICALLY DEFEATING.** It is not only embarrassing but psychologically defeating to put everything you have into the baton, and then end up with just part of it in your hand. It makes the situation worse; instead of controlling the person, it just makes him more angry and violent.

(4) **THE VICTIM USUALLY BLEEDS PROFUSELY.** Even if the break in the scalp is small, it will bleed profusely. Scalp wounds tend to bleed more than wounds elsewhere on the the body. This may gain the sympathy of bystanders and promote charges of police brutality. When the blood runs down over the suspect's face, it looks as if he has received a severe beating even though he may have only been hit once. Today, there is bound to be someone around with a video camera. You will probably see yourself on national television the next day, standing next to a prisoner with blood all over his face.

(5) **IT BRINGS CHARGES OF POLICE BRUTALITY.** Nothing will promote police brutality charges faster than hitting a person over the head with the police baton. Some departments have forbidden the baton to be raised above the head. Activist agitators often have photographers mix with the crowd in hopes that they will be able to photograph an officer with a raised baton. This makes very good copy. When people see a picture of a police officer with a baton raised high above the head, they can almost feel the baton coming down on their own heads. Those who saw the Rodney King video on TV are especially sensitive to this. We in policework don't need any more of that.

(6) **THE PERSON CAN BE LEFT MENTALLY DISABLED.** Because the baton comes down onto the brain, it is quite possible to leave a person mentally disabled for life. There is also an added danger for officers. There have been cases where the person who was hit seemed to gain superhuman strength and it took a large number of officers to control the suspect. This could create a serious menace to both the police officer and bystanders.

(7) **THE OFFICER IS OPEN TO ATTACK.** When the baton is raised above the head, the officer's front is exposed and the officer is open to a number of counter-actions. Strategically, it puts the officer in a bad position.

HOW THE POLICE BATON IS CARRIED, HELD, AND USED

The best "ready" position for the baton is a horizontal position in which the right end of the baton is held in the right hand, palm down, and the left end of the baton is held in the left hand, palm up. When delivering a blow, the baton is snapped from the left hand to the target and is immediately returned. If someone tries to grab the baton, a quick twist will remove his grip. If both hands were gripping the baton, palm down, this could not be done (try it with your partner). When carrying the baton in the police car, it should always be kept in exactly the same position. If it is needed in a hurry, it can be grabbed automatically. Some departments equip all patrol cars with a special baton holder on the side of the door.

OTHER USES FOR THE POLICE BATON

(1) The baton can be used as an aid to come-alongs.

(2) It can be used to break in a window or door when forced entry is required. The firearm should never be used for this purpose.

The unbreakable flashlight can easily be used as a substitute baton. However, if it is used for that purpose, the officer should follow the same rules that apply to the regular baton.

THE YAWARA STICK

Many officers carry a Yawara stick in addition to their police batons. The original Yawara stick had metal spikes at each end and this brought some public criticism. As a result some Chiefs banned its use. This is a shame because it actually reduces complaints. It has the following advantages:

(1) Because it is small, it can be held in the hand and hardly noticed. The officer can have it ready without alerting an opponent. By folding the arms, it can be completely hidden. This reduces the possibility that the officer might have to fight. If an officer comes at someone with a baton in hand, he or she can usually expect a fight. The opponent often feels that he has no choice. There have been fewer charges of police brutality in departments where Yawara sticks have been used, provided officers followed proper training instructions.

(2) It cannot be grabbed from the officer's hand. The size prevents this from happening. When an officer has the stick gripped properly, there is only about an inch showing on either end.

Fig. XII-4; Yawara Stick

BATON POSITIONS

Fig. XII-1a; Single Handed Position: Strong hand grips the baton over the grommet, palm facing toward you. Keep a relaxed grip until making a strike.

Fig. XII-1b; Two Handed Position: Your weak hand grips the baton near the forward end. Grip the baton loosely with the thumb and index finger of your weak hand.

Fig. XII-1c; Overhand Position: The baton is held near eye level with the weak hand gripping the forward end.

Fig. XII-1d; Chopping Position: From the Thrusting Position Grip (see next page, Fig. XII-1e) slide you r weak hand down the shaft until you hold the baton in a grip similar to holding a baseball bat. Your strong hand grips the rear end of the baton. Keep both elbos down, close to your body

Chapter Twelve

Fig. XII-1e; Thrusting Position: Bend your rear arm at the elbow and grip the baton at the end. The baton is a straight extension of your forearm. Hold the front end with your forward hand. Keep both arms and elbows close to your body. Do not extend your arms or the baton toward the suspect.

Fig. XII-1f; Lower Cradle: The stance is the same as the Interview Stance (See Fig. XII-3a & b) and the weak foot is normally forward. With the weak foot forward, the weak hand grips the baton as in the Upper Cradle (See Fig. XII-1g below) palm down near the butt end. The baton is cradled in the strong hand at the grommet. The strong hand is held palm up. The shaft of the baton is held at an upward angle from the weak hand, up toward the strong elbow and the shaft is between the officer's body and the strong arm.

Fig. XII-1g; Upper Cradle: With the weak foot forward, grip the baton with the weak hand near the butt end, palm down. The baton is cradled on the web of the strong hand just above the grommet. Cradle the front end of the baton in the crook of the elbow. The baton shaft is held at an upward angle from the weak hand to the strong elbow.

Fig. XII-1h; Position for Interviewing:The officer positions him or herself in an Interview Stance (See Fig. XII-3a & b): gun side away, forward foot pointing toward the suspect, rear foot turned out at a 45° to 60° angle, weight distributed equally on the balls of the feet. You are ready to move in any direction. Maintain balance and distance. The baton is in the ring between the officer and suspect. The officer's hand rests on the baton in the ring. The hand and baton remain in a relaxed position. The officer is ready to quickly draw the baton if necessary.

BATON POSITIONS, CONT'D.

Fig. XII-1i-A; Striking hand position, left side view

Fig. XII-1i-B; Striking hand position, right side view

Fig. XII-1i; Striking Hand Position: The stance is the same as the Interview Stance (See Fig. XII-3a & b) except that the weak foot is not necessarily forward. The Striking Hand Position is used when the officer feels that the baton may be needed to control the suspect(s), however, the baton is held in a non-threatening position. The officer will hold the baton in the strong hand and stand with the strong leg forward. The baton is held down, along the side of the forward leg. In this position, the baton is unobtrusive, yet ready to use. Grip the baton over the grommet.

TWO COUNT BATON TECHNIQUE

Fig. XII-2a, Two Count Baton Technique: distraction

Fig. XII-2b; Two Count Baton Technique: drawing back

Fig. XII-2c; Two Count Baton Technique: strike to lower leg

STANCES

Fig. XII-3a; Interview Stance—Front

Fig. XII-3b; Interview Stance—Side

Fig. XII-3c; Horse Stance—Front

Fig. XII-3d; Horse Stance—Side

Fig. XII-3e; Front Stance

Fig. XII-3f; Self Defense Stance

NEW DEVELOPMENTS IN POLICE WEAPONS

Never in our history has there been such a need for new developments in the area of police weapons. The United States has the scientific knowledge and ingenu-ity for such an undertaking, but it will be up to the leaders in law enforcement to instigate research and planning in this direction.

Our country has experienced severe riots which, in some cases, may have been triggered by improper use of weapons by police officers. It is essential that the police officer in the United States carry some type of weapon since it appears that, if the present trend continues, our cities will continue to be places of violence and police officers will be caught up in conditions over which they have little control. There are se-veral conditions in our society that illustrate the need for more hu-mane police weapons. Three of them are mentioned here.

(1) **POPULATION CONGESTION.** The more congested our urban areas are, the greater is the chance that innocent bystanders may be accidentally injured or killed by police wea-pons. As the population of our cities conti-nues to increase, this danger will not lessen.

(2) **PUBLIC ATTITUDE AGAINST THE TAKING OF A LIFE.** Whether we agree with it or not, there seems to be an attitude shift against capital punishment taking place. This is reflected in a changing attitude among the general public toward police officers ta-king human life. Citizens are now more likely to question such drastic action. This trend may not reverse itself until such time as crime becomes so prevalent that the average citizen thinks of himself, rather than of the other guy, as the "crime victim." In a democracy the attitude of the people is of paramount impor-tance.

(3) **FEELINGS OF PERSECUTION AMONG MINORITY GROUPS.** Most police officers will readily deny that the police in general carry out prejudicial acts toward people from a minority group. They feel that the accusa-tions are unjust, and are used primarily as a means of rationalizing one's own misdeeds.

The truth of this is not as important as the fact that members of minority groups firmly believe that it is true. If a person believes something to be true, he acts on it as though it were actually true.

Boards of inquiry and the courts have de-clared that officers in several of our major ci-ties were legally justified in shooting criminal violators from minority groups. Yet the ensu-ing disturbances and riots resulted in many deaths and injuries and untold millions of dollars in property damage. The question then arises: "What is the answer?" There is no simple answer! There have been investiga-tions resulting in volumes of written material to address the fact that the problem is much deeper than that of an officer killing a sus-pected criminal from a minority group. Until some answers to this complex problem are found, every time a police officer injures or kills a minority person in the line of duty, the shooting will probably be interpreted by minorities as an overt act of unjust persecu-tion, a use of excessive force, an instance of police brutality, and a violation of civil rights.

There does exist a widespread and firm belief among many minority groups that the police represent the "white establishment," and en-force their "double standard" laws. This makes the police their sworn enemy. This is especially true of Black and Hispanic gangs. Some actually believe that one objective of police departments is to eliminate minorities through curbstone executions. It might seem absurd, but it is accepted by many as fact.

Seldom in the history of American law enfor-cement have the police been subjected to such in-tense criticism as they are today. Apart from some notorious examples of unprofessional police mis-conduct, never in our history have the police deserved it less. Many departments have issued regulations that narrow the use of deadly weapons. Officers cannot fire their weapons unless it is to save a life or prevent great bodily harm.

In this nuclear/space age, our development of personal protective weapons has lagged woefully behind our other great achievements. It has not been until very recently that some effort has been made to update and improve police weapons in line with both our present capabilities and the prevailing conditions of our society. Until now, police weapons have changed very little since those in use at the time municipal police work was instituted.

SUSPECT IDENTIFICATION AND VIDEO CAMERAS

A camera has been developed that is secured permanently in a patrol car. The purpose of this camera is to take pictures of cars and suspects whenever an officer makes a vehicle stop. It has a periscope-type lens that extends up to the windshield level, or can be adapted to other areas of the car. It can be adjusted to take one picture every five seconds for a period of five to ten minutes. This device, developed by Col. Floyd H. Mann, is being used by many agencies. Because of the periscope lens, it is difficult for a suspect to destroy the film. In 1991, a highway patrol officer made a vehicle stop and was shot and killed while being filmed by one of these cameras. It led to the arrest and conviction of the perpetrator. A flash gun will not only provide light for the photograph, but will serve as a reminder to the person being stopped that photos are being taken of his car and himself. Video cameras have also been installed in police patrol vehicles throughout the U.S. The film is used as documentation and evidence.

LIQUID TEAR GAS IRRITANT PROJECTOR

One of the most effective police weapons to be developed in the last thirty years is the liquid tear-gas irritant projector. This device is commonly referred to as "MACE" which is the trade name of the first liquid tear gas projector. This device allows tear gas to be used by the officer in the field as an offensive as well as defensive weapon. The projector is both silent and selective, an advantage not found in the general use of tear gas. Its effect is to temporarily and humanely subdue prisoners and agitators without the traumatic effects of the police baton or the revolver. It leaves no bruises or lacerations to tout around the community as an example of "police brutality." There are no harmful side effects, and the chemical is not toxic to any harmful degree. The effects last about 15 to 20 minutes. By using this device, a violent criminal,

drunk, or emotionally disturbed person can often be subdued without violence on the part of the officer. First unveiled at an International Association of Chiefs of Police conference, this device has been field tested by police departments and prisons across the country. All tests have shown it to be an effective weapon. It has become standard law enforcement equipment throughout the country.

The solution consists of a highly purified combination of liquid tear gas and a skin irritant. This formula takes effect instantly. It is either projected by pumping pressure as is used in the vest pocket model, or by a pressurized charge as is used in the larger device. The skin irritant part of the formula affects the sensitive nerve endings in the skin of the eye area, while the tear gas solution vaporizes to affect the eyes. It is highly selective, even when it is windy. An officer can pick out one person in a group without affecting the others to any extent. It does not have the effect of large area contamination common to regular tear gas. It is necessary, however, to hit the face of the suspect for the most effective results. Unlike other non-lethal weapons, Mace has the capability of firing many shots depending upon the model used.

VEST POCKET MODEL

The vest pocket model delivers eight one-second bursts. Its size makes it good for plain clothes work. It is also good as an off-duty weapon. It is effective up to 10 feet.

THE PRESSURIZED MACE CANISTER

The pressurized Mace cannister delivers from ten up to fifty one-second bursts of liquid tear gas depending upon the model used. The effective range of these liquid bursts is up to twenty feet. Each burst is capable of immobilizing a person. This device is very good when attacked by several persons. The author believes that his life was saved twice by using a can of pressurized Mace.

Fig. XII-5; Small MACE

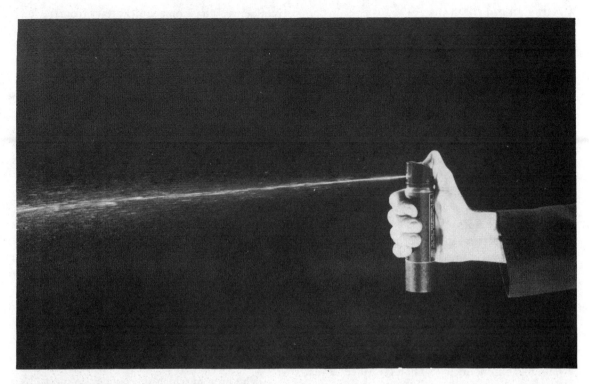

Fig. XII-6; Spray from pressurized MACE cannister

Fig. XII-7; The use of MACE in a dangerous situation   Courtesy: General Ordnance Equipment Corporation

Chapter Twelve

LIMITATIONS OF MACE

Mace is a lacrimal agent. It acts upon the lacrimal glands in the corner of the eyes to cause excessive tearing which, in effect, causes the subject to lose his ability to see. This makes most people very insecure and submissive. However, there are certain types of insanity that can cause these glands to become insensitive. In this case, Mace will not be effective. If the subject is under the influence of a strong narcotic, or PCP, it is possible that the Mace will not work. There have also been cases where a person was so intoxicated, or in such an extreme state of rage, that they were insensitive to normal pain, and therefore not affected by Mace. However, in most cases it will be effective

Mace should be tried first before more extreme measures are taken. An officer should use an escalation policy in the use of weapons. First try physical restraint (unless an officer can reasonably deduce that the size or mental state of the suspect would make it ineffective) Then try Mace. If that doesn't work, try the baton. If the baton doesn't work and it appears that there is a danger of great bodily harm or death, the firearm should be used.

PROBLEMS IN THE USE OF MACE

These devices are not foolproof. The face must be hit in order for the chemical to be most effective; it can be countered by a simple, clear plastic shield. If the officer is attacked by a group of assailants, they can charge with their heads down and attempt to grab the device. In such a case the officer could take evasive action by jumping out of the way, as in bull fighting. If the Mace gets on their clothes, it can have a delayed effect as the fumes rise to their eyes. Another problem is when the officer forgets how many shots have been used. This could be a problem if the officer is attacked by a large group and discovers that there are only two shots left. The newer Mace devices have a replaceable cartridge that can be placed in a glass of water and the level at which it floats indicates by a marked line how many shots are still left in the cartridge.

Although this is an effective and humane weapon in the police arsenal, its indiscriminate use can bring about intense public reaction as did the use of the electric "cattle prod" device. It should only be used when absolutely necessary. Because it is effective, it has come under attack from the "civil disobedience" groups, who cry "gas warfare" or some such terminology in an effort to turn public opinion against its use.

A problem involving the use of Mace is when four or five officers are involved in subduing a prisoner, and one of them uses Mace. Because the officers are so close, it has happened that the officer using the Mace hits another officer rather than the suspect. In one case the officer was wrestling with the suspect and Maced him. In the process of wrestling in close contact, the officer got some of the Mace on his own face and his eyes watered so badly that he could not see. A friend of the suspect then took the officer's baton and began beating him over the head and shoulders. Luckily other officers arrived in time to help the stricken officer.

NON-LETHAL WEAPONS

The area in which the police are most often criticized today occurs when an officer has to kill someone. There is always the question of whether or not the officer really had to shoot the suspect. If the suspect was a minority, the question of racism often arises. Chiefs of Police are often asked "Why don't your officers use non-lethal weapons?"

Few people really understand the pros and cons of non-lethal weapons. There are two types of non-lethal weapons. The first is to be used when the officer's life is in danger. The second is used when a suspect needs to be stopped, but the offense is not life threatening. Most criticism against the police relates to the first type. This occurs most often when the officer believes that the situation is life threatening, but later it is shown that it was not. For example, an officer honestly believes that a suspect is armed and is going to shoot him. He shoots and kills the suspect. It is then discovered that the suspect was, in fact, not armed. With deadly weapons, one cannot correct a mistake in judgment at a later time.

One of the major problems with non-lethal weapons is that the criminal does not carry them. His weapons are all deadly. If a non-lethal weapon were used against a criminal, it would probably not disable him immediately. As a result he would be able to quickly return fire on the officer with his deadly weapon. Most non-deadly weapons are often one-shot devices. If you miss with the first shot, "you're in a heap of trouble."

Despite the problems that must be worked out with a weapon of this type, there has never in police history been a greater need for such a device. Today, criticism of the police is prevalent and sometimes intense. Every time a person is killed by an officer, especially if from a minority group, it can become the spark that sets off a multi-million dollar riot in which many others are either killed or injured. Some of the non-lethal weapons that have been developed are:

(A) FOR NON-LIFE-THREATENING SITUATIONS, USUALLY AGAINST GROUPS

(1) **THE STUN GUN.** A shot filled beanbag is fired from a 40mm shell. It spreads out to a 4-inch pancake that travels about 100 miles an hour. The effective range is about 30-300 feet.

(2) **RICOCHET ROUND.** Each round is fired from a standard 12 gauge shotgun, but round consists of two hard, putty-like slugs which are fired at the ground about halfway to the victim. The slugs do not bounce, but ricochet about 18 inches from the ground hitting the person in the shins.

(3) **HONG KONG BATON.** Fires five wooden slugs that bounce off the pavement and smash into a crowd.

(4) **PLASTIC LOAD SHELLS.** Fired from a regular shotgun, these shells contain sand or plastic buckshot. They inflict severe pain, but no lasting injury.

(5) **RUBBER BULLETS OR SLUGS.** Sometimes these contain a dye that will later identify rioters.

(6) **TASER.** With the appearance of an oversized flashlight. It fires two inch-long barbs which are connected to a battery by long copper and stainless steel wires. The barbs can emit an electrical charge of 50,000 volts which immobilizes the victim but does not kill him. It

can make him unconscious. It is bulky and not too accurate unless used at very short distances. Its sale is controlled by the Bureau of Alcohol and Firearms.

PROBLEMS WITH IMMOBILIZING OR STUN GUNS

Because of the length and size of such a weapon, it could not be used as an emergency "quick draw" weapon. In its present form, it would have to be used as an auxiliary weapon. It could be carried in the police car, or in another holster on the officer's gunbelt.

(B) FOR LIFE THREATENING SITUATIONS

(1) **SEDATIVE SYRINGE DART.** This is the type of device used to sedate dangerous animals. A syringe, containing a sedative, is fired from a large-bore rifle. When the animal is sedated, it is removed to a secure container. The problem with this device is that it can take minutes for the sedative to take effect. During that time a dangerous criminal can do serious harm to others. For best effect, it must hit the target in a prime location. Unlike animals, humans wear clothes and other garments, especially in the winter, that could deflect the dart. Unlike animals, humans will take cover so most of their body is hidden, and the target area is greatly reduced. Weapons of this nature, when perfected, may be an added step in the direction of professional law enforcement.

(2) **LASER-AIMED AUTOMATIC RIFLE** This is a weapon in the police arsenal that is both extremely lethal and at the same time more humane. It can fire 30 of its 22 caliber bullets in one second with the same impact as 11 men shooting at the same target with .45 caliber pistols. It can chop down a telephone pole. It is considered humane because, when it is properly aimed at a person, there is a 3-inch red dot on that person exactly where the bullets will go if the trigger is pulled. The red dot is caused by the helium-neon gas laser. Once the officer sees the red dot on the suspect, he or she knows that there is no chance of missing and hitting an innocent bystander. The firearm is so accurate, that

wherever the red laser dot appears, that is where the bullets will hit. If aimed at the suspect's face, the laser will also temporarily blind him. This increases the chances of his giving up.

This weapon also allows the officer to wound rather than kill. If the red laser dot is on the arms or legs, the officer can pull the trigger and that is where the bullets will go. This reduces the chance that the officer might accidentally kill the suspect.

The company that manufactures these weapons maintains very strict control over who possesses them. They will not sell them to non-law-enforcement agencies. However, this does not preclude the possibility of some of them being stolen.

OFFICER SURVIVAL

Officer survival has become an area of great concern today for both police officers and administrators. In our democratic society, police officers cannot initiate an original dangerous act. They can only react to a situation initiated by the criminal. In cases involving a shooting, officers must wait until they are fired upon before they can return fire. One exception to this would be when the criminal has his firearm drawn and pointed at the officer.

The International Association of Chiefs of Police and the FBI have both been maintaining statistics in this area. With an increase in population and the number of new officers, it should be expected that the number of officers killed in the line of duty will increase. This was true for the 1980's, but in the 1990's it seems to be leveling off.

AMBUSHES

There is no one hundred percent protection against an ambush. There are, however, certain procedures that will greatly improve an officer's chances for survival. Officers, especially those who work in large cities, need to develop certain habits and conditioned responses. Then, if they are ambushed, they will react automatically and immediately in the proper way.

Officers are taught not to follow regular patrol patterns or always have coffee at the same time and place. This is especially true when an officer works on a beat where ambushes occur or are likely to occur. In getting out of the car, the officers should not be so close together that they can both be picked off quickly by the same sniper. Yet they should not be so far apart that they could not offer each other backup in case of an attack. They should maintain a distance which will allow them to keep sight of each other.

There are two theories on the immediate action to be taken when under attack. One is that if the officers are still in the car, they should get out of the area immediately and then call for assistance. This is the safest action for the peace officers. However, if the officers are out of the car, they should take cover where they are best protected. They should then return just enough fire to pin the sniper down until specialized anti-sniper units can arrive.

These types of attacks on police officers are thankfully not common in all cities. They seem to be centered in particular urban communities or districts within certain cities. Criminologists who have studied urban crime and violence indicate that unless something is done to relieve the frustrations of inner city dwellers, riots and ambushes will become a common element of city life. The uniformed officer is a visible representative of the government. Unfortunately, he or she will take the brunt of any social unrest. They will be the "Fine blue line."

PROTECTION FROM SNIPER AMBUSH

It is quite difficult to counter such a diabolical plot as an ambush. The key is good police and government intelligence information. Most sniper attacks occur when someone calls for police assistance. Some measures that will help are as follows:

First, an alert communications officer or desk sergeant, upon receiving a call for assistance, can sometimes sense that something is different about the call. This suspicion should be transmitted to the patrol officer. Often this comes in the form of a hunch. Some calls originate in certain specialized areas such as a ghetto or barrio where the perpetrator feels that he has some local protection and some familiarity with escape routes. Sometimes the instructions as to exactly where the officer should go seem too detailed for a normal call for assistance. A routine "sizing up" of the immediate surroundings before entering a building doesn't take long. It can be a good investment. This is especially true at night.

If there have been other sniper attacks in this area, and cars are available, a backup unit should be assigned to stay back about half a block and view the area with binoculars. Another should cruise the area to look for suspicious circumstances. Although such an incident is difficult to prevent, the fact that the police saturate the area immediately and spare no effort to arrest or shoot the perpetrators, will help act as a preventive measure.

SWAT TYPE TEAMS

When an officer has come under sniper fire, special police sniper teams should be requested immediately. These teams are highly specialized groups that have received extensive training. They are equipped with specialized equipment, including telescopic weapons, and have been very successful in controlling dangerous situations without killing the suspect. They operate in small teams which can be combined into squads or platoons when needed. The FBI has special schools where officers are trained for this type of duty.

Many of these units call themselves SWAT teams (Special Weapons and Tactics units). Other agencies use terms like MERGE (Mobile Emergency Response Groups). There are now television programs that use SWAT experiences for their plots.

POLICE OFFICERS SHOOTING POLICE OFFICERS

One of the saddest types of police officer shootings is one where an officer is accidentally shot by another officer. Those studying police tactical procedures wonder why it hasn't happened more often. This can happen in many ways. Some of the following are examples:

(1) **CROSSFIRE.** Because of panic firing, especially at night, it is unfortunately common for a situation like this to occur. After a long pursuit, a large number of officers finally surround the armed suspect. When the suspect shoots at one of them, they all open fire with everything they have, seemingly unaware that there are officers on the other side of the suspect. The authors are aware of one situation involving an officer shooting where the suspect escaped and was finally surrounded by about fifty officers from varying jurisdictions. When the suspect refused to give up, all fifty officers, who were in a circle around the suspect, began shooting their firearms. St. Michael, the guardian saint for policemen, was working overtime that night. None of the officers were hit by the tremendous crossfire.

(2) **POLICE OFFICERS WORKING UNDERCOVER.** Officers who work narcotic and other investigative details often have beards and dress shabbily. When the officer is wearing a beard, even friends might not recognize him. There have been numerous incidents where officers, responding to bar fights, have mistaken undercover officers as perpetrators and have attacked them with their batons. Sometimes their disguises are so good that even their ex-partners would have difficulty in recognizing them. The key here is proper communication. It is important to notify beat officers of any undercover activity on their beats.

In Houston, Texas, an officer responded to a report of shots being fired in a bar. Someone mentioned that the action was in the rest-room. The officer barged into the rest-room with his firearm drawn. Inside was an undercover officer holding a gun on some suspects. When the door burst open, he instinctively turned to the door with his firearm in hand. The uniformed officer shot the undercover officer holding the gun before he had the chance to identify himself as a police officer.

(3) **LACK OF INTER-AGENCY COMMUNICATION IN TRAINING SESSIONS** It is common for an agency to conduct realistic role-playing training exercises without notifying other agencies and/or other divisions within their own agency. This has resulted in unfortunate and embarrassing confrontations.

In one case, police training officers were conducting officer survival training at the county fairgrounds using weapons containing blank ammunition. A highway patrol officer just happened to be driving by and observed that one of the student officers was chasing an instructor dressed as a suspect. Blanks were being fired. The highway patrol officer stopped his car, jumped the fence and began also firing at the "suspect" but with real ammunition. Luckily no one was shot. The highway patrol officer had received no information about the training session despite the fact that his beat was in that area.

In a similar situation, a juvenile officer of an agency was driving by the location of a training exercise. He was unaware that a training exercise was in progress. He notified radio control (who also had not been notified of the exercise), and then jumped out of the car with his firearm drawn and proceeded to assist in the apprehension. Again, luckily, no one was shot.

There have also been cases of officers injured when blanks have been fired too close to their faces. This is usually the fault of the training officers. In training, safety should be top priority.

(4) **FAILURE TO NOTIFY OTHER AGENCIES OF OPERATIONS CLOSE TO THEIR AREA** Those planning a tactical operation or arrest exercise should inform all agencies in the area of their general plans.

This happened in Largo, Florida where the police failed to notify the Sheriff's department with dangerous results.

GENERAL OFFICER SURVIVAL INFORMATION

Based on considerable past studies and experience, training officers have come up with some basic tactics that will assist the patrol officer in staying alive in dangerous situations. Some considerations are:

PERSONAL CONTACT

It is not just any person who tries to kill police officers, or to kidnap or hold them hostage. He is different from the general population. In most cases, he is a person of dangerous mentality who can be both vicious and calculating. His law is the "law of the jungle." He believes that survival of the fittest is the only law. He will brag to his friends about the fact that he was able to steal a little old lady's pension check, a thing that most people would find reprehensible. To him it shows that he is a more capable person.

THE CRIMINAL His action is usually involved with a crime of some sort. His original purpose is to commit a crime. If, for some reason this objective is thwarted, his new objective is to escape by any means possible.

He is often a socio/psychopath whose values and conscience are different from those of the average person. He has usually spent time in jail or prison and is not anxious to return. If there is more than one person involved, the others will usually go along with the one who is the most vicious. In many cases it is out of fear. He is usually the leader.

THE EMOTIONALLY DISTURBED PERSON This person's motivation is usually based on fear. It is a fear caused by a mental delusion that some person or group is about to harm or kill him. As a result, he must do everything in his power to counter this. Even to the point of killing one or more persons. He is usually familiar with the uniformed officer. This is the person who has taken him into custody in the past. This is the person who is responsible for his being taken to a mental institution. Studies show us that of all the officers shot, emotionally disturbed persons are responsible for only 10%.

It is difficult to talk with this type of person on a logical basis because his thinking processes are presently warped. However by listening to him you can usually determine what his basic mental delusions are. From this the officer can then plan a course of action. It should be based on the assumption that these delusions are actually true. Too many officers try to convince this person to take a course of action based on reality. To the emotionally disturbed person, the delusions are very real and no amount of argument from an officer can convince him otherwise.

If handled correctly, the emotionally disturbed person will often go along with an offer of protection because he sometimes associates the police with protection. Naturally this would not apply if he has had some prior negative experiences with the police.

CAUSES OF OFFICER DEATHS

Pierce R. Brooks, in his book <u>Officer Down, Code Three</u>, lists ten deadly errors that he has found to be the major causes of officer deaths. These not only apply to the United States, but to all countries. The ten are listed as follows:

(1) **Failure to Maintain Proficiency and Care of Weapon, Vehicle and Equipment.** If you have learned to shoot, will your firearm respond when you pull the trigger? Will your vehicle respond when you need it?

(2) **Improper Search and Use of Handcuffs.** Many police fatalities here.

(3) **Sleepy or Asleep.** How well can you react?

(4) **Relaxing too Soon, or Letting Guard Down.** Usually at those "false" silent alarm calls.

(5) **Missing the Danger Signs.** Miss or don't recognize them; they can be fatal either way.

(6) **Taking a Bad Position.** Write a citation or an FI card with your back turned to the subject. Or, while confronting a barricaded gunman, be casual or curious from your place of concealment rather than careful and cautious from a place of cover.

(7) **Failure to Watch Suspects' Hands.** Where else can the subject hold a gun, or a knife, or an impact weapon?

(8) **Tombstone Courage.** Why wait for a backup?

(9) **Preoccupation.** Worrying about personal problems while on duty may be a deadly way to solve them.

(10) **Apathy.** A deadly disease for the cynical veteran police officer.

To these ten the authors would like to add an eleventh:

(11) **Making Deadly Assumptions.** Rationalizing an observation by thinking of some legitimate reason for why the condition exists or the person is engaging in a particular action. If your assumption is wrong, you can be DEAD WRONG.

SOFT BODY ARMOR

No one can argue the importance of soft body armor in view of the increasing number of attacks upon peace officers. However the best type and make of soft body armor for patrol duty has caused a continued and heated argument. Rather than taking sides in this issue, this chapter will cover it from a general standpoint.

The major considerations in the use of soft body armor should be the practical versus the theoretical. Naturally the best type of body armor would be rigid, high quality steel. Yet from a practical standpoint, the patrol officer could not function wearing body armor of such specifications. The knights who fought in the Crusades were at a great disadvantage because of the limitations of their rigid armor. If they were knocked off their horses they were unable to get up.

Despite various preferences, it is generally accepted that the best type of armor is a soft body armor. It is generally made from a synthetic fiber similar to Kevlar which is woven into a cloth.

The fact that an officer was shot while his body armor was in the trunk of his patrol car, brings up a very important consideration. It is more important than the argument as to which armor vest has the best stopping power. That consideration is simply "what good is body armor if it is not worn?" If a body armor is too heavy, too uncomfortable, or too hot to wear normally, will it be worn? What if, when the armor was worn, it interfered with the normal functions of the officer's duties. If this happened, it is doubtful that the patrol officer is going to wear the armor.

The answer then seems to lie in finding a "happy medium." Today there are light weight, flexible bodily armors that are good enough to prevent fatal injury. They can result in some minor injury, but they offer practical comfort which is an important plus. There can be no doubt that these vests have saved many lives, and that officers have lost their lives because they have failed to wear them.

BULLETPROOF CLIP BOARDS

Another safety device that could assist an officer who is suddenly surprised by an armed person during a traffic stop is the bulletproof clip. It is best at short ranges because it is then able to deflect most angle shots. Most of these clipboards can stop a .38 caliber bullet at four inches.

THE MAGNA TRIGGER SAFETY RING

A new device that won the IACP award for police safety devices after it had undergone extensive testing by their Police Equipment and Technology Center is the Magna Trigger Safety Ring. This device was developed by Mr. Joseph Smith, of Sunnyvale, California. He had read of the increasing number of accidental shootings and wanted to do something about it. He was also concerned about the FBI report showing that one of every six officers shot was shot with his own gun. After reading newspaper articles that stated "the drunk and belligerent suspect took a policeman's gun and shot three of the officer's comrades" (Milwaukee, Wis.). "The officers took him to a conference room for questioning, but he apparently wrestled Marks' gun away and shot both officers through the head" (Oakland, Calif.). Smith decided that he would do something about the problem. He developed a device that makes it almost impossible for officers to be shot with their own guns.

Basically the device is a safety lock that prevents the firearm from being fired unless the person holding the firearm is wearing a special magnetic ring that releases the lock. Mr. Smith spent years developing this device, even selling his home to finance the research. The firearm has to be re-tooled to a certain extent which in no way affects its firing ability. Any model firearm can be so adapted. The major disadvantage is that the officer must give up the firearm for a few days while it is machined and modified.

The natural question is "if the suspect obtains a ring, can he fire the gun?" The answer to this is yes. However, studies have shown that the majority of officers killed by their own firearms have been in situations that were unplanned. The next question is "What if the officer is wounded in the hand containing the magnetic ring?" When the officer has the weapon modified, two rings are issued, one for each hand. The magnetic ring is made of Samarium Cobalt, and does not lose its power. The locking device is inside the weapon, and cannot be easily removed. If this device were to be installed during the manufacturing process, it would add only about $45 to the cost of each firearm.

Apart from the protection of police officers, this device could save the lives of untold numbers of children who accidentally shoot a playmate or themselves with daddy's gun. Many officers with children are concerned about having firearms in the house. One way to secure a stored weapon from being accidentally fired is to lock a pair of handcuffs behind the trigger and around the trigger guard. This will prevent the trigger from being pulled all the way back. The keys must be kept secured, however. Children are not attracted to keys as much as weapons.

STATISTICS ON OFFICER SURVIVAL

Probably the most important single statistic dealing with officer survival is that 85% of all officers who gave up their weapons were later shot. Knowledge of these odds should make officers hesitant to give up their weapons. Other significant statistics are:

(1) 73% of officers shot were accompanied by one or more other officers, THEY WERE NOT ALONE.

(2) 28% of officers shot were dealing with criminals in buildings (more training is needed in the proper tactics of building searches.)

(3) 90% of the people who assaulted officers had been drinking prior to the attack according to the National Association of State Directors of Law Enforcement Training.

(4) 37% of officers shot were answering "robbery or burglary in progress" calls. This was more than any other type of call.

(5) Next to the above, the most dangerous type of call for officers being shot was the "disturbance" call. (25%)

(6) 80% of the officers shot were in uniform.

(7) The most dangerous shift is midnight to 8:00 a.m., and the next most dangerous is the 4:00 p.m. to midnight shift.

(8) Carelessness per se was not a major factor in most shootings. Officers made mistakes, but at the time they felt that they had made the right decision. It was not just carelessness.

(9) More officers were shot in business sections of town than any other area.

(10) The average officer shot was 31 years old, had 5 years of service, and was shot at a distance of less than 10 feet.

PRE-PLANNING FOR EMERGENCY SITUATIONS

WHEN THE SUSPECT HAS A HOSTAGE

First consider why he has the hostage. Next try to evaluate something about his personality. Usually, the purpose for a hostage is to facilitate an escape. In some cases, however, it gives the hostage taker a needed sense of power and importance. Deals with this type of person should be avoided if possible. If any deals are made, very little of the deal should be made based on trusting this person. Since the deal will involve the safety of the hostage, the officer must learn to bargain for as much of an advantage as possible, keeping in mind the ultimate safety of the hostage. It lays a terrible responsibility at the feet of the officer since the suspect can be playing a bluffing game. The stakes are too high to

involve second-guessing. As a result, it is best to call for an expert hostage negotiator, if one is available. Each department should have at least one trained negotiator. In the meantime, be a good listener.

Bargaining is also a delaying factor. Time usually works against the suspect. He should be told that the officer's superior is the only one authorized to make bargains. This is a good delaying technique. The line should be definitely drawn when the criminal suspect uses the hostage as a means of demanding that officers disarm themselves. Such an action can only compound the problem. The suspect should be told that absolutely, under no conditions, will the officers disarm themselves. If the hostage is killed, the suspect will definitely be shot to death. Since most suspects are gamblers, the odds, as he sees them, would deter such an action. There are some hostage takers who actually want to be shot to death. They want to commit suicide but are afraid to do it themselves. However, they are somewhat rare. Their usual action is to run out toward the officers with firearm in hand.

HOSTAGE NEGOTIATIONS

Over the years, the techniques used to handle hostage takers has changed greatly. When hostage taking first became common, many police leaders were military veterans. It was natural for them to take the "military assault" approach when dealing with hostage takers. The police would simply charge the hostage taker with guns firing. With this type of approach, it was common for the hostage to be killed, either by the hostage taker or the heavy police firepower. The hostage taker and one or two police officers were probably killed as well. Today the police use a unique technique in handling hostage situations. No longer do we have the "Gang Busters" or military assault approach. After the massacre of Israeli athletes at the Munich Olympics in 1972 by terrorist hostage takers, it was decided that a new approach must be developed. In New York City, where hostage taking was probably more common, Dr. Harvey Schlossberg, a police officer for 12 years, and the Director of Psychological Services for the New York Police Department, developed an approach to deal with persons who hold hostages. His approach was called "dynamic inactivity," and is based on the premise that if given enough time, one of four things will happen:

(1) The suspect will fall asleep.

(2) The hostage will be able to escape.

(3) Having ventilated his problems in negotiating, the suspect will surrender.

(4) In time, the suspect's anxiety level will drop to a level where he will listen to reason.

Dr. Schlossberg also has some suggestions about the negotiations:

(1) Don't call relatives or a pastor. They are often the cause of the problem.

(2) Use an impartial negotiator.

(3) Don't try to use hostages for help. They are often unable or unwilling.

(4) Never give the hostage-holder something for nothing, such as a cigarette or something to drink. Condition him to bargain for everything. Give him something in exchange for one of the hostages.

(5) Never place a time limit on conditions. Don't tell him "We'll give you exactly one hour to surrender or else."

(6) Try to initiate the first contact by telephone or loudspeaker. When he has had time to cool down, it might then be advisable to stage a face-to-face contact.

(7) If you do make face-to-face contact, wear plain clothes with lightweight body armor.

Dr. Allen Bristow of Los Angeles State University did a study on hostage negotiation based on limited reports for a 5 year period. He found that there were usually five reasons for a person taking a hostage. They were:

(1) To escape arrest.

(2) To promote political ideals. It gets a lot of free publicity.

(3) For reasons of political extortion (release certain political prisoners or else.)

(4) The hostage-holder is emotionally disturbed.

(5) The hostage-holder wants to commit suicide, but is afraid to do it himself. He hopes the police will shoot him.

His study seemed to indicate that hostage negotiation does work. In 79% of hostage-negotiation incidents, the hostages were released unharmed. If the persons on the hostage-negotiation team have been specially trained, there is even less possibility of hostages being harmed. Although the study showed 100% effectiveness in this regard, the sample was too small to be statistically significant.

Training and discipline are very important. One "hot-head" officer can ruin the whole operation. It is always best, if possible, to use trained teams to handle these situations. Regular patrol officers should be assigned to perimeter control.

WHEN THE SUSPECT HAS NO HOSTAGE, BUT HAS A SUPERIOR TACTICAL POSITION.

Through thought conditioning, officers must, at a previous time, have made up their minds as to what they will do in such a situation. Decisions made under pressure, during an emergency, are usually not the best. If the suspect wanted to kill the officer right then he would have done so. He is seeking some further advantage. Think about what it might be and try to use it to your own advantage.

When officers give up their guns, we know that there is an 85% chance that the suspect will later "execute" them. With this statistic in mind, the best rule is NEVER GIVE UP YOUR WEAPON. The officer who gives the suspect his or her firearm also gives him a hostage and probably a life. If the situation does result in an exchange of fire, the officer should consider the following factors that are in his favor:

(a) The suspect might miss.
(b) His firearm might misfire.
(c) If shot, not all wounds are fatal (all executions are).

(d) In an exchange of fire, the suspect is taking a chance of getting shot. (Although not true, most people think police officers are all expert shots). Officers should wear their shooting badges on their uniforms. Even if the badge is just for "marksman" rating, it can have a definite psychological effect and may help back up a verbal bluff that the officer is an excellent shot.

If there are two or more officers, the suspect should be told that he can only get one officer. The other will surely shoot him. He should be told to drop his gun and save his own life.

WHEN AN OFFICER IS SHOT

There is some controversy on this point. Some departments have established the policy that an officer should forget the natural tendency to stay with a wounded partner, and should instead call for help and an ambulance and immediately pursue the perpetrator. The reasoning is as follows:

(a) The perpetrator may harm others.

(b) No one is better able to pursue and apprehend the perpetrator than the partner.

(c) If it is a well-known department policy, suspects will know that they will be relentlessly pursued under any condition. This may have a deterrent effect.

(d) In most cities, ambulances and other patrol units can respond to assist the wounded officer in a very short time.

On the other side of the coin is the fact that if the officer is unconscious and bleeding, he or she could easily bleed to death without the partner staying to apply pressure to the wound. Sound judgment and discretion should help resolve this controversy. Still an officer must be able to overcome the feeling of guilt about leaving or "abandoning" a partner. If the wound is not serious and the officer is conscious, he or she can apply pressure to the wound. Citizens or witnesses offering to help may also alter the situation. In these cases immediate pursuit could be the best answer.

ROLE-PLAYING OF DIFFICULT SITUATIONS

Officers, in their training sessions, could use role-playing techniques. If they are repeated often enough, it would help establish memory or habit patterns that would condition each officer's response. The conditioned officer would then respond in a proper manner when actually faced with both the pressures and decision responsibilities of a real life situation. The officer's mental processes will recall the prior decision made in the role-playing situation and use that as a basis for the present decision.

In any role-playing situation involving the use of real firearms, each member of the group, and the instructor, should examine the firearm carefully to be sure it is not loaded. As an extra precaution, special guns may be used that have the barrels welded shut and the grips painted red so that other guns won't be accidentally substituted. Welding the barrel shut at the cylinder end and leaving the end toward the "victim" open would lend realism to the exercise. People who have been held up at gunpoint have commented upon the traumatic experience of looking down what seems to be a very large barrel.

Although realism in role-playing is important, safety cannot be stressed enough. One of the finest police training divisions in the United States had a very tragic shooting when somehow a loaded firearm ended up in a role-playing exercise.

DISCRETION IN DANGEROUS SITUATIONS

There are two old sayings that are very appropriate for patrol officers. First "Fools go where angels fear to tread" and second, "Discretion is the better part of valor." The officer who must take unnecessary chances just to show the suspect or other officers that he or she is not really afraid should seek some professional counseling to resolve this problem.

An officer should never be afraid of being afraid. Fear is a necessary part of the human response cycle and serves an important purpose. It is not synonymous with cowardice. Some officers show fear more than others, but all police officers are subject to fear.

Let us illustrate an example of discretion. Several years ago, an officer on patrol, working alone, stopped a suspicious car in an isolated area. When he talked to the three passengers he became convinced that something was definitely wrong. He then noticed that they were moving out in an effort to out-flank him. He quickly smiled and told the suspects that everything seemed OK and for them to go on their way. He then returned to his patrol car and called for help and a road block.

The suspects were later stopped with appropriate personnel. It was then found that they were escapees who had recently committed several felonies and were in a stolen car that had not yet been reported. All of the suspects were heavily armed. They later admitted that they were trying to outflank the first officer so they could kill him. Had he tried to handle the situation alone the first time he probably would not have lived to tell about it.

SALESMANSHIP IN NEGOTIATION

Every day of the year people are sold things that they don't necessarily want, so we know that salesmanship is a technique that can and does work. An officer's life may be placed in danger often. For example, someone is holding a gun on that officer. In cases like this, the officer should try many different subterfuges and techniques to eliminate the danger. Salesmanship is one of the safest.

The first step is to determine the suspect's immediate needs, and then his long range needs. It is these that usually motivate his actions. Any form of conversation is also a means of stalling for time. Time is nearly always on the side of the officer. The following approaches should be attempted in an effort to talk the subject into surrendering.

(1) **RELIGIOUS APPROACH.** The officer might ask if he is a religious person, and if a minister or priest could possibly be called in to mediate the situation.

(2) **RELATIVES OR LOVED ONES.** People do things for others that they would not do for themselves. The mere mention of their mothers or loved ones could cause their thinking or attitude to change. The officer should tell the suspect not to do anything that might further hurt or bring shame to the family. In some cases this subject can cause them great agitation. Here the subject of conversation should be immediately changed.

(3) **LOGICAL APPROACH.** If the suspect does not appear intoxicated or emotionally diturbed, the officer might try a logical approach. This should be based on what the suspect hopes to gain by all of this. A good approach should be based on his present fears and needs. He should be sold on the obvious merit of giving himself up. Other pointers could be "Don't make things worse by unnecessary killing. Nothing will be solved by harming innocent victims. You will get fair treatment. You will not be hurt if you surrender. We will see that someone hears your side of the story. Nothing good can come of your present actions" and so on.

(4) **EMOTIONAL APPEAL.** If cold logic does not work, any number of emotional appeals can be made. Religion and family can both be very emotional topics for many people. He could be told that it takes courage to make the right decision in a tight situation like this. That he is too intelligent to throw away his life for something like this.

(5) **CONVINCE HIM OF THE FUTILITY OF THE SITUATION.**

Some of the points to be brought up are:

(a) Escape is impossible.
(b) The area is completely surrounded.
(c) The Sniper Squad has him in their telescopic sights.
(d) The police are heavily armed.
(e) The others will absolutely not make deals for one officer's life, and will shoot the suspect if he fires his weapon.
(f) The officers have bulletproof vests (this will detract from the overall value of his weapon).

COUNTERMEASURES: PREVENTIVE AND EVASIVE ACTION

Officers who find themselves covered with a gun and are told to surrender their weapons can do one or all of the following, but under no circumstances should they give up their weapons. An exception might be when the officer has a hideaway firearm that could be drawn when the suspect is off his guard. There can be other situations, but they must serve a very definite advantageous purpose.

(1) Look off in one direction and yell. This will not only startle the suspect but will probably cause him to look in the same direction to see what is there. It is an old ruse, but very hard to resist. This is especially so if the suspect is emotionally disturbed.

(2) Shout to nonexistent officers to hold their fire for a while.

(3) Throw something at the suspect. Watch for him to look away for any reason. Just staring over his shoulder can cause him to do so.

(4) Place your hand on your heart and pretend to collapse.

(5) If the firearm is in the suspect's right hand, kick his gun hand and then jump to the left. A firearm held in the right hand usually jerks to the left or to your right.

(6) If close enough, quickly slap the firearm in the direction of his palm. This can usually be done before he can pull the trigger.

(7) If close enough, grab the cylinder of the revolver. If it is not already cocked, it will not fire if the cylinder will not turn. If it is cocked, jam a finger between the hammer and the pin. Wrap the rest of your hand around the cylinder. With help from your other hand, bend the firearm toward the palm of his hand, removing the firearm from his grasp.

(8) If close enough, and the firearm is a military type .45 caliber automatic, a hand pushed against the barrel will engage the safety device and prevent it from firing.

(9) Use a pencil or pen to stab the suspect in the eye or jugular vein.

(10) Pretend to surrender and take off your gunbelt. Instead of letting it drop, swing it at the suspect's gun hand toward the back of the hand. The gunbelt is quite heavy and can easily knock the firearm from the suspect's hand. If it doesn't, it can injure the hand so that the firearm cannot be properly fired.

(11) If the officer has a "hideaway" gun, it should be used at the first opportunity WITHOUT ANY WARNING. This can be difficult for an officer who has been raised with ethical standards and has a sense of "fair play." Unfortunately, any other way could cost the officer's life. That price is too high to pay.

THE PUBLIC SAFETY OFFICER'S BENEFITS ACT OF 1976

The federal government, recognizing the dangers involved in public safety work, has supported this recognition by passing the Public Safety Officers' Benefits Act of 1976. This act authorizes the payment of $100,000.00 to the families of peace officers and firemen who have given up their lives in the line of duty. It applies to any public safety officer, regular or reserve, who died or suffered an injury that later resulted in death, while on duty. Although it can never replace the loss of a loved one, it does serve as one indication that our elected leaders do recognize the service performed by these officers. The original amount was $50,000, but congress can and has increased this amount. Often on a yearly basis.

THE NEWHALL SHOOTING INCIDENT

Although the Newhall shooting incident occurred some years past, it can still serve as an example that officers need constant training and should develop good survival habits.

This incident started next to a gas station in the Newhall area, just north of Los Angeles. Four Highway Patrol officers lay dead from gunshot wounds. In the prior four and one half minutes, more than forty shots were fired. Fifteen of them by three of the four dead officers, and the rest by two heavily armed suspects in a vehicle stop. The incident occurred in a well-lighted area. there were over thirty witnesses, and neither the first, second, or third two-officer patrol cars involved were caught completely by surprise.

Throughout the West, officers received the news with disbelief. Was it an ambush? How could this possibly have happened? A short rundown of this incident is given in the hope that from this tragedy, we can find some lessons that will save the lives of future police officers.

At 11:20 p.m., a red Pontiac violated the right of way of a car containing a serviceman and his wife. The serviceman pulled alongside the Pontiac and reprimanded the driver, who in turn pointed a revolver at him and called him a "smart punk." The serviceman hurriedly drove off and in about 15 minutes found a phone booth where his wife reported the incident, giving the license number and description of the car. A check by the Highway Patrol revealed that it was registered in the south Los Angeles area, and that there were no wants on the car. Since Newhall is a rural area where some hunting is done, and reports of persons brandishing weapons is not uncommon, the incident was broadcast to the Highway Patrol unit in the immediate vicinity.

Seventeen minutes later, at 11:45 p.m., unit 78-8, with Officer Gore driving and officer Frago as his partner, spotted the suspect vehicle and requested backup, which would indicate that they felt it was something more than a traffic stop.

The Pontiac, containing two male adults, pulled off the freeway into a well-lighted gas station/restaurant complex which contained at least thirty persons who were to become witnesses to the tragic incident.

Units 78-12 and 78-16R responded to the backup request, but when unit 78-12 reported that they were almost there, unit 78-16R abandoned the response and returned to patrol.

As the Pontiac pulled off the freeway, unit 78-8 displayed its red light and stopped the vehicle at the driveway approach to the gas station. Officer

Frago turned the white spotlight on the Pontiac and then exited the patrol vehicle with his shotgun, taking a position at the side of the vehicle's right front headlight. The driver, Officer Gore, drew his .357 Magnum and went to the front left of the patrol vehicle where he leaned over the fender for protection with his firearm extended. Officer Gore then ordered the suspects three times in a loud and clear voice to "get out with your hands up," and "We told you to get your hands up." This was certainly no ordinary vehicle stop. We must assume that the officers saw some furtive movements on the part of the suspects, probably involving the guns that they were carrying.

The suspect driver got out of the car and was ordered to lean against the car in a search position. The passenger suspect remained in the car. At this point, Officer Gore moved forward to begin a search of the driver suspect. At the same time, Officer Frago moved up to the right front door of the suspect vehicle with his shotgun at "point arms." As he reached the door, it was believed that the passenger suspect suddenly opened it and produced a gun. Witnesses heard Officer Frago yell "hold it." However, in the criminal trial, it was brought out that Officer Frago's fingerprints were on the door handle which would indicate that he opened the door himself. The passenger suspect quickly turned in his seat and fired two shots from a four inch .357 Magnum, killing Officer Frago instantly.

At the sound of the shots, Officer Gore turned toward the passenger suspect and found he was now under fire from him. He immediately returned the fire but missed. With his attention distracted, the driver suspect drew a two inch .38 revolver from his waist and began firing at Officer Gore, killing him instantly with two shots in the chest.

At this moment (11:56 p.m.) unit 78-12, with Officer Pence driving and Officer Alleyn as his partner, arrived at the scene and found themselves under fire. They immediately called in a code 30 — "shots fired" to which both Highway Patrol and Sheriff's units responded. The passenger suspect emptied his revolver and went back to the car to get another .45 automatic, but this time he exited on the driver's side. At the same time, the driver suspect picked up a 12 guage sawed-off shotgun from the car and began firing at unit 78-12.

Officer Pence, the driver of unit 78-12, got out of the car and, using the left front door as a shield, returned fire. At the same time, Officer Alleyn exited on the right side with a shotgun. He chambered a round and moved up to the rear of the first patrol car. From there he moved to the open right front door of unit 78-8 and fired three rounds penetrating the rear window of the Pontiac and causing a slight wound on the passenger suspect's forehead. Finding his shotgun empty (he apparently forgot that he had one in the chamber when he moved up and cranked out a live round the first time) he withdrew to the rear of unit 78-8 and began firing with his service revolver. As Officer Alleyn moved to the rear of the police vehicle, the driver suspect outflanked him and mortally wounded him with the sawed-off shotgun. At the same time, Officer Pence was exchanging fire with the passenger suspect who was near the left front of the suspect vehicle, using it for cover.

At this time, Officer Pence ran out of ammunition, ejected the spent cartridges, and retreated to the rear of his vehicle (78-12) to reload. He was just finishing reloading when the passenger suspect moved up along the left side of the patrol car, raised himself up over the fender, and fired at close range, hitting Officer Pence four times and mortally wounding him. The driver suspect then took Officer Frago's revolver from the fallen officer's holster and began firing at officer Alleyn, even though he was down and mortally wounded.

A passing motorist saw the gun battle and, after parking his car, ran over to drag the fallen Officer Alleyn out of the line of fire. He grabbed a shotgun, but it was empty. He then took Officer Alleyn's revolver and fired a shot at the driver suspect. It hit the suspects' car and splintered, with fragments hitting the suspect in the chest. He tried to fire again, but the gun was empty. Then he heard a loud report and turned to see the passenger suspect standing over the downed Officer Pence yelling something like "I got you now," and then shooting him through the back of the head, killing him instantly.

At 11:59 p.m., unit 78-16R arrived and was immediately fired upon. When the officers returned fire, the suspects jumped into their car, accelerated through the service station and drove about 150 yards. They then abandoned the vehicle and ran off in different directions.

The driver suspect followed a river bed until he came upon a parked pick-up camper containing a sleeping male adult. He ordered him out of the camper and fired a shot into the side of the camper with the revolver which he had taken from Officer Frago. It was the last shot, so when the owner of the camper came out, the driver suspect beat him severely with the empty revolver. He then drove off in the camper. When the owner of the camper reported the incident to the police, a Sheriff's unit set up a road block and stopped the camper with the suspect in it. He came out with his hands up and surrendered.

The other suspect escaped detection until 4:45 a.m., when he entered a home and took one of the occupants hostage. The house was surrounded and through the use of the telephone, deputies were able to engage the suspect in a conversation and try to convince him to release the hostage. he talked about killing Officer Frago and stated "*He got careless, so I wasted him.*" The suspect later released the hostage, but refused to give himself up. When officers finally charged the house, he took the Highway Patrol shotgun and blew his own head off.

When the suspect vehicle was first stopped, it contained the following weapons: one .38 caliber revolver, one four-inch .357 Magnum revolver, two .45 caliber automatics, one 12 guage sawed-off shotgun, one .44 Magnum Ruger automatic rifle and an 18 inch machete. The suspects also took several guns from the downed officers.

CRITIQUE OF NEWHALL

It is easy to be "Monday morning quarterbacks" and say from our secure armchairs that officers should have done this or that. We must remember that things are quite different at night and under fire.

No amount of criticism will bring these officers back. Yet we must not let this unfortunate incident be repeated if it can, in any way, be prevented. The very essence of education and training is to profit from the mistakes of others and begin where they left off. The main question is how can we improve our police training to prevent a similar incident? Let us begin by covering a list of both errors and possible errors:

(1) Although it seems likely that two two-officer cars could handle most car stops, filling units should not cancel backup just because other units seem closer. Even seconds can be important. There is also a certain safety in numbers.

(2) Officers should not advance toward a suspect vehicle until all suspects are out of the car. The suspects must be in plain view with their hands up or on their heads, and facing away from the officers.

(3) Never let your attention be so distracted by one suspect as to completely ignore a suspect in another known location. In combat conditions this is very difficult, but its importance cannot be stressed enough.

(4) Officers should have extensive practice with the shotgun on a regular basis. The mechanics of handling the shotgun should be automatic with little thought process involved. This would reduce the chance of a live round being cranked out because the officer was not sure whether one was in the chamber.

(5) Range practice should involve more practical combat shooting rather than the bulls eye target type of practice. Today most departments or agencies have corrected this problem.

(6) Departments should have extensive "simulated combat" training exercises to help officers avoid panic firing. This would train officers to count their shots and not empty their firearms unnecessarily.

(7) Officers should carry an extra firearm (possibly a hideaway). Many officers have been in policework for twenty years and have never used their firearms in combat. If they have, it has been on a rare occasion. You only need that extra firearm once to save your life. In the Newhall incident, the large number of firearms at the suspects' disposal was a decided advantage.

(8) Officers should carry at least one extra cartridge/slide holder (speed loader), and practice using it for quicker reloads.

(9) Officers should train in "simulated combat" situations. The use of practical tactics and defensive movements should be taught. Firing the weapon is important, but tactics are as well. In the Newhall incident, the officers were out-maneuvered.

(10) Two-officer cars should practice operating as teams in combat situations. Tactical procedures such as protecting each other's flanks should be practiced

Let the word **NEWHALL** mean more than just a location where four officers were killed.

Never approach until safe

Evaluate all possible dangers

Work as a team

Hold off until backup arrives

Always maintain tactical (and safety) advantage

Load quickly from proper coverage

Live longer by not taking unnecessary chances

STUDY QUESTIONS for Patrol Operations

CHAPTER 12

1. The case that stated that a city is responsible for training an officer in the use of dangerous weapons is:

    a. _ Weston v. NY   b. __Linda Peer v. Newark
    c. _ Harrison v. Calif.   d. __none of these

2. The purpose of the gun is to:

    a. _kill someone.   b. __wound a suspect.
    c. _injure someone.   d. __scare a suspect.

3. Most citizens mistakenly believe that an officer can shoot a gun out of a suspect's hand.   **T or F**

4. An officer can never shoot a suspect when the crime is classed as a _____.

5. From a practical standpoint, an officer should use a gun in two situations:
    (a) _____
    (b) _____

6. Give an example used in the book where a person was killed by an officers mistaken belief.
    _____

7. Most departments allow officers to shoot at stolen cars since it is a felony.   **T or F**

8. An officer must be very careful not to become involved in "panic firing." When this happens the officer usually _____ the gun.

9. Name one reason why warning shots should not be used. _____

10. What is the best type of ammunition to use in "dispatching animals"? _____

11. If it is necessary to shoot a badly injured animal, it is best to first do what to it? _____

12. What material can be used to do this? _____

13. Never shoot an animal in _____.

14. Why not? _____

15. Rather than shooting the injured animal, you can also _____
    which is much safer.

16. If an officer accidentally shot a bystander during a gun battle, he or she could be sued civilly if the jury believed that _____ was not exercised.

---

17. There is a problem in policework with officers who fail to use their guns when they should. **T or F**

18. "Buck Fever" refers to the officer who is overanxious to use his gun. **T or F**

19. What is the police baton used for? _____

20. If you intend to kill the suspect, you should use your gun. **T or F**

21. The baton seldom knocks a suspect unconscious. **T or F**

22. Improper use of the police baton is a major cause of charges of police brutality. **T or F**

23. Using the baton to hit a suspect over the head opens the officer to numerous counter moves. **T or F**

24. Name two places in which it is acceptable to use the police baton.
    (a) _____
    (b) _____

25. One of the best places to use the baton is on the head. **T or F**

26. Name a place you can use the baton where the bone is not close to the skin. _____

27. The Yawara Stick can be hidden until an emergency arises, and then it can be brought from **T or F**
    under the arm into immediate use.

28. If people believe the police misuse their weapons, it can be just as bad as if the officers **T or F**
    actually do misuse them.

29. A U.S. Supreme Court decision has restricted the use of deadly force by the police when **T or F**
    no one's life is in danger.

30. The term "police brutality" can be difficult to define. **T or F**

31. What is the term for the device that projects a stream of liquid tear gas? _____

32. Name two limitations of MACE.
    (a) _____
    (b) _____

33. Match the following.

    (1)___stun gun   A. barbs give 50,000 volts
    (2)___Hong Kong baton   B. shot filled bean bag
    (3)___plastic load shells   C. wooden slugs that bounce on pavement
    (4)___rubber slugs   D. plastic buckshot
    (5)___taser   E. dyed slugs

34. The American Arms Company has produced an automatic rifle that ensures accuracy. When
    the officer sees a _____ on the subject, that is where the bullet will _____.

35. If a suspect obtains an officer's Magna Trigger Safety Ring, he can fire the officer's gun.   T or F

36. The "Magna Trigger Safety Ring" can save children's lives.   T or F

37. When officers find themselves in an ambush and they are in the car, they should immediately get out of the area.   T or F

38. Name one of the four situations in which police officers are likely to shoot other police officers.
_____

39. SWAT means: _____

40. When an emotionally disturbed person becomes violent it is usually caused by _____.

41. Of all police officers shot, only _____% are shot by emotionally disturbed persons.

42. You should first tell an emotionally disturbed person that you are there to _____ him.

43. By making assumptions, an officer can be _____ wrong.

44. Name three of the ten "deadly errors".
    (a) _____
    (b) _____
    (c) _____

45. The best body armor is made of a soft synthetic fiber similar to:

    a. _ krypton   b. _ kevlar
    c. _ syptic   d. _ cotton

46. What percentage of officers who give up their guns are executed? _____

47. Seventy-three percent of officers who were shot were not alone.   T or F

48. The most dangerous type of call as far as being shot is _____.

49. The next most dangerous call is the _____.

50. The most dangerous shift for being shot was _____.

51. The average distance at which officers were shot is less than _____ feet.

52. If the suspect has a hostage, it is best to give up your gun.   T or F

53. The reason you bargain with a suspect holding a hostage is to gain _____.

54. Under the theory of "dynamic inactivity", if you stall long enough, the suspect will probably
_____

55. Relatives and pastors are the best people to call when a person is holding a hostage.   T or F

56. Never place a time limit on the suspect holding a hostage.   T or F

57. In _____ % of hostage negotiations incidents, the hostages were released unharmed according to Dr. Bristow of LASU.

58. If the suspect has the drop on you, it is best to give up your gun.   T or F

59. If the suspect has the drop on you, you could stab him in the eye with _____.

60. An officer who has a "hideaway" gun, and because of this gives up his duty gun because a   T or F
    suspect "got the drop on him", should draw the "hideaway" and shoot the suspect without
    giving any warning.

61. According the 1976 Public Safety Officers Benefits Act, the federal government will pay the family
    of a police officer killed in the line of duty.

    a. _ $100,000   b. __$20,000
    c. _ $60,000   d. __$50,000

62. The above law also applies to reserve officers.   T or F

63. The "Newhall Shooting Incident" occurred in a well-lighted area with over thirty witnesses.   T or F

64. Why was the report of persons brandishing weapons not taken seriously in the Newhall Incident.

    _____

65. In the "Newhall Incident", Officer Frago approached the suspect passenger with his shotgun at
    "_____ _____".

66. How do we know that Officer Frago opened the suspect passenger's door? _____

    _____

67. What mistake did Officer Alleyn make with his shotgun? _____

68. Because Officer Pence ran out of ammunition and couldn't reload before he was executed, a
    new device has been developed called the "_____ loader".

69. In the Newhall Incident, a passing motorist stopped his car, grabbed a dead officer's gun   T or F
    and shot at the suspects.

70. The suspect who escaped and held the occupants of a house hostage, stated over the phone
    that he killed Officer Pence because he got _____.

71. The above suspect finally killed himself with a _____ shotgun.

72. The Newhall Incident stressed the need for more bull's eye target type of shooting courses.   T or F

CHAPTER XIII

TACTICS BY TYPE OF CALL — GENERAL CALLS FOR SERVICE

The techniques and tactics used for each type of call are topics of great controversy. With few exceptions, there is no one set procedure or technique that must be used in handling calls for police service. As stated in the Introduction of this book, the techniques mentioned here are not gospel. They are the result of the varied experiences of many officers. They also involve extensive research on the part of the authors and, of course, personal opinion.

HOMICIDES AND DEATH CASES

If the department is large enough to have a special investigative division, the duties of the patrol officer at the scene of a homicide are quite limited. However, these duties are extremely important. Even in departments that have their own detective or investigative divisions, they seldom operate twenty-four hours a day. After 1:00am or 2:00am there are usually no investigators on duty. It is up to the patrol officer to carry out all of these duties.

ESTABLISHING DEATH

In all other crimes, the first step of the patrol officer at the scene is to protect the scene. In reported death cases it is to establish death. Many of the cases that are reported as deaths, are reported by persons who are in a highly emotional state. Because of this, it is possible that the victim is really not deceased, but either injured or in a coma. Therefore, the first job of the patrol officer on arriving at the scene of a reported homicide or deceased person is to establish whether the victim is, in fact, dead. This is not always easy. There have been cases of medical doctors who have pronounced a person dead, only to have the person come to life on the mortician's table

Evidence is extremely important in cases of homicide. Because of this, some investigators feel that preservation of evidence is of the utmost importance. However, in a homicide, if the victim is not really dead, the officer can call for medical assistance that can save the victim's life. What better evidence could you have than a live witness who can point out the person who shot him?

CONDITIONS THAT SIMULATE DEATH

There are certain conditions that will cause a person to appear dead when he is in fact not dead. Some of the more common are:

(1) Electric shock. (Look for wires or electrical appliances.)

(2) Prolonged immersion. (Drowning)

(3) Poisoning from drugs. (Look for bottles and containers.)

(4) Prolonged disease. (Typhoid is an example. Relatives can usually substantiate this.)

(5) Barbiturate poisoning. (Sleeping pills are the number one cause. Look for bottles.)

(6) Deep hypnosis. (There will often be little else to indicate the cause of the comatose state.)

METHODS OF ESTABLISHING DEATH

The following are some of the more common means of determining or establishing death:

(1) Lack of breathing. Hold a mirror to the mouth and nostrils. (Watch for fogging.)

(2) Absence of heart beat. (Feel pulse in wrist and neck, and put ear to heart.)

(3) Loss of flushing of fingernails. (Pinch the fingernail against the fingertip and then release it. If it changes color, the person is alive.)

(4) No reaction of pupils to light. (Shine flashlight across the eyes to see if there is any change in the size of the pupil. Any contraction is an indication that the victim is alive.)

(5) Dull appearance of the eyeball. (It has a dull sheen like the eye of a fish that has been out of the water for a while.)

(6) Lack of tension in the eyeball. (Close one eye, and press a finger gently against your eyelid. The tension is noticeable. In a deceased person, it feels like a rotten grape.)

(7) Obvious signs. (The body has been eaten by insects or animals, or it is crushed, decapitated or bloated, and the death of the person is obvious. Discoloration is also a sign of death, but not a positive one. Persons with heart trouble and circulatory ailments can show discoloration when they are unconscious.)

Never assume death. Officers should always check victims for the possibility that they could be alive. A book could be filled with examples of officers who have been greatly embarrassed when they have assumed death and later the victim showed some sign of life. It is always worse when someone else brings this to the officer's attention.

PROTECTING THE SCENE

When death is obvious, the first duty of the patrol officer is to protect the scene. Since officers are usually the first persons at the scene, this duty naturally falls on their shoulders. The fact that they are in uniform also suits them for the task. The importance of protecting the crime scene cannot be overemphasized. From whom must the officer protect the scene?

(1) **HIMSELF.** By touching objects, and by walking over evidence, the officer can do irreparable damage to the crime scene.

(2) **FELLOW OFFICERS.** Whenever something big goes down, there are many patrol officers who rush to the scene just to satisfy their curiosity. They went into police work for excitement. Unfortunately they can easily get in the way and destroy evidence.

(3) **RELATIVES OF THE VICTIM.** They feel that they have the God-given right to be there and to look around. After all, the case involves their relative. They will also steal everything in sight because "Uncle Fred always promised them they would get it when he died."

(4) NEIGHBORS AND PASSERSBY. It is not uncommon to have evidence, especially weapons stolen by someone in a crowd of onlookers.

How can the scene and evidence be protected? The first step is to evaluate the scene and determine if more assistance is needed. Then what special equipment might be needed such as rope and barriers. There are three ways to protect the scene.

(1) COVERING THE EVIDENCE. This can be done by putting boxes over footprints and similar types of evidence. Chairs and saw horses can be put in front of or around other evidence.

(2) SECURING THE CRIME SCENE. If the area is suited for this task, it should be roped off with red or orange fluorescent plastic tape. The tape should have printing on it that tells the public that they are not to trespass beyond the tape. Most patrol cars have a roll in the trunk. If there are permanent posts or trees on which to tie the tape, this procedure should be used. In an open field, it might not be suited. For a temporary situation, the tape might be laid on the ground around the area containing the evidence.

(3) PHYSICALLY MOVING PEOPLE AWAY. Often the patrol officer has to be firm to the point of using physical force to remove sightseers or move them back. Crowds can be difficult to control. At first the officer should try to be courteous but firm. If this doesn't work, a slow changing of the tone of voice might get people to respond. Unfortunately, some onlookers may actually have to be arrested in order to remove them from the scene. In some areas of large cities, they might just be looking for an opportunity to start something.

OTHER DUTIES

Apart from protecting the scene, officers should also try to obtain the names, addresses and phone numbers of as many witnesses as possible. They should also record the location of various pieces of evidence, but not touch or remove them. Statements can be obtained from witnesses. A dying declaration may be taken from the victim. In order for a declaration to be accepted in court, the victim must have made it under the belief that he was dying, and that there was no hope of recovery. The declaration must pertain to the circumstances leading to his injury or the person causing it.

Homicide investigations can be quite involved. Officers from small departments where there are few homicides should read and study one of the many textbooks on homicide investigation. They will have to do everything themselves, and there is a lot of knowledge needed to properly investigate this type of crime. Most states have a special investigative agency that will come to the aid of small jurisdictions when they have a serious case that requires special skills. In the meantime, proper location, recording and preservation of evidence can be of great assistance to these special investigators.

DUTIES OF THE CORONER

The laws regarding deceased persons are becoming more involved. Every patrol officer should become aware of the legal duties the coroner has in cases of death. Usually he has total authority.

BURGLARY

THE IMPORTANT ELEMENT IN BURGLARY

The most important element in burglary and the one that makes the offense a felony instead of misdemeanor trespassing, is the element showing intent to enter the building to commit theft or some felony. The law does vary to a certain degree in different states. Too often, officers who catch a burglar inside the building will think that they have him cold as far as a conviction is concerned. In court, the officer receives a lesson in criminal law. When the burglar is caught inside, he often feels that all is lost, and at this time it is usually very easy to obtain a statement as to why he broke in. Later when he talks to his attorney, his attitude will change. In court he will explain that he didn't have a place to sleep and was cold, so he broke in just to keep warm. If one member of the jury believes him, you will not get a burglary conviction. But if the officer takes the stand and tells the jury that the defendant admitted that he broke in to steal a typewriter, the important element of intent is proven, and chances are that a conviction will result.

COMMERCIAL BURGLARIES

There are two classifications of commercial burglaries as far as the patrol officer is concerned. The first is the late reported burglary and the second, the burglary in progress.

THE LATE REPORTED BURGLARY

This is the burglary that is usually reported by the owner or janitor when they arrive at the place of business in the morning. The duties of the officer depend upon whether the case is to be handled by a team of investigators. If this is the case, the prime duties of the officer involve the protection of the scene until the investigators arrive. The officer should also obtain all of the information for the offense report.

If the crime is reported on a Monday morning in a large city or town, there will be a large number of such burglaries for investigators to cover. As a result, the officer may have to spend hours waiting for their arrival. In the meantime the owner of the business is anxious to clean up and prepare for his customers. The officer will have to be a good salesman to convince him to leave things as they are unless the amount taken is quite sizable, and the owner is anxious to have the burglars caught. Since the patrol officer is the first at the scene, he or she usually obtains the information for the offense report. If the burglary is a safe burglary, the officer should have some idea of the various types of techniques used in perpetrating a safe burglary.

CLASSIFICATION OF SAFES BY PURPOSE OR USE.

There are two types of safes, the burglar proof and the fireproof.

(1) **BURGLAR PROOF.** The burglar proof safe is expensive because it is made of solid steel. Because of this, it is usually small. Its main purpose is to protect money and small valuables. It can have elaborate anti-burglar devices built into the safe. They can range from tear gas devices to mechanisms that jam the lock when the extreme heat of an acetylene torch is detected. Breaking into this safe requires a considerable amount of skill.

(2) **FIREPROOF.** The fireproof safe is made of two thin sheets of steel. Between these is placed about four inches of asbestos. The sole purpose of the fireproof safe is to protect its contents from fire. It is less expensive than the burglar-proof safe and is therefore larger. It is usually quite impressive, and because of this many businessmen fool themselves into thinking that these safes are really burglar proof. Their purpose is to protect important papers from fire. They were never intended to be burglar proof. A novice with basic knowledge could probably break into this type of safe with a large can opener.

TYPES OF SAFE JOBS

It is important for the patrol officer to know the different types of safe jobs. The offense reports for these crimes go to a central state records center. Here the safe burglaries are classified by type. This is a step towards identifying the safe burglar through modus operandi. Unless the officer encloses photographs of the safe job, they may not be able to determine the exact classification apart from the general term "Safe Burglary." Some of the major types of safe jobs will be covered as follows:

(1) **THE PUNCH JOB.** The "punch job", or "drift job" as it is sometimes called, involves knocking the dial off the front of the safe with a sledge hammer. The spindle, or pin that is attached to the locking gears is then exposed. The perpetrator uses a center punch to drive the spindle into the interior of the safe. This disengages the locking gears so the safe may

Fig. XIII-1; A punch job

be opened. More recent safes contain a special spindle that is thicker in the center, and cannot be punched out. Because safes are expensive, most of them are the old type that have been in use for years. A businessman is reluctant to replace a safe as long as it is still in working order. Replacement can be quite expensive. (See Figure XIII-1, prev. pg)

(2) **THE RIP JOB.** In the "rip job", the perpetrator knocks or drills a hole in the back, bottom or front of the metal surface of a fireproof safe. The bottom is usually the weakest part. He then takes a tool similar to a large blade-type can opener, and inserts it in the hole. By lifting up and down, he rips the metal open just as a can is opened by a can opener. (See Figure XIII-2)

Fig. XIII-2; A rip job

When two meeting lines have been ripped, the metal is pulled or bent back, and the asbestos is pulled out. The perpetrator uses the same technique on the inner wall. He can then reach in and take out the contents.

The patrol officer should be especially aware of this technique since the asbestos has a tendency to stick to the perpetrator's clothing. During a field interrogation, the officer may notice fine particles of white asbestos on the suspect's clothing or shoes, and know that the suspect is a possible safe burglar.

(3) **THE CHOP JOB.** The "chop job" is similar to the "rip job," only instead of ripping the metal, the safe is pushed over, and an axe is used to chop through the bottom.

(4) **THE PULL JOB.** The "pull job" or "drag job" as it is sometimes called, involves the use of a device similar to a wheel puller. It is attached to the dial on the surface of the safe, and its screws are tightened until the dial and the spindle are pulled out. The gears are then disengaged and the safe may be opened.

(5) **THE PEEL JOB.** The "peel job" is used on fireproof safes. The upper corner of the face plate is chiseled with a hard cold-steel chisel. This will break it away from the corner rivet. It is then chiseled down and to one side to break some of the other rivets. A clamp device is attached to the loose corner plate and the plate is forcibly peeled down like the top of a sardine can. The asbestos is then pulled out to expose the locking mechanism. By shining a light on the locking mechanism, the tumblers can be observed. The dial is turned until the tumblers are all lined up, and the safe will open. Sometimes the locking bars can be manipulated.

Fig. XIII-3; A peel job

(6) **THE BURN JOB.** The "burn job", sometimes referred to as a "torch job", involves the use of an acetylene torch or similar type of cutting device. It is usually used on burglar proof safes. The safe is usually attacked in one of two ways: by cutting the locking mechanism out, or by cutting a hole large enough to reach through and take the money or valuables. This type of safe job is not as popular as it used to be because of the severe penalties attached to the offense. Today, safes do not contain as much cash as they did in the past. They often contain mostly checks, and the increased penalty is not worth it.

Fig. XIII-4; A burn job

Many of these jobs are perpetrated by a person who has taken a high school course in welding. He thinks he can easily open a safe because of his skills. What often happens is that he burns up all the money and papers in the safe. He usually ruins the safe, and really doesn't get anything.

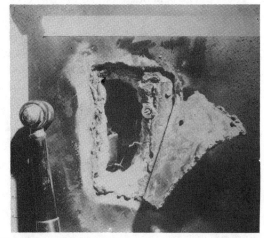

Fig. XIII-4; Another burn job

(7) **THE SOUP JOB.** The "soup job" involves the use of explosives ("soup" is a nickname for nitroglycerine) on burglar proof safes. In the case of nitroglycerine, a small soap or clay dam is made along the edge of the safe door. Into this is poured a small amount of nitro. Capillary action draws it into the crack. Because this is a dangerous operation, the perpetrator will usually attach a very long fuse to the nitro so it can be lit from another room. Another means is to attach one end of an electrical wire to the nitro, and the other end to a light switch in the next room. The perpetrator can then set it off electrically from a safe position.

Because nitroglycerine is so sensitive and unpredictable, this type of safe job is dangerous both to the perpetrator and to the patrol officer. Many perpetrators are blown up while trying to pull this type of job. More important is the danger to the patrol officer. The fuse can be faulty. The perpetrator can be frightened off by the patrol officer who has discovered the break-in. In this case the officer might walk into the room just as the fuse catches, and be killed by the explosion. Another possibility is that the officer will turn on the light switch to check the room, not realizing that it is wired to the safe. This would blow up the safe and possibly the officer.

Patrol officers who discover a break-in, and find a safe that has been set up for a "soup job," should take extreme care not to light matches, turn on light switches or slam doors. Above all, an officer should never stand in front of the safe door. The deactivation of a safe should be handled by experts. If there are no experts available, the nitroglycerine may be neutralized by mixing one pound of sodium sulphite with a gallon of wood alcohol, and then spraying all areas that might contain the nitro. When this is done, it should be left for at least one half hour, and the process repeated until all the solution has been used up. The application of the solution should be generous. Steps should be taken to cover the floor with some type of cover, or the solution might damage it.

ROBBERY

Robbery, like rape, is often falsely reported. Because of this, the patrol officer should be cautious when taking robbery reports. Especially those in which an officer is alerted by the so-called sixth sense. It is a feeling that something is wrong. You don't know what it is, but you sense it. Often a few well directed questions can confirm the officer's suspicions. There are many motives for falsely reporting a robbery. The main motive is to cover up a loss of money. There have also been cases reported just because the so-called victim wanted attention. When taking the report, the officer should listen for meta-communication. Meta-communication is the term for the hidden messages that we often transmit when we speak. It is usually different from the spoken word. A person can say, "All right", but tone of voice and facial expression may indicate that they really mean the opposite. Often we do not fully hear the exact words a person is saying, but from his tone of voice and the expression on his face, we fully understand his feelings in the matter. In the field of law enforcement we have a tendency to become overly word conscious. This is because exactness is required in our work. The importance of verbatim testimony in court cannot be overemphasized. Yet we should also try to look behind the words into the person saying them. We should seek and understand the true motivations behind these words. The best way to learn this is to sit in on a group conversation and fix your attention on the person talking. Don't listen to the words that the person is saying, just devote your full attention to the speaker. Try to sense the speaker's feelings. With a little practice, you will be able to gain a deep insight into meta-communication.

Why does a person falsely report a robbery? If you talk to him enough, you can often ferret it out. By knowing the most common motives, you can use them for bait. A person who has spent his paycheck at a downtown bar and at a card-room will want to avoid discussing his activities before the robbery. When he is asked if he had been to a bar or a card-room, he will try to change the subject. Probably the main motive in such a case would be the fear of his wife knowing the truth. In such cases, it is usually not the victim who originally called the police, but his wife. Second person reports should always alert an officer's suspicions. The so-called victim would just as soon the police not be involved. His tone of voice will often transmit this message.

THEFT CASES

The key to theft investigation is talking to everyone connected with the case, and the proper interrogation of the suspects. If fingerprints are used in determining the perpetrator, the officer should try not to let him know. Use other bluffs. Otherwise the next time he will use gloves. The use of police records can often produce a suspect. All persons connected with the case should have their names run through the records division.

If state law does not allow arrest for misdemeanors not committed in the officer's presence, other action must be taken. In most cases, the vic-

tim is willing to make a private person's arrest (citizens arrest) and turn the suspect over to the officer. The alternative would be to properly identify the suspect and then obtain a criminal complaint from the D.A. The average citizen does not know the law, and when he observes someone stealing things belonging to him, he will call the police demanding that they arrest the suspect. The officer should explain the process of a private person's arrest, and have the victim or complainant make the actual arrest, first making sure that the facts are true and that the case appears to be sound.

When a petty theft has occurred and a witness has observed and recorded the license number, a local all points bulletin is broadcast. If the car is spotted by a patrol unit and the items taken are found in the car the officers usually make an arrest, and book the suspects. Nothing is said, but the process is illegal. It is an arrest made for a misdemeanor not committed in the officer's presence. The legal procedure would be to confiscate the evidence, identify the suspects and then obtain a complaint from the District Attorney. In some cases the victim can be brought to the scene to make a private person's arrest. Some states allow officers to arrest juveniles for misdemeanors not observed when there is probable cause.

SHOPLIFTING CASES

In most shoplifting cases, the officer is just a means of transportation. The clerk or store detective has observed the theft and has made the arrest. An officer should not overlook the possibility of clearing other cases by talking to shoplifting suspects about turning over a new leaf and starting out clean. This is especially true with juveniles.

If possible, leave the evidence at the store and have the store officer or clerk bring it when he testifies in court. It saves overcrowding police storage and property lockers. If the evidence is perishable, the police department does not usually have a very large refrigerated storage capacity. The store or victim usually does. In such cases, the chain of evidence is not too important. The victim can even bring in a similar item. In court the victim can testify that the item was the same as the one taken. If the shoplifted item is to be kept at the store, the officer should instruct the victim to initial and date it.

SEXUAL OFFENSES

Sexual offenses are commonplace to police officers. Yet most officers are often not fully aware of how many cases have a sexual basis. These cases are hidden by apparent conditions or circumstances. This does not mean that officers should become Freudian psychologists and find a sexual motive for everything. It does mean that we should prepare ourselves for the possibility that there could be a sexual motive for certain types of offense. The patrol officer should be aware that sex is not strictly a physiological exercise. Although for most persons, it is difficult to experience sexual pleasure without the sexual organs in some way being involved, there are many forms of perversion where the person attains a complete sexual climax without the sexual organs being touched.

Every officer should be familiar with the more common types of sexual offenses and the technical name given these offenses. Officers who use street terms for sexual offenses in their reports will come under criticism in court. Defense attorneys will try to convince jurors that the officer is a vulgar person. Some of the more common are:

ADULTERY: Sexual intercourse by married persons with others than those to whom they are married. (Not illegal in all states)

ANTHROPOPHAGY: The sexual pleasure derived from eating the victim's flesh.

BESTIALITY: The sex act between a human being and an animal.

BUGGERY: Intercourse with the anus or rectum of either sex. Also called sodomy.

CUNNILINGUS: Use of the mouth on the sexual organs of the female, but not the breast. Also referred to as oral copulation of the female sexual organ.

EXHIBITIONISM: Sexual pleasure obtained by exhibiting self in the nude, or by showing sexual organs. This person usually makes obscene phone calls as well.

FELLATIO: Use of the mouth on the sexual organ of the male. Also referred to as oral copulation of the male sexual organ.

FETISHISM: The sexual satisfaction obtained from certain objects or parts of the human body, especially clothing. These people are prone to stealing or cutting the crotch out of women's underclothing. Some like to sniff women's shoes. This is called a "shoe fetish." The range of objects that can arouse sexual stimulation in some people is unlimited. Nearly all fetishists are males.

FLAGELLATION: This can either be the sexual satisfaction obtained by the masochist who has a passion to be whipped, or the sadist who likes to whip others. Sometimes a brutal murder can result when a masochist and a sadist get together. They both get pleasure out of the beating and continue the act until the victim dies. The city of San Francisco averages one death a month resulting from this act. In order to reduce the deaths, the coroner of that city has started classes to show how the act can be performed without killing the victim and has come under criticism for doing this.

FORNICATION: Sexual intercourse between unmarried males and females over 18. Not a crime in all states.

FROTTAGE: Sexual gratification derived from rubbing against a woman when she is fully clothed. This type of deviate is usually found in cities containing crowded transportation conditions. He usually prefers to rub against a woman's buttocks.

INCEST: Sexual relations with a relative who is within the degree of consanguinity (blood relationship). Most common between father and daughter, especially where there is incompatibility between husband and wife.

KOPROLAGNIA: Sexual pleasure in handling or eating human excrement.

MASOCHISM: The sexual pleasure derived from being beaten and humiliated. More common in women than in men, common in male homosexuals. Also the desire to be kidnapped, bound and imprisoned. Houses of prostitution will cater to these people.

NECROPHILIA: The desire to have sexual intercourse with dead bodies.

PEDERASTY: The act of sodomy by a man against a boy.

PEDOPHILIA: The sexual desire to fondle children or sexually violate them.

PIQUERS: Those who receive sexual satisfaction from sticking sharp objects into their victims and drawing blood, or tearing their flesh. A form of sadism.

SADISM: The sexual satisfaction derived from the infliction of pain on others. This includes mental pain and humiliation.

SODOMY: Intercourse with anus or rectum.

TRANSVESTISM: The desire to dress in the clothing of the opposite sex. Some males go so far as to let their hair grow long, and actually live as women. Some hang out in bars and this can cause fights when a man picks up a transvestite and later finds that "she" is male. This is a perversion of both sexes. Not all transvestites are homosexuals.

TRIOLISM: The desire to be involved in a sexual act with several partners, or in the presence of numerous persons. Usually a perverted act.

UROLAGNIA: Sexual stimulation from the sight and odor of urine. Two common variations of this are the "Golden Fountain" where the person gets into a bathtub and has a partner urinate on him, and the "Golden Rinse" where the person desires to have someone urinate in his mouth. Usually the partners are propositioned in a bar, and paid for performing the act.

VOYEURISM: The receiving of sexual pleasure from watching women undress or watching persons engaged in sexual intercourse (The Peeping Tom). This person is often unable to perform a normal sexual act, so seeks gratification in peeping.

ZOOPHILIA: The sexual gratification from handling, fondling, petting or stroking animals.

THE HANDLING OF COMMON SEXUAL OFFENSES

EXHIBITIONISM (INDECENT EXPOSURE)

Witnesses and modus operandi are most important in indecent exposure cases. The "M.O." will often enable the officer to establish a pattern and even make possible the identification of the perpetrator. Exhibitionism is a male trait. There are cases of women exposing themselves, but the motive is usually drunkenness or mental illness. The motivation is not sexual. The male "exposure artist" however, receives a definite sexual pleasure from not only exposing himself, but from shocking women by doing it. There might be a borderline of sadism involved in the desire to shock and humiliate women

The greatest problem in cases of this type is getting victims to testify in court. Women are usually very embarrassed at having been involved. This is especially true if the suspect has done a good job of picking his victim. He is turned on mostly by victims who are shocked, so he tries to pick women whom he believes will be upset and embarrassed by the act. As a result, a good defense attorney can easily get this victim confused when on the stand.

There is a certain amount of planning involved in these cases. Many perpetrators will try to aim the exposure at one particular group or person. Occasionally there will be unnoticed witnesses who can provide valuable information as to the license number or vehicle description. They can give information as to the escape route taken by the perpetrator. Because of this, the officer should go door-to-door in the immediate area in an attempt to locate witnesses.

Officers must be careful not to think of the exhibitionist as a stereotypical character. Don't expect him to look odd or "crazy". Neither is he necessarily effeminate. Lance Rentzel, the football star has suffered this condition and, at the request of his psychiatrist, has written a book titled <u>When All the Laughter Died in Sorrow</u> (Bantam Books). It gives great insight into this sexual aberration.

Exhibitionism can often be a symptom of a defeat or loss that challenges a person's manhood. It must be regained in some overt manner. It is apparently an ego bolstering act. When men suffer a period of impotence, which is a blow to their male ego, many find some other method of compensating until the problem is solved. The exhibitionist finds that his ego and self image are bolstered when he is able to frighten or shock a woman or girl through exposing his sex organs. In our society, a man's worth and masculinity are too often tied up with his sexual prowess, or lack of it. By this act, some psychologists believe, the exhibitionist seeks to restore a damaged ego. The officer should understand that this type of person can be of any social class or occupation. The only sure category into which he can be placed is that of being a male.

Modus operandi. There are several "methods of operation" that seem to be common to this type of sexual offense. One technique is for the perpetrator to park his car next to the curb and to sit on the passenger side of the front seat. He will often hold a newspaper over his lap as though he is reading it. He will be fully dressed from the waist up, and the newspaper will hide the fact that he is naked from the waist down. When a woman passes by, whom he feels will be a good subject, he will open the door, stand up and call to her. When she sees him exposed and screams (he hopes), he then jumps back into the car and drives off.

Another technique used by the habitual exhibitionist is to wear a long overcoat which hides the fact that his trousers come only up to his knees. They are held up by a suspender type device. When he finds a person who he feels is a good subject, he simply opens his overcoat As far as location is concerned, it can happen any place. Public libraries seem to have an attraction to this sort of person. During or just before exam time, colleges and universities experience a very high rate of indecent exposures. This could very likely be due to the pressure of exams.

There is a very high degree of recidivism among exhibitionists. We don't seem to have a cure for it. As a result, most of them have been arrested at one time or another. This means that their photographs are in the sexual offender's "mug book." Witnesses and victims should be shown this book in an effort to make positive identification. When they are shown the book, they should be told that not all of the pictures in the book are sexual criminals, nor for that matter criminals; that they will probably see pictures in there of people they know. It can be explained that the purpose of this is to help prevent a person from just identifying anyone. It can be further explained that many of the non-criminal pictures are put in the book because the person has particular features. They are different and can aid the police if a victim were to say that the perpetrator looked something like one of them. The purpose for this subterfuge is to prevent unjust neighborhood gossip when a victim or witness sees one of their neighbors in the book. This has caused a problem in the past.

MOONING

There is a form of exhibitionism called "mooning." It is practiced by teenagers and college students as sort of joke. It involves driving down the street in a vehicle with the window rolled down. As they pass a group of girls on the street, one of the passengers will stick his bare buttocks out the window. The pleasure in this act seems to be derived from the act of shocking someone. Because of this, there is a feeling among some that, in the majority of the cases, it is really a sexual offense that is passed off as a joke.

As in all cases where the perpetrator confronts the victim, a bluff during a lineup can often be used effectively. Since the perpetrator knows that the victim saw him, he is ready to accept the fact that the victim will identify him. In many cases, however, the victim was so shocked that she would be unable to make positive identification. Some of the old time recidivists in this type of offense are aware of this and are very hard to bluff.

Only a very small number of indecent exposures are actually reported. It is very difficult for women to report such things to the police. Apart from the personal embarrassment, many do not want to become involved in a criminal trial.

Many exhibitionists will keep a diary. When things are slow, they can look over the it and relive their experiences. Because of this, all sex offenders should be asked about their sex diaries. An officer who can obtain one will receive quite an education.

OBSCENE PHONE CALLS

Obscene, abusive and irritating telephone calls are increasing throughout the nation. A national study by the Bell Telephone system showed 568,000 complaints of abusive or obscene calls in a year. It must be remembered that these are not the total number of such calls, but only the total number of those reported.

Whenever a person is arrested for indecent exposure, he should also be asked about the phone calls he has made. The two usually go together. Modus operandi is most important in offenses of this type. Like indecent exposure, the perpetrator can often be identified by what he said, or the way that he said it. The exact wording is very important, and if the victim is embarrassed to repeat the words to the officer, she should write it down on paper or tell her husband or boyfriend so he can repeat the words to the officer.

There are two types of obscene phone calls. The classification is based on the ultimate objective. One type of call is made by a normal but crude male for the purpose of lining up a sexual date. His feeling is that if he calls enough women, he is bound to find one that would like to be his sexual partner. Sometimes he has observed a particular woman who interests him and he calls and propositions her. The ultimate objective here is not the phone call but the date. This person can be dangerous. He can let fantasy replace reality. The other classification is the person whose ultimate objective is the phone call itself. He receives his pleasure from using obscene language to a woman over the phone. He will sometimes make a date, but the majority of these individuals are incapable of normal sexual relations. Their main pleasure is in the vulgar language used over the phone. They also receive pleasure from shocking the victim.

Like indecent exposure, very few victims actually call the police when they are victimized. When they do, it is usually after a second or third call is made. Here the victim becomes concerned about her safety, or the safety of her family. Often an attempt is made to trace the phone call, but there is a great misconception in the area of tracing phone calls. Most of the public think that a quick call to the phone company will result in an immediate tracing. On the average, tracing a phone call will take from fifteen to twenty minutes. It is important that the officer requesting the tracing go about it in the right way. The first person to be contacted is the Special Agent. The Special Agent is the enforcement officer for the telephone company. If he is not available, the senior operator or the supervisor should be contacted. Officers should not call the operator since she can do very little but refer the call to someone else. Many wasted minutes can be spent on explaining the purpose of the request to a person who can do nothing about it.

The chairman of the Federal Communications Commission recently told a Senate Commerce Subcommittee that the problem of obscene and abusive phone calls has become "a matter of serious concern." Because of this problem, new procedures and techniques in tracing calls are being developed. One is a new device that will record information about the caller every time a certain number is called. Departments should contact the Chief Special Agent for the phone company in their area to determine when this equipment will be installed. They should also find out under what conditions the phone company will install it.

THE VOICEPRINT SOUND SPECTRO-GRAPH

An innovation in the area of voice identification is the Voiceprint Sound Spectrograph. This piece of criminal detection equipment was developed by Dr. Lawrence Kersta, for many years a scientist at the Bell Telephone Laboratory. This method of voice identification is an important aid in helping law enforcement authorities identify criminals who use the telephone to make obscene phone calls, as well as bomb threats, extortion threats, and ransom demands.

Much like fingerprint identification, which uses the unique features in the inked impressions of people's fingerprints, voiceprint identification uses the unique features in the spectrographic impressions of people's utterances of 10 commonly used English words. The cue words used are: the,

FIGURE 3

IDENTIFY A VOICE — which "you" has a double? These six voiceprints were made of five different speakers' utterances, of the word "you." One of the speakers said it twice. Which two voiceprints are from the same speaker? Answer below.

The voiceprints at upper left and at lower right.

Fig. XIII-6; Voiceprints

to, and, me, on, is, you, I, it, and a. Perpetrators cannot escape identification by whispering, muffling, noseholding, or even filling the mouth with marbles. This is based on the fact that the voiceprint is a result of the combination of physical characteristics unique to each individual's vocal cavities (the throat, mouth, nose, and sinuses), and the manner of manipulating the articulators (the lips, teeth, tongue, soft palate, and jaw muscles). An expert mimic can usually fool the human ear, but not the Voiceprint Sound Spectrograph.

In the many thousands of tests that have been made so far, the results have been better than 99 per cent successful in providing positive identification. There have been many cases where the voiceprint has been used to prove the identity of the perpetrator. In many cases the suspects pleaded guilty when presented with evidence, so it wasn't until 1966 that the Voiceprint was first accepted into evidence in a criminal trial in White Plains, New York. However, the U.S. Court of Appeals in Washington, D.C. ruled that the voiceprint may not be used as evidence in that court. The court ruled that "whatever its promise may be for the future, voiceprint identification is not sufficiently accepted by the scientific community as a whole to form a basis for a jury's determination of guilt or innocence." This rule, however, is binding only in the federal courts in the District of Columbia, but could have a great effect on future cases. It is still a good investigating tool.

An important aspect of the voiceprint that should not be overlooked is its part in proving innocence. This was graphically demonstrated in a Connecticut death threat case where the suspect was tentatively identified by the victim. The voiceprint was used to prove his innocence. Because of this, the investigation was continued and the real perpetrator was apprehended.

Small departments that cannot afford the Voiceprint Sound Spectrograph can, for a fee, send a tape recording of the perpetrator's voice along with a tape of the suspect's voice to the Voiceprint Laboratory in Somerville, New Jersey, and they will make the determination. This service normally takes a week. Voiceprint Laboratories also offers a two-week course for law enforcement officers. Today there is a computer attached Voiceprint Spectrograph. Since the voiceprint may be classified and stored by the computer, the voice of all arrested "phone call" offenders can be filed in the computer. Then, whenever a "phone call" offense is reported and recorded, it may be fed into the computer to search for prior classifications of the same voice, and thus identify the perpetrator.

UNDERCLOTHING THEFTS

Underclothing thefts are more common than the average police officer thinks. The reason for this misconception is the fact that few thefts are reported. Yet when a person is arrested for this offense, and investigators check his home, they may find hundreds upon hundreds of items of women's underclothing hidden in a closet or in the garage. Since sex offense investigators are anxious to clear as many past offenses as possible, they check back through the reported thefts to see if the arrestee might have committed any of them. They seldom find that more than a fraction of the recovered undergarments have been reported to the police as stolen. Women are a little hesitant about calling the police and reporting that a pair of panties or a brassiere has been stolen. Although with the increased costs of such items today, women are making more reports.

Because of this, when there have been a few underclothing thefts reported, the officer can be sure that there are really more. As a result, the area should receive a close watch. As in most sexual offenses, modus operandi is important. An officer can plot the reported offenses on a map and can sometimes arrive at a pattern that will help in the arrest of the perpetrator. It is common for underclothing thieves to occasionally wear a pair of woman's panties. An officer who stops a suspicious person loitering in the vicinity of a series of underclothing thefts might keep this in mind. If an officer arrests a person, and during booking it is found that he is wearing a pair of women's panties, a judge might issue a search warrant for his residence.

A file check will sometimes reveal a past record for this offense. Sometimes, male juveniles who have are beginning puberty will have an intense interest in all things sexual. They can get hung up on this offense. They are usually from families where sex is a bad word. A mysterious atmosphere has been created around women's underclothing or "unmentionables" as they were once referred to.

MOLESTERS

A molester can be the most dangerous type of sexual criminal. This is not just because of the traumatic emotional damage that is done to the child, but because he will sometimes kill the victim.

Some psychologists contend that it is not a serious offense. They feel that it is the parents and the court that cause such emotional trauma. It is their belief that the molester does nothing to the child that other children have not already done while playing "Doctor" or in normal childhood experimentation. Recent studies have shown that the majority of children molested have been molested by a relative. New officers find it difficult to believe that a parent, grandparent or other relative could do such a thing. When such cases are discovered, they are seldom reported to the police because of the shame that it will bring upon the family.

There are usually two reasons for killing the victim. One, when molesters have achieved sexual climax, their minds are no longer clouded with emotion. Thinking clears to the point where the realization dawns that they have committed a very serious offense. They know they will be treated harshly if caught and thus feel that the victim must be killed to eliminate an important witness.

If the victim starts to cry or scream, the perpetrator may kill in an effort to keep him/her quiet. The second major reason for killing the victim would be in the case of a normally respectable person who has a strong abnormal sexual drive. He or she is able to control it most of the time, but when, in a weak moment, this person does molest a child, he or she will later be quite remorseful and resentful of the child who was such a temptation. They can then rationalize that it was the child's fault that they gave in to such a terrible thing. Therefore the child should be punished. They will sometimes kill the child as a form of punishment to satisfy their own deep personal guilt feelings. To counter the argument of some that the offense is not serious, one need only read the newspapers to see the number of children who have been killed.

Since young children are most often the victims, officers should be very careful when questioning them. Children have wild imaginations. Children are very susceptible to suggestion. A person's life could very easily be ruined just because he or she wanted to be nice to a child. The officer should not use the "Did he do this?" approach. This is too suggestive. The best approach would be "Just what did he do?" Proving innocence is as much a part of a police officer's job as arresting guilty persons. Suppose the charges were later dropped as being false. The person accused would have to state on applications that he or she had been arrested for child molesting, which is true. There are those who will always think the worst and feel that the person might have gotten off the hook because of politics, a payoff or a loophole.

Since the molester is attracted to children, the patrol officer must be quite watchful when patrolling areas where children normally play. Parks, public pools, playgrounds and school grounds should receive special attention. When officers spot a person loitering in such a place, they might stake out from a distance and watch the suspect. They can also grab the bull by the horns and approach the suspect. Many times it may be the parent or grandparent of one of the children. Because of this, the officer should be somewhat tactful in the approach. Once the officer has the suspect's name, it can be checked with records. Molesters usually have a prior record of some sort. Many are sex offenders who are supposed to register, but have not.

When male molesters hang around children, they often have their hands in their pockets. This enables them to play with their own sexual organs while watching the children. They are quite prone to carrying obscene pictures in their pockets or wallets. This is sometimes used as a means of exciting curiosity or stimulation in their victims. Because they often masturbate, it is common for their handkerchiefs to be stiff with dried semen. They often have holes in their pockets. Patrol officers need to learn these and other signs in order to be alert to the presence of such persons.

When an officer patrols areas where children congregate, and politely asks questions of the adults present, it has a tendency to curb the molester's activities. When molesters hang out near children, the last person in the world they want to see or talk to is a police officer. Even though the officer is extremely polite and an arrest is not made, merely stopping and talking to the suspect has a deterrent effect.

Officers who have a few extra minutes on a quiet shift should look over the Sex Offender Registration book. They will see many persons whom they observe on the streets or loitering near parks. Each state has a Sex Offender Registration law. Most require that convicted sex offenders register in the city or town where they are staying. Recidivism is extremely high for sexual offenders. Next to narcotic violations, this offense has the highest rate of repeat offenders. We simply do not know how to cure them. Because of this, the registration requirement law is a great help to law enforcement agencies in protecting the community.

HOMOSEXUALS

Some officers, who have had few dealings with homosexuals, have many misconceptions. Some believe that it is illegal to be a homosexual. No one knows what causes homosexuality and therefore no one should condemn another for being this way. Most homosexuals have little or no official contact with the police. They find a partner and live together in a fairly peaceful lifestyle. Those of us in policework see only a certain element of the homosexual community. We see the worst element, and it is too easy for humans to judge a whole group by a few.

MALE HOMOSEXUALS

There are two general types of male homosexuals as far as policework is concerned. The "soliciting active" and the "passive." The soliciting active homosexual not only practices his sexual preference, he is extremely promiscuous. He feels the need to solicit as many partners for his acts as possible. There are certainly some heterosexual males in this category as well. Rather than hang out in Gay bars and meet other gays, he will loiter around public rest-rooms and parks. Some will stop every male they see on the street and solicit him for a homosexual (sodomy or oral copulation) act or other perverted act (usually involved with masochism and sex fetishes). Most of those who solicit partners for fetishes do so in public bars. When this happens, those solicited usually either complain to the police department or beat up the solicitor. They feel that they should be able to go to a bar, public rest-room or park without being solicited. If there is a complaint or a fight, it then becomes a police problem. This problem is best handled by undercover officers, but it doesn't hurt for patrol officers to make their presence known in areas where there are numerous complaints.

Another misconception is that homosexuals are child molesters. Most child molesters are married heterosexuals. Many of them are relatives of their victims. Although most homosexuals are adamant about not being child molesters, many do try to seduce young heterosexual males when they reach puberty. Many feel that there is nothing wrong with this. They would certainly get a lot of argument from the general public.

The laws of some states make sodomy and oral copulation illegal. Others allow it between consenting adults. All states have laws prohibiting sexual acts with minors, and all states have laws against Soliciting Lewd Acts. This is the law that most officers will be called upon to enforce. These laws are the same for homosexual and heterosexual alike. If a male heterosexual solicits a woman for a sexual act, he can be arrested. Male homosexuals often complain that the law is unfair to them. The law is the same for everyone.

The passive homosexual is discreet and minds his own business. He is seldom a problem to police officers. He often lives in the community and his sexual preference is unknown to others. If he is not overly effeminate, he is probably present in some police departments, especially the larger ones. The modern professional police officer must look upon the homosexual as a human being. He is a person who can and does contribute to the society in which he lives. Not all homosexuals are effeminate. Homosexuals have been around throughout recorded history. So far we have not been able to arrive at any solution or reason for the occurrence of homosexuality. Since homosexuals are a contributing part of our society, we, as professional law enforcement officers, must accept them as part of our society. This does not mean that we have to accept their lifestyle if it goes againt our own religious beliefs. There are many people in our lives with whom we disagree, but still accept as members of the communmity. Sometimes our own children do things we cannot accept, still we do not reject them as members of our family. Accepting homosexuals as part of our community does not mean that we accept illegal soliciting. The active homosexual will argue that he has as much of a right to practice his own form of sex as heterosexuals have to practice theirs. The argument sounds good, but what the active soliciting homosexual is really asking for is free rein for his sexual behavior. This is a privilege that is denied to all persons.

FAMILY FIGHTS

Family fights do occur when two male homosexuals live together. The causes of the fights are usually the same as the causes of heterosexual family fights. One partner is drinking too much. One partner is fooling around on the side. One partner claims his lover doesn't love him any more. Officers should handle a family fight involving two homosexuals the same as other family fights. The basic underlying reasons for the fight are the same.

FEMALE HOMOSEXUALS (LESBIANS)

It is very seldom that police officers are officially involved with lesbians. They are usually very private persons. It is quite rare for them to solicit sex on the street. It is just as rare for neighbors to call the police because of a "family fight" involving two lesbians living together. On occasion, the police will be called to a lesbian bar. It will usually be a case of a male heterosexual trying to pick up a lesbian's girlfriend (or "fem"), and she is trying to "punch his lights out."

STRONG ARM ROBBERY OF HOMOSEXUALS

Apart from soliciting sex, the male homosexual is often the victim of strong arm robbery. There are people in our society who feel that there is nothing wrong with "Gay bashing." Acts such as this are clear examples of robbery. The minute officers enforce the law for one category of citizen and not the other, we are on the verge of losing any semblance of professional status. Robbery is robbery.

When the police allow the practice of "Gay bashing," they are asking for trouble. Where does one draw the line? Any hoodlum, when arrested, could accuse the victim of propositioning him. It would in effect be legalizing strong-arm robbery. Officers soon learn that they cannot tell a homosexual just by looking at him or for that matter talking to him. Some homosexuals are very masculine. Many are married and have several children.

STATUTORY RAPE OR UNLAWFUL INTERCOURSE

In dealing with "statutory rape" cases, the patrol officer should take many things into consideration. The purpose of the law is to protect young innocent girls from fast operators or older men who could easily impress a young girl with fancy cars and a lot of money. Society feels that the act of sexual intercourse is a serious matter, and can have far reaching effects on the life and emotional well-being of those involved. The law is strictly statutory and makes no distinction between an innocent 14 year old virgin, and a 17 year old divorcee with three children. An arrest involving the latter "victim" is not always the best answer. The patrol officer should use a lot of discretion in cases of this sort. In preparing a case for court, the patrol officer should take the following steps :

(1) Separate the parties and interrogate both of them with the bluff that the other has already told all. Use the sympathize-minimize technique and be careful to appear understanding and, above all, not condemning.

(2) Make a recorded statement of the confessions, and in the statement make sure that the subject knows the meaning of all the words in the statement. An admission of having intercourse is worthless if, in court, the victim states that she thought intercourse meant "French kissing." There is no law stating that a person must know the meaning of all words. If there was we would all be criminals. Think of every possible excuse that might be used in court. Then try to counter it with good questions. Make sure that the conversation is recorded. The victim who might be very cooperative at the time of arrest will often have a different story at the time of trial.

(3) Since penetration is the essential element of rape, the victim should be taken to a city or county doctor to be examined. There are cases on record where confessions were obtained and yet the doctor reported that the girl was a virgin. It is very possible that they were involved in an act of oral copulation and were ashamed to admit it. Many states have recently changed the title of this offense to Unlawful Intercourse, because it never was really a rape.

FORCIBLE RAPE

Forcible rape is sometimes falsely reported. This is due to many factors. In our society, we have a double standard in relation to sex. It is all right for the man to run around, but not the woman. Yet women are human beings as well as men. Occasionally a situation will arise, aided by the use of alcohol, where a woman will find herself compromising a man who is not her husband. If she has had a "proper" or religious upbringing, she might later have feelings of guilt. It is also natural for her to rationalize her part in the affair. If she is remorseful enough, she may actually convince herself that it must have been a rape. After all, she is just not that type of woman.

Another situation familiar to experienced officers is the husband who leaves town on business. His wife takes this opportunity to go "out-on the-town." After she has had her fling, she becomes concerned about the possibility of becoming pregnant or of contracting a venereal disease. This weighs heavily on her mind, and when the husband returns home, he senses that something is wrong, and keeps after her until she feels that she must tell him something. It is natural for her to justify the situation by sobbing and telling her husband that she was raped. He immediately calls the police. These situations must be handled delicately or they can result in a divorce. Officers should look upon "second day reported" rapes with suspicious concern. This is the type of case where listening to a message other than the actual words can be important. A sharp officer can sense that something just isn't right.

The possibility of a false rape report is an important consideration because society looks upon this crime as a serious and heinous offense. To falsely brand a person with such an offense would be a travesty of justice. In most legitimate reports of forcible rape, there is usually ample evidence of its being forcible. In the handling of such cases, officers should follow the following procedure:

(1) Comfort the victim. She is often in a state of shock. Keep her warm with blankets.

(2) Try to obtain a description of the suspect from the victim or witnesses. Realize that the victim is in a highly emotional state and consequently the description may not be accurate.

(3) Rush her to the county hospital for a sedative and an examination to determine whether penetration had actually been made. In some cases, the rapist has become so excited by the act that he reaches a sexual climax before penetration. Because of this, penetration was not actually made, and the crime of rape did not legally occur. The case is one of Attempted Rape. While at the hospital, the doctor can administer a douche to prevent possible conception or give medication to prevent a venereal disease. It is rare for a rapist to use a pro-phylactic (condom), so preventative steps should be taken.

(4) When the victim is feeling better, she should be shown the sex registration book. She may be able to identify the suspect from the pictures of known rapists. Her mental condition should be taken into consideration on any possible identifications. When she is finished, the witnesses, if any, should be given an opportunity to go over the book.

UNREPORTED RAPES

Today most cities have established Rape Crisis Centers where a victim of rape can talk over the phone with a counselor who has also been the victim of a rape. Because of her experience, the counselor can listen to the victim's story with genuine sympathy. Since these centers have been established, we are learning that about half of all rapes are not reported to the police. This failure to report such a serious crime is based on many conditions.

First of all, it is an extremely personal emotional trauma. The victim is also very hesitant to discuss it with a male officer. Because of this, many departments are now using women rape investigators. This has been successful. Their women's intuition is also good in detecting false reports.

SOME RAPE STATISTICS

Sociologist Menachem Amir, in his book <u>Patterns of Forcible Rape</u>, brings out the fact that in over 30 percent of rapes, the victim and attacker knew each other, or had at least met each other. One third occur indoors and most often in the victim's home. Seventy five percent are not impulsive crimes. They have been planned in advance.

MALICIOUS MISCHIEF OR VANDALISM CASES

Vandalism calls are a common experience of the patrol officer. They are usually committed by juveniles who live somewhere in the vicinity. The modus operandi of the offense will often indicate that it was perpetrated by juveniles. Footprints and handprints can also indicate whether juveniles were involved. Sometimes a theft will accompany the malicious mischief and the very nature of the item taken will indicate that the perpetrators were juveniles.

If it is obviously a juvenile case, the officer should go door-to-door in search of witnesses. If this fails, he or she should go to the nearest schools. There are usually some youngsters who hang around the school yard after classes are out. If the officer handles them right, information can often be obtained. If the youths do not know anything, but appear to be trustworthy, the officer can leave a card with them and ask them to call if they hear of anyone bragging about the offense. They may later hear rumors about who committed it. In checking the neighborhood, an officer should always check the house directly behind where the offense occurred. Often a person in that house might be looking out the kitchen window when the offense occurred, or when a group of juveniles passed by. If the offense occurred during school hours, the nearest school should be contacted for a list of absences. This technique pays off quite well.

In talking to juvenile suspects, it is important to minimize the value of the damage. It is easy for a juvenile to do hundreds or thousands of dollars worth of damage in a very short time. To the average juvenile, a hundred dollars can seem like a lot of money. If the officer tells the juvenile suspect that the damage amounted to hundreds of dollars, he may be so scared that he would never admit to the damage. By minimizing the value, it makes it easier for the juvenile to admit his guilt. After he has admitted his part in the offense, he should then be told the truth about the costs.

If the case appears to be one perpetrated by an adult, the officer should look for a motive. The victim usually has a pretty good idea who the suspect might be in a case of this sort. He knows who has it in for him. Many times the victim knows the reason for the offense, but is reluctant to discuss it because he has done something deserving of this retaliation. Watch the expression on the victim's face when he is asked about who might have committed the offense. The officer can often sense that the victim is holding something back. In a case of this sort, the victim should be questioned in a place away from his wife. Ask him to come out to the patrol car for a minute. The officer should convince the victim that he or she is an understanding person. He may confide in them and the truth may be obtained. He might admit that he has been seeing another man's wife and that he is sure that her husband is the perpetrator. He might mention that he had threatened to throw a brick through the victim's window if he didn't stop seeing his wife.

INTOXICATION CASES

In larger cities, intoxication accounts for over half of all arrests. Drinking itself is associated with the majority of crimes in one way or another.

ILLNESSES THAT RESEMBLE INTOXICATION

A common cause of false arrest suits is the person who appears to be intoxicated but is in fact suffering from some emotional or physical illness. This is of great concern to most officers. There are many illnesses that could cause a person to appear intoxicated. We shall consider those most often encountered by the law enforcement officer. It must be remembered however, that in each one of the following cases, the suspect may have in fact been drinking, and have the odor of alcohol on his breath. This could easily lead the officer to jump to the conclusion that the suspect is intoxicated.

Officers should understand the following conditions. With this knowledge, the officer should also develop a routine of thoroughness. This will go a long way in correcting the error of falsely judging a person to be intoxicated.

(1) **PHYSICAL INJURY.** Because of accidents or even criminal action, a person may appear to be intoxicated. His disorientation is really due to physical injury. This can be caused by blows to the head from:

    (a) Criminal attack.
    (b) Automobile injury.
    (c) Tripping over unseen objects.
    (d) Objects falling on victim.

The officer should look for both head injuries and the possible cause of such injuries. Sometimes the injuries are caused because the person is intoxicated and fell down.

(2) **STROKES.** Strokes usually occur in persons of middle age or older. As a matter of routine, an officer should examine the eyes of all intoxication suspects. Persons suffering from strokes will have one pupil larger than the other.

(3) **REACTION FROM ALLERGIES.** Some people have anaphylactic or immediate negative reaction to certain foods and medications. Sometimes the reaction is delayed up to several weeks. Ten percent of all people have some type of allergy to Tetanus shots. A common reaction is for the person to go into acute shock. This can appear to be advanced stages of intoxication.

(4) **ACCIDENTAL POISONING**

    (a) **GASES** A person who has been subjected to natural gas or carbon monoxide can easily appear to be intoxicated. The officer should search the immediate area for gas leaks or escaping fumes of one type or another.

(b) MEDICATIONS. A great many of the 11,000,000 arthritics and rheumatics are taking cortisone, hydrocortisone, or ACTH. After shock or injury, without one of these drugs, complications could be serious. Many of the 10,000,000 cardiovascular patients take daily medications that must be counteracted by other drugs, or continued in emergencies. Other heart patients are highly vulnerable to most common anesthetics, stimulants and sedatives. The investigating officer should look carefully on the victim's person for evidence of medications. If the person is at home, talk to others and check medicine cabinets.

(5) DISEASES

(a) FAULTY KIDNEYS. Persons with faulty kidneys do not normally drink. Their kidneys do not properly pass off the poisons in liquor, and they suffer an exaggerated "hangover." In such cases, the breath has an odor of ammonia.

(b) DIABETES. There are 2,000,000 known diabetics in the United States. Although they are not supposed to drink, they often do. Diabetes is a condition in which the person's body does not supply enough insulin to properly break down the sugar in the blood. To overcome this, the person may diet to limit the sugar. They may also take insulin by hypodermic each day to make up the loss. If a person has been taking insulin for some time, his thigh will be tough and leathery to the touch because this is where he usually takes his injections. An officer would do well to feel the thighs of a suspected intoxicated person who might really be a diabetic. Another clue might be small pieces of sugar cube or candy in the persons pockets. The diabetic is subject to two types of reaction because of this illness.

INSULIN SHOCK. If too much insulin is taken, or if the regular dose is taken, but less than the usual amount of food is eaten, the person may go into "insulin shock." In this condition, the blood sugar level becomes too low. It is treated by administering sugar to the victim orally or intravenously. In insulin shock the person may become extremely confused mentally. His condition easily resembles alcoholism or drug addiction. He may even become unconscious for a variable period of time. Insulin shock frequently occurs suddenly, with little warning. Because of this, the person may not have time or presence of mind to take sugar to prevent it. Some of the symptoms of insulin shock are: weakness, sweating, hunger, double vision, blurred vision, appearance of being intoxicated, and stupor. Some of the signs of insulin shock are: pallor, shallow respiration, pulse normal, eyeballs normal, and sweating.

DIABETIC COMA. This too, may be confused with acute alcoholism or drug addiction. The symptoms of impending diabetic coma are: thirst, headache, nausea, vomiting, abdominal pain, dim vision and shortness of breath. The signs of diabetic coma are florid face, rapid breathing, dehydration, rapid pulse, soft eyeballs, paralysis and finally coma. The breath will also have an acetone odor.

Either of the previous conditions may result in death. People who have not received proper treatment have died. If a diabetic person spends a few hours in jail because an officer believes that alcohol is the cause of that person's mental confusion or unconsciousness, that person may die. Today, no jailer will accept an unconscious prisoner without first having a doctor or nurse check him out.

(c) EPILEPSY. Epilepsy is a condition in which convulsions occur suddenly and repeatedly. They can last for several minutes. They are followed by a variable period of unconsciousness and/or mental confusion. This mental confusion may last for several hours. The unconsciousness or period of mental confusion has been frequently mistaken for acute intoxication or drug addiction. In the past it has resulted in an afflicted person spending several hours in jail. There are at least 1,500,000 known epileptics.

(6) **EMOTIONAL DISTURBANCE** Since it is common for persons suffering from emotional problems to drink, it is easy to assume that, because they have alcohol on their breath, they are intoxicated. In the acute stages of psychosis a person can go into a semi-coma or coma that could be interpreted as intoxication. Certain mild spastics and persons who are "punch drunk" from injuries can appear to be intoxicated. Patrol officers should take pains to learn of such people who frequent their beats and pass the word on to other officers. They sometimes hang around skid row and may associate with winos. Because of this, it would be easy for an officer to assume such a person is intoxicated because of his associations.

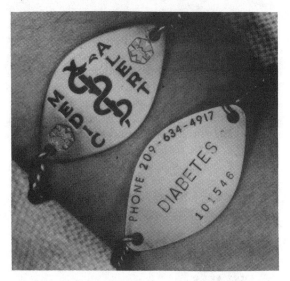

Fig. XIII-7; Medic Alert bracelet

MEDIC ALERT

An innovation that can be of great help to the police officer is the Medic Alert bracelet or neck chain. When dealing with those who appear to be intoxicated but are really suffering from some illness, the officer can look for a Medic Alert tag.

The Medic Alert Foundation is an international, nonprofit organization dedicated to educating and encouraging individuals to wear on their person an identification tag. This tag lists any medical problems that should be known in the event of an emergency. The foundation, which was formed in 1964 by Dr. Marion C. Collins, has been endorsed by the International Association of Chiefs of Police.

To help those who have an existing medical problem, the foundation distributes a metal emblem that bears the staff of "Aesculapius", symbol of the medical profession. The words, "MEDIC ALERT", are emblazoned in red on the face of the emblem. In addition, there is also the universal symbol for medical identification adopted by the American Medical Association. Many police officers having allergies wear MEDIC ALERT tags. On the reverse side of the emblem is engraved the immediate medical problem or problems of the wearer such as: DIABETES, ALLERGIC TO PENICILLIN, TAKING ANTI-COAGULANTS, WEARING CONTACT LENSES, NECK BREATHER, EPILEPSY.

The foundation maintains a central file which accepts, on a 24 hour a day basis, collect calls from anywhere in the world. They are able to give the caller information from the file which pertains to the wearer. Each emblem is registered and the serial number is engraved on the reverse side, as is the telephone number of the Central File. The number which can be dialed from anywhere is (209) 634-4917. More than 200,000 persons wear Medic Alert emblems. More than 1800 join monthly. One of the difficulties is to get those having medical problems to overcome the fear of wearing any symbol that will make them seem "abnormal". Statistics in the United States show us that, on the average, one person in every family has a medical problem. It is hoped that with proper publicity this fear will be overcome and people will rightly place their own safety over their personal pride.

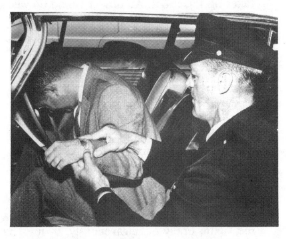

Fig. XIII-8; Officer checking Medic Alert bracelet

Apart from the person's blood type and the name of any special doctor, the emblem can present important information to the police officer. This is especially true if the officer is the first person at the scene. The back of the emblem has information in three general categories: "ALLERGIC TO", listing special allergies, "I AM TAKING", listing the special medicines that the person must take, and "SPECIAL CONDITIONS" listing special problems of the wearer. Under the last category there are two worth mentioning:

CONTACT LENSES. Officers should be aware that a person who is quite sick or even intoxicated can suffer permanent damage to his eyes if contact lenses are not removed. In some cases they can cause a corneal abrasion or a corneal tear. As a general policy, police officers should examine the eyes of all suspects with a flashlight. A side or oblique light on the eyes will reveal the presence of contact lenses.

NECK BREATHER. If this term is on the back of an emblem, it means that the wearer has had his larynx or voice box removed due to cancer (Laryngectomy). Due to the operation, there is a hole in the front of the neck where the larynx was previously located. This person breathes through the hole rather than his mouth. An officer who is unaware of this could, with good intentions, wrap the victim up tightly in a blanket to help prevent shock, and as a result cause suffocation.

PROBLEMS WITH INTOXICATED PERSONS

Because an intoxicated person can seldom reason correctly, it is difficult to appeal to their sense of logic. Intoxicated persons are very unpredictable, and officers should not let themselves get into the frame of mind that they are just handling "another drunk". Since so many arrests are for intoxication, it is easy to become lax when handling them. This is especially true if the person is a transient or "wino." Always be alert to the possibility that the person is not intoxicated but sick. The odor of alcohol alone is not proof of intoxication. Juries continually find a defendant "not guilty" because the officer's main proof was the smell of alcohol on the defendant's breath. There can be many explanations for this, and a smart attorney knows them all.

IS THE PERSON REALLY INTOXICATED?

It is not only possible, but it does happen, that a suspicious person feigns intoxication. Why? Because we excuse many actions when people have been drinking. We say that they are not really responsible for what they say and do.

We excuse their acts by saying that it is the liquor and not the person. The law does not excuse responsibility of an action because of the use of alcohol. In some states it can affect the element of specific intent. Since general crimes require criminal intent, the law will often take into consideration the use of alcohol when considering the extent of criminal intent. Criminals know this, and will often take a few drinks just before a crime so that they will have the smell of alcohol on their breath. They also do this to bolster their courage. They will then feign intoxication in an effort to escape the consequences of their actions. It is also a good ruse for a criminal or a lookout. This explains why he is alone in an alley or behind a building in the middle of the night.

Whenever an officer arrests a suspect for a felony, and the suspect acts as though he were intoxicated, the officer should obtain a blood sample from him so that the exact amount of alcohol in the blood can be determined. When the defendant is in court and tells the jury that he was intoxicated and didn't know what he was doing, the prosecution can show scientifically that this was not the case.

It is not a violation of either the Fourth or Fifth Amendment to take blood from a suspect. It can be taken and later used in court. The key is that it is legal if done in a medically approved manner. (Schmerber v. California 384 US 757 (1966))

Some District Attorneys advise against forcibly taking blood from suspected intoxicated drivers. They feel this action might prejudice the jury against the police. it could be looked upon as being too excessive for the class of offense. It could also be seen as being brutal. Felony cases would be different.

HOW DO WE KNOW IF A PERSON IS INTOXICATED?

One of the best ways to tell whether a person is really intoxicated is to feel his heart and the pulse in his wrist. The normal pulse in an adult is 72 beats per minute. It should be counted for 15 seconds and then multiplied by four. If the suspect is pretending, his pulse beat will be faster than normal. This is because he is trying to deceive the officer and is nervous. If the beat is below 40, it is possible that he is under the influence of heroin. A person who has just injected heroin can have a pulse as low as 15 beats per minute. If he is really intoxicated to the point where he is not in possession of all of his faculties, then his pulse will be quite slow. The eyes should also be checked with the flashlight. The Nystagmus test (which will be covered later) should also be administered. If the suspect is really as intoxicated as he pretends to be his eyes will often be bloodshot.

PROCEDURE OF ARREST

Intoxicated persons can be either extremely easy to handle, or extremely difficult. It is best to try a little psychology and subterfuge in dealing with intoxicated persons before actually resorting to force.

Officers should never take what they say or do personally. They should think of it as the liquor talking rather than the person. This philosophy makes it a little easier to stomach the intoxicated person. Sometimes an officer must have the patience of Job in dealing with intoxicated persons. Both their comprehension and response are affected by the amount of alcohol in their system. Generally speaking, intoxicated persons are susceptible to flattery and sympathy. Officers should not be afraid to apply generous amounts of both when dealing with this type of person. The philosophy of "wearing your badge on the tip of your tongue" can be well applied when handling an intoxicated person. The normal respect that can be associated with the authority of a badge is soon lost through the gen-erous use of alcohol.

Intoxicated persons should not be beaten up to "teach them a lesson." The next morning they might not remember a thing. The only purpose served by the beating would be the satisfaction of the officer's own ego. However, his or her self respect would take as much of a beating as that given the intoxicated person. Many times an intoxicated person will offer so much abuse that it is all an officer can do to stop from punching him right in the mouth. Any normal citizen in the officer's place might do just that. But officers who are striving for professional standards must remember that it is not a gift. It must be earned.

Officers should not feel reluctant to handcuff an intoxicated person. Always remember that when a person is arrested for intoxication, that person becomes the officer's personal responsibility. Anything that he does to himself or to others while in custody becomes the responsibility of that officer. The officer can be sued for any damage done by a prisoner if it can be shown that the officer was negligent in controlling the prisoner.

SHOULD AN OFFICER ARREST ALL INTOXICATED PERSONS?

Sometimes an officer feels that justice would be better served if an intoxicated person were not arrested. If the officer knows the person, should he be put him in a cab and sent home? Should the officer ever take the person home? In most states, the law allows an officer to release an intoxicated person from custody when it is felt that the circumstances warrant it.

There are times when an officer is about to go off duty and he or she observes an intoxicated person walking down the street. Under these circumstances the officer is quite prone to be merciful toward the intoxicated person and not arrest him. However, the officer should be aware of the legal responsibility in this situation. Suppose the officer tells the intoxicated person to go to his room. Under these orders he turns and proceeds towards his room or a creek where he normally sleeps. In doing this, the intoxicated person steps off of the curb in front of a car and is injured. Can the officer can be successfully sued? If the intoxicated person was killed, can the officer be held criminally liable on a charge of involuntary manslaughter (failure to perform a legal duty)? Sometimes an act of intended kindness can backfire. Officers must be aware of their legal responsibilities and then act accordingly.

INTOXICATED WOMEN

Male officers with years of experience seem to agree that one of the most difficult arrests can be an intoxicated woman. Even with our advances toward sexual equality, society demands a certain respect for womanhood. Human society has created a situation in which man by his very nature, as the sexual aggressor, is apt to take advantage of a woman. In lower animals, this urge is the key to the continued propagation of the species. It is biologically necessary that one member of a species take this role. However, in civilized societies the rules of behavior establish certain accepted ways of acting. This distinguishes us from animals.

Women, like men, do not want to be arrested. If they are normal, they will try to avoid arrest. If they cannot avoid arrest they will try to establish grounds for winning the case in court. It is natural that they will use whatever means is at their disposal to achieve either of these goals. Most women arrested for intoxication are not only aware of this, but will take full advantage of it. It is always best to call for the assistance of a female officer. Sometimes one is not available. In this case the male officer should follow certain procedures that will protect him and enable him to carry out the arrest.

Male officers who have not been married, nor had the experience of handling intoxicated females, should be aware of what appears to be a common pattern. When first arrested the female will try to charm the male officer. If that doesn't work, the next step is the crying routine (which can be very effective). If this doesn't work, the officer should be on guard for the next step can be dangerous. At this point intoxicated females can turn into wildcats. They can scream, fight, scratch, cuss and kick the officer in the shins and other sensitive parts of his anatomy. The male officer must be firm and yet fair. He must let her know that he is definitely in charge, and will not give in to her tactics.

Officers arresting intoxicated women should be constantly aware of public relations. The public is very sensitive to the mistreatment of women, even if it just appears that way. The public can be fooled by appearances. If the officer smiles and talks to her gently, even though he is nearly breaking her arm, the public will probably accept the action. It is important that she be made aware that she can't take advantage of the officer because he is a gentleman. An officer should not be afraid to handcuff a woman, especially an intoxicated one.

When the author was a rookie, he arrested an intoxicated woman and was taking her to jail. It was a warm night and the windows were down. As the police car drove through the crowded downtown area, the woman stuck her head out of the window and screamed "Rape, rape, rape, rape." Needless to say, this was quite embarrassing. After putting a finger-lock on the arrestee and applying pressure, she realized that her tactic was not working became quiet

If the female prisoner shows any signs of being combative, it would be wise to place another set of handcuffs on her ankles. The plastic ones are best suited for this. This saves a lot of wear and tear on the officer's shins. If a woman is wearing shoes with pointed toes or spiked heels, she can cause considerable damage to whatever or whomever she kicks. It would be best to remove the shoes.

For protection, male officers should always radio in the location and speedometer mileage when transporting a female prisoner. When the officer arrives at the jail, the mileage should again be given to communications. This prevents her from accusing him of stopping and molesting her on the way to jail. The department now has a record of the distance and time the officer took while bringing in the prisoner.

INTOXICATED PERSONS WITH THE "DT'S"

When an intoxicated person has the "DT's" (delirium tremens), he is in need of medication. The most common type of medication for this particular condition is Paraldehyde. He should be taken to a city or county doctor for this medication. Without it, the prisoner can present quite a problem in jail. Watching a prisoner go through the DT's can be a traumatic experience. There is no doubt to those watching that his hallucinations are very real to him. Those giant spiders and snakes might as well be real. His fear is so great that he can cause a lot of damage. The real wonder of this situation is how this person can ever again take a drink after going through that experience. In this condition, he is a danger to himself and the other prisoners. If possible, a "paddy wagon" should be used to transport the prisoner since this will prevent the police vehicle from being damaged. It will also eliminate the possibility of the prisoner vomiting all over your vehicle. It is easy to wash out the paddy wagon with a hose. When a prisoner has just received a shot of paraldehyde, it is wise to roll the windows down, as the fumes from this medication are quite powerful.

DRIVING UNDER THE INFLUENCE OF ALCOHOL

Because intoxicated drivers are potentially very dangerous, society has demanded stricter laws and punishments for this offense. But because many of society's prominent citizens are often guilty of this offense, and they can afford better attorneys, there are an increasing number of "not guilty" pleas. There are also more court trials for this particular offense. The fact that the punishment greatly increases with each successive offense makes it worthwhile for the defendant to hire an attorney and take the case to court. Added to this is the possibility that the defendant might lose his driver's license. In many cases, the defendant has little to lose by taking the case before a jury.

It seems to most officers that, in cases involving intoxicated drivers, it is the arresting officer who is on trial. Because of this, an officer must give careful attention to the evidence and proper procedures in a Driving Under the Influence case, more than in other misdemeanor charges. Attorneys have written books on ways to beat cases involving intoxicated drivers. Police officers have to be aware of these techniques so that in handling the case, they may be able to counter any possible maneuver by the defense attorney. Both drinking and the number of cars on the highway are increasing. This offense has become one of the most serious in the nation. Punishment is not the sole answer. Recidivism for this offense is high. The problem must also be attacked from the mental health standpoint.

At one time Massachusetts lowered the legal drinking age from 21 to 18. In the eight months that followed the new law, the number of teen-age highway deaths increased 136 percent. Michigan and Wisconsin also experienced similar increases in teen-age highway deaths after their legislatures lowered the legal drinking age.

Today we are averaging about 55,000 deaths on our highways each year. It has been estimated that 20,000 of these deaths in some way involved what would be called "problem drinkers".

North Carolina is trying an approach where liquor stores give away free breath-test kits. In this way party-goers can test themselves before leaving the party. If they fail the test, they sit around a while until the blood alcohol ratio drops.

Ann Arbor, Michigan is trying a system where the person convicted for driving under the influence is given a choice of escaping a jail term or a fine by taking one anti-alcohol pill each day. When the person takes the pill, it makes him ill to ingest any alcohol. This forces him not to drink.

When an officer stops a suspected intoxicated driver, he or she should make sure to note in their report that the suspect exited the car from the driver's side. This will help counter the excuse in court that the defendant was really a passenger and not the driver.

WHEN IS A PERSON UNDER THE INFLUENCE?

The best and most accurate way of determining whether a person is under the influence of alcohol is through a blood test. This will show the blood-alcohol relationship. Some states have set a certain blood-alcohol relationship as being prima facie evidence of intoxication. It has been written into law. There has been a move in various states to lower the amount required for legal intoxication.

Research findings at the University of California at Berkeley and other centers, have shown that even one drink can cause temporary but important changes in vision. It decreases the drinker's ability to see fine details after exposure to bright lights. The recovery from such glare takes up to 50 percent longer than it would for persons who have had nothing to drink.

TESTING DRIVERS SUSPECTED OF BEING UNDER THE INFLUENCE

There are many other types of field tests. They are usually based upon the reaction of the suspect's alcohol saturated breath on certain chemicals contained in a glass tube. The reaction is determined by a change in color of the chemicals which gives an estimate of the degree of alcoholic influence. These tests are not as accurate as the blood-alcohol test, but are a good means of testing suspects in the field. Many times a suspect is involved in an accident, and the officer is not sure whether the suspect's actions are due to alcohol or a head injury as a result of the accident. The simple field chemical tests can be of great assistance.

Most intoxicated drivers are either apprehended because they became involved in an accident, or because of their extremely erratic driving. If an officer makes an arrest on the latter, it is most important that detailed notes be taken as to exactly what the driver did that was wrong and caused the officer to stop him. The defense attorney will dwell on this so the officer should prepare ahead of time by making adequate and detailed notes.

TESTS AT THE SCENE

At the scene it should be determined whether or not the person is under the influence of alcohol. This can be done by administering one of the field chemical tests such as the "balloon test." It can also be done by a test of physical agility. It is wise to use both. The most common field agility test is to have the suspect walk a straight line heel-to-toe. When first talking to the subject, the officer should make sure that the suspect is not using anything for support. There have been cases where the subject appeared to be quite steady due to the fact that he had his hands behind his back, and was pushing his extended fingers against his automobile. When removed from the proximity of the automobile, he would fall flat on his face.

The officer may use any number of tests at the scene, providing they are not so complicated that the average person would have difficulty in performing them. Many officers have devised a series of their own special obstacle tests. This should be avoided. The test is merely to determine whether the person is too intoxicated to drive. If he is, a simple test will usually do the job. Some "smart" officers have been quite embarrassed in court. The defense attorney would ask them to perform the same feat in court that they used on the defendant in the field. They were unable to do so.

THE NYSTAGMUS TEST

A good preliminary test for intoxication is the Nystagmus Test. Nystagmus means a jerking of the eyes. It has been found that if a person is under the influence of alcohol, and that person is asked to follow a finger moving horizontally, the eyes at some point will start to fluctuate. The sooner the eye fluctuates, the greater is the blood alcohol concentration (BAC). It should be noted that a blow on the head can cause a nystagmus reaction.

Many times a driver will be involved in an accident and will have the odor of alcohol on his breath. Yet he will not appear to be unduly under the influence. Some drivers can respond to simple acts while under the influence, but cannot perform multiple acts which are often required while driving in heavy traffic.

PROCEDURE

Fig. XIII-9; Officer testing subject for intoxication

During daylight hours, the officer's finger can be used. During darkness, a small pen light should be used. The suspect stares straight ahead while the officer holds a finger 12 to 15 inches from the suspect's eyes (12 inches seems to be more common.) The suspect is asked to follow the officer's finger with his eyes. The finger is then moved from the center outward. The finger should be moved slowly so eye fluctuation can be detected at the angle that would indicate the right BAC. Both eyes should be tested from the center outward.

Because narcotics will often cause an eye to react to a vertical test, officers should routinely test for both horizontal and vertical nystagmus. When a pen light is flashed across the retina of a person suspected of smoking marijuana, the pupil will close and open again (oscillate.) If a person is not under the influence of marijuana, the pupil will just close. They white of the eye will also be very bloodshot if the suspect has been smoking marijuana. If a person is under the influence of PCP, he will often react to both horizontal and vertical testing.

If the nystagmus reaction occurs at 40 degrees from center, the BAC is about 0.10%. A nystagmus reaction at 35 degrees from center would indicated a BAC of about 0.15%. If it occurs at 30 degrees, the BAC would be about 0.20%. If the suspect has a BAC of over 0.20%, his eyes may not be able to follow a moving object. The formula for determining BAC is to first determine the angle (or degree) of when the eye first oscillates, based on the point where the officer's finger first started. (straight ahead) Then multiply that by 0.01. Then subtract it from 0.50. For example: The left eye oscillates at 35 degrees from straight ahead. This is multiplied by 0.01 which equals 0.35. Subtract that from 0.50 and you have a BAC of 0.15.

Officers who are assigned to traffic enforcement and use this procedure frequently, become quite good at estimating BAC. In fact some officers become competitive about it. They make bets as to who can guess what the BAC will be when the results of the blood test return from the lab.

TESTS AT HEADQUARTERS OR THE ACCIDENT INVESTIGATION BUREAU (AIB)

When the suspect is brought to headquarters, a further series of tests should be given to substantiate the officer's beliefs. Officers should never be afraid to release the suspect at headquarters if they feel that maybe the first judgment was wrong. Anything else would be a miscarriage of justice. It is difficult for people to admit that they are wrong. It takes a person of strong character to do this. Some officers will go ahead and book the suspect because they fear a civil suit if they release the person. Officers have nothing to fear if they release a person whom they feel is "borderline". If there is probable cause for stopping the driver in the first place, it is proper and legal to conduct a test in the field and

later at headquarters. Here the proceedings may not be under the pressure of a watchful crowd, and can be different. An officer should never rationalize an unjust arrest by stating "We'll just let the jury decide." Officers should be firmly convinced and have no doubts in their minds that the subject is intoxicated. It should be remembered however, that when a person is arrested in the field and taken to headquarters, because he is scared, it can stimulate the adrenalin glands to the point where he does not appear to be as intoxicated as he was in the field.

TESTS FOR INTOXICATION

BALANCE TESTS

One of the most common balance tests is that of walking a straight line. In the field, the dividing line of the sidewalk can be used. At headquarters or AIB, there should be a special line painted on the floor for this purpose. It should be wide enough so that it may be properly seen by a person who has poor vision. If a person wears glasses, he should be allowed to wear them during the tests. If the jury realized that the defendant was not allowed to wear his glasses, they would discount the evidence of his inability to perform the tests.

When officers have a suspect walk a line, they should follow the movements of that person by tracing them on a sheet of paper. Two parallel lines should be drawn on the paper. one for walking away and one for coming back. When the subject is walking, his movements and path can be recorded by moving a pen or pencil in relation to the lines. For example:

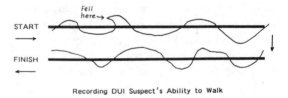

Recording DUI Suspect's Ability to Walk

Fig. XIII-10; Diagram of DUI suspect's ability to walk

The officer should first perform the test as an example for the subject. This shows him how it is to be done and can clear up any misunderstanding. The officer giving the test should have another officer as a witness.

DRIVER UNDER THE INFLUENCE ARREST – INVESTIGATION REPORT	ARRESTING AGENCY: _____		CASE NUMBER

TIME-DATE OF INCIDENT	LOCATION OF INCIDENT			BEAT	TIME-DATE REPORT STARTED

BOOKED ☐ NO ☐ YES	CITATION NUMBER	DATE AND TIME BOOKED	LOCATION OF ARREST	WHERE BOOKED

ACCIDENT ☐ NO ☐ YES	FORMS USED BY FORM #	CHARGE(S)

A. **SUBJECT**

NAME LAST, FIRST, MIDDLE	HAIR	EYES	HEIGHT	WEIGHT	SEX	RACE	BIRTHDATE	AGE

RESIDENCE ADDRESS	CITY	PHONE #	BUSINESS ADDRESS	PHONE #

DRIVER'S LICENSE #/SOC. SEC. #	STATE	LICENSE STATUS	DATE & TIME DDL INFO REQUEST SENT	METHOD SENT ☐ TT ☐ MAIL ☐ PHONE

B. **VEHICLE INFORMATION**

VEHICLE LICENSE #	STATE	YR. OF VEH.	MAKE	BODY TYPE & MODEL	COLOR	VEHICLE REPORT COMPLETED? ☐ NO ☐ YES

REGISTERED OWNER	☐ SAME AS DRIVER	R/O ADDRESS	☐ SAME AS DRIVER

NAME OF GARAGE/RELEASED TO	ADDRESS

C. **WITNESSES (INCLUDING OFFICERS AND PASSENGERS)**

AGE	NAME LAST, FIRST, MIDDLE	ADDRESS	CITY	PHONE RES/BUS	WITNESS LOCATION	OBSERVED DRIVING	INDICATIONS	
							SCENE	FACILITY

D. **OFFICERS NARRATIVE/REMARKS**

PROBABLE CAUSE FOR STOP OR CONTACT:

IN WHAT MANNER CAN SUSPECT BE PLACED BEHIND WHEEL IF NOT DIRECTLY OBSERVED?

DISTANCE OBSERVED DRIVING: CLOTHING WORN/CONDITION AND DESCRIPTION:

USE SUPPLEMENTAL REPORT IF NECESSARY

Fig. XIII-11a; Driving Under the Influence report (front)

E. | **ADMONITION**

1. YOU HAVE THE RIGHT TO REMAIN SILENT.
2. ANYTHING YOU SAY CAN AND WILL BE USED AGAINST YOU IN A COURT OF LAW.

3. YOU HAVE THE RIGHT TO TALK TO A LAWYER AND HAVE HIM PRESENT WITH YOU WHILE YOU ARE BEING QUESTIONED.

4. IF YOU CANNOT AFFORD TO HIRE A LAWYER, ONE WILL BE APPOINTED TO REPRESENT YOU BEFORE QUESTIONING, IF YOU WISH ONE.

THE ABOVE STATEMENT WAS READ TO THE ARRESTEE BY: _____ WHERE: _____ TIME: _____

DO YOU UNDERSTAND EACH OF THESE RIGHTS I HAVE EXPLAINED TO YOU? ☐ NO ☐ YES

HAVING THESE RIGHTS IN MIND, DO YOU WISH TO TALK TO US NOW? ☐ NO ☐ YES

SUBJECT'S WAIVER STATEMENT

ARE YOU SICK OR INJURED? ☐ NO ☐ YES - DESCRIBE

DO YOU HAVE ANY PHYSICAL DEFECTS? (FEET, LEGS, ANKLES OR HIPS)? ☐ NO ☐ YES - DESCRIBE.

ARE YOU DIABETIC OR EPILEPTIC? ☐ NO ☐ YES
DO YOU TAKE INSULIN? ☐ NO ☐ YES

ARE YOU UNDER CARE OF DOCTOR OR DENTIST? ☐ NO ☐ YES - WHOM? | ADDRESS

WHEN DID YOU LAST SLEEP? | HOW LONG? | WHEN DID YOU LAST EAT? | WHERE? | WHAT DID YOU EAT?

WERE YOU DRIVING THE VEHICLE? ☐ NO ☐ YES IF NO, WHO? | WHERE WERE YOU GOING? | TIME STARTED? | WHERE DID YOU START DRIVING?

HAVE YOU BEEN DRINKING? ☐ NO ☐ YES - WHAT? | HOW MUCH? | TIME STARTED? | WHERE? | TIME STOPPED? | WHERE?

DO YOU FEEL THE EFFECTS OF THE DRINKS? ☐ NO ☐ YES - DESCRIBE | WITH WHOM WERE YOU DRINKING?

HAVE YOU TAKEN ANY MEDICINE OR DRUGS? ☐ NO ☐ YES - WHAT? | HOW MUCH? | TIME OF LAST DOSAGE? | OBTAIN SAMPLE? ☐ NO ☐ YES | WEARING GLASSES? ☐ NO ☐ YES CONTACT LENSES ☐ NO ☐ YES NORMALLY WEAR GLASSES? ☐ NO ☐ YES CONTACT LENSES ☐ NO ☐ YES

DO YOU FEEL THE EFFECTS OF THE DRUGS? ☐ NO ☐ YES DESCRIBE | WHERE ARE YOU NOW?

WHAT IS YOUR OCCUPATION? | DATE AND HOURS LAST WORKED? | HAVE YOU BEEN DRINKING SINCE INCIDENT? ☐ NO ☐ YES - WHAT? | WHERE?

DID YOU GET A BUMP ON THE HEAD? ☐ NO ☐ YES | DO YOU HAVE AN EXPLANATION FOR HOW YOU PERFORMED THE TEST? ☐ NO ☐ YES - EXPLAIN

DO YOU HAVE AN EXPLANATION FOR HOW YOU WERE DRIVING? ☐ NO ☐ YES - EXPLAIN

DO YOU KNOW OF ANYTHING MECHANICALLY WRONG WITH YOUR VEHICLE? ☐ NO ☐ YES - DESCRIBE

F. | **SOBRIETY TESTS**
ALL TESTS TO BE GIVEN AT SCENE AND AT FACILITY

	AT SCENE		AT FACILITY		LINE WALKING: HEEL TO TOE/SHOES REMOVED AT OPTION OF ARRESTEE.
ODOR OF ALCOHOLIC BEVERAGE?	YES ☐	NO ☐	YES ☐	NO ☐	AT SCENE / AT FACILITY
ATTITUDE					
EYES					
PUPILS					
NYSTAGMUS					
SPEECH					
WALKABILITY					
ORIENTATION: LOCATION & TIME					

FINGER DEXTERITY: TOUCHING EACH FINGER TO THE THUMB OF ONE HAND IN BOTH DIRECTIONS

AT SCENE	AT FACILITY

△ L. FOOT   ○ R. FOOT

BALANCING ON ONE FOOT: SUBJECT BALANCES ON ONE FOOT FOR TEN SECONDS.

AT SCENE	AT FACILITY

LINE WALKING DESCRIPTION

DESCRIBE TEST LOCATION, SURFACE, WEATHER AND LIGHTING:

G. | **CHEMICAL TEST**

☐ BLOOD ☐ BREATH ☐ URINE ☐ REFUSAL   TIME TAKEN 1. _____ 2. _____ _____   DRUG RESULTS REQUESTED? ☐ YES ☐ NO

RESULTS, IF AVAILABLE: INITIAL BREATH RESULTS _____ % _____ % _____ %   DRUG SUSPECTED _____

IF REFUSED, WHAT DID SUBJECT SAY?   (IF BREATH RESULT UNDER .10, ALWAYS INDICATE DRUG SUSPECTED IN LINE ABOVE.)

NOTE: ALSO USE DMV FORM DL 367 IN ALL REFUSAL CASES.

LOCATION WHERE TEST CONDUCTED	DISPOSITION OF SAMPLE	NAME AND TITLE OF PERSON GIVING TEST OR TAKING SAMPLE		
ARRESTING OFFICER NAME & RANK	I D NO	TIME, DATE REPORT COMPLETED	BY:	I.D. NO.	CASE NUMBER

Fig. XIII-11b; Driving Under the Influence report (back)

THE RHOMBERG TEST

.The Rhomberg test is a balance test where the subject stands with feet together and eyes closed, then tilts his head back. The subject may first be allowed to use his arms for balance, then with his hands at his side. The officer giving the test should stand close to prevent the subject from falling and injuring himself. While the subject is in the officer's custody, he or she is responsible for his safety.

THE PICKUP TEST

In this test, the officer drops something on the floor and asks the subject to pick it up. If the subject is quite intoxicated, he can fall flat on the floor. Again the officer should be concerned with the safety of the subject. The use of coins on the floor is not the best test, because even a sober person has trouble picking up coins that are laying flat on the floor. The defense attorney could make this test backfire by asking members of the jury to try it.

JUDGMENT TESTS

The judgment tests are varied. For example, asking the subject if he knows what time or date it is. He may be asked to touch the tip of his nose with the end of his finger while his eyes are closed.

MANUAL DEXTERITY TESTS

In the manual dexterity tests, the officer asks the subject to do something involving the use of his hands. One of the most common is to have the subject write his name or draw a circle. When the subject is released, his signature is obtained in return for his property, and it is used to compare with the signature taken at the time of the test.

Fig. XIII-12; Officer administering a manual dexterity test

RECORDING THE SUBJECT'S VOICE

The use of the tape recorder during the test can have many advantages. First it can show the demeanor of the officer during the test. Secondly it will often show how vile the subject's language and behavior is. Thirdly, the subject's voice will indicate that he was in fact intoxicated.

PHOTOGRAPHING THE TEST OR THE SUBJECT

The subject can be photographed with both still and video cameras. The still camera can show the intoxicated expression, and the disorder of the subject's clothes.

The video camera can record the subject's lack of coordination and balance. Those who do not advocate the use of the video camera claim that in some cases the person can have a high blood-alcohol, and yet may not appear intoxicated in the video. This is true, but only in a very small percentage of cases. Those who use videos as a part of their testing, claim to have a very high degree of guilty pleas. As a result they save the community a considerable sum of money that would normally be spent on trials.

Fig. XIII-13; Photopraph of manual dexterity test

In conducting these tests, Officers should take detailed notes. They should not just indicate that the subject failed or passed the test. If the subject fell or wavered, it should be recorded. If he slipped or tripped, it should be recorded. Details are important in trying to convince a jury. Officers should try to mentally create the test in the juror's minds.

TESTING FOR INTOXICATION WHEN SUSPECTS ARE INJURED OR CLAIM TO BE

There are times when a person suspected of being under the influence of alcohol will either have or claim a disability to avoid a test for intoxication. Below are some examples of tests that can be used as substitutes. The officer should first demonstrate the proper way to perform each task.

(1) **TIME ORIENTATION.** Ask him to tell you when 15 seconds are up after you slap your hands together.

(2) **ASK HIM TO RECITE THE ALPHABET.** (make sure he went to school) Don't wait until you are in court to find out. Some people are very sensitive about a subject like this. They will tell you they can read and write when they really can't.

(3) **HAVE THE SUSPECT COUNT HIS FINGERS** by placing his thumb first on index finger, then middle finger, then on ring finger and lastly on the little finger. Then go backwards. Repeat on both hands.

(4) **NYSTAGMUS TEST.** Even though the suspect might be injured, the test can be valid. It should not be used when the suspect has a head injury.

OBTAINING BLOOD.

Obtaining a blood sample is the best and most accurate method of determining the actual degree of intoxication. Because of this, officers should develop techniques for obtaining samples. Once a person has been arrested for driving under the influence, his attorney will tell him never to give blood again. There are also those persons who have a fear of needles. This means that a job of salesmanship is often needed in order to obtain a sample of blood.

The law is quite clear on the right of the police officer to forcibly take blood from a suspect. Most district attorneys, however, advise against taking blood by force. This is because it will prejudice the jury against the officers. In the long run, it would be ill advised.

Officers should not ask for permission to take blood. They should approach the subject with the attitude that it is just a routine matter. They should show surprise that the subject even objects. A little psychology goes a long way. The officer might use a little subterfuge by referring to the technician as the "doctor." This will ease the subject's fear somewhat and give him more confidence in the technician.

The officer can appeal to the subject's manliness by stating, "You mean that a big strong man like you is afraid of a little needle? Boy, what is the world coming to? Heck, we had a little old lady here an hour ago, and she wasn't the least bit afraid." This should be done only if he objects. Otherwise officers should try to make as little of the matter as possible. They might casually mention that a small blood sample is now going to be taken for his own protection. Actually this is true. It can be for his own protection if he is not intoxicated. There are many cases that have been dropped when the blood-alcohol report came back too low.

If the subject refuses to give blood, the officer should try to obtain a urine sample. Many times a person has been advised by an attorney not to give blood if arrested for driving under the influence, and he will refuse. However, he will give a urine sample because he is unaware of its significance.

IMPLIED CONSENT LAWS

Most states today have "implied consent" laws relating to suspected intoxicated drivers. This type of law states that every person driving a vehicle in the state has given his consent to be tested when stopped for driving under the influence. The alternative is not to drive. Driving a vehicle is a privilege not a right.

The three most common tests are: blood, breath or urine. The person arrested has the right to select any one of the tests. The penalty for failure to consent to such a test is the suspension of one's driving privilege for a set number of months. The legal elements of such a law are:

(1) Did the officer have reasonable cause to believe that the person arrested had been driving while under the influence of intoxicating liquor?

SAMPLE IMPLIED CONSENT FORM

On _____ at _____ AM – PM,
             Date   Time

at _____
                   Location

I arrested _____ _____ _____
                    Name   Citation #   Violation

Address _____

Dr. Lic. # _____ DOB _____ Vehicle Lic. # _____

At the time of arrest, I had reasonable cause to believe the person arrested had been driving a motor vehicle upon a highway while under the influence of intoxicating liquor. Among those actions which led me to that belief were: _____

_____

_____

_____

I read the following statement to the arrested person:

> You are requested to submit to a chemical test to determine the alcoholic content of your blood. You have a choice of whether the test is to be of your blood, breath, or urine. A refusal will result in the suspension of your driving privilege for a period of six (6) months.

The person arrested refused to submit to any such test. His refusal was evidenced by: _____

_____

_____

_____

Blood, breath, or urine sample was taken after refusal: Yes _____ No _____

I certify, under penalty of perjury, that the foregoing is true and correct.

Date _____ City _____ County _____

Signature of Officer: _____ Badge # _____

Agency: _____

Address: _____
          Street   City   Zip Code

Fig. XIII-14; Sample Implied Consent Form

(2) Was the driver placed under arrest?

(3) Did the officer request that the driver take a chemical test?

(4) Did the driver refuse to take the test?

(5) Did the officer then tell the driver that such refusal would result in a suspension of his driving privileges?

To properly ensure the fifth element, it is best for the officer to read a prepared statement to the suspect. If challenged in court, a copy of this statement can be presented. An example of such a statement is as follows:

"You are requested to submit to a chemical test to determine the alcohol content of your blood. You have a choice of whether the test is to be of your blood, breath, or urine. A refusal will result in the suspension of your driving privilege for a period of six months."

EXCEPTIONS

Persons suffering from certain medical conditions are exempt from the blood test. These two conditions are as follows:

(1) Is he afflicted with hemophilia? (A condition where bleeding is difficult to stop.)

(2) Is he taking an anti-coagulant for a heart condition under the direction of a physician.

If the suspect should answer yes to either of these two conditions, the officer should obtain the name and address of the physician treating him for this condition. He should also be asked when he last saw the physician. It must be remembered that these conditions do not prohibit the taking of breath or urine samples.

POINTERS IN ADMINISTERING THE TEST

(1) If the suspect requests a Breathalyzer test, and the reading is very low or negative when he appears to be intoxicated, he may be on drugs. It is then advisable to obtain a blood

test in order to test for the presence of drugs. Try TALKING him into a blood test even though court decisions allow the forcible taking of blood (it does not violate the 5th Amendment). If he refuses, try to settle for a urine test. Although the blood test is better, urine will show the presence of drugs as well.

(2) The law allows reasonable privacy in the taking of a urine sample. However, this does not mean complete privacy. It simply means that he should not be subjected to the indignity of having to urinate in a bottle in front of a group of people. Where complete privacy is allowed, the following two evasive actions have been common:

(a) The suspect would put the bottle into the urinal or toilet bowl and half fill it with water, and would then urinate into the bottle. The result would be a watered down sample of urine and a very low indication of alcohol.

(b) A trick common among college students is to urinate into a test tube, cork it and tape it to the leg before going out drinking. If they are stopped by police and a urine test is requested, they reach into their trousers and tip the contents of the test tube into the bottle. The test results will naturally be negative.

(3) What about a suspect who claims to be cooperative, but in reality is trying to thwart the test? He should be reminded that lack of cooperation is the same as refusal. Examples would be the person who requests the urine test and then states that he just can't seem to urinate. Another is the person who requests the breath test, but does not fully blow or only pretends to blow into the mouth piece.

(4) All suspects must be kept under very close observation from the time of their arrest. They should not be allowed to put anything into their mouths. If this happens, the person could testify in court that the alcohol reading of the test was caused by some type of alcohol taken after the arrest. If so this would not be a true indication of intoxication while driving. If the officers observe a suspect put anything into his mouth, they should immediately be on the alert and find out what it was.

Some people have been known to carry a vial of strong alcohol or mouthwash in their pockets. Just before taking the breath test, they take out a handkerchief containing the vial and turn away, pretending to blow their noses. They drink the liquid and hold it in their mouth as long as possible. They then blow into the mouthpiece. The result is such a high reading that they would have to be unconscious or dead to have so much alcohol in their system. It then becomes easy for the defense attorney to attack the evidence by showing that the equipment must be faulty. If such a situation is suspected, the officer should have the person wash out his mouth with water, and then wait a little while before giving another test.

REFUSING THE TEST

There are many reasons why a person will refuse to take one of the required tests. Some feel that it is better to lose their license for six months than to be convicted for a third or fourth DUI offense. Here the fine is large, and a jail sentence may be mandatory. Others refuse out of drunken stubbornness. For those that do refuse, one of the best defenses is that the officer did not explain or fully make clear that the suspect could lose his license. To prepare against a defense of this nature, and to lay the legal groundwork for suspending the license of the person refusing the test, a standard form is made available to departments. It sets forth the conditions of the arrest and lists the legal warning of responsibility. It must be remembered that a form of this nature may be used in court as grounds for prosecution. In view of this, the officer filling out the form should give the wording much thought and consideration. The key to this problem is detail and description. When it asks why the person was arrested, the phrase "he acted drunk" is not sufficient? Examples might be "head laying on steering wheel, drove up on curb, drove over white line, ran into parking meter," etc.

Another section covers why he refused the test. Again, detail is important. The phrase "he said no" is not enough unless he absolutely refuses to say another word. If at all possible, the reason should be listed. For example: "Subject stated that he would not take any test because 'No damn cops are gonna make me do nuthin.'" "Subject refused tests on the grounds that they violated his constitutional rights." "Subject refused test on the grounds that the tests violated his religious beliefs." If the arrestee does not give a reason, the officer should make some effort to obtain one though it can take time and patience. It is very important should the arrestee contest the driving suspension.

LIQUOR LAW VIOLATIONS

In those states having a separate enforcement unit for alcoholic beverage violations, there is a tendency for patrol officers to avoid the enforcing of these laws. This is because they feel they are treading on someone else's territory. There is also the feeling that this is a specialized area that might be outside the expertise of the average patrol officer. It is also common for an officer to seek assistance when confronted with a case involving alcoholic beverage laws. This is an unfortunate misconception. Of all the divisions of a police department, the patrol division has the greatest opportunity to handle liquor law violations. This is because they are out in the field where they occur.

Many of the violations that patrol officers observe involve juveniles. In departments that have a specialized Juvenile Division, the patrol officer usually turns juvenile cases over to this unit. Since many juvenile cases involve the use of alcohol, this can further promote the feeling that this is a specialized area outside their domain.

The facts are these. The patrol officer is usually the first to observe the violation, and is also the first to make contact with the perpetrators. The officer is in a position to "make or break" the case through success or failure in obtaining important facts and gathering important evidence. He or she is present at a crucial time when this evidence is relatively easy to obtain. This alone warrants the patrol officer having the knowledge necessary to properly handle violations of the state's liquor laws.

In many states it is a misdemeanor for an officer to fail to enforce any alcoholic beverage control law. The reason for this law is that no small special enforcement unit could effectively police a whole state. Their main purpose is to handle some of the more technically involved cases. They serve as advisors and follow-up units to the regular police enforcement of such violations.

Because patrol officers have frequent occasion to come into contact with some of the more common liquor law violations, they can more effectively serve the community and criminal justice if they become familiar with some of the investigative techniques used in violations of this nature. Evidence laws are becoming more technical and restrictive. Because of this, patrol officers must make observations and gather evidence in the prescribed manner or the whole case may be lost. To assist the patrol officer in this area, investigative techniques will be first covered in a general, over-all approach. Then they will be covered by type of case.

GENERAL INVESTIGATIVE TECHNIQUES

Officers who have spent any time on the witness stand, subjected to the lashing tongue of a sharp defense attorney, soon learn what should have been done in the initial stages of the investigation. After this experience they seldom make the same mistakes twice. However, through proper information and training, the patrol officer can learn from the mistakes of others and avoid unnecessary humiliation on the stand.

To properly observe and gather evidence, the officer must first know the elements of the offense. These are the points that must be proved in court in order for a conviction to be obtained. These are the points that the defense attorney will attack. If the state fails to prove, beyond a reasonable doubt, any of the elements of the offense charged, a conviction will not be obtained.

Today there are so many laws and statutes on the books that it is difficult for the patrol officer to know the exact elements of each and every crime. This means that the officer must learn to use the penal code. It should be carried in the patrol car at all times. In this way, if the officer is not sure of the elements of a particular offense, It can be quickly checked.

Often, a little common sense and conscious effort on the part of the officer can predetermine the questions a defense attorney will ask in court. When things are slow on the beat, officers would do well to make mental exercises out of pre-guessing the various ways in which a particular element of a crime may be attacked.

COMMON ELEMENTS IN LIQUOR AND ALCOHOL OFFENSES

The following are some of the most common elements in violations of alcohol beverage or liquor laws:

TIME

Many offenses refer to specific times when certain actions are prohibited. An officer can count on the defense attorney attacking the reliability of the officer's timepiece. To counter this, the officer should call communications and ask the radio operator to call the telephone company or Western Union and verify the time. If the radio operator can plug the desk officer into the incoming call, there can be two witnesses to the time check. Officers can, if they wish, call the phone company or Western Union themselves. This way, however, provides no witnesses.

Problems often occur when the zone in which the officer works changes from Daylight Savings Time to Standard Time or vice versa. Usually there is some confusion as to when the bar should close on such days. If closing time is normally 2 a.m., the bar must close two hours after 12 Midnight of the preceding day. This is the simple rule. The time on the clock after it has been adjusted, has no bearing.

Bar clocks are often set ahead to help expedite customers in finishing their drinks before legal closing time. Because of this, an officer should not assume that a violation automatically exists because of the time on a bar clock. An officer should, however, record the time indicated on the bar clock if it is the same as the time given by the radio operator. This will corroborate the fact that a violation has in fact been committed.

ALCOHOLIC BEVERAGE

The term "alcoholic beverage" can present a problem regarding proof. To properly prove that the liquid or drink in question did in fact contain alcohol, a sample must be obtained for the laboratory. Then it may be officially analyzed for presentation in court. The patrol officer does not normally carry the containers to preserve such evidence. Because of this, the officer's own ingenuity must be used.

When a suspected liquid is seized, the officer should record the data from the label. This can be prima facie evidence regarding the alcoholic content. The officer should first sniff the contents of the bottle or glass. The next step is to touch the tongue to the liquid. The officer can then testify in court to both the sense of smell and taste. This should be done right away in case the bartender or suspect should accidentally (or intentionally) spill or knock over the drink. The liquid should be first smelled in case the suspect might have urinated in the bottle just prior to the officer's arrival. As in general crime scene evidence, the suspected liquid must be protected from contamination on its way to the lab where it will be scientifically examined and identified. If there are ice cubes in the drink, they should be removed. They will dilute the alcohol content.

Officers should obtain verbal or written statements from all parties, as to the contents or identification of the liquid. If handled right, statements can be easily obtained from those involved. For example, an officer might ask, "Is this a Martini?", or "Is this imported beer?" They will usually respond by saying "No, it's a Manhattan." or "No, it's a Bud." Later, on the advice of their attorney, they will deny it and claim that the drink was non-alcoholic.

SELLING OR GIVING

Many liquor law violations have the element of selling or giving an alcoholic beverage to another. This can be proved through observation, cash register receipts, or statements and admissions of the persons involved.

Regarding observation, officers should remember the pointers mentioned under "Identity of Persons." If the cash register receipt is to be used as evidence, it should be shown to the person who received the alcoholic beverage with the question "Under what condition did you obtain this receipt?" If they state that it was obtained when they bought the beverage, they should then be asked to point out the person selling them the beverage. Be careful not to make specific suggestions such as "Did he sell it to you"? and then point to a particular person. In court the defense attorney can attack this on the grounds that the witness made the identification as a result of suggestion rather than a voluntary choice. This admission will

corroborate the officer's observation along with the receipt itself. Most receipts have the name of the establishment printed on the top. If there are several employees, they will often use code keys that print on the receipt to show who made the sale.

If the recipient of the alcohol is cooperative, he should be asked to personally confront the person who did the selling or giving. When this happens, the suspect will often make an admission of guilt along with some excuse. Not only will this statement be damaging in court, it will produce another witness apart from the officer.

The officer should always be alert to the possibility of a minor falsely identifying a clerk or bartender in order to seek vengeance. The clerk or bartender may have refused to sell him liquor in the past. There are cases of minors threatening grocery clerks that if they didn't sell them beer, they would tell the police that he did. Foreign-born clerks are especially subject to this type of extortion.

Sometimes the parties involved will not cooperate. The evidence in the case might be "borderline" so a conviction could be doubtful. In this case the officer should turn all of the information over to plainclothes investigators, or State agents. then the suspected establishment may be "staked out" for violations. They can also have a minor undercover agent make a "buy" from the suspect.

EVIDENCE OF AGE AND IDENTITY

Age and identity are two different aspects of identification. The law requires that those selling or dispensing alcoholic beverages, make a reasonable effort to establish both.If they do make an effort, it is a defense to criminal prosecution. Whenever it is obvious that the identification presented does not establish either or both, a case should be prepared. Ideal identification should contain the following:

(1) Height and weight.
(2) Color of hair and eyes.
(3) Sex.
(4) Age and/or date of birth.
(5) Signature.
(6) Picture or fingerprint.

Most documents of identification establish either age or identity but not both. For example, a birth certificate establishes age but not identity. Any person of the same sex could present it as their own. The best examples of documentary evidence of age and identity are:

(1) Driver's License
(2) Draft Card
(3) Armed Forces ID Card

Most other documents indicate identity only.

When the officer stops a suspected minor in possession of an alcoholic beverage, his identification should be checked not only for age and identity, but for possible alterations. One of the best ways to detect document alteration is to place the document over the headlight of the police car. A headlight is strong enough to penetrate most identification cards, and will show up erasures and alterations. Next, the physical description on the card should be compared with the person in possession of the identification. If the description is obviously not that of the person possessing the document, he should be asked if the alcoholic beverage was obtained by showing the identification in question. If it was used, then this is prima facie evidence that the person selling the alcoholic beverage did not comply with the requirements set forth by law.

Compare all evidence of age and identity in the suspect's possession. Many times the suspect will have a false or altered driver's license that he will use to make illegal purchases. Ask him for all identification in his wallet. The rest of his identification may be legitimate and will not match the false or altered identification. Seldom will a person selling alcoholic beverages ask for more than one piece of identification, or ask to look at other identification in the person's wallet. They will ask for more identification if a check is being cashed. Especially if the purchaser looks young.

When a minor identifies a clerk as the one who sold him the alcoholic beverage, the officer should ask the seller if he did in fact make the sale. If he did, what type of identification was used. He should then be shown the identification in question.

At times an officer will find indications of false age presentation, but will want to check further. The following methods are suggested, but remember that this is only prima facie evidence.

CHECKING AT NIGHT

(1) A call to the parents or guardians, without giving the nature of the offense. If they know, they might lie.

(2) The minor's place of employment, if open.

(3) A call to next-door neighbors (If at a reasonable hour). This can be done by checking the address section of the city directory, and then obtaining their phone number from that.

(4) Check police and juvenile records to see if suspect has prior arrests or traffic offenses.

CHECKING DURING THE DAYTIME

(1) All sources previously mentioned.

(2) The suspect's school office.

IDENTITY OF PERSONS

Identity of persons is often a problem in the administration of criminal justice because of human error and fallibility. If a crime was witnessed by a group of people, how certain are we that the person they accused was in fact the real perpetrator? A good defense attorney can often ask questions that might make the officer testifying unsure of the identification. This is especially true if proper procedures were not followed by the officer during the initial stages of the investigation.

The fact that most bars are dimly lit adds to the possibility of error in a positive identification. When an officer observes a suspect violate a liquor law, he or she should jot down the physical and clothing description of the suspect as soon as possible. It may be almost a year before the case goes to court. The officer's memory can suffer during that period of time. Later, in court, this will greatly help in convincing the judge or jury that the suspect was in fact the person observed.

It is common procedure for officers to ask a suspect for identification after they have observed him commit some suspicious act. Unfortunately, officers commonly fail to follow through with a thorough examination of the suspect's identification. Is this person really the same person on the identification? If the suspect borrowed his brother's ID and the officer failed to notice this, the mistake would certainly be brought up in court. This could have disastrous results for the successful prosecutor of the case.

If the bottle or glass seized as evidence is handled properly, it is possible that fingerprints may be obtained. This is one way to prove the identity of the person possessing the alcoholic beverage.

An officer should never overlook the possibility of having witnesses or friends of the suspect help with identification. By talking to these people alone and away from the group, and by using proper interviewing techniques, or even subterfuge, the sharp patrol officer can further establish the suspect's true identity. (See Chapter X.)

Statements of the person buying the alcohol, as to who sold it to them, are often used in court and can be very damaging. The defense attorney will undoubtedly attack the identification on the grounds that the person making the identification was under the influence of alcohol and not capable of making a good identification. Since the case involves the receiving of alcohol by the person making the identification, it is logical for the judge or jury to assume that this could be possible. This may be contradicted by giving the witness a simple sobriety test just prior to the actual identification. If the case were important enough, he could be given a blood alcohol test, and this would show the exact degree of alcoholic influence.

Many times the minor knows the seller by name or nickname. He should always be asked if he does, in fact, know the seller's name. If he does, it should be recorded as corroborative evidence of the seller's identity. The fact that the minor knows the name of the seller might indicate that he has made prior purchases there. Always ask the minor if he has made prior purchases from this person. List the exact number of sales, what type of alcohol was purchased, and the date and time of the sale.

GENERAL TECHNIQUES COMMON TO LIQUOR LAW OFFENSES

(1) Confront all suspects with evidence as soon as possible, then try to obtain a positive statement regarding the evidence. This should, if at all possible, be done again in the presence of witnesses after the initial admission is obtained. Witnesses present during initial questioning may make the suspect hesitant to talk.

(2) Handle all alcoholic beverages as evidence by preventing contamination and by maintaining a good "Chain of Possession" (Chain of Evidence). Have the suspect initial the container or evidence tag if possible. Remove ice from the glass if it is a mixed drink.

(3) When sales tags have been found and seized as evidence, the officer should obtain a "Standard of Comparison." This can be done by obtaining a sample cash register receipt. It should be from the same register from which the original receipt was obtained.

(4) Be sure to obtain full information on all witnesses (occupation, place of employment, work number.) This will save follow-up officers considerable time as they usually begin their follow-up during normal working hours.

(5) Obtain a detailed description of the place where the violation occurred. The defense attorney will dwell on this. He will try to discredit the officer's testimony and place suspicion in the jurors' minds by suggesting that a mistake was made in identifying the location.

(6) Obtain a detailed account of the happenings surrounding the sale. For example:

(a) Number of persons present.
(b) Full description of the person selling or dispensing the beverage.
(c) Time that the sale took place.
(d) Monetary details of the transaction.

(7) Secure signed statements whenever possible. The longer the time span between the offense and the statement, the more difficult it will be to have it signed.

(8) Write down the identification numbers and names on all licenses and permits in the bar or liquor store. This will help counter the defense's accusation that the officer identified the wrong establishment.

INVESTIGATION OF LIQUOR LAW VIOLATIONS BY TYPE OF VIOLATION

SALES, POSSESSION AND CONSUMPTION BY MINORS, INCLUDING VIOLATIONS INVOLVING VEHICLES.

(1) When stopping vehicles containing minors at night, look for beer cans and bottles being thrown out of windows. By observing this an officer can establish possession. The officer could also add violations of the Litter Laws.

(2) Become familiar with Vehicle Code laws pertaining to open alcoholic beverage containers. Know other sections not found in the regular Alcoholic Beverage Control Laws.

(3) Since officers seldom observe actual consumption, they should confront minors with half empty beverage containers in hopes of obtaining an admission of consumption. When containers are found in a car with minors, admissions are fairly easy to obtain. The juveniles should be immediately separated before questioning. Officers should be cautious about threatening to dust the containers for fingerprints except as a last resort. This is because it will train the suspects to be more fingerprint cautious during the next offense. The next offense might be of a more serious nature.

(4) Be cautious when minors identify the person who sold them the beverage. Ask them for complete details. It is very common for juveniles to state that they paid some transient or wino a dollar to buy the alcoholic beverage for them. They will say that they have never seen him before. This is an easy out for them. It also helps them protect their source. In cases of this type, the juveniles should be separated and asked for minute details. This will usually reveal discrepancies that can be brought to their attention. The techniques discussed in Chapter Ten can be helpful.

SALES TO HABITUALLY OR OBVIOUSLY INTOXICATED PERSONS

This is a law that is seldom enforced by patrol officers, yet most of them know the habitually intoxicated persons on their beats. In cities they can amount to over half of all arrests. These arrests can be very time-consuming, and sometimes unpleasant for patrol officers. They can keep the officer out of service when some real emergency arises. Enforcing the law against selling alcoholic beverages to habitually or obviously intoxicated persons will not always stop them from obtaining them. It can, however, curb their consumption enough to make the patrol officer's job a lot easier.

The element that is most difficult to prove is found in the term "Habitual Drunk." There are two common ways to prove this element:

(1) By the suspect's reputation in the neighborhood or community.

(2) By prior arrests for intoxication. Some courts will accept three arrests in a six-month period as satisfying this requirement. However, this is not a set rule, and will vary from community to community.

It should be noted that there is some legal question as to the enforceability of this particular section, and your local prosecutor should be consulted for a legal opinion.

When patrol officers observe a habitually intoxicated person leave a bar or liquor store, they should take him back into the store and warn the proprietor that this person is a "habitual drunk" and has been arrested several times. They should be told that if he is sold alcoholic beverages in the future, prosecution will result. This action, though borderline legal, will help the prosecution in overcoming the defense's contention that the proprietor was unaware that the person was a habitually intoxicated person. It helps counter the defense that no intent or criminal negligence was involved.

Another difficult element to prove is that the person served was "obviously" intoxicated. A blood test or chemical test may show intoxication, but not "obvious" intoxication. Different people react in different ways when under the influence of differing amounts of alcohol. The following are some of the things that, when combined, will help to prove obvious intoxication. They are, however, not indications when they are taken alone.

(1) Condition of clothing and hair.

(2) Inability to walk properly.

(3) Falling off the bar stool.

(4) Difficulty in pronunciation.

(5) Bloodshot eyes.

(6) Inability to pick up change.

(7) Poor muscle coordination. Suspect bumped against walls. had difficulty with door.

(8) Knocked over drinks.

(9) Periods of passing out or unconsciousness.

DISORDERLY HOUSES

Most states have sections on Disorderly Houses in their Penal Code and Alcoholic Beverage Control Law. This type of law allows the District Attorney to condemn any building which has been used for unlawful activity for an extended period of time. It also includes any building that has become a public nuisance to the neighborhood.

Patrol officers tend to look upon this as an administrative procedure having little to do with patrol duties. Yet the patrol officer plays a very important part in this procedure. In order for the District Attorney to begin legal proceedings, the conditions leading to this action must be fully documented. If an establishment where liquor is served is becoming a problem in the community, the patrol officer should fully record each call, the number of officers who responded to the call, the number of persons arrested and a list of violations that occurred.

If it is believed that criminals are patronizing this establishment, officers should write down all license numbers of vehicles parked at the location. Later record checks can document this belief.

The beat officer should warn the proprietors that there have been too many fights or disturbances at their establishment. It is important that all of the details of this warning be recorded. The time, date, location and name of the person to whom the officer spoke. This information can be very important in court when the defendant claims that he was not warned about the situation.

It is important to show that there is a relationship between the establishment and increased criminal activity. The patrol officer can do this by keeping track of all activity in the vicinity. All fights, stolen cars, and vandalism in the immediate vicinity should be recorded. The time is important because it might show that these problems only occur when the establishment is open.

Evidence of gambling, narcotics, prostitution and other vices should be passed on to respective investigative units. They can do a better job of undercover investigation than an officer in uniform.

OTHER OFFENSES

By developing good contacts and informants, patrol officers often receive information or they make observations that would indicate that the liquor laws are being violated at a certain location. This information, when turned over to the proper agency, can result in a successful investigation and prosecution.

For example, it is common for taxi cab drivers to make a few extra bucks by selling liquor to tourists after hours. Bellhops and waiters will sometimes do the same. Patrol officers will often receive a tip that this activity is going on. The patrol officer is limited in what can be done to investigate liquor law violations while in uniform. Yet he or she is in the best position to play a team role in controlling this type of activity. Other types of alcohol related offenses are:

(1) Sales and consumption after hours.
(2) Illegal, after hour, "bottle clubs."
(3) The use of "B girls" in certain bars.

MISSING PERSONS

MISSING CHILDREN

Fig. XIII-15; Officer with found missing child

Missing children present a dangerous potential. Because the majority of them are soon found or come wandering home, the average police officer takes a missing child case very lightly. If it turns out that the child is injured or is found dead at the hands of a molester, any hesitancy on the part of the police officer to start an initial search would be most severely criticized. Yet from a practical standpoint, the department does not have enough personnel to start a large-scale area search every time a child is reported missing. An officer may seek a happy medium through proper evaluation of the situation. Prime considerations are the age of the child, both chronological and mental, and the length of time he or she has been missing. The longer the child has been missing, the more involved the police department should become. As time stretches out, other agencies should be called in, including the media.

Even if the officers have already handled four other similar cases that same day, they must convince the mother that they are sincerely interested in the case, and will do everything in their power to find the child. It is difficult to convince a distraught mother that it is really nothing and happens all the time. In an effort to build good public relations officers should use the approach that the child will definitely be found because they and the whole police department will do everything possible to locate the child. As time passes and the child is not found, this promise should definitely be brought into action. If one hour passes, and the child is not found, the juvenile units and the district sergeant should be notified, since the majority of lost children are usually found within this time. After two hours units from other areas should be diverted to look for the child. After three hours the Chief should be notified because this sort of situation can develop into a political bombshell. This is especially true in light of the fact that most lost children are located within the first three hours. The Chief will then decide whether the radio and television stations should be notified. Many times information broadcast over the radio and television stations has resulted in finding the child. A listener may remember seeing a young child fitting the description at a certain location.

Children under five years old usually take naps in the afternoon, and they are not too particular where they take them. It is common for them to crawl into a closet or under a bed, or even under the house while playing, and then fall asleep. Officers who take a report of a missing child in this age group, should begin the search right in the home, and then on the immediate property. The mother will often insist that she has searched the home, but the officer should still check the house.

Fig. XIII-16; "Missing" child found asleep in closet

This author was involved in one case which developed into a major search. The police reserves were called out, and newspaper and television reporters were swarming all over the place. Neighbors were forming search parties to assist the police. While television cameras were focused on an interview with the sobbing mother in her bedroom, the sleepy-eyed, "missing" child crawled out from under the bed. It was certainly embarrassing both to the mother and to the police. It could have been prevented if the first patrol officer answering the call had thoroughly searched the home. In one case the patrol officer searched under all of the beds, in the closets, under the house and in the garage in an attempt to locate a missing 2-year old boy. Just as he was about to give up and initiate a major search, he went to the laundry room and found the tot asleep in the dryer.

MISSING CHILDREN OVER FIVE

If the child is over five, Officers should obtain certain information before initiating the search.

(1) The mental and physical condition of the child. Sometimes parents are reluctant to mention that their child is mentally handicapped, yet it is important information to the planning of the search. An illness that may leave the child unconscious would indicate that a more thorough search of out-of-the-way places must be made.

(2) Who are their friends and where do they live? Young children make friends easily and their age makes them naturally irresponsible. They think nothing of wandering off to their friend's house even if it is some distance away. The patrol officer should enlist the aid of children in the neighborhood in either locating the lost child, or in providing information as to who his friends are.

(3) Where are their favorite play areas? The mother won't know all of them, and she has probably already looked in the places she knows. This information is usually obtained from playmates. Favorite play areas change according to various conditions. The creek bed might be a good place in the summer because it is dry. A certain field might be better in the spring because the grass is higher. A new freeway overpass might have created a huge mound of dirt that the kids have discovered which is unknown to their parents. There may be a new group of apartments that are being built several blocks away. They are fun to play in when the workers are gone.

(4) What and where are the attractive hazards? Most areas have attractive hazards such as water holes, abandoned houses, wells, large trees and tree houses. Patrol officers should be aware of these places as a matter of general information. They should not fail to ask the local children because they are bound to know of some new places.

MISSING ADULTS

It is the policy of many departments to take a full missing person report when the adult has been missing for twenty four hours. If there are extenuating or suspicious circumstances connected to the disappearance, immediate action should be taken. In an effort to promote good public relations, the officer should take the basic information on the report. When it appears that the case is legitimate, a full missing persons report should be filled out completely, and if possible a photograph attached.

Often a wife will call the police when she knows that her husband has stopped at the local bar and is late in coming home. She will do this in order to teach him a lesson. She hopes that he might be stopped by the police while he is intoxicated, and in this way break him of his bad habits. There are a high number of missing persons reported around the first of the month and on Fridays. This undoubtedly has some connection with paydays. It would indicate that the validity of many of these reports could be questioned.

When officers take what appears to be a legitimate missing person report, they should check the teletypes or computer messages for any unidentified bodies that would fit the general description of the missing person. By talking to the neighbors on all sides, valuable information might be obtained as to why he might be missing. Neighbors might even know where he is located.

MISSING ELDERLY PERSONS

Elderly persons should be treated almost the same as children. The police receive many reports of elderly, senile persons who have walked off from rest homes or from relatives who are caring for them. They seldom get into trouble, but they occasionally are hit by passing automobiles. They can also fall and cause injury.

A lost child will cry and attract the attention of persons passing by, but the elderly person will not. Someone in the neighborhood might think that the elderly person is lost. He seldom asks him for fear of hurting his feelings. They usually don't go far because they are not physically capable of walking long distances and they seldom have money for taxi or bus fare. Door to door inquiries are often productive. Many times the elderly person will stop and chat with someone in their front yard, and will be invited inside for a cup of tea. At times the elderly, senile person can be very lucid and carry on a good conversation. Because of this, it is possible for them to be missing for longer periods of time than the lost child without attracting attention.

RUNAWAYS

Runaways present many problems to the police. They need to be protected from those who would victimize them. Just as often, the general public must be protected from them. They must eat to live, and since they are seldom old enough to obtain a good job, they often obtain these necessities by criminal means. The patrol officer must be continually alert for possible runaway juveniles.

When a runaway is picked up, he should not be taken home. The condition that caused the child to run away in the first place should first be checked. A full investigation by the juvenile authorities should be instigated. If not, the juvenile will probably run away again. The overall situation is important. A child that has been away for only two hours, and is from a good home environment, and requests to return home should more than likely be released to his parents after a good "talking to".

Runaway girls have usually been involved in some type of sexual activity. Because of this, they should be booked until a health check can be made. It is common for runaway girls to become infected with a venereal disease. Since those girls often have a disrespect for adults, they will often take pleasure in naming adults with whom they have had affairs during their absence. Sometimes they will even keep a little diary that includes license numbers of the cars that gave them a lift when they were hitchhiking. A male officer who picks up this type of runaway should be most careful that he doesn't find his name added to her list. He should always give radio control the location and mileage reading when he picks up a female runaway. This will help protect him in the event that she accuses him of stopping on the way and molesting her.

BICYCLE ENFORCEMENT

Bicycle enforcement is a very important part of the patrol officer's job. Yet the average officer spends little time and effort working in this area. WHY? It is often due to the feeling that it is "petty" and "kid stuff." Why should an officer enforce the bicycle laws?

(1) It is part of an officer's patrol duties.

(2) Failure to obey bicycle laws can result in injury to the bike rider, and to pedestrians who might get in the way. It can also cause serious damage to automobiles if they collide.

(3) To develop good vehicle operating habits and learn the Rules of the Road. If a person learns to obey traffic laws when young, he is that much better when he begins to drive a car. "As the twig is bent, so grows the tree." In the long run it makes the officer's job easier.

(4) Bike citations also serve as Field Interrogation cards. Later, when a crime is discovered that appears to be a "juvenile job," the bike citations issued in that area might provide suspects for the follow-up detective or juvenile officer.

(5) If the bicycle cited is stolen, it will be discovered when the bike bureau follows up on the citation. All serial numbers on citations are checked against the stolen bike files.

(6) Citing for bicycle offenses has excellent deterring effects. The juvenile has to report to court with a parent. Because of this. less than five · percent of all juveniles cited are ever cited again.

(7) A juvenile who is arrested for bike theft will usually clear many other cases. Officer who make an arrest for bike theft, should also interrogate the suspect on other crimes that he might have committed.

(8) Many Juveniles who get away with bike thefts because of poor enforcement, later commit auto theft. Bicycle enforcement serves to lower other crime rates.

CONTROLLING BIKE THEFTS

(1) Bike license numbers and serial or frame numbers can be checked with communications the same as car license numbers. Records has a file on stolen bikes, and registered owners. The officer doesn't have to use the radio. This information can be checked at the end of the shift. Very few Juveniles are going to leave town.

(2) Once a bike has been licensed, a small "bug" is stamped next to the frame number. Each

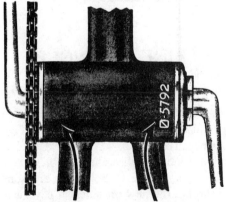

Under side of | Number stamped on side
Crank Bearing | away from sprocket where bearing is re-inforced

Stamp numbers at point indicated as this is heaviest section of bearing where there is no danger of damage to vehicle.

Fig. XIII-17; Bike frame number

city or community has a different symbol. Some juveniles will state that they have owned the bike since it was purchased. They say they just haven't been able to buy a license yet. On checking the bike, the officer notices that a bug has been stamped on the frame. This would indicate that the person is lying. The stamp is part of the registration process. A check of the symbol list will reveal which community has registered the bike. A phone call to the police department of that community can quickly obtain the registered owner's name. Many times the juvenile will tear off the license and repaint the bike in an effort to escape detection. However, the bug stamped next to the frame number will still be there, showing that it has been registered at one time.

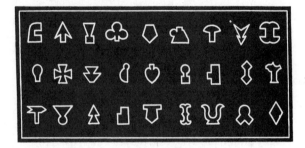

Fig. XIII-18; "Bugs" stamped on bike frames

(3) If beat officers would stop and check just one bicycle rider each day, this would probably reduce the number of stolen bikes on that beat by 50 percent. Juveniles know very quickly that the police are checking bicycles in their neighborhood, and the thefts drop. The Cranford, New Jersey, Police Department reduced their bicycle theft rate by 40 percent after instituting an enforcement and education program in that area.

(4) Encourage bicycle licensing. Have "Licensing Days" at the local schools. Have Fire Departments and stations also license bikes. Make it easy to have the bike licensed. Once the bike is licensed, and the special bug is stamped on the frame, its legal owner can be located. It is very unfortunate, but every six months, most police departments have to auction off a large roomful of bicycles. These bicycles belong to somebody. The police have no crystal ball that tells ownership if the bike has not been licensed.

(5) Many states have established a state licensing law. When this is done, a central records bureau is formed to hold all license information. California (with over 6 million bicycles) has established mandatory bicycle licensing laws. This information is placed in state-wide computers, making determination of the owner of any bicycle a quick and easy task.

FIRE CALLS

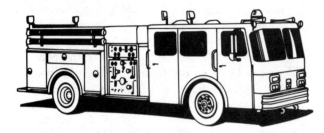

Fig. XIII-19; Firetruck

Officers with any seniority have handled numerous fire calls, yet it is a task in which they have little knowledge. Properly assisting the fire department requires officers to have some basic knowledge about this field. This lack of knowledge is usually caused by two things. First officers do not fully understand the role they are supposed to play in this relationship. Second, they fail to understand the firefighter's duties and responsibilities, and the problems that confront them. The U.S. has the highest fire death rate of all industrialized nations. Because patrol officers are already mobile, and because they are usually in the immediate vicinity, they are often the first public officers at the scene of the fire. Many times it is the officer who actually discovers the fire. This places an important responsibility on an officer's shoulders. Officers who arrive at the scene first should do three things:

(1) Evaluate the extent of the fire in case more fire equipment, police cars or ambulances may be needed. This includes requesting traffic control at certain intersections or locations. This initial report should include the type of structure, its size and the exact and obvious extent of the fire. For example: "Wooden three story house, flames coming through roof, houses situated on both sides."

(2) Decide on a course of action and notify communications of this action in case a superior officer might want to suggest changes.

(3) Execute the plan of action, making sure that the police vehicle is not in a position to be an obstruction to responding fire vehicles

The protection of life and limb is a very important part of the police officer's job. Because of this, it is natural and proper for officers to consider the saving of lives a first priority. Yet ignorance of the team concept in a fire fighting operation, and of the mechanics of a fire, can result in the loss of life, including that of the officer.

THE CHEMISTRY OF FIRE

A crime is made up of certain elements, each and all being essential for a conviction. In the same way a fire is made up of elements that must be present in order for fire to exist. This is sometimes referred to as the "fire triangle," and a normal fire cannot exist without these three elements.

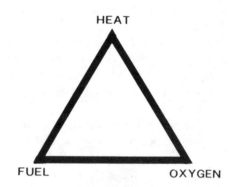

FIRE TRANGLE

Fig. XIII-20; The Fire Triangle

If a patrol officer were to see a trash-can on fire, and could put a lid on the top of the can, the fire would soon extinguish itself for lack of oxygen. This is because it is one of the essential elements needed for a normal fire. On the other hand, if it had the lid on and were smoldering, and someone lifted the lid, the new presence of oxygen would cause it to flame up again. If an officer sees someone run from a burning building with their clothes on fire, he or she should stop them from running as this just fans the flames. Rolling them on the ground or covering them with a coat or something like a blanket will prevent oxygen from getting to the flames, and they will be extinguished.

Fires have been discovered that have extinguished themselves because the building was fairly airtight and the oxygen was used up and the fire could no longer burn. A dangerous situation occurs when there is just barely enough oxygen in the building to allow the fire to smolder and heat up the building without actually putting the fire out. In a situation like this, an officer, unaware of the chemistry of fire, could easily open a door or window, and allow oxygen to rush in and literally cause the building to completely burst into flames or even blow up. Police officers opening a door to such a building, have been blown back like cannon balls, causing injury or death. There have been recent cases where police officers have opened doors in order to rescue one or two people, but in opening the door they caused the ultimate death of many others in the building who were on upper floors.

Because officers are usually the first public officials at the scene of a fire they should examine the scene carefully. If it is a two story wooden house and no actual flames are observed, but there is pulsating smoke that is yellow brown to black in color coming out of cracks, the officer should stay clear of the house. The officer's main duty at this time should be keeping others away. The roof, if it is made of shingles, will probably be pulsating like a living thing. This "breather" is the most dangerous kind of fire for it is oxygen-starved. It can literally explode when a door or window is opened. When a house-fire reaches this stage, the lack of oxygen has already suffocated all life. There is little hope of saving anyone inside. The incomplete combustion in a fire like this produces carbon monoxide, and carbon monoxide will explode at a temperature of 1004°. A normal house fire generates temperatures of between 1400° and 1800°.

Some other signs of an oxygen starved fire are:

(1) Discolored, rattling windows.

(2) Walls and doors hot to the touch.

(3) Pale or sickly yellow flames.

(4) Smoke escaping from the building in puffs.

(5) Whistling sound from oxygen on the outside being sucked in through cracks.

THE FIRE QUADRANGLE

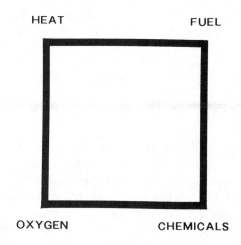

Fig. XIII-21; The Fire Quadrangle

In most fires, knowledge of the fire triangle is sufficient. Today however, it is becoming more common for fires to have an added element: chemicals. In our increasingly industrialized society, new chemicals are ever present in plants and buildings. If these buildings catch fire, all previous rules go out the window. What can commonly occur is the uninhibited chemical chain reaction. It is not only difficult to control, it is dangerous. Fire departments are trained to deal with this catagory of fire. Police officers are not. When officers respond to a large plant fire, and they are assigned to control traffic in the immediate vacinity, they should watch carefully for the type of clothing worn by fire fighters. The danger to officers from chemical fumes far exceeds any danger from criminals. If an officer notices that fire fighters are donning special protective equipment, it would be advisable to move the traffic control point back a considerable distance. At this point the fire fighters are usually "up to their asses in alligators," and they seldom have time to warn the traffic control officer to move back.

Although chemicals do come under the classification of fuel, the rules are so different that a new side has been added to this graphic equation making it a quadrangle rather than a triangle. For one thing, the ignition point for fire is considerably lower when chemicals are involved. Some chemical fires do not respond to the use of water. Some chemicals can ignite without heat. Just being near or combining with other agents can cause ignition. Chemical fires can also continue slow combustion without overt signs of a fire.

If an officer is the first at the scene of a fire, and the resident reports that he has already put out the fire, do not cancel the fire units. Many times a fire that has been "put out" by amateurs kindles and starts again. It is best to let the experts examine the fire scene and take proper measures to ensure that the fire is, in fact, out and will not rekindle.

THE POLICE OFFICER'S JOB AT A FIRE

The job of the police officer at a fire can depend upon the situation and such things as time of arrival, who else is coming and when. If it is late at night or early in the morning and there is no need to worry about immediate traffic congestion, the officer can use precious time to warn people in the neighboring houses. As far as saving persons in the building is concerned, officers should remember the information about the dangers of openeing doors and windows in an oxygen starved fire.

SAVING LIVES. First of all an officer is not dressed in protective clothing and does not have the proper equipment for such rescues. Instead of saving others, the officer may die. Each situation can be different depending upon the type of fire. Few rules can be established. In many cases an officer could do more good by standing outside in case babies or young children are dropped from windows as commonly occurs during fire panic. Officers who are outside a burning building should not try to break the fall of older persons. They could be seriously injured and then become another liability at the scene. If older persons do jump and are injured, the officer can drag or carry them away from the immediate danger of fire or falling debris. In most cases, the fire department will arrive in a short time, even seconds after the officer. They are trained to handle rescue operations.

The electronic siren and the police car's loudspeaker system can be used to warn sleeping residents of the fire. They should be warned in such a way as not to cause them to panic. The officer's tone of voice is probably the best way to accomplish this. A high, tense, excited voice will always tend to cause others to respond accordingly. The same information given in a firm, calm voice can result in a different reaction.

ENTERING A BUILDING OR STRUCTURE THAT IS ON FIRE. If an officer does decide to enter the structure, communications should first be notified. In this way, other police and fire units will know you are in the building.

There are certain facts which an officer should know before entering a structure that is on fire. First of all, there are many things in the average home that produce poisonous gases when burned. Both wool and vinyl objects can produce deadly gas. If the oxygen in the structure falls below 17 percent, thinking becomes difficult and coordination slows down. An officer could easily become so confused that he or she would not be able to find the way out of the building. One way to help correct for this hazard is for officers to crawl with their faces literally on the floor, not just crawling on hands and knees. The closer an officer's nose and mouth are to the floor, the more oxygen will be available.

If officers are going to enter a building on fire, they should always take flashlights, even in the daytime. The smoke inside will make visibility very poor. Always touch a door before opening it. Also listen for sounds of rumbling, cracking or hissing. This may indicate that the structure is about to collapse. Avoid standing in front of windows as they may blow out like a shotgun.

An officer should stop people leaving the building and ask them if they know of anyone else inside, and if so, if they know the location. If the room can be determined, most people will be hiding under a bed, table or other piece of furniture, or in a closet.

In fires and bomb scares, the owners of nearby hotels and buildings might refuse to evacuate their buildings because of the trouble or loss of work that it might involve. A police officer does not have the authority to force these people to evacuate a building if they want to be stubborn. Firemen, however, have the authority by law to call a fire drill at any time in any building. They should be summoned if trouble of this nature develops.

TRAFFIC AND CROWD CONTROL. If the fire is in the daytime, or in a downtown area, the officer's major concern should be traffic and crowd control. If the officer fails in this duty, it is possible that traffic congestion could prevent fire equipment arriving at the scene of the fire. This could result in greater death and destruction. The parking area just across the street from the fire should be kept clear if the building is tall. The ladder or snorkel truck needs to put its ladder up at an angle and cannot park on the same side of the street as the fire. To properly do their jobs, firefighters need plenty of space. It is the officer's job to provide it.

Once intersection controls have been set up and enough fire equipment has arrived, the next problem is crowd control. When people become tightly packed together at a scene where there is a state of high excitement, like most mobs, they lose their individual identities and sink to the level of the lowest person in the group. At times the emotion of the situation and the leaping flames and screaming sirens seem to hypnotize onlookers until they have no regard for their own safety. Sometimes they just stand there in a trance, oblivious to the danger. In situations like this, they can become very hard to control. If they are tightly packed, the ones in the front cannot move back when ordered. It is impossible to physically push them back with only one or two officers. Most fire vehicles and many police vehicles carry long lengths of rope or orange florescent tape that can be used to rope off areas and set limit lines for crowds. A good rope and one officer can do the job of over a half dozen officers who are trying to keep a crowd back by holding up their arms. If the crowd continues to push against the lines and cannot be controlled and is slowly edging closer to the danger area, the officer should first warn them of the dangers. They should be politely told to move back. If this doesn't work, the officer can mention the possibility of getting accidentally sprayed by the hoses. If this doesn't work, the officer might request that the firefighters give an occasional spray in the direction of the crowd. If lack of control due to carelessness or poor judgment could be proved, and a citizen happened to be injured, the city could be held liable. Even if contributory negligence is proven, it could still cost the city a lot of money. Sometimes a responsible citizen can be used to assist in crowd control, roping off areas, and taking messages to superior officers or command cars.

Along with the problem of crowd control is the problem of theft control. There are those who are always ready to take advantage of the misfortunes of others for their own personal gain. At fires there is often a feeling that everything from the building is "up for grabs" People who could never think of stealing from their neighbor think nothing of taking things at the scene of a fire. Many feel that it is all covered by insurance, and that the owner will really suffer no loss.

Added to other problems are the "gate crashers." These are those persons with lots of nerve, who represent themselves as being news media representatives, owners, relatives of the owners, insurance men, and so on, just to get by you and get a closer look at what is going on. It can be very important for some people to get past the officer and inform the firefighters of the location of certain dangerous chemicals or explosives in the building. Officers cannot just stop everyone from passing a control point. The use of proper interrogating techniques can be of great help in situations of this nature. If an officer at a fire scene has an important message, the ranking firefighter should be contacted. The "chain of command" procedure is not only courtesy, but a means of ensuring that delivery of the message is expedited.

FIRE HYDRANTS AND HOSES. It is an officer's job to keep space clear near fire hydrants so that hoses may be quickly attached. Pumping engines need to be parked close to the hydrants. Once the hoses have been attached and are filled, they must be protected from vehicles that may run over them. This is not only to protect the hoses from damage, but to protect firefighters on a roof, holding the nozzle end of the hose. If the firefighter is standing on a roof or at the top of a ladder, the sudden change in the high pressure in the hose caused by a car running over it could whip the fire fighter off balance and cause injury or death. Hose crossing plates or boards are usually located in the metal boxes on the rear sides of ladder trucks. The firefighters might be so busy after first arriving at the fire, that they don't have time to set up the hose crossing plates. It is also important for the police officer to know that fire hydrants directly in front of the building are not normally used, as the fire could burn the hoses or damage the engines parked there. In view of this, the officer must plan on clearing the street at the next nearest hydrant.

RANKS ON PROTECTIVE CLOTHING

How can a police officer recognize firefighting ranks at the scene of a fire when everyone is wearing protective clothing? Most fire departments throughout the country have standard markings on protective clothing that will indicate rank. Generally speaking, the firefighter will have black protective clothing and a black helmet. As the rank increases, the helmet and jacket will have more white or yellow. It can be in the form of stripes or half of the Jacket or helmet.

RANKS ON DRESS UNIFORMS

Unlike police officers, who use military symbols, firefighters use thin trumpets as rank symbols. Rank usually starts with parallel trumpets and as rank increases so do the trumpets except they cross in the center in spoke fashion. The hat band also changes from silver to gold, and in higher ranks the hat bill will have "scrambled eggs" like the military.

REQUESTING FIRE DEPARTMENT EQUIPMENT FOR POLICE EMERGENCIES

There are times when an officer can be greatly assisted on the job by requesting the services and equipment of the fire department. The following pieces of equipment are common to most fire departments. After each piece of equipment will be listed the way in which it may be used by the police.

(1) **Rescue Apparatus Unit.** The Rescue Apparatus Unit is equipped with tools for use in cliff rescue, vehicle accidents, and railroad accidents. Iit has a front-mounted power winch. Since they are usually Civil Defense units, they are equipped with enough apparatus to handle most emergencies.

(2) **Light and Salvage Units.** The Light and Salvage Units are equipped with 7500 watt or 5000 watt light generators for use in illuminating an area in night rescue work and in illuminating an area where the police must conduct a detailed search. Two of these units, each located at diagonally opposed corners of a block can illuminate the whole block. These units also have tools for forcible entry during rescue work, and they usually carry large salvage covers for protection against exposed materials that might be dangerous to the public.

(3) **Aerial Ladder Units.** Aerial ladder trucks carry a variety of ground ladders ranging in length from 10 to 15 feet. They can be used for many general public services and can be of great use to the patrol officer who must check out a report of a suspicious person on the roof of a house or building. They can be used to check for evidence on buildings where the point of entry was made by sawing or drilling through the roof. In situations where a roof must be examined for a possible dangerous criminal, it is suggested that a "Snorkel" unit be requested, since this device will lift the officer to the edge of the roof and allow him to have both hands free to use the shotgun or revolver, should they be needed. The hydraulic-operated extension ladders that are permanently mounted on this unit can allow the officer to gain access to exceptionally high places. This could offer many tactical advantages in the apprehension of wanted persons.

This unit also carries small light generators of the 1500-2500 watt capacity as well as various sizes and lengths of rope. Most units also carry forcible entry tools.

Fig. XIII-22; Rescue apparatus unit

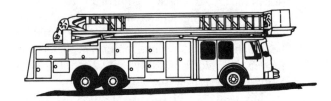

Fig. XIII-23; Aerial ladder unit

(4) **Engine Companies.** The engine company is the unit that usually responds to an automobile accident for a "wash-down" when there has been gasoline spilled in the street. Most engine companies carry an auxiliary water supply of 500 gallons. This is enough water to wash down most spills of oil, gas or debris in the street. Engine companies also carry a resuscitator that can be used in most cases involving respiratory problems. Fire fighters assigned to this engine are top rated paramedics and can often arrive at the scene before an ambulance.

(5) **Tanker Trucks.** Tanker trucks carry 1200 gallons of water. This is best used on highway accidents where large spills result from commercial vehicle collisions and rollovers. These accidents often occur in an area where there are no adequate water supplies.

CIVIL CASES

Of all the general types of cases that cause new patrol officers trouble, the civil case is one of the most prominent. Deputies from the Sheriff's Department will handle civil cases when under the direction of a judge's orders. Municipal police officers are concerned solely with criminal law, yet they are constantly confronted with a battery of civil cases that are couched in criminal attire.

The borderline civil case demands that the officer have some knowledge of the limitations in this area. In an era when people are so conscious of their civil rights, an officer is treading on thin ice by taking criminal action in a case that is civil in nature. With all of the laws on the books today, an officer cannot possibly know them all. Even attorneys must look up most laws. An officer's best hope is to know something of the more common civil laws, and be well grounded in criminal law. Basically, an officer should judge a case by the existing criminal code and refer all cases outside that code to the District Attorney's office.

The main task of the patrol officer when called to a civil case is to prevent it from becoming a criminal case. This will occur when one complainant assaults the other. It requires tact and patience and sometimes the wisdom and judgment of Solomon.

The average citizen is unaware of the fine distinction between civil and criminal law. Some people believe that the police can resolve any problem. Because of his vested interest in the matter, the citizen feels that it is the officer's place to assist him. A failure to act could be looked upon as a flagrant violation of duty. On the other hand, there are those businessmen who are aware of the law, and yet try to use the police department to further their own financial ends. They will threaten a person with police action, or actually call the police. Some of the more common examples are:

BAD CHECKS

Many merchants will accept a check knowing that there are not sufficient funds in the bank. Legally this is not a criminal offense, but a civil debt. The merchant will often take such a check and later threaten the person writing the check with criminal prosecution if payment is not made immediately. In many foreign countries the police can handle civil offenses. This causes confusion with some of the foreign born residents in this country. The elements of the offense of issuing bad checks are numerous, and if one is missing, it is likely that it is not a criminal offense.

LANDLORD/TENANT DISPUTES

When a landlord owns a piece of property and rents or leases it, it is natural to be concerned about the care and condition of that property. However, many complaints are referred to the police when the landlord's interest becomes an outright matter of snooping. A resident will call and claim the landlord is trespassing, or invading his privacy. In most cases, a landlord has no legal right to enter rented or leased premises without permission even though he or she feels quite justified in their action. Most of these cases can be mediated at the scene by the patrol officer. If they cannot, it is suggested that the matter be referred to the District Attorney's office, or the complainant's attorney.

Often a landlord will call the police in an effort to force a tenant to pay his rent. In some states there are laws on defrauding proprietors. Usually one of the elements of that crime is that the perpetrator leave without paying. So unless the intent is quite obvious and the person tries to leave, it is best to refer these cases for civil action. Equally as common is the request by a landlord for the police to immediately evict one or more of his tenants. The police have to be very careful that they are not used as bouncers at the whim of some landlord.

FAMILY RELATIONSHIP PROBLEMS

The patrol officer is often confronted with family problems that are represented as being criminal cases, but are really civil when all of the facts are known. It is important to listen for all of the facts. At times the complainant will base his complaint on religious or moral grounds rather than criminal grounds. When parents have raised a daughter for eighteen years, it is sometimes difficult for them to voluntarily relinquish the reins. If she has arrived at an age of legal independence, there is little the officer can do except explain that the parent can violate the law by beating the daughter. When an argument takes place and the daughter leaves home, the parent is likely to call the police stating that his daughter has run away, and that he wants her picked up.

It is not uncommon for a husband to instruct the police to go to a certain bar and arrest his wife who will not come home when he tells her. Again there is the feeling on the part of the citizen that moral and criminal law are one.

Child custody cases can be difficult to handle. Concern for the child and the legal status of the case are both important. There are two main factors to consider when dealing with these cases. One is whether the court has legally awarded the child to one particular parent. This can be determined by asking for the legal court papers. The other is whether the parents are legally married or divorced. If neither parent has obtained a court order to establish custody, the child belongs to one parent as much as the other.

Often the parents will tell the officer that they are divorced when it is really a separation. When this occurs, they will often come to an agreement among themselves, regarding custody. Later one of the parents will back out of the agreement. If the parents appear to have common decency and really care for the child, one tactic might be to threaten to take the child to a children's shelter until such time as they reach an agreement. This may shock them into making a decison. These cases

usually occur as the result of drinking or a heated argument, and the problem may be temporary. The officer should try to talk the parents into leaving the situation as it was prior to the argument, and then re-evaluating it in the morning when tempers have receded. An appeal to them through the emotional health of the child will sometimes work.

SMALL CLAIMS COURT

The Small Claims Court can be the solution to potential fights. Sometimes one party feels that the other party owes them money or property and they are going to "punch out someone's lights" if they dont get it. When the officers arrive, they should explain how the Small Claims Court works.

Resolving the matter without taking criminal action should be the officer's objective. The matter can often be resolved by explaining to the person wronged what civil action he can take. In order for there to be a criminal offense, there must be criminal intent or negligence. If it appears that a window was broken by accident, it would be wrong to arrest the perpetrator for vandalism. The proper course of action would be to mediate an on-the-spot financial settlement. Officers can often make some arrangement that is satisfactory to both parties. If a person becomes aware of a way in which he can receive monetary satisfaction, it can prevent a physical fight.

Small Claims Courts are held by Judges of the Justice or Municipal courts in most states. They are restricted to cases involving a certain amount of money. In many states a person can go to Small Claims Court for any amount under $1,000. Usually the amount is raised each year. It is the fastest and cheapest means of resolving small monetary matters legally. The plaintiff, or person bringing the action, may start the proceedings by filing an affidavit with the Judge or clerk of the court. This affidavit must state that the defendant is indebted to the plaintiff through contract obligation, rental of property, or through injury to person or personal property. There is a small filing fee and a writ of execution fee for each defendent served. A judgment in favor of the plaintiff will include these costs. Neither party may be represented by an attorney. They may however present evidence and witnesses on their behalf. Small Claims Court is sometimes referred to as the "poor man's court."

MECHANICS AND BAGGAGE LEINS

Mechanic's liens, are legal steps to recover monies for work performed. Baggage liens give keepers of certain establishments the right to seize baggage and property for non-payment of rent. When one person tries to carry out one of these liens, it can present perplexing problems. The officer is often called for a theft or burglary complaint when in reality it is a matter of property being seized under one of these laws. Similar to this is the repossession of automobiles or property of which the ownership has never been relinquished by the seller. When it is seized, the purchaser calls the police and reports that the property has been stolen.

To further complicate matters, the purchaser of the property that has been seized under a lien law will often steal or surreptitiously retake the property. This could be a criminal action. Even where it is suspected that the action is criminal in nature, it is wise to treat the borderline case as civil. Refer the parties to their own attorneys. These types of cases often require legal interpretation and research.

One way to cool down the demands for immediate action by one of the parties in a borderline civil case is to take the party to one side for a confidential talk. He should be informed that any mistake or error made in a spur of the moment decision could result in a sizable lawsuit. It should be explained that the officer is not an expert in civil law, and the safest action would be to consult with someone who is. Advise them to go to the District Attorney, or the person's own attorney. At no time should an officer attempt to give legal advice in civil cases unless it is to inform the plaintiff of his right to use the courts to settle the problem.

STUDY QUESTIONS for Patrol Operations

CHAPTER 13

1. The main quality needed by officers when handling police calls is common sense.　　　T or F

2. In most crimes one of the officer's first concerns is the protection of evidence. In homicide cases it is to _____.

3. Name one of the conditions or illnesses that can simulate death. _____

4. There are many methods of establishing death, but one of the best is to examine the _____ _____.

5. To assist the investigators, an officer should gather the evidence and place it on a table or in　T or F one location for the investigator to examine.

6. Officers who find that the victim of homicide is not dead, and is conscious, should try to obtain a dying _____.

7. The most important element in burglary, and the one most difficult to prove in court but the one that is easier for the patrolman to obtain is _____.

8. There are two major types of safes, (1) fireproof and (2) _____.

9. Match the following types of safe jobs with the technique involved.

   (1) ___punch job　　　(A) nitroglycerine is used
   (2) ___rip job　　　　(B) the spindle is knocked into the safe
   (3) ___chop job　　　(C) the safe is opened with a large "can opener"
   (4) ___peel job　　　 (D) the plate on the front of the safe is taken off like a sardine can
   (5) ___burn job　　　(E) an acetylene torch is used
   (6) ___soup job　　　(F) an axe is used on the bottom of the safe

10. When officers are handling a juvenile reckless driving complaint, even though they cannot cite for a misdemeanor not committed in their presence, they can at least talk to the juvenile's parents. If the parents are uncooperative, they can threaten to talk to _____.

11. When investigating a theft case, the officer lifts fingerprints that match with the suspect.　　T or F It is best not to use that evidence in obtaining a confession.

12. Since most theft cases are petty theft (misdemeanor), an officer cannot legally arrest the　　T or F suspect at the scene.

13. Sex is not strictly a physical exercise.　　　T or F

14. Match the following sexual terms with their definitions.

(1) ___buggery	A. sexual gratification from fondling animals
(2) ___cunnilingus	B. sexual stimulation involving urine
(3) ___fellatio	C. sexual stimulation involving human excrement
(4) ___koprolagnia	D. sexual intercourse with the anus or rectum
(5) ___necrophilia	E. the desire to wear clothing of the opposite sex
(6) ___pedophilia	F. sexual desire to fondle children
(7) ___transvestism	G. sexual intercourse with dead bodies
(8) ___urolagnia	H. the desire to peek through windows at undressing women
(9) ___voyeurism	I. use of the mouth on the sexual organs of a female
(10)___zoophilia	J. use of the mouth on the sexual organ of a male

15. It appears that the exhibitionist gets his pleasure from _____ women by his actions.

16. Exhibitionists do not seem to fit any simple category. The only sure category is that they are all _____.

17. Name one of the common types of places where there seem to be more indecent exposures.

_____

18. Many times exhibitionists can be identified by having victims look at the _____

_____.

19. A common type of exhibition that is practiced by college students, as a sort of joke, where they expose their bare buttocks is called _____.

20. It is common for the exhibitionist to also commit the offense of _____.

21. When trying to trace a telephone call, you should first contact the _____ of the telephone company.

22. There is a device that can identify a person by his voice. It is called the:

a. _voice activator   b. __voice analyzer
c. _voice sound spectrograph   d. __voice analysis spectrolizer

23. When an officer books a suspect and finds that he is wearing women's underclothing, he could be a transvestite, but he should also be suspected of being _____.

24. There is a controversy among experts as to the real danger of child molesters.   T or F

25. In child molesting cases, the officer has to be very careful not to lead the child   T or F
by suggestions when questioning him/her.

26. It is not against the law to be a homosexual.   T or F

27. Male homosexuals all have very feminine mannerisms.   T or F

28. Promiscuous male homosexuals tend to spread sexual diseases because they have many sex partners. 　　**T or F**

29. It is legally permissible for a person to hit a male homosexual if he makes a sexual proposition to him. 　　**T or F**

30. When dealing with statutory rape cases the officer should use a lot of discretion and consider the legislative intent of law. 　　**T or F**

31. Forcible rape is often falsely reported. 　　**T or F**

32. What percentage of rapes are not reported to the police? _____%

33. According to the book <u>Patterns of Forcible Rape</u>, over _____ of the victims of rape knew the attacker.

34. _____% of rapes are not impulsive crimes. They are planned in advance.

35. Most cases of vandalism are committed by _____.

36. If adults are the perpetrators of vandalism, the officer should look for the _____ in the case.

37. In larger cities intoxication accounts for over _____ of all arrests.

38. Name an illness that can resemble intoxication. _____.

39. If a person has suffered a stroke, one _____ will be larger than the other.

40. A person who suffers faulty kidneys can have a breath odor of _____.

41. A person who has diabetes can either go into insulin _____ or into diabetic _____ if they have too much or too little insulin.

42. A person who is wearing a diabetic tag, appears to be on the verge of unconsciousness, and whose pulse is normal is probably suffering from _____.

43. The above person whose pulse is rapid and skin is dry is probably suffering from _____ _____.

44. A person who is suffering from insulin shock should be given _____.

45. It is now very common for persons suffering from various illnesses to wear a tag that indicates what the illness is and has a toll-free number where further information can be obtained. It is called a _____ tag.

46. Statistics in the U.S. show that, on the average, one person in every family has a medical problem. 　　**T or F**

47. If an officer finds a person with a tag that indicates neck breather, care should be taken not to bundle him up tightly because he has had his _____ removed and breathes through his neck.

48. How can you tell if a person is pretending to be intoxicated? _____

49. The normal pulse in an adult is _____ beats per minute.

50. Generally speaking, intoxicated persons are susceptible to _____ and _____.

51. When a male officer arrests an intoxicated female and is taking her to jail, he should give communications the _____ and his _____.

52. The abbreviation "DT's" stands for:

    a. _ drunk test   b. __delirium tremens
    c. _ don't tell   d. __delirium testicles

53. A person arrested for drinking while driving is more likely to go to court than is common for **T or F** other offenses.

54. In states that have lowered the drinking age, there has been a noticeable increase in traffic   **T or F** deaths.

55. All persons are under the influence of alcohol when their blood-alcohol relationship is

_____.

56. Officers who have developed complicated field sobriety tests have been embarrassed when

_____.

57. The problem with using a movie camera or video camera to photograph suspected intoxicated persons is that _____.

58. Give an example of an intoxication test to use on an injured person who claims he cannot walk.

_____

59. To overcome resistance in taking blood, you should mention that you are doing it for his own

_____.

60. Under the implied consent law, a driver who refuses to submit to a test for intoxication will lose his license for _____.

61. Give an example of a person who is not legally required to consent to a blood test. _____

_____

62. If a suspect agrees to a breath test, but does not cooperate and barely blows into the tube,   **T or F** it is the same as a refusal.

63. The best test from a scientific standpoint is the _____ test.

64. Officers tend to avoid enforcing ABC Laws because they feel that this is the jurisdiction of   **T or F**
the ABC agents.

65. If an officer is enforcing a law that depends upon the exact time, how should it be obtained?
_____

66. It is the Saturday night when time changes from standard time to daylight savings time. When
does the bartender turn back the clock, or when does the new time take effect? _____

67. The bar closes when? _____

68. Bar clocks are usually set a little slow.   **T or F**

69. In the offense of selling to a minor, the officer must prove two things relating to the minor.
They are _____ and _____.

70. Most documents of identification establish either _____ or _____ but not both.

71. Most identification cards list height and weight, color of hair and eyes, sex, age or date of birth,
and signature. However, the best positive evidence of identification is either a _____
or _____.

72. One of the best ways to detect an alteration on a document is for the officer to place the card or
document over the _____ of the police car.

73. When an officer asks a person for identification, it is always best to also ask him for other   **T or F**
identification as well.

74. Why should this be done? _____

75. How can an officer double check a young person's age
a. at night? _____
b. in the daytime? _____

76. A minor arrested for buying alcohol should be asked if he has made prior purchases from   **T or F**
the same clerk.

77. When an officer arrests a minor for possession and observes a sales tag in the bag with the
beer, he or she should go to the store where the beer was purchased and obtain a sample tag
from the same machine. This is called a _____ of _____.

78. An officer who makes an arrest involving an off-sale business should obtain the _____
_____ from the wall of the business.

79. If an officer observes beer cans being thrown out of a parked car, apart from ABC violations,
the suspects can also be cited for _____.

80. What is the most common answer from juveniles when asked where they bought the beer?

   _____

81. You observe a habitually intoxicated person being served by a bartender in violation of the ABC Laws. How do you prove that the person served is a habitually intoxicated person?

   _____

82. A blood test can prove obvious intoxication in court.   T or F

83. Name a person who will often sell liquor after hours on the side, as mentioned in the book.

   _____

84. A bar has become a hangout for criminals and prostitutes, yet there have been few violations of the ABC laws reported. The bar can still be closed down as a _____ house.

85. It is illegal for bars to have "B" girls. "B" girls are:

   a. _ girls who are prostitutes.   b. __ girls who tend bar.
   c. _ girls who solicit drinks.   d. __ girls who tally the bills.

86. Most lost children are located within a few hours.   T or F

87. Name one of the locations in a house where children under five might be located when they are reported missing. _____

88. After you have talked to the parents of a missing child, to whom do you then talk to obtain further information? _____

89. About _____ % of missing adults show up within 24 hours.

90. When a runaway child is found, he should be immediately returned to his parents.   T or F

91. If an officer finds an open door and there is no fill available, he or she should go in alone.   T or F

92. If officers find an open door, they should call the owner. If the owner does not want to   T or F
    come down, in the interest of community relations the officer should lock up for the owner.

93. When a bicycle is licensed, a symbol is stamped next to the _____.

94. Give one reason why officers are often negligent in enforcing bicycle theft. _____

95. Enforcing bicycle licensing laws cuts down on bicycle thefts.   T or F

96. The three elements necessary for fire are called the "fire _____."

97. They consist of (1) fuel, (2) _____, and (3) _____.

98. When an officer observes a wood-frame house from the cracks of which brown smoke is coming and the house seems to be pulsating, he or she should not open a door or window because it is an oxygen-starved fire. It is nicknamed a:

    a. _ sucker.   b. __pulsator.
    c. _ breather.   d. __none of these

99. In the above type of fire, all life in the house has already expired due to the lack of oxygen.   T or F

100. An officer who suspects a house is on fire should always _____ the door before opening it.

101. The job of a police officer at the scene of a fire is to save lives by rushing into the building.   T or F

102. The quickest way for an officer to warn the people in houses next to a house on fire is to
_____.

103. Officers who do enter a building on fire should take a _____, even if it is in the daytime.

104. An officer in a burning building should stay near windows in order to make a quick   T or F
escape.

105. An officer in a burning building should stay as close to the floor as possible, even   T or F
if it restricts movement.

106. An officer's main concern at a fire should be _____ and _____.

107. Why should an officer stop cars from driving over fire hoses that are full of water? _____
_____

108. Fire hydrants directly in front of the building on fire are not normally used by firefighters.   T or F

109. A good rope and one officer can do the job of over a half dozen officers in crowd control at   T or F
a fire.

110. Theft is a problem at fires.   T or F

111. An officer who needs to know which firefighter is in charge should know that as the rank increases, the helmet and jacket will have more _____.

112. Unlike police officers who use bars for rank, firefighters use _____.
The more they have in a crossed form, the higher the rank.

113. An officer investigating a report of a child who has fallen into a well should request that the fire department send its _____ unit.

114. An officer who has some evidence that a burglar might be on the roof of a building should request communications to send a fire department _____ unit so that the top of the roof can be examined.

115. Of all of their units, the _____ unit is best for the above job.

116. Engine companies often respond to cases like heart attacks because they carry a _____ and are trained in its use.

117. An engine company is also called to certain accidents involving vehicles. It is so they can do a _____ of the gasoline that is leaking and prevent fires.

118. Two cannery trucks loaded with tomatoes have a collision and the road is covered with tons of tomatoes. The fire department can help by sending a _____ truck. It carries 1200 gallons.

119. The main task of a patrol officer when dealing with civil matters is to prevent them from becoming criminal matters.   T or F

120. If a merchant accepts a check from a customer knowing that there is a lack of funds in that account, it is still a criminal violation.   T or F

121. A renter calls the police regarding the landlord trespassing in his apartment. When you arrive, the landlord admits he was in the apartment. Since he is the landlord, there is no violation.   T or F

122. Private citizens often confuse moral law with statutory law.   T or F

123. A couple have separated without any involvement with the courts. When you arrive at their apartment, they are arguing about custody of the child. The father states that he is going to take the child to the movies. The mother states that he is not; that they agreed that she was to have custody. From a legal standpoint, who has custody? _____

124. In **YOUR** state, the small claims court handles cases involving amounts under $_____.

125. In the small claims court only the defendant is entitled to an attorney.   T or F

126. The law on mechanics and baggage liens comes under criminal law.   T or F

CHAPTER XIV

TACTICS BY TYPE OF CALL — HIGH RISK CONTACTS

RESPONDING TO SILENT BURGLAR ALARMS

The silent burglar alarm is a very common call. Unfortunately it is so often false that officers tend to let their guards down when they receive it. There are many things that can cause a false burglar alarm. The rain and wind are the most common. This is especially true during the year's first rain. The dust of the summer has gathered on the windows, and the first rain can dampen the dust and other particles to make electrical contact which sets off the alarm. Another reason for false alarms is the presence of cats or other animals who hit windows or doors, or cross the path of an electronic beam. Sometimes it is a custodian who inadvertently sets off the alarm.

In many cases, the police department will call the establishment to confirm whether the alarm is accidental. Since it might be the burglar who answers the phone, he would naturally tell the police that it was an accidental tripping of the alarm. Sometimes the operator can ask questions that a burglar would not normally know.

BURGLARIES IN PROGRESS

The following is one example of how patrol officers should respond to a burglary in progress, whether initiated by alarm or human observation.

(1) UPON RECEIPT OF THE CALL

Officers should practice set procedures. This is to prevent the panic reaction that can occur when officers receive a call suggesting "something big might he going down." Habits are developed through practice.

(a) Make sure your seat belts are on.

(b) If you are not familiar with the beat, check a map for the exact location. Keep a map available as a reference for the best approach. Check for streets that dead end and creeks that may be near by. They can be avenues of escape. Check for other important pieces of tactical information.

(c) If the patrol car is parked, make sure that it is safe to pull out. Too often the driver of a patrol car will, upon receiving an important call, pull out into the street as though no other cars were there. If there are other drivers on the street, they are not mind readers.

(d) Remember that the important thing is to get there. Speed can be important, but it is not the essential factor.

(e) While en route, it would be good to check emergency equipment such as flashlights, shotgun, and red lights.

(f) Develop a strategy. If it is your beat, and you will probably be the first car there. In your mind, develop some type of strategy. What will you do upon arrival? If you have a partner, what will your partner do? If the call is being supported with fill cars, just what should their duties be? Who should go where. When burglars have been arrested and later questioned, they have often reported that, while hiding, they observed several patrol cars covering the same area while not one of them checked the area where they were hiding. Proper coordination prevents duplication.

(g) Advise communicaitons of your plans (or your field sergeant, if available).

(h) If it is not your normal beat, ask communications for the cross street. The address should tell you what side of the street it is on. Usually one side of the street has odd numbers and the other side has even numbers.

(i) Drive defensively. It greatly insures that you will arrive at the scene. Getting there, after all, is the immediate objective.

(j) Don't drive Code 3 to a silent alarm. The idea is to catch the suspect, not to scare him away.

(2) TWO TYPES OF APPROACH

(a) **THE "GANG-BUSTERS" APPROACH** When there is a surplus of patrol cars, this approach involves getting to the scene as quickly as possible, blocking off all exits, lighting up the area and then using loudspeakers to negotiate the surrender of the suspect or suspects. Entry and search is a last resort. Police dogs are of great value in this tactic. They are prompted to bark loudly. The suspect(s)who are inside, are then told to come out or the dogs will be let loose.

(b) **THE "SILENT" APPROACH** In this approach, patrol cars sneak up on the building, hopefully without the perpetrator(s) being aware of the officers' presence and "stake out" the area waiting for the suspect to exit the building with the properety in his arms. This approach has an added safety factor because the officers do not have to enter the building, which can be dangerous. However, racing engines and squealing tires ruin the surprise factor in this approach.

(3) THINGS TO LOOK FOR ON THE APPROACH

The officer first sent to the scene of the silent alarm SHOULD NOT STOP ON THE WAY (an emergency would, of course, be an exception.) If the responding officer sees something that is suspicious while responding to the call, it should be reported to radio control or another car asked to check it out. The officer (or partner, if a two-person car) should have pen and paper available so that they can jot down important information and clues. For example, license numbers of parked cars that are observed on the way to the call.

(a) **LOOKOUTS** Since it is common for criminals, especially burglars, to have lookouts, the patrol car responding to a silent alarm should be alert to this possibility. The lookout does not wear a sign that says "lookout." Some of them are ingenious in their attempts to disguise the fact that they are lookouts. Because handy-talkies are so available and reasonable in price, it is becoming more common for lookouts to possess them. Some of the ruses that have been used by lookouts are:

(i) A male and female embraced in the front seat of a car pretending to be lovers.

(ii) A parked car with the hood up and a lookout looking under the hood as though he were trying to determine the cause of his engine trouble.

(iii) A person walking a dog.

(iv) A person who has no apparent business in the area, but pretends to be extremely intoxicated and not sure of where he really is. If an apparently intoxicated person is stopped for questioning, the officer should take his pulse. A person who is pretending to be intoxicated will have a rapid pulse. The highly intoxicated person will have a slow pulse.

(b) **PROCEDURES FOR RESPONDING OFFICERS** On the way to the scene, be alert for lookouts. It doesn't take but a few seconds to write down the license numbers, car descriptions or descriptions of persons in a car. When this is done, a request should be made through communications to have another car check out the suspected lookouts. If they are gone, a follow-up can easily be done based on the license number and description.

(4) UPON ARRIVAL AT THE SCENE

Most buildings can be secured from the outside by two cars. By using the headlights and the spotlights when positioned at one corner, two sides of the building can be lighted. The headlights cover one side, and the spotlight covers the other. Any person running from the building can be spotted. The other car can cover the remaining two sides from the diagonally opposite corner.

Once the building has been covered from the outside, the next car to arrive can then circle the building and examine all locks and windows with its spotlights. This is not as good as a search on foot, but is a good beginning.

Next a search should be conducted on foot. The foot officer should avoid being silhouetted when passing windows and glass doors. The officer should also walk as close to the building as possible. His or her progress should be covered by one of the officers in the parked patrol cars. The officer in the car can provide protective fire if the foot officer is fired upon.

Sometimes pry marks can be seen by a foot officer and not from a patrol car. If there are no visible pry marks or other signs of forced entry, the officers should always consider the possibility of a "roof job." Sometimes shining a light through a window onto the ceilings will reveal a roof entry. When there is good reason to believe that entry was made through the roof, the fire department can be called. Their ladders or snorkel can be used to inspect the roof.

(5) DISCOVERY OF AN ILLEGAL ENTRY

Once an illegal entry has been discovered, officers should call for the use of police dogs. They are the safest and most efficient means of locating a person who may be hiding in a building. The supervising sergeant should also be notified for additional assistance and resources.

(6) SEARCHING THE PREMISES

Whether or not evidence of entry is found, the police or the owners should make entry of the building to make sure. This can be done in two ways. A representative of the alarm company will have a key to the building. He can let the officers in. The owner of the building should also be called. He knows where the lights are, and he also knows where the best hiding places might be.

If the building is a very large department store, and it has been sealed off, reserve officers or officers from other jurisdictions can be requested to assist in the search. although police dogs are better suited for this type of search. A little psychology is very helpful in the use of dogs. You can warn the suspects that you do have police dogs, and that they will soon be released. Then have the dogs growl or bark into the "bull Horns." This tends to help persuade them to give up.

WARNING: When you have discovered or located one or more suspects hiding in the building, or if they have given up, DO NOT ASSUME THAT THEY ARE THE ONLY ONES.

Tell the ones who have been located that you are going to use police dogs for a continued search. They might tell how many others are still in the building to save them being bit. Sometimes they will even give you the names of those persons. This has great psychological effect when you make an announcement over the loudspeaker using the names of those still hiding. If a helicopter is available the sound of it hovering over the area has a strong psychological advantage. It also tends to discourage attempts at escape. If the helicopter is carrying a FLIRS unit, its infra red sensor can often tell you if someone else is still in the building and in which part of the building they are hiding.

OTHER POINTERS IN SEARCHING THE PREMISES

(1) **HAVE A PLAN.** The search should be organized by your supervisor. Officers should be assigned to search one particular area.

(2) **ENTERING A ROOM.** When opening doors, slam them open in case someone is standing behind them. Don't stand too long in the doorway, keep low and dart around to the side. If you have a partner, go one at a time.

(3) **CROSSFIRE.** Always make an effort to avoid being in a position where, if a suspect were to pop up, you would be in your partner's line of fire, and vice versa.

(4) **AVOID UNNECESSARY CONVERSATION.** Use hand signals to communicate with your partner. Don't give yourself away.

(5) **TURN ON THE LIGHTS IF POSSIBLE.** It reduces the chance of being shot, and increases the chance of the suspect giving himself up. It also reduces the chance of officers shooting each other (yes, it does happen.) Officers should still remember the possibility that a light switch has been connected to explosives in a safe. Quickly shine a flashlight on the light switch. look for wires leading from the switch.

(6) **FLASHLIGHT USE.** Hold the flashlight away from your body to distract a person who might use it as a target. Don't leave the flashlight on all of the time. Use it sparingly. If you do spot something, quickly change your position in case the suspect fires in the direction of the light. The flash of his gun will give you a target at which to aim.

(7) **SEARCHING PRISONERS** When suspects have been arrested, search them at the scene. Make sure to identify items taken from them not only by name of suspect, but from which pocket they were taken. In some cases a weapon will be found that will add to the suspect's sentence. Because there can often be confusion at the scene during the search and arrest, re-cording the exact location can be overlooked. Months later in Court, under cross examination, it can be of the utmost importance.

(8) **LOCATING THE SUSPECT'S CAR** How did the suspect get to the scene? Locating the vehicle can be very worthwhile. Important evidence can be found in the car. It may also contain evidence of other crimes.

Unless the suspect had someone drop him off, with instructions to pick him up at a later time, the car will be somewhere in the general vicinity. The hood will often he warm because the engine has not yet had a chance to cool down.

In case he has been dropped off by a friend, it would be well to check all cars that are circling the area. Especially if the car takes off in a hurry when the driver spots a patrol car.

BURGLARY IN PROGRESS

Sometimes a neighbor or passerby will notice something suspicious, such as a light flicker, inside a building that is closed for the night. They may even notice jimmy marks on a door or window. They may also hear a noise inside a house or building where no one is supposed to be. This type of report will usually come over the radio as a "Burglary in Progress." For all practical purposes, it to be treated the same as a "Silent Burglar Alarm."

RESIDENCE BURGLARY

If a residence burglary is reported some time after it has occurred, it will be handled the same as a late reported commercial burglary. If it is a burglary in progress, then patrol officers must be careful to approach the scene quietly. Someone should cover the back yard from the other street since it is quite easy for the perpetrator to jump the fence and run out to the other street. All persons in the area should be stopped and checked to determine their business in the area. Each person stopped should be treated in a courteous manner.

Police cars should not be parked in front of the residence. It is best to park at least one door down. The complainant should be contacted right away. He might have vital information as to the exact location or description of the burglar.

When patrol officers find that a burglar is operating on their beat, they should pay particular attention to his M.O. or "method of operation." From this they might be able to establish the type of residence he prefers to hit. Officers can then give extra attention to places fitting that description.

It is important that officers stop and question all strangers on their beats when a burglar is operating in their area. If a field interrogation card is filled out on each person, it is possible that the detectives might find some information to link one of them with the offenses. When a person is stopped, officers should not give the suspect the impression that he is under suspicion. Don't say "Hey you. Come here." Play the information seeker. "Pardon me sir, have you seen any strangers loitering around the neighborhood today (or this evening)?" If he says no, the next question would be "In which house do you live?" If the person does not live in the neighborhood, then the questioning can narrow down to the possibility of that person being a suspect.

Officers should never miss the opportunity to learn a few things from their adversaries. Many times a criminal, when first apprehended, will freely talk about his exploits. Sometimes it is a form of bragging. It can also be an attempt to show how dumb the police really are. At any rate it's an excellent opportunity to learn some tricks-of-the-trade.

The following are a few observations and techniques as told by a residential burglar who committed nearly 800 burglaries and avoided arrest for over a year:

(1) Nearly all police officers follow a fixed pattern. You don't have to watch an area too long to see how much coverage it gets and how attentive the officer really is when he checks out the beat.

(2) It is easy to tell the progress of a police search by the noise. Tires squealing, backing out of a driveway to make a turn, and so on.

(3) I never worried about foot searches because police officers seldom leave their cars, especially if it is cold out.

(4) In observing officers shaking down an area, it appeared that either they believed I had already left or that the call was a phony. They seemed to be just going through the motions of a search because it was expected by the person calling. Many times flashlights passed across me without the officers seeing me.

(5) When the officers left, I always listened for car doors to slam. If I heard only one, I knew an officer was staying behind, so I stayed put.

(6) A good hiding place is where it is dirty. Officers don't like to get their uniforms dirty, so they avoid these places.

(7) For some reason the police look under everything, but they never look up. Whenever I heard the police coming, I would go up the nearest tree or try to get on a flat roof.

(8) The average police officer really doesn't check things out carefully when he stops a car. I've often been stopped and given citations when I was in a stolen car. I would just remain calm and act nonchalant and at ease, and the police figured I was okay. Many times I would have a stolen registration or driver's license. One time the license I had was for a guy over 200 lbs., and I don't even weigh 140 lbs.

(9) I always dressed nice so I wouldn't look out of place in a neighborhood.

(10) I wore shoes with thick rubber soles that were about two sizes too big so they couldn't match me to any footprints.

(11) All I carried in the way of tools was a three-bladed knife and a small flashlight. The police expect burglars to carry a big jimmy.

(12) I would steal license plates and keep them till they were off the "hot sheet", and then put them on a stolen car.

(13) I liked patio doors the best, other doors next, and then side windows. I found that many people don't even lock their doors.

(14) If I had to flee, I never used alleys or streets. I would go over fences and hedges for blocks, always paralleling the streets being searched.

(15) I would always figure out what the police would probably do, and I would do the opposite. It seemed to work.

STAKEOUTS

One of the most boring jobs in law enforcement can be the stakeout. Most stakeouts occur when the department has information that a suspect will try to commit a crime at a certain location. Sometimes an informant will tell the police that a wanted person will be at a certain location within a certain time period. Sometimes careful examination of a series of crimes will indicate that a serial criminal will probably try again. The pattern of prior crimes can point to a certain location and the M.O. can possibly help with a time frame.

For the stakeout to be effective, the officer must be quiet and still. If the suspect spots the stakeout, the game is over. Although some stakeouts are manned by detectives, most of them are handled by patrol officers. The stakeout can be very effective in catching criminals if it is properly han-dled. The key to a good stakeout is preparation. Some stakeouts are organized on a moment's notice. Most of them, however, are known ahead of time so some planning can take place.

The two most important questions for a patrol officer to ask are:

(1) What is the type of location? Is it indoors or outdoors. This can make quite a difference in the clothing worn. If it is winter, it can make a great difference.

(2) How long will the stakeout last? If it is to be just a few hours, much less preparation is needed. Sometimes this is difficult for those in charge to determine. If the time cannot be estimated, the officer should plan on its being a long time. Most stakeouts require that officers not be in uniform. There are some exceptions where it is important that when the officer comes out of hiding, he or she be immediately and readily identifiable. If the officer is given enough time to pick up things at home, the following list is suggested:

(a) Warm/cool clothing (weather?) and a hat.
(b) Rain gear if it's outside. (again, weather?)
(c) Large-mouth jar (in case nature calls)
(d) Binoculars.
(e) Food and drink. (Thermos bottle)
(f) Small plastic sheet.
(g) Off-duty gun and handcuffs.
(h) Foldup air cushion. (hard surfaces)
(i) Flashlight and penlight.
(j) Soft shoes that do not squeak.
(k) Notebook and pens.
(l) Police radio (off until help is requested.)
(m) Photo of suspect and all info. available.

AT THE SCENE OF THE STAKEOUT

(1) It is best to be dropped off near the location by an unmarked police car. If using another vehicle, don't park in front of the location. Park a few doors down and walk quietly to the location. Sometimes riding a bicycle is the most quiet way to approach.

(2) If you are in a building, find the location of:

(a) The telephone
(b) The light switches
(c) Fire extinguishers

(3) If in a vehicle, park under a tree if possible.

(4) If in a vehicle, notify communications and the beat officer that you are on a stakeout, so you will be left alone.

(5) Prepare yourself mentally for what could happen. Ask yourself, "What would I do if someone came through that window? What action would I take if such and such a thing happened?" By thinking about it ahead of time, you will be better prepared.

RESPONDING TO ROBBERY CALLS

A common fault of patrol officers in responding to a robbery call is that too many of them respond to the immediate scene. By the time the patrol cars arrive, the perpetrator will be long gone. Cars are needed to watch possible escape routes and to look for abandoned escape vehicles. The only time more than two cars should respond to the scene is when there is a robbery in progress.

The thing of immediate importance in a robbery call is obtaining a description of the perpetrator(s). When a victim calls the department to report a robbery, the communications officer should first obtain the name of the victim and the address of the business. The victim should then be told to hold the line for 30 seconds. A call should be broadcast to patrol cars on the beat so that they may respond immediately. The cars will be alerted to stand by for further information. The communications officer will then resume talking to the victim. By using a description check-off sheet, the police communications officer will obtain as many details as possible over the phone and broadcast this information to the patrol officers. In the meantime, the supervising sergeant in charge of the district will set up a quadrant search. If the sergeant is out of service for some reason, the senior radio operator will set up the search.

THE QUADRANT SEARCH

In order to achieve maximum tactical efficiency in a holdup, the quadrant search should be set up as soon as possible. Time is most important. That is why the senior radio operator should take over in the absence of the field sergeant.

The quadrant search involves a division of the city into four parts or quadrants originating at the crime scene. This division is usually along existing street systems rather than by compass headings. One car is assigned to each quadrant. Sometimes the apex of the quadrant does not make the division easily understood because of uneven or dead end streets. In this case, either the sergeant or the radio operator can quickly establish the street boundaries of each quadrant, and give the quadrant officer a more detailed set of instructions.

The duties of the quadrant car involve first responding to the apex of the quadrant. Then a street-by-street search, in an outward direction, for the suspect vehicle. The reason for this is twofold. First, it prevents three or four cars covering the same area. When this happens, it usually means that some areas are not covered at all. Second, many armed robbers will park their own cars a few blocks away and use stolen cars to actually perpetrate the crime. They will then drive to the location of their own cars and abandon the ones used in the robbery. If the quadrant car can locate the vehicle used, the officer can then quickly question neighbors and possibly find someone who saw the perpetrators change cars. Someone may have seen a car being parked where the stolen car is found. A description of this car can greatly assist police units watching possible escape routes .

As soon as a patrol car has been assigned to the scene and to each quadrant, other available cars should be assigned to major intersections and main roads leading out of town. While this is being done, another police radio operator should be notifying nearby police agencies of the holdup and the available description of the suspects. Often a single stakeout by one of these agencies located on the main route of travel will pay dividends.

When the patrol units are responding to their quadrant area stakeout assignments, it is important that they hurry. But as they are responding, they often observe cars that are suspicious, but do not fit the description originally broadcast of the suspect vehicle. When this occurs officers should write down the license number and description of the car, and the direction in which it was traveling. Later, should the quadrant car discover that the perpetrators have switched cars, this information could be quite important. It takes only a few seconds to jot down a license number or two.

PURSE SNATCHES — STRONG ARM ROBBERY

In the case of a "Strong Arm Robbery", the perpetrators often remain in the vicinity because they usually have no transportation. Since most of these robberies occur in the lower sections of town, a thorough search of the nearby bars and cheap hotels can often give results. Cafes and restaurants are also good places to check out.

"Purse Snatches" are usually perpetrated by a lone male juvenile, but often, there are several of his buddies nearby, and when searching for the perpetrator, the officer should look for groups of ju-veniles rather than just one. If a vehicle is stopped, it should be thoroughly searched. Juveniles who snatch purses seldom throw them away. Usually the purse and all of the contents can be found hidden in different places in the vehicle.

DISTURBING THE PEACE

Disturbing the peace calls are one of the most frequent in patrol service. This type of call can test an officer's tact and ability more than any other.

NOISE DISTURBANCES

Even in Roman times there were laws to protect citizens from excessive noise. These laws prohibited chariots on the city streets after dark. The clickety-clack of their wheels on the cobble stones would wake sleeping residents. In 18th century England, there are records of lawsuits involving noise abatement. It is believed that Boston was the first city in the United States to pass an ordinance that prohibited disturbing the peace.

The major problem in handling complaints of noise disturbance has been the fact that it is a highly subjective evaluation. When is noise actually too loud? This is difficult to put into law to fit all situations at all times. Let us take a woman just out of the hospital after a serious operation. She is still in pain and overly sensitive to noise. Naturally she would feel that a particular noise was excessively loud. Her neighbors, however, might not even be aware of the noise. In cases of this nature, the patrol officer must act as a mediator, and hopefully arrive at a suggestion that will make all parties satisfied.

Demanding that the noise cease because one person feels that it is too loud, may not always be just. The answer is seldom easy.

Today, the issue of industrial noise pollution has become a popular cause. As a result, laws have been passed that actually establish a limit to noise based on decibels of sound. There are several companies that now produce sensing devices for use by law enforcement officers to measure neighborhood noise.

Fig. XIV-1; Noise meter

In absence of noise meters, the officer's best bet is to obtain written or tape recorded statements from neighbors. Then, if possible, tape record the noise itself. The distance of the recording device from the noise and the number on the volume knob should also be recorded in the officer's notebook.

In loud noise calls, the officer should not come on like "Gang Busters" and demand that the noise be stopped right now "or else." Most of these cases can be resolved at the scene without further action. The soft approach is best. When an officer challenges a person's ego, a belligerent response should be expected. This is especially true in communities where males tend to be on the "macho" side. It is the professional officer who understands the feelings of others and will allow people to save face.

NOISY PARTIES

This type of call can often be difficult because most persons at the party have been drinking. Because of this, it can be difficult to reason with them. The stereo can be turned down, but a short time after the police leave the scene, someone is bound to turn up the volume again. Shortly, another citizen complaint will be received. In a call of this nature, there is usually someone who is in charge of the party. Usually it is the owner of the house or renter of the apartment. They are the hosts, and are busy seeing that everyone is properly served. As a result, they are often not as intoxicated as the rest. Because of this, they should be given the responsibility for keeping things quiet. Mass arrests are usually the least acceptable solution. Other less severe possibilities could be removing a part from the stereo; turning off the lights or removing a fuse; having the owner of the house lock up the booze, or suggest they all go someplace for a bite to eat.

An officer's duty is to keep the peace. It is not to start fights or become involved in them. The key to this type of call is to wear your badge on the tip of your tongue. It takes no ability or tact to become involved in a fight. Any fool can do it. There are times when an officer has no choice but to fight. Yet most departments have at least one officer who seems to be involved in a fight on every other call of this nature. Police administrators who want to avoid civil suits are very sensitive to this type of officer. Each time it occurs, a notation is placed in the officer's personnel file. Some departments require that a special report be made out each time an officer is actually involved in a fight. The purpose is twofold. First, it provides information in the event that the officer and the department are sued. Second, it can be put in the officer's personnel file so frequency can be noted. Once the officer has been warned of the problem and it continues, this can become the basis for disciplinary action.

It is easy to be a "Monday morning quarterback" and state that an officer should or should not have become involved in a fight. No one but the officer really knows the circumstances that led to the fight. However, there are certain officers who seldom become involved in fights. They handle as many if not more calls than those officers who seem to be constantly involved in fights. This condition usually involves a personality or emotional problem on the part of the fighting officers. Sometimes professional counselling can be of great help.

FAMILY FIGHTS

One approach to family fights is separation. When two adults are so highly emotional that they are fighting, the officer will have difficulty in resolving the matter while they are both in each other's presence. The officer should take one person to one room and the other officer should take the other person to another room. When the two parties are separated, they can be calmed down to some extent. The chance of reasoning with them is now greatly increased. While they are together it can be most difficult.

In a family fight, both feelings and pride have been hurt. If the officer will briefly listen to each party, it will tend to decrease the tension. However, officers must remember that they are not trained family counselors. They should not expect to solve a problem in one night that has been years in developing. The officer's job is to preserve the peace. This should be done with understanding, tact, and an awareness of one's limitations. Naturally, officers cannot spend all night listening to the complaints of the parties involved and offering advice. There are many other citizens who might need assistance. The officer should know the various agencies that assist families with problems, and refer the persons involved to those agencies.

CASES OF WIFE BEATING

In the past, too many male officers tended to "kiss off" cases of wife beating unless the wife was hospitalized. The thought seemed to be that if it was that bad, she would leave him. This is easier said than done. Especially if there are children and the wife is not employed. Because of important studies involving the beating of spouses, and because of televised reports on cases involving serious officer neglect in such cases, some states have enacted very strict laws pertaining to family fights involving wife beating. According to the FBI, a woman is beaten every 18 seconds. About 3,000 are beaten to death each year.

THE MINNEAPOLIS STUDY

The City of Minneapolis conducted a six month study on the effect of the way in which officers handled wife beating cases. In this study the victims were interviewed six months after officers responded. The calls involved a family fight in which the wife was beaten. First, Investigators determined what action the officers took. Second, they determined whether or not the husband repeated the beating after the first incident? The results of the study showed:

(1) Of suspects sent away by officers, 24% beat their wives again.

(2) Of suspects sternly warned, 19% beat their wives again.

(3) Of suspects arrested, 10% beat their wives again.

Because of this study, as well as national TV specials on cases involving serious injury, compounded by officer neglect, attention was focused on this problem. Women's groups coordinated an intensive effort to have legislators enact strict corrective laws. A few states did pass laws in this area. and more seem to be following suit. The first laws passed made it mandatory that an officer arrest the suspect in ALL cases involving the beating of a cohabitant.

Any professional officer knows that the interests of justice are not always served by arresting the suspect. As in most cases where officer discretion has been taken away, the acts, or failures to act, of a small number of officers have been responsible. States that enacted laws at a later time have responded by requiring that officers submit a report on all cases involving wife beating. If the suspect is not arrested, the officer must state in writing why he was not arrested.

Many states have set up special marital counseling centers. They also mandate that officers hand out information pamphlets to victims. The pamphlets explain the laws that protect them and what legal steps they can take. They give phone numbers and addresses of people to contact for help or assistance. Some states also require officers to tell the wife when she can expect the husband to be released from jail. It comes as a shock to some that the husband can post bail and be back in a few hours. If they are not familiar with the legal system, the officer should explain the system briefly. This will allow the wife to take some protective measure once she is aware of how the system works.

Some states have established centrally controlled record keeping centers that document the number of times a suspect has beaten his spouse or cohabitant. So far, evidence indicates that more aggressive handling of wife beating cases reduces the number of times the offense is repeated. Something needs to be done to break the cycle of violence.

FAMILY CRISIS INTERVENTION

Throughout the country departments are using a newer approach to handling family fights. It is called Family Crisis Intervention. It involves a considerable amount of training. Some departments provide this training to all of their patrol officers. Others train specialized teams to intervene in family fights. Some wear blazers rather than uniforms. This is to reduce a negative attitude that some may have toward police officers. Especially if officers have taken them to jail in the past.

The basic theory of this approach is to send someone who is properly trained in handling family fights to handle these calls. These officers intentionally spend considerable time trying to resolve the basic issues of the problem. It is believed that this approach might reduce the number of calls received by officers from a particular family. The theory is that, in the long run, there will be a smaller number of hours spent by police officers dealing with a particular family. This is opposed to the common philosophy of solving the immediate problem within fifteen minutes or booking someone if they can't.

Some departments trying this approach, have specially trained two-officer cars that respond only to family fights. In areas containing a high ratio of minority races, these special cars contain one white and one minority officer. The justification for training officers to use this approach is twofold. First, there are fewer repeat calls. Second, and more important, is the fact that fewer officers are hurt or killed while handling family fights. FBI statistics show that one out of every four officers killed on duty is killed trying to settle a domestic argument.

A study by the Kansas City Missouri police department showed that 40% of the murders in that city were spouse killing spouse. It also showed that, in 85% of the cases, the police had been called at least once before. In 50% of the cases the police had been called five or more times. The authors have found nothing to show that these statistics do not apply to cities throughout the United States.

As part of Family Crisis Intervention training, officers are given a good grounding in the psychological principles of problem resolving. They are also given the opportunity to participate in role playing situations involving family crisis problems. By videotaping the role playing situations, the officers can later see how they actually reacted to the various problems presented by the actors.

In family disturbances, the patrol officers are too often the persons doing all the talking. They sometimes feel that they have to give advice to others. The reason is probably that in general police work, the public looks to the officer for guidance. In emergencies, someone must take control of the situation, and the officer is best suited for that job. In Family Crisis Intervention, however, officers are taught to listen for a change. This can be a difficult skill to develop for those who have always taken the verbal initiative. Yet this is a very effective means of allowing the parties involved in the fight to "defuse" their emotions. Cities experimenting with this approach have reported an increase in good police-community relations. The police are looked upon as helpers rather than "head bashers."

Another skill taught in this special training is to quickly get to the real cause of the conflict. Each partner will give numerous reasons why the fight started, but they are seldom the real basic problem. Until the parties involved face up to the real underlying causes, there will seldom be a lasting solution.

Some of the techniques in FCI training are similar to regular family fight procedures. A partial list of these techniques is as follows:

(1) Separate the parties involved by taking them to different rooms.

(2) Allow only one person to talk at a time.

(3) Do not take sides.

(4) Listen to the stories.

(5) Ask questions that really get to the "heart" of the matter. If one person makes an important statement, repeat it to them. Ask if what you heard was a correct interpretation of what they really meant. This goes a long way toward clearing up misunderstandings.

(6) Determine the previous history of their domestic problems.

(7) Bring them together so they can repeat their stories in front of each other. Do not let one interrupt the other. Tell the other person that he or she will have a chance to rebut any statement made after the first party has completed their statement.

(8) Ask both parties what they see as a solution to the problem.

(9) Have both parties commit themselves to conditions under which they would accept at least a temporary truce.

(10) Tell them that you will drop by in a few days or a week and see how they are resolving the problem. This places some responsibility on their shoulders. It also shows a personal interest in them as human beings.

(11) Have cards available with the names, addresses and phone numbers of follow-up agencies. Just telling them to see a marriage counselor is not enough. Make sure that they have the phone number, and then follow up to see that they did make contact.

Officers should remember that there is more than one side to every story. When listening to the story of one party, do not jump to conclusions until hearing the other person's side of it. When two officers respond to a family fight, each officer should take one party off to the side to hear their version of what happened. However, they should be very careful not to take sides. There have been cases of the officers themselves becoming involved in an argument because each officer thought that the other person was at fault and should be booked.

An officer need not be a psychologist to understand human nature. He or she should use a little introspection, and put themselves in the other person's place. By doing so, they might at least understand some of that person's emotions and feelings. Asians have not cornered the market on "saving face." It is part of all basic human nature. This becomes very important in the family fight because a person does not want to be humiliated in front of his family. He will often put on a big front while in their presence, and will be as meek as a lamb after he is in the patrol car and away from the house. An officer should realize this, and allow the person to save a little face in front of his family. If an officer cannot consider the circumstances and take a little more guff from the suspect, a change of career should be considered. Not taking the suspect's words personally and considering the source can make an officer's job a lot easier.

In dealing with family fights, officers should be aware that "blood is thicker than water." The victim(s) of a family fight will often call the police, and want the offending family member arrested and thrown in jail. If the suspect is abusive to the officer, that officer may have to use force to control that person. If this happens, it is very common to find the whole family, victims included, climbing on the officer's back. In a family fight where the husband is booked at the insistence of the wife, it is usually the wife who is down at the jail the first thing in the morning to bail him out. Some officers will use a technique in which they get both parties mad at the officers so they forget their own fight. This will often work, but it is not the best solution.

It is common for a husband and wife who are fighting, to try and win the support of the responding officers to their side. This is done by telling them every rotten thing that their partner has done, not during the day, nor week, but during the last twenty years. Because of this, the patrol officer will obtain access to a considerable amount of very private information. This is just one reason why law enforcement must become a profession. For only when police officers are professional will this type of information be kept confidential rather than being spread around the community in the form of ripe gossip. Any information of this sort, obtained as part of an officer's duties, should be remembered but not repeated. We all have some part of our past that we would like to have forgotten. The officers who repeat private information obtained as part of their duties are violating a sacred trust.

GANG FIGHTS

In dealing with a gang fight, the tone of voice is important. Next to that is attitude and posture. The officer who rushes up to a gang fight with baton raised in a stiff and rigid posture and yells in a high pitched and excited voice, is bound to end up involved in a fight. Most gang fights occur as a result of group pressures. Gang members who have been interviewed privately by psychologists have revealed that they were really scared to death, and that they were happy when the police came to break up the fight. It allowed them to stop the fight and save face. It is common for members of a gang, about to become involved in a fight, to call the police and give them the location and time of the fight, hoping that it will be broken up.

An officer receiving a "gang fight" call should find out what other units are responding. The second concern should be whether or not weapons are involved. One officer can seldom stop a gang fight. He or she can get stomped into the ground very quickly though. If the officer is the only one responding to the call, it is best to proceed quickly toward the scene, but slow down the last few blocks. If alone, a good tactic is to sound the siren at full volume and proceed slowly. By doing this, chances are that the gang will disperse. The peace will have been preserved, which is the officer's duty, and the officer will be safe. If the officer arrives at the scene and finds that the gang is still there, it is best to park in a spot that is not too noticeable and watch for leaders in the gang until the arrival of other units. Communications can be advised of the extent of the situation and whether dogs or tear gas might be needed. Witnesses may also be identified who could later be questioned.

THE HOLDING TACTIC

The "Holding Tactic" or "Holding Quadrant" as some agencies call it, is used when patrol cars are assigned to any type of gang or crowd problem. This is used where the people involved have the reputation of attacking a lone officer or throwing rocks at the first patrol car that arrives. Usually the type of area will determine the need for this tactic.

In this tactic, communications notifies the cars responding to maintain a one block distance from the scene, and to report when they are in a holding position. When all of the cars responding are one block from the scene, they are given a key command such as "execute", and all of them move in on the scene at once. Having all of the cars arrive at the scene at once seems to have a better effect as far as police safety is concerned.

In gang fights it is common for the participants to carry some sort of weapon or "equalizer." Should they be observed using these weapons, a charge of "Assault With a Deadly Weapon" can be added to other charges. Just swinging a baseball bat over their heads is usually enough to uphold such a charge. Some of these weapons are illegal to possess and the person carrying the weapon can be arrested for possession alone.

BARKING DOG DISTURBANCE

Although this type of call can seem minor to a patrol officer, it can often be a most difficult case to handle. The improper handling of the case, or "kissing it off", can seriously damage public relations in the neighborhood. The problem is simple. The neighbors want the dog to stop barking. However, they don't want to become involved in a neighborhood quarrel so they usually refuse to give their name when calling. They still want satisfaction, since it is a disturbance of the peace.

Too many officers will drive by, and if they don't hear the dog barking, they forget about it. Many times an officer cannot find the dog, and leaves. When the officer leaves, it starts up again. The patrol officer should not look at the barking dog complaint as being petty. Because they often have to try to sleep during the day, officers, above all people, should know the tortures of being awakened by an irritating noise.

If the dog is found locked in the house and the owner is not home, it can become a very touchy matter. Should the officer break into the house? If the people living there are slightly deaf, or are sound sleepers, would they shoot at the officer thinking it was a prowler. Suppose the officer breaks in and takes the dog, but is not able to properly lock the house again. Would the officer be responsible for any article stolen from the house. In cases like this the officer should seek the sage advice of the supervising sergeant. If a town or city has an Animal Control Officer, a phone call to that person's office might solve the problem. The Animal Control Officer is usually on call at night. In real life, however, they don't always answer the phone in the middle of the night.

VEHICLE DISTURBANCES

The motorcycle, automobile and go-cart that causes a neighborhood disturbance can be similar to the barking dog complaint because few people want to give their names. Yet they feel justified in demanding service. Because they don't want to give hints as to their identity by giving their exact location, they are usually vague as to the location of the disturbance. Most states have laws that only allow officers to arrest or cite for misdemeanors committed in their presence. Some states have laws that allow the arrest of a juvenile for a misdemeanor when there is probable cause. The vehicle driver cannot be cited without a formal citizen complainant. Most people do not understand this. They believe that an officer either has, or should have, the power to resolve any problem once a citizen complains. Even if the officer locates the vehicle, the driver cannot be cited for reckless driving because the officer did not observe that violation.

Not realizing the legal processes of the law, citizens want the noise stopped and don't care how it is done. It is also potentially a more dangerous situation. If it continues, a child might be run over or killed. Even if the driver is not cited, the officer can stop him and "read him the riot act." Threatening the driver with having his license taken away can, in some cases, curb the problem. Since most perpetrators of this offense are juveniles, this tactic usually works. If not, a call to the parents will often result in them taking away the juvenile's driving privileges. If the parents are uncooperative, a threat to call their insurance company can work wonders.

PROWLER CALLS

Prowler calls can be the result of many things, both serious and harmless. The following is a list of some of the more common reasons for a person prowling on another's property:

(1) **SEXUAL PSYCHOPATH** The most common is the voyeur, usually referred to as a "Peeping Tom." He receives sexual satisfaction from looking into windows. Panty thieves also come under this heading. They steal undergarments from clotheslines while prowling. However, they are usually not voyeurs.

(2) **THE RAPIST** His purpose is to catch a woman alone in a house and rape her.

(3) **THE THIEF** He is trying to steal something from the yard. It can be a bicycle or any item left outside. Sometimes this person can be a juvenile stealing cherries or apples from trees.

(4) **THE BURGLAR** He intends to burglarize the home. He's prowling in order to find a good point of entry or escape route if he's caught.

(5) **THE TRESPASSER** Usually a young person who is taking a "short cut" through someone's backyard. It is often hard, at first, to tell the voyeur from the kid who is truly taking a "short cut." A voyeur will have a hundred different reasons for being in someone's yard.

(6) **THE JEALOUS SPOUSE OR LOVER** This person is checking up on his wife or girlfriend because he suspects her of seeing another person. This also includes ex-husbands who are paying alimony. They feel that as long as they are paying alimony, their ex-wives have no right to see other men. They can present a problem because they feel that they have a God-given legal right to be there.

(7) **THE "PRIVATE EYE"** He or she has been hired by a husband to find out who has been visiting his wife while he is out of town. This also applies to suspicious wives.

SUBTERFUGES USED BY PROWLERS

Since most prowlers commit their acts with some preparation (even if on a subconscious level), they will often use some type of subterfuge. Some of the more common are as follows:

(1) **THE DOG WALKER** His excuse is that sometimes the dog gets away from him and he has to chase it between houses.

(2) **THE DRUNK** He claims that he is so intoxicated that he does not really know where he is. Always check his pulse. If he is faking, his pulse rate will be high.

(3) **THE JOGGER** He says that he was jogging and had to "take a leak real bad," so he just ran in between two houses to do his thing. He didn't want to expose himself in public.

(4) **THE PERSON WITH CAR TROUBLE** He has his car hood up. He says that he just went between two houses looking for a faucet in hope of borrowing some water for his radiator.

Prowler calls have one of the lowest rates of apprehension of all types of criminal calls. Why? Some of the answers are:

(1) There was never a prowler there in the first place. The victim is the nervous type, and when the wind blows branches against the window, or when a cat runs across the roof, they convince themselves that it is a prowler.

(2) If there actually is a prowler, he is difficult to catch. He has usually staked the place out and has found the best place to hide. He also knows the best escape route. He can use darkness to aid him in hiding, unless the officer has a dog.

(3) The average police officer does not know how to properly respond to a prowler call. That includes searching for a prowler.

FAULTS IN RESPONDING TO PROWLER CALLS

The best way to describe the faults of an officer in responding to a prowler call is to see the approach from the position of a prowler. The following would be what the prowler might see and hear during the average response to a prowler call.

(1) The screeching of brakes. Sound travels far at night.

(2) The racing of engines from blocks off.

(3) The flashing of spotlights all over the neighborhood as officers try to find the address.

(4) The blaring of loud police radios.

(5) The slamming of doors and flashing of brake lights.

(6) The jingling of keys and police whistles on the officer's snap ring.

(7) Loud commands from one officer to another.

(8) The heavy thump of running feet.

Under these conditions, a prowler would have to be a low grade imbecile to be caught in someone's backyard by surprise. Either that or the object of his attention must be extra special.

HOW TO RESPOND TO A PROWLER CALL

(1) **APPROACHING THE SCENE** When approaching the scene, it is important that the officer have a good idea just where the victim's house is located. Most communities have the even numbers of addresses on one side of the street and the odd numbers on the other. An officer Who knows the beat, will not only know what side of the street the house is on, but will have a pretty good idea of which block. During the last few blocks, the officer should slow down to prevent the noise of a racing engine, and the screeching of brakes. If more than one car is responding, some form of rough strategy might be

planned. For example, having one car take the next street in case the suspect goes over the back fence. If he does, it is sometimes best just to park the police car in as dark a place as possible and watch and wait.

To assist in finding the exact address, the officer should only use the spotlight on the opposite side of the street. If the officer is looking for 1112, the spotlight should be used on the odd side of the street until the address 1109 is located. Then the officer knows that the address 1112 is almost across the street. The use of the spotlight does not give the officer away with this technique.

(2) **ARRIVING AT THE SCENE** As the officer approaches the victim's house, the engine should be turned off to let the car coast to within one or two houses of the destination. Use only the hand brake to stop the vehicle, since it does not cause the brake light to go on. The radio should be turned down or off. The car door should be opened slightly before stopping. This is to prevent noise. When the vehicle has stopped, the officer should remove the car keys and secure them and the whistle in a handkerchief. This should be placed in a front pocket. The door of the police car should be left slightly ajar to prevent any noise caused by the door slamming shut. The approach to the victim's house should be from the neighbor's lawn rather than the sidewalk, where the footsteps can easily be heard.

(3) **THE SEARCH.** Communications between officers during the search should be conducted through hand signals. Any verbal communications should be in a whisper. Flashlights should be held out from the body in the non-gun hand and should be used sparingly. Besides locating things, they also give away an officer's presence. At night, officers might protect their faces from injury by raising their gun hand up in front of their faces. Officers have nearly broken their necks by running into thin wire clotheslines. The raised hand would protect them from this fate. In the dark, it is hard to see a thin wire. Officers should stand close to the building or house. They should keep as low as possible so as not to make large silhouettes.

(4) HANDLING THE COMPLAINANT AND NEIGHBORS Nothing can shake up a neighborhood more than the belief that there is a prowler on the loose. Officers should be very tactful and try not to alarm people. They should search for positive evidence of the presence of the prowler such as footprints in the dirt next to the house, or in the dew on the grass. They might also suggest to the neighbors that it was probably an animal to reduce their fears. An officer should also be prepared for the possibility of a neighbor hearing about the prowler and then grabbing his gun and joining the "posse." He could be mistaken for the prowler, and when officers spot the gun, a panic shooting could occur.

When a cursory search has been made, the complainant should be contacted to see if a prowler was actually observed. If so, a description should be obtained.

THE USE OF DOGS

Since dogs have such a keen sense of smell, they can be invaluable in locating prowlers. It must be remembered that, in most states, prowling is a misdemeanor. A dog should not be set loose on a misdemeanant if he should try to run away. If the dog is well trained, it might be used to run herd on the suspect and possibly bluff him. But that is all. To do otherwise would require good probable cause to believe that the suspect had, in fact, committed a felony.

THE STAKEOUT

Sometimes officers will find evidence, such as fresh footprints, that indicate that a prowler was in fact present. If he has not been found, chances are he is hiding some place nearby. In this case a stakeout is warranted. Two procedures can be followed. One, the officers can loudly state that the suspect must have gone. One of them noisily gets into the car and slams both doors. Another way is for one officer to slam a door from the outside and then make a dive for some bushes or some type of cover. That officer will then hide as the police car drives off. The driver will go a few blocks off and park. When the prowler believes that the police have left the scene, he will emerge from hiding. The hiding officer will then arrest him.

The other procedure involves the officers actually leaving the scene. One of them returns on foot from around the corner and across the lawns until a good hiding place is found. The driver, as before, parks the police car a few blocks down the street with the lights out and the radio down. By parking under a tree, the police car is less likely to be noticed.

EMOTIONALLY DISTURBED PERSONS

A common part of the police officer's job is the handling of emotionally disturbed persons. Officers should know their limitations regarding the committal of such persons and under what conditions this can be done. Under the Welfare and Institutions Code or similar codes (They are different in each state), officers are generally allowed to commit a person under an emergency committal if:

(1) That person is, from all appearances, a danger to himself, (and/or)
(2) He is a danger to other persons.

When officers commit a person, it is important to list in detail all the conditions that led them to believe the person to be emotionally disturbed. Many times the person will have spells of disturbed behavior. The next morning when the psychiatrist talks to him, he may be quite lucid and appear normal. As a result he is released with the feeling that the officer must have used bad judgment. If, however, the officer gives a detailed account of the person's actions and conversation, the psychiatrist may be able to recognize symptoms. These may be used to justify further detention and treatment even though the subject now appears to be all right.

There are times when officers are called to investigate a situation where a person appears to be behaving strangely. They must remember that a person can be eccentric or neurotic and not come within the emergency committal section. To be committed the person must present a clear and present danger to himself or others. If we were to commit people because they acted odd or strange, it would be a miscarriage of justice. It would also require the building of thousands of new mental institutions because most people act a little strange at one time or another. This is especially true of elderly persons.

SYMPTOMS OF EMOTIONAL DISTURBANCE

The following are some of the symptoms that an officer should look for as an indication that an individual is in need of professional psychiatric care.

DISORDERS OF SENSATION OR PERCEPTION

THE HALLUCINATION A hallucination is the sensing of an object or person when there is nothing really there to stimulate the sense. For example the person hears voices when there really are no voices. The person sees red devils when there are none there. More common types of hallucinations with which law enforcement officers deal, is where the person hears the voice of God, and those where the person hears radio messages in his head.

The latter is probably a form of rationalization. The person hears voices, and yet has enough contact with reality to know that only radio waves can carry voices, so arrives at the conclusion that they are radio transmitted. There is a common fixation among the emotionally disturbed concerning electronics and secret inventions. They are often the victims of electric rays and electronic beams that strange people shoot at them. The sad part is that these imaginary rays hurt the person as much as if they were real.

THE ILLUSION The illusion differs from the hallucination in that there is some physical basis for disorder. It really amounts to a false interpretation of a stimulus. The person may see a child crawling on the grass, and their senses perceive the child as a dog. An undershirt on the clothesline may be interpreted as a ghost. This is deeper than the average misconception that most people occasionally experience. It is not a case of looking like something else, to the person, it actually is something else. They may be fully convinced that the officer is a person from outer space, and that the police car is a space ship.

DISORDERS OF CONSCIOUSNESS

CATATONIA When life becomes so terrible, some people are able to mentally dissociate themselves from the world. They go into what is called a catatonic state. They are completely oblivious of what is going on around them. They will just sit motionless and stare. In lesser forms, they will be in a dream state or a state of confusion. Here they might answer you but without meaning or understanding. This is may be a sign of catatonic schizophrenia, a serious mental disorder.

DISORDERS OF JUDGMENT

DELUSION A delusion is a false belief which cannot be corrected by an appeal to reason. It is usually quite obvious to others that there is no foundation for the belief. In fact the person's intelligence and education are often at odds with the belief. Delusions are different in various forms of emotional disturbance. For example: Delusions of grandeur. He might think that he is a king, or Napoleon. Then there are delusions where everything is wrong and bad. The person feels that he is no good and unworthy. It goes in cycles. Paranoia, a delusion that others are persecuting you, is commonly referred to as a persecution complex. This can be dangerous because the individual can injure others in an attempt to protect himself from those he believes are his enemies.

OBSESSION An obsession is an idea, emotion or impulse that persistently forces itself into a person's mind even though he may recognize it as abnormal or foolish and would like to get rid of it. The obsessive person will repeatedly perform certain rituals, such as handwashing. He may become upset if these activities are curtailed for any reason.

PHOBIA Phobias are very common in the milder form. Many people are afraid of heights, small enclosed areas, animals and any number of other things. When the fear becomes so great that it impairs a person's ability to function in what would be considered a "normal" manner, it may be a sign of a serious emotional disturbance.

DISORDERS OF ASSOCIATION AND ATTENTION

A person suffering from these disorders will not be able to keep his attention on one thing. While a normal person can keep his ideas in some orderly fashion, and develop them toward some goal, the disordered person will talk in circles and each group of words may not be associated with the preceding or following words. For example: 'Well, I don't, that is, are you sure? Well is it new? Well I guess it could. Oh, well ummm, no I guess it was the other one." Often this person cannot give the officer more than twenty seconds of attention. When asked to repeat what was just said, he would be unable to do so.

DISORDERS OF EMOTION

ANXIETY Anxiety is usually associated with neurosis. It is a feeling of impending danger and is expressed by extreme nervousness and irritability. It is also expressed by body twitches and strange facial expressions as well as other finger and body movements.

APATHY There is a complete inability to express any emotion, sadness or happiness. The face is often blank. The subject is indifferent to emotional stimuli.

IMPAIRMENT OF AFFECT The person will show extreme elation when it is not warranted. He can go into hysterics over nothing. It can start as a giggle and then develop into a laugh. He may often try to hold it back, and that makes it worse.

MANIC DEPRESSION A person who is manic depressive will exhibit wild, and sometimes violent, mood swings. These mood swings will not have any discernible external cause. One moment, the person will feel on top of the world, almost god-like. This is the manic stage. The next moment, the person will be plumetted into the depths of despair and could even become suicidal. This is the depressive stage.

DISORDERS OF ACTION

IMPULSE The person will have irresistible impulses that are beyond his control to do certain acts. They may be simple, involving things we associate with superstition, such as knocking on wood or stepping on cracks in the sidewalk. Here the subject will go down the street knocking on all the wood he passes. In kleptomania, the impulse is to steal. In the more serious forms it can be dangerous because the impulse might have sexual associations. This can cause the subject to grab the breast of each woman he passes as he walks down the street. It is closely associated with compulsion, which is stronger than impulse. Compulsion can naturally be more serious.

STEREOTYPY In stereotypy the person will repeat words and actions without apparent cause or reason. Sometimes the actions will be like that of a mechanical man. Each movement will be exactly like the other. This is also called echolalia.

TERMINOLOGY RELATING TO EMOTIONALLY DISTURBED PERSONS

Officers should be very careful about the terminology they use. Never refer to an emotionally disturbed person as a "nut." Refer to the mental hospital as the state hospital rather than the "puzzle factory" or the "funny farm." Emotionally disturbed persons can be very sensitive to the use of improper terminology. Most of an emotionally disturbed person's aggressive action is due to fear. It may not appear that way on the surface, because true feelings are often hidden. Because of this, many emotionally disturbed persons will seek the help of the police, or welcome it if it is offered. An officer should be very generous with the words "help" and "protect." They are often the key to establishing rapport with the subject. It is not unethical to use subterfuge when dealing with the emotionally disturbed. Do not, however, tell them outright lies. They can be told that they are going to the police departrment for protection until the matter can be straightened out. This will reduce the chance of the person going wild when you arrive; he expects it. Many psychotics who come to the attention of the police have some delusion regarding electronics and radio waves. Because of this, the officer might tell them that he is going to headquarters where an expert in these matters can help him.

APPROACHING THE EMOTIONALLY DISTURBED SUBJECT

The first and best approach to use is that of a non-threatening, "We're here to help you" or "How can we help you" approach. No weapons should be in hand. If the person has not had a lot of negative association with the police, he may look upon them as persons who can help him. He may even say "Thank God you're here. They have been trying to kill me for a week." If he is paranoid, he sincerely believes that someone is trying to kill him and wants protection. He may even ask that you call for more assistance because there are so many of "them" out there. This does not mean that you should not remain alert. You must be extremely alert and yet give the impression that you are completely relaxed and not a threat. If this approach doesn't work, then you must physically restrain the person so that he does not harm others or himself.

RESTRAINING THE EMOTIONALLY DISTURBED

Restraining the emotionally disturbed can sometimes be quite a task as they often have increased strength as a result of an obsessive drive. If they show signs of violence they should always be handcuffed, hands behind their backs. If they return to normal and appear relaxed, do not take off the handcuffs even if they assure you that they are all right.

One of the best ways to control an emotionally disturbed person who is violent is to cut off his air supply. It seems to temporarily bring them to their senses. This can be done with a short jab to the stomach, knocking out the air. Another way that might even be better is the cutting off of the blood supply to the brain by applying pressure to the carotid artery. This can be done with the thumb and index finger when facing them, or may be accomplished from behind by wrapping the arm around the subject's neck, with the elbow even with the Adam's apple. By flexing the muscles, pressure is applied to the carotid arteries and unconsciousness will soon result. This seems to temporarily bring them to their senses because of a change in blood flow to the brain. Officers should not apply pressure to the Adam's Apple. This can result in serious injury.

If the subject is in a room, the officer may be able to obtain a blanket and wrap him in it. This serves as a do-it-yourself strait jacket. Another thing that may be used in place of a blanket is a rug. If the subject can be held on the floor near the edge of the rug, the edge may be lifted over him, and he can be rolled up quite securely.

THE MOON AND EMOTIONAL DISTURBANCE

The word "lunatic" is from the Latin word for moon. The origin of the word dates back to the ancients whose observations led them to conclude that emotionally disturbed persons became more so during the full moon. Many experienced officers noticed that when there was a full moon, emotional disturbance calls and crimes of violence seemed to increase. If they dared mention this to anyone with a scientific background, they were laughed at. Today it is the scientist who is touting this theory. Researchers at Duke, Northwestern and other universities have come up with evidence that would indicate that the moon does, in fact, affect human emotions. Since the human body is electrochemical, some scientists theorize that solar radiation reflected from the moon changes the electrical nature of the atmosphere. More ionized particles are bounced toward the earth when the moon is full.

Criminologists who have studied police records both in Europe and the United States have not only found an increase in crimes of passion at times of the full moon, but have found a 50% increase in murders during this time. In New York City it was found that there was a 100% increase in arson cases during the full moon, and that many of them were attributable to emotionally disturbed pyro-maniacs. Dr. Leonard Ravitz of Duke University and Dr. Harold Burr of Yale, have both found incontrovertible evidence that the moon influences the voltage of currents that constantly flow from one place to another in both plants and animals. Studies of 1000 cases in Florida have shown that 82% of the bleeding crises in these cases took place in the period around the full moon. They also found that almost all attacks of bleeding ulcers occurred during the same period. Research at the University of Miami revealed in a study of 2,000 murders in Dade County, that homicide rates coincided with phases of the full and new moon.

HOW CAN THESE STATISTICS HELP THE PATROL OFFICER?

By anticipating, or being prepared for such conditions, officers can better perform their duties. Administrators can adjust assignments to ensure better coverage during these times. They may also assign as many two-person patrol cars as possible.

ATTEMPTED SUICIDES AND SUICIDES

ATTEMPTED SUICIDES

An attempted suicide is a "cry for help." It is an attempt to stop or avoid an intolerable existence. The statements "I can't stand it anymore," "I just can't go on," "There is nothing to live for," reflect the feelings of despair that drive a person to attempt suicide. The patrol officer can play a very important part in helping such a person. First the officer must become alert to the signs of a potential suicide when on patrol duty.

BECOMING AWARE OF THE CONDITION

In his book Preventing Suicide, E. S. Schneidman states that the basic prerequisites for a person to become aware of a potential suicide are simply sharp eyes and ears. Having good intuition, a pinch of wisdom and the ability to act appropriately are also helpful. Since these are also prerequisites for patrol officers, they should be suited to the task.

Officers usually become aware of the potential suicide because a person has reacted in an overt manner to his or her inner feelings. Something happens that triggers an emotional response. It can be the death of a loved one, one married person leaving another, a family fight, or a great material loss. Since these situations do not cause all persons to attempt suicide, they are obviously just triggering factors. Persons about to commit suicide must have a pre-disposition toward not being able to resolve problems by themselves. The situation is simply the "straw that breaks the camel's back."

WARNINGS OF AN IMPENDING SUICIDE

In almost all suicides there are warning signs or hints that the person is contemplating such action. They can be verbal such as "I want to die" or "I can't live without her," or they can be behavioral in the form of preparations to die. Giving away prized possessions, obtaining extra insurance, attempting to put affairs in order or phoning a distant friend or relative are a few. Along with the verbal and behavioral warnings there is usually some pre-existing condition that has laid the emotional foundation for this state of mind. It can be the death of someone close, a terminal disease or even financial pressures. These conditions can be discovered by interviewing those closest to that person. Probably relatives and neighbors.

When officers come in contact with a person who is suicide-prone, unless they have had previous dealings with that person, or the call indicates an attempted suicide, they come into the situation with little supporting background information. They must therefore be alert to symptoms that might indicate the person's intent.

Studies have shown that most suicides were preceded by obvious symptoms; symptoms that were very often ignored. These symptoms could be in the form of statements like those previously mentioned. They could be obvious preparations such as the recent purchase of a gun or ammunition, or the sealing of cracks in the garage with rags. The writing of suicide notes is also an act of preparation. So is the giving away of personal property. The most obvious hints will come from verbal statements. Because of this, it is important for the officer to engage the suspect in conversation as much as possible once a clue or hint of his intentions is revealed.

WHAT TO DO WHEN A POSSIBLE ATTEMPT AT SUICIDE IS INDICATED

(1) Where the victim is making threats and possesses a weapon. This includes persons in precarious positions making threats to jump.

(a) Stall for time. Talking seems to work best.

(b) Try to find out why the person is doing this.

(c) Appeal to basic or perceived needs. Tell the subject that "it will all work out. Tomorrow is another day. It is always darkest before the dawn. Help will be found. Don't hurt loved ones." If a woman, appeal to vanity. "Do you want people to see how you look after you do it?" Try flattery, e.g.: "You're too intelligent a person to do such a foolish thing. A person as good looking as you doesn't need to do this."

(d) Ask if there is someone they would like to talk to before they do the act (e.g. family member, religious advisor, psychiatrist).

(e) Consider the reasons why they haven't already done it. The fact that they have not already done it might be due to fear of pain. Maybe the whole action is a "cry for help", and they really want someone to present arguments that will change their mind.

(f) See that the fire department is called. They have useful equipment to help in this situation.

(g) Try to remove him or get him to move away from the dangerous situation.

(2) Where the victim has already taken some dangerous action.

(a) **Poisons and pills.** Rush victim to the hospital by ambulance, and then search the scene for bottles or containers. If they are found, phone the name of the drug to the hospital so they can know what antidote to administer. If there will be a delay in the arrival of an ambulance, the officer should prepare an emetic unless the victim has swallowed a very strong agent that will further burn the throat when it comes up again. In this case have the victim drink as much water as possible. Two of the most common and easily obtainable emetics are salty water and soapy water.

(b) **Attempts by Cutting.** Administer first aid by stopping the bleeding. Use towels from the bathroom. If the victim resists, use handcuffs as a means of restraint. If there is any adhesive tape that can be located, it will make an excellent restraining device. If the victim is still trying to continue the attempt, remove any object that might be used as a cutting agent.

(c) **Attempts by gunshot.** Stop bleeding and remove weapon from immediate vicinity.

(d) **Attempts by hanging.** Cut down immediately. Lower head and administer mouth-to-mouth resuscitation after placing handkerchief over mouth.

ATTEMPTS AT SUICIDE IN AN EFFORT TO GAIN SYMPATHY

There is no doubt that some attempts to commit suicide are really attempts to gain sympathy. There is no sure way to determine this. Often there are hints. The man whose wife has just left him might state as soon as you arrive, "Does my wife know about this?", or "Did you call my wife yet?" or "Is my wife coming over?" When a human life is at stake, an officer cannot play games or guess about the person's true motives. All attempted suicides should be treated as the real thing.

If the person states that he has taken pills, he should be taken to the hospital to have his stomach pumped. This is an unpleasant experience, and often discourages a person from playing that game again. Sometimes there are cases where a person actually commits suicide without intending for the act to be completed. He misjudges the time it will take for help to arrive, or the means which he uses to make the attempt look convincing. The person who expects the police to arrive in time to take him to the hospital and have his stomach pumped probably doesn't expect the car to have an accident, or for there to be no cars available. The person whom they call to tell of their intentions might feel that this is just another false alarm and forget the matter rather than tell the police like they have in the past. As a result, the person dies by accident rather than by intent.

Police officers have a terrible responsibility in dealing with attempted suicide cases. Should they commit the subject to a mental institution or not? If they were to commit all persons who have attempted or have indicated they might attempt suicide to a mental institution, the institutions would not be able to hold them all. Yet if the officer were to release the person, and later that person were to commit suicide, the officer might be held legally responsible for failing to perform a legal duty. The answer several communities are using is a mental first-aid station. Here a person can be examined by trained psychiatric personnel who can recognize a legitimate case of emotional disturbance. This tends to relieve the police officer of the responsibility of deciding whether to commit the person or not. In one study in California, it was found that over half of all persons committed to the local state mental hospital by police officers, were released the next morning. It was felt that they were not emotionally disturbed enough to commit. The hospital officials seemed quick to condemn the police officer for unnecessary commitments, but they failed to understand the legal responsibility on the officer's shoulders. If the officer were not to commit the person, and someone were later injured by that person, or if that person committed suicide, the officer would be responsible.

INVESTIGATIVE PROCEDURE ON COMPLETED SUICIDES

When a patrol officer arrives at the scene of a reported suicide and finds the victim dead, certain steps must be taken.

(1) **Protect the scene.** A reported suicide can actually be a homicide. Because of this, the patrol officer should be very careful to protect any evidence at the scene. It is common for members of the family to destroy suicide notes. They do this for three reasons. First the note might blame some member of the family as being the person who drove the victim to commit the act. Second, they don't want anyone to know that a member of their family committed suicide. In Western society, suicide is looked upon as a cowardly way out. This reflects negatively on the family. Some feel that the person committing suicide might be mentally ill, and that people would think that it is an inherited family trait. In some families the religious factor is very important. Some religions will not allow a suicide victim to be buried in a church cemetery. They feel that this is an honor for members in good standing only. A third reason is the insurance factor. Some insurance companies will not pay off on a suicide.

(2) **Talk to witnesses.** Gather as much information and as many witnesses' names as possible.

(3) **Survey the scene.** Write down the location of important pieces of evidence. Do not collect them unless a detective will not arrive at the scene for follow-up or further investigation.

OPEN DOOR CALLS

When a citizen or a foot patrol officer finds an open door, they will call the police department. A patrol unit will then be dispatched to the scene. Because open doors are so common, officers have a tendency to treat them too lightly. Open doors present a valid potential danger to officers. The only way to guard against that danger is to establish a set procedure when checking out an open door. The following steps will help ensure that a police officer will live long enough to retire.

(1) Cover all exits and size up possible escape routes.

(2) Check all around the building for any possible forced entry.

(3) If signs of forced entry are found, call for assistance. Also tell police communications to have a unit check the area for a parked vehicle that could belong to the perpetrator. Also have that unit check for a partner driving around the block with the intent of picking up the perpetrator when he is finished.

(4) Park the patrol car in front of the entrance and put the spotlight high on the door that was found open, at about shoulder height.

(5) Assign areas of search when the building is entered. This will prevent duplication of coverage and the possibility of some area being missed. Break it up by sides.

(6) Enter through the door, keeping low and under the spotlight. Don't make a silhouette at any time. Once inside, spread out. Stop for a minute and size up the area. Do not talk. Communication should be carried on through hand signals.

(7) Call for a dog unit if warranted.

(8) Try to turn the lights on, but be alert to wires leading from the switch box. Keep low when they are turned on.

(9) When going through doors, slam them back hard in case there is someone behind them.

(10) If, after checking the building, it is felt that it is a matter of the owner leaving the door unlocked, he should be called and asked to come and verify that all is in order. Sometimes the owner will not want to come, and will ask the officers to lock up. This should never be done. Make the owner come down. It is possible that someone did enter the building and had left before the officers arrived. If the owner finds something missing in the morning, he might blame it on the police.

STOLEN VEHICLES

In the early 1990's, according to the Consumer Reports News Digest, auto theft became the number one property crime in the United States. In 1991, there were 1.6 million vehicles reported stolen. Auto thefts total more than $7 billion a year. It accounts for over half of the total value of all property lost through criminal means. A Consumers' Research study found that 80% of stolen cars were unlocked, and more than 40% had the keys left in the ignition. In taking stolen vehicle reports, the first consideration is whether or not the vehicle was actually stolen. The following are some of the situations where people will report a vehicle as stolen when it was actually not.

(1) The vehicle was repossessed. This is the most common reason. The officer should always ask the complainant whether he is making payments on the vehicle, and when the last payment was made. Some companies will wait like vultures for the owner to miss a payment so they can repossess the car and charge the owner a high repossession fee. Most agencies that repossess vehicles will sneak the car off to avoid a possible fight. Since they hold the papers on the car, it is a legal process. Most agencies notify the police within so many minutes after it is repossessed. Some cities require this by law.

(2) The vehicle was taken by another member of the family without notifying anyone. This is usually one of the children.

(3) The victim knows who has the car, but won't mention it to the officer because he is mad at the party and wants him thrown in jail.

(4) The victim loaned the vehicle to someone, who didn't return it promptly. This is a borderline civil case, and the victim should be referred to the District Attorney who will issue an embezzlement complaint rather than an auto theft complaint. Used car lots often report this type of offense.

(5) Either the wife or husband got mad and took off in the car. In states that have community property laws, this is not an offense.

PREVENTION OF AUTO THEFT

The key to controlling stolen vehicles is prevention. This means making it difficult for a car thief to first, get into a car, and second, to start the car. Cities that have passed ordinances making it mandatory to lock cars and not leave keys in the ignition, have reduced their auto theft considerably.

SPOTTING HOT CARS

There are certain signs that will enable the patrol officer to detect a car that might be stolen. If the patrol officer is constantly alert to these, it will greatly increase the number of stolen vehicles re-covered. Some of these "attention getters" are:

(1) Actions of the driver or passengers. Often the driver, on seeing a police car, will stiffen up or have a scared look on his face. He may look straight ahead and pretend that the police car is not there. Many times one of the passengers will look back, see the police car and quickly tap the driver and point in its direction. Other passengers will quickly look back with expressions of fright. If an officer states that the driver and passengers "Just didn't look right," this will not hold up in court as probable cause. The description of what happened must go into enough detail to convice a person who was not there.

At times the driver will seem to be unfamiliar with the car. He may drive off without the lights on because he cannot find the light switch. On close examination the driver might not fit the car. A young juvenile badly needing a haircut and driving an expensive new car should certainly arouse suspicion.

At one time in our history it was popular for drivers to wear gloves. No longer. Wearing gloves by itself is not probable cause, but if the driver is wearing gloves along with other indications, it should make the officer suspicious. This is especially true in hot weather.

The majority of vehicles are stolen by Juveniles. They are often under age, and lack driving skills. The officer's attention may be first alerted by the poor way in which the car is being driven. Often the juveniles are after a thrill and will drive the car in a reckless manner in order to achieve this goal. If the officer observes a violation, there is no need for probable cause. Asking for the vehicle registration will soon establish ownership.

(2) Condition of the vehicle. A new car in good condition will seldom have a window broken. The owner of the car would have the window fixed right away. Because of this, any damage to a new vehicle in otherwise good condition, is an indication that the car should be checked out. Even if it is not a stolen car, it could have been involved in a hit and run accident.

Whenever a vehicle is stopped for a traffic violation, officers should automatically look for the ignition keys. If they are missing, they should call for assistance and remove the occupants from the car. A check should be made under the dashboard for a jumper wire or some form of hot wiring. Sometimes tinfoil or a gum wrapper will be wrapped around the back of the ignition plug. The hot wire or "jumper wire" as it is sometimes called can simply be a piece of radio wire with an alligator clip on each end.

(3) License plate discrepancies. To avoid being picked up because of the license number, many thieves will steal or borrow a set of license plates which they change with the originals. This will allow them to drive around town without the average officer being alerted to the fact that the car is stolen. When different plates are attached to a stolen vehicle, there are usually certain characteristics that can alert an officer.

(a) The condition of the license plate is not harmonious with the condition of the car. Plates are often stolen from wrecking yards, and are in bad condition. The vehicle stolen is usually newer. However, in some states the license plate is transfered by the owner from car to car and may be in bad shape.

(b) The plates are often wired on rather than being bolted because it is a faster operation and can be done quickly in the field.

(c) Sometimes the new plate will be fastened on over the old one.

(d) Sometimes the perpetrators will attempt to alter the numbers on the license rather than change plates. they might do this as a temporary measure until they are able to obtain another set of license plates.

(e) Bugs and debris on back plate. Thieves will often steal just the front plate from another car and then attach it to the rear of the stolen car. The owner of the original car may not even notice that his front plate is missing. However, front plates often become splattered with bugs and other debris such as road oil and tar. This does not happen to the back plate. If a back plate does have bugs or debris splattered on it, the car should be investigated.

CONFIRMING OWNERSHIP

When an officer stops a vehicle because he or she senses something wrong, the first objective is to find proof of ownership. There are many little ways in which an officer can find out whether the driver is lying when he states that the car is his own.

(1) Ask the driver when the car was last lubricated, and at which station. There are usually papers in the glove compartment or a sticker on the inside of the door frame.

(2) Ask the driver what articles are in the glove compartment.

(3) Ask the driver to step out of the car, then ask him the approximate mileage of the vehicle.

(4) Ask the driver for information regarding the type of jack in the trunk.

If there are several people in the car when it is stopped, they should be separated and interviewed individually. If something is wrong, it can soon be determined by the evasiveness of the answers and by the discrepancies in their stories. Whenever something said indicates that all is not right, police communications should be requested to phone the person to whom the car is registered. Many times the driver will state that the vehicle is not his own, that it was lent to him by his cousin or a buddy at work. These excuses should always be checked out.

THE USE OF STATISTICS AND AUTO THEFT

When an officer is having a series of auto thefts, or a large number of stolen cars abandoned on the beat, a spot map should be developed in order to show a pattern. A person who steals cars is usually lazy. However, he is not completely stupid. He tries to seek a happy medium. He doesn't want to dump the car right in front of his house, yet he doesn't want to walk too far. He usually dumps it about a block from his house or where he is going. The next time he will also dump the car about a block away but in a different direction. If the patrol officer were to plot the location where each car was abandoned, a pattern would develop showing the approximate location of the suspect's home.

By use of the address file in the Records division, a check may show which persons live in that immediate area who have been arrested for similar offenses. A mug shot of the suspect(s) should be obtained from records. While patrolling the beat, the officer can look for the suspect driving a vehicle. Especially if it is around the time that most of the cars are stolen. If the suspect is spotted, the vehicle should be checked out thoroughly.

Plotting where the cars are stolen will often give clues as to the identity of the perpetrator. The time that they are stolen will also help. A little follow-up may reveal that there is only one place in the vicinity where the employees get out at the time the cars are stolen. and a further check might reveal which employees do not have cars, and which employees have been arrested on prior occasions.

JOYRIDING

The majority of cars taken are stolen by juveniles for the purpose of "joy riding." Because of this, the vehicles will remain in the immediate vicinity or will be en route to, or at, a nearby hangout for juveniles such as a beach. Alert officers can often catch them while they are driving around. Many times they will leave the vehicle for a while, and will return to it later for more driving. This happens frequently around schools where the perpetrators, who are truant, will give rides to their friends during the lunch hour and after school. They are also prone to stealing a car for transportation to sporting events such as a boxing match or hardtop racing. They will usually take the same car back home. Patrol officers should always check cars parked near sporting events. It usually pays off in recovered vehicles. When a stolen car is found at one of these locations, it should be staked out in hopes of catching the perpetrators when they return. To prevent their escape, the officer might pull a couple of the ignition wires. When officers find a stolen car parked with no one in it, the hood and exhaust pipe should be immediately checked to gain an idea of how long it has been there. The amount of heat present will roughly tell when it was last driven. This will help the officer in deciding whether to stake out the car.

ELECTRONIC HOMING DEVICE RETRIEVAL SYSTEMS

There are two major electronic homing devices that have been developed to help retrieve stolen cars and apprehend the perpetrators. They both require the owner to install special equipment in the vehicle. The first is LOJACK. With this system, the owner immediately reports to the LOJACK headquarters when his car has been stolen. They send out a radio signal that activates a transmitter within the car. The car then emits a continuous radio signal. When two or more police cars with special receivers pick up the signal, they can obtain the car's location through triangulation. This device also gives the description of the stolen car and the name of the legal owner. The second is TELETRAC. It works only when the car is hot wired. Since most cars are stolen via this method, it is quite effective. When the car is hot wired, it automatically activates the transmitter. The signals are picked up by TELETRAC receiving antennas located in major cities. The signal is displayed on a city map in a computer. The position is updated every ten seconds as the car moves. The control operator then gives the police the exact location of the stolen car.

NARCOTIC CASES

The patrol officer is seldom assigned to narcotic cases. Still there is an opportunity to make many field arrests for offenses associated with narcotics. In past times, before restrictive court decisions, the patrol officer could make many narcotic arrests just by stopping known narcotic users and searching them. Today, officers must rely more on their wits and five senses.

The patrol officer will still have occasion to come in contact with narcotic offenders because they do not confine their activities to narcotic abuse and are often arrested for other offenses. It is when this type of arrest occurs that the patrol officer should be aware of common narcotics paraphernalia found on their persons during the booking search. Officers should be especially alert to the possibility of the suspect disposing of evidence en route to booking. When the patrol officers suspect that a person might be a narcotics offender, they should watch him very closely. There are many signs that can alert the officer to this possibility. One of them is the terminology used by the suspect.

LANGUAGE AND TERMS USED

Today the use of narcotics is so widespread in this country that the terminology for narcotics and paraphernalia differ by area and change with time. Because of this, a list of terms will not be included in this chapter as it was in the past. Updated lists of narcotic terminology are readily available in most departments and through state narcotic agencies. An alert patrol officer can pick up the terms from "dopers" with whom he or she deals daily.

PHYSICAL REACTIONS & OBSERVATION OF PECULIARITIES IN NARCOTIC USERS

The first thing that officers should check when they suspect that a person is under the influence of a dangerous drug is the eyes. The eyes seem to react to drugs more noticeably than other parts of the body. Also check for needle marks on inner arms or where veins are close to the skin. Reactions to drugs will be covered by general class of drug.

I. **THE OPIATES.** There are at least 27 derivatives of opium, but the average patrol officer comes across about three. They are Heroin, Morphine and Codeine. The reactions to the drug are basically the same, except that they are more intense with Heroin.

(A) Effects of opiates

(1) Pupils of the eyes are pinpointed.
(2) Insensitivity to pain, fatigue and hunger.
(3) Eyelids are droopy.
(4) Feeling of euphoria or well being.
(5) Slower breathing
(6) Mouth is very dry.
(7) No sex drive
(8) Constipation
(the last two are not readily observable.)

(B) Symptoms of withdrawal

It has been noticed that initial heroin withdrawals are similar to having a cold. Then going to the flu and finally ending up with pneumonia.

(1) Profuse sweating.
(2) Running of nose and eyes.
(3) Dilation (or widening) of pupils.
(4) Severe hot flashes alternating with chills.
(5) Involuntary muscle twitching.
(6) Sneezing and goose pimples.
(7) Severe cramps of legs, stomach, etc.
(8) Nausea, diarrhea, vomiting, headaches.
(9) Yawning.
(10) Increase in breathing & blood pressure.
(11) Inability to sleep.

II. GOOFBALLS (Amphetamines/Barbiturates)

(A) Effects of Amphetamines (stimulants)

(1) Dilated pupils of eyes (eyes bright/shiny.)
(2) Excitation and hyperactivity.
(3) Restlessness, talkativeness.
(4) Feeling of well being.
(5) Relief from fatigue.
(6) Bad breath and dry mouth.

(B) Effects of continued use.

(1) High blood pressure
(2) Hallucinations, panic, psychoses.
(3) Tremors and dizziness.
(4) Increased sweating.

(C) Effects of Barbiturates (sedatives)

(1) Drowsiness.
(2) Constricted pupils of eyes.
(3) Appears intoxicated, no alcohol odor.
(4) General feeling of euphoria or well being.
(5) Slow reflexes and coordination.
(6) Irrational behavior.

(D) Effects of continued use.

(1) Slow confused thinking.
(2) Emotional disturbance and belligerence.
(3) Tremors/involuntary oscillation of eyes.

III. COCAINE AND SPEED (METH)

Although Cocaine is of vegetable origin and Speed is a synthetic, they are both stimulants and have the same effect. They are sometimes injected, so arms should be inspected for needle marks. Cocaine is also sniffed through a glass tube from a mirror. These items should alert an officer to possible cocaine use. These drugs are not physically addictive but they can be highly psychologically addictive.

Crack cocaine has basically the same effects, but is more concentrated, acts faster, is more addictive, and has far greater negative psychological effects.

(A) Effects of Cocaine or Methamphetamines

(1) Removes pain, hunger and fatigue.
(2) Movements are quick, almost jerky.
(3) Eyes are dilated. (Affects perception)
(4) Hyperactivity/amphetamine use symptom

(B) Effects of continued use

(1) Periods of depression and exaltation.
(2) Symptoms of paranoia
(3) Severe anxiety or fear.
(4) Tremors and hallucinations.
(5) Fixed stare.

IV. HALLUCINOGENS (Mind Altering Drugs)

(A) Effects of Marijuana

(1) Enlarged pupils.
(2) Yellowish bloodshot eyes.
(3) Droopy eyelids.
(4) Intoxicated appearance/no alcohol odor.
(5) Distorted perception.
(6) Loss of sensitivity to pain.
(7) The final effect of continued use is sleep (Final effect is depressant.)

(B) Effects of Peyote (Mescaline — non-addicting)

(1) Similar to Marijuana, except that it tends to produce color and musical fantasies.

(C) Effects of LSD (Lysergic Acid Diethylamide) (Acid)

(1) Dilation of pupils
(2) Sensations over-intensified.
(3) Perceptions distorted.
(4) Illusions, delusions, hallucinations.
(5) Loss of drive and initiative.
(6) Lack of concern about nudity.
(7) Desire for self-mutilation (emasculation, or cutting off of penis)
(8) Severe depression if on "bad trip".
(9) Can have Grand Mal seizures.
(10) Suicidal tendencies if on "bad trip".
(11) Excitation and hyperactivity.
(12) Irrational behavior and rambling speech.
(13) Increased sweating and tremors.

NARCOTIC INFORMATION IN GENERAL

The main types of narcotics and associated equipment will be covered under the general narcotic headings:

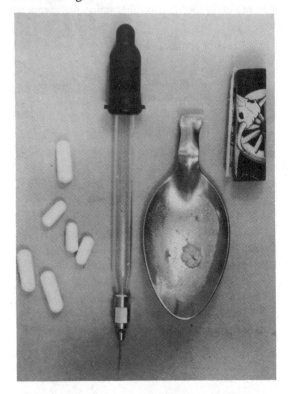

Fig. XIV-2; Narcotic user's paraphernalia or "kit"

OPIATES

(1) **HEROIN.** The most common form of opiate with which patrol officers deal in their work is heroin. It is the favorite drug of addicts in the United States. Heroin is a white powder like milk sugar. On the street, it is sold in capsules (caps) and bindles or folded papers. When arrested, the suspect will often try to swallow the evidence. The "kit" or "outfit" is the paraphernalia need-ed to prepare the narcotic for solution and to inject it into the subject's veins. It contains the following items:

(a) Eye dropper. This is preferred over the hypodermic syringe because it may be used with one hand. The corner of a dollar bill is often used as a needle gasket. It has the added advantage of being easily available. Possession of a hypodermic syringe can be illegal.

(b) Needle. Sometimes a rubber band is used to hold it onto the eyedropper.

(c) Spoon. The spoon is used to cook the heroin because it will not dissolve in water without being heated. The spoon will be black on the bottom from the carbon of the match flames.

(d) Match book. The match book is used to heat the heroin, and also to hold the needle.

(e) Tie rag. The tie rag is used to tie off the circulation of the vein and make it swell. This makes injection easier. A handkerchief can be used.

(f) Cotton. The cotton is used to filter the heroin solution before the injection. It is placed in the spoon, and the eye dropper is placed on top of it.

GOOFBALLS

"Goofball" is the term used for the many types of synthetic stimulants and depressants that are sold through prescription on the legitimate market. They are usually brightly colored and many-shaped. Most police departments have a sample board of these pills and capsules which can be used for comparison. Color charts may also be obtained from the Federal Food and Drug Administration. Suspected "goofballs" should be seized as evidence to be analyzed later.

AMPHETAMINES (Stimulants or Pep Pills)

Amphetamines are legal prescription drugs that are used as stimulants and aids to weight reducing. On the street they are referred to as "Uppers", and the most common are Benzedrine (Bennies) and Dexedrine (Dexies). Sometimes they are mixed with a depressant drug and called a "Speedball". They come in many colors and are found in capsule or in pill form. In pill form there are many shapes. The color and shape often determine their "street" name. Common names are Peaches, Hearts, Whites, Footballs, and so on. There are many Over-the-Counter drugs that have a similar appearance. There are simple field-test kits that can quickly test a suspected pill or capsule.

CRACK COCAINE

Crack is a form of freebased cocaine. It is made by way of a chemical process rather than the previous use of flammable solvents. The end result of this process is a rock-like substance. While cocaine is usually snorted, Crack is smoked in various kinds of glass pipes. It is usually packaged in small sealed or "zip-loc" baggies or other plastic bindles.

Crack takes effect rapidly, often within five seconds. Those who have used cocaine on occasion report that their need for Crack is constant. Because Crack is easily manufactured, can be sold at reasonable prices, and quickly builds up an addictive tolerance, it is a very lucrative business. As a result, gangs have taken over its manufacture and distribution. Competition has resulted in gang wars in which great numbers of people have been killed. Crack tends to cause increased paranoia and violence in its users. It also causes crime to increase because those addicted to it are usually poor and must resort to crime in order to support their habit. Although it is heavily used in poor minority areas, it is also widely used by persons in the movie and television industries. It is not uncommon for it to become a contractual element in large movie deals.

Along with numerous medical complications, the use of Crack can cause depression, irritability, loss of sex drive, memory loss, suicidal tendencies and extreme paranoia. It can also induce a state of psychosis similar to schizophrenia.

CRACK HOUSES

Crack is sold on the street and in Crack Houses. Whenever dealers open a Crack House, there is usually a great increase in crime in the immediate area. The most effective way, at present, to eliminate a Crack House is for the District Attorney to close the house as a public nuisance. In order for this to happen, the patrol officer must keep careful records of every incident that occurs in the immediate vicinity. This includes incidents in which no arrests have been made. Field interrogation cards should be filled out on all known criminals who frequent the house. When customers stop their cars in front of a Crack House, they should be approached and warned that there have been numerous crimes and robberies at this location and for their own safety, they should avoid it.

BARBITURATES
(Hypnotics/Sedatives--Addictive)

Barbiturates are also legal prescription drugs that are used as sleeping pills or sedatives. On the street they are referred to as "Downers." The most common are Seconal (reds), Tuinal (Rainbows), Nembutal (Yellow Jackets), and Doriden (Cibees). They are the most popular type of dangerous drug among teenagers because they are cheap, don't have the tell-tale odor of alcohol, and are readily available. They are also the most dangerous because they can become addictive. Like amphetamines, there are many over-the-counter drugs that have the same appearance as barbiturates.

METHAQUALONE

Popular with youths is a "downer" called Methaqualone. Its street name is "sopor" or "quaalude." Originally it was thought to be non-habit forming, but experience in Europe and elsewhere indicate that the drug has a strong potential for causing dependence and has a severe with-drawal syndrome. It has also been called the "love drug."

Medically, it is a non-barbiturate hypnotic that is prescribed by doctors to induce sleep. It is legal with a prescription, and can therefore be legally possessed in cases where it has been prescribed by a doctor. When taken in excess, it acts like alcohol. The person taking it will have a loss of motivation and motor coordination.

The Journal of the American Medical Association reports that the abuse of this drug has reached a "silent epidemic" proportion among students and other young persons in the United States. They seem to be caught up in the "love drug" mystique, and are unaware of its potential dangers. Staff members of the Haight-Ashbury Free Medical Clinic in San Francisco report that methaqualone has become as popular as the barbiturate (Reds), and that it appears to have the same addictive qualities.

HALLUCINOGENIC DRUGS
Marijuana (Marihuana)

The Marijuana bush will grow in almost any climate except the arctic. It is the oldest known narcotic in the world, with a history going back 4,000 years in the Mid-East. The patrol officer should be aware of its appearance. The leaf always has an odd number of leaves, with tips similar to the Japanese Maple except that the Japanese Maple leaf joins together at the body. Marijuana leaves come to a point at the stem.

Fig. XIV-3; Marijuana leaf

Smell. The smell of burning marijuana is quite distinctive, and is often the first thing that arouses suspicion that a narcotics offense has been committed. Every officer should learn this distinctive odor. It has a tendency to stick to clothing and upholstery, so the odor will remain after the "joint" has been smoked.

Seeds. As the marijuana cigarette is smoked, the seeds will pop out. A careful examination of the floorboard in an automobile will often result in the finding of seeds. When the seeds are found, the officer has probable cause for a more thorough search. Uusually a butt or two can then be found.

Shape. Manicured marijuana is very loose, and will pour out of the end of the cigarette if the end is not twisted or tucked in. Because the marijuana is rough, two cigarette papers are needed to wrap it. The person who prepares the cigarettes usually rolls the cigarettes in brown paper, but today there are papers of many colors and even flavors.

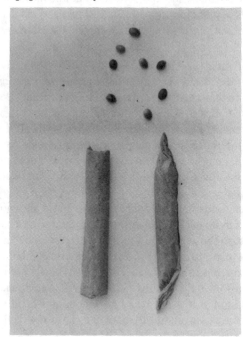

Fig. XIC-4; Marijuana seeds and cigarettes (joints)

LSD (Acid; Lysergic Acid Diethylamide 25)

The great increase in the use of hallucinogenic drugs such as LSD 25 (d-Lysergic Acid diethylamide), DMT (Dimethyltryptamine) and Mescaline or Peyote, has caused many problems for the patrol officer. At one time LSD lost popularity, but in the 1990's it has become popular again. Since it is odorless, colorless and tasteless, it presents quite a prob-lem in field identification. At present, the best means of identifying the drug is through the Infra-red Spectrophotometer. This equipment and the special dyes necessary to its use are not always readily available. A kit to be used for field testing has been developed by the Bureau of Drug Abuse Control, but this is for field tests only, and cannot be used as positive identification for court purposes. LSD 25 can cause temporary insanity. If this happens, the user should be treated as an emotionally disturbed person and committed under emergency conditions to a state hospital or local psychiatric ward. A jail is definitely not the place for persons under the influence of LSD as they can become uncontrollable. If the person is committed, the officer should obtain all pills and drugs from the suspect's belongings. They can later be submitted for examination.

Although the advocates of hallucinogenic or psychedelic drugs promote them as being the cure for all of man's ills, and sell or give them to college and high school students as being "mind expanding", there has been no objective scientific evidence to back up this claim. On the contrary, the scientific investigation of Doctors Ungerleider and Fisher of the Department of Psychiatry at U.C.L.A. shows just the opposite. All scientific experiments undertaken since the effects of LSD were first discovered in 1943, show its use to be definitely dangerous and its effect upon the user to be unpredictable.

Originally LSD came as a clear liquid in the form of medical ampules. The only legal manufacturer was Sandoz Laboratories. Because of widespread misuse of the drug, Sandoz Laboratories stopped production, even for medical purposes. To-day it is made in makeshift laboratories and illegally sold throughout the country. The original ap- plication was to place a drop on a cube of sugar, but today it is found in many forms. One of the most common is a white pill similar to aspirin. In the liquid form it comes in every color imaginable, depending upon the person making it. Until the new field testing kits are more widely used, it is advisable to book "high" suspects as emotionally disturbed persons. All pills and liquids taken from their immediate possesion should be seized as possible evidence for examination by the crime lab. Some of the dangers of this drug are as follows:

(1) Its effects can recur any time without the necessity of taking further doses. These recurrences can even occur a year later. This is referred to as a "Flashback."

(2) Experiments with animals who have been given LSD have shown evidence of brain damage. We can assume that the danger of such damage exists for humans as well.

(3) Since the drugs are illegally manufactured, there is no control over impurities.

(4) It is extremely difficult to measure LSD or to determine proper dosage so too much could easily be taken.

(5) It causes faulty judgment of time, motion and space, making the user accident prone.

(6) A person who is emotionally unstable can easily become suicide prone. The effects normally last about 10 to 12 hours and the "taper off" can take days.

OTHER HALLUCINOGENIC DRUGS

In local communities, students will often discover that certain plants, seeds, or species of vegetable matter can "turn them on", and because of this, cause a local police problem. The effects are usually obtained by smoking or chewing the drug containing substance. Local departments must do all they can to prevent undue publicity. There will be many students who, not being aware of the potential danger, will try it. Common examples are certain Morning Glory seeds, Nutmeg, Hawaiian Woodrose, and others.

There are also cases of juveniles who have found ways in which to alter common household products or over-the-counter drugs and get "high" on them. We cannot possibly eliminate every product that might be harmful to humans. The American Medical Association estimates that in the U.S. there are a staggering 250,000 products for use in the home which are potentially harmful.

THINGS TO WATCH FOR (signs of drug use)

(1) Apparent intoxication, no alcohol odor.

(2) Extremely bloodshot eyes without the odor of hangover breath.

(3) Parked automobiles with small groups in them. Marijuana smokers like company.

(4) Cars that have the windows rolled up in the summer (to keep the smoke inside) or cars that have the windows rolled down in the winter after being stopped by a police car (to get the smell of marijuana out of the car).

(5) Pupils that show no reaction to light. Heroin will cause the eyes to contract to a pinpoint. Marijuana and Cocaine will cause the pupils of the eyes to dilate. Officers should use their flashlights to check for these signs. When a heroin addict starts his withdrawal, his eyes will dilate.

(6) In dealing with narcotic addicts, be careful to wash your hands afterwards since many not only have venereal diseases, but also infectious hepatitis.

(7) Next to male homosexuals, the highest rate of AIDS occurs in intravenous drug users. These persons require special handling. Officers should be careful to avoid getting any of the suspect's body fluids in cuts or open sores.

IDENTIFICATION OF DRUGS

The identification of drugs can present quite a problem to the patrol officer. There are so many OTC (over-the-counter) drugs that look like dangerous drugs, that it is difficult for the officer to know whether or not the suspected drug is in violation of the law.

To assist in this endeavor, Eli Lilly company, a major producer of drugs in the United States, is now placing a code letter and number on each of their prescription drugs. A booklet is available to police departments that will give the formula for each number. This will enable officers to make an identification simply by radioing the number to headquarters where it may be located in the Identi-Code booklet. Should the officer find drugs where the number has been scraped off, it would be reasonable to suspect that they were illicit.

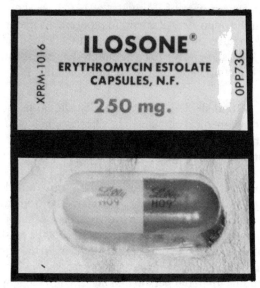

Fig. XIV-5; Drug identification

STUDY QUESTIONS for Patrol Operations

CHAPTER 14

1. A problem with burglar alarms is that there are so many false alarms, officers tend to treat   T or F
    them all as false after a while.

2. Speed is not the essential factor in responding to a burglar alarm.   T or F

3. In your town the even numbers of an address are usually on the _____ side of the street.

4. Officers should drive code three to silent alarms.   T or F

5. If an officer who is responding to a burglar alarm spots what appears to be a lookout, he   T or F
    should stop and check him out.

6. Name a common ruse used by lookouts so as not to attract attention. _____
    _____

7. Most buildings can be secured from the outside by _____ police cars.

8. When a burglar uses a tool to pry open a door or window, the mark is called a _____.

9. When a burglar breaks through the ceiling, it is called a _____ job.

10. When entering a room, the door should be slammed open against the wall.   T or F

11. In court you may have to tell which items came from which prisoner during the search.   T or F

12. In trying to locate a burglar's car, you find a car parked nearby. You should check what on
    the car to see if it has been used recently. _____

13. In responding to a burglary-in-progress call, you should park the police vehicle in front of   T or F
    the residence in case you need it for an emergency.

14. The burglary-in-progress call is basically so simple that no special tactics are involved.   T or F

15. A professional burglar gave information about what he observed when the police responded
    to a call. Which of the following is false (write "F" after each false statement)

    (a) Nearly all police officers follow a similar or fixed pattern. ____
    (b) Most police officers act like they believe the burglar call was false. ____
    (c) Officers don't mind searching where it is dirty. ____
    (d) Officers always check the physical description on a driver's license against the driver's physical
        appearance. ____
    (e) Officers make a lot of noise when they respond to a call. ____

16. In searching for suspects, officers look under things but seldom look _____.

17. Robbery, like rape, is many times falsely reported.   T or F

18. One of the greatest faults of patrol officers in responding to a robbery call is that too many   T or F
    of them respond to the immediate scene.

19. When an area is divided into four sections for the purpose of searching for the getaway car
    after a holdup, the tactic is called a _____.

20. In the above tactic, it is best to begin the search on the outskirts and then move in towards   T or F
    the location of the holdup.

21. One of the most common examples of strong-arm robbery where no weapon is used, is the
    offense of (slang) _____.

22. What type of criminal commits the above type of crime? _____

23. Disturbance of the peace is one of the most common types of calls for patrol service.   T or F

24. Laws concerning disturbance of the peace go back to Roman times.   T or F

25. The first city in the United States to pass a law against disturbance of the peace was the city of
    _____.

26. There are devices available that can measure the loudness of sound. They measure loudness in
    _____.

27. In the case of loud parties, the best approach is mass arrests.   T or F

28. The key to disturbance of the peace calls is to wear your badge on _____.

29. The key to family fights is _____ when you first arrive.

30. Family crisis intervention training takes about six hours.   T or F

31. According to FBI statistics, one out of every four officers killed on duty was killed trying to
    settle what type of crime _____.

32. A Kansas City study showed that 40% of the murders in the city were _____ killing
    _____.

33. In cases involving murders during family fights, it was found that in _____ % of the
    cases officers had been called for fights five or more times.

34. In family crisis intervention classes officers are taught to _____ for a change.

35. Asians are not the only humans interested in "saving face."   T or F

36. Most gang fights are the result of group pressure.   T or F

37. Who is it that often calls the police to let them know that a juvenile gang fight is about to be held? _____

38. When officers are responding to a large mob, it is best to use the tactic where all of the cars stay back a block and then move in all at once on a given command. This is called the

_____.

39. Name three of the reasons listed as to why a person might be prowling on someone else's property.
    (a) _____
    (b) _____
    (c) _____

40. Name two excuses that prowlers give as to why they are at the place they have been stopped.
    (a) _____
    (b) _____

41. Prowlers have one of the lowest rates of apprehension of all types of criminal calls.   T or F

42. List three reasons why the above is so.
    (a) _____
    (b) _____
    (c) _____

43. Why should an officer hold his or her hand or gun up in front of his face when searching back-yards for prowlers at night? _____

44. If a two-officer unit responds to a prowler call and finds evidence that a prowler was actually there but can't locate him, what could they do? _____

45. The laws pertaining to emotional disturbance are found in the:

    a. _ Health and Safety Code.   b. __ Welfare and Institutions Code.
    c. _ Penal Code.   d. ___ Government Code.

46. A peace officer can take an emotionally disturbed person into protective custody when (1) he is a danger to others, and (2) _____.

47. Match the following symptoms of emotional disturbance with the terms used for them.

    (1) ___ hallucination   A. compulsive repetition of words
    (2) ___ illusion   B. compulsive repetition of actions
    (3) ___ catatonia   C. violent mood swings
    (4) ___ delusion   D. response to persons or objects that are not real
    (5) ___ obsession   E. belief that others are trying to harm him
    (6) ___ phobia   F. a fixed, motionless state
    (7) ___ stereotypy   G. inappropriate response to real persons or objects
    (8) ___ paranoia   H. false belief that cannot be corrected by reason
    (9) ___ manic depression   I. unreasonable fear of something

48. When first approaching a suspected emotionally disturbed person, you should use the phrase (1 of 2) _____.

49. Since emotionally disturbed persons can often exhibit great strength, the officer will often have to (1) knock the wind out of them by a blow to the stomach or (2) _____
_____

50. An emergency strait jacket can be made from a blanket or a _____.

51. There is no evidence that the full moon affects emotionally disturbed persons.   T or F

52. A study of Europe and the U.S. found that there was a(n) _____ in murders during the full moon.

53. A New York study found a _____ % increase in arsons during the full moon.

54. Studies in Florida have shown an increase in bleeding ulcers during the full moon.   T or F

55. An attempted suicide is a _____ for _____.

56. Name one thing a person contemplating suicide might do or say that would give you a hint of his intentions. _____

57. In handling an attempted suicide, stall for _____.

58. You believe that a person has taken drugs to commit suicide. You call for an ambulance and when they leave, you search for _____.

59. Name one household item that can be used as an emetic when mixed with water. _____

60. Name a case where you would not want to administer an emetic. _____
_____

61. What should you do before you administer mouth-to-mouth resuscitation? _____
_____

62. If you think a person is faking an attempted suicide just to get attention, you should still take them into custody.   T or F

63. A study done in California showed that over _____ % of all persons committed to psychiatric wards under emergency conditions by police officers were released the next day because it was felt that they were not sufficiently disturbed emotionally to warrant admission.

64. Why should you protect the scene at a suicide? _____

65. Name one reason why families will often hide evidence of the fact that a relative committed suicide.
_____

66. Stolen vehicle reports are sometimes false.   T or F

67. Name one of the reasons stolen vehicle reports are sometimes false. _____

_____

68. Enforcing laws against leaving keys in the ignition has little effect on the number of   **T or F**
    stolen cars.

69. Name an attention getter that would cause you to suspect that a car might be stolen. _____

_____

70. Name a condition of license plate that would make an officer suspect the car is stolen.

_____

71. Name one way in which the officer can confirm that the driver of the car is really the owner of
    that car. _____

72. What is the term used when juveniles take a car temporarily for fun or transportation and not to
    permanently steal? _____

73. An officer is staking out a stolen car. How can the suspect be prevented from showing up and
    driving off with the car? _____

74. One of the first places to check on a person suspected of using narcotics is _____.

75. If a person is suspected of using opiates, his eyes will have _____ pupils.

76. If a person is suspected of using a stimulant type drug (speed, coke), the pupils of his eyes will
    be _____.

77. An officer arrests a suspect who was trying to hold up a liquor store. The suspect is sneezing and
    has runny eyes and nose. He should be suspected of beginning to go through _____
    _____.

78. A person under the influence of barbiturates (reds) will have _____ pupils.

79. Cocaine is a: ____ depressant. ____ stimulant. ____ hallucinogen. ____ sedative.

80. If a person is under the influence of cocaine, his eyes will have dilated pupils.   **T or F**

81. The final effect of marijuana is as a depressant.   **T or F**

82. A person under the influence of LSD will have dilated pupils.   **T or F**

83. Under the effects of LSD, males often want to emasculate themselves. This means:

    a. _ putting out one's eyes.   b. __cutting off one's nose.
    c. _ cutting off one's ears.   d. __cutting off one's penis.

84. When a powdered narcotic is folded up in a small piece of paper, it is referred to as a _____.

85. A heroin addict will carry a book of matches to heat up the heroin solution and also to carry the _____.

86. A combination of a stimulant and depressant drug is called a _____.

87. Marijuana is a hallucinogenic drug.   T or F

88. Marijuana always has an _____ number of leaves.

89. Marijuana grows anywhere in the world except the Arctic.   T or F

90. The finding of marijuana seeds gives probable cause to search further in the car in which   T or F
    they are found.

91. Dr. Ungerleider has found some evidence that LSD does, in fact, expand your mind.   T or F

92. The effects of LSD normally last about how long?

    a. _ six hours   b. __eight hours
    c. _ five hours   d. __twelve hours

93. The American Medical Association estimates that about how many products for household use
    are potentially harmful?

    a. _ 1,000   b. __10,000
    c. _ 100,000   d. __250,000

94. When a heroin user starts to go through withdrawal, his eyes will _____.

95. It is common for narcotic users to have venereal diseases and _____.

CHAPTER XV

COURTROOM TESTIMONY AND DEMEANOR

COURTROOM TESTIMONY

Courtroom testimony is not only a challenge to the police officer, it is one of the best means of measuring an officer's true ability. It measures self control, obedience, personal conduct, bearing and tact. It also shows the ability of officers to express themselves and be understood by others. An officer's testimony will indicate the quality of work done in the field. It is here that an officer's work will be challenged and must be defended.

As an active participant in the American system of jurisprudence, the modern police officer should not fear this role. It should be looked upon as a challenge. It is here that officers participate in the search for justice. By testifying in court, a professional police officer must face the great paradox of humanity: that man will never find true justice on this earth, yet must continue to seek it. Man's fallibility makes him incapable of true justice. Yet because of his dignity and higher calling, it must be sought as if it were actually attainable. If life is indeed a stage and we are but the players, we must be judged by performance rather than by plot.

The American courtroom is also a stage, and our concern should also be the performance rather than the plot or the verdict. A police officer soon learns that a good performance will certainly affect the verdict. If an officer does well on the stand, his or her job is done. The verdict is the jury's job.

It is very natural for officers to take a personal interest in the case, and firmly believe in the defendant's guilt. They must never forget that justice is not one person's opinion. They must understand that the very purpose of our democratic court system is to protect people and their rights from the opinions or convictions of one person or one group. This is not always easy, but neither is policework. Those who feel that it is, should reevaluate the situation with the view of either changing their minds or their jobs.

FEAR OF TESTIMONY IN COURT

Court testimony is an essential part of the patrol officer's job. It is not always a pleasant task because of the pressures and tensions under which officers find themselves when on the stand. Yet it can be even more unpleasant when officers are ignorant of the true objectives of the trial. Especially if they do not understand court procedures.

Officers should have an understanding of the courts and how they operate. They should also understand the officer's true relationship within the system of jurisprudence. Once they do, they will find that this task can be faced with less trauma.

A SIMPLIFIED TRAIL PROCEDURE FOR WITNESSES

(1) **Direct Examination** Direct examination is used to introduce the witness. The attorney who introduces the witness will ask the court to call the witness. If it is the prosecuting attorney, the first witness will probably be the officer. His or her name will be called, and they will approach the bench to be sworn.The presenting attorney will ask questions such as name, address and occupation. Questions will be asked to show that the witness has relevant information regarding the case. At first the question and answer approach will be used because it is the best method for bringing out specific information. Once the competency of the witness has been established, the narrative approach will most likely be used. For example, "Officer Smith, would you please tell us, in your own words, what happened when you arrived at 1134 north 14th street on January the fifth?"

(2) **Cross Examination** Once a witness has testified under direct examination, the attorney for the other side gets a chance to ask questions of that witness. This is called cross examination. It is one of the rights listed in the sixth amendment of the Bill of Rights. This is the time that officers really earn their pay. It is the job of the attorney conducting the cross examination to impeach (discredit) witnesses whose testimony can be harmful to his case. They may ask questions that are phrased in a way that demands a yes or no answer. The rules of evidence today do not allow an attorney to ask questions such as "Have you stopped beating your wife? Answer yes or no." However they seem to come pretty close.

(3) **Re-direct and Re-cross Examination** During questioning, statements are made that need further clarification. This is done through the re-direct and re-cross examination. It is an opportunity for attorneys to ask new questions of a witness. It can be an opportunity to impeach or rehabilitate the witness. If, under cross examination, a witness is made to look bad because he or she answered a question without an opportunity to explain why, the re-direct examination will allow that witness to explain the answer.

(4) **Resting the Case** Once the attorneys have presented the best cases of which they are capable, and they have cross examined all witnesses to the fullest extent, they will "rest their case." This means that they are through. The only thing left is closing arguments.

It is natural for the new officer to feel uneasy about court testimony. As humans, we have a tendency to fear things we know little or nothing about. Although knowledge and experience will do much to reduce the fear of testimony, it will never completely elimiate it. This is because fear is part of human nature and the body's way of reacting to possible danger. The danger mentioned is not physical, but an emotional or psychological danger. It is the danger of having our testimony challenged, or being berated or even called a liar in front of other people. It is also a fear of making fools of ourselves.

Humans react to all types of danger in the same way physically. Psychologists and physiologists refer to the physical symptoms of fear as the "fight or flight" reaction. It is part of man's basic nature. Its purpose is protective. When man senses danger, he has two alternatives, fight or flight. In order to prepare for either action, certain physiological changes take place in the body. The adrenal glands stimulate muscular reaction and give energy. The body becomes alert. Without an active outlet, this physiological state is expressed as nervousness. Blood starts draining from the extremities to the vaso-cavity in the center of the body. This is a protective reaction that prevents the person from bleeding to death in the event that he is attacked or injured. This in turn causes dryness of the mouth, and a dropping of the body temperature because there is not enough blood to warm the tissues. This causes chills and possibly shaking.

The heart, preparing for increased physical action, pumps harder, and this causes the sensation of palpitations of the heart. Alertness causes tension in the muscles and the throat, and vocal cords contract to make the voice higher than usual. When these symptoms are acute, the body goes into a state of shock and unconsciousness can result.

Under normal circumstances, however, these symptoms can be controlled by the individual, at least to where they are not obvious to others. Because of this, the new officer often looks in reverence toward the veteran officer who, while testifying on the stand, appears to be so calm. Officers new to the experience of testifying, do not realize that the reactions experienced are common to everyone, despite outward appearances. These feelings can actually help officers in the long run by making them more alert. Yoga breathing about twenty minutes before testifying is a good way to reduce nervous tension. It can be practiced without anyone else noticing it.

FREQUENCY OF COURT APPEARANCE

Officers who do their jobs properly will have to testify in court. It goes with the job. The frequency of going to court can be another matter. Going to court too often can be an indication that the officer is doing something wrong. Traffic officers would be an exception. They deal in traffic offenses which are routinely contested. The number of citations issued and traffic accidents investigated far exceed those of the average patrol officer.

There are at least two reasons for frequent court appearances. First is the frequency of court appearance in relation to the number of cases handled. Second is frequency in relation to the number of court appearances by fellow officers under the same circumstances. Both police administrators and court judges are concerned about an officer who is in court too often.

Most of a patrol officer's court appearances are for traffic citations rather than serious crimes. A great number of people who go to court on traffic citations go because of the conduct of the officer. Their pride is hurt and because of this, they often base their whole defense on the misconduct of the officer rather than on the validity of the citation.

Fig. XV-1; Proper bearing and attention in court are essential

Fig. XV-2; Improper bearing and gun showing have a negative effect on the judge and jury.

Fig. XV-3; This reflects little interest in the trial and gives a bad impression

Photos courtesy of Trinidad State Junior College, Colorado

Judges do not like to see the same officers before them continually, and in cases where the defendant is claiming officer misconduct. This cannot help but affect the judge's opinion of the officer. Sooner or later the judge will tend to disbelieve a lot of the officer's testimony and decide in favor of the defendant. In the locker room, these officers, who lose so many cases, will rationalize and present all kinds of excuses to other officers as to why they have lost so many in court. They will blame it on the judges, the court rules or anything else they can think of. Their fellow officers will usually nod in agreement so as not to offend them. However, the supervisors and administrators who must evaluate the officer's performance, will not accept these rationalizations. When officers find themselves in this position, they should seek help from their sergeant. He or she can offer good advice on performance both in the field and in court. They can usually suggest some adjustment in behavior and approach to improve the officer's techniques.

A third area of concern is the rate of conviction in cases where the officer is the main witness. There are innumerable factors that enter into every court decision. The best officer on the department is going to lose some cases. It depends upon the frequency and degree of certain factors. Our forefathers purposely stacked the system against the prosecution and law enforcement officers. It was felt that the power of the state was so great against a lone individual, that the rules should be in his favor. However, a police administrator cannot help but be concerned about an officer who continually loses cases in court. This is especially true if the officer is the main, or only, witness in the case. Most prosecutors are busy, and are reluctant to take officers aside to reprimand them for a poor presentation on the stand. They often feel that this is the job of the police supervisor or training officer. Sometimes they feel that there is no hope for the officer, and don't want to get involved in fighting city hall.

New officers usually suffer from a misconception about courts and justice. Being idealistic, they feel that the case should be decided by evidence alone (and it should.) They fail to realize that the judge and jury are human beings. They cannot help but be influenced by their own feelings. They must often weigh conflicting statements and points of view on their impressions of the person. In most cases, the improper conduct of officers on the stand is simply a matter of ignorance. They have never been properly instructed in court demeanor except through watching old movies and television. In the police academy little time was devoted to this topic. They have never really tried to use sympathetic introspection to see themselves through the eyes of others. These are the officers who can profit most from proper instruction in court testimony. It is to these officers, and those who have the desire to improve, that this chapter is directed.

COURT PREPARATION

When an officer receives a court notice, there are certain procedures that should be followed in order to properly prepare for court:

(1) Check field notebook and radio log for the case being tried. Often these records will contain little bits of information that will not be found in the offense reports. Sometimes they can be important because the defense attorney is not aware of them.

(2) Obtain copies of all reports from the Records Division, including a "mug shot." It may be needed later to identify the defendant. Many times the officer arrests a defendant for the first time. The officer is with the defendant for a very short time under conditions that make him look different than he does in court. Seeing the "mug shot" just before the trial will help ensure identification. Sometimes the defense attorney, knowing the circumstances of the short contact, will ask the officer on the stand if he can point out the defendant in the courtroom. It is be embarrassing if the officer is unable to do so.

(3) Find out who else is involved with the case. They can accompany the officer when seeing the District Attorney. If they are on vacation, have the D.A. try for a delay in the case.

(4) Make a list of all the evidence in the case and its location and storage numbers so it can be quickly obtained when needed. It is wise to check with the property officer ahead of time to make sure that the evidence is still there. If it is not, there will be time to trace it. If an attempt was made to pick up the evidence just before the trial and it could not be found, the case might have to be dismissed.

(5) Make a list of witnesses, including their addresses and phone numbers. If it is important that the District Attorney listen to their testimony, make arrangements for an appointment and transportation if needed.

(6) Sign the copy of the trial notice and return it to the District Attorney's office so they know that you have received it.

(7) Make arrangements for a conference with the District Attorney or the Deputy District Attorney assigned as the prosecutor. This enables him to properly plan a strategy in court. This will give the officer and the prosecutor an opportunity to meet if they have not worked on a prior case together.

(8) Have subpoenas made out for all witnesses. Some officers talk to the witnesses and receive their verbal agreements to appear, and do not obtain subpoenas. If the witness should fail to show under these circumstances, there is nothing that could be done to the witness. It is possible that the case might be lost. The subpoena is a form of insurance. If witnesses knows that they can be found in contempt of court, they will make every effort to appear when ordered.

(9) Calendars should be marked with the date of the court appearance. They should be marked both at work and at home. the notation should include the time, exact location, and judge. The location should include the number of the courtroom.

(10) The day before the trial, witnesses should be called to remind them of the date. It is an extra effort, but it pays off in a greater percentage of convictions. If they do not have transportation it would be wise to offer them a ride. It will further insure that they show up in court. The case often rests on their testimony.

PRELIMINARIES JUST BEFORE THE TRIAL

(1) Call the court to make sure the trial has not been postponed. If it has been, call the witnesses.

(2) Pick up all evidence from headquarters. If there are several officers involved in the case, one officer should be assigned this task. Judges are not sympathetic to the excuse "I thought Officer Jones was picking up the evidence."

(3) Pick up any witnesses who do not have transportation, or arrange for the beat car to bring them to court.

(4) Check to be sure there have been no last minute changes in the location of the courtroom. With the large number of cases in courts today, many changes are made at the last minute.

(5) Check if the prosecutor has been changed at the last minute. If so, it is important that a short conference be held. This would enable the prosecutor to read the offense report and discuss possible tactics. This author had one case where the prosecutor was changed four times before the trial actually started. The fourth one was assigned a half hour before the trial began.

(6) Locate witnesses and try to make them feel more comfortable and at ease. Give them moral support and try to boost their confidence. Tell them a joke. Humor and laughter are good outlets for nervousness. Let them know that you will be there watching, and for them not to worry. Many times the entire case can rest on one witness. It is therefore quite important that proper care and attention be given this witness. If the witness has never testified in court before, it would be worthwhile to briefly go through the procedures with them. They should be told that their nervousness is natural; that officers who have been on the department many years still have that feeling. It could be a terrifying experience for them, and they need any encouragement the officer can give.

(7) Try to locate the defendant in court. He may look quite different than he did when he was arrested. If you can't locate him, the prosecutor might be able to help. He knows the defense attorney, and can point him out. Usually the attorney for the defense will be coaching the defendant, or the defendant will be sitting close to him. If he still can't be identified, the prosecutor can go over to the defense attorney on the pretense of seeing if he has changed his plea, and while there try to locate the defendant. Defense attorneys will sometimes have the defendant sit in a different location. Then when the officer is on the stand, he or she will be asked to point out the defendant. The mug shot of the defendant could be used here. As was mentioned, many attorneys will purposely ask an officer to identify the defendant in court. This is in hopes that he looks different from when he was first arrested. If the officer cannot make the identification, he or she can be impeached in the eyes of the jury. The defense attorney will then suggest that the defendant is innocent and has been wrongly charged with the crime.

(8) Let the prosecutor know that everything is in order, and that all the evidence and witnesses are in court.

THE OFFICER'S APPEARANCE

The officer's appearance is often as important as his or her testimony. This is one of the faults of the jury system. A trial often boils down to opposing witnesses telling different versions of what supposedly happened. How is the jury to decide which witness to believe? Obviously the one who makes the best impression will tend to be believed over the one who makes a poor impression. It is a part of human nature to judge people by appearances rather than by facts. We see evidence of this every day. The defense attorney is well aware of this and will take great pains to properly groom his client for the trial. He will personally see to it that the defendant has a haircut and is wearing a nice conservative suit with a clean or new shirt. He will see to it that his shoes are shined to perfection. He knows that this is a sign of neatness, pride in possessions, and responsibility. It will go far in convincing the jury that he is not deserving of the negative picture presented by the prosecution.

If only police officers would do the same. It is sometimes said that the police are more on trial than the defendant. If this is true (and there is plenty of evidence to support the claim) then officers should spend as much time on appearance as defendants. But do they? The following are suggestions for the officer appearing in court:

(1) Don't wear casual or "loud" clothes. A conservative suit is best. If the department requires that a uniform be worn, make sure that it is clean and neat. Since officers are supposed to be impartial witnesses (although they certainly are not) it is felt by some that they should be in civilian clothes rather than in uniform. This could further the impression of impartiality. Officers should never mix uniform pieces and civilian clothes when testifying in court. This is true even if the officer is just getting off work.

Shoes should be conservative and shined. Socks should not be loud in color. There should be no bulges in the officer's pockets or anything else that could distract from the testimony. Cigars stuck in a lapel pocket are often offensive to members of the jury.

(2) No badges, rings, or pins representing particular lodges or religions should be worn. It's possible that a member of the jury has strong feelings against that particular organization, and would discount the officer's testimony.

(3) Don't be visibly armed. This has a negative effect on the jury, and can make them receptive to suggestions from the defense that the police were brutal. It could also support a claim that the defendant was intimidated to make a confession. Some officers like to expose their sidearms. It makes them feel important. This is an example of "macho" behavior and is usually not pleasing to the jury.

(4) Male officers should be clean-shaven with neatly cut hair. All officers should have clean fingernails. Nothing will impeach an officer's character like noticeably dirty fingernails or a general slovenly appearance.

(5) Don't smoke or chew gum. Because the officer is nervous there is a strong need for one of these outlets. The psychological advantage gained by releasing tension in this manner are far outweighed by the poor impression received by the jury.

THE TRIAL

TAKING THE STAND

When an officer's name is called, he or she should walk to the bench and face the court clerk. Posture should be erect. However, the officer must not appear too casual, but sincere and interested in the oath. Officers must impress the jury that they are very concerned with the process. They should give the impression that this act is as important as being sworn in as President of the United States. All eyes of the jury will be on the officer at this time. If they sense any insincerity regarding the oath, they may discredit the officers testimony.

The clerk will raise his or her right hand and recite the oath. The officer will raise his or her right hand in a military manner. The upper arm should be parallel to the floor with the forearm at a right angle to it. The palm should be flat and facing the clerk. When the clerk has finished reciting the oath, the officer should attest, "I do" in a manner that indicates firm conviction. Because the court clerk recites the oath so often, he or she has a tendency to run through it in a speedy and bored manner which could set the tone for the officer's answer. The prosecutor will then ask the officer to be seated and will introduce the officer to the court by means of basic questions such as as name, occupation and department.

To set the stage and qualify the officer, the prosecutor will ask whether the officer was working at the particular time that the crime was committed or when the defendant was arrested. When the officer replies "yes," the prosecutor will usually ask him or her to relate their part in the investigation or incident. On the preliminary questions, the officer should direct the answers to the court recorder who might ask for the correct spelling of the officer's name and other pertinent information. After this, responses should be directed to the questioning attorney.

While on the stand, officers should keep their feet flat on the floor. They should try to curb the display of nervous habits. They should sit up straight in the chair and not scratch or rub their faces or pick at their nails. They should lay their hands in their laps or on the arm of the chair. Although this is untrue, jurors can misinterpret nervous signs on the stand as an indication that a person is not telling the truth.

COMMUNICATING WITH THE JUDGE OR JURY

The sole purpose for officers being on the stand is to serve as witnesses and to communicate certain facts to the jury. In order to do this, it is important that they be both heard and understood. Volume must be gauged by watching the expressions on the faces of the jury. If they are straining to hear the testimony, it will be obvious. Officers should avoid shouting or talking too loud. If the volume is too low, it can be increased without yelling, by concentrating on speaking from within the stomach rather than just with the mouth. It takes a little practice, and really amounts to a form of forced breathing from the stomach while talking. A sergeant in the military soon learns this technique when commanding subordinates.

Enunciation should be clear and the modulation controlled. If the defense attorney is asking the questions, the officer should look at him, but increase the volume slightly so the jurors can hear each word. The officer may face the attorney during the question, and then turn halfway between the attorney and the jury to give the answer.

Should officers be asked to repeat a statement containing vulgarities, they should make this known with an apology to the jury before actually repeating the words: "Yes sir, I can tell you exactly what he said. But first I would like to apologize to the ladies and gentlemen of the jury for the vulgarities contained in this statement." If the officer appears embarrassed at having to repeat the vulgarities, it tends to convince the jury that the officer is a decent sort of person. Vulgarities should never be used unless they are part of verbatim statements.

Officers should avoid terminology that would normally be unfamiliar to the jury. It is quite easy for an officer who uses police terminology as a part of normal conversation to unconsciously use it in court testimony. Some officers do this intentionally in order to impress the jury. All it does is break down communication and make the testimony ineffective. The officer's purpose on the stand is to effectively communicate with the Trier of Fact (judge or jury).

ANSWERING QUESTIONS ON THE STAND

When asked questions on the stand, officers must remember that they are JUST WITNESSES AND NOT PROSECUTORS. When on the stand, they are like puppets and the prosecution pulls the strings. As witnesses, officers must answer all questions and do so in a manner that is fair to both sides. All answers should be brief and cover ONLY THAT WHICH WAS ASKED. The greatest mistake an officer can make is offering too much information. At times the prosecution will be saving a particular piece of testimony for the right moment in order to gain the best psychological effect. He will not appreciate the officer's volunteering this information ahead of time in the belief that the prosecutor forgot it. If the officer believes that the prosecution has left out something important, he or she may quietly notify him after leaving the stand. The prosecutor can then recall the officer to the stand if it is felt to be necessary. A witness can be recalled to the stand any time before the attorneys "rest their case."

Many times the defense will ask questions that put the officer on the spot. The best tactic here would be to hesitate slightly as though thinking of the answer and then reply to the best of the officer's ability. This hesitation gives the prosecution a chance to object should the question be out of line. Officers should not engage the defense in a battle of wits. Chances are the defense attorney is a smarter person, and more capable at this sort of thing. It is always best to allow the prosecuting attorney to come to the rescue. Should the defense attorney ask questions that are unfair and make the officer look bad, the prosecuting attorney can later recall the officer to the stand. This will allow an explaination showing the circumstances of the unfavorable answer.

An officer should always tell the truth, even if it means losing the case. The officer's reputation is worth far more than just winning a case. It means the officer's own self respect, and that can't be measured. When officers lie on the stand (and some do) they are taking the chance of being caught in their own lies, (and some are.) An officer who is caught lying in court is not only subject to criminal prosecution, but might as well get out of law enforcement. The word will quickly get around among judges that this particular officer lied under oath. Even if it could not be proven, the judge, in his own mind, may discount this officer's testimony in all future cases. The officer might as well forget about going to court again. It would be foolish to even attempt doing so. Under these conditions, an officer might as well leave the department before asked.

It is natural for officers to feel strongly about cases that they are presently handling and consider them to be the most important cases in the world. Years later, if they were to look back, they might not even remember simple details of the cases. Officers must remember that they will handle a thousand or more cases before retiring and that it is not worth jeopardizing all of these cases just to win the one now being tried.

Occasionally, the defense attorney will catch the officer in an innocent mistake. If the officer becomes defensive and tries to justify the error, it could lead to impeachment in the eyes of the jury. It is very difficult for humans to say they are wrong. Because of this, when a person admits to a wrong, that person gains the respect of others because they know the difficulty of such an admission. When officers make a mistake on the stand, they should frankly admit that it was an error and apologize. If this is done in a sincere manner, it will work in the officer's favor. It can convince the jury that the officer respects truth even at the expense of his or her own embarrassment. For example, an officer makes an arrest on a Tuesday. On the stand the officer mistakenly states that the arrest was made on a Wednesday. When the defense attorney brings this to the court's attention, the officer should simply state "Did I say Wednesday? I'm sorry. It was clearly Tuesday."

There are times when the defense attorney will purposely reword an officer's prior testimony. The purpose is to distort its meaning or confuse the officer into thinking that he or she said the wrong thing. If the officer is sure that this is the case, the proper response would be, "I'm sorry sir, but I believe you misunderstood me. I don't believe that I said that because it's not true. May we have the recorder read that statement back?" Should the court recorder read it off just as the defense attorney stated it, the officer has no choice but to apologize by saying, "I stand corrected and must apologize for misstating the fact the first time."

GENERAL POINTERS IN TESTIFYING

(1) Say "yes sir" and "no sir" to the defense as well as the prosecuting attorney. Being respectful to both sides impresses the jury with your personal qualities and your interest in justice. When addressing the judge, refer to him or her as "your honor." Always give the judge the respect that is his or her due. This can be done by using phrases such as "with your honor's permission" whenever appropriate. An example would be leaving the stand to demonstrate something for the jury, or asking for permission to refer to notes.

(2) If a question is not clear, or if the officer feels that the prosecutor is asleep on the objection, the best response is, "I don't fully understand the question sir, would you mind repeating it?" Nothing makes a dramatic attorney more angry than this technique. Often this question has been used at just the right psychological moment to obtain a special effect. If the officer were to hedge on the question, it would still have the desired negative effect. But when the officer sincerely asks for the question to be repeated to make sure of the content and give the best possible answer, it takes away all the effect. It is like asking an actor to repeat some of his lines right in the middle of the play.

(3) Answer only the question at point. Often an attorney for the defense will ask a question and then stare at the officer in anticipation. It can easily give the witness a feeling that there should be more to the answer. When officers fall into this trap, they will continue to talk,

feeling that it is somehow expected. The more officers talk, the more material the attorney will have to entrap them in later questioning. It is better to err on the side of saying too little than too much.

(4) Sometimes a defense attorney will ask an officer if the case has been discussed with anyone prior to this trial. It will be presented in a tone of voice as though the officer were asked if he or she had masturbated last night. Under this type of questioning, the officer can easily assume that this must be a very terrible thing and state that the case was discussed with no one. The best answer is that the case was discussed with the District Attorney and the victims and witnesses. The defense will then probably suggest that this was a big plot or conspiracy. It will be suggested that the witnesses were coached. The officer may then reply that the facts discussed with the District Attorney are the same as those brought out in court. Nothing has been altered because the officer really has no reason to do so.

(5) Notes may be used in court with the judge's permission if the court is satisfied that they were made when the material was fresh in the officer's mind. The notes should be on loose-leaf paper only. Only those notes to be used in the trial should be brought to court. If looseleaf notes are not used, then the whole book would have to be submitted as evidence and could be examined thoroughly by the defense attorney. If he is handling another case referred to in the notebook, this could allow him to obtain special information. There have also been cases where the defense attorney found items in the notebook that were personally embarrassing to the officer. This can serve to impeach the officer in the eyes of the jury. When officers redo notes for clarity, they should keep the originals. In this way, the defense cannot accuse the officer of purposely destroying the old notes because they contained the "truth" that the officer is trying to keep from the jury.

(6) Officers should never become personally involved in a battle with the defense attorney. He is just a good actor and will try to make the officer angry. When we are angry we will

say things that would ordinarily not be said. This is because emotion blocks proper thinking. If officers show any emotion at all, it should be a slightly hurt expression because of the unjust verbal beating they are taking. This will cause the jury to feel sorry for the officer. The American public is noted for its sympathy for the underdog.

(7) Don't be afraid to say things that are favorable to the defendant. The jurors may have an idea in their minds that the officer is set against the defendant and would do anything to see him convicted and in jail. This is usually true because when an officer goes to court, he or she has generally done their best to prepare the case against the defendant. The District Attorney has reviewed the case and found it to be sound, otherwise, it would have never reached court. The officer usually has other information, such as the defendant's prior record, that cannot be brought into court because of the rules of evidence. Officers are personally involved because a "not guilty" verdict would seem to say that the defendant should not have been arrested. It is difficult not to take the case personally.

Officers have to be good actors. They also have to be careful not to show bias. Nothing can harm the case more. Many people have an innate suspicion of the police. Some of them feel that police officers get carried away in the performance of their duties. It doesn't take much to confirm this suspicion when people look hard enough. Nothing can destroy the image of a so-called "prejudiced officer" more quickly than for the officer to say something favorable about the defendant.

(8) Don't violate court rules at the expense of the defendant. Court rules are implemented for a purpose. These rules protect the rights of the defendant during the trial. Sometimes an officer feels that the defendant is obviously guilty and should have no rights in the trial. If the officer were on trial it would certainly be different. Defense attorneys may violate or twist these rules to benefit their clients, but this does not mean that the police should degrade their own professional status to compensate. Two wrongs do not, nor will they ever, make a right. Probably the most

common violation in this area is the rule of Undue Prejudice. It is usually forbidden to bring into court the past record of the defendant. (There are some exceptions.) Just because a person has committed a crime before is not a sure sign that he has committed the offense with which he is presently charged.

Although not just, it is human nature to judge people on past experience. In its effort to protect the rights of citizens, the law has made it illegal to bring up past criminal offenses during a trial, except under special circumstances. In the past, certain officers would devise various schemes to bring this past record out in court. The defense would object and the judge would instruct the jury to forget what the officer had said and that it should be stricken from the record. The officer would smirk to himself, and say, "Let the jury just try to forget it." The officer would be right. It would be very difficult for jurors to wipe this sort of information from their minds. The trial would continue with one strike against the defendant. Such tactics in court can damage a judge's impression of the testifying officer and may affect future decisions the judge will make in cases where the offending officer is involved.

Recent trials have shown that this tactic will no longer be tolerated. In cases today, the defense will simply ask for a retrial on these grounds and one will be granted. This has placed the burden of an unnecessary expense on the public and it has not helped the prosecution one bit. Neither has it helped the officer, apart from flattering his or her ego at having pulled a fast one on the defense attorney. If, by the questions presented, an officer has the opportunity to slip the defendant's past offenses into the trial, it should be explained to the questioning attorney that the question cannot be answered without causing undue prejudice against the defendant. The officer should then ask for time to think about the answer so as to avoid this error. The officer might even ask the judge for advice. For example, "Your honor, could I consult with you on a point of law?" This would not only impress the jury with the officer's objectivity, but the judge as well.

(9) During the recesses, stay clear of the members of the jury. At times the officer will be out in the hall at the same time as members of the jury. If some member of the jury was not instructed properly, that member might want to ask a question of the officer. If the defense attorney sees the two talking, he may ask for a mistrial on the grounds that the officer tried to influence a juror. It is best to simply avoid that entire situation. The officer should not even talk to the defense attorney. There have been cases where the defense attorney purposely struck up a conversation with one of the testifying officers. It was done when he knew that the members of the jury could see. Later, under cross examination, the attorney would ask the officer, "When you were talking with me outside the courtroom during the recess, didn't you offer to change your testimony?" The officer would deny it, and the defense attorney would drop the matter. Some members of the jury might wonder why the question was asked in the first place if there were not some truth to it. Fortunately, today this type of tactic is not tolerated by judges. Still officers have to be on their toes against such a possibility.

(10) A difficult task for an officer testifying on the stand is to give the defendant the benefit of the doubt. Some officers feel that they are somehow being traitors by doing so. Actually this works in reverse. Nothing will make a juror discount the testimony of an officer faster than the feeling that the officer is playing the prosecutor, or wants to see the defendant "hung." It is natural for the officer to take a personal interest in the conviction of the defendant. However, according to court rules, the officer is just a witness. According to the rules of human psychology, the officer can harm the defendant more by being fair towards him. Sir Bernard Spilsbury, the famous pathologist of Scotland Yard, won a reputation for being objective in his testimony and giving the defendant the benefit of the doubt. As a result, juries accepted his testimony verbatim, and he hurt the defendant more than if his testimony had been prejudiced in tone. Court records reveal many cases where there was good evidence against the defendant but the case was lost. This was because the jury sensed that the officers were against him, and they discounted most of the police testimony as being prejudiced. They felt that it was presented in an effort to persecute rather than prosecute.

(11) Leave the courtroom when finished. When officers have finished testifying, the attorney will tell them that they may step down. If it appears that the officer's testimony is finished, the prosecutor should be quietly asked if it is OK to leave the courtroom. The prosecutor will ask the defense attorney if he wants to further cross examine the officer. If the defense agrees, the officer will be given permission to leave. Hanging around the courtroom might indicate to the jury that the officer is "waiting for the kill." It could give them the feeling that the officer can hardly wait to see the defendant "hung." This could cause one or more members of the jury to see the officer and his or her testimony in a negative light. It is best not to take chances.

In the American system of jurisprudence, a criminal conviction requires that all twelve members of the jury be convinced beyond a reasonable doubt that the defendant is guilty. Because we are all different it can sometimes be a difficult task to convince all twelve persons. Today there is talk of either reducing the size of juries or allowing an 11 to 1 decision for a conviction. (Except capital offense cases).

(12) Come to court prepared. Any officer of normal intelligence can anticipate most of the questions that will be asked. If a question is asked and you do not know the answer, you should be able to answer it by referring to your notes.

(13) Do not volunteer information. Use "yes" and "no" when possible. When asked to explain something, keep it brief.

(14) Do not shake your head as a substitute for "yes" or "no." This puts the court reporter on the spot. It requires interpretation.

(15) If the defense attorney asks "isn't that so?" and you are not sure or do not agree. Do not answer "yes."

(16) Do not answer a question before the attorney is finished asking it, even if you are sure that you know what he is asking and know the answer.

(17) If you are asked a question, always pause a moment to allow the prosecutor to object. If the prosecutor objects, hold your answer until the judge rules on the objection.

(18) Keep answers short and to the point. Don't elaborate unless you are asked to. Again, keep the elaboration short and to the point.

(19) Always look at the person asking questions.

(20) If you do not understand a question, always tell the attorney asking it. Ask for clarification or to have the question rephrased.

(21) If you do not know the answer to a question, state that you do not know the answer.

(22) If you cannot remember the exact wording, when quoting a statement, be sure to state that it is not exact. Declare that to the best of your knowledge it carries the intended message.

(23) Do not be confused by the fact that direct examination proceeds in chronological order, while cross examination jumps from topic to topic, seemingly with no apparent order.

(24) Listen carefully to questions but do not answer them quickly. Give them some thought. Don't let the defense attorney harangue you into giving an answer before you have thought about it.

(25) If you are asked a question that could be embarrasing, do not say that you can't remember. Especially if it can be shown that you should reasonably remember such an answer. Telling the truth is more important than saving face.

USING THE CHALKBOARD

Since the basic purpose of court testimony is communication between the officer and the jury, the use of the blackboard can be most beneficial. The Chinese proverb that "one picture is worth a thousand words" could never be more true than in the courtroom where every effort must be made to properly transmit ideas. The following pointers can assist an officer in successfully getting a message across to the jury.

(1) Stand to one side so the jury can see the board. Use a pointer if you have to reach across it.

(2) Draw straight lines by laying the chalk on its side and then sliding it across the board along its long axis. This makes it much easier to draw straight lines.

(3) Use colored chalk for clarity. Whenever it is important to show differences in objects that are close together, draw each object in a different color.

(4) Since a jury is made up of persons of varying I.Q., gear all explanations and demonstrations toward the lower end of the scale. It is essential that all members understand the point being presented. Colored drawings will help in this task. Look for expressions on faces of the jurors. They will often indicate whether the message is getting across.

(5) Identify everything with either letters or numbers so it may be referred to without having to give the full description again. Always show North with an arrow. Orient the sketch so that North points as directly to the top as possible.

STUDY QUESTIONS for Patrol Operations

CHAPTER 15

1. An officer must look upon the courtroom as a stage in which he or she is an actor.   T or F

2. An officer who is afraid and nervous on the stand has no business being in police work.   T or F

3. All humans react the same way physically when fear is present. There is an increase in adrenalin, the heart beats faster, and fluids leave the extremities. The term used for this is the "_____ or _____" reaction.

4. An officer who appears in court all the time will impress his or her superiors because they will know that he or she is working hard.   T or F

5. In many cases the improper conduct of officers on the stand is simply a matter of _____.

6. Before going to court, an officer should stop by records and obtain a _____ of the suspect.

7. It is best not to subpoena friendly and willing witnesses, as it might offend them.   T or F

8. Getting witnesses to laugh is a good way to help them release tension.   T or F

9. An officer's appearance in court can be more important than what he has to say.   T or F

10. If an officer has a choice between wearing uniform or civilian clothes, the uniform should be worn.   T or F

11. An officer testifying in civilian clothes should make his or her gun visibly noticable so that the jury will know that he or she is really a police officer.   T or F

12. Because testifying is hard on the nerves, it is permissible for an officer to smoke while on the stand.   T or F

13. When testifying, an officer should wear noticeable religious or lodge badges or rings just in case one or more of the jurors are also members and will be impressed.   T or F

14. When on the stand during the preliminary part of questioning, the officer should direct answers to the court recorder and not the jury.   T or F

15. The sole purpose of the officer being on the stand is to serve as a witness.   T or F

16. How can an officer on the stand know whether or not he or she is talking loudly enough?

_____

17. If an officer on the stand is asked to repeat a statement that includes vulgarities, he or she should first apologize to the jury and then state the vulgarities verbatim.   T or F

18. It impresses the jury when an officer uses police terminology during testimony.   T or F

19. If an officer notices that the D.A. has forgotten to ask an important question, the D.A.   T or F
    should be reminded from the stand.

20. When officers feel it is important, they should not only answer the questions of the attorney, T or F
    but should expand on the answer to show the jury what they know.

21. When an officer needs the judge's permission to do something, the expression "_____
    _____ " should be used.

22. The best response to an attorney who is very talented in cross examination, dramatic in
    presentation, and who builds up to certain questions for dramatic effect, is to ask him or her
    _____.

23. Some attorneys will try to make an officer emotional during questioning on the stand.   T or F

24. Today, when an officer slips in the defendant's past record in violation of the rules of evidence,
    the judge is likely to _____.

25. During a recess period, it is permissible for an officer who is a witness in the trial to talk to   T or F
    members of the jury.

26. Although it is difficult, an officer should always give the defendant the benefit of the doubt   T or F
    during testimony.

27. If the prosecutor says it is permissible, officers should leave the courtroom when they have   T or F
    finished testifying.

28. When drawing something on the chalkboard for the jury, how should a straight line be drawn?
    _____

29. If you are explaining something by using the chalkboard, look at the _____
    on the faces of jurors to check your effectiveness.

30. You are identifying several autos and a body on the chalkboard so that the jurors will understand
    the accident better. How do you identify individual items? _____

Index

A

The ABC's of Radio Transmission: 138
  accuracy: 138
  brevity: 138
  clarity, the second "c": 139
  courtesy: 138

AIDS
  prostitution: 237
  transvestites: 238

Aids to Better Communication: 142
  Bell Telephone Company: 142
  standard phonetic alphabet: 142
  standard phonetic alphabet for numerals: 142

Aids to Clarity
  phonetics: 139
  radio interference and distortion: 139
  semantics: 139
  squelch control: 139

Air Patrol: 99
  advantages of helicopter patrol: 100
  City of Lakewood, California: 101
  disadvantages of helicopter patrol: 100
  Eglen Hovercraft: 102
  fixed wing aircraft: 101
  FLIRS: 100
  Forward Looking Infra Red System: 100
  Helicopters: 100
  Hughes helicopter: 101
  Los Angeles County Sheriff's Department: 101
  Project Sky Knight: 101
  remote piloted miniblimp: 102
  remote-controlled air patrol: 101
  Remotely Piloted Vehicle: 102
  Telecopter: 106

AMIS: 154

APCO: 134
  137
  146
APCO Ten Code: 149

Harry Arons: 220

At-the-scene Identification: 216
  People v. Floyd: 216
  Spencer v. Turner: 216

Attention Getters: 173
  rationalization: 176
  Terry v. Ohio: 175

Aural Sense
  See: Hearing

Automobile Patrol: 87
  advantages: 88
  horse drawn wagons: 87
  No-Doz: 90
  one-officer cars (advantages): 93
  paddy wagons: 87
  police call booths: 87
  President's Crime Commission: 88
  procedures: 89
  the San Diego Study: 93
  team concept in one-officer patrol cars: 93
  two-officer cars (advantages): 92
  unmarked car patrol: 94
  Wichita, Kansas: 93
  AUTOSTATIS.: 154

B

Babylonians
  See: Ethics: The Code of Hammurabi

Badge: 50
  60
  See also: History
  public trust: 23
  symbol of public faith: 23

Basic Duties
  preparation of reports: 79
  preservation of evidence: 78

Baton
  considerations in the use of: 292
  how to use: 292
  introduction to: 291
  other uses: 293
  positions: 294
  target areas to avoid: 292
  target areas to strike: 292
  Yawara Stick: 293

Beat: 83

Beat Patrol: 83
  informants: 91
  the TABS Program: 92

Roger Bennett: 239

Bicycle Enforcement: 362
  controlling bike thefts: 363

Bicycle Patrol: 103
    Military Police: 103
    Military Police at Fort Dix: 103

Bill of Rights
    amendments to the U.S. Constitution: 29
    assistance of counsel: 30
    Constitutional Democracy: 27
    cruel and unusual punishments: 30
    due process of law: 29
    eighth amendment: 286
    excessive bail: 30
    Executive branch of government: 29
    fifth amendment: 227
    first amendment: 236
    See also: Fourteenth Amendment
    Fourth Amendment: 29
    227
    . . . . 229 - 230
    freedom of speech: 29
    impartial jury: 30
    independent Judiciary: 29
    indictment: 29
    legislative intent: 27
    letter of the law: 27
    right to a speedy and public trial: 30
    sixth amendment: . . . . 215 - 216
    227
    420
    spirit of the law: 27
    Supreme Court: 29
    unreasonable search and seizure: 29
    unreasonable searches and seizures: 29
    warrants: 29

Bluffing: 249
    criminal "code of honor": 250
    indirect bluff: 249
    Miranda: 249
    physiological bluff: 249
    separation bluff: 249

Boat Patrol: 102
    Harbor and Navigation Code: 103
    harbor patrol: 102

Allen Bristow: 244
    310

Peirce R. Brooks
    "Officer Down, Code Three": 307
    ten deadly errors: 307

Charles Brown: 69

Burglary: 323
    commercial burglaries: 324
    important element: 323
    late-reported burglaries: 324
    modus operandi: 324
    safe jobs, types: 324
    safes, burn job: 325
    safes, chop job: 325
    safes, peel job: 325
    safes, pull job: 325

safes, punch job: 324
safes, rip job: 325
safes, soup job: 326

Burglary in Progress: 384

Dr. Harold Burr: 399

C

The Call Box: 150

Checking Out the Vehicle:
    123 Cherry Hill, New Jersey: 69

Civil Cases: 369
    bad checks: 369
    baggage liens: 371
    family relationship problems: 370
    judges of the justice or municipal courts: 370
    landlord/tenant disputes: 369
    mechanic's liens: 371
    poor man's court: 370
    small claims court: 370

CJIC: 154

Code of Conduct
    See: Police Code of Conduct

Dr. Marion C. Collins: 340

Communication of Transients: 155
    Dr. Hans Gross: 155
    transient symbols: 156

Communications History: 131
    Albany, New York Police Department: 132
    APCO: 134
    Robert L. Batts: 133
    Alexander Graham Bell: 132
    Chicago Police Department: 132
    church bell: 132
    Cleveland Police Department: 134
    Detroit Police Radio System: 134
    Detroit, Michigan Police Department: 132
    Differential Squelch Circuit: 134
    FCC: . . . . 133 - 134
    FCC control of police radio comm.: 134
    Federal Radio Commission: 133
    first FM mobile two-way radio system: 134
    first mobile two-way radio system: 134
    first police call box: 132
    first police motorcycle radio: 134
    first state police radio system: 134
    first workable mobile radio receiver: 133
    first workable police radio system: 133
    FM (Frequency Modulation): 134
    Paul Gavin: 134
    hand sets: 134
    handi-pack radios: 134
    hue and cry: 131

Indianapolis Police Department: 134
Michigan State Police: 134
Motorola Police Radio: 134
New York Harbor Police: 132
Daniel E. Noble: 134
Pennsylvania State Police: 133
point-to-point radio telegraph: 133
William P. Rutledge: 133
station WBFS: 133
telephones: 132

Complaints of Communications Officers: . . 140

Computer Directed Patrol: 92
game theory applied to police patrol: 92
New Orleans Police Department: 92

Computer Messages: 150

Computerized Composites: 210
Compusketch: 211
Identi-Kit vs.: 210
Visatech: 211

Computerized Sources of Info: 154
AMIS: 154
AUTOSTATIS: 154
CJIC: 154
NCIC: 154
PIN: 155

Computerized Switching Systems: 154

Computers, other uses: 155
Dick McDonnel: 155

Constitution
See: Bill of Rights

Control of Vehicle Occupants: 257

Conventional Communications & Command Center: 135

Court Decisions/Field Interrogatn.: 227
Harris v. New York: 228
Michigan v. Mosley: 228
Miranda v. Arizona: 227
Owens v. U.S.: 228
U.S. v. Castellana: 228
U.S. v. Rinka: 228

Court Decisions/Stopping & Frisking
Terry v. Ohio: 23

Court Decisions/Vehicle Search
Carroll v. U.S.: 229
Chambers v. Maroney: 229
Gustafson v. Florida: 229
New York v. Belton: 229
U.S. v. Robinson: 229
U.S. v. Ross: 230

Court Decisions/Warrantless Search
Chimel v. California: 231
Mapp v. Ohio: 230

Court Preparation: 422
officer's appearance: 424
subpoenas: 423
trial preliminaries: 423

Courtesy Services: 72
assisting other city agencies: 78
courtesy information card: 73
deadbolt: 74
death messages: 76
escorts: 75
general information: 73
house and vacation checks: 76
invalids: 75
lockouts: 73
locksmith: 73
picking locks: 74
police escorts: 75

Courtroom Testimony: 178
. . . . 419
cross examination: 420
direct examination: 420
fear of testifying: 419
fight or flight reaction: 420
five stages of testimony: 177
frequency of court appearance: 421
impeaching the witness: 420
re-cross examination: 420
re-direct examination: 420
rehabilitating the witness: 420
resting the case: 420
simplified trial procedure: 420
sixth amendment: 420
sympathetic introspection: 422

Criminal Records
See: History

Criminal Traits: 241
bums, traits common to: 242
narcotic addicts: 242
narcotic addicts' tattoos: 242
recidivism: 241
Sherlock Holmes: 241
"snake": 242
tattoos: 242
"track": 242
Youth Authority facility: 242

Criminologists' study: 4
Spot maps: 4

CYMBALS: 146

D

Description of Property: 217
    in-car identification system: 219
    microfiche: 219
    pictures of property: 219
    property lists: 218
    ultra microfiche: 219
    UMF Systems: 219

District Attorney: 21

Disturbing the Peace: 388
    animal control officer: 393
    barking dogs: 393
    See also: Family Fights
    See also: Gang Fights
    noise disturbances: 388
    noisy parties: 389
    vehicle disturbances: 393

Documents of Identification: 244
    alien identification card: 246
    alien laborer's permit: 246
    bootleg identification: 245
    breeder document: 245
    Allen Bristow: 244
    driver's license: 245
    false information: 244
    FBI: 244
    "Field Interrogation": 244
    Patricia Hearst: 245
    immigration identification: 246
    Immigration Service: 245
    Mexican nationals: . . . . 246 - 247
    minor's driver's license: 246
    operator's license: 245
    "papeles": 247
    "The Paper Trip": 245
    RR employees' social security card: 246
    social security card: 246
    Symbionese Liberation Army: 245
    temporary driver's license: 246
    3M Company: 245
    tombstone theory: 245

Dog Patrol: 96
    Allegheny County Police: 98
    bomb detection dogs: 98
    Lackland Air Force Base: 98
    NAACP: 97
    narcotic detection by use of dogs: 98
    privately owned security dogs: 99
    Savannah, Georgia: 98
    Sergeant Blitz: 98
    ultrasonic dog chasers: 99
    U.S. customs inspectors: 98

Drunkenness
    See: Intoxication

E

Egyptians: 169
. . . . 203

Emergency Calls for Service: 71

Emergency Vehicle Procedures: 125
    caution in emergency driving: 127
    civil liability: 125
    code 2/code 3 time difference: 126
    code 3 driving, dangers: 126
    code 3 vehicle passing: 127
    criminal liability: 126
    difficulty in stopping: 127
    duty to yield right of way: 126
    fire alarms: 125
    hot pursuits: 125
    siren audibility: 126
    sound barriers: 127
    what is an emergency vehicle?: 125

Emotionally Disturbed Persons: 396
    anxiety: 398
    apathy: 398
    approaching: 399
    Dr. Harold Burr: 399
    catatonia: 397
    delusion: 397
    disorders of action: 398
    disorders of association: 398
    disorders of consciousness: 397
    disorders of emotion: 398
    disorders of judgment: 397
    disorders of perception: 397
    echolalia: 398
    hallucination: 397
    illusion: 397
    impairment of affect: 398
    impulse: 398
    lunatic: 399
    manic depression: 398
    the moon and: 399
    obsession: 397
    persecution complex: 397
    phobia: 397
    Dr. Leonard Ravitz: 399
    restraining: 399
    stereotypy: 398
    symptoms of disturbance: 397
    terminology relating to: 398
    University of Miami study: 399

Enhanced 911 (E911): 136

Ethics: 3
    acting officiously: 15
    animosities: 16
    Badge of Office: 23
    See also: Bill of Rights
    bribery: 24
    The Code of Hammurabi: 9
. . . . 24 - 25

Code of Ethics: 6
cooperation w/authorized agencies: 25
corruption: 24
Detroit Chief of Police: 25
discredit to agency: 11
divorce rate: 26
enforce the law courteously: 16
finders keepers: 24
"firm but fair": 17
friendships: 16
gratuities: 22
hypocrisy: 27
immoral standard: 26
in the face of scorn or ridicule: 14
information of a confidential nature: 15
Internal Affairs: 25
International Assoc. of Chiefs of Police: 3
. . . . 8
IRS: 24
King Charles I; Articles of War, 1629: 17
knowledge and competence: 25
Lambda Alpha Epsilon: 26
The Law Enforcement Code of Ethics: 5
. . . . 8
. . . . 27
letter of the law: 16
. . . . 27
Los Angeles Co. Sheriff's Dep't.: 24
maintain courageous calm: 14
The Metropolitan Police: 6
moral fiber: 23
morals: 26
Gene Muehleisen: 8
narcotics: 24
"new breed": 4
no compromise for crime: 16
Sir Robert Peel: 6
See also: Peel's Principles
"people's police": 4
personal feelings: 16
plea bargaining: 25
police unions: 25
political beliefs: 16
prejudice: 16
private life: 11
professional courtesies: 12
Professional Policing Ethics: 8
right to liberty, equality and justice: 10
rules: New York police dep't., 1872: 11
"Salus Populi est Suprema Lex": 10
San Diego Evening Tribune: 12
self restraint: 14
serve the community: 8
special narcotics investigation team: 24
speed reading: 27
spirit of the law: 16
. . . . 27
standard of professional performance: 25
State Comm. on Peace Officer Standards: 8
teaching through example: 12
to protect to innocent: 9
to safeguard lives and property: 9
traffic citations: 12
See also: Unnecessary force or violence
vice investigation: 24
"White Paper": 24

Excessive force
See: Unnecessary force or violence

F

Family Fights: 389
family crisis intervention: . . . . 390 - 391
FBI statistics: 391
Kansas City, Missouri Police Dept. study: 391
Minneapolis study of wife beating: 390
wife beating: 389
wife beating, Minneapolis study: 390

Faults in Observation: 176
Battleship Missouri: 177
distraction: 177
factors that affect observation: 178
five stages of testimony: 177
mechanics of faulty perception: 177
Hugo Münsterberg: 176
Münsterberg Experiments: 176
sound determination: 177
time judgment: 176
Toulouse-Lautrec: 178
visual perception: 176

FBI: 244
officer survival: 304

The Field Telephone: 150

Field Interrogation: 225
the Burger court: 226
discretion: 226
fishing trips: 234
Miranda: 226
police philosophy: 226
purpose of: 232
shakedowns: 226
. . . . 234
warrantless vehicle searches: 229

Field Interrogation & Miranda:227

fifth amendment (self incrimination): 227
fourth amendment: 227
"in custody": 227
Miranda & the field stop: 227
Mirandize: 227
probable cause for arrest: 227
reasonable cause: 227
rights warning under Miranda: 228
sixth amendment: 227
stop and frisk cases: 227
waiver of rights: 227

Field Interrogation & Rinka
voluntariness of confession: 228

Field Interrogation (FI) Cards: 233
. . . . 232

Field Note Taking
chalk: 186
chronological style: 192

Codes of Civil Procedure: 183
compass or map: 185
equipment needed: 184
graph paper: 185
how: 190
map or compass: 185
narrative style: 192
notebook: 184
notebook, care and use of: 186
photograph information: 200
printed forms: 185
procedures in: 191
purpose of: 183
question and answer style: 192
styles of note taking: 192
tape measure: 185
tracing paper: 185
what: 190
what notes to take: 190
when: 190
when to take notes: 188
where: 190
who: 190
why: 191
writing implements: 185

Fingerprints: 215

Fire Calls: 364
breathers: 365
chemistry of fire: 364
crowd control: 367
entering a structure that is on fire: 366
fire hydrants: 367
fire quadrangle: 365
fire triangle: 364
police officer's job at a fire: 366
ranks on dress uniforms: 368
ranks on protective clothing: 368
saving lives: 366
traffic control: 367

Fire Equipment/Police Emergencies: 368
aerial ladder units: 368
engine companies: 369
light and salvage units: 368
rescue apparatus unit: 368
tanker trucks: 369

Firearms: 285
buck fever: 291
deadly force in arresting felony suspects: 286
dispatching injured animals: 290
8th U.S. Circuit Court of Appeals: 286
eighth amendment (excessive punishment): 286
failure to use: 291
legal aspects of use: 286
liability: 291
panic shooting: 289
People v. Newsome: 286
practical aspects of use: 287
purpose: 285
See also: Shooting at Juveniles.
warning shots: 289
warning shots, an exception: 289

Five Stages of Testimony: 177

FLIRS: 100
. . . . 384

Foot Patrol: 84
advantages: 85
Des Moines, Iowa: 85
foot patrol procedures: 86
"Metro" plainclothes foot patrol: 94
public attitude: 85
San Jose, California: 85

Fourteenth Amendment
life, liberty or property: 30

Frisking
definition of: 231

G

Gang Fights: 392
holding quadrant: 393
holding tactic: 393

Gen'l Descriptions of Persons: 211
breakdown of descriptions: 213

Gustatory Sense
See: Taste

H

Handcuffing: 278
one officer: 280
plastic strip handcuffs: 279
two officers: 280

Hearing: 169
ancient Egyptians: 169
blind persons: 169
direction and distance: 169
hearsay testimony: 169
"tell a secret": 169
things affecting what we hear: 169
voice identification: 169

Highway Patrol: 68

History
ancient police: 34
Astor Place Riots: 57
Augustus Ceasar: 50
Babylonians: 34
badges: 38
banishment: 52
beak: 42
Beak Runners: 42
bellmen: 38

Bible: 34
Blind Beak": 42
Blue Devils: 46
bootlegging: 60
Boss Tweed: . . . . 55 - 56
Bossism: . . . . 54 - 55
Boston: 53
Bounty Hunters: 39
. . . . 53
Bow Street Court: 40
. . . . 42
Bow Street Horse Patrol: . . . . . 42 - 43
Bow Street Patrol: 44
Bow Street Runners: . . . . 40 - 45
Canada: 53
capital punishment: 45
the Charlies: 38
Chicago: 53
Chief Tamanend: 56
Chief Tythingman: 37
Cincinnati: 53
Citizen Night Guard: 50
City of London Day Police: 47
Civil Service: . . . . 60 - 61
Civil Service protection: 60
Civil Service system: 57
Code of Ethics: 48
colonial U.S.: 52
Columbian Order of New York City: . 56
constable: 44
. . . . 48
. . . . 50
. . . . 52
Constable system: 52
Continental Police: 47
cop, word origin: . . . . 33 - 34
copper: 33
corruption: 54
criminal records bureau: 42
curfew: 38
James Curley: 55
Louis-Marie Debelleyme: 52
Democratic political machine: . . . 56
Dirty Papists: 46
dossier: 50
Draconian Code: 45
Dutch colonists: 52
Egyptians: 34
emergency rescue services: 52
Emperor Augustus: 35
England: 37
English Metropolitan Police system: 53
European watchmen: 36
Sir John Fielding: . . . . 39 - 42
Fielding's People: 41
Fieldings: 47
Fit justitia ruat coelum: 54
Frankpledge: 37
French police: 50
. . . . 52
French Revolution: 50
G.I. Bill: 61
gangster: 60
gansterism: 60
George III: 39
graffiti: 45
gratuities: 22
Major A. Griffins: 57
Frank Hague: 55

Headborough of the Night: 39
High Constable: 37
. . . . 41
highwaymen: . . . . 43 - 44
Home Office: 46
Horse Patrol: . . . . 43 - 44
house numbers: 52
hue and cry: 37
Hue and Cry (police gazette): . . . 47
hundredman: 37
hundreds: 37
Indus Valley: 34
Industrial Revolution: 45
Intermediate period U.S.: 53
Irish Constabulary: 44
Andrew Jackson: . . . . 55 - 56
Jacksonian philosophy: 54
Keepers of the Peace: 37
King Richard: 37
Korean War: 61
Richard Lapthorne: 38
Law Enforcement Education Program: . 61
Leatherheads: 53
LEEP: 61
Lexow Commission: 57
Liberty or Death: 46
local control: 54
the London Times: 49
loyalty oath: 52
Machine: 55
. . . . 57
. . . . 60
Lord Mansfield: 54
marching watches: 38
Marine Police: 45
marshals: 54
Medjay: 35
Merchant Police: 38
. . . . 45
Metropolitan Police: 40
. . . . 44 - 45
. . . . 48 - 49
. . . . 52
Metropolitan Police Act, 1829: . . 45
Metropolitan Police Department: . . 58
Middle Ages: 35
Modern period U.S.: 60
Mounties: 53
Municipal Police Department: . . . 58
Thomas Nast: 56
the New York Times: 56
New Breed: 61
New Orleans: 53
New Police: 42
. . . . 45 - 47
. . . . 49
New York: 53
New York City: 56
. . . . 58
New York City police dep'ts (battle): 58
New York Herald: 57

Headborough of the Night: 39
High Constable: 37
. . . . 41
highwaymen: . . . . 43 - 44
Home Office: 46
Horse Patrol: . . . . 43 - 44
house numbers: 52
hue and cry: 37
Hue and Cry (police gazette): 47
hundredman: 37
hundreds: 37
Indus Valley: 34
Industrial Revolution: 45
Intermediate period U.S.: 53
Irish Constabulary: 44
Andrew Jackson: . . . . 55 - 56
Jacksonian philosophy: 54
Keepers of the Peace: 37
King Richard: 37
Korean War: 61
Richard Lapthorne: 38
Law Enforcement Education Program: 61
Leatherheads: 53
LEEP: 61
Lexow Commission: 57
Liberty or Death: 46
local control: 54
the London Times: 49
loyalty oath: 52
Machine: 55
. . . . 57
. . . . 60
Lord Mansfield: 54
marching watches: 38
Marine Police: 45
marshals: 54
Medjay: 35
Merchant Police: 38
. . . . 45
Metropolitan Police: 40
. . . . 44 - 45
. . . . 48 - 49
. . . . 52
Metropolitan Police Act, 1829: 45
Metropolitan Police Department: 58
Middle Ages: 35
Modern period U.S.: 60
Mounties: 53
Municipal Police Department: 58
Thomas Nast: 56
the New York Times: 56
New Breed: 61
New Orleans: 53
New Police: 42
. . . . 45 - 47
. . . . 49
New York: 53
New York City: 56
. . . . 58
New York City police dep'ts (battle): 58
New York Herald: 57
Newgate Prison: 47
Night Watch: . . . . 52 - 53
Night Watchmen: 38
Nubians: 35
Officers de Paix: 52
Old Testament: 34
Parish Police: 45
patrol wagons: 52

patrol, word origin: 34
patrouiller: 34
pawn shops: 52
payoff: 60
Sir Robert Peel: 42
. . . . 44 - 45
. . . . 47
. . . . 52
Peel's Bloody Gang: 46
Peel's Metropolitan Police: 52
Peelers: 44
. . . . 48
Thomas Pendergast: 55
Pendleton Act: 55
. . . . 60
Philadelphia: 53
Pinkerton: 54
police ambulances: 52
police dogs: 35
Police Science: 61
police, word origin: 33
politeia: 33
politia: 33
posse: 53
Posse Comitatus: 53
Prefect of Police: 52
Prohibition: 60
Ratlewacht: 52
rattle: 35
. . . . 39
Reeve: 37
riot at Parliament, 1780: 44
Robin Redbreasts: . . . . 42 - 43
Royal Guard: 50
Abraham Ruef: 55
Runners: . . . . 41 - 42
Saint-Louis: 50
San Francisco: 53
. . . . 60
San Francisco Committee of Vigilance: 54
General Sanford: 58
Scandinavian watchmen: 36
Scotland Yard: 45
Sergeants de Ville: 52
Seventh New York Regiment: 58
Sheriff: 37
Sheriff system: 52
"Shiver and Shake Watch": 38
Spoils system: 55
St. Martin's Le Grand Church: 38
State Comm. on Peace Officer Stds: 61
Statute of Winchester: 38
stolen goods brokers: 40
street lighting: 52
street signs: 52
Tammany Hall: . . . . 56 - 57
Tammany Society: 56
the Thames River Police: 40
the Thief Takers: . . . . 39 - 41
William Thompson: 55
"to the victor go the spoils":: 55

patrol, word origin: 34
patrouiller: 34
pawn shops: 52
payoff: 60
Sir Robert Peel: 42
. . . . 44 - 45
. . . . 47
. . . . 52
Peel's Bloody Gang: 46
Peel's Metropolitan Police: 52
Peelers: 44
. . . . 48
Thomas Pendergast: 55
Pendleton Act: 55
. . . . 60
Philadelphia: 53
Pinkerton: 54
police ambulances: 52
police dogs: 35
Police Science: 61
police, word origin: 33
politeia: 33
politia: 33
posse: 53
Posse Comitatus: 53
Prefect of Police: 52
Prohibition: 60
Ratlewacht: 52
rattle: 35
. . . . 39
Reeve: 37
riot at Parliament, 1780: 44
Robin Redbreasts: . . . . 42 - 43
Royal Guard: 50
Abraham Ruef: 55
Runners: . . . . 41 - 42
Saint-Louis: 50
San Francisco: 53
. . . . 60
San Francisco Committee of Vigilance: 54
General Sanford: 58
Scandinavian watchmen: 36
Scotland Yard: 45
Sergeants de Ville: 52
Seventh New York Regiment: 58
Sheriff: 37
Sheriff system: 52
"Shiver and Shake Watch": 38
Spoils system: 55
St. Martin's Le Grand Church: 38
State Comm. on Peace Officer Stds: 61
Statute of Winchester: 38
stolen goods brokers: 40
street lighting: 52
street signs: 52
Tammany Hall: . . . . 56 - 57
Tammany Society: 56
the Thames River Police: 40
the Thief Takers: . . . . 39 - 41
William Thompson: 55
"to the victor go the spoils":: 55
Townsend: 42
truncheon: 43
William Tweed: . . . . 55 - 56
Tweed Ring: 56
tythings: 37
the United States: 52
William Vare: 55
Vigilance Committees: 54

vigilantes: 45
Vigilat ut Quiescant: 50
Vigiles: 35
Chief George Walling: 57
wanted poster: 53
ward: 55
warrant card: 50
. . . . 52
Watch and Ward: 45
Watch and Ward Act: . . . . 38 - 39
Watch system: 52
watchman's equipment: 39
watchmen: . . . . 34 - 35
. . . . 37
. . . . 39
. . . . 41
. . . . 44
. . . . 50
. . . . 52 - 53
watchmen's equipment: 35
General Wellington: 45
Westminster Bridge: 45
Whitechapel division: 46
Whitehall Place: 45
Jonathan Wild: 40
Fernando Wood: 58
World War II: 61

History of Criminal Identification: 203

ancient Egyptians: 203
Alphonse Bertillon: . . . . 204 - 205
. . . . 207 - 209
Bertillonage: 205
composite drawings: 209
criminal anthropometry: 205
ear identification: 209
Father of Police Photography: 204
first composite device: 209
Grand Duchess Anastasia: 209
Identi-Kit: 209
Leavenworth Prison: 207
Los Angeles County Sheriff's Office: 209
Hugh C. McDonald: 209
Metropolitan Police: 205
photography: 204
Portrait Parle: . . . . 207 - 209
Prefect of the Paris Police: 205
. . . . 207
Prefecture of Police: 207
prisoner resisting photo taking: 204
rogues' gallery: 203
Will West: 207

Homicides and Death Cases: 321

conditions that simulate death: 322
coroner, duties of: 323
establishing death: 321
methods of establishing death: 322
protecting the scene: 322

Horse Patrol: 95

Hostage Situations: 309

Dr. Allen Bristow: 310
dynamic inactivity: 309
Los Angeles State University: 310
Munich Olympics, 1972: 309

negotiation: 309
New York Police Department: 309
Dr. Harvey Schlossberg: 309

Hypnosis and Identification: 219
Harry Arons: 220
LAPD: 219
Captain Mike nielsen: 220
Dr. Martin Reiser: 219
Winter Park, FL, Police Department: . . . . . . 219 "Hypnosis in Criminal
Investigation": 220
Society for Inv. & Forensic Hypnosis: 220

I

IACP
See: IACP

Impound/Inventory Vehicle Search: 230
Colorado v. Bertine: 230

Informants: 91

Initial Contact: 239
Roger Bennett: 239
deception and lying: 239
Dr. Paul Ekman: 239
friendly approach: 240
Dr. Wallace Friesen: 239
Ohio State University: 239
rapid blinking: 239
signs to watch for: 239
subterfuge: 240

INSLAW: 232
study on patrol arrests: 232
tangible evidence: 232

Internal Affairs: 20
. . . . 25
. . . . 94

IACP
MACE: 300
Magna-Trigger Safety Ring: 308
officer survival: 304

Intoxication: 338
AIB 346
arrest procedure: 342
BAC: 345
BAC, formula for determining: 346
balance tests: 346
blood test, Schmerber v. California: 341
Breathalyzer test: 352
D.T.'s (delirium tremens): 343
diabetes: 339
diabetic coma: 339
driving under the influence: 344
epilepsy: 339
how to recognize intoxication: 342
illnesses resembling intoxication: 338
implied consent laws: 350

insulin shock: 339
intoxicated women: 343
is the person really intoxicated: 341
judgment tests: 349
See also: Liquor Law Violations
manual dexterity tests: 349
See also: Medic Alert
multiple DUI convictions: 353
nystagmus test: 345
obtaining blood: 350
persons exempt from blood test: 352
photographing the subject: 349
pickup test: 348
problems with intoxicated persons: 341
reaction from allergies: 338
recording the subject's voice: 349
refusing the test: 352
Rhomberg test: 347
should all be arrested: 342
strokes: 338
testing drivers: 345
testing when suspects are injured: 349
tests at AIB: 346
tests at the scene: 345
tests for: 346
when under the influence: 344

K

Dr. Lawrence Kersta: 331

Kevlar: 307

Rodney King:
See: Unnecessary force or violence

Dr. Lyle Knowles: 69

L

LEEP: 61

Lineup Identification: 215
blank lineup: 216
Kirby v. Illinois: 216
People v. Guerea: 216
sixth amendment: 215
U.S. v. Banks: 216
the Wade decision: 215
Wade, Gilbert, and Stovall: 215
Wade, modification by Kirby: 216
Wade, when it doesn't apply: 216

Liquid Tear Gas Irritant Projector
See: MACE

Liquor Law Violations: 353
alcoholic beverage: 354
Alcoholic Beverage Control Law: 359
chain of evidence: 357
chain of possession: 357

disorderly houses: 359
elements of alcohol offenses: 354
evidence of age and identity: 355
habitually intoxicated persons: 358
identity of persons: 356
investigative techniques: 353
minors: sales, poss. , consumption by: 358
Penal Code: 359
selling or giving: 355
standard of comparison: 357
techniques in liquor law offenses: 357
time: 354

Los Angeles: 106
. . . . 209
. . . . 261

Los Angeles Police Department: 69
. . . . 219

M

M.O.: 189

MACE
IACP: 300
limitations: 302
PCP: 302
pressurized MACE cannister: 300
problems in the use of: 302
vest-pocket models: 300

Magna-Trigger Safety Ring: 308
IACP: 308
Joseph Smith: 308

Making an Admission of Guilt Easy
avoid discussing punishment: 249
avoid sensitive words: 248
minimize the crime: 248
sympathize with the suspect: 248

Malicious Mischief
See: Vandalism

Col. Floyd H. Mann: 300

Dick McDonnel: 155

MDT's: 137

Medic Alert: 340
Dr. Marion C. Collins: 340
Medic Alert Foundation: 340
Medic Alert tag: 340

MERGE : 305

"Metro" Plainclothes Foot Patrol: 94

The Metropolitan Police: 68
. . . . 205

Miranda: 215
. . . . 226 - 227
. . . . 249

Missing Persons: 360
adults: 361
children: 360
children over five: 361
elderly persons: 362
runaways: 362

Mobile Display Terminals: 137

Mobile Teleprinters: 137

Modern Computerized Comm. Ctr: 135
CAD: 135
City of New York: 135
Computer-Aided Dispatch System : 135
Enhanced 911 (E911): 136
E911 (Enhanced 911): 136
911: 136
President's Comm. on Law Enforcement: 136
PSAP 136
Public Safety Answering Point: 136
typical CAD system: 136

Most dangerous occupations: 14

Motor Scooters and Mopeds: 103

Motorcycle Patrol: 104
Health Insurance Institute: 104
scooters: 105
three wheel motorcycles: 105

Hugo Münsterberg: 176

Münsterberg Experiments
See: Faults in Observation

N

Narcotic Cases: 406
acid: 407
. . . . 410
American Medical Association: 411
amphetamines: 408
barbiturates: 409
benzedrine (bennies): 408
bindles: 408
Bureau of Drug Abuse Control: 410
cocaine: 409

cocaine and speed (Meth): 407
crack cocaine: 409
crack houses: 409
dexedrine (dexies): 408
downers: 409
Eli Lilly Company: 412
flashback: 411
general information: 408
goofballs: . . . . 407 - 408
Haight-Ashbury Free Medical Clinic: 409
hallucinogens: 407
. . . . 410
heroin: 408
Identi-Code booklet: 412
identification of drugs: 412
Journal of the AMA: 409
kit: 408
language and terms used: 406
LSD: 407
. . . . 410
marijuana: 407
. . . . 410
mescaline: 407
. . . . 410
methaqualone: 409
opiates: 406
. . . . 408
OTC drugs (over the counter): 412
other hallucinogens: 411
outfit: 408
paraphernalia: 408
peyote: 407
. . . . 410
physical reactions in users: 406
Sandoz Laboratories: 411
signs of drug use: 411
speedball: 408
Ungerleider and Fisher: 411
uppers: 408

NCIC: 137
. . . . 154

The Newhall Shooting Incident: 313
critique: 315

911: 136
Enhanced 911 (E911): 136
E911 (Enhanced 911): 136

Non-Lethal Weapons: 302
electric cattle-prod device: 302
Hong Kong baton: 303
laser-aimed automatic rifle: 303
life-threatening situations: 303
non-life-threatening situations: 303
plastic load shells: 303
ricochet round: 303
rubber bullets: 303
sedative syringe dart: 303
stun gun: 303
stun guns, problems with: 303
TASER: 303

O

Observation
definition of: 164

Observation and Perception
Houdini: 163
tachistoscope: 163

Obtaining Information: 188

Obtaining Information for Patrol: 120
announcements: 120
beat file: 120
bulletin board: 120
daily arrest sheets: 120
daily offense bulletin: 120
mail slots: 120
missing persons: 120
offense report file: 120
pin maps: 122
wanted persons: 120
watch notices and schedules: 120

"Officer Down, Code Three": 307
ten deadly errors: 307

Officer Survival: 285
. . . . 304
ambushes: 304
Pierce R. Brooks: 307
bulletproof clipboards: 308
criminals, contact with: 306
crossfire: 305
deadly assumptions: 307
emotionally disturbed persons: 306
FBI: 304
general information: 306
inter-agency communication: 305
IACP: 304
Kevlar: 307
"law of the jungle": 306
Magna-Trigger Safety Ring: 308
officer deaths, causes of: 307
officers shooting officers: 305
personal contact: 306
protection from sniper ambush: 304
soft body armor: 307
statistics: 308
SWAT type teams: 305
SWAT, FBI schools: 305
ten deadly errors: 307
undercover work: 305

Olfactory Sense
See: Smell

Open Door Calls: 402

Operating the Police Radio: 143
the electronic console: 144
multiple channel radio: 143

single channel radio: 143
two channel radio: 143

P

Panhandling: 236
   Berkeley, city of: 237
   civil rights suits: 237
   1st amendment right to free speech: 236
   laws on vagrancy: 237
   the Middle Ages: 237

Patrol
   See: History; patrol, word origin

Sir Robert Peel: 68
   See also: History Peel's Principles

Phonetic Alphabet: 150

Photograph Identification: 216
   mug shots: 216
   Nassau County: 217
   sixth amendment: 216
   talking rogues' gallery: 216
   3M Sound Slide System: 217
   U.S. ex rel. Reed v. Anderson: 216
   U.S. v. Ash: 216

Photographing the Crime Scene: 198
   admissibility of photos as evidence: 199
   cameras: 198
   instamatic cameras: 198
   instamatics, common problems: 199
   notebook information: 200
   polaroid cameras: 199
   professionsl photographers: 199
   testimony on photographs: 200
   Harris Tuttle: 200
   types of photographs: 198

Physical fitness
   physical agility examination: 26
   physical conditioning: 25

Pimping: 237
   AIDS: 237

PIN
   Police Information Network: 155

The Police Officer's Locker: 118
   flashlight : 118
   handkerchiefs: 118
   shaving gear and toothbrush: 118
   shoe laces: 118
   thermos bottle: 118
   underwear: 118
   wide-mouthed jug: 118

Police Brutality
   See: Unnecessary force or violence

Police Chief: 69

Police Code of Conduct: 8

Police Observation: 171
   binoculars, the use of: 171
   infra-red illumination: 172
   light-intensifying binoculars: 172
   night viewing device: 172
   observation from a patrol car: 171
   portable lights: 173
   spotlight, using the: 172

Police Reserves: 72

Police Unit Identification: 144
   all number computer ID system: 145
   function letter: 144
   individual and dep't ID system: 144
   key number: 144
   personal number: 144

Police Weapons
   minority groups: 299
   new developments: 299

Pre-Planning for Emergency Situations
   309
   "discretion is the better part of valor": 311
   discretion in dangerous situations: 311
   "fools go where angels fear to tread": 311
   See also: hostage situations
   never give up your weapon: 310
   no hostage, superior tactical position: 310
   officer shot: 311
   preventive and evasive action: 313
   role-playing difficult situations: 311
   salesmanship in negotiation: 312

Preparation for Patrol: 115
   before leaving home: 116
   before leaving the locker room: 117
   Deputy Dale E. Curry: 119
   fingernails: 116
   full length mirror: 119
   haircuts: 117
   inspection: 122
   leaving the squad room: 122
   locker calendar: 117
   locker cleaning: 117
   uniform cleaning: 117
   white collar workers: 116
   writing implements: 116

Preventive Enforcement: 67
   93
   234
   Charles Brown: 69
   Cherry Hill, NJ Dept. of Pub Safety: 69
   Highway Patrol: 68
   house and vacation checks: 76
   Indianapolis Police Department: 68
   Kansas City: 69
   Kansas City preventive patrol: 69
   Dr. Lyle Knowles: 69

Los Angeles Police Department: 69
The Metropolitan Police: 68
off duty police car plan: 68
Sir Robert Peel: 68
Police Chief: 69
Police Foundation: 69
police reserves: 76
proactive beats: 69
proactive patrol: 69
reactive beats: 69
reactive patrol: 69
role playing: 71

Priority Codes: 145
code 1: 145
code 2: 145
code 3: 145
no code (code 0): 145

Proactive Patrol: 69

Protective Weapons: 285
Linda Peer v. City of Newark, NJ: 285
police training academies: 285
State Comm on Peace Officer Stds: 285

Prowler Calls: 394
dogs, use of: 396
faults in responding to: 395
how to respond: 395
panic shooting: 396
peeping tom: 394
stakeout: 396
subterfuges used by prowlers: 394
trespassers: 394

Public Safety Officer's Benefits Act: 313

Public Telephones
use of: 150

Purpose of Field Interrogation
crime prevention: 234
development of informants: 232
development of suspects: 234
identification: 232
preventive enforcement: 234

Purpose of Police Patrol: 67
basic duties: 67
courtesy services: 72
emergency calls for service: 71
police reserves: 72
preventive enforcement: 67
routine calls for service: 72
selective enforcement: 70
traffic enforcement: 70

R

Radio Procedures: 145
abbreviations: 147
APCO: 146

APCO Ten Code: 149
Communications Act of 1934: 146
CYMBALS: 146
Lakewood, Colorado: 149
phonetic alphabet: 150
preferred words and phrases: 149
subject classification: 147
Ten Code: 149
Ten Code Experiment: 149

Ramming the Suspect Vehicle: 261
Monday morning Review Board: 261

Dr. Leonard Ravitz: 399

Reactive Patrol: 69

Residence Burglary: 385
burglar who committed 800 burglaries: 385
FI card: 385
M.O.: 385

Robbery: 326
meta-communication: 326

Robbery Calls
purse snatches: 388
quadrant search: 387
responding to: 387
robbery in progress: 387
strong-arm robbery: 388

Role Playing: 71

Routine Calls for Service: 72

Royal Ulster Constabulary
See: Ethics

S

Salus Populi Est Suprema Lex: 257

Dr. Harvey Schlossberg: 309

E. S. Schneidman: 400

Searching & Handcuffing Suspects: 270
body search: 271
clothing search: 271
considerations in searching: 271

Selecting the Subject: 234
"jungle": 235
loitering persons: 236
older males w/young females: 238
out of place persons: 235
panhandlers: 236
peeping toms: 235
persons acting strangely: 236

persons carrying suspicious objects: 235
persons stopping people on the street: 236
pimps: 237
reasonable cause: 234
skid row: 235
stolen goods, sellers of: 237
transvestites: 238

Selection of Officers
"Cross Examination" by A.L. Cornelius: 4
The Metropolitan Police: 5
George Orwell: 5
standards of recruitment: 5

Selective Perception, External: 164
contrast: 164
intensity and size: 164
movement: 164
proximity: 165
repetition: 164
similarity: 165

Selective Perception, Internal: 165
conditioning: 165
personal drives: 165
personal interests: 165

Sellers of Stolen Goods: 237
five and dime stores: 237
search warrant: 238

The Senses
See: sight, smell, etc.

Sexual Offenses: 328
Menachem Amir: 337
Chief Special Agent/phone company: 331
exhibitionism: 329
FCC: 331
female homosexuals: 335
forcible rape: 336
gay bashing: 335
golden fountain: 329
golden rinse: 329
handling of: 329
homosexuals: 334
indecent exposure: 329
lesbians: 335
male homosexuals: 334
molesters: 333
mooning: 330
obscene phone calls: 331
"Patterns of Forcible Rape": 337
peeping tom: 329
Rape Crisis Centers: 337
Lance Rentzel: 330
Sex Offender Registration Book: 334
shoe fetish: 328
soliciting lewd acts: 335
statutory rape: 336
strong-arm robbery of homosexuals: 335
underclothing theft: 333
unlawful intercourse: 336
unreported rapes: 337
See also: Voiceprint
"When All the Laughter Died in Sorrow": 330

Sheriff
See: History; sheriff

Shifts: 83
See also: the Ten Plan

Shooting at Juveniles: 288
headline happy media: 288
joy riding: 288
monday morning quarterbacks: 288
public pressure groups: 288

Shoplifting: 327

Sight: 165
the blind spot: 166
color: 167
color blindness: 165
Dalton's dichromatism: 165
Daltonism: 165
Dr. Samir Deeb: 166
Dr. John Mollon: 166
the Müller-Lyer illusion: 167
night vision: 167
optical illusions: 167
Lord Rayleight: 165
recognition of persons: 166
rods and cones: 165
visual acuity: 166

Silent Burglar Alarm
arriving at the scene: 383
burglaries in progress: 381
code 3 driving: 382
crossfire: 384
flashlight use: 384
FLIRS units: 384
gang-busters approach: 382
illegal entry, discovery of: 383
lookouts: 382
responding to: 381
roof jobs: 383
searching the premises: . . . . 383 - 384
silent approach: 382
suspect's car, locating: 384

Sketching the Crime Scene: 192
best type of sketch: 194
computerized sketching: 198
cross projection sketch: 194
exploded sketch: 194
floor plan sketch: 194
format of the crime scene sketch: 197
how the sketch may be used: 193
materials: 193
measurement, rules of: 196
measurements, scales used in: 197
measuring, methods of: 196
outdoor plan sketch: 194
plane lines: 196
polar coordinates: 196
purpose of sketching: 192
rectangular coordinates: 196
rough sketch: 193
thrust lines: 196
triangulation: 196

Skin Senses
  See: Touch

Smell: 169
  chloral hydrate: 170
  marijuana: 170

Joseph Smith: 308

Soft Body Armor: 307
  Kevlar: 307

Spanish Surnames
  problems in identification: 214

Special Paraphernalia: 242
  consent search: 243
  criminally associated business cards: 244
  gambling devices: 244
  glue-sniffing apparatus: 243
  hot wires: 243
  jump wires: 243
  lock-picking devices: 243
  narcotics: 243
  narcotics, LSD (foil-wrapped): 243
  narcotics, marijuana seeds: 243
  obscene pictures: 243
  244
  obscene pictures showing sadism: 244
  obscene pictures, pedophile: 243
  obscene pictures, sexual sadist: 243

Sir Bernard Spilsbury: 429

Stakeouts: 386
  M.O.: 386

Standard Phonetic Alphabet: 142
  Bell Telephone Company: 142
Numerals: 142

State Comm. on Peace Officer Stds: 61

Stolen Vehicles: 403
  attention getters: 403
  confirming ownership: 404
  Consumer Reports News Digest: 403
  Consumers' Research study: 403
  electronic homing devices: 405
  hot wire: 404
  joy riding: 405
  jumper wire: 404
  LOJACK: 405
  prevention of auto theft: 403
  spotting hot cars: 403
  statistics and auto theft: 405
  TELETRAC: 406

Stopping and Frisking: 231

Stopping the Vehicle: 261
  Watts riot: 261

Suicide
  attempted suicide: 400
  attempts to gain sympathy: 401
  becoming aware of the condition: 400
  investigative procedure: 402
  "Preventing Suicide": 400
  E. S. Schneidman: 400
  warnings: 400

Suspect Identification Cameras: 300
  Col. Floyd H. Mann: 300

SWAT units: 305

T

The TABS Program: 92

Tactile Sense
  See: Touch

Taste: 170
  four qualities of: 170

Team Concept of Patrol: 94
  beat commander system: 94
  neighborhood police team system: 94

Techniques in Radio Comm.: 138

Techniques of Interrogation: 247
  bluffing: 249
  communication: 247
  don't give more information: 250
  making an admission of guilt easy: 248
  meta-communication: 247
  salesmanship: 248
  tone of voice: 247
  use presumptive questions: 250

Teletype : 150
  examples of messages received: 153
  examples of messages sent: 152
  format of teletype messages: 151
  sources of teletype information: 153

Television Patrol: 105
  Desert Storm: 106
  Rodney King: 106
  LLLTV: 105
  LLLTV photos: 107
  Los Angeles: 106
  narcotic "safe houses": 106
  Orleans PD: 105
  Orleans, New York: 105
  Telecopter: 106
  Watts riot: 106
  West Germany: 105

The Ten Plan: 83
   advantages: 84
   disadvantages: 84
   Huntington Beach: 83

Ten Code: 149
   experiment: 149

Terry v. Ohio: 175

Theft: 327
   citizen's arrest: 327
   private person's arrest: 327

Touch: 170
   cold: 170
   heat: 170
   pain: 170
   pressure: 170

Traffic citations: 12

Traffic Patrol: 104
   George Cugnot: 104
   first speeding ticket: 104
   first vehicle accident: 104
   Jacob German: 104
   New York City: 104

Transients, Communication of
   See: Communication of Transients

Transvestites: 238
   AIDS: 238

The Trial: 425
   answering questions on the stand: 426
   communicating with judge or jury: 425
   impeachment of witnesses: . . . . 426 - 427
   notes: 427
   Sir Bernard Spilsbury: 429
   taking the stand: 425
   testifying, general pointers: 427
   trier of fact: 426
   undue prejudice: 428
   using the chalkboard: 430
   vulgarities: 425

Harris Tuttle: 200

24-Hour Time: 192

U

Unnecessary force or violence: 21
   blackmail: 21
   Christopher Commission Report: . . . . 19 - 20
   confessions: 21
   cost: 19
   District Attorney: 21
   See also: Escalation of Force Policy

   fear: 22
   "Fight or Flight": 21
   Internal Affairs: 20
   See also: Rodney King
   L.A.P.D.: 19
   See also: Los Angeles
   methods of interrogation: 21
   See also: misconduct suits
   Mobile Digital Terminals (MDT's): 20
   number of complaints: 18
   the "third degree": 21

V

Vandalism: 337

Vehicle Care: 123

Vehicle Pursuits: 257
   AAA Foundation for Traffic Safety: 257
   aggressive response: 258
   blind intersection: 260
   emotional involvement during: 258
   passing vehicles at intersections: 260
   police advantages in: 258
   pursuit considerations: 258
   tactical considerations: 259
   turn signals: 261

Vehicle Search & Chambers
   contraband: 229
   search incident to arrest: 229

Vehicle Search & Gustafson
   probable cause for arrest: 229

Vehicle Search & Robinson
   fourth amendment: 229

Vehicle Search & Ross
   closed containers: 230
   expectation of privacy: 230
   fishing expedition: 230
   independent probable cause: 230
   nexus (legal connection): 230
   probable cause: 230
   scope of search: 230
   warrantless search: 230

Vehicle Search/Motor Homes: 230
   California v. Carney: 230
   fourth amendment: 230

Vehicle Stop Techniques
   California Highway Patrol study: 263
   immobilizing suspect vehicle: 268
   removing suspects from vehicle: 269
   removing suspects/high risk: 270
   removing suspects/non-hazardous: 269

Vehicle Stop Techniques, General
approaching the vehicle: 263
contact with the driver: 264
pre-planning: 262

Vehicle Stop Techniques, High Risk
leaving the police vehicle: 268
method 1: 266
method 2: 266
method 3: 266
methods of stopping: 266
notifying communications: 265
observing the suspects: 265

Vehicle Stop Types
high risk stops: 262
investigative stops: 262
traffic stops: 262

Vehicle Stops: 257

Video Cameras
mounted in patrol vehicles: 300

Visual Sense
See: Sight

Voiceprint
Bell Telephone Laboratory: 331
Dr. Lawrence Kersta: 331
voiceprint sound spectrograph: . . . . 331 - 333

W

Warrantless Search: 230

Warrantless Search & Chimel
exceptions to Chimel: 231
exceptions to Chimel: automobiles: 231
exceptions to Chimel: emergencies: 231
exceptions to Chimel: hot pursuit: 231
exceptions to Chimel: plain view: 231
lunge and reach rule: 231
reach rule: 231

Warrantless Search & Mapp
Civil Rights Act of 1968: 230
exclusionary rule: 230
fourth amendment: 230
reasonable cause: 230

Warrantless Vehicle Search
Chimel v. California: 229
search incident to arrest: 229

Watts Riot: 106
. . . . 261

Women in Law Enforcement
Attorney General of the U.S.: 109
Crime Control Act: 109
EEOC:: 109
Equal Employment Opportunity Act: 109
Equal Protection, 14th amendment: 109
Equal protection under the law: 109
federal funding: 108
Fourteenth amendment: 109
glass ceiling: 109
history of women and patrol: 108
Indianapolis Police Dep't: 108
LEAA: 109
LEAA funds: 109
legal basis for hiring female officers: 109
Police Foundation: 108
police matron: 108
reverse discrimination: 109
Dr. Lewis J. Sherman: 108
Title VII, Civil Rights Act of 1964: 109
University of Calif. v. Allan Bakke: 109
University of Missouri: 108
Urban Institute Study: 108
World War I: 108

Y

Yawara Stick: 293